Methods of Educational Research

Methods of Educational Research

Max D. Engelhart

DUKE UNIVERSITY

Rand McNally and Company
Chicago

RAND McNALLY EDUCATION SERIES

B. Othanel Smith, Advisory Editor

Cover: Courtesy Boulevard Photographic for
Burroughs Corporation

Second Printing, 1972

TO WALTER S. MONROE

Distinguished Pioneer in Educational Research

Foreword

Educational research is barely in its infancy if we count Rice's studies in the 1890's as its birth. Yet its methodology is sophisticated. Rice used simple procedures to collect his data and simple arithmetic to handle them. But by 1904 the methods and procedures of educational research had become complex enough for the publication of an extended volume on the subject. That year Thorndike published his *Introduction to the Theory of Mental and Social Measurements.* A little more than a decade later, in 1917, appeared Rugg's *Application of Statistical Methods to Education.* Then in 1923 the first work on experimentation in education—McCall's *How to Experiment in Education* —was issued. Thus in the short span of approximately twenty-five years, research in education was launched and its methods and procedures formulated so that all could see what it was about. Following in the tradition of these epoch-making volumes a number of distinguished books have appeared through the years. This book is to be counted among these outstanding works.

Dr. Engelhart's approach to the methods of educational research is broad and yet intensive. He is familiar with the philosophy of science and he brings his knowledge of this aspect of methodology to bear upon the problems of educational research. He comes to grips with a gamut of basic theoretical problems—definitions, constructs, assumptions, fallacies, or whatever. Then he delves into the tasks of data collection and interpretation and moves into the ways of studying relationships among variables. Nor does he stop there. He also deals with methods and procedures of collecting and interpreting data about the past and of coping with questions about what ought to be, as in curriculum research. Finally he faces the question of the role of the computer in educational study.

The need for capable research workers in education is perhaps greater today than ever before. All sorts of innovations are being urged upon the profession of teaching, some of which have been tried before and found wanting. They are often put forth with neither a theoretical nor research basis. Cleaning up after the innovators is an almost overwhelming job in itself, to say nothing of developing new knowledge for the profession. If the history of education in this century teaches anything, it is that progress in teaching and learning is more apt to come from research than from romantic innovations. If this book contributes to the development of an increasing number of courageous and insightful research workers, it needs no other justification.

Dr. Engelhart writes out of an extensive background of experience in research at both the university and public school level. He knows what it means to face a research problem and wrestle with it to a successful conclusion. His intimate knowledge of research problems and methods equip him to prepare a book valuable to anyone who desires either to understand or to undertake research in education.

B. Othanel Smith
Advisory Editor

Preface

This book is designed primarily as a basic text for an introductory course on the methods and techniques of research in the study of educational problems. It has use secondarily as a guide for school administrators and teachers who wish to apply the findings of educational research to their own professional problems. While these active school workers are not expected to possess detailed knowledge of research techniques, they should recognize the hallmarks of dependable research and the warning signs of poor research. Such understanding can contribute to wiser decisions in educational practice.

The initial chapters introduce the reader to the patterns and levels of scientific inquiry in the physical and behavioral sciences. The treatment is both historical and philosophical. It provides a basis for better understanding of fundamentals important in conducting educational research.

Students taking an introductory course in research methods, both master's and doctoral candidates, and, increasingly, advanced undergraduates majoring in education, may have limited knowledge of the procedure of thesis writing, and less knowledge of the language and concepts of statistics. Accordingly, early in this text definition of problems, location of previous research pertaining to a selected problem, and various methods of collecting data are discussed. Later chapters deal successively with differing types of research. Almost one-half of the book is concerned with statistical techniques: descriptive statistics, statistical inference, correlation analysis, analysis of variance and analysis of covariance. Applications of these techniques to survey research and to studies of relationships, including causal ones, are demonstrated.

For readers who have had one or more courses in statistical methods, these chapters may be a review, but those who have not had the benefit of such courses should find later advanced study less formidable. While they may not seem so to the novice, the chapters are introductory and elementary. Practice exercises for developing statistical skills are included. Most of the chapters have lists of questions for study or discussion, suggestions for further reading, and lists of selected references.

Chapters 4 and 16 will be helpful to those graduate students who still need to acquire skills useful in locating information and in writing adequate reports of their investigations. Chapter 14 on historical studies and Chapter 15 on curriculum inquiry are offered for the many students interested in research that is not exclusively scientific. Then, recognizing that the computer is revolutionizing both education and educational research, the text concludes with a brief chapter on data processing.

More than twenty years of teaching methods of educational research, and many years of experience in administering testing programs and conducting institutional research in the City Colleges of Chicago have prompted me to include both the practical and theoretical in this book. In addition to imparting the knowledge and intellectual skills implied above, a course in research methods should inculcate scientific attitudes, an abiding interest in research, and a faith in its value to our society.

Acknowledgment is gratefully made for suggestions and encouragement given by former colleagues Macklin Thomas, Theodore G. Phillips, Samuel T. Mayo, and Henry Moughamian and by my present colleagues W. Scott Gehman, Jr., William J. Katzenmeyer, and Peter Carbone. Helpful suggestions were made by Evelyn J. Harrison, Librarian, Woman's College Library, Duke University, who carefully read Chapter 4; Ned A. Flanders, Donald M. Medley, and Harold E. Mitzel who read all or parts of Chapter 6. Charles E. Werts brought me almost up-to-date on "path analysis."

Herman G. Richey of the National Society for the Study of Education, Oscar E. Shabat and James J. Zigerell of the City Colleges of Chicago, and Virginia G. McDavid of the *Illinois Schools Journal* gave me permission to draw upon certain of my earlier writings without repeated special citations. To the authors and publishers of all quotations cited gratitude is here expressed for permission to reprint. Apart from quotations, other sources of information and ideas are also appropriately cited.

The sources of the statistical tables are cited in the Appendix. I am indebted to the Literary Executor of the late Sir Ronald A. Fisher, F.R.S., to Dr. Frank Yates, F.R.S. and to Oliver & Boyd Ltd., Edinburgh, for permission to reprint in abridged form Tables III and IV from their book *Statistical Tables for Biological, Agricultural and Medical Research.*

The very tangible encouragement of William H. Cartwright, Allan S. Hurlburt, and Dean Harold W. Lewis of Duke University is also deeply appreciated.

I am very grateful to my editors: Edward Bowers, Jr. and Charlotte Iglarsh of Rand McNally, and to B. O. Smith, now of the University of South Florida, and for many years of the University of Illinois.

Finally, I appeal to the reader and critic of this book with the concluding words of the great scholastic philosopher, Anselm of Canterbury, from his reply to the monk Gaunilon:

> I thank you for your kindness both in your blame and in your praise for my book. For since you have commended so generously those parts of it which seem to you worthy of acceptance, it is quite evident that you criticized in no unkind spirit those parts which seemed to you weak.[*]

MAX D. ENGELHART
May 1971

---

[*] From Sidney Norton Deane's translation of Anselm's *Apologetic,* a defense of his faith.

Contents

List of Tables

List of Figures

1

Introduction

We live in a time of rapid change in most aspects of our culture. Scientific advances and technological developments inevitably create social problems. The knowledge explosion, the population explosion, automation, the migration of people to urban centers, the changing values of the younger generation, and international tensions are all factors contributing to the present troubled state of our civilization. In a static society the function of education can be largely that of transmitting the cultural heritage. In a dynamic society education is expected to play a much greater role. This role includes efforts to aid in solving the social problems implied above, and in contributing to the reconstruction of society. For education to perform this function, as well as its traditional role efficiently, educational research is essential. It is needed to formulate decisions as to which educational practices can most effectively be used.

What is educational research?

The ultimate purpose of educational research is the discovery of generalizations relating to the various aspects of education. Such generalizations help us to decide what we should do, or attempt to do, in educating children and adults. Many educational researchers have as their immediate purposes the determination of what the characteristics of education have been in the past, what the characteristics of educational practices and conditions are in the present, and what the effects of introducing different practices will be in the future. The tested knowledge thus obtained contributes to solving the problems of what should be done in education. Problems of this "what should be done"

1

type transcend those concerned with what has been, is, or will be, by introducing questions of values. Such problems are not exclusively scientific, although certain philosophers do not agree.

A person confronted with an educational question may accept an answer without giving the question much serious thought. He may derive an answer from experience or casual observation. He may consult other persons in regard to the answer. He may seek his answer in the published opinions of others. Means, such as these, to answer educational questions are *not* those of educational research. In contrast, educational research is the total procedure employed in collecting, organizing, summarizing, and interpreting data for the purpose of arriving at dependable answers to questions about education. This statement requires modification when educational research is regarded as including the philosophical type of inquiry. The conclusions of philosophical educational research and decisions based, in part, on historical as well as scientific research in education, are in the domain of "what should be."

The questions with which educational research should be concerned are questions requiring critical thinking. The routine collection of educational data necessary to the administration of schools is not educational research. To justify this designation there must be a novel problem and the collection and interpretation of data appropriate to the problem.

Educational research and the graduate student in education

Most graduate students in education are expected to accomplish research on a suitable thesis problem. Obviously, these students have an incentive to acquire understanding of the methods and techniques of educational research; and even those who do not engage in thesis research benefit from the type of understanding just mentioned. Professional training for school administration, guidance, and counseling necessitates the reading of research reports whether in texts or in the journals. Such reading should be critical reading characterized by sensitivity to limitations in the material read.

A growing number of graduate students in education are becoming aware of opportunities in full-time educational research. More and more researchers are devoting themselves to research which requires extended professional training. Training of the scope exemplified in this and other introductory texts on educational research techniques is far from enough. Understanding of psychological, sociological, and educational theory is essential. In certain areas of educational research a strong mathematical background is needed, not merely an introductory course in largely descriptive statistics. Courses in experimental design, multivariate analysis, and in computer applications are growing more and more necessary. Only the philosophical and historical educational researchers may safely neglect such training.

Educational research and the school administrator, counselor, and teacher

There is much to be said for including some research experience in the training of administrators, counselors, and teachers. There is also much to be said for a continuing interest in educational research on the part of such persons. Improvements in educational practices are most likely to occur when teachers and administrators use research findings intelligently in making decisions regarding their educational practices.

An understanding of educational research may be valuable from another standpoint. More and more administrators, counselors, and teachers are participating in large-scale educational research by collecting data in survey or prediction studies or by offering experimental instruction. Frequently a knowledgeable teacher or administrator can make suggestions which will improve the quality of the research.

Action research

Some years ago "action research" became quite popular. Teachers were encouraged to participate in research studies, and it is probable that action research did motivate teachers to more professional efforts in instruction. The major criticism of action research was directed at the tendency toward inadequate planning. Problems were ill-defined and necessary control of relevant factors was neglected. The findings were seldom sufficiently dependable to warrant long-term decisions or to be regarded as an even minor contribution to the science of education. Despite all this, as was stated earlier, participation by school personnel in educational research activities should be promoted. Teachers and administrators may acquire greater understanding of what is involved, and may make more intelligent use of the findings of the large-scale researches now being conducted. Such use is essential if the vast expenditures by the foundations and by the federal government are to be justified. Finally, where administrators and teachers conduct research in efforts to solve immediate local problems, simple but appropriate techniques and generalizations restricted to the local situation can be of adequate dependability for decisions. Rarely, of course, should the reports of such studies appear in other than a local school publication.

Institutional research

Many of the larger school systems and numerous higher institutions have long had bureaus or divisions engaged in "institutional research." Usually such offices are expected to solve problems stemming from instructional and administrative practices. The studies conducted may be extremely helpful to administrators in formulating decisions with respect to administrative policies. These studies may be of the survey type summarizing facts concerning pupil and teacher personnel, trends in enrollments, characteristics of school buildings, and socioeconomic attributes of school districts. Or, they may evaluate achievement resulting from innovations in curriculum materials or instructional methods. On occasion, such problems may be more appropriately studied by means of controlled experimentation. Prediction studies may be conducted to determine what tests or other measuring instruments are likely to be most useful in solving problems of guidance and placement. Institutional research which must have as its major goal the study of problems relevant to the educational program of a school system or higher institution is seldom regarded as also contributing to the development of a science of education. Whether or not this attitude is justified will be considered in the next chapter.

Educational research financed by the federal government and by foundations

Expenditures for large-scale educational research have expanded enormously in recent years. Millions of dollars in grants have been and are being made available by the great foundations and by the federal government. Universities and city school systems are conducting educational development and research to an extent undreamed of not long ago. While such efforts to improve educational practices are generally to be applauded, the magnitude of these undertakings creates misgivings with reference to the quality of the research phase of the programs. One major source of apprehension is that the research will be isolated from theory and, hence, will not contribute explanatory principles. It is also feared that adequately trained educational research workers, still in very short supply, directing such programs of research and development will spend too much of their time in promotion of the development aspect and in the dissemination of findings. Hence, they will have little time for creative thought. There is danger that the promotional aspects will make difficult the maintenance of objectivity. Administrators of city school systems and possibly of universities, too, often expect results reflecting credit to their systems or institutions. Negative results or nonsignificant differences are seldom welcome. Small differences, though statistically significant, may be used as justification for the promotion of "fads." Let us hope that this is too pessimistic an outlook.[1]

---

[1] For a challenging discussion of these matters see Lee J. Cronbach, "The Role of the University in Improving Education," *Phi Delta Kappan* 47:539–45 (June 1966).

PLAN OF THIS TEXT

Chapter 2, "Methods of Inquiry," deals with the various ways of seeking solutions to educational problems. Not all questions or problems are scientific ones, but most of the chapter is devoted to scientific methods of inquiry with special emphasis on the applications of such methods to educational problems.

In keeping with the assumption that all research should begin with a problem, Chapter 3 focuses on the selection and definition of educational research problems. This chapter aims at helping the graduate student or other educational researcher to write a plan for research on a problem. For the graduate student this plan may be a thesis proposal. Locating and summarizing earlier research on a problem is also essential. This is a means of relating a problem to theory, of discovering hypotheses to be tested, and of acquiring understanding of methods which may be useful in a contemplated project. A critical summary of previous research is usually a desirable part of the report of a new research and is often expected in a thesis. Useful procedures in locating and summarizing previous research on a problem are discussed in Chapter 4.

Basic techniques for collecting educational research data are described in Chapters 5–7. Chapter 5 explains procedures for obtaining data from records and published sources and from questionnaires and interviews. Chapter 6 deals with collection of data through systematic observations of pupil and teacher behaviors in classrooms and through use of content analysis. All of Chapter 7 is devoted to discussion of data collection by means of tests and other instruments of measurement.

In Chapters 8 and 9 the student is introduced to techniques useful in organizing, summarizing, and interpreting numerical or quantitative educational research data. The techniques explained are those of elementary descriptive statistics and of statistical inference.

For a comprehensive treatment of the history and present status of educational research consult the following reference: *Educational Research and Development in the United States.* National Center for Educational Research and Development, Office of Education, U.S. Department of Health, Education, and Welfare. Washington: U.S. Government Printing Office, 1970.

This source contains detailed information concerning the role of the U.S. Office of Education, other government agencies, and the great foundations, in the management and financial support of educational research and development. It deals extensively with the R & D centers.

Since the publication of the reference just cited, a National Institute of Education has been proposed which would be coordinate with the Office of Education and would ultimately absorb and broaden its educational research functions; see James J. Gallagher, "A National Institute of Education: Promise and Problems," *Educational Researcher* 21:1–4 (September 1970). (Other articles in this issue deal with the same proposal.)

It should be noted that Chapters 5 through 9 are concerned with techniques or "tools" useful in efforts to solve a variety of educational research problems. Along with Chapter· 3, they are in a sequence which follows the general pattern of scientific inquiry. This sequence begins with the selection and definition of a problem, continues through the collection of data appropriate to the problem, and concludes with the summarization and interpretation of the data.

Chapters 10 through 15 discuss research methods in the study of different types of educational problems. Chapter 10 is concerned with methods useful in investigating present practices and conditions and Chapters 11–13 with the study of relationships between variables. If scientific methods are broadly defined, Chapters 10–13 are in the realm of scientific educational research. Certainly the label is justified for research concerned with relationships between variables in which correlation analysis or experimentation are the methods used.

Chapter 14 introduces the student to some of the methods of historical research or historiography. Some of the most interesting problems of educational research are those concerning the past in education. The solutions of such problems contribute greatly to the thought required in making decisions dealing with current educational practices. They also contribute to the area of philosophical research in education. Many apparently historical researches in education, especially certain biographical studies, are both historical and philosophical.

Philosophical research, seeking answers to questions of values, is concerned with both means and ends of education. Determination of objectives of education is the basic problem of curriculum planning and development. Educational philosophers also engage in critical studies of scientific methods and of scientific contributions to education. Some even doubt the possibility of a science of education! These matters are discussed in Chapter 2, and again in Chapter 15.

Chapter 16 covers the reporting of educational research. Many an otherwise excellent research project suffers from inadequate reporting. A well-written report is essential if important findings of dependable generalizations are to be of use to others interested in their applications, in their further study as part of theory, and in their assimilation to the science of education.

Chapter 17 describes the impact of the computer on education and on educational and psychological research. Its applications include organization and summarization of factual data, analysis of research data, and computerized instruction.

Questions for study and discussion are included in Chapters 2–15. The concluding pages of most of these chapters have suggestions for further study. Each of the chapters, with the exception of Chapter 8, ends with a list of selected references. (The references at the end of Chapter 9 are for both Chapter 8 and Chapter 9.)

At appropriate intervals in Chapters 8, 9, 10, 11, and 13, practice exercises are inserted, requiring application of the previously explained statistical techniques to data. Solution of these problems should enhance the student's understanding of the techniques. Answers to the practice exercises are listed in the Appendix, which also contains several statistical tables explained in the chapters listed above.

Tables, figures, formulas, and practice exercises are numbered to correspond with the chapter number and succession of the same items within the chapter. For example, Formula 8.9 is the ninth formula of Chapter 8 and is so referred to on other pages of Chapter 8 and in later chapters.

No educational researcher, from graduate student to professional, should depend on this introductory text alone, but let us hope that the reader will acquire not only some of the skills of a scholarly educational research worker but some of the scientific attitudes as well.

2

Methods of Inquiry

There are three general types of scholarly inquiry in education: (1) scientific inquiry, (2) philosophical inquiry, and (3) historical inquiry. All three types have certain attributes in common—critical thinking, collection and interpretation of data, and the quest for generalizations. The kinds of questions with which they deal are different. Scientific inquiry in education provides generalizations useful in explanation, prediction, and control of educational processes and conditions. Philosophical inquiry in education has as one major aim the solution of problems of goals or ends of education. Historical inquiry in education has as its function investigation of educational ideas and events of the past. All three methods of inquiry contribute more than is usually recognized to the thinking which precedes decision making in the practice of education.

This chapter will deal largely with the methods and levels of scientific inquiry. It is assumed that an understanding of these matters is one of the major objectives in the training of educational research workers who expect to undertake scientific educational research. Potential educational philosophers should also find this material of value since the philosophy of science is another major domain of their discipline. Any discussion of the methods of scientific inquiry is within this field. Finally, prospective researchers in the history of education should seek such understanding in order to better deal with the history of education of the past seventy years, a period characterized to an important degree by the development of educational research.

An understanding of the methods of scientific inquiry should be a part of general education. Scientific thinking and critical thinking are so synonymous that understanding the former should contribute to undertaking the latter. We may, at least, hope for transfer!

METHODS OF SCIENTIFIC INQUIRY

A definition of science

A science is often defined as organized and tested knowledge of natural phenomena in some field. A science includes facts, hypotheses, theories, and generalizationś, or laws. The latter are useful in explaining events or phenomena known to occur, in establishing relationships between events or phenomena, in predicting events which have not as yet occurred, and in promoting control of events. According to Braithwaite:

> This function of establishing general laws is common to all the natural sciences; it is characteristic also of those parts of psychology and of the social sciences which would ordinarily be called scientific as opposed to philosophical. If the science is in a highly developed stage, as in physics, the laws which have been established will form a hierarchy in which many special laws appear as logical consequences of a small number of highly general laws expressed in a very sophisticated manner; if the science is in an early stage of development—what is sometimes called its 'natural-history' stage—the laws may be merely the generalizations involved in classifying things into various classes.[1]

Psychology and sociology

The science of psychology has not reached the status of physics in its development, but it does include systems of laws or theories analogous to those of physics. This may be illustrated by four of twenty principles of learning stated by Hilgard and Bower:

> *Frequency of repetition* is still important in acquiring skill, and in bringing enough overlearning to guarantee retention. One does not learn to type, or to play the piano, or to speak a foreign language, without some repetitive practice.
> *Reinforcement* is important; that is, repetition should be under arrangements in which desirable or correct responses are rewarded. While there are some lingering questions over details, it is generally found that posi-

---

[1] Richard B. Braithwaite, *Scientific Explanation* (Cambridge: Cambridge University Press, 1953), pp. 1–2. Reprinted with permission of author and publisher. See also F. S. C. Northrop, *The Logic of the Sciences and the Humanities* (New York: Macmillan, 1947), Chapter III.

tive reinforcements (rewards, successes) are to be preferred to negative reinforcements (punishments, failures).

Divergent thinking, which leads to inventive solutions of problems or to the creation of novel and valued products, is to be nurtured along with *convergent* thinking, which leads to logically correct answers. Such divergent thinking requires the subject to perceive himself as potentially creative through appropriate support (feedback) for his tentative efforts at originality.

Anxiety level of the individual learner may determine the beneficial or detrimental effects of certain kind of encouragements to learn. The generalization appears justified that with some kinds of tasks high-anxiety learners perform better if *not* reminded of how well (or poorly) they are doing, while low-anxiety learners do better if they *are* interrupted with comments on their progress.[2]

Similarly, sociology has its theories and generalizations, or laws justifying its designation as a science. An example is the generalization that widespread and rapid social change in material culture is usually accompanied by relatively unchanging nonmaterial culture, justifying the prediction that introduction of laborsaving farm implements will be more quickly accepted by a primitive society than that change will occur in their rituals or ceremonies thought to insure good crops. The phenomenon described by this generalization is termed "cultural lag."

Is there a science of education?

Over the years educational research workers have been and still are being criticized for inadequate training, lack of understanding of the nature of scientific evidence, overemphasis on descriptive studies, and so on.[3]

At this point, the student may ask, "Is there a science of education?" Certainly the practice of education is an art and, with the proliferation of audio-visual aids, teaching machines, and televised instruction, a technology as well. Since laws and generalizations from the fields of psychology and sociology are applied to the solution of instructional and other educational problems, many contend that education is only an "applied" science. Nevertheless, whatever the sources of the laws and generalizations thus applied, there is a growing body of organized and tested knowledge. Research is also directed

---

[2] Ernest R. Hilgard and Gordon H. Bower, *Theories of Learning,* 3rd ed. (New York: Appleton-Century-Crofts, 1966), pp. 562–64. Reprinted with permission of authors and publisher.

[3] See, for example, Michael Scriven, "The Philosophy of Science in Educational Research," in "The Methodology of Educational Research," *Review of Education Research* 30:422–29 (December 1960).

toward solution of educational problems without immediate concern for application of generalizations or laws thus established. Whether the research he is engaged in stems from psychology, sociology, or education may be of little concern to the researcher. There is a science of education and there has been work toward its development since 1900; and this development parallels the development of other sciences.[4] Before 1900, it was almost exclusively characterized by deductions from philosophical ideas. Later, and even now, it came to be mainly based on data largely descriptive of conditions or factors in educational practice. More recently it has become increasingly characterized by findings from application of hypothetico-deductive patterns similar to research in other natural sciences, although most of such research may also be classified as psychological or sociological.

The problems of education are as challenging as any other scientific problems. More effective techniques are being developed for seeking solutions to educational problems, and research workers are becoming increasingly sensitive to the necessity for higher standards.[5]

Is there a universal scientific method?

Most contemporary philosophers of science disagree with Karl Pearson's claims that "the scientific method is one and the same in all branches and that method is the method of logically trained minds," and that *"the unity of all science consists alone in its method."*[6] The disagreement would seem to be with the concept that there is a single scientific method universally applicable regardless of the problem and to the stage of the inquiry. Nevertheless, scientific methods or procedures and patterns of scientific thinking, though varying from science to science or problem to problem, have much in common. Few will quarrel with the assertion that a research is "scientific" which (1) starts with a problem, (2) is characterized by hypotheses deduced

---

[4] For discussion of the early history of the concept of a science of education, see Walter S. Monroe and others, *Ten Years of Educational Research, 1918–1927,* University of Illinois Bureau of Educational Research Bulletin No. 42 (Urbana: University of Illinois, 1928), pp. 30–87; Walter S. Monroe and Max D. Engelhart, *Experimental Research in Education,* University of Illinois Bureau of Educational Research Bulletin No. 48 (Urbana: University of Illinois, 1930), pp. 7–17; B. Othanel Smith, "Science of Education," in W. S. Monroe, ed., *Encyclopedia of Educational Research,* 2nd ed. (New York: Macmillan, 1950), pp. 1145–52.

[5] This view is supported by Leslie D. McLean, "Design and Analysis Methodology—An Overview," in "Methodology of Educational Research," *Review of Educational Research* 36:491–502 (December 1966).

[6] Karl Pearson, *Grammar of Science* (London: J. M. Dent and Sons, 1937), pp. 15, 16. (Originally published in 1892.)

from theory, (3) proceeds to the empirical testing of the consequences deduced from the hypotheses by observation or experiment, and (4) concludes with generalizations or laws useful in explanation and prediction, inferred from these tests. This is a hypothetico-deductive model. Its general methodology is characteristic of research in a variety of sciences and on a variety of problems, even though within this frame, special methods and techniques differ from science to science and from problem to problem.

Another model or general methodology, also scientific, is common from science to science on the "natural history" or descriptive level of inquiry. Let us consider some of its aspects.

Research on the natural history or descriptive level of inquiry

Much research in education and in other fields is largely limited to observation, description, and classification. Such research is exemplified by the natural history stage of biology in the observation and description of plants and animals and in their classification in categories ranging from phyla to genera and species. In geology, an example is observation, description, and classification of rocks as igneous, sedimentary, and metamorphic. In astronomy, it may be exemplified by observation, description, and classification of such things as planets, stars, and galaxies. In psychology and sociology there have been very numerous descriptive studies of traits and of environmental conditions. Educational research, largely descriptive in character, may have such titles as "Individual Differences in the Reading Ability of College Students," "Mistakes Which Pupils Make in Spelling," "The Duties of Elementary School Principals," "The Social Composition of Boards of Education," and "Characteristics of Teacher-Pupil Classroom Interactions."

All research, whether on the descriptive or hypothetico-deductive level, begins with the recognition of a problem or, in the words of John Dewey, a problematic situation. The situation may be an encounter with some hitherto unexplained or inadequately explained phenomenon. Analysis of the situation or phenomenon may reveal that traditional beliefs or theory do not suffice and that the immediate problem is determining which facts are relevant, rather than the formulation of hypotheses as tentative solutions. The next stage on the descriptive or natural history level of inquiry is inductive and largely empirical. It includes the inspection or observation of the relevant facts and relations and the description and classification of what is apprehended. According to Northrop this ends the natural history stage of inquiry.[7]

It was noted earlier that application of the hypothetico-deductive

---

[7] Northrop, *Logic of the Sciences,* p. 35.

model may result in generalizations or laws useful in explanation and prediction. The results of observation, description, and classification of facts on the natural history level may be summary statements or descriptive generalizations. The process can reveal the components and structure of a phenomenon. Given this knowledge the phenomenon is better understood. While descriptive generalizations have less capacity for explanation and prediction than the laws resulting from the testing of hypotheses deduced from theory, this is a matter of degree.[8] The apprehended, described, and classified facts provide an organized, if not complete, pattern. The process and the relations observed may disclose sequences of events and similarities between observed phenomena so that awareness of analogies with other more familiar phenomena suggests explanations. The descriptive generalization can tell not only *what* and *how* but *why*.

After terming explanation a "concatenated description," a putting together of one fact or law into relation with others, Kaplan observes:

> Because of the concatenation, each element of what is being described shines, as it were, with light reflected from all the others; it is because they come to a common focus that together they throw light on what is being explained. We see why something happens when we see better— in more detail, or in broader perspective—just what does happen.[9]

Similarly, according to Scriven:

> The point . . . is that understanding is roughly the perception of relationships and hence may be conveyed by any process which locates the puzzling phenomenon in a system of relations. When we supply a law, we supply part of the system; but a description may enable us to supply a whole framework which we already understand, but of whose *relevance* we had been unaware. We deduce nothing; our understanding comes because we see the phenomenon for what it is, and are *in a position* to make other inferences from this realization.[10]

It should be noted that what has just been quoted applies with equal force to inquiry on the hypothetico-deductive level, augmenting the explanatory capacity of theoretical laws.

---

[8] See Abraham Kaplan, *The Conduct of Inquiry* (San Francisco: Chandler, 1964), p. 114.

[9] *Ibid.,* p. 329. Reprinted with permission of author and publisher.

[10] Michael Scriven, "Explanations, Predictions, and Laws," *Minnesota Studies in the Philosophy of Science* Vol. 3 (Minneapolis: University of Minnesota Press, 1962), p. 193. Reprinted with permission of author and publisher.

Descriptive or empirical generalizations can be a basis for predictions even when they do not provide explanations. Ancient astronomers made accurate predictions concerning total eclipses and positions of the planets without possessing satisfactory explanatory theories.[11] Many descriptive or "survey" studies in education are used in making predictions in educational practice. Usually these predictions are limited to the immediate future and to the local situation before conditions change.

Possibly the greatest contribution of research on the descriptive level is the basis it provides for research on the hypothetico-deductive level. These matters are considered further in Chapters 6 and 10.

Scientific inquiry on the hypothetico-deductive level

We may think of a theory as containing a network of interrelated generalizations or laws. The generalizations or laws are deductively connected with each other. The theory may be headed by definitions of basic terms and by assumptions or axioms. If we visualize a theory as having a vertical organization, the definitions and axioms or assumptions will be placed at the top. Near the top we may also place postulates or propositions. The theorems of the theory will be placed nearer the bottom of the sequence and will be regarded as the hypotheses most immediately to be tested. It is, of course, accepted that all scientific laws and generalizations are to some extent hypothetical and subject to modification as new evidence makes it necessary. If the theorems or hypotheses deduced from the axioms or laws are justifiably rejected when tested empirically, then the axioms or earlier established laws must be modified. If, however, such hypotheses or theorems are confirmed empirically, they are explained by the axioms and earlier established laws. The hypotheses thus tested and explained serve to predict events or conditions which have not as yet occurred. Beyond that they may contribute to the control of anticipated events and conditions.

Consider Brodbeck's example of the laws of motion:

> A theory is a deductively connected set of laws. It thus has the logical form of an explanation. Some explanations, those that explain statements of individual fact, contain both laws and statements of individual fact as premises. In a theory *all* the statements, both explained and explaining, are generalizations. Those that do the explaining are called the *axioms* of the theory. The laws that are explained are the *theorems* of the theory. The axioms are such only by virtue of their place in a theory. Neither

---

[11] Kaplan, *Conduct of Inquiry*, p. 349.

self-evident nor otherwise privileged, they are empirical laws whose truth is, temporarily at least, taken for granted in order to see what other empirical assertions, the theorems, must be true if the axioms are true. An axiom in one theory may be a theorem in another. Thus, what is an axiom in Galileo's theory about the free fall of bodies on earth is a theorem in the Newtonian theory of gravitation which explains Galileo's law.[12]

It is interesting to note that the sequence of axioms to theorems is not the sequence in which they are formulated. Galileo established his laws concerning freely falling bodies and of projectile motion long before Newton formulated his laws of gravitation and of motion. Similarly, the laws of Newton explain Kepler's three laws concerning the motions of the planets. It should also be noted that Newton's law of gravitation served to predict the existence of the planets Uranus and Neptune. All of this exemplifies how a comprehensive theory such as that of Newton serves to organize and unify scientific knowledge. The laws of Galileo and Kepler, and other laws later established, have become special cases of Newton's more general ones.[13]

In the following section some of the characteristics of hypothetico-deductive theory are discussed in an elementary fashion.

Axioms and assumptions

The axioms of a deductively formulated scientific theory are not now considered self-evident truths. They are empirical laws or generalizations, the truth of which is tentatively accepted. From such axioms, basic postulates, propositions, and hypotheses are deduced. If the hypotheses are confirmed, the consequences predicted by the hypotheses are explained by the axioms, as, for example, Newton's law of gravitation explains why the orbits of the planets are ellipses. If the hypotheses deduced from axioms are not confirmed, the truth of the axioms is challenged.

In the stage of inquiry characterized by induction it is assumed that the world of nature exists, that it possesses consistency, and that it is observable. In deductively formulated theory, the same assumptions are relevant when the theory is tested empirically. One seldom finds, however, explicit statements of such assumptions since their truth is so usually taken for granted.

---

[12] May Brodbeck, "Logic and Scientific Method in Research on Teaching," in N. L. Gage, ed., *Handbook of Research on Teaching* (Chicago: Rand McNally, 1963), p. 68. Copyright © 1963, American Educational Research Association. Reprinted with permission of author and copyright holder (AERA).

[13] *Ibid.*, p. 70.

Frequently, the assumptions or axioms which function as working premises and from which postulates, propositions, theorems, and hypotheses are deduced are not labeled as axioms or assumptions in a report of research. In summarizing the earlier research on his problem and other relevant theory, the author of the report may cite generalizations from such sources. He may actually use such generalizations as axioms from which his own hypotheses are derived. Numerous examples of this can be found in the literature of educational research. Occasionally, a research report does present a formal statement of basic definitions, basic assumptions, subassumptions or postulates, and propositions or hypotheses. Possibly the best example of this is the David Ryans report of his research on the characteristics of teachers.[14] Some of these statements are quoted in Chapter 3 of this text.[15]

Assumptions are frequently made and often stated in reports of research concerning the techniques used in collecting and interpreting data. In experimental evaluation of differing methods of instruction, the assumption may be made that random assignment of pupils to groups taught by the different instructional methods will serve to control or equalize the effects of irrelevant factors. Certain statistical tests of hypotheses assume that the variable measured has a normal distribution in the population from which the samples are drawn, and to which generalizations inferred from the data are to apply. Another assumption is that, in spite of departures from the normal in the population, sample statistics have distributions which approach the normal more and more closely as sample size increases. As sample size increases the mean of a sample approaches the mean of the population. These assumptions when more precisely stated are referred to in texts on statistical method as the "Central Limit Theorem" and the "Law of Large Numbers."

The place of a problem in deductively formulated theory

It is generally agreed that research begins with a problem. In the case of research in the natural history stage of inquiry, a problem may call for observation, description, and classification of facts. The method is inductive and the generalizations obtained predominantly empirical.[16] To have such a generalization is to have a theory from which hypotheses can be deduced. Where there is, however, a theory

---

[14] David G. Ryans, *Characteristics of Teachers, Their Description, Comparison, and Appraisal* (Washington, D.C.: American Council on Education, 1960).

[15] See pages 52 to 53.

[16] Northrop, *Logic of the Sciences,* p. 36.

of greater complexity a problem may still initiate a research, but its place may be visualized as intermediate between the generalizations acting as axioms and the theorems or hypotheses whose consequences are to be tested. A researcher may start with a problem stemming from his experience, formulate hypotheses based on generalizations arrived at inductively and then discover that his problem is best studied in the context of a deductively formulated theory of which he was not earlier aware. This may lead the researcher to realize the importance of identifying the axioms and assumptions relevant to the theory and to the study of his problem. The axioms may be generalizations or laws established by earlier research and stated in the reports of the research or in relevant discussions of theory.

Problems and hypotheses

Research on the natural history stage of inquiry is seldom characterized by explicitly stated hypotheses. In survey or other descriptive studies in education problems may be merely declarative statements of the purpose of the research; or they may be general questions followed by subordinate questions. Although the questions may imply hypotheses or tentative solutions, such solutions are seldom stated in connection with the statement of the problem. The answers are in the data later reported and summarized. In theory-related research, the problems may also be stated as questions, but these are usually immediately followed by hypotheses—tentative solutions to the questions raised.

Consider the following hypothesis:

If pupils are praised, they will learn more efficiently.

If praise is considered a type of reinforcement, this hypothesis can be deduced from the second of the generalizations quoted from Hilgard and Bower on page 9. The hypothesis also exemplifies the "If A, then B" type of conditional frequently described in discussions of hypotheses. It expresses a relationship between two variables: praise and learning, both of which can be observed and measured quantitatively. Consequences can be deduced from the hypothesis and thus tested. The relationship between praise and learning can be explained by motivational and learning theory. One can also predict that if pupils are praised they will learn more efficiently. If the prediction is correct the hypothesis is confirmed and the truth of the general principle from which it was deduced receives support. The hypothesis and the consequence predicted can be written in the form of a syllogism:

Major premise: If pupils are praised, they will learn more efficiently.
Minor premise: The pupils learn more efficiently.
Conclusion: Therefore, the hypothesis is true.

This all seems very logical, but in actuality one of the rules of logic has been violated. To suppose that such a minor premise, even though correct, guarantees the truth of the major premise is the "fallacy of affirming the consequent." (Here the "consequent" is the part of the major premise which says "they will learn more efficiently.") The pupils in a given sample may have learned more efficiently because of causal factors other than praise. Furthermore, while the pupils observed may have learned more efficiently as a result of praise alone, these pupils may not be representative of all types of pupils. In Chapter 3, a research is cited which reports that retarded pupils regard praise as a threat and that the consequence of praise for such pupils is that they learn *less* efficiently.[17]

The moral to be drawn from all of this is that the confirming of hypotheses does not guarantee their truth. Even when further data are collected to verify it, a hypothesis is still considered as only probably true. When a hypothesis has been thus confirmed, its confirmation in a variety of situations may increase the probability of its truth and, hence, our confidence in it.

Consequences are deduced from hypotheses. The testing of a hypothesis is the testing of a relationship expressed in the form "If A, then B." The conclusion drawn from this testing is an inductive inference. Thus we see that induction has a double role in the development of deductively formulated theory. "Statistical inference" is discussed in Chapter 9 of this text. It is the kind of inductive inference associated with the statistical testing of hypotheses.

If, in a theory, the axioms are true, the hypotheses deduced from them are necessarily true. In a simple theory the axiom may be a single hypothesis deduced from a single descriptive generalization. It has been noted that axioms are not privileged. When one or more hypotheses derived from them are disconfirmed, the axioms themselves must be discarded or modified. (It is assumed that the disconfirmation of the hypotheses is supported by adequate evidence.) It can be accepted that the disconfirmation or rejection of hypotheses is an essential factor in the growth of science. Scientists are thus motivated to seek more adequate explanations of phenomena.

It follows from what has just been said that a scientist should formulate several alternative hypotheses as tentative explanations of the phenomenon he is investigating.[18] If he thus becomes interested in several contrasting hypotheses, he is less likely to become so

---

[17] See pages 50 to 51.

[18] See Thomas Crowder Chamberlin, "The Method of Multiple Working Hypotheses: Reprint from *Science* 1890," *Science* 148:754–59 (May 7, 1965).

attached to a single hypothesis that he is reluctant to discard it even though his data warrant its rejection. If, however, several contrasting hypotheses are proposed and tested and only one of them is not disconfirmed, confidence in the probable truth of that one is more greatly increased. This has been termed "strong inference."[19]

In concluding this discussion of hypotheses, it should be noted that terms appearing in hypotheses frequently refer to unobservables. In psychological and educational research these terms are constructs pertaining to traits within individuals. The A of "If A, then B" may be a trait such as "liberal attitude." The B of the hypothesis may specify behaviors that can be observed or measured. The behaviors may be responses to items keyed as liberal in an attitude inventory, for example, the *Scale of Beliefs* of the Progressive Eight Year study. One of the items states that "public regulation of business and industry is necessary in order to protect the interest of the general public."[20] An affirmative answer to this item is one of the evidences of possession of a liberal attitude. A hypothesis having the form and kind of content described above is an *operational definition.*[21]

Concepts and constructs

In the physical sciences, constructs include mass, force, energy, proton, electron, and photon. In psychology and education, examples of constructs are intelligence, creativity, reading ability, self-concept, and anxiety. These cannot be directly observed, but are inferred from behavior. In sociology, social class and cultural lag are important constructs, of a kind more directly based on observables than are traits or intervening variables. They are empirical generalizations that summarize observation of facts and of the relationships between them. Social class necessarily presumes that various levels of social status have been categorized.

Cultural lag and social class might almost as justifiably be called concepts. Concepts and constructs are both abstractions, but the latter are more abstract than the former. In general, concepts are more directly based on observations of particulars than constructs. They are a result of inductive thinking and are descriptive generalizations. They may be facts whose derivation from experience is relatively simple and direct. Hypothetical constructs, on the other hand, are not

---

[19] John R. Platt, "Strong Inference," *Science* 146:347–53 (October 16, 1964).

[20] For more information about this inventory, see E. R. Smith, R. W. Tyler and the Evaluation Staff, *Appraising and Recording Student Progress* (New York: Harper, 1942), pp. 209–29.

[21] See pages 20 to 21.

directly related to the world of particulars or to experience. A construct is a type of concept postulated or proposed as one of the links in a network of theory. A construct is not, however, without connection to the world of experience or phenomena. These connections may be through the operational definitions explained later and less directly through association with concepts and other constructs.

The following discussion of anxiety as a hypothetical construct illustrates both what is meant by such constructs and their usefulness.

> Assuming the theoretical framework is reasonably well stipulated, meanings of the term and research results are more easily assessed and compared with those of other studies when anxiety is used as a hypothetical or theoretical construct. Used in this way, anxiety is assumed to be an entity or process that actually exists (but is not at present fully observable) and which gives rise to measurable phenomena, including phenomena other than the observables that led to hypothesizing the construct. Thus anxiety, inferred from one aspect of the child's behavior (e.g., stating his feelings on a questionnaire), is conceived of having certain other predictable consequences (e.g., interference with performance on a complex learning task); which follow from the role of the construct in its theoretical framework.[22]

One of the major types of test validity discussed in Chapter 7 is "construct validity." A test is judged to have satisfactory construct validity if it effectively measures the *trait* it is postulated to measure. As noted above, reading ability, intelligence, and creativity are examples of constructs. These refer to traits presumed to exist within individuals and which account for the scores they earn on tests so labeled. If we think of the trait as varying in magnitude with the size of test score we have an example of what Northrop terms epistemic correlation—a functional relationship between unobservables and observables.[23] Such correlations between the abstract and the concrete should not be confused with the kind of relationships between variables of which the ordinary correlation coefficient is an index. They are not restricted to the relationships between test scores and the traits they measure, but may be thought to label the relationship between any construct and the phenomenon with which it is associated by means of

---

[22] Britton K. Ruebush, "Anxiety," *Child Psychology.* The Sixty-second Yearbook of the National Society for the Study of Education, Part I (Chicago: University of Chicago Press, 1963), pp. 461–63. Reprinted with permission of author and publisher. Ruebush also discusses anxiety as "an empirical construct," as a "state variable," as a "process variable," and in a number of other ways.

[23] Northrop, *Logic of the Sciences,* Chapter VII.

an operational definition. The term *epistemic* comes from epistemology, an appropriate source, since epistemology is the branch of philosophy concerned with the nature of human knowledge.

Operational definitions

Constructs like intelligence can be defined constitutively through use of other constructs or concepts such as "mental ability" or "general scholastic aptitude." In a network of laws, certain constructs not explicitly related to observables are thus defined. For such constructs to have meaning, however, they must be connected with constructs more closely related to observables through operational definitions. An operational definition is one that gives meaning to a construct by specifying how it is to be measured or manipulated.[24]

The construct "liberal attitude" and one possible operational definition of it have already been briefly described. In the case of intelligence, a given researcher may define his use of the term by stating that it is the trait measured by a well-established intelligence test, for example, the *Otis-Lennon* or the *Lorge-Thorndike.* If the construct pertains to a less familiar variable or is to be measured in some novel way, its operational definition will need to be more detailed. The researcher may describe and illustrate the instrument used and present evidences of its validity, including its construct validity. The graduate student may also find it appropriate to include a copy of the instrument in the appendix of his thesis.

In an experimental evaluation of instruction designed to promote scientific attitudes in high school students of chemistry, the experimenter may describe in detail the characteristics of instruction, hypothesized to promote acquisition of this trait. He may also describe in detail just how acquisition of the trait is to be measured. No matter how measured or manipulated, intelligence, creativity, scientific attitude, and anxiety are constructs. We know them only through the variables which we measure or manipulate and through the relationships of these variables to other variables.

The very great importance of operational definitions in research should be emphasized. Unless some of the elements or links of a theory are related to the world of experience through operational definitions, the theory is without value in explanation or prediction. When the constructs or terms used in hypotheses are operationally defined by one investigator, other investigators can verify the original researcher's findings with respect to his hypotheses. Unless the same

---

[24] See Fred N. Kerlinger, *Foundations of Behavioral Research* (New York: Holt, Rinehart, and Winston, 1965), pp. 33–49. See also Brodbeck, Chapter 2 in *Handbook of Research on Teaching.*

operations of measurement or manipulation are used, different hypotheses are tested.

Cause and effect

The meaning of the term *causation* is one of the most controversial of philosophical problems.[25] To empiricists since the time of David Hume, saying that A causes B is only to say that B follows A, or that they are connected by a series of intermediate events. To metaphysicians, however, there is more to cause and effect than this. They hold that some force analogous to a push or other necessary connection literally ties A and B together. When A occurs, B *must* follow. When I raise my arm to lift an object, the force is experienced. Similarly, we think causal relationships between emotional states and related behaviors are better understood because of similar self-observation or introspection.[26] In the physical world, justifiably or not, we intuitively conceive some force connecting events. Because of such a conception, Newton's contemporaries hesitated to accept the idea of gravitation since it implied "action at a distance" with nothing in between.

If we accept the empiricist view that all we can say about B is that it follows A or is connected to A by intermediate events, how can a sequence of events be considered causal rather than accidental? Madden states that the "way we distinguish those constant conjunctions which *are* causal from those which are *not,* says the empiricist, is by reference to an overall deductive context, not by invoking an unobservable force."[27]

When we state such "indicative conditionals" and "subjunctive conditionals" as, for example:

> If a gas is heated, it expands.
> If this gas were heated, it would expand.

we need not make further observations and engage in induction to accept them as expressing causal rather than accidental relationships. This is so because the law from which they were deduced is one of the well-established laws of physics.

The contention is sometimes made that subjunctive conditionals are

---

[25] See Edward H. Madden, ed., *The Structure of Scientific Thought* (Boston: Houghton Mifflin, 1960). The student will find this anthology an excellent source concerning this and other problems of the philosophy of science. Especially helpful are Madden's introductions to each chapter.

[26] See "The Operation Called 'Verstehen' " by Theodore Abel in Madden, *Structure of Scientific Thought.*

[27] Madden, *Structure of Scientific Thought,* p. 203. See also Brodbeck's chapter in the *Handbook of Research on Teaching* earlier cited and all of Madden's Chapter 4.

more helpful than indicative conditionals in distinguishing lawful or cause and effect relationships from accidental ones. We seem to be better able to predict that *any* gas we heat in the future will expand. While we seem to know this intuitively, this is not empiricist doctrine. Some authorities also contend that it is useful in distinguishing lawful from accidental relationships to assert a corresponding "counterfactual inference" or "contrary to fact" statement:[28]

If this pencil were a gas, it would expand when heated.

This may be contrasted with:

If this pencil were on my desk, it would be blue.

Even if all of the pencils on my desk are blue, there is no necessity for another pencil placed upon it to be blue. The pencils on my desk are a finite or limited class of pencils. There is, however, a nonfinite or indefinitely large class of gases. At the same time, if *all* instances of a finite class are observed, it is possible to state laws applicable only to these instances.

A major problem in studying causal relationships is that A may not be a cause of B, or B a cause of A, even though they are associated in ways earlier described. Both may be the effects of a common cause or causes. For children varying in age from five to fifteen, mental age increases as the children increase in height. For children all of the same age, however, there is no such concomitant variation. Mental age is not a cause of height nor is height a cause of mental age. The two variables are due to age, or more precisely, to all the multiplicity of factors in physical and mental growth with which age is associated. In Chapter 11, relationships between numerous variables important in education and psychology are studied by calculation of correlation coefficients and similar indices of concomitant variation. Chapter 12 emphasizes the point that which variable is cause and which effect, or whether they are related through a common cause or causes, must be determined by evidence separately derived from observation or experiment. Experiment is considered more effective than observation in identifying factors as causes because the variables hypothesized as causes are introduced or manipulated by the experimenter. The experimenter can more legitimately believe that A is the cause of B, if he is responsible for the occurrence of A; he can more justifiably conclude that A is at least an immediate cause of B.

Many scientists prefer to speak of functional relationships rather

---

[28] For a critical view of this claim, see "Law Statements and Counterfactual Inference" by Roderick M. Chisholm in Madden, *Structure of Scientific Thought*.

than cause-and-effect relationships. Instead of saying, for example, that *X* is a cause of *Y,* they say *Y* is a function of *X.* Empirical data may be used in obtaining an algebraic equation expressing the functional relation, or the equation may be deduced from theory and then tested empirically. Predictions of *Y* for various values of *X* can be compared with actual occurrences of *Y.*

It is said with reference to such equations that *Y* is a function of *X* or, if not of *X* alone, of several variables in combination. *X* and other such variables are termed the *independent* variables. *Y* is termed the *dependent* variable, since its magnitude depends on that of *X* or on the magnitudes of several independent variables. While independent variables may not be referred to as causes nor the dependent variable referred to as an effect of these causes, this is surely implied. It is certainly implied when the relative importance of the independent variables is estimated from the weights given to them in a prediction equation.[29]

The dependent variable in one research may become the independent variable in another. High school grade point average may be the *Y* where the problem is that of predicting such averages from tests given on entrance to high school. The same grade point averages may become an independent variable when the problem is that of predicting college achievement.

Models and paradigms

The meanings of the term "model" in everyday life are in some respects analogous to the meanings given the term in science. A fashion model may hopefully resemble an idealized version of feminine beauty. A toy airplane may picture for a small boy many of the characteristics of a real airplane. Rutherford's concept of an atom with its nucleus of protons and its orbital electrons is analogous to the sun and its planets. A theory in one science may serve as a model for a theory in another science. In psychology, the field theory of Lewin was an effort to use field theory in physics as a model. Algebraic equations fitted to data or deduced from theory are models; the normal curve is another model. Such models are idealized versions of phenomena. They are useful in thinking about a theory, even though the theory thus portrayed may not correspond in detail to the model.

A paradigm is a less idealized type of model which illustrates, usually in graphic fashion, the elements of a theory or processes relevant to it. Kerlinger presents excellent examples relating constructs to

---

[29] Proportions of the variability (or variance) of a dependent variable may be assigned in terms of the squares of such weights. See pages 340–341.

each other and to observational data through operational definitions.[30] Among numerous other examples of paradigms, Gage reproduces and discusses paradigms constructed by Stolurow to show the analogies between those of a teacher in directing learning and those of an "adaptive" teaching machine.[31]

Figure 2.1 exemplifies a paradigm illustrative of the explanatory and predictive functions of theory. The arrow at the left assumes that the phenomenon has first occurred and is to be explained. The arrow at the right assumes that it has not as yet occurred, but is predicted.

Figure 2.1   A paradigm

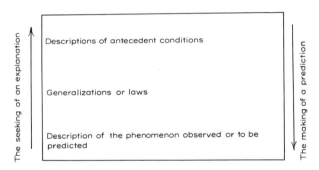

This is a simplification which departs somewhat from its model in "Studies in the Logic of Explanation" by Carl G. Hempel and Paul Oppenheim. In the original a downward arrow at the left depicts the occurrence of the phenomenon as logically deduced from antecedent conditions and general laws.[32]

In planning an experimental or other educational research the researcher will often find it useful to construct a paradigm of his research design. When perfected it may serve as a kind of "production chart" scheduling his mental and other operations.

It may be helpful to the student to turn from the explanation of methods, levels, and other characteristics of scientific inquiry in order to trace actual developments of theory in physics and in the psychology of learning. The student should observe and take some comfort from

[30] Kerlinger, *Foundations of Behavioral Research,* pp. 36–37.

[31] N. L. Gage, "Paradigms for Research on Teaching," in N. L. Gage, ed., *Handbook of Research on Teaching* (Chicago: Rand McNally, 1963), pp. 130–31.

[32] Simplified with the assistance of Hemple and Oppenheim from the original in *Philosophy of Science,* 15:138 (1948). © 1948 by The Williams & Wilkins Co., Baltimore, Md. Reprinted by permission of authors and copyright holder.

the fact that no single scientist did more than make a partial contribution to the theory with which he was concerned. The student in his own research will have made a contribution also, if his research provides a link, albeit a minor one, in the network of theory which may some day be truly a science of education.

ILLUSTRATION OF THEORY BUILDING IN PHYSICS

On a simple level, the pattern of scientific thinking in physics is illustrated by descriptions of a sequence of observations and experiments stemming from initial testing of the hypothesis that air has weight, first suggested by observation of the fact that a suction pump cannot lift water more than 34 feet.[33] In 1643, Torricelli, a disciple of Galileo, invented the simple mercury barometer shown in Figure 2.2. He found

Figure 2.2
A simple mercury barometer

that the weight of the air above the barometer, the atmospheric pressure, would hold up between 29 and 30 inches of mercury. (A water barometer would need to be at least 35 feet high. Mercury is 13.6 times as heavy as water; hence, comparable results are obtained with an instrument a little more than 30 inches high.)

The contributions of Pascal

The great French philosopher and scientist, Pascal, confirmed the truth of Torricelli's hypothesis using the simple mercury barometer. He further hypothesized that since air has weight, its pressure should vary with altitude. In 1648 his brother-in-law Perier tested this hypothesis at different altitudes on the Puy de Dôme mountain in central France while another person checked the height of the mercury in a barometer at the foot of the mountain in order to observe that there was no change. Other checks were made to be sure that changing altitude was the only factor causing the change in the height of the mercury taken up the mountain. Such checks included the taking of barometric readings at different times and places at the top of the mountain, in sunlight and in shade, and inside and outside of an enclosure. These steps amounted to control of variables other than altitude.

---

[33] My sources for the sequence of discovery from Torricelli to Boyle include James B. Conant, *Science and Common Sense* (New Haven, Conn.: Yale University Press, 1951), pp. 63–96; Gerald Holton and Duane H. D. Roller, *Foundations of Modern Physical Science* (Reading, Mass.: Addison-Wesley, 1958); and Edward H. Madden, *Structure of Scientific Thought*, pp. 3–7.

The contributions of Otto von Guericke

About 1650, Otto von Guericke, Mayor of Magdeburg in Germany, actually made a water barometer which projected above the roof of his house. A wooden image floating on the top of the water could be seen by passers-by when the atmospheric pressure was high, but not when it was low. Although this was useful in foretelling fair weather and bad, von Guericke's fellow citizens supposed him to be in league with Satan. Von Guericke invented a vacuum pump and further tested the hypothesis that air has weight and exerts pressure, subsequently discovering that a thin-walled container collapsed from the pressure of the atmosphere when his pump removed most of the air inside the container. He then experimented with large heavy-walled copper hemispheres which were so held together by atmospheric pressure when exhausted by his pump that two teams of eight horses each were unable to pull them apart. They easily fell apart, however, when air was admitted through a valve.

The contributions of Robert Boyle

In 1659 Robert Boyle of Oxford, England, having read of von Guericke's vacuum pump, manufactured one for himself and continued the testing of Torricelli's hypothesis. He sealed the lower part of a mercury barometer inside a spherical glass container connected to a vacuum pump. As the air was progressively exhausted from the container, Boyle observed the fall of the air pressure as measured by the barometer. Later, having observed the relationship qualitatively, he became interested in the problem of finding the quantitative relationship between air pressure and air volume. Boyle formulated the hypothesis that the volume of air is inversely proportional to the pressure (the greater the pressure, the smaller the volume, or the converse). In mathematical form, the relationship may be expressed $PV = K$, where K is a constant. It is assumed that the mass of the gas and the temperature remain unchanged.

Boyle tested his hypothesis using a U-shaped glass tube, the shorter leg of which was sealed. At the start of the experiment, the mercury had the same level in both legs. Therefore, the pressure of the air in the closed leg equaled the pressure on the surface of the mercury in the open leg, which was the atmospheric pressure as measured with a barometer, for example, 29 inches. Then, when enough additional mercury was poured into the open leg of the U-shaped tube to double the pressure, the volume of air in the closed leg decreased by one-half. This experiment is illustrated by the two diagrams in Figure 2.3.

Continued experimentation, varying the height of the mercury and measuring the changing volume, provided further evidence confirming Boyle's hypothesis and justifying its designation as Boyle's Law.

Figure 2.3 Boyle's quantitative experimental investigation of the relation between air pressure and air volume

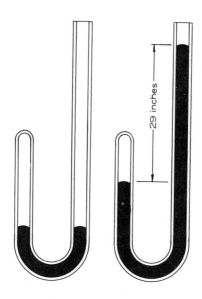

29 inches

The contributions of Charles and of Gay-Lussac

French scientists Jacques Charles in 1787 and Joseph Louis Gay-Lussac in 1802 independently discovered the related law that change in the volume of a gas is directly proportional to change in temperature while the pressure remains unchanged. (The temperature is now measured in absolute degrees, a scale whose zero is −273 degrees centigrade.)

Unifying the laws of Boyle and of Charles or Gay-Lussac

More recently, the two laws discussed above were combined in a mathematical equation from which, given the original volume, absolute temperature, and pressure, the new volume that would result from change in temperature or pressure, or both, can be computed. But this was not the end of the story. The gas law just mentioned is a mathematical model to which only "ideal" gases conform. Its equation is $PV = RT,$ where the constant R pertains to a mass of one mole[34] of the

---

[34] A mole is one gram molecular weight. For example, 2 grams of hydrogen, H_2, 32 grams of oxygen, O_2, or 44 grams of carbon dioxide, CO_2. At standard conditions the volume of each of these gases is 22.4 liters.

gas and to its volume and pressure at standard conditions. *T* is the absolute temperature. Given high pressures and resulting small volumes of highly condensed gases, modification of the law is necessary to take into account the volumes of the gas molecules themselves and their attractions for one another.[35] Thus modified, the ideal gas law becomes van der Waals' Law as represented by the equation:

$$(P + \frac{A}{V^2})(V - B) = RT$$

The terms added are respectively the corrections for molecular attractions and molecular volumes. Van der Waals' equation does not work perfectly, but it does work much more nearly perfectly for high pressures than does the ideal gas law. The preceding discussion illustrates a sequence of discoveries in physics instrumental in organizing and testing hypotheses in one part of that field. The same pattern of scientific methods also occurs in psychology in the development of theories of learning.

ILLUSTRATION OF THEORY BUILDING IN PSYCHOLOGY

As long ago as 1885, Hermann Ebbinghaus, one of the great pioneers of experimental psychology, graphed observational data obtaining points falling along a curve to which he fitted a logarithmic equation containing constants derived from his data. In later years, other experimental psychologists similarly fitted curves to empirically obtained learning data.

Learning curves deduced from theory

While empirically obtained curves are descriptive of learning, they do not tell much about why learning occurs in the ways illustrated. It is now more generally accepted that a mathematical equation should be deduced from theory and then tested with empirical data. For example, in 1930 at the University of Chicago, Professor L. L. Thurstone developed an equation based on assumptions related to Thorndike's law of effect and other theoretical considerations. Predictions based on his equation were satisfactorily confirmed by empirical data. In 1934, Gulliksen further developed the theory, adding constants for "initial strengths of correct and incorrect responses, a constant for the strength added by repeating and rewarding a correct response, and a constant for the strength subtracted by repeating and punishing an

---

[35] These volumes and attractions are constructs. They are not directly observable.

incorrect response."[36] Figure 2.4 is an example of the closeness of fit of empirical or experimental data to Gulliksen's equation:

Figure 2.4 The curve of Gulliksen's equation fitted to data for two rats [Quoted by Hilgard from Harold Gulliksen, "A Rational Equation of the Learning Curve Based on Thorndike's Law of Effect," *Journal of General Psychology* 11:420 (1934).]

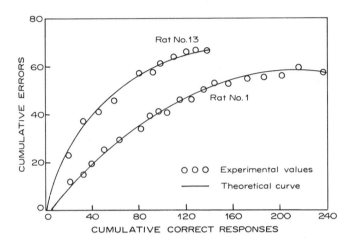

In 1938, Gulliksen and Wolfle extended the equation to cover discrimination learning and subjected it to experimental tests.[37] Note the phraseology of one of their deductions: "The difficulty of a problem, as measured by the maximum level of accuracy attainable, is inversely related to the distance separating the two configurations to be discriminated."[38] Observe that the equations and the modifications obtained by the adding of constants are derived from theory rather than merely from empirical data, though the latter, or experience, is certain to have made contributions in the initial stages of the development of the theory. According to Hilgard the "papers of Thurstone, Gulliksen, and Gulliksen and Wolfle represent a kind of succession, in which each equation is somewhat more general than the preceding one, and the earlier equations can be considered special cases of the later ones."[39] Finally, note the analogy to the development of the theory pertaining to

---

[36] This discussion follows Ernest R. Hilgard, *Theories of Learning,* 2nd ed. (New York: Appleton-Century-Crofts, 1956), pp. 369–75. (Note the 2nd ed. is cited, *not* the 3rd ed.) Reprinted with permission of author and publisher.

[37] Harold Gulliksen and Dael L. Wolfle, "A Theory of Learning and Transfer." *Psychometrika* 3:127–49 and 225–51 (1938).

[38] *Ibid.,* p. 147.

[39] Hilgard, *Theories of Learning,* p. 374.

gases and especially to the formulation of van der Waals' equation or Law. Karl Pearson, indeed, had a point.

THEORY BUILDING IN EDUCATION

The preceding examples have illustrated a parallel between the development of theory in physics and in psychology. Does the parallel extend to education? It is most evident that such a parallel exists in educational psychology and educational sociology, but theory building in education is not restricted to these areas. In recent years it has also begun to characterize research in school administration and in curriculum development.

Although too much descriptive research in education deals with trivial and ephemeral problems, this does not minimize the value of properly conducted descriptive studies. Such research provides a foundation for the development of theory, suggests problems, and provides facts useful in identifying assumptions, postulates, and hypotheses. While the facts obtained in descriptive studies are helpful in the making of educational decisions, the dependable generalizations inferred from adequate testing of hypotheses become even more useful in decision making. They reduce the need for proliferation of descriptive studies on essentially the same problem.[40]

Both facts and generalizations are necessary to decision making in the practice of education. But, in addition, the making of decisions involves the making of value judgments. Our discussion of methods of inquiry will conclude with a look at this aspect of educational research.

Scientific educational research deals with educational problems concerning "what is" and "what will be." Historical educational research presumably is concerned with "what has been." In contrast, philosophical educational research concerns itself, for the most part, with problems of the goals or objectives of education; in other words, with problems of "what should be." In solving curriculum and related instructional problems the "what should be" or values aspect is comparatively easy to see, especially in the case of formulating objectives of instruction and in the selection of instructional materials and methods contributing to these ends. Further discussion of historical and philosophical inquiry in education is postponed to Chapters 14 and 15, but it is desirable at this point to indicate how questions of values and of moral issues are factors in conducting other types of educational research.

The educational researcher is a social scientist. The problems he

---

[40] See Lee J. Cronbach, "The Role of the University in Improving Education," *Phi Delta Kappan* 47:539–45 (June 1966).

selects to study are in part determined by his conception, and the contemporary conception, of what is regarded as socially important. Consider, for example, the contemporary popularity of investigating problems relevant to the education of the culturally disadvantaged.

It is contended that social scientists should "abandon the pretense that they are free from all bias, and that instead they state their value assumptions as explicitly and fully as they can."[41] This, of course, applies as much to the interpretation of data as to the selection of problems for investigation and to educational researchers as much as to other social scientists.

In educational and psychological research, moral issues are involved both in manipulating the subjects of research, and in so collecting personal data as to be guilty of unwarranted invasion of privacy.[42] This should be of concern to any educational researcher collecting data from school pupils. Is one ever justified in asking pupils to provide information concerning family income, attitudes toward parents, or personal sexual problems? To what extent does maintaining security of such data insofar as individual pupils are concerned make such data collecting legitimate?

There is much contemporary discussion of "accountability" and of "performance contracts." The issues present many problems for measurement, descriptive, and experimental research, but essentially they concern *what should be done.* Experts in educational measurement have misgivings about valid measurement of important objectives transcending knowledge or habitual skills and the reliable measurement of gains.

Value judgments are also involved in the making of statistical tests of significance of differences. How high a standard to set depends on how important a decision based on the data will be. A lower level of significance may be acceptable in adopting a method of instruction involving no greater expenditure of time or effort than another method. A high level of significance may be demanded where a decision may crucially affect the future of a student; or example, whether or not he should enroll in an engineering curriculum or major in psychology. These matters are again considered in Chapters 9, 11, and 13.

It is often contended that the social scientist can study objectively the values of his or other cultures. Even here, however, there are the subtle influences of his own values or those of his culture which make

---

[41] Ernest Nagel, *The Structure of Science: Problems in the Logic of Scientific Explanation* (New York: Harcourt, Brace & World, 1961), p. 489. See also his pages 485–502 and Chapter 7 of Madden's anthology, "Science and Values."

[42] This problem has been the subject of congressional investigation. See the November 1965 and May 1966 issues of *American Psychologist.*

it difficult to produce purely descriptive or factual statements. Consider in this connection the frequent appearance in supposedly fact-finding studies of such words or phrases as "maladjusted," "gifted student," "appropriate counseling procedure," and "administrative bureaucracy." If it is any comfort, the physical sciences have their value problems also.

Finally, mention should be made of increasing interest in "process-oriented research," in which the pupils participating in a descriptive or experimental study are observed and tested repeatedly to discover, not only what they have achieved or produced, but the way they have behaved during the period of data collection. Another important change in the realm of educational research is the attention now being shown to educational problems by experts in disciplines other than the professional field of education—psychology, social psychology, sociology, and even anthropology.

Questions for
Study and Discussion

1. What characteristics should a school survey have to be called scientific research?

2. Formulate an hypothesis in the form of an indicative conditional from the last of the generalizations quoted from Hilgard and Bower on page 10.

3. Change the hypothesis you have formulated into a subjunctive conditional. Next, change it to a "counterfactual inference."

4. How would you defend theory from the accusation that it is impractical?

5. Why cannot instructional objectives be determined by scientific research in education alone?

6. What is meant by the terms "metaphysics," "epistemology," and "logical empiricism"?

7. A hypothesis is *deduced* from theory and the relationship between variables it expresses is tested. Why is the conclusion thus obtained called an *inductive* inference?

8. Criticize the statement: Scientific or basic research as contrasted with applied research seeks eternal verities.

9. Why should an operational definition of a construct be called an hypothesis?

10. Devise a paradigm portraying the various elements of a network of theory.

Suggestions
for Further Study

The student is urged to begin thoughtful and continued study of such books and articles as those cited among the selected references concluding this chapter. Writings on the philosophy of science are both technical and controversial. They are challenging, however, and their study contributes to the understanding of science which should characterize those who engage in educational research.

In his reading the student should seek understanding of what is meant by "hypothetico-deductive," "operational definitions and operationism," "models and paradigms," "logical empiricism," "conditional or if-then statements," "contrary-to-fact statements," "reduction sentences," "nomological networks," and "constructs and intervening variables." Certain words used in ordinary speech acquire added and technical meaning in the philosophy of science. Such words include "induction," "deduction," "prediction," "explanation," "causation," and "values."

The selected references listed at the end of each chapter are not an assignment of readings, although it is hoped that the student will soon begin to read the articles and books cited. It is also hoped that the student will continue such reading in the years to come, interested in and alert to new publications of similar content.

Selected References

Benjamin, A. Cornelius. "Is There a Scientific Method?" *Journal of Higher Education* 27 (May 1956): 233–38.

Bergmann, Gustav. *Philosophy of Science.* Madison: University of Wisconsin Press, 1957.

————, and Kenneth W. Spence, "Operationism and Theory in Psychology." *Psychological Review* 48 (January 1941): 1–14.

Braithwaite, Richard B. *Scientific Explanation.* Cambridge: Cambridge University Press, 1953.

Brodbeck, May. "The Philosophy of Science and Educational Research." In "Methodology of Educational Research." *Review of Educational Research* 27 (December 1957): 427–40.

————. "Logic and Scientific Method in Research on Teaching." In *Handbook of Research on Teaching,* edited by N. L. Gage, pp. 44–93. Chicago: Rand McNally, 1963.

Carroll, John B. "Basic and Applied Research in Education: Definitions, Distinctions, and Implications." *Harvard Educational Review* 38 (Spring 1968): 263–76.

Cohen, Morris R. and Ernest Nagel. *An Introduction to Logic and Scientific Method.* New York: Harcourt, Brace & World, 1934.

DiRenzo, Gordon J., ed. *Concepts, Theory, and Explanation in the Behavioral Sciences.* New York: Random House, 1966.

Ennis, Robert H. "Operational Definitions." *American Educational Research Journal* 1 (May 1964): 183–201.

Feigl, Herbert and May Brodbeck, eds. *Readings in the Philosophy of Science.* New York: Appleton-Century-Crofts, 1953.

Frank, Philipp. *Philosophy of Science, the Link Between Science and Philosophy.* Englewood Cliffs, N.J.: Prentice-Hall, 1957.

————, ed. *The Validation of Scientific Theories.* New York: Collier Books, 1961.

Gage, N. L. "Paradigms for Research on Teaching." In *Handbook of Research on Teaching,* edited by N. L. Gage, pp. 94–141. Chicago: Rand McNally, 1963.

Hempel, Carl G. "Fundamentals of Concept Formation in Empirical Science." In *International Encyclopedia of Unified Science,* vol. II, no. 7. Chicago: University of Chicago Press, 1952.

Kaplan, Abraham. *The Conduct of Inquiry: Methodology for Behavioral Science.* San Francisco: Chandler, 1964.

Kerlinger, Fred N. *Foundations of Behavioral Research, Educational and Psychological Inquiry.* New York: Holt, Rinehart, and Winston, 1965. Chapters 1, 2, and 3.

Langer, Susanne K. "On the Relations Between Philosophy and Education." *Harvard Education Review* 26 (Spring 1956): 139–41.
This issue contains other important articles on the same topic.

Maccia, George S. "Hypothetical Thinking in Education." *Educational Theory* 10 (July 1960): 182–86.

Madden, Edward H., ed. *The Structure of Scientific Thought.* Boston: Houghton Mifflin, 1960.

Nagel, Ernest. *The Structure of Science, Problems in the Logic of Scientific Explanation.* New York: Harcourt, Brace & World, 1961.

Northrop, F. S. C. *Logic of the Sciences and the Humanities.* New York: Macmillan, 1947, or Meridian Books, 1959.

Popper, Karl R. *The Logic of Scientific Discovery.* New York: Basic Books, 1959.

Schoeck, Helmut and James W. Wiggins, eds. *Scientism and Values.* Princeton, N.J.: Van Nostrand, 1960.

Scriven, Michael. "The Philosophy of Science in Educational Research." In "Methodology of Educational Research." *Review of Educational Research* 30 (December 1960): 422–29.

———. "Explanations, Predictions, and Laws." *Minnesota Studies in the Philosophy of Science.* vol. 3. Minneapolis: University of Minnesota Press, 1962.

Skinner, B. F. "A Case History in Scientific Method." *American Psychologist* 11 (May 1956): 221–33.
Also in his Cumulative Record. *Appleton-Century-Crofts, 1959. Pp. 76–100.*

Travers, Robert M. W. *An Introduction to Educational Research.* 3rd ed. New York: Macmillan, 1969. Chapters 1 and 2.

Van Dalen, Deobold B. *Understanding Educational Research, An Introduction.* 2nd ed. New York: McGraw-Hill, 1966. Chapters 1–4, 7–8, and Appendices B–H.

3

Selecting and Defining
an Educational
Research Problem

The selection of a problem is the initial step in conducting an educational research. Usually, a number of problems are identified, analyzed, and evaluated before one of them is chosen for investigation.

When a suitable problem has been selected, it should be carefully stated. The problem statement may be a general question followed by subsidiary specific questions or by one or more hypotheses. More than a formal problem statement is needed, however, to clarify the implications of the problem.

The problem statement should be supplemented by definitions of the technical terms it contains. If hypotheses are listed, they should be related to theory. Relevant assumptions and postulates should be stated and explained, usually prior to the problem statement. It is often desirable to specify limitations on the scope of a problem. Finally, there should be specification of the sources of data and the techniques to be used in collecting and interpreting them.

Most of the process here outlined may be called "stating and defining a problem." The total process begins with the selection and stating of a problem and ends with a plan for its research. In written form such a plan can be most or all of the content of a thesis proposal. It can later become the major source of content in the first chapter of a thesis. Similar planning should characterize educational research other than thesis research.

SOURCES OF THESIS PROBLEMS

The graduate student in education, expected to produce a thesis in partial fulfillment of the requirements for his degree, usually finds it a most difficult task to select a suitable problem for his thesis. This is especially true if he is not participating in some general research project in which the project director may permit a choice among several problems subordinate to the project's general one. The student working independently may arrive at a problem through discussion with the professor who is to act as his thesis advisor. Usually during such discussion, the advisor will encourage effort on the part of the student himself to propose one or more potentially suitable thesis problems for evaluation.

Educational literature as a source of problems

Consideration is given here to the kinds of reading useful in discovering a problem, in judging its suitability, and in relating it to earlier research and theory. Acquainting students with sources to be consulted when searching for a thesis problem and in planning a thesis or other research will be further developed in Chapter 4.

The values of wide reading

The graduate student in education seeking a problem for his own thesis research will find it extremely helpful to read widely in the area of his interests, always alert to content which may help him to identify a suitable problem. This reading should include textbook discussions, the later chapters in the *Handbook of Research on Teaching,* yearbooks of the National Society for the Study of Education, articles in the *Encyclopedia of Educational Research,* and summaries of research in the *Review of Educational Research.* In the case of the *Encyclopedia of Educational Research* the student should not restrict himself to the most recent edition. He may find it useful to supplement his reading in the 1969 edition, for instance, by reading articles on the same or related topics in the 1960 or earlier editions. Similarly, if the student has found a particular chapter in a recent issue of the *Review of Educational Research* helpful in his exploration for a problem he should seek similar chapters in earlier issues on the same general topic, knowing that such issues have usually occurred in three-year intervals. When the student has decided upon a problem, the sources just mentioned become those most useful to him when compiling his own bibliography.

The fields of psychology and sociology have contributed importantly to the solution of educational problems and to the development of a science of education. The study of instructional problems is aided by an understanding of learning and motivational theory. In seeking solutions to instructional problems of the culturally disadvantaged, for example, an understanding of relevant sociological theory is a necessity. Wide reading in the fields of psychology or sociology will not only provide background knowledge useful to the graduate student who has already selected an instructional or learning problem, but can help a student to discover a suitable problem for his own research.

Similarly, in preparation for research in the field of school administration, the student may benefit from background knowledge in political science and in economics. The solution of curriculum problems, especially problems of formulating educational objectives, requires a background in educational theory or philosophy. The solution of historical problems requires knowledge of the general history of the period, the history of education of the period, and understanding of the techniques of historical research or historiography.

The values of intensive study

Critical reading of research studies may alert the student to the need for replication of a certain study using improved or superior techniques. Sometimes the replication may be the conducting of a similar study, but with a different population or in a different subject field. Often the last paragraph of a report of research will suggest a need for further related research. While such reading of research studies can thus be helpful, similar reading of theoretical discussions can also be a means of discovering a problem. Furthermore, as a student narrows his focus on a problem, relevant theory helps to formulate an adequate problem statement. Study of theory also aids in the stating of assumptions and postulates, the formulating of hypotheses, and the defining of terms. Intensive study of the earlier research on a problem may enable the student to identify hypotheses whose further confirmation or whose rejection will contribute to theory building. Study of earlier research also aids in planning new research concerned with sources of data and techniques to be used in collecting, summarizing, and interpreting such data.

A critical summary of earlier research is usually expected in a thesis and—more briefly—in a thesis proposal. References to earlier studies, to separate discussions of theory, and to the notes taken while reading them are useful materials in writing such a summary. See pages 80–82 for more information on this topic.

Professional experience as a source of thesis problems

Often graduate students who have had professional experience in school administration, counseling, or teaching are interested in undertaking thesis research on some problem originating in their professional experience. Wide reading as described above, which ranges over discussions of contemporary educational events and issues, is very useful in supplementing professional experience. Such reading accompanied by intensive study of relevant theory and research can help to clarify the problem originally stemming from professional experience, and will sometimes result in the selection of a related, but more suitable problem.

Interest and ability as factors in selecting a problem

The student's degree of interest in a problem is of great importance in motivating his efforts to solve it. Interesting problems, however, are difficult problems. Much of the thought and effort required in their solution is sufficiently challenging and rewarding to sustain interest, but most of the work is not so enjoyable. Frustrating difficulties arise from time to time. The time-consuming chores of tabulating and computing may be necessary. The student's interest and motivation must be high and of such permanence as to maintain continuous effort to the end.

More than interest needs to be considered, however. A student may select a problem inappropriate to his abilities. Obviously, without a reading knowledge of some foreign language, he should not undertake a historical educational research for which ability to read the language is a necessity. Similarly, a graduate student should not undertake research on certain educational problems requiring a high level of understanding of advanced psychological or sociological theory unless he is willing to devote the time necessary to acquiring such understanding. Sometimes an ill-advised graduate student collects data and then finds that he does not have command of the statistical techniques required for organizing and interpreting them. Acquisition of such skills should be anticipated before the graduate student commits himself to such thesis research.

Although a student may expect his data to be computer analyzed, he should acquire understanding of what the machine does for him. If, for example, the student supplies the computer with series of scores on several tests and is later supplied with means, standard deviations, regression coefficients, a multiple-correlation coefficient, and a standard error of estimate, he should be able to demonstrate his understanding of the theory of such an analysis of his data and the meaning of each of the statistics named. Primarily he needs to know why the computer supplied the results obtained rather than how it was able to do so. In this connection, it should also be said that the educational researcher who anticipates that his data will be analyzed for him by a computer should consult a computer specialist *before* collecting his data, preferably when planning his study, so that the data will be collected in such form as to facilitate analysis by the computer. Even the student so trained in data processing that he can write his own program will benefit from consultation with professional data processors.

Practical considerations in selecting a problem

When selecting a problem the student should carefully decide whether or not the time he can devote to a solution is sufficient for the scope of the problem. He must consider whether or not he can expend the effort required for the collection and analysis of the necessary data. He must judge whether or not he can afford the expense involved in the data collection and in their analysis. Test material and test scoring, for example, are expensive. Finally, the student must know, prior to committing himself to a problem, whether or not the data can be obtained from appropriate sources.

If interviewing is to be used in collecting data, can the student afford the time and travel expense necessary? Collecting of data from school records, or through administration of tests or questionnaires to school pupils or to school personnel, necessitates obtaining permissions from school administrators. The securing of cooperation of other school personnel including teachers is also essential. Investigation of some problems requires consent of the subjects' parents for the collection of certain types of data. In conducting a historical educational research the student may find that the data he must collect are not readily available, but can only be collected in another state or country. All of these matters should be considered before the student commits himself to a problem. A typical statement in a graduate school catalogue is that the thesis title may change, but the problem never!

Must a thesis research be a contribution?

It is often emphasized that a thesis research should be "an original contribution." Although the skeptic is probably justified in holding that few theses actually deserve this label, the student should strive toward this goal. However, what the thesis research does for the student is equally important. If the thesis research serves to enhance the student's understanding of his professional field, gives him an abiding interest in his problem and a stimulus to further research in the area, and results in knowledge and appreciation of scientific methods and attitudes, his degree is deserved.

SOURCES OF PROBLEMS FOR CITY SCHOOL AND COLLEGE BUREAUS OR DEPARTMENTS OF RESEARCH

Some mention should be made of sources of problems studied by bureaus of research in city school systems or by divisions of institutional research in colleges or universities. Such organizations do not usually originate the problems they investigate. In general, administrative or instructional staff members propose the problems. They may be administrative or instructional ones; or they may be relevant to admissions, placement, and guidance. They may concern evaluation of the comparative effectiveness of differing instructional methods or materials. They may be problems whose solution will improve the tests given at the time of entrance, or those given to evaluate achievement in order to determine more valid and reliable course marks. They may be problems requiring the testing of hypotheses deduced from theory whose solution will contribute to the science of education. The major criterion, however, in the selection of problems is the relevance of the problem to the educational program of the school system or higher institution.

Promoting awareness of institutional problems

While all or most of the problems to be investigated should originate with administrative, instructional, or counseling personnel it may be helpful to indicate some of the kinds of problems with which the research organization can be usefully concerned. For example, some years ago, I distributed the following problem suggestions to stimulate interest in institutional research in the Chicago City Junior College (now the City Colleges of Chicago). It was assumed that decisions with reference to which of the problems should most immediately be studied would be made by the administrative officers or other personnel of the College:

1. What factors are related to student retention in the College? To what extent is retention related to student abilities as measured on entrance to the College? To what extent do superior students transfer to other institutions prior to obtaining a junior college certificate of graduation or associate in arts degree? To what extent are below-average students retained?

2. To what extent do the instructional staffs in the required courses in the program of general education have clearly defined instructional objectives? To what extent do instructional objectives range from information or knowledge, through intellectual or critical thinking skills, to attitudes, ideals, and interests? To what extent is there coordination of instruction in the various general courses within each branch and within the College as a whole?

3. How useful are the data collected on entrance in the placement and guidance of junior college students? What improvements can be made in testing at the time of entrance?

4. What are the possibilities of team teaching in the junior college? Should such teaching characterize instruction in the general courses? What use should be made of TV instruction for resident students? Should greater use be made of audio-visual aids and programed instructional materials?

5. What are the characteristics of parttime and evening students? What proportion of such students continue to graduation from the junior college? What are the special problems of such students?

6. Should there be greater differentiation of instruction for stu-

dents of below-average, average, and above-average ability on entrance to the junior college? Should there be a uniform program of basic or remedial instruction in all branches for less able entrants? Similarly, should there be higher level instruction for superior entrants?

7.   What happens to students graduating from the College? What is their success in higher institutions? What is their vocational success? What is their evaluation of the education they received in the College?

Distribution of a similar list may stimulate interest in research in a city school system. School administrators, teachers, and counselors can be made more alert to problems whose solutions will contribute to improvement of their own educational programs.

Promoting the cooperation of school personnel

It should be pointed out that nothing is more likely to promote cooperation in the collection of data in public schools or in higher institutions than a clearly and completely defined problem. It should include precise specifications referring to just what data need to be collected and just how much time and effort will need to be supplied by administrators, teachers, and pupils or students. No unanticipated additional requests for data should be made during the conducting of a research study. In general, there is no better way to irritate a school administrator. Large city school systems, for example, Chicago's, insist that a research proposal to be considered for clearance include the above-specified information. In process-oriented research, the researcher should indicate at the start that he may discover need for additional data, but he should clear again when such need arises.

After the data have been collected the participating school administrators and teachers should receive a summary of the findings and the thanks of the researcher. What is said above is applicable to thesis research as well as to research conducted within a school system or higher institution.

WAYS OF STATING A PROBLEM

An educational research problem may be stated in declarative or question form, either form implying a question to be answered by the study. For example:

The purpose of this research is to investigate the relative effectiveness of team teaching and single-teacher instruction in the sixth grade.

What is the relative effectiveness of team teaching and single-teacher instruction in the sixth grade?

As indicated above, problems can usually be stated more concisely in question form. This form seems preferable to the declarative one, unless there is good reason to use both with respect to the same problem. In such cases, the declarative statement may serve to introduce the question. This is illustrated by the following example from the report of an experiment conducted by Cameron:

> The primary purpose of this study was to determine the effect of feedback in learning principles of educational psychology. A basic question was: What will be the differential effect of systematically informing one group of students of the correctness and incorrectness of their classroom responses, and not providing such information for a control group?[1]

It may be noted that the question elaborates on the problem. It implies the hypothesis to be tested.

An illustration of the use of a series of questions

In a descriptive or survey type of research a series of questions is useful in planning a questionnaire, an interview schedule, or in deciding what tests to use in collecting data. The use of a declarative statement of purpose accompanied by a series of specific questions is illustrated in a survey-type study reported by Horton:

> The major purpose of this investigation was to study the problems of beginning principals as a basis for improving the program for the preparation of school principals. The data obtained centered upon the following:
>
> (1) What are the nature, scope, and frequency of the problems encountered by beginning principals as recognized by teachers, principals, and superintendents?
>
> (2) How do the problems of beginning principals compare when viewed by teachers, principals, and superintendents?
>
> (3) How universally are the problems felt?
>
> (4) What changes in the nature and frequency of problems occur during the year? . . .[2]

---

[1] Howard K. Cameron, "The Effectiveness of Feedback in Teaching Principles of Educational Psychology," *Journal of Experimental Education* 34 (Spring 1966), p. 53. Reprinted with permission of author and publisher.

[2] Ben Horton, "A Study of the Problems of Beginning Principals as a Basis for Improvement of the Program for the Education of Principals at Appalachian State Teachers College," *Educational Administration and Supervision* 44 (September 1958), pp. 261 and 262. Reprinted with permission of publisher.

An illustration of the use of several hypotheses

After stating that his research was "designed to examine, in an explorative fashion, both the sociocultural and psychodynamic factors involved in withdrawal from the academic milieu"[3] or, more simply, factors in dropping out of high school, Cervantes listed the following hypotheses:

> (1) The dropout is reared in a family that has less solidarity, less primary relatedness, and less paternal influence than the family in which the graduate is reared.
>
> (2) The dropout is brought up in a family that has fewer close friends and fewer "problem-free" friends than the family in which the graduate is brought up.
>
> (3) The dropout's personal friends are typically not approved by his parents. The resulting "independent youth culture" of the dropout is in sharp contrast to the youth culture of the graduates, whose friends are approved by his parents and thus integrated with the adult culture.
>
> (4) The dropout was in trouble at school when he terminated his education and was but slightly involved in any school-related activities throughout his academic career.
>
> (5) Our hypothesis is that the phantasy life of the dropout as manifested by the TAT is more characterized by unrestrained Id themes and that of the graduate more characterized by restrained superego themes. The youth culture of the dropout will prove to be a culture of revolution, aggression, frustration, and protest; in the words of Conant, it will be found to be "explosive . . . it is social dynamite."[4]

In an experimental evaluation of materials or methods of instruction the subordinate questions or hypotheses may designate the kinds of educational achievement to be evaluated; for example, (1) knowledge and understandings, (2) critical thinking skills in the area, and (3) attitudes, ideals, and interests. In a well-written research, conclusions in the same order will constitute the investigator's answers to the questions stated or implied at the beginning of his report whether the research is an experiment, a survey, or some other type. Where several hypotheses are listed in a problem statement, conclusions in the same sequence may be restatements of the hypotheses, accompanied by information concerning their confirmation or rejection.

---

[3] Lucius F. Cervantes, *The Dropout: Causes and Cures* (Ann Arbor: University of Michigan Press, © 1965), p. 6. Reprinted with permission of publisher.

[4] *Ibid.,* p. 8. For a brief summary see my review in *Science* 148 (May 7, 1965), pp. 788–89.

Illustrations of research hypotheses and null hypotheses

The following hypotheses are quoted from the report of Hani Van De Riet's experimental study of the effects of praise and reproof on paired-associate learning in educationally retarded children:

> For educationally retarded children, praise results in a significantly larger number of trials to reach criterion on the second task than does reproof because success constitutes a threat.
>
> For normal children, praise results in a significantly smaller number of trials to reach criterion than does reproof.[5]

Hypotheses of the type just illustrated may be called research hypotheses. Such hypotheses represent tentative solutions to a problem and are of service in thinking about the problem. They constitute ideas to be tested through the collection and interpretation of data. They are best deduced from theory relevant to the problem.

Hypotheses as conditional statements or propositions in the form "if A, then B" were discussed in Chapter 2. The two hypotheses quoted above imply this form though they are not explicitly stated in this way. The first of the two hypotheses can, for example, be rephrased: "If retarded children are praised rather than reproved, more trials will be required to reach criterion because success constitutes a threat."

Often the hypotheses listed in the statement of a problem are stated as "null" hypotheses.[6] Such hypotheses are useful in the testing of the significance of differences and need not appear in the statement of a problem. The research or tentative solution type of hypothesis may be, for example, that some new method of instruction is more effective than a method currently used. The corresponding null hypothesis would be that there is no difference in their effectiveness. If the statistical analysis justifies rejection of the null hypothesis, it may be inferred that the alternative hypothesis—the tentative solution—can be accepted as supported by the data and, hence, will become a conclusion in the report of the research. In presenting his interpretation of his data, an experimenter may write "we reject the null hypothesis," without explicitly stating it. He may then continue with a restatement of his tentative or research hypothesis noting that it is supported by his data.

Despite the above, however, null hypotheses are sometimes listed

---

[5] Hani Van De Riet, "Effects of Praise and Reproof on Paired-Associate Learning in Educationally Retarded Children," *Journal of Educational Psychology* 55 (June 1964), p. 139. Reprinted with permission of author.

[6] For further discussion of null hypotheses see Chapter 9.

in problem statements. In the report of an experiment they conducted, Bartz and Darby state:

> The present study was designed to investigate the effects of a programed text under traditional and independent study techniques for an entire college semester upon the achievement of students enrolled for credit in a mathematics course. It was hypothesized that the achievement of students who used a programed text would *not* differ from the achievement of students using a non-programed text. Further, it was hypothesized that the achievement of students under traditional and independent study would *not* differ. (Italics mine.)[7]

It can be argued that it is more objective to present a null hypothesis in a problem statement than one of the tentative solution type. The experimenters cited above show no bias in their problem statement toward any of the compared methods of instruction. Some authorities advocate the formulation of alternative hypotheses as a means of avoiding excessive commitment to a single hypothesis. Use of the null hypothesis and the "two-tailed" test of significance is similar in effect to stating alternative and contradictory research hypotheses—one favoring each method.

Must hypotheses be stated?

In many reports of survey-type research hypotheses are not stated. Where the problem is one of describing practices or conditions without concern for relationships, the problem does not call for the testing of hypotheses. In reports of such studies, problems are typically found in question or declarative form followed by subordinate questions. If a survey involves study of relationships between the variables measured, or generalizations are drawn from samples to a larger population, hypotheses are stated or implied.

The absence of explicitly stated hypotheses is characteristic of reports of historical or philosophical research in education. This does not mean, of course, that researchers in these fields do not formulate and test hypotheses. They do, but the reader of the reports of their research often must infer the nature of the hypotheses tested from the generalizations stated.

The title of a thesis or other research report

A title should convey to a reader sufficient information to enable him to decide whether it is relevant to an area in which he is interested. The title should imply or suggest the problem of a research. I recall a mono-

---

[7] Wayne H. Bartz and Charles L. Darby, "The Effects of a Programed Textbook on Achievement Under Three Techniques of Instruction," *Journal of Experimental Education* 34 (Spring 1966), p. 46. Reprinted with permission of authors and publisher.

graph publication of a Ph.D. thesis entitled "Educational Insurance." On locating the monograph it was discovered to be a study of the effect on English composition achievement of high school students resulting from the basing of their marks in English on ratings of their writings in high school courses *other than English.* This device *insured* greater English composition achievement. Consider the reaction, however, of administrators interested in the problem of insuring school personnel after taking the trouble to locate this publication.

The time to decide on a title is after a problem has been stated in final form. The key words or phrases in the problem statement will usually provide the basis for a brief, but adequate, title.

DEFINING OR CLARIFYING A PROBLEM

Defining terms in a problem statement

While it is essential to phrase problem statements, questions, and hypotheses with care, the meanings of certain important terms may need to be clarified by precise definitions following the problem statement. For example, consider the problem: "What are the relative contributions of intelligence, educational opportunity, and socioeconomic status to individual differences in educational achievement?" This problem appears to have fairly definite meaning, but no typical single research study conducted in an attempt to solve it would provide a general solution. If several investigators attempted to answer the question, it is probable that their conclusions would vary considerably. Much would depend on the various definitions that they gave to the terms "contribution," "intelligence," "educational opportunity," "socioeconomic status," and "educational achievement." Differing meanings would have influenced the nature of the data collected and the techniques used in collecting and interpreting them. The problem as stated says nothing concerning the population studied. It seems to imply that the solution will apply to pupils in general. The variation in conclusions may thus be the resultant of collection of data pertaining to different populations, none of which is representative of "pupils in general."

In the case of the problem just suggested the investigator may give meaning to the terms "intelligence" and "educational achievement" by naming the tests he plans to use. Similarly, he may give meaning to "educational opportunity" and "socioeconomic status" by specifying the kinds of data he plans to collect. "Contributions" may be clarified by specifying that they are to be evaluated as proportions of the variation, or variance, of the dependent variable "educational achievement," to be attributed to the other, or independent, variables named.[8] Finally,

---

[8] For explanation of such analysis see Chapter 11, pages 339 to 341.

the researcher may specify the pupil population from which the pupils participating are drawn at random. Given such additional information the reader of the research report is better able to judge to what type of pupil population the conclusions or generalizations apply.

Defining variables studied in terms of the tests or other instruments used in collecting data may suffice where their validity is well established but, where this is not the case, it is often necessary to present or refer to evidences of validity.[9] It is frequently desirable to give an explicit definition of the trait, or traits, studied. In her study of creativity in educational administration, Elizabeth Antley defined "creativity" as follows:

> *Creativity:* A behavior pattern which includes the following factors: sensitivity to problems, perception, fluency, novel ideas, flexibility of mind (ease with which one changes set), synthesizing ability, analyzing ability, reorganizational or redefinition ability, complexity or intricacy of conceptual structure of which one is capable, motivational factors, attitudes, and temperament.[10]

Similarly, in experimentation with differing educational treatments these should be defined in behavioral terms. (Just what behaviors are expected by the teacher and the pupils.) Observational records obtained during the experiment may require modification of the original definitions used in directing the experiment. This is further discussed in Chapter 12.[11]

Relating hypotheses to theory

When the statement of a problem includes hypotheses deduced from theory it is advisable in defining the problem to relate the hypotheses to the theory. For example, in Hani Van De Riet's study of the effects of praise and reproof, the first hypothesis earlier quoted suggests that praise may *not* motivate the learning of educationally retarded children. She points out:

> If need to fail is present in children with learning disabilities, then it would be expected that praise of their performance would be experienced

---

[9] See page 54 for an example.

[10] Elizabeth Martin Antley, "Creativity in Educational Administration," *Journal of Experimental Education* 34 (Summer 1966), p. 21. Reprinted with permission of publisher. Her definition is based on J. P. Guilford, "Creativity," *American Psychologist* 5 (September 1950), pp. 444–54.

[11] See page 388.

as threatening and would act as a detriment to further learning. Indeed, the factor of level of achievement may be one of the uncontrolled variables which contributes to the contradictory results of prior research on the effects of praise and reproof on learning.[12]

An appropriate place to relate a problem to theory is in conjunction with a summary of the previous research on a problem,[13] either with the statement and definition of the problem, or in the second chapter of a lengthy research report or thesis. The former is illustrated in Cameron's study of the effectiveness of feedback in teaching principles of educational psychology:

> Among psychologists there is widespread acceptance of the principle that immediately provided feedback has a positive influence on learning and/or performance of students. According to Greenspoon and Foreman, immediate feedback is thought to reduce the possible interference which might result if the interval between response and feedback were of a longer duration. Chansky states that the schedules and types of feedback students receive are significantly related to verbal learning. It has also been stated that feedback among or between students can lead to desirable changes in behavior in the same manner as feedback from the classroom instructor.
>
> Skinner believes that feedback is influenced in controlling the probability of subsequent student behavior, and suggests various feedback schedules for specific learning conditions and objectives. Michael and Maccoby summarize their data by stating that students who received feedback scored significantly higher on a test measuring knowledge of a film viewed than students who received no feedback. In reviewing experimental studies concerned with the influence of feedback in motor learning (under laboratory conditions) Bilodeau and Bilodeau state: "Studies of feedback of knowledge of results (KR) show it to be the strongest, most important variable controlling performance and learning. It has been shown repeatedly, as well as recently, that there is no improvement without KR, no progressive improvement without it, and there is deterioration after its withdrawal. A number of studies show that performance is seriously disrupted or made impossible by lags in feedback of even less than 1.0 second." Not only is it considered important to provide feedback for the responses of students, but several of the investigators above emphasize that if it is to be effective, it should immediately follow the response. These studies also indicate that the role of feedback depends on how frequently a given response receives feedback. In the study reported herein provisions will be made for ensuring the existence of frequent and

---

[12] Van De Riet, "Effects of Praise," p. 139.

[13] See Chapter 4 for further discussion of this topic.

immediate feedback for experimental subjects via the teaching technique and class size.[14]

Recognizing assumptions

In clarifying a problem and in relating it to theory, it is desirable to give explicit recognition to assumptions. This is admirably illustrated in David G. Ryans' report of his research on characteristics of teachers. After defining the term "teacher behavior," Ryans states as his first basic assumption, "Teacher behavior is a function of situational factors and characteristics of the individual teacher."[15] He then lists and explains several postulates related to this assumption, for example:

> Teacher behavior is characterized by some degree of consistency.
> Teacher behavior is characterized by a limited number of responses.
> Teacher behavior is a function of general features of the situation in which it takes place.
> Teacher behavior is a function of the specific situation in which it takes place.[16]

Ryans then states as his second basic assumption, "Teacher behavior is observable" and lists three postulates:

> Teacher behaviors are distinguishable.
> Teacher behaviors are classifiable qualitatively and quantitatively.
> Teacher behaviors are revealed through overt behavior and also by symptoms or correlates of behavior.[17]

The two assumptions and related postulates are followed by a series of "propositions" illustrative of the kinds of hypotheses tested by data collected in the *Teacher Characteristics Study*. For example:

> General classes of teacher classroom behaviors fall into relatively homogeneous clusters characterized by substantial intercorrelation of behaviors within a cluster. Teacher behavior *in toto* may be described in terms of a limited number of such major clusters of behaviors.
> The major clusters or families formed by teacher behaviors have the

---

[14] Cameron, "Effectiveness of Feedback," p. 53. Quote from Edward and Ina Bilodeau, "Motor Skill Learning," *Annual Review of Psychology* 12 (1960), p. 250, is reprinted with permission of publisher.

[15] David G. Ryans, *Characteristics of Teachers,* Washington, D.C.: American Council on Education, 1960, p. 16. Reprinted with permission of author and publisher.

[16] *Ibid.,* pp. 19 and 21.

[17] *Ibid.,* pp. 21–23.

characteristics of *dimensions*. Individual teachers, in their manifestations of a particular behavior pattern, vary along a continuum between two behaviorally describable poles.

Reliable estimates of teacher behavior constituting a major cluster (positions along a major dimension) may be obtained through assessments derived from the observations of trained observers.[18]

The beginner in educational research may feel that the illustrative material just cited makes the recognition of assumptions a formidable task. For less elaborate researches than the *Teacher Characteristics Study* much less attention to assumptions may be appropriate, but essential ones should be stated. In addition to those relevant to the problem and its related theory, assumptions and postulates need to be recognized with reference to the collection and interpretation of data. Ryans' second assumption and its postulates are clearly relevant to the collection of data. Similar examples may include the assumption that "intelligence" is measured by a typical group intelligence test and the assumption that an objective achievement test in arithmetic measures arithmetical "ability." (Ability is inferred from data relevant to arithmetic achievement, an overt behavior.) In interpreting data it is expected that the statistical formulas used will be appropriate in terms of assumptions concerning the data. As will be explained in Chapter 13, application of the analysis of variance and covariance techniques implies that the data satisfy (or reasonably satisfy) the assumptions of "normality," "homogeneity of variance," and "homogeneity of regression." The careful researcher tests his data to determine how well such assumptions are satisfied.

Limiting the scope of a study

In addition to clarifying the meanings of the terms included in the statement of a problem, to relating hypotheses to the theory with which they are associated, and to giving recognition to assumptions, it is sometimes important to specify limitations to the scope of the problem. Such a restriction in the scope of a problem appears in Lehmann's report of his research on changes in critical thinking, attitudes, and values during four years of higher education:

> The purpose of this paper is not to demonstrate whether college aids or facilitates the development of attitudes and values, nor are we concerned at this time with identifying those factors which might have an impact upon student personality development. We are primarily concerned with studying what changes, if any, occur in college students' critical thinking

---

[18] *Ibid.,* p. 25.

ability; attitudes of stereotypy and dogmatism; traditional value orientation; and religious, social, and political views from their freshmen to senior years.[19]

OTHER ESSENTIALS IN A RESEARCH PROPOSAL
Specifying techniques used in collecting data

The nature of Lehmann's research is further clarified by his excellent descriptions of the instruments used to collect his data:

Inventory of Beliefs (American Council on Education, 1950)

Test of Critical Thinking (American Council on Education, 1953)

Differential Values Inventory (Prince, 1957)

Dogmatism Scale (Rokeach, 1960)

Experience Inventory (locally constructed)

Each of these measuring instruments is discussed separately with emphasis on characteristics relevant to its validity. The second of these statements can serve as an example:

> A second instrument used was the Test of Critical Thinking (American Council on Education, 1953) which consists of 52 verbal, situational type problems designed to measure five factors thought to be involved in critical thinking: the ability to (a) define a problem, (b) select pertinent information, (c) recognize stated and unstated assumptions, (d) formulate and select relevant hypotheses, and (e) draw valid conclusions. It would be expected that an effective general education course would cause students to raise their scores.[20]

Similar brief specifications should appear in a research proposal with reference to other data-collecting techniques. A student may state, for instance, that his data are to be collected by means of a questionnaire distributed under the sponsorship of the state educational association, and that the questionnaire data will be supplemented by interview data to evaluate the representativeness and reliability of the questionnaire data.

Specifying sources of data

In addition to describing the tests or other means used in collecting data, it is essential in adequately defining a problem to designate the

---

[19] Irvin J. Lehmann, "Changes in Critical Thinking, Attitudes and Values from the Freshman to Senior Years," *Journal of Educational Psychology* 54 (December 1963), p. 306. Reprinted with permission of author.

[20] *Ibid.,* p. 306. From the description quoted above one might suppose that this instrument could be used as a pretest and posttest for students studying this chapter.

prospective sources of data. Such information enables the reader of a thesis or other research proposal to judge the kind of population of schools, teachers, or pupils to which the generalizations later derived from the data will apply. The researcher may say, for example, "Three groups of 35 sixth-grade pupils each in a random sample of 15 of the 92 elementary schools of Metropolis, Ohio, will participate in this experiment. The groups in each school will be assigned at random to the compared instructional methods . . . " In a survey-type study the researcher may say "Data will be collected by means of a questionnaire sent to the superintendents of schools in all cities in the United States with populations ranging from 25,000 to 100,000." In an historical research, the investigator may say "The data concerning subjects offered by private school masters in colonial Massachusetts will be obtained by reading all of the advertisements of such school masters in newspapers published in Massachusetts between 1750 and 1775."[21]

Specifying the techniques to be used in interpreting data

In a thesis research of the historical or philosophical type, a student may satisfy his advisor that he is ready to undertake such research without specifying in advance just how his data will be interpreted. For a survey-type study, however, a student can explain how his numerical or quantitative data will be organized and summarized to yield descriptive generalizations. If there are to be hypotheses tested, relevant to variables which will be quantitatively measured, it is desirable to specify the type of analysis to which the data will be subjected if, when collected, the data can satisfy certain assumptions. In the case of an experimental research, the student may specify that methods by levels analysis of variance will be used. Often, in such cases, a section of the proposal will be given the title "Experimental Design" and the plan of the analysis will be explained in some detail so that it can more readily be evaluated by a thesis advisor, or other persons concerned about the contemplated research.

Specifying data limitations

The educational research worker should seek to collect the best data obtainable for the solution of his problem. Even so, however, the data are likely to be in some respects faulty. There may be variable errors of measurement and of sampling, or systematic error of measurement, validity, and sampling. The data may be, in whole or in part, a substitute for data impossible to collect which would be more appropriate in solving the problem. The researcher should recognize and evaluate the possible effects of these data limitations on the dependability of his

---

[21] For a reference to an example of such research see pages 455–456.

conclusions. For example, a decision with respect to the size of the sample to be studied requires consideration of the relation of sample size to the magnitude of sampling errors. It should be the purpose of the investigator to reduce or account for data faults so that the conclusions he derives will be defensible. When defining a problem, mention should be made of anticipated limitations of the data and in the report of the research, as just suggested, the data limitations should be taken into account.

Distinguishing between conclusions and recommendations

A very important consideration in defining certain educational research problems concerns the distinction between the scientific and the philosophical. Many educational problems are both scientific and philosophical. Consider the question, "Should ability grouping be employed as a means of dealing with individual differences?" The scientific aspects of this problem pertain to the nature and amount of the effects of ability grouping on individual differences. When the effects of ability grouping have been determined, whether or not ability grouping *should* be used depends upon the values attached to the effects identified and measured. The application of the conclusions of educational research to the practice of education almost always involves a transformation of the problem to the practical and immediate concern with what should be done.

When recommendations are included in a report of research, they should follow conclusions or generalizations based directly on the data. In stating the problem of the research, such words as "ought" and "should" are to be avoided. If the making of recommendations is an objective of the research, this should be noted apart from the statement of a scientific problem in a thesis or other research proposal.

CONCLUSION

Clearly stated problems in reports of educational research promote the development of the science of education. They aid future researchers to synthesize the findings of earlier research. They facilitate the identification of the studies whose conclusions should be brought together and critically evaluated in arriving at a generalization supported by the research thus analyzed. Such generalizations become a part of theory until modified or discarded by future research. Meanwhile they remain a portion of the body of tested knowledge comprising the science of education.

Questions for
Study and Discussion

1. Why are hypotheses often absent from the problem statements of survey-type educational research?

2. List several problems that might be investigated by the research bureau of a small city school system.

3. Give some examples of terms which might appear in a problem statement for which operational definitions would be appropriate.

4. What kind of generalizations would result from confirmation of Cervantes' hypotheses?

5. How would you state Cervantes' hypotheses in the form of "If A, then B" statements? If the hypotheses were thus stated, how would you go about testing them?

6. Select some area of interest to you—administration, supervision, counseling, or some school subject—and list several problems or issues that you feel need research.

7. In what circumstances do you feel that a research report can appropriately include a list of recommendations?

8. List in appropriate order the topics you think should characterize a well organized thesis proposal.

9. Consider the problem—"What is the effect of weekly tests on school achievement?"
   (a) Restate this problem in a way which will limit its scope.
   (b) State one or more hypotheses relevant to your reformulated problem.
   (c) To what psychological theory is your reformulated problem related?
   (d) What type of research is most appropriate for investigating this problem?

10. Discuss the major themes of *Research for Tomorrow's Schools: Disciplined Inquiry for Education* including "Some Paths for Future Inquiry."

Selected References

Carmichael, Leonard, and others. "Child Development Research: The Next Twenty-five Years." *Child Development* 31 (March 1960): 191–208.

Carroll, John B. "Neglected Areas in Educational Research." *Phi Delta Kappan* 42 (May 1961): 339–46.

Cartwright, William H. "The Teacher in 2065." *Teachers College Record* 66 (January 1965): 295–304.

Chansky, Norman M. "Problems of Research in Reading." *Journal of Developmental Reading* 7 (Winter 1964): 102–19.

Coladarci, Arthur P., and others. "Research Priorities in Educational Administration." *Journal of Educational Research* 47 (April 1954): 625–30.

Cronbach, Lee J., and Patrick Suppes, eds. *Research for Tomorrow's Schools: Disciplined Inquiry for Education.* New York: Macmillan, 1969.

Knox, Alan B. "Current Needs in Adult Education Research." *Journal of Education* 147 (February 1965): 21–31.

Leonard, Regis J. "Guidance in 1975." *Journal of Educational Sociology* 36 (January 1963): 229–36.

Price, Roy A., ed. *Needed Research in the Teaching of the Social Studies.* National Council for the Social Studies Research Bulletin No. 1. Washington, D.C.: National Education Association, 1963.

Ryans, David G. "Possible Directions for Teacher-Behavior Research." *Theory into Practice* 2 (April 1963): 105–12.

Seeman, Julius. "Organizing a Thesis Proposal." *The American Psychologist* 9 (December 1954): 794–97.

Vander Werf, Lester S. "Needed Research in Vocational Education." *Phi Delta Kappan* 46 (April 1965): 405–10.

4

Locating and Summarizing
Previous Research
on a Problem

In the preceding chapter, wide reading of theoretical discussions and reports of research was strongly recommended to the graduate student as a means of discovering a suitable problem for his thesis research. It was also suggested that such relevant reading should enable the student to evaluate the feasibility of conducting research on some problem he has tentatively selected. It will help provide answers to questions such as:

Are the hypotheses I have formulated testable?
Are they appropriately and precisely stated?
Have I considered all of the variables which should be manipulated or controlled?
What instruments or procedures should be used in collecting the data?
From what sources should the data be collected?
What techniques are appropriate in organizing and interpreting them?
What limitations of research similar to mine can I avoid?

Often as a result of such reading, a problem first selected is modified or discarded. Except with reference to the discovery of a problem, this is equally applicable to the professional educational researcher.

This chapter has five major objectives: (1) to present information useful in improving library skills; (2) to cite general and specific guides, indexes, and other important aids in locating reports of educational research and publications helpful in conducting it; (3) to describe practices useful in compiling a bibliography; (4) to suggest effective

59

note-taking processes; and (5) to aid the student in writing a critical summary of the previous research on his problem.

IMPROVING LIBRARY SKILLS

The efficiency with which a graduate student, or professional educational research worker, is able to locate theoretical discussions and research relevant to a problem depends considerably on his knowledge of the library of his institution, or other nearby libraries. Much time is wasted if the student is not aware of what resources are available in the library, and of their locations. A card catalog may be casually used for years without clear understanding of the types of cards used, the specific kinds of information they contain, and precisely how they are filed.

The main card catalog

The main card catalog of a library has at least two cards for each book in the library, but often there are three or more—an *author* card, a *title* card, and one or more *subject* cards. A library may obtain author cards from the Library of Congress such as Figure 4.1 illustrated below:

Figure 4.1   Typical Library of Congress author card

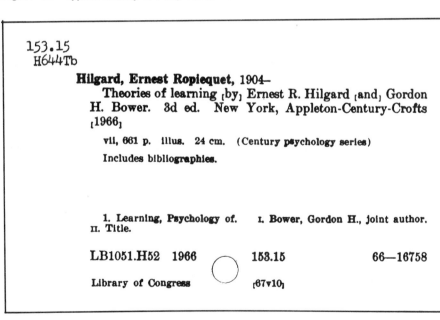

While numerous Library of Congress Cards have information indicative of the contents of a book, many libraries use cards obtained from

the H. W. Wilson Company which give a brief annotation concerning the book to which the card applies. Such an annotation may indicate the extent to which the book has been revised since its first publication and may include more definite information concerning the theme of the book than is indicated by its title.

In the upper left corner of the cards pertaining to a given book the library usually enters the call number of the book according to the Dewey Decimal System, although some libraries use the Library of Congress System. Graduate students in education most often encounter the former and soon learn that call numbers ranging from 370 up through 379 apply to books in the field of education. Often a second card pertaining to a given book is filed according to title in the same general card catalog. (The title of the book is typed at the top of the card following the call number and filing is according to the first important word in the title.) One or more additional cards may be filed as subject cards. On each such card the subject is typed above the printed title and to the right of the call number. The cards are then filed in alphabetical order by subjects in the same general catalog used for author and title cards. Subject cards are now tending to supplant title cards; hence, failure to find a title card for a book does not necessarily mean that the library does not have it. The book may be filed by author and subject. Some libraries maintain separate subject catalogs.

Most of the items shown on the *author* card are self-explanatory. The entry, 24 cm., indicates the size of the book in terms of its height. On the lower part of the card the entries of chief interest to the user of the library are the headings under which other cards pertaining to the book are filed—the subject, or subjects, and the title. The names of one or more joint authors also appear here indicating that other cards with such names typed above the printed titles are filed accordingly in the general catalog. Books *about* an author also have his name typed at the top. In a card catalog containing cards filed by author, title, and subject, such cards follow the author cards of books written by the author himself. Title cards are useful in locating books where one is uncertain of an author's name. Author cards alone are not much help if all the student knows is that someone named Smith is the author of an anthology in the field of philosophy. If, however, the student looks for a title card using "philosophy" or "philosophers" as key words he should soon find one for T. V. Smith's *Philosophers Speak for Themselves.*

Subject cards are useful when the student is uncertain with reference to both author and title, especially when a vaguely recalled title is not as definitive as it could be. A student interested in historical research knowing only that an important book on this topic was published a few years ago by two professors at Columbia University might more quickly locate *The Modern Researcher* by Jacques Barzun and Henry F. Graff by consulting subject cards classified under "historiography." (It is also cataloged under "authorship," the joint author Henry Franklin Graff, and the title.) When cards classified under a given subject heading are being used to locate a particular book, the student can also discover references to other books he should consult and possibly include in his bibliography. *Cross reference* cards placed at the end of a series of cards on a given subject will inform the student of other subject headings pertaining to books he should "see also."

Special card catalogs

In addition to its author-title-subject card catalog, or author-title and subject catalogs, most libraries have a number of special catalogs. These include separate catalogs of periodicals, reference books, and books put on reserve by professors teaching various courses. While a student can learn from a card in the main catalog that the library has a certain periodical, the card for that periodical in the periodical catalog will tell him which volumes are available in the library. If, for example, the library does not have the first few volumes, or does not possess one or two more recent volumes of *Educational and Psychological Measurement,* he quickly learns from the periodical catalog that the missing volumes must be sought elsewhere. While the call number on the card for a given reference book in the general card catalog will have an "R" above it, thus indicating that it is to be found in the reference room, a special reference catalog in the reference room will more quickly aid the student in locating such books. Similarly, the special catalog for books on reserve will help the student find a needed book that is missing from the regular stacks by informing him, for example, that the book he seeks is among those set aside for the students of Education 243. Another special catalog is the "shelf list" which records all of the publications possessed by the library in order of call number. Some research libraries use such a list in place of subject cards. If, for example, a student or other library user knows the call number pertaining to "data processing," he can quickly obtain information concerning all of the books and periodicals in the library which deal exclusively with this subject. He will not learn, however, that the journal *Educational and Psychological Measurement* has articles dealing with this topic in a special section.

Reference, reserve, and periodical rooms

It has been pointed out that the student should know where in his library various publications are available. He should know, for example, the locations of the reference, reserve, and periodical rooms. A walk along the shelves of a reference room will reveal to the student just where he will find various encyclopedias, *Readers' Guide, Educational Index, Dissertation Abstracts,* and such sources of biographical information as *Who's Who in America.* A survey of the books on the shelves in a reserve room will help the student to discover important books in his fields of interest. If, for example, the student is interested in problems of the culturally disadvantaged, professors of psychology and of sociology are certain to have placed books dealing with this subject on reserve for the students of their courses. Other students can also study the books within the reserve room. A survey of the journals on the shelves in a periodical room will disclose the locations of recent issues of journals which the student should consult in bringing a bibliography up to date.

The library stacks

The graduate student should obtain the card which permits him to visit the stacks. In addition to learning and observing the rules which govern the use of the stacks, he should also familiarize himself with the organization of the stacks and be able quickly to reach the shelves containing books in the educational, psychological, sociological, and other professional fields. He should know that the first of the symbols below the call number of the book he is seeking refers to the first letter of its author's last name. This letter enables the student to find the particular book he wants among all the books shelved according to a given call number (if it is not on loan to someone else). Such access to the stacks may also serve to make the student aware of other books on the subject in which he is interested, since these may be adjacent to the book he is seeking. Finally, it is extremely important that the student learns and appreciates the many ways in which members of the library staff can aid him in obtaining the books, periodicals, and other publications he needs.

LOCATING SOURCES OF EDUCATIONAL INFORMATION

How to Locate Educational Information and Data by Carter Alexander and Arvid J. Burke[1] has long been of great value to graduate students and to professional educational research specialists for its help in locating sources of educational information and in acquiring library utilization techniques. Among the general aids in locating information listed in this book, or elsewhere, are the following:

---

[1] Carter Alexander and Arvid J. Burke, *How to Locate Educational Information and Data,* 4th ed. (New York: Bureau of Publications, Columbia University, 1958). This book has been revised as Arvid J. Burke and Mary A. Burke, *Documentation in Education* (New York: Teachers College Press, Columbia University, 1967).

*Reference Books: A Brief Guide for Students and Other Users of the
Library* by Mary Neill Barton
The New Library Key by Margaret G. Cook
How and Where to Look It Up: A Standard Source of Information
by Robert W. Murphey
Basic Reference Sources: An Introduction to Materials and Methods
by Louis Shores
Guide to Reference Books by Constance M. Winchell

Persons who make frequent use of a library should be alert to revisions of or supplements to the guides just mentioned. Recent issues of the *Review of Educational Research* on the "Methodology of Educational Research" have chapters largely concerned with newly published aids in locating educational literature or information. For example, Margaret R. Sheviak and Haynes McMullen in their chapter "Research Tools: Access to the Literature of Education" discuss not only "the newer conventional bibliographies and reference aids which are primarily useful in the study of education in the United States" but include information with reference to "educational systems outside the United States" and the "development of machines and systems of searching which permit quick access to ideas and combinations of ideas not easily located through conventional bibliographies, indexes, or abstracts."[2] Again, the student should be on the lookout for similar chapters in later, but comparable issues of the *Review of Educational Research.*

More specialized than the five guides just listed is Gillooly's *The Literature Search, Document Retrieval in The Behavioral Sciences.*[3]

The New York University List of Books in Education, compiled and edited by Barbara Marks, Head Librarian of the School of Education, contains annotated references to 2,857 books classified under 178 subject headings with numerous cross references. Some of the subject headings are Academic Freedom, Administration of Schools, Child Development, Computers in Education, Programed Instruction, Statistical Methods, and Urban Problems and Education. Most of the titles appeared in the 1950s and 1960s, but some appeared earlier. Under

---

[2] Margaret R. Sheviak and Haynes McMullen, "Research Tools: Access to the Literature of Education" in "Methodology of Educational Research," *Review of Educational Research* 30 (December 1960), p. 487. In addition to *Dissertation Abstracts International,* described in detail later in this chapter, University Microfilms of Ann Arbor, Michigan, has developed a service called *Datrix.* Given the appropriate key words, this computerized system searches through more than 240,000 post-1938 dissertations on file, retrieves relevant titles and prints out the desired bibliography.

[3] William B. Gillooly, *The Literature Search, Document Retrieval in the Behavioral Sciences* (Somerset, N.J.: Mariner Press, 1969).

History of Education and Educators and Philosophers are titles of a few books published in the 1800s.[4]

It was noted in the preceding chapter that the graduate student in education seeking a thesis problem will find it useful to read widely in such sources as the *Handbook of Research on Teaching,* yearbooks of the National Society for the Study of Education, summaries of research in the *Review of Educational Research,* and articles in the *Encyclopedia of Educational Research.* As the student reaches the point of identifying a few potentially appropriate problems for his own research, or a single problem in which he is seriously interested, certain special aids become of great help to him. The more important of these are discussed below.

The Phi Delta Kappa compilations of titles of educational research reports

Study of the lists of titles of doctoral dissertations in a particular area of interest in the Phi Delta Kappa compilations[5] is useful to the student when seeking a problem for his own research or when preparing his own bibliography of earlier research. After titles of interest have been identified, information concerning possible publication of the research may be obtained in one of the research journals by consulting *Education Index, Psychological Abstracts,* or *Sociological Abstracts.* Given titles of doctoral dissertations since 1953, the student will find more comprehensive abstracts in *Dissertation Abstracts.* The Phil Delta Kappa *Research Studies in Education,* where possible, cite the *Dissertation Abstract* number with each title.

Education Index

The *Education Index* has been published since January 1, 1929 by the H. W. Wilson Company. Until June, 1961, it was "a cumulative *author* and *subject* index to a selected list of educational periodicals, books, and pamphlets." In July, 1961, this specification of its coverage was changed to "a cumulative *subject* index to a selected list of educational periodicals, proceedings, and yearbooks." In July 1969 it again became an *author* and *subject* index. In addition to indexing 242 educational journals, it presently covers proceedings of meetings and yearbooks of the important educational associations including the various

---

[4] Barbara S. Marks, ed. *The New York University List of Books in Education* (New York: Citation Press, 1968).

[5] See Mary Louise Lyda, and others, *Research Studies in Education,* 1953–63. Edited by Stanley Elam (Bloomington, Ind.: Phi Delta Kappa, 1965). There were earlier and there are later compilations of the titles of doctoral dissertations and field studies published by Phi Delta Kappa, a professional education fraternity.

departments of the National Education Association and practically all publications of the U.S. Office of Education. In Volume 20 for July 1969 through June 1970, about eleven double-column pages are devoted to references classified under the major subject heading "READING" and further classified under 35 subheads in alphabetical order including "Achievements, Student"; "Activities"; "Administration"; "Aims and Objectives"; "Bibliography"; "Correlation with other subjects"; "Curriculum"; "Motivation"; "Remedial teaching"; "Research"; "Teacher education"; and "Teaching." The items under "Teaching" are, for example, further subdivided according to educational levels, types of schools, bibliography, evaluation, and research. The last references under the subhead "Teaching" are classified by states and several foreign countries.

In the same volume, five and one-half double-column pages follow the major subject heading "MATHEMATICS" and again there are numerous subheads. Closely following the major heading is a list headed "See also" to direct the reader to other pages of the *Index.* These include "Algebra," "Algorithms," "Conic sections," and the like. Figure 4.2 is an excerpt from a part of one of the columns mentioned above. Note the italicized subheads. They identify references relevant to the topic of the preceding subhead. For example, *Research* identifies an article concerning the psychology of mathematics. "Research," on the other hand, identifies an article (or articles) relevant to the major heading, MATHEMATICS. Again, the subhead *Bibliography* identifies bibliographical material relevant to research in mathematics education rather than to mathematics education in general. In the *Education Index,* references listed under the subheads "Research" or *Research* are relevant to periodical articles which are research reports as well as articles about research.

In using *Education Index* it is desirable for the student to begin by listing key words relevant to the problem (or problems) in which he is interested. Such key words may serve to identify the subject headings and subheadings he should locate in successive volumes and recent issues of the *Education Index.* The list of key words may be replaced by the headings which serve to reveal to the student references which he should consult. Similarly, names of persons known to have written articles of interest in the past should be sought in the current volume or, if not in the current volume, should be sought in earlier volumes. The references listed in the excerpt also appear elsewhere in the same volume according to the names of their authors.

If the student has a problem in the field of educational psychology, for example, *Psychological Abstracts* should be used in conjunction with *Education Index.* A similar suggestion can be made with reference to *Sociological Abstracts* and indexes in other fields if the student's problem has relevance to a field besides education.

Figure 4.2 Excerpt from *Education Index* 20 (July 1969–June 1970), p. 472 [Reprinted by permission of the H. W. Wilson Company.]

Programmed teaching

Comparative effects of ability and presentation mode in computer-assisted instruction and programmed instruction. W. Dick and R. Latta. AV Comm R 18:33-45 Spr '70

Computer-extended instruction: an example. W. S. Dorn. il Math Teach 63:147-58 F '70

Construction and evaluation of a programed course in mathematics necessary for success in collegiate physical science. R. B. Collagan. J Res Sci Teach 6 no4:358-65 '69

Effects of logical and scrambled sequences in mathematical materials on learning with programmed instruction materials. J. L. Brown. bibliog J Ed Psychol 61:41-5 F '70

Experimental program in computer-assisted mathematics. H. S. Hughes. Nat Assn Sec Sch Prin Bul 54:85-90 F '70

Instructional system for computer assisted instruction on a general purpose computer. E. G. Kerr and others. Ed Tech 10:28 Mr '70

Time-shared computer: a teaching tool; Dartmouth college and South Portland, Me, high school. K. K. Thompson and A. Waterhouse. Nat Assn Sec Sch Prin Bul 54: 91-8 F '70

Using a small computer in the college mathematics curriculum. G. B. Swartz. Ed Tech 10:31-2 Mr '70

Projects

To make a million. G. C. Muehl. il Instr 79:48 N '69

We made it and it works! the classroom construction of sundials. M. S. Wahl. il Arith Teach 17:301-4 Ap '70

Psychology

Longitudinal study in mathematics attitude. R. G. Anttonen. bibliog J Ed Res 62:467-71 Jl '69

Research

Nonintellective variables and mathematics achievement: directions for research. L. R. Aiken, jr. bibliog J Sch Psychol 8 no 1:28-36 '70

Remedial teaching

Math lab. F. J. Mueller. Sch & Com 56:44-5 N '69

Three-by-five card plus an opaque projector plus an ice pick. G. D. Schiele. Arith Teach 16:533-5 N '69

Research

Science and mathematics education; ed. by J. M. Atkin and T. A. Romberg. bibliog R Ed Res 39:377-511 O '69

Bibliography

Research on mathematics education, grades K-8, for 1968; comp. by C. A. Riedesel and M. N. Suydam. Arith Teach 16:467-78 O '69

Psychological Abstracts

Psychological Abstracts has been published since 1927 by the American Psychological Association. Its subtitle is "Nonevaluative summaries of the world's literature in psychology and related disciplines." In addition to containing abstracts or brief summaries of purely psychological periodical articles and books published in the United States and in other countries, there are abstracts of psychologically relevant articles in such journals as: *American Journal of Sociology, Child Development, College Board Review, Educational and Psychological Mea-*

surement, *Journal of Social Issues, Peabody Journal of Education,* and *Journal of Experimental Education.* Articles judged to be of interest to psychologists in *Harpers, Atlantic Monthly, Science* and other such magazines are also abstracted. The abstracts, printed in double columns, are classified under 12 general headings including "Educational Psychology." Under this heading are the subheads "Programed Learning," "Attitudes and Adjustment," "Testing," "Physical Education," "Special Education," "Guidance," and "Personnel."

Each December issue has an author index and a subject index of all the abstracts that appeared in all of the issues of that year. The researcher should begin his search with key words as in the case of *Education Index,* possibly largely the same ones. (Study of the subject index may suggest other key words or the omission of those used earlier.) It is always advisable to use "bibliographies" as one of the key words. Figure 4.3 is an example of one of the abstracts appearing in

Figure 4.3 Excerpt from *Psychological Abstracts* 40 (July 1966), p. 761 [Reprinted by permission of the American Psychological Association.]

PROGRAMED LEARNING

8047. **Bartz, Wayne H., & Darby, Charles L.** (U. Florida) **The effects of a programed textbook on achievement under three techniques of instruction.** *Journal of Experimental Education,* 1966, **34**(3), 46–52.—This research was designed to investigate the achievement of college students using programed or non-programed texts under traditional or independent study techniques of instruction. The Ss, 147 students enrolled in a mathematics course, were assigned to 12 groups differing in the type of text used, instructional techniques employed, and instructor. An achievement test was administered at the beginning and end of the semester; in addition, a questionnaire was administered at the end. The results show that Ss under the traditional instructional technique performed significantly higher on the achievement test than did Ss under independent study (.05 level of significance). Also, Ss using the non-programed text performed significantly higher (.05 level) than did Ss using the programed text. Other results are reported and discussed.—*G. F.*

Psychological Abstracts, an abstract relevant to a research cited on page 48 of Chapter 3.

It should be evident that such a summary or abstract is more useful than a bibliographical reference alone in helping the student decide whether to include an article or book in his bibliography and to obtain the original itself for study.

Dissertation Abstracts

The longer abstracts of doctoral theses in *Dissertation Abstracts* are extremely valuable, and may indicate to the researcher the need to order one or more microfilmed or xerographic copies of the dissertation itself for intensive study. *Dissertation Abstracts* has been published since 1938 with the cooperation of 240 or more higher institutions. Each volume has a long section in the field of Education and since 1961 has prepared abstracts of research reports of short-term projects conducted by professors, instructors, and graduate students that are financed by grants under Title VII of the National Defense Education Act (NDEA). In *Dissertation Abstracts* the printing is also in double columns.

One rather long abstract is shown in Figure 4.4 on pages 70–71. It may be useful as a model to the student faced with the problem of preparing an abstract of his own dissertation. If it were written in the present tense and the conclusions omitted, it would also illustrate an effective statement and definition of a problem. (One might wonder why there is no mention of random selection and assignment of subjects.)

Examination of the abstracts themselves may reveal to the student that the research he contemplates will duplicate too closely some previous research and may indicate to him that he should discard or modify his problem. Examination of an abstract may also justify the student in omitting a citation of it from his own bibliography and excluding the particular dissertation from further consideration.

Frequently, carefully taken notes on an abstract will suffice when writing a summary of the earlier research, but in the case of very relevant dissertations the student should order from University Microfilms a microfilmed or xerographic copy of the dissertation itself for intensive study. The Phi Delta Kappa compilations of titles, and *Dissertation Abstracts,* with its duplicating service, have become important factors in contemporary educational research. Until a few years ago, unless published as a book or summarized in journal form, the research embodied in doctoral dissertations was not generally known or considered in later researches. The duplicating service, through payment of a modest fee, makes it possible for a student to obtain and keep a copy of the dissertation itself. This is obviously more satisfactory than having the thesis for a few days on interlibrary loan.

New educational research information services

In 1967, the U.S. Office of Education of the Department of Health, Education and Welfare started a new publication, *Research in Education,* a monthly abstract journal published by ERIC (Educational Research Information Center, more recently, Educational Resources Information Center), containing abstracts of reports of educational research both completed and in progress. This publication is not restricted to doctoral dissertations. Its abstracts, however, are generally much shorter than those in *Dissertation Abstracts.*[6]

The Bureau of Research of USOE also began publication in 1969 of a new monthly *Current Index to Journals in Education,* CIJE, indexing by title, subject, author, and descriptive index title articles appearing in over 200 educational and related journals.[7] Also initiated by the Bureau of Research is *Putting Research into Educational Practice,* PREP, a service that develops and distributes materials which synthesize and interpret research, developments, and current practices.

The Educational Researcher, the official newsletter of the American

---

[6] Subscriptions to ERIC are $11.00 per year. They can be obtained from the Government Printing Office in Washington, D.C.

[7] Published by CCM Information Corporation of New York, a subsidiary of Crowell-Collier and Macmillan in cooperation with USOE.

Figure 4.4 Excerpt from *Dissertation Abstracts* 26 (February 1966), p. 4345 [Reprinted by permission of the author and University Microfilms, Inc., of Ann Arbor, Michigan.]

A COMPARISON OF THREE TEACHING PROCEDURES
TO DEVELOP CREATIVITY IN WRITTEN EXPRESSION

(Order No. 65-12,233)

Ruth Lucille Rees, Ed.D.
University of Oregon, 1965

Adviser: C. W. Schminke

    The purpose of this study was to determine which of three teaching methods would be most effective for developing creativity in written expression. Answers were sought to the following questions:

1. Which of three experimentally designed methods is most effective for developing creativity in written expression?

2. What is the relative effectiveness of each of the three experimentally designed methods on children of designated intelligence quotients for developing creativity in written expression?

3. Which of three experimentally designed methods is most effective for developing creativity in written expression of boys; of girls?

4. What is the reaction of each teacher toward the relative effectiveness of the method used with his group for developing creativity in written expression?

5. What are the pupils' reactions toward the especially designed written experiences used in this study?

Three approaches to the development of creativity in written expression were prescribed. These were the Structured Systematic Method, Method A, Unstructured Developmental Method, Method B, and Structured Developmental Method, Method C. Method A was characterized by its formality. The pupils wrote on an assigned topic, during an assigned time limit and their papers were checked for the mechanics of writing. Two grades, one for the mechanics of writing and the other for the development of the plot, were placed on these papers. Method B was characterized by its laissez-faire format. Pupils selected their topics, wrote any time during the week when "in the mood" and received a comment on the development of the plot. Method C pupils developed an assigned topic which emanated from the weekly social studies during an assigned forty-five minute period. Comments were made by the teacher toward the development of the plot.

This study was completed in the Portland, Oregon Public School District. Nine teachers and nine classes of fifth grade pupils participated in the ten week study.

Participants had been administered the Lorge Thorndike Test during the fourth grade by the school psychologist. Intelligent quotients, as determined by this test, were used in implementing Lindquist's treatments by levels design.

Torrance's Imaginative Stories pre-test and post-test were administered to 216 pupils at the beginning and ending of the experiment. The statistical techniques used to analyze the test data was analysis of variance in which the groups-within-treatment was used. The results of the pre-test were used as the control measure.

The pupils reacted to a questionnaire and the teachers to a short answer questionnaire at the completion of the study. An analysis was made of these two questionnaires.

Within the limitations of this study, the data obtained warrant these conclusions:

1. Obtained "F" value for effect of teaching methods, significant at the 1% level of significance, favored Method A Structured Systematic Method for developing creativity in written expression.

2. Obtained "F" value for effect of teaching methods on sex, significant at the 5% level of significance, indicated that the girls made greater growth than the boys.

3. Both sexes developed creativity in writing to a greater degree with Methods A and B than with Method C.

4. Obtained "F" value for interaction among the intelligence levels within groups, significant at the 5% level, favored Method B for children in the higher intelligence level and Method A for those in the middle and low levels.

5. Analysis of pupil questionnaires indicated pupils want mechanics of writing corrected; want to select their own topics; and do not want a time limit imposed for writing.

6. Teachers were helped to identify pupils with writing ability they might have missed and were given better insight into some of their pupils.

Microfilm $3.00; Xerography $5.80. 120 pages.

Educational Research Association, appears monthly except in July and August. It is the best source of information concerning current events in the field of educational research.

Phi Delta Kappa, with the aid of a Kettering Foundation grant, has instituted the School Research Information Service (SRIS). This service will disseminate reports of research or of innovative practices originating in school systems or educational institutions. It is also equipped to identify reports in the USOE information retrieval system, ERIC. According to a bulletin concerning this service:

> Inquiries addressed to SRIS will be answered with relevant SRIS documents and a listing of relevant ERIC documents.... A document of up to sixty pages can be stored on a single microfiche card, costing twenty-five cents for the card, postage and handling. Paper copies of the reports are available at greater expense (ten cents per page plus postage).[8]

Dissertation Abstracts and other services of University Microfilms of Ann Arbor, Michigan, ERIC of the U.S. Office of Education Information Service, and SRIS of Phi Delta Kappa should enable educational researchers of the future to more easily identify and have access to reports of research than in the past.

Other sources of special interest

The preceding section dealt with sources of greatest interest to educational research. Certain other sources may be mentioned briefly, but the guides and textbooks earlier cited should be consulted for more comprehensive and detailed information. If the contemplated research is to deal with some current issue in education for which both lay opinions and facts are needed, *Readers' Guide, International Index, The New York Times Index,* and *Facts on File* will be useful. Similarly, if the problem requires information about various prominent persons of the present or the past, *Biography Index, Who's Who in America,* and directories of professional associations will be helpful. In defining terms, occurring in the statement of a problem or elsewhere in a thesis or other research report, and in understanding technical terms used by others, Good's *Dictionary of Education* should be consulted.[9] Reviews in various educational journals and abstracts of reviews in the *Book Review Digest* can be useful to the student or other researcher in evaluating books relevant to his problem. If tests are to be used in collecting

---

[8] Reprinted with permission of Phi Delta Kappa Research Service Center, whose address is Eighth and Union, Bloomington, Indiana, 47401.

[9] Carter V. Good, *Dictionary of Education,* 2nd ed. (New York: McGraw-Hill, 1959).

data, the same may be said of the Buros *Mental Measurements Year-books.* Finally, in completing bibliographic data concerning books, the *Cumulative Book Index* and earlier compilations of the same kind, like the *United States Catalog,* can be helpful. In the *Cumulative Book Index* complete book references are cataloged by author, title, and subject in one alphabetical list. Very recent books are listed in *Publishers' Weekly. Books in Print* lists the publisher, the price of a given book, and whether it is still in the market and can be ordered.

A student compiling a bibliography may find it useful to consult the *Bibliographic Index* published by the H. W. Wilson Company since 1938, or earlier bibliographies of bibliographies, such as the one compiled by Monroe and Shores.[10] In an effort to keep his bibliography up to date the student should continue to examine new issues of the indexes he is using and recent issues of journals that publish reports of research or discussions of theory in areas relevant to his own problem.

COMPILING A BIBLIOGRAPHY

The importance of a record of sources consulted

It is very important to keep a record of just what sources have been consulted while compiling a bibliography. If the search for discussions of theory relevant to a problem, and of the earlier research on a problem, has begun with examination of such publications as the *Encyclopedia of Educational Research,* particular yearbooks of the National Society for the Study of Education, the *Handbook of Research on Teaching,* certain issues of the *Review of Educational Research,* or any of the numerous anthologies now proliferating, the 3″ x 5″ bibliography cards described below may suffice as a record of the articles, chapters, or selections examined. A brief note may be added to the references that conclude with a bibliography which needs to be checked more closely. None of the cards should be discarded since each card testifies to a source examined.

In the case of *Education Index, Psychological Abstracts, Dissertation Abstracts,* ERIC, and similar sources, while the 3″ x 5″ bibliography cards containing references later to be located and read are important, another type of record is also needed. It is desirable to keep a running record or checklist of the volumes and more recent unbound issues of the sources above-named which have been consulted for references. It is also a good plan to record the headings and subheadings under which relevant references are to be sought. A checklist form may be

---

[10] Walter S. Monroe and Louis Shores, *Bibliographies and Summaries in Education to July 1, 1935* (New York: H. W. Wilson, 1936).

used having columns labeled with volume numbers or dates of unbound issues below a title such as "Education Index." The rows may
be labeled at the left with the headings and subheadings just mentioned. A check in a particular cell will record that one or more bibliography cards have been made for references listed in the specific
source. An X may record that the specific source listed no useful
references.[11]

A record of just what sources have been consulted must be kept;
otherwise time is wasted in going back to the same sources again and
again. In addition to saving time, such records will forestall embarrass-
ment for the student when his advisor asks, "Just where have you
looked?"

Bibliography cards

It is recommended that 3″ x 5″ index cards be used when compiling
a bibliography and that 5″ x 8″ cards be used in taking notes when
reading relevant articles, books, or other publications. The student
should make tentative judgments of the relevance of reference to his
own problem while consulting *Education Index, Psychological Abstracts,*
and other such sources. Similar judgments should also be made while
reading the bibliographies at the ends of articles in the *Encyclopedia
of Educational Research,* at the ends of chapters in the *Review of Educational Research,* or at the ends of other articles on research or theory. It is usually wise to record a reference on a bibliography card even
though its relevance seems somewhat doubtful. It may or may not be
discarded at the time the references themselves are read. As reading
goes forward concepts of relevance are likely to change with minor
changes in the problem being studied. Often references not truly relevant to one's problem may suggest techniques or points of view worth
considering. It is usually best to copy accurately all, or almost all, of
the information as actually given in the source, indicating with a check
that the copying is accurate. Writing each reference according to the
forms required for thesis writing in the student's institution or for publication in a particular journal or in a monograph or book should be
postponed until the publication has been obtained. Then, the reference
may be rewritten at the top of the 5″ x 8″ note-taking card according to
the forms later required. It was noted earlier that a record should be
kept of all the sources consulted even though certain references may
be discarded after reading definitely indicates that they are not relevant. It is a desirable practice, however, to keep a separate file of the

---

[11] For such a checklist form, see Walter R. Borg, *Educational Research, an Introduction*
(New York: David McKay, 1963), pp. 48–50.

discards in the event such a reference recurs in bibliographical sources later consulted.

When a referenoe in *Education Index* or other source is copied on a 3″ x 5″ bibliography card, all of the information should be recorded as given. In order to alphabetize correctly, however, the last names of authors should be given first. For example, the second reference in Figure 4.2 may appear on a bibliography card (Figure 4.5) as:

Figure 4.5   Bibliography card

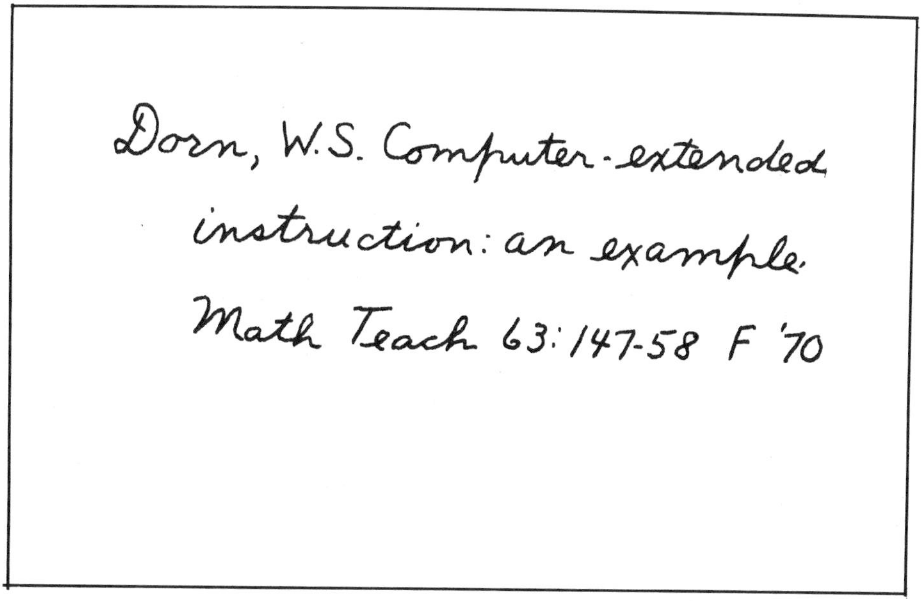

In the case of *Psychological Abstracts* names of authors can be copied as given. Copying the name of an author's institution may seem unnecessary, but such information is useful in writing for a reprint. Copying the number of an issue of a journal is seldom essential, although some publishers recommend its inclusion in footnote and bibliographical references. Usually the volume number suffices. *Psychological Abstracts,* the *Annual Review of Psychology,* and other publications omit the month (or season) in which journal articles appeared. If such information is needed, it can be obtained when reading the reference itself.

Note-taking cards

It may be mentioned again that the reference as written at the top of a 5″ x 8″ card should be according to forms later required. Examples of such forms are given in Chapter 16 on reporting educational research. One can, of course, abbreviate the name of the journal, for example, *J. Ed. Meas.* for *Journal of Educational Measurement* or even *E.S.J.* for *Elementary School Journal,* so long as the abbreviations can be readily translated. It should not be assumed that the reference as given on the bibliography card is necessarily accurate. For journal articles check the spelling of the authors' names, the title of the article, the name of the journal, the volume number and range of pages, the month or season when the article appeared, and the year, against the original. Certain journals have Spring, Summer, Fall, and Winter issues and weekly or bimonthly journals give the day of the month. The issue number should also be checked. In the case of books authors' names, titles, date of publication, publisher, and location of publisher should be verified. If the date of publication is not on the title page, the date of copyright appears on the next page. The fact that the book is a revised, second, third, or other edition should also be recorded. In the case of an article or chapter in a yearbook or similar association publication, the name of the series should also be cited, for example, *Sixty-third Yearbook of the National Society for the Study of Education,* Part II. This might be abbreviated, of course, as *63d Yrb. N.S.S.E.* II. The names of editors of books, yearbooks, and other such publications may be needed also.

After the reference at the top has been carefully verified as described above, a check mark or OK should precede the reference. In the case of book references it is wise to record the call number, and it is often useful to note where a given periodical or yearbook series may be found, especially where several libraries are used.

Determining relevance

After a reference to a research has been located and obtained, a quick look at its statement of a problem may suffice to indicate the extent of its relevance to one's own problem. Sometimes it is necessary also to skim the presentation of data and the findings or conclusions. A theoretical article or one containing opinions on some issue may have a revealing first paragraph or a concluding summary useful in judging relevance. When discarding a reference, it is good practice to enter a note on its card giving the reason for rejection before placing it in one's discard file. When references to earlier research are being read, the publication should be identified as a report of research. The hallmarks of research are, of course, a statement of a problem, the presentation of data, the interpretation of data, and findings or conclusions.

The determination of relevance and, then, the actual reading of the publication itself, should be guided by one's own statement of the problem with its subordinate statements, questions, or hypotheses. It is so easy to waste time in reading material not especially relevant to one's problem just because it is interesting.

Identifying content worthy of notes

The entire report of a research should first be skimmed rapidly, identifying the location of items of such importance as to justify notes. After a first such skimming, the entire report should be read critically, in order to be certain that nothing significant has been overlooked and to acquire enough knowledge of its content to evaluate it critically. The same process is applicable to a theoretical article or to some other relevant publication.

If the book, issue of a journal, or bound volume is the property of the student or researcher, checks can be made in margins, or sentences underlined. If, however, the publication is on loan from a library, or other source, no marks should be made. Alexander and Burke suggest using slips of paper about 1″ wide and long enough to reach from the bottom to the top of a page. A pencil mark is made near the top of the slip which is placed at the left of a page with the mark in line with the top of the page. Checks or brief comments can then be entered in line with the content to which they refer. The front of the slip may contain marks relevant to a left-hand page. The other side of the slip can function for the right-hand page. The page numbers should be entered at the top of the slip. When the book is returned to the library, or other source, the slips may be appended to the bibliography card.[12]

Characteristics of good notes

Note-taking should *not* be a copying of isolated words or phrases, nor should it be copying of long sentences unless such sentences are crucial. Acquiring skill in paraphrasing or summarizing in the student's own words is important. The paraphrase or brief summary is checked against the source to make sure that the precise meaning of the source has not been distorted, and a check mark is placed before the note. The page or pages referred to should also be entered adjacent to the note to facilitate a return to its source and to make it easier to write a proper footnote reference or other specific citation.

While relatively few notes should be direct quotations, it is often wise to quote problem statements, hypotheses, and findings or conclusions in full. This is especially desirable where criticism of findings or conclusions is anticipated. When this is the case, it is also desirable to quote rather than paraphrase details of content justifying the criticism; for example, a formula inappropriate for the data analyzed. To avoid the unintended plagiarism which occasionally and embarrassingly occurs in theses, and sometimes elsewhere, it is important that notes which are direct quotations should begin and end with quotation marks. Ellipses are useful where omissions are made within quotations—three

---

[12] Alexander and Burke, *How to Locate Educational Material,* p. 177.

spaced dots for omitted words or phrases . . . and four dots where the omission occurs at the end of a sentence, or where one or more sentences are omitted. Errors in a quotation may be indicated by [sic], but it is better to correct obvious typographical errors. Sometimes, it is appropriate to correspond with an author to clarify phraseology where it seems apparent that a phrase or sentence is not consistent with what the author really meant to say. Again, as with other notes, the page, or pages, of a quotation should be recorded and checked. The page numbers of quotations are useful in obtaining permissions to quote from authors and publishers and in preparing precise footnote citations.

The following is an excellent summary of the characteristics of a good note:

> A good note may be any one of these things: a *statement* so clear that its meaning cannot be questioned; an *illustration* so given that it can be substantially reproduced; a *collection of data* that can be used as evidence; the *essentials of the author's point of view;* the *exact question raised by the author;* or *one's reaction to something,* so definitely expressed that it would be perfectly clear to another person.[13]

Notes on a 5″ x 8″ card may be in order of the content of the source. It is better organization, however, to record notes relevant to research reports under certain headings. These may vary according to the types of research reports studied, but the following are generally useful:

1. *Problem*
2. *Sources of data*
3. *Collection of data*
4. *Interpretation of data*
5. *Findings and conclusions*
6. *Evaluation.*

Such headings facilitate the comparison of different researches and help to insure collection of information essential to such comparisons. These headings need not be written on each card; the numbers alone will suffice.

Under the first heading the general problem, any subordinate problems, and any hypotheses may be quoted or briefly summarized. Under the second heading, mention may be made, for example, that "two

---

[13] Alexander and Burke, *How to Locate Educational Material,* p. 170 or Burke and Burke, *Documentation in Education,* pp. 60–61. Reprinted with permission of authors and publisher.

classes of 5th-grade pupils in each of nine schools were assigned at random to the compared methods of instruction." Under *Collection of Data,* tests or other measuring instruments used in collecting data and the times when the tests were given may be indicated. Under *Interpretation of Data* the kind of analysis undertaken may be specified, for example, groups-within-treatments analysis of variance or analysis of covariance. Under *Findings and Conclusions* notes may be made concerning the levels of significance at which null hypotheses were rejected (or accepted). This information should be supplemented by relating such data to corresponding research or other alternative hypotheses.

It is useful to interject in brackets adjacent to descriptive notes of the types described above, one's own brief comments. Such comments may refer to aspects deserving of special commendation or criticism like [improper formula] or [no mention of randomization]. Such comments are useful in writing the notes under the heading *Evaluation.*

Evaluative notes

Interjected phrases of the kind just described are definitely evaluative notes. Under the heading of *Evaluation* additional specific comments may be listed, either criticizing or commending aspects of the report being read. A final note may be a general evaluation of the research, but, as noted below, this evaluation should be tentative.

How effectively a graduate student, or other educational researcher, will evaluate a research report is directly proportional to his knowledge, experience, and attitudes. It is often necessary to resort to explanation of techniques in advanced texts in statistical method to determine whether or not a particular procedure is justified. Comparison of the techniques used in several studies of the same problem is helpful as are the published critical summaries of the researches he is evaluating in such publications as the *Encyclopedia of Educational Research, Review of Educational Research,* and *Psychological Bulletin.* Careful study of the later chapters of this text and similar texts should be of value.

Such limitations in a report of research as failure to state and define a problem clearly and completely are probably easier for the less experienced educational researcher to identify. Sources of data are often not specifically noted or described. The author may not indicate whether or not random sampling was employed. Differences between means may be reported without mention of evidences of their significance. It may be obvious to a student that important variables considered in other studies are neglected in the one at hand. Sometimes, the student may identify evidences of excessive zeal or bias. It may seem to the student that the author of a research is enamored of an hypothesis and anxious to prove it true. The student should soon acquire as part of his own scientific attitude the idea that judgment should be suspended until additional study of theory and techniques and of similar researches justifies definite praise or condemnation. The evaluation that is recorded when one is taking notes on a research report should usually be a tentative evaluation.

The six headings enumerated ought to prove useful in note-taking of research reports even though the kinds of notes recorded will vary with the type of research being read. In the case of survey or descriptive studies, it may suffice to list the general problem, or question, rather than all of the subordinate ones. While the sources of data should be explicitly noted, mention of the fact that the data were collected by questionnaire or interview may be sufficient. Similarly, it may be noted that the data are presented in tables or graphs and the conclusions may be briefly summarized. One should, of course, note the occurrence of unusual procedures or methods of interpretation.

In the case of historical or philosophical researches quite different note-taking procedures may be employed. It is often recommended that each significant note be written on a separate card to facilitate sorting prior to their use in writing. Again, such notes should conform to the criteria for a good note quoted on page 78. This will be considered further in Chapter 14.

Use of more than one note-taking card

It is recommended that notes be made on only one side of note-taking cards and that, if more than one card is needed, the name of the author may suffice at the top of cards other than the first. If, however, there are several references to the same author an abbreviated title or the date of publication may be needed. In any case, it is wise to number the cards 1, 2, 3, etc., and clip or staple them to the first card. If there are numerous references or notes on separate cards pertaining to different topics, subject heads at the tops of the note-taking cards will be useful in the sorting preparatory to writing a summary. For very important earlier research, it is advisable to have the reports immediately available, as reprints, for example, or as xerographed or otherwise duplicated copies. Even in this case, however, the production of notes as described above should not be omitted. The taking of such notes, involving as it does analysis and evaluation, is a major factor in understanding the research of others.

WRITING A CRITICAL SUMMARY

A student may be tempted to postpone the writing of a critical summary of the previous research on his problem until he has completed his own research and is about to write his entire thesis. There are benefits, however, to preparing at least a first draft prior to undertaking the collection and interpretation of data. The reading of earlier researches, the taking of notes including tentative evaluations, and the recording of ideas concerning theory, sources of data, and techniques useful in organizing and interpreting them need to be synthesized not only in the mind of the student, but on paper. Ideas are clarified, gaps filled and, in this way, a coherent understanding of one's own problem is acquired. Assimilation and understanding of previous research and relevant theory may result in problem modification and in the selection of more appropriate sources of data and techniques.

A summary of previous research should not be a succession of brief notes on one research after another in chronological order. Rather, it should be based on a carefully prepared outline. Several researches on essentially the same problem and reporting similar or disparate conclusions may be grouped together. Often, the more important researches may be treated in separate paragraphs summarizing the information recorded about them in terms of the headings earlier listed: (1) the problem, (2) the sources of data, (3) the procedures used in the collection of data, (4) the techniques used in their interpretation, and (5) the findings and conclusions. Evaluative comments may appear next, or such comments may be grouped into a concluding section, which presents a general evaluation of the previous research. In some cases, it is desirable to conclude such a discussion of one or more recent and important researches by citing similar or less important researches very briefly; as, for example, "similar findings are reported by Davis (8), Edmunds (16), Green and Hudson (23), etc.," where the numbers refer to enumerated references in the bibliography of the thesis or other report of research containing the summary. Often, citing of this type is done at the beginning of one or more paragraphs of a summary followed by detailed discussion of several of the references cited. The graduate student should, of course, determine whether such a method of citation is permitted in his higher institution. It is certainly well accepted in educational and psychological publications.

While many critical summaries deal separately with various reports of research, or as mentioned above, the various reports are grouped for concurrent discussion, an effective summary is one that concludes with a general evaluation of the quality of the earlier studies and a synthesis of the earlier findings or generalizations along with judgments respecting their dependability. The various earlier researches may be compared with reference to definitions of their problems, sources of data utilized, and techniques used in collecting and interpreting the data. In such an evaluation it may be necessary to make such statements as, for example: "There has been little agreement among the experimenters as to what constitutes team teaching." "In only one of the experiments were the pupils assigned at random to the compared methods." "It was evident that the differences reported can largely be attributed to lack of control of such factors as the zeal and skill of teachers." "Only one of the experimenters undertook to discover whether or not team teaching was more effective than individual teaching in developing critical thinking skills." If the studies summarized are characterized to a large extent by such limitations it will be difficult to synthesize dependable general conclusions. The effort, however, may be worth while in revealing the present status of our knowledge concerning the problem and in justifying further research on the problem. Much critical judgment is required, however, in writing such a concluding section of a summary. What has been dependably established should be recognized and a researcher should not exaggerate the faults of his predecessors. After his own research has been completed, the first draft of the critical summary should be considered again in the light of the researcher's own experience in the collecting and interpreting of his data.

Suggestions
for Further Study

It is suggested that the student visit his institutional library following the procedures earlier mentioned in seeking a better understanding of the library resources available to him. He should familiarize himself with the card catalogs referred to and study the various kinds of cards; he should locate and examine *Education Index, Psychological Abstracts, Dissertation Abstracts,* and other aids in locating information; and he should locate journals containing reports of educational research such as:

*American Educational
  Research Journal
Educational and Psychological
  Measurement
Educational Research Bulletin
  now Theory Into Practice
Elementary School Journal
Harvard Educational Review
History of Education Quarterly
Journal of Educational
  Measurement
Journal of Educational
  Psychology*

*Journal of Educational Research
Journal of Educational
  Sociology
Journal of Experimental
  Education
Journal of Research and
  Development in Education
Journal of Teacher Education
Measurement and Evaluation
  in Guidance
School Review
Teachers College Record* now
  The Record

The student should also examine one or more editions of the *Encyclopedia of Educational Research* and recent yearbooks or proceedings of professional educational organizations like the National Society for the Study of Education, including such recent volumes as *Social Studies in the Elementary School, Child Psychology,* and *Theories of Learning and Instruction.* The student should, of course, become familiar with recent titles in the *Review of Educational Research.* If the student anticipates thesis research in the field of educational psychology, he should acquaint himself with such journals as *American Psychologist, Journal of Applied Psychology, Psychological Bulletin* and *Psychological Review,* in addition to *Psychological Abstracts* and *Journal of Educational Psychology* earlier mentioned.

It is an excellent learning experience for the graduate student tentatively to propose a thesis problem for himself, compile a bibliography of several recent researches relevant to the problem selected, locate these researches, read them, and make the kinds of notes previously described. Then, after studying some of the summaries of research listed among the selected references at the end of this chapter, he can attempt a critical summary of the recent researches he has read. All of this will contribute to his selection of a problem and the writing of a thesis proposal for evaluation by his advisor, or his committee of advisors. Such a proposal often includes, in addition to the statement and definition of a problem, and the specifications of sources of data and techniques to be used in collecting and interpreting them, a brief, but critical summary of some of the previous researches on his problem. This summary need not be exhaustive to demonstrate to an advisor or graduate committee that the student is ready to begin his own research in earnest.

Selected References

The references listed include a variety of educational or psychological research summaries relevant to educational problems. Almost all of the summaries cited are concerned with very general problems or fields of research, but sections of them deal with more specific problems. While not all of the summaries truly deserve to be called "critical," they represent some of the more important sources of summaries with which the student should become familiar. The summary entitled "A Critical Evaluation of Experimental Studies Relating to Supervised Study," written by the junior author, then a graduate student, is old, indeed, but it does illustrate the type of organization earlier discussed—individual descriptions of important researches, general evaluation of the techniques, and an effort to synthesize the findings of the researches summarized.

Anastasi, Anne. "Cultural Differences." In *Encyclopedia of Educational Research,* edited by C. W. Harris, pp. 350–58. 3rd ed. New York: Macmillan, 1960.

Birkmaier, Emma M. "Modern Languages." In *Encyclopedia of Educational Research,* edited by C. W. Harris, pp. 861–88. 3rd ed. New York: Macmillan, 1960.

Bloom, Benjamin S. *Stability and Change in Human Characteristics.* New York: Wiley, 1964.

Blough, Donald S., and Richard B. Millward. "Learning: Operant Conditioning and Verbal Learning." *Annual Review of Psychology* 16 (1965): 63–94.

Bretsch, Howard S. "Boards of Education." In *Encyclopedia of Educational Research,* edited by C. W. Harris, pp. 150–54. 3rd ed. New York: Macmillan, 1960.

Gallagher, James J., and William Rogge. "The Gifted," in "Education of Exceptional Children." *Review of Educational Research* 36 (February 1966): 37–55.

Getzels, J. W. "Creative Thinking, Problem-Solving, and Instruction." *Theories of Learning and Instruction.* Sixty-third Yearbook of the National Society for the Study of Education. Part I. Chapter X. Chicago: University of Chicago Press, 1964.

———, and P. W. Jackson. "The Teacher's Personality and Characteristics." In *Handbook of Research on Teaching,* edited by N. L. Gage, Chapter 11. Chicago: Rand McNally, 1963.

Hilgard, Ernest R., and Gordon H. Bower. "Learning and the Technology of Instruction." In *Theories of Learning,* Chapter 16. 3rd ed. New York: Appleton-Century-Crofts, 1966.

Kennedy, Wallace A., and Herman C. Willcutt. "Praise and Blame as Incentives." *Psychological Bulletin* 62 (November 1964): 323–32.

Lumsdaine, A. A. "Instruments and Media of Instruction." In *Handbook of Research on Teaching,* edited by N. L. Gage, Chapter 12. Chicago: Rand McNally, 1963.

Marx, Melvin H. "Motivation." In *Encyclopedia of Educational Research,* edited by C. W. Harris, pp. 888–901. 3rd ed. New York: Macmillan, 1960.

Michael, William B., and Ernest L. Boyer. "Campus Environment." In "Higher Education." *Review of Educational Research* 35 (October 1965): 264–76.

Monroe, Walter S., and Max D. Engelhart. "A Critical Evaluation of Experimental Studies Relating to Supervised Study." In *Experimental Research in Education,* Chapter IV. University of Illinois Bureau of Educational Research Bulletin No. 48. Urbana: University of Illinois, 1930.

Renner, K. Edward. "Delay of Reinforcement: A Historical Review." *Psychological Bulletin* 61 (May 1964): 341–61.

Russell, David H., and Henry R. Fea. "Research on Teaching Reading." In *Handbook of Research on Teaching,* edited by N. L. Gage, Chapter 16. Chicago: Rand McNally, 1963.

Smedslund, Jan. "Educational Psychology." *Annual Review of Psychology* 15 (1964): 251–76.

Sprinthall, Norman A., and David Tiedeman. "Guidance and the Pupil." *The Changing American School.* Sixty-fifth Yearbook of the National Society for the Study of Education, Part II. Chapter III. Chicago: University of Chicago Press, 1966.

Wallach, Michael A. "Research on Children's Thinking." *Child Psychology.* Sixty-second Yearbook of the National Society for the Study of Education, Part I. Chapter VI. Chicago: University of Chicago Press, 1963.

Withall, John, and W. W. Lewis. "Social Interaction in the Classroom." In *Handbook of Research on Teaching,* edited by N. L. Gage, Chapter 13. Chicago: Rand McNally, 1963.

5

Collecting Data:
Records, Questionnaires,
and Interviews

An educational research begins with the selection of a problem. The analysis of the problem should result in a carefully formulated statement of the problem which includes questions to be answered or hypotheses to be tested. The more elaborate definition of the problem, as in a thesis proposal or other design for a research, includes specification of the sources of data and the procedures to be used in collecting and in interpreting them. The next three chapters will be devoted to discussion of data-collecting methods.

The suggestions made with reference to locating sources of educational information, especially the sources to be consulted in preparing a critical summary of the earlier research on a problem, pointed out that this activity may also be useful in learning what sources of data and research methods have been used by other investigators of the same or similar problems. Such study often results in the modification of a problem tentatively selected and in some cases to the selection of a different problem.

The value of pilot studies
Before making a final commitment to a problem, it is desirable to investigate the feasibility of collecting the data needed to solve it. Unless a research is a "follow-up study," or a replication of earlier research by the same researcher, a "pilot study" is strongly recommended whether data are to be collected from records, through use of interviews, by means of systematic observations, or through administration of tests. Such trials of the procedures later to be used in earnest are extremely useful. For example, experiences in making classroom observations

can do more than help the researcher become more efficient in collecting observational data; they also may alert him to previously unconsidered aspects of his problem which need investigation or may even suggest a change to a more important problem.

Pilot studies or preliminary efforts to collect data are additionally useful in planning the procedures to be employed when the data are organized for the solution of the problem. If machine tabulation and analysis are to be applied to the data later collected, a hand tabulation of the pilot study data will enable a computer expert to offer suggestions. These suggestions should insure that the data later collected will more readily become computer "input." The expert may also suggest the kinds of analyses and printouts that will best provide a problem solution.

The problem as a guide to the collection of data

The statement and definition of a problem should guide the collection of data. They suggest what kinds of data are needed to answer questions or to test hypotheses stated in the problem. Decisions with reference to this aspect of the problem are among the most important decisions to be made in conducting an educational research. The researcher must collect the best data that he can in his efforts to solve his problem. He is also obligated to recognize that even the best data he can collect will have limitations which ought to be accounted for in his interpretation of them.

Although a number of procedures are described, it should not be supposed that educational research can be reduced to a mechanized routine. At every stage, educational research worthy of the name is characterized by critical and creative thinking. Systematic collection and handling of data may become routine in the sense that procedures are uniformly and continuously applied for a considerable time after thoughtful planning. But thinking is also required in maintaining the necessary uniformity and in meeting unexpected difficulties. Finally, critical thinking, often of a very high order, is needed in interpreting the data collected.

Desirable characteristics of data

Relevance to the problem is the basic criterion in deciding what data should be collected. Hypotheses deduced from theory and study of earlier research on the same or similar problems may indicate relevant and appropriate kinds of data. In survey-type researches not clearly related to theory study of similar researches may point to the kinds of data required. In such studies the questions listed in the statement of the problem themselves suggest what data are needed to answer them.

Suppose that the problem is one of investigating the comparative effectiveness of two instructional methods. Data concerning teacher attitudes toward the methods being compared are relevant to the problem, but test data collected in the experiment, if not more relevant, are more appropriate or essential in testing hypotheses concerning the effectiveness of the methods. Similarly, data collected by interviews may be more effective than data collected by questionnaires in studying a survey-type problem.

Closely related to the criterion of relevance is that of validity. A test will collect relevant data if it is valid for the purpose implied by the problem. With reference to data collected by tests or other measuring instruments, validity is considered in Chapter 7.

Similarly, consideration should be given to the reliability of the tests or other measuring instruments considered for use in the collection of data. While high reliability should be sought, a relatively unreliable test may have adequate reliability for group comparisons. Unreliability is a limitation, but it is a limitation that can be taken into account when interpreting the data.

Another fundamental criterion concerning the quality of data is representativeness. Data are usually obtained from samples of the population or universe to which the generalizations inferred from the data are to apply. If, for example, all of the sixth-grade pupils in a city school system are tested with a given achievement test, the mean of the scores is the mean of the population of pupils tested. If, however, only a sample, preferably a random sample, of sixth-grade pupils are tested, the sample mean is an estimate of the population mean. Chance operates to cause such samples to differ in representativeness. Even if a sample is perfectly representative of the pupil population from which it was drawn, this fact is unknown. Given a random sample, however, it is possible to generalize from the sample to the population and to estimate the possibility of error in such an inference. In the example just given, it is possible to estimate at a specified level of confidence the range within which the population mean is most likely to be located. An elementary explanation of how this estimate is made is given in Chapter 9.

Such estimates of error take into account both the effect of chance in limiting the representativeness of random samples, and the effects of chance or variable errors of measurement due to unreliability of tests or other instruments used in collecting data. Such statistical techniques do not take into account systematic errors which bias the data. (In large-scale investigations where data are collected from numerous groups or subsamples, systematic errors may become randomized or, more simply, compensating.) More often, however, biasing due to systematic errors cannot be adequately dealt with in organizing and interpreting data after they have been collected. Yet careful planning prior to the collection of data may prevent the amount of biasing that would limit the dependability of the generalizations later derived from the data. Such planning can provide for training interviewers and observers to be less likely to bias the data they collect. Planning may also provide for instruction to teachers so that time limits of tests are precisely observed. When a descriptive study or an experiment is begun in a large school system, the participating schools should be selected at random. Random selection prevents the biasing likely to result when schools are chosen for participation because their principals are enthusiastic about the research. It also prevents the biasing likely to occur when some schools are excluded because they are characterized by low achievement. Even in historical research lack of representativeness may be a limitation, biasing the data. Consider a study of subjects taught in colonial America that neglects to include data concerning the course offerings of the private school masters.

Frequently in educational research it is not possible to collect data that are representative of the population to which the researcher would like to have his generalizations apply. The data may pertain to a random sample of pupils in a particular school system, or to students entering some particular college. Strictly speaking, the generalizations should be restricted to the given school system or college. The researcher may, however, provide other data which tend to characterize or define the population from which his principal data are drawn. This may justify application of the findings to other school systems or colleges. The reader of the research report may discover, for example, that the level and range of ability of the pupils or students studied are comparable in level and range of ability to the pupils in his own school, school system, or college where the same test, or test battery, has been given. Such efforts to characterize or define populations investigated should occur much more frequently than they do in reports of educational research. Too often research reports imply that the conclusions apply without qualification to "sixth-grade pupils in general" or to "college students in general."

Objectivity of data and of the researcher

It is often said that educational research data should be "objective." Responses to questionnaires or to questions asked in interviews are frequently deprecated as "subjective" if they are expressions of judgments or of opinions. Such data may, however, be exactly the data appropriate to a problem. It is much more useful to think of objectivity or subjectivity in terms of the extent to which the person or persons collecting the data can influence them. Some kinds of data can be collected without being influenced by their collector if the work is done systematically and uniformly with careful checking. Numerical data in published reports, counts of pupils in classes, or numbers of correct answers on objective tests can be obtained with perfect agreement among different persons obtaining the data. Such data may be justifiably called objective. Certain other types of data can only be regarded as subjective. Different persons will assign different scores to essay responses or to ratings of traits of pupils or teachers whose behaviors are being observed. While some amount of subjectivity may be unavoidable in collecting data relevant to a problem, a researcher may be able to demonstrate that subjectivity is not a significant factor limiting the dependability of his findings and that his conclusions or generalizations are justified in spite of the faults in his data. To accomplish this acceptably the researcher himself must be objective, earnestly seeking not to go beyond his data or "overgeneralize." If his generalizations are capable of verification by another competent investigator it is evident that he has been objective and characterized by scientific attitude.[1]

The balance of this chapter is devoted to discussion of three general methods of collecting educational research data: (1) Copying data from records or published sources; (2) Constructing and using questionnaires; (3) Collecting data by interviews. Other general methods are discussed in Chapters 6 and 7. These include collecting of data by direct observation of pupil and teacher behaviors, by analysis of the content of oral and other communications relevant to educational problems, and by means of tests and other measuring instruments.

Methods of collecting data and types of problems

Before beginning to discuss general methods of collecting educational research data, it should be pointed out that methods of data collecting do not define types of educational research. These are better defined in terms of kinds of problems, for example, historical educational problems, problems concerning the status of present educational practices or conditions, and problems of experimental evaluation of the effects on school achievement of instructional methods, materials, and other factors. In conducting historical research or in studying present practices or conditions, data may be copied from records. In studying or surveying educational practices or conditions, questionnaire, interview, observational, and test data are the types of data collected. In an experimental evaluation of instructional methods test data copied from permanent or cumulative pupil records are often useful; while interview and even questionnaire data obtained from participating teachers may

---

[1] See the discussion of "intersubjectivity" in relation to repeatability and objectivity in Abraham Kaplan, *The Conduct of Inquiry* (San Francisco, Cal.: Chandler, 1964), pp. 127–28.

be a valuable supplement to the test data. Systematic observation, as will be emphasized later, is a valuable technique in maintaining the kinds of instruction specified for the various groups or classes participating in the experiment. At the same time such observations may also yield insights concerning effects on learning of the compared methods not evident in the test data. The test data may reveal the relative effectiveness of the methods; the observational data may help explain why the methods differ in effectiveness.

An educational researcher as he thinks about his problem should consider what type, or types, of data collecting are most appropriate to the problem. The truly creative researcher is one who discovers for himself a problem of unrecognized importance and then invents or adapts data collecting procedures in order to solve it. It is a rare researcher who can create for the first time a technique as novel as the Q sort or the semantic differential, but all researchers can thoughtfully seek out and often improve methods of data collecting appropriate to their problems.

COPYING DATA FROM PUBLISHED SOURCES OR RECORDS

Many of the suggestions made in the preceding chapter are relevant to the method of collecting data from records and published sources. Determining just which data of this type may be useful requires that a problem be well defined. It is essential that such data be copied accurately and that the copying be checked. Check marks should be entered adjacent to each entry to indicate that this has been done.

Copying quantitative or numerical data

In many cases, the quantitative or numerical data to be copied are single isolated items or groups of items. Any and all such items copied from a table or the context of a report should be accompanied by the words or phrases which give them meaning. These words or phrases may be derived from the title of a table and its column headings or subheadings. It is usually desirable to supply more than a mere label. For example, instead of recording $5,258 as the average salary for beginning teachers with bachelor's degrees, it is important to note that this datum refers to such beginning teachers in 156 of the largest school systems of the United States for the school year 1966–67.[2] The information needed later in citing the publication from which the datum (or data) came should also be recorded.

---

[2] "Increases in Scheduled Salaries, 1965–66 to 1966–67," *NEA Research Bulletin* 44 (December 1966), p. 110.

In copying numerical data from several columns of a table in a published report or similar source, a strip of cardboard or the edge of a large card can be used in following a row of figures across the table. If one or more of the columns do not contain relevant data, a notched strip of cardboard or a notched card may be used to reveal relevant items and to mask irrelevant ones. In copying numerical data it is desirable to anticipate how the data are later to be organized and summarized. The form on which the data are copied may be similar to an anticipated table. Items from several sources may be copied on the same form. Blanks or empty cells on the form may indicate the need for further search for relevant items. Again it is essential that the data copied be appropriately labeled. Headings and subheadings of tables are usually brief and it is often necessary to seek their precise meanings in the context of a report, or elsewhere. Where data are copied from different sources it is necessary to know whether or not such a label as "expenditure for teachers' salaries" has the same meaning from one source to another. In some cases, teachers may be restricted to classroom teachers. In other cases, counselors, librarians, and other school personnel may be included. Where the data copied are percentages, it is important to know what bases were used in their computation. Percentages of college entrants receiving remedial instruction in reading and in English composition have little meaning unless the criteria used in their selection are also known. Such criteria vary from college to college.

Checking accuracy of sources

In addition to checking the copying of all entries on a copying form and using care in their accurate labeling, it is essential that the accuracy of the sources be checked. Efforts should be made to compare the data from one source with data reported in an independent source. The researcher should follow the example of the historical investigator attempting to obtain affirmations of independent witnesses. On some occasions, the researcher will discover evidences of the unreliability of a source. Data from one year to another may not reveal a consistent trend—one or more figures may seem greatly "out of line" with other figures. Other sources, or the original investigator, may need to be consulted.

Obtaining clearance for student data

For some problems data will need to be collected from student records. It is essential in such cases to secure clearance, not from a school principal or teacher, but from the superintendent of schools. In other cases, clearance will need to be obtained from the appropriate college administrator. In obtaining such clearances, the superintendent, or other administrator, should be provided with statements indicating the importance of the problem and clearly defining it. Especially useful is a series of questions in nontechnical phraseology that the study, hopefully, will answer. It is essential to tell the administrator that the data will be treated confidentially, and sometimes it is necessary to assure the administrator that the data will not be so reported as to reflect discredit to his school system or higher institution. Where the data are likely to be uncomplimentary to their source, the administrator may still decide to grant clearance when he is assured that the data from several sources will be pooled without identification of the individual sources. Finally, the administrator must be promised that a report based on pupil data will not disclose the names of the pupils even though the names will need to be recorded for certain research purposes such as the computation of indices of relationship (for example, the coefficients of correlation explained in Chapter 8).

In obtaining clearance it is also important to make clear to the administrator just who is to copy the data from the school records. Some administrators may insist that such copying be done by school personnel. Other administrators may prefer that the work be done by the researcher himself, or by his trained assistants. In any case, it will need to be indicated that the data collecting will not interfere with usual school activities. Finally, the researcher should assure the administrator that he will receive a summary of the data in the report of the study and should keep this promise. Study of the report by the cooperating administrators prior to its publication may result in suggestions contributing to its improvement.

Where random sampling of schools or colleges has been done it is important to obtain clearance for *all* such sources of data to maintain the sampling as random. In this connection, emphasizing the fact that the data are to be pooled as described above may be a crucial factor in obtaining clearance.

Securing cooperation of school personnel

In collecting data from pupil records, the researcher will need to consult school personnel. The researcher should attempt to ease the burden on the school person who is showing him where to find the data and the labels which give them meaning. If assistants are used, the researcher should accompany them on their first visit to a school and should check their initial efforts to copy the needed data. The work should be planned so that it will be accomplished systematically, uniformly, and as unobstrusively as possible. Entering a school during the first minutes of a school day is usually unwise. It is better to wait until the principal is sure that all classrooms are manned by teachers and instruction is well begun.

Copying data from student records

When collecting data from pupil records, individual cards containing appropriately placed and labeled blanks are likely to be more useful than larger forms. If the items to be copied are test scores, or derived measures such as the standard scores or percentile ranks explained in Chapter 8, it is essential to record the title and form of each test and the date on which it was given. Data from different tests or forms of tests may create a problem of establishing comparability of such measures from time to time for the same pupil or from group to group of different pupils. This problem is much less likely to be encountered where a city school system has a well-administered citywide testing program. When school marks are recorded, copy the precise course titles or have them printed in advance on the data cards. If it is anticipated that grade-point averages will be computed, it is necessary to record also the numbers of credit hours earned in each course. When the data are teacher ratings of pupil traits, descriptions of pupil attainments and maladjustments, and other evidences of pupil behaviors, small data cards may not suffice. What is said in the pupil record should be copied accurately and appropriately labeled. The researcher will have problems in determining the extent to which such data are comparable from pupil to pupil, teacher to teacher, and school to school. These kinds of data may be among the most important data to collect in investigating certain problems; they are also the data most necessary to treat confidentially.

Conclusion

In concluding this discussion of the collecting of data from published reports or school records, it should be emphasized that accuracy of copying and labeling entries is essential, as is keeping a complete record of the sources consulted. A record of this kind makes it possible to locate the source more easily if additional data are needed, or if the accuracy of the data collected needs further checking. Such a record is also necessary in writing the research report in order to give adequate and accurate citations of the sources of the data. Finally, for reasons of accuracy, the collection of data as described above should always be considered as preferable to the collection of the same data through the use of a questionnaire.

CONSTRUCTING AND USING QUESTIONNAIRES

The collecting of data by means of questionnaires has long been criticized. Consider this comment made in 1839, "It is impossible to expect accuracy in returns obtained by circulars, various constructions being put on the same question by different individuals who consequently classify their replies upon various principles,"[3] or that voiced by E. L. Thorndike in 1911, "One vice of statistical studies in education today is the indiscriminate use of lists of questions as a means of collecting data by correspondence."[4]

Many more such critical comments have been made from 1911 to the present time.[5] For example, after noting that the mail questionnaire is in popular use in education in spite of its serious limitations when not used with other techniques, Kerlinger states, "Two of these defects are possible lack of response and the inability to check the responses given. These defects, especially the first, are serious enough to make the mail questionnaire worse than useless, except in highly sophisticated hands."[6]

Necessity of questionnaires in wide-scale data collection

Despite the foregoing, it is evident that competent use of the questionnaire in the investigation of important problems cannot be condemned. Obviously, widespread collection of data by the United States Office of Education, the Research Division of the National Education Association, and other such governmental divisions or professional organizations can be accomplished in no other way. The cost of collecting data by interview would be prohibitive. There is usually a much higher proportion of response to questionnaires originating from such sources than from independent educational researchers including graduate students. When a graduate student *must* use a questionnaire, it should be sponsored by his institution or some educational association.

Obtaining representative returns

In many questionnaire studies less than 50 percent of the recipients complete and return the questionnaire received. Such a small percentage of return would not be so serious a matter if the sample of respondents were representative of the population to which the questionnaire is sent. Unfortunately the representativeness of the respon-

---

[3] "Report of a Committee of the Manchester Statistical Society on the State of Education in the County of Rutland in the Year 1838," *Journal of the Statistical Society of London* 2 (October 1839), p. 303.

[4] Edward L. Thorndike, "Quantitative Investigations in Education," *School Review Monograph*, Vol. 1, 1911, p. 43.

[5] For a brief history of the early use of questionnaires in educational investigations, see Walter S. Monroe and others, *Ten Years of Educational Research*, University of Illinois Bureau of Educational Research Bulletin No. 42 (Urbana: University of Illinois, 1928), pp. 36–38.

[6] Fred N. Kerlinger, *Foundations of Behavioral Research* (New York: Holt, Rinehart and Winston, 1965), p. 397.

dents is seldom known and one can usually safely assume that the sample is biased. It is widely accepted that questionnaires sent to the alumni of a university are less likely to be returned by those who are relatively unsuccessful. Factors other than level of success may also cause questionnaire recipients to differ in their willingness to respond. The seriousness of this problem is evidenced in the following statement from the *NEA Research Bulletin* earlier cited:

> A recent NEA Research Division study found that until 90 percent of those queried have responded, the results often do not reflect accurately important characteristics of the entire group from which the sample is drawn. Therefore, the Division usually makes five follow-up requests at two-week intervals. In some cases telegrams are sent.[7]

Even a professional association with such prestige as the National Council of Teachers of English in conducting a study supported by funds supplied by the United States Office of Education under contract with the University of Minnesota had difficulty in obtaining a satisfactory proportion of response:

> Of the 1,683 questionnaires mailed to administrators in colleges, schools, and other agencies, 810 came back, a return of 48 percent. But of these AQ's [administrator questionnaires], only 510 or 30 percent, contained sufficient information to justify their inclusion.[8]

In a scholarly discussion of the representativeness of his data, Allen mentions his inability to obtain cooperation from the superintendents of schools of Chicago and San Francisco, two cities with large numbers of non-English speaking children and adults. No reply was received from Chicago, in spite of follow-up requests. The superintendent of the San Francisco schools contended that "lack of time and personnel prevented a response."[9] Similarly, several college administrators included in the sample failed to respond because they did not consider foreign students' difficulties with English a problem. While the superintendents and other administrators referred to possibly should have been more alert to the importance of the research just cited, it

---

[7] "Increases in Scheduled Salaries," p. 109. Reprinted with permission of publisher.

[8] Harold B. Allen, *Tenes, A Survey of the Teaching of English to Non-English Speakers in the United States* (Champaign, Ill.: National Council of the Teachers of English, 1966), p. 5.

[9] *Ibid.*, p. 6.

should be recognized that the high incidence of poorly constructed and complex questionnaires asking for data relevant to trivial problems has made unwelcome even superior questionnaires. Furthermore, unless clearance has been properly obtained, most principals and teachers will be reluctant to respond.

For these reasons the use of questionnaires should be limited to worthwhile inquiries for which the needed data cannot be obtained by other means.

Questionnaire request for necessary and readily available information

The recipient of a questionnaire is most likely to respond to requests for simple factual information, either in his possession, or easily accessible to him. A questionnaire that requires the recipient to spend much time in collecting the requested information is not likely to be very successful and should be used only when the problem is one of considerable importance. The recipient should not be asked to do work which the investigator can do himself, such as computing totals, averages, or percentages. The questionnaire should be just long enough to secure the necessary facts or opinions, but the investigator must make certain that he has anticipated all of his needs. If the data required for the problem are not thus anticipated, the investigator may find it necessary to do without important information, or to impose a second questionnaire on his respondents.

Writing a questionnaire

The statement of the problem of the research, especially if it lists subsidiary questions, will suggest the content of the questionnaire items and a logical organization for the questionnaire. The researcher should anticipate the kind of thinking necessary for effective response. Before proceeding to the items, however, the questionnaire should start with labeled blanks for name, institutional affiliation, date, sex, and other necessary background information. A decision will need to be made on whether or not the questionnaire should be signed by the respondent. In my opinion an unsigned questionnaire does not, on that account, produce honest answers. There may be occasions, nonetheless, when it seems desirable not to ask for the respondent's signature. A statement such as the following may overcome reluctance of respondents to give their names:

> While you are asked to give your name, your individual answers will be treated confidentially. The name is necessary because we wish to classify the questionnaires for analysis in terms of other data.

The questions should be stated clearly to minimize misinterpretation. Technical words and other unusual terms should be explained. Efforts should be made to so word questions that they will less often suggest or bias the answers.

The use of "open-end" or essay type questions

It is sometimes desirable to use "open-end" questions. For example, in collecting data relevant to testing programs in a large and random sample of cities and higher institutions, a brief questionnaire of five such questions was used, for example, "What tests are used to collect the data used in counseling?" It was felt that these questions would obtain more honest answers than questions whose listed answers might suggest practices worth marking even though not actually employed. The answers were not particularly difficult to classify when several hundred respondents replied. The same technique is useful in obtaining judgments or opinions even if the classification of answers is subjective. Frequently, in questionnaires where most of the items are of the "fixed-alternative" or objective type some questions are included for which written answers are expected.[10] When this is the case, each such question should be followed by enough widely spaced blank lines for an adequate answer.

Open-end questions, discussed in the last part of this chapter, are extensively used in interviewing.

The use of "fixed-alternative" or objective type items

In most questionnaire studies, however, it is best to use questions calling for responses involving as little writing as possible. Questions calling for numerical data, for "yes" or "no" responses, underlining, or checking are most desirable in questionnaires where answers are to be entered on the questionnaire itself. Since the 1940's, the development of machine methods of scoring and analysis has made it possible to construct questionnaires formulating the questions as illustrated below, but preceded by directions specifying that the answers are to be recorded on an answer sheet or mark-sense card. This is later discussed under the heading "Tabulating Questionnaire Data."

Several years ago, in the course of conducting an institutional research which definitely contributed to curriculum revision in the Chicago City Junior College, the author administered a questionnaire containing items of two types to graduating students. Since the respon-

---

[10] The two types of questions, whether in questionnaires or in interviews, are often referred to as "open" and "closed."

dents were a "captive audience," an almost 100 percent response was obtained. The first series were of the fixed-alternative type usually requiring a single response:

23. In which of the following general courses do you think that you learned the most about the scientific method?
A. Biology
B. Humanities
C. Physical Science
D. Social Science

Some items of this type permitted a multiple response. For example:

28. For which of the following general courses did you receive credit?
A. Biology
B. Humanities
C. Physical Science
D. Social Science
E. All of the above courses

Where the number of alternatives exceeded five, two or three successive items were used with the instruction to the student to mark *one* answer for the group of items. This was necessary since the answers were recorded on answer sheets with five answer spaces after each answer sheet number. If answers are marked on the questionnaire itself, on a specially designed answer sheet, or on a mark-sense card, the alternatives may exceed five. In the institutional research mentioned above, such items were used to obtain data with reference to which higher institution the students planned to attend after graduation or which profession or vocation they expected to enter. One of the answers to items of this type whether given as single items or groups of items should be a last alternative, "None of the above."

An amusing sidelight with reference to item 23 quoted above occurred when the highest percent of the graduates, by far, indicated that they thought they learned the most about scientific method in *social* science. The chairman of the physical science department, assuming that physical science by its very nature makes the greatest contribution to this important objective, protested, asking the students how they could give the credit to social science. The answer was invariably, "But the social science instructors talk about scientific method all of the time!"

The questionnaire also included a series of numbered statements for which the graduating students were to answer A to indicate agreement, B to indicate disagreement, and C to indicate neither agreement nor disagreement. Three of the statements in a second such study are listed:

19. The trimester plan has enabled me to speed up my junior college education.
21. Competent students should be permitted to substitute specialized courses in the same general field for the general course in that field.
28. The trimester plan has caused me to slow down my junior college education.

Items 19 and 28 exemplify items or questions which will provide an estimate of the reliability of the questionnaire data. The data collected by them were, in this instance, in close agreement. The sum of the two A percents approximated 100. Items with more than three alternatives can also be used in obtaining such estimates.

Three categories of response were given for the series of items just illustrated. For certain problems, it is useful to provide a scale of five categories in collecting attitude data.

Improving a questionnaire through criticism and trial

The first draft of a questionnaire should be submitted to competent persons for criticism and be given a preliminary trial by persons typical of the proposed mailing list. Criticism and trial often reveal inadequacies not apparent to the author of the questionnaire. For example, it may be found that certain questions are easily misinterpreted. Analysis of these questions may show that the terms used are more technical than necessary or are in need of definition. Attempts to tabulate the data secured in a trial may suggest changes which will make tabulating easier. Even in cases where the questionnaire data will later be tabulated by means of data processing equipment, *hand* tabulation of the pilot study data is desirable; the researcher is more likely to sense the ambiguities and other defects of his questions. It has already been suggested that such tabulations of data will be useful to the expert in data processing when planning later machine tabulation and analysis. The expert may also have suggestions with reference to the item forms used and the directions given to the persons who will respond on the questionnaire itself or on an answer sheet or mark-sense card.

Duplicating the questionnaire

An attractive-looking questionnaire is much more likely to receive a good response than one that is unappealing. If possible, the questionnaire should be printed; respondents can more easily write legibly on a printed page. When it is more than two or three typewritten pages in length and several hundred copies are required, offset printing is no more expensive than mimeographing.

The questionnaire should have a heading which includes an institutional or associational designation, and a title. As noted earlier, where responses are to be entered on the questionnaire itself, blanks should be provided for name, institution, date, sex, and other background data. The questions should be spaced with care, ample room being allowed for written responses. Respondents are less likely to overlook items when they are spaced effectively. The typing should be free from error and unsightly corrections. The size of the questionnaire should be one that is convenient for handling and filing. Letter size (8½ by 11) is recommended. Legal size sheets are inconvenient.

The covering letter

When it is mailed, a questionnaire should be accompanied by a tactful covering letter.[11] Such a letter should inform the questionnaire recipient of the nature of the problem and of its importance. The discussion of the nature of the problem should be a concise summary statement rather than the elaborate one that lists numerous subordinate questions characteristic of a complete statement of the problem. (The questionnaire itself informs the recipient of such questions.) The discussion of the importance of the problem should also be relatively brief and should imply that a satisfactory solution of the problem will be important to the recipient. Mention should *not* be made that the solution of the problem is of importance to the graduate student because it will enable him to obtain his master's or doctor's degree. It is advisable to have the letter signed by the sponsor rather than by the graduate student. Many persons unwilling to respond to a questionnaire from an unknown person will respond to one signed by someone affiliated with a respected institution or professional organization.

Something may be said in the covering letter to indicate why a response from the recipient is essential. For example, it may be implied that he is among those whose position is uniquely such that his judgments or the information he alone can supply is indispensable. It is a good tactic to point out that little time will be required in responding.

It is frequently desirable to send the questionnaire to the chief administrator of a school system or college, suggesting in the covering letter that he delegate the responsibility of responding to the person in his school system or higher institution best able to reply. If this suggestion is heeded by the chief administrator, he is relieved of the work of responding, clearance is obtained, and the delegation of the work will be regarded by the subordinate as a command. Thus, the percentage of response will be increased. In my survey of testing mentioned earlier this strategy was used with generally effective results.

---

[11] For a good example of the kind of letter described above, see Walter R. Borg, *Educational Research, an Introduction* (New York: David McKay, 1963), pp. 214–15.

In the case of one higher institution the professor to whom the task was delegated, an enthusiast for testing, wrote a bitter letter to his president stating that, in spite of his years of pleading, their institution had no testing program worth telling anybody about. This letter was the response received!

The covering letter may conclude with a promise to supply the respondent with a summary of the questionnaire data when available. This promise will, of course, be kept. Attention can also be called to the enclosed self-addressed return envelope and to the desirability of a prompt reply.

Preferably the letter should be printed rather than mimeographed with space left at the upper right for the name and address of the recipient, later typed in with the same typewriter used in typing the body of the letter prior to its printing. Space may also be provided in the usual place for the sponsor's handwritten signature above his typed name and title. The signature may be added later in other than black ink. (In large-scale studies a facsimile of the signature or the typed name alone may be printed.) Such a letter can be typed on a letterhead for photographing in offset printing.

Distributing the questionnaire

The questionnaire should be mailed to all, or to a representative sample,[12] of the persons, schools, school systems, or higher institutions to whom the findings or generalizations derived from the data are to apply.

Before sending out a very elaborate questionnaire the willingness of the prospective recipients to respond should be determined by a preliminary inquiry. When this precaution is taken, greater interest is likely to be stimulated. Furthermore, some of the expense of sending the elaborate questionnaires to individuals disinclined to respond will be avoided. Those willing to respond, however, may still be a nonrepresentative sample.

The questionnaire should be mailed at an opportune time, accompanied by a self-addressed stamped envelope for its return. Seasons of vacation or periods of excessive activity should be avoided. For example, it is unwise to mail out a questionnaire just prior to the Christmas holidays or at the beginning or close of a semester.

One or more follow-up letters should be sent to those who fail to respond. Frequently, a tactful follow-up will greatly increase the percentage of responses. It may be worthwhile to record the number of

---

[12] See pages 294–295, 308–314, of Chapter 10 for a discussion of sampling techniques applicable in the collection of questionnaire and interview data.

questionnaires returned daily and to mail the follow-up cards or letters when the number falls off abruptly.

Hand tabulation of questionnaire data

If data are to be tabulated by hand, a tabulation form must be designed. The questions, or their numbers, may be listed along the left margin followed by appropriately labeled blanks or cells in which tallies can be entered. For example, a fixed-alternative item like item 23 on page 100 may be provided for by a row of cells on the tabulation form:

	A	B	C	D	E
23.					

Items having three alternative responses will have three cells labeled A, B, and C. Where responses are brief, written answers and these can be categorized, a row of appropriately labeled cells may suffice. A last large cell may be set up for unusual answers which do not fit any of the categories. If the sample of questionnaires has been numbered serially, the relevant questionnaire numbers may be entered in this cell so that the researcher can later pull out these returns and summarize the various responses.

It is most efficient to tally all of the responses on a given questionnaire return before beginning another. If the data are to be recorded for subgroups, use a separate form for each subgroup. The hand-tally form, whether used to tabulate only the data in a pilot study or all of the data later collected, suggests, if properly designed, the organization of tables which will ultimately appear in the report of the research.

Machine tabulation using 80-column cards

For many years, questionnaire and other data have been coded and punched by a key-punch operator into 80-column cards for later machine sorting and tabulating.[13] A single column of such a card suffices for as many as ten categories or intervals of a variable.[14] If the cate-

---

[13] According to Fattu, "machines for sorting cards were invented before 1890 . . . Hollerith saw that the next census of 1890 would not be completed before the 1900 census was started, and proposed a mechanical system for such tasks." Nicholas A. Fattu, "Processing of Data," in C. W. Harris, ed., *Encyclopedia of Educational Research*, 3rd ed. (New York: Macmillan, 1960), p. 1051.

[14] There are actually 12 positions in each column, but the two or three at the top of the column are used for other purposes including, for example, the recording of the letters of a name. Figure 17.2 on page 508 illustrates how information is recorded in an 80-column IBM card.

gories are mutually exclusive, a single hole may be punched in one of the standard 0 through 9 positions in a given column. For some variables, more than one hole may be punched. Suppose, as an example, student respondents to a questionnaire are asked to indicate the extracurricular activities in which they participate. When the number of categories of each of a number of variables is no more than five, each of the columns can provide for two variables. Where the categories are more than ten, two or more columns are used. For example, 349 will be punched as holes in the third, fourth, and ninth positions of three successive columns. After the cards have been punched by a key-punch operator and verified, they are machine sorted by variables and categories within variables. The data are then machine tabulated and printed. A major advantage of such machine sorting and tabulating is that data relevant to different subgroups can be sorted, tabulated, and printed separately. Another major advantage is that the data relevant to pairs of variables can be printed so as to reveal the relationships between them. Such printouts resemble the correlation charts shown in Chapter 8.[15]

In order to punch cards as described above, a key-punch operator needs a code[16] to transcribe the data from a questionnaire, or other record, to successive columns and positions within columns of each card. Sometimes a researcher or one of his assistants facilitates the process by entering the code on each item of data entered in each of the questionnaires returned. For instance, 27–3 would indicate that a hole should be punched in position 3 of column 27.

An alternative to the procedure described above is to so design a questionnaire that the code is inherent in the questionnaire itself. A row of 25 squares may be printed at the top so that the respondent can enter the letters of his name. Then the questions can be numbered to correspond with the numbers of later columns of the card. The questions should also be preceded by parentheses for the recording of answers by the respondents. For example:

38 (   )   Write the number from 0 to 5 which best indicates the total college credit hours you have earned to date: (1) 1 to 11; (2) 12 to 28; (3) 29 to 44; (4) 45 to 63; (5) 64 or more.

39 (   )   What high school did you last attend? (Select the proper code number from the list at the upper right.)

---

15 See pages 221 and 223.

16 Robert S. Casey and James W. Perry, eds., *Punched Cards; Their Applications to Science and Industry* (New York: Reinhold, 1951); Harry P. Hartkemeir, *Punched Card Methods* (Dubuque, Iowa: William C. Brown, 1952).

41 (   )   What is your reason for enrolling in college courses this semester? Choose the one response from the list at the right which best designates your reason.

Note that the second and third items listed above require two columns of the card since the code numbers to be entered in the parentheses are two-digit numbers. Holes are punched in columns 39 and 40 and in colunms 41 and 42. The questionnaire from which these illustrative items were taken was administered to obtain data in a survey of the characteristics of students registering in September 1963, at Chicago City Junior College.

Carefully phrased directions to the respondents should precede questions of the type illustrated above. The first draft and the revised drafts of such a questionnaire should be very carefully evaluated, especially by the expert in data processing, prior to its duplication in final form. A last trial prior to final revision with several persons responding in the presence of the researcher will help to identify details still in need of modification.

When such a questionnaire is administered to groups of students, those supervising the students should be as well trained as if they were proctoring an examination. Even under the best of circumstances the filled-out questionnaires should be inspected by the researcher or his assistants prior to card punching and tabulation. These precautions also apply to questionnaires requiring responses to be recorded on an answer sheet, rather than on the questionnaire itself.

Tabulation of questionnaire data on answer sheets

After the IBM 805 electric scoring machine became available around 1940, a "graphic item counter" was added to the machine to facilitate item analysis.[17] This device was useful, not only for this purpose, but in the tabulation of questionnaire data where the questionnaires consisted of fixed-alternative items of the kinds illustrated on pages 100 and 101. If, for example, there were 18 questions each with five alternative answers, 100 answer sheets could be put through the machine in about 12 minutes. The machine would then print a bar graph. The length of each of the 90 bars indicated the number of respondents giving that answer. Students when so directed could mark more than one answer space for a given question of from one to five alternative answers. When the questionnaire contained more than 18 items, or more precisely, more than 90 different alternative answers, the process was repeated the required number of times. When there were more than 100 answer sheets, the data in successive bar graphs were com-

[17] See pages 361 to 366 of Chapter 11.

bined by hand. If data for different subgroups were desired, the answer sheets were first sorted by subgroups and the bar graphs were later appropriately labeled. Contemporary data processing has made the above procedure obsolete. Modern electronic equipment is very much more rapid and accurate.

The relatively new IBM 1230 electronic scoring machine scores test answer sheets at the rate of 1200 an hour. When the machine is connected to a key punch the data on the answer sheets are automatically punched into 80-column cards. The IBM 1231 transfers the answer sheet data to magnetic tape, whether for a roster of scores or for analysis by other data processing equipment. Various models of the Digitek scoring machine transfer the test or questionnaire data to punched cards, punched paper tape, or magnetic tape. Such machines are becoming more widely available.

While standard answer sheets containing questionnaire rather than test data can be "read" by the "optical scanners" mentioned above, it is better to use a specially designed answer sheet. Such an answer sheet can have both the questions and spaces for recording answers printed on it. A researcher planning to design his own special answer sheet should obtain samples to serve as models. He should also keep abreast of further progress in the development of machine methods for handling questionnaire and other data.

Conclusion

Studies based on questionnaire data can, but seldom do, contribute significantly to the science of education. Institutional research of the kinds described in the preceding paragraphs using questionnaire and other data are, however, of considerable value to administrative officers, counselors, and teachers involved in decision-making. Such decisions may relate to course offerings, placement and guidance practices, and other aspects of the educational program of the institution. Why not in this way give students and graduates a voice in policy-making?

It should be reiterated, in concluding this section on the collection of data by questionnaire, that the problem should be an important one for which it is impractical to obtain data from widespread sources in any other way. Background data on the questionnaire and data from other sources should be used to evaluate the representativeness of samples of respondents. Where this cannot be done, the researcher should at least summarize the questionnaire background data so that the reader of his report can infer the kind of population to which his findings do apply. Such data may include age, sex, vocation, and present geographical location of respondents. Finally, an effort should be made to collect the same kind of data by interview in order to validate those collected by questionnaire. The population interviewed should be a population comparable to the questionnaire population *sampled,* not a biased population comparable to the population of the questionnaire respondents. The collection of data by means of interviews is further discussed below.

COLLECTING DATA BY INTERVIEWS

As is true of all research, the data collected by interviews should be relevant to the problem of the research, should be as reliable as possible, and should be sufficiently representative to justify generalizations. In common with questions on questionnaires, questions in interviews should be characterized by vocabulary or phraseology appropriate to the level of understanding of the respondents. Sponsorship and clearance are often desirable or essential. Both fixed-alternative and open-end questions may be used. In collecting data by interviews it is essential to try out a schedule of questions prior to collection of data in earnest; such trials are means of acquiring skill in interviewing which requires more time, effort and skill than data collection by questionnaire.

Superiority of the interview to the questionnaire

When data are collected by interview it is possible to reduce, if not eliminate, one of the major limitations of the questionnaire technique— lack of response due to inability of the respondent to understand the questions. The level of understanding of the respondent can be assessed and necessary explanations provided. On occasion, appropriate questioning may reveal that a respondent is not competent to respond. As will later be discussed at length, interviewing makes possible collection of data "in depth." Finally, repeated efforts to interview all of the persons in a sample may contribute data much more representative than the data solicited by a mailed questionnaire.

In contrast to data collection by questionnaire, data collection by interview is deservedly becoming much more highly regarded as a tool in scientific behavioral research. Interviews can be used in the first stages of an inquiry to identify variables and relations between variables. Such relations may later be formulated as hypotheses for subsequent testing with observational or experimental data. The interview itself may also be used to collect data for the testing of hypotheses. The questions may be so formulated that the data collected measure the variables quantitatively. Such questions are scale items calling for varying degrees of agreement or disagreement or varying degrees of attitude. When this is the case, the questions become parts of a psychometric instrument rather than merely a means of collecting information.[18]

General characteristics of effective interviewing

To collect interview data effectively, the interviewer must be well prepared for his task. The training and experience in interviewing possibly obtained in a pilot study are helpful in this preparation. An important phase is that of determining what questions are to be asked and in what order. It is essential that the questions be relevant to the problem. Relevance to the problem is important not only to the solution of the problem; it is also a factor in maintaining rapport with a respondent. After the interviewer has motivated the respondent by interesting him in the importance and purpose of the research, presenting him with questions without apparent relevance is likely to reduce the respondent's willingness to communicate. When a respondent clearly understands the general purpose of the questions, he is more likely to answer with an appropriate frame of reference.

The language level of the questions, in both vocabulary and sentence structure should be compatible with the level of understanding of the persons interviewed. This does not mean that the interviewer should try to talk as the respondent does. Such an attempt could decrease the respondent's respect for him in his role as interviewer. It is more important that the respondent be made to feel "that the interviewer is an empathic individual, a person who can understand him."[19]

Fixed-alternative or open-end questions?

A major decision in the preparation of a series of questions, or interview schedule, is whether to use fixed-alternative items or open-end questions. The fixed-alternative type of item is widely used in opinion polling where the purpose is to classify the persons interviewed. In educational research, the following fixed-alternative item might be used in a survey of teacher opinion of team teaching:

> Numerous elementary schools in this area are experimenting with team teaching. Do you favor this method of organizing instruction?
>
> Yes_____
>
> No_____
>
> Undecided_____

While items of this type are useful in promoting uniformity in the collection of data and in obtaining responses readily tabulated, in con-

---

[18] Kerlinger, *Foundations of Behavioral Research*, p. 468.

[19] Robert L. Kahn and Charles F. Cannell, *The Dynamics of Interviewing* (New York: Wiley, 1957), p. 112.

trast to open-end questions they do not reveal *why* respondents answer as they do. Consider several teachers who answer "Yes" to the above item. The first teacher may do so because of experience with the method in which she was in charge of the team, a status very satisfying to her ego. The second teacher may more genuinely feel that team teaching has merit because it capitalizes on the varied abilities of a group of teachers. The third teacher may answer "Yes" because she has observed certain values to the pupils thus taught. Finally, a fourth teacher with no team teaching experience may answer "Yes" because it seems to be growing in popularity. Examples could also be given of why teachers might respond negatively. One teacher may genuinely feel that traditional instructional organization is superior to team teaching, while another teacher answers "No" because she resents the fact that she was not included in the team.

In a somewhat similar illustration from industrial interviewing, Kahn and Cannell state:

> The open question appears to be more appropriate when our objective is not only to discover the respondent's attitude toward some issue, but also to learn something about his level of information, the structure or basis on which he has formed his opinion, the frame of reference within which he answers the question, and the intensity of his feelings on the topic.[20]

In this connection, imagine how the teachers mentioned above might have answered the open-end question:

How do you feel about team teaching?

Fixed-alternative items seeking factual information assumed to be in the possession of the respondents are often used in collecting data by interview. They may precede the asking of open-end questions to obtain essential "background" data. If interviewing is used to validate data collected by a mail questionnaire, as earlier suggested, and the questionnaire contains fixed-alternative items, the interview questions must be identical. Finally, if the fixed-alternative items are "scale" items calling for varying degrees of agreement or disagreement, or varying degrees of attitude, as exemplified by the items on p. 178, the interview schedule becomes a psychometric instrument.

Funnel-type questioning

The interviewer may start with a broad general question and continue with increasingly specific ones. According to Kahn and Cannell this de-

---

[20] *Ibid.,* p. 135. Reprinted with permission of authors and publisher.

vice yields information useful in determining the respondent's frame of reference and prevents the "early questions from conditioning or biasing the responses to those which come later." Sometimes the questions in such a sequence begin with open-end ones and conclude with closed or fixed-alternative items, for example, those of the scale item type which measure degrees of attitude toward some specific issue. On occasion, the funnel is inverted. Starting with the specific questions may encourage the respondent to think his way through to an expression of a previously unformulated point of view.[21]

Probing questions

When using a sequence of open-end questions it is frequently desirable for an interviewer to supplement a primary or initial question on some new topic or issue with secondary or probing questions.[22] This requires great skill. Such probes should motivate communication without biasing the respondent's attitudes. They should elicit valuable information concerning the respondent's frame of reference. Examples of "neutral" probes in addition to "I see" and "um-hm" include:

How do you mean?
I'd like to know more about your thinking on that.
What do you have in mind there?
I am not sure I understand what you have in mind.
Why do you think that is so?
Why do you feel that way?
What do you think causes that?
Do you have any other reasons for feeling as you do?
Anything else?[23]

After completing such a series of probing questions, it is usually desirable for the interviewer to recall to the respondent the earlier expressed purpose of the interview.

Using funnel and probing types of questions
to measure variables

Measurement of variables in interview data can be accomplished with other types of items than the scale type earlier referred to in which the fixed alternatives range over degrees of agreement and disagreement. In an unusually challenging research in which data were collected by

---

[21] *Ibid.*, pp. 158–60.

[22] *Ibid.*, pp. 205–210.

[23] *Ibid.*, p. 207.

interviews, Richard Wolf described his measurement of specific environmental factors:

> It was noted earlier that the focus of our investigation was what parents did rather than what parents were in terms of status, economic well-being or some demographic variable. The questions in the interview schedule were carefully designed to elicit information about what parents actually did insofar as general achievement and academic achievement were concerned.
>
> One process characteristic which was measured, for example, was the parents' educational aspirations for the child. In the course of the interview, the parents were asked how much education they wished their child to have, how much education they actually expected their child to receive, and the minimum amount of education they felt their child must have. In response to these questions, a number of parents indicated that they hoped their child would receive a college education. Later in the interview, the topic was brought up again, and parents who had indicated that they hoped their child would go to college were queried as to what plans had been made to finance a college education. The answers to this latter question were most illuminating in differentiating a seemingly homogeneous group—parents who had hoped that their child would have a college education. The responses ranged from the total absence of any plan to the most elaborate of plans. At the high end of the scale were several parents who had already established trust funds earmarked for their children's college expenses. It may be noted that parents who rated high on the planning for the attainment of educational goals were also the ones who indicated that education was frequently discussed in the home, and that the child was aware of the educational plans that had been made.[24]

Wolf's total environmental ratings correlated + .69 with measured general intelligence and + .80 with total scores on an achievement battery, much higher correlations than those obtained when general measurements of environment are used.

Decreasing the anxiety of interview respondents

If the data collected by interview from pupils, parents, teachers, principals, and even superintendents of schools are likely to seem threatening or embarrassing, the interviewer is confronted with delicate situa-

---

[24] Richard Wolf, "The Measurement of Environments," in Anne Anastasi, ed., *Testing Problems in Perspective* (Washington, D.C.: American Council on Education, 1966), pp. 495–97. This paper was first published in the *Proceedings of the 1964 Invitational Conference on Testing Problems* (Princeton, N.J.: Educational Testing Service, 1965). It is quoted with the permission of the author and both publishers.

tions. Anxiety in adults may be reduced by a statement that the data will be treated confidentially. Another generally helpful device is to use a question which focuses the respondent's attention on some person other than himself. Often a question may ostensibly concern some hypothetical person or group of persons. Instead of asking a superintendent of schools "How do you exert leadership in school administration?" it is both less threatening (and more discreet) to ask, "In what ways do you feel that school superintendents can exert leadership in school administration?" A sequence of questions following the one just given with reference to decision-making in his school system may elicit responses answering the unasked first question. Indirect questioning is particularly useful where threatening or embarrassing data are to be collected from pupils. It is usually wiser to ask a high school dropout why he thinks boys drop out of high school before confronting him with a question which asks specifically why he dropped out. Kahn and Cannell describe an indirect approach using cartoons in which the respondent completes a blank cartoon "balloon." In the first example given, the respondent is expected to write in a reply a boy might make to the pictured father's admonition, "Be sure to be home by ten o'clock. We are going out ourselves and will be late getting back." In the second example, the boy is with friends in a drugstore where a clock shows that it is 9:57 P.M. The boy says, "I have to go home now," while a friend replies, "Oh, stick around. Your folks aren't home anyway." Quoting Kahn and Cannell:

> The interviewer presented this picture to the respondent and asked him what the boy decided to do. Again the responses were readily given. They were used to infer the extent to which the adolescent boys had internalized the parents' standards. Would they obey, even when the risks of disobeying were pretty well eliminated?[25]

Other characteristics of effective interview questions

The wording of questions should be free from ambiguity. For example, a question containing the phrase "democratic school administration" may be criticized since the phrase has no truly clear operational meaning. Long and complex questions are usually characterized by ambiguity. A respondent can get lost in the verbiage. Care should be exercised that questions do not promote insincere socially desirable responses nor present the respondent with the dilemma of giving a socially undesirable one. The desired data may be obtained through use of indirect

---

[25] Kahn and Cannell, *Dynamics of Interviewing*, p. 145.

questioning, other subtle means, or postponing direct questioning until rapport has clearly been established. Leading questions should also be avoided. Asking "Do you prefer trimesters to semesters?" encourages a respondent to give an affirmative answer while a fixed-alternative item or an open-end question, "What is your attitude toward the trimester?" is less likely to do so.[26]

Recording interview data

The method used by an interviewer to record responses may vary from the recording of answers out of the presence of the respondent after the interview has ended, to the use of a tape recorder. Postponing the recording of data may be necessary on occasion when interviewing young children. It may also be desirable when interviewing adults where obvious recording would seem an added threat. Postponed recording has the disadvantage that important details may be forgotten and the interviewer may unconsciously bias the data. With older children and mature adults and where appropriate means have been used to establish rapport, overt recording of responses is less likely to have a detrimental effect on the data collected. As a matter of fact, mature respondents usually have greater respect for an interviewer who engages in systematic recording of answers. They become more confident because what they actually said is on record. If printed or mimeographed forms are used which list primary questions and provide spaces for answers, the data collected are less often incomplete. As in questionnaire studies, answer sheets or mark-sense cards can be filled out by the interviewer or the respondent under his supervision. Answers to fixed-alternative background questions and to scale items can be so recorded.

Bucher, Fritz, and Quarantelli[27] describe some of the kinds of interviewing for which tape recording is effective. They contend that such recording does not increase respondent resistance or significantly affect the interview data. Tape recording enables the interviewer to give his full attention to the respondent. Another advantage of tape recording is the complete recording of what is said, thus eliminating bias due to conscious or unconscious selection by the interviewer of what to record. Finally, tape recording facilitates evaluation of the reliability

[26] For an excellent brief discussion of these matters, see Kerlinger, *Foundations of Behavioral Research*, pp. 473–75.

[27] Rue Bucher, Charles E. Fritz, and E. L. Quarantelli, "Tape Recorded Interviews in Social Research," *American Sociological Review* 21 (June 1956), pp. 359–64. If this journal is not readily available, see Carter V. Good, *Introduction to Educational Research*, 2nd ed. (New York: Appleton-Century-Crofts, 1963), pp. 300–01. Quotations in Good are from the article cited above.

and validity of interview data. Different listeners to the tape can compare their interpretations. The interview process itself can also be evaluated.

Conclusion

A decision to collect interview data requires acquisition of skill in formulating questions, in organizing an interview schedule or sequence of questions, and in obtaining experience in interviewing. There should also be effort to understand the problems of interviewer-respondent interaction.[28] Planning is necessary in order to promote the interviewing of a representative sample of respondents, preferably a random sample. (More will be said about this matter in Chapter 10.) Consideration should be given in planning to receiving sponsorship and clearance. Interviewers should be persistant but considerate in making appointments and diligent in keeping them. Repeated efforts should be made to obtain data from all persons included in the sample. In interviewing school personnel, interviewers should avoid interference with normal school activities. Finally, during interviewing, interviewers should be alert to the possibilities of discovering unanticipated hypotheses deserving further research.

---

[28] For thorough discussion of such problems consult the text by Kahn and Cannell and study the research reported in Herbert H. Hyman and others, *Interviewing in Social Research* (Chicago: University of Chicago Press, 1954).

Questions for
Study and Discussion

1. Formulate a list of criteria which an effective questionnaire should meet.
2. Critically evaluate the following questionnaire item: Which of the following parts of a newspaper do you read regularly?
    a. International news articles
    b. News articles concerning local, state, and national politics
    c. News articles relevant to crime
    d. Editorials
    e. Society news
    f. Financial or business pages
    g. Comic strips
    h. Sports news
    i. Articles and editorials concerning controversial social issues
    j. None of the above
3. What would be the advantages and disadvantages of stating the foregoing question as an open-end one?
4. Ask one or more school administrators of your acquaintance about the number of questionnaires they receive and their attitudes or behavior toward them.
5. For what types of data collecting might it be more effective to use a questionnaire with open-end questions rather than interviews?
6. To what extent is interaction between interviewer and respondent a problem because of differences in race, religion, or social status?
7. Assume that you are to conduct a study of the high school dropout problem collecting data by means of interviews. How would you select your sample? Where would you best interview the dropouts? What would you do to establish rapport? What types of questions would you ask and in what order?
8. What would be the advantages of using two interviewers to interview each respondent?
9. What would be the advantages and disadvantages of interviewing groups of respondents rather than individual respondents?
10. In what type of research would it be legitimate to collect data which are value judgments?

Selected References

Cannell, Charles F., and Robert L. Kahn. "Interviewing." In *The Hand-book of Social Psychology,* edited by Gardner Lindzey and Elliot Aronson, pp. 526–95. Vol. II. 2nd ed. Reading, Mass.: Addison-Wesley, 1968.

Conrad, Herbert S. "Clearance of Questionnaires With Respect to 'Invasion of Privacy,' Public Sensitivities, Ethical Standards, Etc.: Principles and Viewpoint in the Bureau of Research, U.S. Office of Education." *Journal of Educational Measurement* 4 (Spring 1967): 23–28 (Supplement).
One of the papers in a symposium on Invasion of Privacy in Research and Testing *sponsored by the National Council on Measurement in Education.*

DiVesta, Francis J. "Problems in the Use of Questionnaires for Studying the Effectiveness of Educational Programs." *Educational and Psychological Measurement* 14 (Spring 1954): 138–50.
Comparison of signed and unsigned questionnaires and data on reliability of scale-type items.

Fischer, Robert P. "Signed Versus Unsigned Questionnaires." *Journal of Applied Psychology* 30 (June 1946): 220–25.

Franzen, Raymond and Paul F. Lazarsfeld. "Mail Questionnaire as a Research Problem." *Journal of Psychology* 20 (October 1945): 239–320.
Comparison of questionnaire with interview.

Goslin, David A. *Teachers and Testing.* New York: Russell Sage Foundation, 1967.
Questionnaires well worth studying as models are presented in Appendix II and Appendix III.

Heberle, Rudolph. "On the Use of the Questionnaire in Research: An Open Letter to Graduate Students." *American Sociological Review* 16 (August 1951): 549.

Hyman, H. H., and others. *Interviewing in Social Research.* Chicago: University of Chicago Press, 1954.

Kahn, Robert L., and Charles F. Cannell. *The Dynamics of Interviewing.* New York: Wiley, 1957.

————. "The Collection of Data by Interviewing." In *Research Methods in the Behavioral Sciences,* edited by Leon Festinger and Daniel Katz, pp. 327–80. New York: Dryden, 1953. Chapter 8.

Kerlinger, Fred N. *Foundations of Behavioral Research, Educational and Psychological Inquiry.* New York: Holt, Rinehart, and Winston, 1965. Chapter 26.

Brief, but excellent discussion of interviews and interview schedules.

Kornhauser, Arthur. "Constructing Questionnaires and Interview Schedules." In *Research Methods in Social Relations, With Special Reference to Prejudice,* edited by Marie Jahoda, Morton Deutsch, and Stuart W. Cook. Part II. 1st ed. New York: Dryden, 1951. Chapter 12.

Koos, Leonard V. *The Questionnaire in Education.* New York: Macmillan, 1928.

This is old, but still worth reading.

Lenski, G. E., and J. C. Leggett. "Caste, Class, and Deference in the Research Interview." *American Journal of Sociology* 65 (March 1960): 463–67.

Maccoby, Eleanor E., and Nathan Maccoby. "The Interview: A Tool of Social Science." In *Handbook of Social Psychology,* edited by Gardner Lindzey. Vol. I. Cambridge, Mass.: Addison-Wesley, 1954. Chapter 12.

Mouly, George J. *The Science of Educational Research.* New York: American Book Company, 1963.

Good discussion of questionnaires and interviews on pp. 238–78.

Nixon, John E. "The Mechanics of Questionnaire Construction." *Journal of Educational Research* 47 (March 1954): 481–87.

Norman, Ralph D. "A Review of Some of the Problems Related to the Mail Questionnaire." *Educational and Psychological Measurement* 8 (Summer 1948): 235–47.

Summarizes studies on factors related to proportion of questionnaire returns and bias in returns.

Payne, Stanley L. *The Art of Asking Questions.* Princeton, N. J.: Princeton University Press, 1951.

Romine, Stephen A. "Criteria for a Better Questionnaire." *Journal of Educational Research* 42 (September 1948): 69–71.

Sheatsley, Paul B. "The Art of Interviewing and a Guide to Interviewer Selection and Training." In *Research Methods in Social Relations, With Special Reference to Prejudice,* edited by Marie Jahoda, Morton Deutsch, and Stuart W. Cook. Part II. 1st ed. New York: Dryden, 1951. Chapter 13.

6

Collecting Data:
Systematic Observation
and Content Analysis

Methods of data collection other than from records and by means of questionnaires and interviews or by the use of tests and other measuring instruments, treated in earlier chapters, include the collecting of data by means of systematic observation of behaviors as they occur and through the use of content analysis. Content analysis, in addition to its other applications, is increasingly applied to transcripts of tape and other recordings of classroom discourse.

The nature of observation

Observation is much more than the reception of stimuli by the nervous system. The reception of stimuli is an essential part of the process, but the giving of meaning to what is received, the perceptual or cognitive part dependent on prior experience, is also essential. We hear a sound and infer that it is the bark of a dog. Had we never seen a dog and heard it bark, the sound would be meaningless. All observation involves cognition or inference, the amount of inference or thought varying with the kind of observation made. Most often the process of giving meaning to stimuli occurs immediately, automatically, and apparently without conscious effort. The casual observations of everyday life may be contrasted to the observations made by a scientist. For the scientist, according to Kaplan, "Observation is purposive behavior, directed toward ends that lie beyond the act of observation itself: the aim is to secure materials that will play a part in other phases of inquiry, like the formation and validation of hypotheses."[1]

---

[1] Abraham Kaplan, *The Conduct of Inquiry* (San Francisco: Chandler, 1964), p. 127. Reprinted with permission of author and publisher.

If an observer's purpose is merely to observe and record what he sees or hears, the inferential element in the observation may be limited to identifying it as an instance of some particular object or event. The identifying characteristics of the object or event may be familiar to all observers in our culture. Many observations made of the behaviors of teachers or pupils are of this character. The observation that the teacher praised a pupil is an example. If, however, the observation of a teacher or pupil behavior is to be used as evidence of the manifestation of a construct pertaining to some personality trait, the role of inference is more important. Two observers of the same behavior may infer quite different constructs. Suppose, for example, one observer, deeply concerned about the education of the culturally deprived, observes for the first time, instruction in an "inner city" school. Such an observer may infer that certain behaviors of a teacher in the school may be interpreted as "dominating," "authoritarian," or as "hostility." Another less idealistic and more experienced observer may consider the same behaviors of the teacher no more than necessary efforts to secure and maintain conditions conducive to learning. The initial judgments made by the first observer may create a "halo," causing him to ignore other behaviors of the teacher that, in another classroom milieu, he would regard as "supportive," or positively motivating. This hypothetical example implies the need for controls to minimize error when observational data are collected in research.

While the major purpose of this chapter is to introduce the student to methods used in the collecting of observational data, it is desirable to begin by noting the kinds of educational research for which such data are appropriate.

Types of educational research using direct observations of behavior

Direct observations of the classroom behaviors of teachers and pupils have long been employed in efforts to study pupil participation in classroom lessons and to identify effective teacher behaviors. More recently, the emphasis in classroom observation research has been the study of "teacher-pupil interactions" or "classroom climate." Such research is especially relevant to the social-emotional, affective, or motivational aspects of classroom learning. Most recently, observational data have been obtained in studying the cognitive aspects of learning and instruction in a classroom setting. In some recent research, both the cognitive and affective have been studied concurrently.

Data obtained through direct observation of behaviors outside the classroom have also been used in studies of the dynamics of small groups, the behaviors or traits of atypical children, interactions between counselors and pupils or students, and interpersonal relationships within families. Observational data are obviously valuable in studying the home, community, and non-classroom school environments of pupils, especially in view of the present concern for the "culturally disadvantaged."[2]

The kinds of research mentioned above have been termed sociopsychological and process oriented. The terms "multiple-criterion," "multiple-dimension," and "multi-aspect" have been used in efforts to describe and explain the behaviors observed. Instruction is a global phenomenon. According to Withall, in order better to understand, control, and predict such a global phenomenon ". . . all-encompassing and relatively meaningless concepts have to be broken down into manageable, discrete, describable operations or behaviors."[3] Although tests and other measuring instruments may be used, direct observation of specific operations or behaviors is crucial. The observational data alone may suffice. In studies of the relationships between variables, both observational data and test data may be needed. For example, Medley and Mitzel urge the collection of observational data in experimental research on methods of teaching:

> Direct observation should play a crucial part in the most fundamental kind of research on teaching—the search for effective patterns of classroom behavior—the type of research most worthy of the name *methods research.* . . .
>
> The classic design for methods research requires that one (or more) classes be taught by an experimental method and one (or more) by a "control" method. The dependent variable is a measure of the gains of pupils in each class on an appropriate test. The classic design does not involve any observation of the teaching in either class to find out whether —and to what degree—the method supposed to be applied actually is applied.[4]

It is quite likely that the frequent failures to obtain significant differences in experiments of the type described above are largely caused by inattention to identifying just what specific changes in pupil achieve-

---

[2] For such a classification of different types of studies and of observational category systems, see Robert D. Boyd and M. Vere DeVault, "The Observation and Recording of Behavior" in "Methodology of Educational Research," *Review of Educational Research* 36 (December 1966), pp. 532–33.

[3] John Withall, "Research Tools: Observing and Recording Behavior" in "Methodology of Educational Research," *Review of Educational Research* 30 (December 1960), p. 496.

[4] Donald M. Medley and Harold E. Mitzel, "Measuring Classroom Behavior by Systematic Observation," in N. L. Gage, ed., *Handbook of Research on Teaching* (Chicago: Rand McNally, 1963), p. 249. Reprinted with permission of authors and copyright holder (AERA).

ment are related to just what specific patterns of teacher behavior. An ill-defined method of instruction may be only distantly related to actually occurring changes in pupil behaviors or in the cognitive and affective traits not measured by forms of the standardized achievement test used as a pretest and a posttest.

Levels of inquiry in research using observational data

While many reports of educational research using data obtained by direct observation in classrooms or elsewhere are characterized by the testing of hypotheses and other efforts to relate the research to theory, some of the important studies are on the natural history or descriptive level. These studies contrast in quality with most of the survey studies less kindly regarded in education. They contribute facts concerning both overt teacher and pupil behaviors in classrooms and factors and conditions outside of classrooms affecting pupil learning and motivation. They contribute through analysis of what is directly observed or recorded (on tape, or otherwise), to an understanding of instructional strategies directing and motivating cognitive classroom learning. Such studies contribute "some degree of explanation even in the early stages of inquiry"[5] and they help to develop more adequate "conceptual frameworks" for theory-related research. Although the term is not used in describing these studies, they are also examples of process-oriented research.

What has been said above applies to research using observational data obtained in classrooms and elsewhere. The next section of this chapter deals specifically with the collection and analysis of classroom observational data.

OBSERVING, RECORDING, AND ANALYZING
TEACHER AND PUPIL BEHAVIORS

Much preparation is necessary prior to the systematic collection of observational data in the study of classroom learning. The observer needs to acquire a general understanding of learning and motivational theory.[6] There should be serious study of relevant theory and research in social psychology and in the philosophy of science.[7] Study of re-

---

[5] See pages 12–13 of Chapter 2 and Milton O. Meux, "Studies of Learning in the School Setting," in "Growth, Development, and Learning," *Review of Educational Research* 37 (December 1967), p. 541.

[6] An excellent source to consult is *Theories of Learning* by Hilgard and Bower, first cited on page 10 of Chapter 2.

[7] See the references earlier cited to Kaplan, Scriven, and Meux. The chapter by Meux is an excellent and particularly relevant introduction.

ports or summaries of earlier research using classroom observational data will provide knowledge of the kinds of problems investigated, the observational schedules or category systems which have been used, and the procedures employed in analyzing and interpreting the data collected. This kind of preparation will contribute to the development of the conceptual framework needed to focus on a problem and to make decisions when attempting to solve the selected problem.

A number of representative studies are briefly summarized in the following paragraphs to illustrate the characteristics of research using observational data. For most of these summaries, emphasis is placed on the methods used in obtaining the data.

Early studies of classroom behaviors

Ernest Horn in his 1914 study of pupil participation in recitations had observers record small circles on a seating chart for each request to recite and small squares for each response to the request.[8] In 1928, R. C. Puckett used such symbols as ⊙, ⊙, ⊙, and ⊙ on a seating chart to record such pupil behaviors as "pupil raised hand, was called on by the teacher, and made a single-word response," ". . . a fair response," ". . . a good response," and ". . . a very good response."[9] In their brief summary of this study, Medley and Mitzel state that this recording procedure "is particularly ingenious, since each mark made refers to a single behavior, or aspect of behavior," but they are somewhat dubious of "requiring the recorder to quantify the merit of the pupil's response."[10]

The earliest comprehensive research effort to identify the teaching behavior patterns of effective and ineffective teachers was reported by A. S. Barr in 1929.[11] The observational data included counts of such motivating behaviors as "nods approval" and "interests and experiences of pupils utilized." Questions asked by teachers were classified as requesting "recall of facts," "memorized judgments," "expository answers (explain, define, illustrate, etc.)," and "real judgments." The teachers were classified as "good" or "poor" by their supervisors rather than in terms of measures of pupil achievement.

---

[8] Ernest Horn, "Distribution of Opportunity for Participation Among the Various Pupils in Classroom Recitations," *Teachers College, Columbia University, Contributions to Education,* No. 67, 1914.

[9] R. C. Puckett, "Making Supervision Objective," *School Review* 36 (March 1928), pp. 209–12.

[10] Medley and Mitzel, "Measuring Classroom Behavior," in *Handbook of Research,* pp. 254–55.

[11] A. S. Barr, *Characteristic Differences in the Teaching Performance of Good and Poor Teachers of the Social Studies* (Bloomington, Ill.: Public School Publishing Company, 1929).

In 1934, Wayne Wrightstone reported a study in which such symbols as 5a, 5c, and 5f were recorded after pupils' names on a class roster to indicate such teacher behaviors as "allows pupil to make a voluntary contribution," "proposes a question ... for pupil or class," and "discourages or prohibits a pupil contribution." Each of the behaviors was defined in a few sentences.[12]

Beginning in 1939, and with associates in 1945 and 1946, H. H. Anderson reported studies in which dominative and integrative teacher behaviors were observed and classified in 26 categories, for example, "DC–5, disapproval, blame or shame directed toward the child as a person" and "IT-Helps child to define, redefine, or advance a problem." Certain pupil behaviors were related to the teacher behaviors, thus leading to the conclusion that pupils subjected to the integrative teacher behaviors were characterized to a greater extent by spontaneous and cooperative behaviors and to a lesser extent by nonconforming ones.[13]

The studies summarized above emphasize the observation of overt behaviors. They do illustrate, however, a growing interest in teacher-pupil interactions, teacher personality traits, and the beginning of interest in observing cognitive aspects of instruction.

Later efforts to observe and measure teacher-pupil interactions or "classroom climate"

In 1949, John Withall reported a truly influential study of "social-emotional" classroom climate. He formulated seven categories ranging from "learner-centeredness" to "teacher-centeredness." These were used in coding typewritten transcripts of sound recordings of teacher verbal behaviors alone. For example: "2) *Acceptant and clarifying statements* having an intent to convey to the pupil the feeling that he was understood and help him elucidate his ideas and feelings" and "6) *Reproving* or deprecating remarks intended to deter pupil from continued indulgence in present 'unacceptable' behavior."[14]

Cornell, Lindvall, and Saupe reported a study in 1953 for which they developed an observation system to measure eight dimensions of classroom behavior. The dimensions were:

---

[12] J. Wayne Wrightstone, "Measuring Teacher Conduct of Class Discussion," *Elementary School Journal* 34 (February 1934), pp. 454–60.

[13] Harold H. Anderson, "The Measurement of Domination and Socially Integrative Behavior in Teachers' Contacts with Children," *Child Development* 10 (June 1939), pp. 73–89. (See also *Applied Psychology Monographs*, Nos. 6, 8, and 11. The co-authors are Helen M. Brewer, J. E. Brewer, and Mary F. Reed.)

[14] John Withall, "Development of a Technique for the Measurement of Socio-emotional Climate in Classrooms," *Journal of Experimental Education* 17 (March 1949), pp. 347–61.

A. *Differentiation* (provisions for individual differences)
B. *Social Organization* (group organization, leadership, and inter-action)
C. *Pupil Initiative* (teacher domination and control and pupil and teacher participation)
D. *Content* (textbooks and other instructional materials)
E. *Variety* (instructional teacher and pupil learning activities)
F. *Competency* (9 positive and 9 negative instructional behaviors, for example, "was thorough in explanation" and "explanation seemed to leave pupils puzzled.")
G. *Climate—Teacher* (11 positive and 11 negative behaviors, for example, "gave special evidence of patience" and "corrected and criticized excessively.")
H. *Climate—Pupils* (6 positive and 6 negative behaviors, for example, "responded eagerly in recitation" and "were restless, gazed about, doodled, daydreamed.")[15]

Between 1955 and 1959, Medley and Mitzel developed the Observational Schedule and Record, OScAR, by modifying, simplifying, and combining the items earlier formulated by Withall and by Cornell, Lindvall, and Saupe.[16] During the first five-minute period of a total thirty minutes of observation, an observer checks once, in the *Activity Section* of the form, each activity observed of 44 listed activities. Examples of these activities are "teacher questions and pupil answers," "teacher illustrates at board," and "pupil ignores teacher question." The observer next marks in the *Grouping Section* the nature of the groups observed, for example, "at least one-half class in group with teacher" and "2–3 pupils in group without teacher." He then marks in the *Materials Section* such items as "Audio Aid" and "Supplementary Reading Material." The observer also enters plus signs in the appropriate row of the *Signs Section* to record the occurrence of such behaviors as "teacher shows affection for pupil," "pupil shows hostility to the teacher," and "teacher yells." After marking the area of instructional activity of the first five-minute period (reading, mathematics, language arts, etc.), in the *Activity Section,* the observer spends the second five-minute period tallying each statement made by the teacher according to the five categories of the *Expressive Behavior Section:* "Pupil Supportive," "Problem Structuring," "Miscellaneous," "Direc-

---

[15] F. G. Cornell, C. M. Lindvall, and J. L. Saupe, *An Exploratory Measurement of Individualities of Schools and Classrooms* (Urbana, Ill.: University of Illinois, Bureau of Educational Research, 1952).

[16] For a more detailed discussion of OScAR, a facsimile of it, and references to its development and later use, see Medley and Mitzel, "Measuring Classroom Behavior," pp. 278–86.

tive," and "Reproving." After entering a check in column II of the *Activity Section* to record the area of instructional activity of the second five-minute period, the procedure described above is repeated for the third and fourth five-minute periods and again for the fifth and sixth.

An interesting feature of OScAR is the use of abbreviations in the rows of the form so that teachers looking at it will not too readily be aware of what behaviors are observed and recorded. The first three examples given above appear as "t qu, p ans," "t illus at bd," and "p ign t qu."

In order to facilitate the analysis of the data recorded on OScAR, 20 scoring keys were developed by combining the data for various items which seem to belong together. Six keys were discarded as not yielding reliable differences between the mean scores in different class-rooms. The scores obtained from the remaining 14 keys were used in a factor analysis.[17] These scores were:

1. Time spent on reading
2. Problem-structuring teacher statements
3. Autonomous administrative groupings
4. Pupil-leadership activities
5. Freedom of movement
6. Manifest teacher hostility
7. Supportive teacher behavior
8. Time spent on social studies
9. Disorderly pupil behavior
10. Verbal activities
11. Traditional pupil activities
12. Teacher's verbal output
13. Audiovisual materials
14. Autonomous social grouping[18]

The factor analysis of the data led to the conclusion that OScAR measures "three relatively discrete dimensions of classroom behavior."[19] After the names given to each of the three, I have identified by number the most closely related of the 14 scores with their "loading" on the given factor:

Emotional Climate (2) + .54, (4) + .55, (6) − .76, (7) + .63, (9) − .73
Verbal Emphasis (1) + .85, (3) + .59, (8) − .60, (10) + .65
Social Organization (3) + .49, (5) + .48, (12) − .60, (13) + .55, (14) + 72.
   or *Structure*

---

[17] See pages 343 to 350 of Chapter 11.

[18] Donald M. Medley and Harold E. Mitzel, "A Technique for Measuring Classroom Behavior," *Journal of Educational Psychology* 49 (April 1958), p. 90.

[19] Medley and Mitzel, "Technique for Measuring Classroom Behavior," p. 91.

A factor loading is the correlation between a variable and the factor. It may be inferred from the data above that scores 2, 4, and 7 are positively related to *Emotional Climate,* while 6 and 9 are negatively related. It is difficult to understand why time spent on social studies should be negatively related to *Verbal Emphasis* and teacher's verbal output negatively related to *Social Organization.* Possibly a teacher who talks excessively leaves little time for grouping.

A very ingenious observation system has been developed by Flanders to record classroom behavior.[20] In using this system teacher and student communications are coded according to the categories briefly identified at the left side of Figure 6.1 on page 129. They are separately defined at greater length, for example:

1. ACCEPTS FEELING: accepts and clarifies the feeling tone of the students in a nonthreatening manner. Feelings may be positive or negative. Predicting or recalling feelings are included.

7. CRITICIZING OR JUSTIFYING AUTHORITY: statements intended to change student behavior from nonacceptable to acceptable pattern; bawling someone out; stating why the teacher is doing what he is doing; extreme self-reference.

Training in the use of the system includes memorization of the categories as defined above and practice in applying the system both in classrooms and to tape recordings. During a period of observation, the observer simply lists the numbers coding the behaviors observed successively and rhythmically at the ends of three-second intervals. Although Flanders states "There is NO scale implied by these numbers," categories 1 to 4 are relevant to teacher behaviors which encourage student participation and freedom of action, while categories 5–7 are relevant to teacher behaviors which increasingly control student behaviors and concentrate the authority of the teacher.

The numbers listed are tallied in pairs in the cells of the matrix or chart of 10 rows and 10 columns shown at the right side in Figure 6.1 (the now lettered areas indicate the locations of tallies differently interpreted). Suppose that 9, 3, 4, 8, 2, . . . are some of the numbers listed. The first pair, 9 and 3 calls for a tally in the cell in row 9 and column 3. The next tallies would be in the cell in row 3 and column 4; in row 4 and column 8; and in row 8 and column 2. This is a recording of the

---

[20] Ned A. Flanders, *Teacher Influence, Pupil Attitudes, and Achievement.* U. S. Department of Health, Education, and Welfare, Office of Education, Cooperative Research Project No. 397 (Minneapolis: University of Minnesota, 1960). Also reported as Cooperative Research Monograph No. 12 (Washington, D.C.: Government Printing Office, 1965). Reprinted with permission of the author.

observation that a student offered an idea used by the teacher who next asked a question and praised the student who answered it.

The kinds of interpretation that can be made of the data recorded in various areas of the interaction matrix and in many of the individual cells indicate the value of this method of observing and recording classroom data. The sums of the tallies in columns 1–7, Area A; in columns 8 and 9, Area B; and in column 10, Area C reveal the proportions of teacher talk, student talk, and silence or confusion. The ratio of indirect to direct teacher influence can be obtained by comparing the sums of the tallies in columns 1–4 with the sums of the tallies in columns 5–7. Comparisons of the sums of columns 1–3 with those of 6 and 7 give an index more independent of subject matter emphasis. A comparison of the relative numbers of tallies in Areas D and E may contrast a teacher who makes much use of indirect influence with one who makes possibly excessive use of direct influence. Flanders states with reference to Area D:

> When a teacher accepts, clarifies, or makes constructive use of a student's ideas or feelings, when he praises or encourages student behavior, and when he asks questions, he will usually be increasing the freedom of action of the student.[21]

Presumably such a teacher would also provide greater motivation for student learning—praise, knowledge of progress, and feedback. Flanders refers to Area E as the "vicious circle":

> The vicious circle gets its name from the sequence in which the teacher gives some directions, the students resist, the teacher criticizes and then gives more directions, the students resist even more, and so it goes.[22]

The tallies in Area F and Area H are evidence respectively of how the teacher reacts to student talk and what kind of teacher talk stimulates student talk. The tallies in Area G are indicative of the amount of student intercommunication. A comparison of the tallies in rows 8 and 9, or columns 8 and 9, are further evidence of the degree of teacher use of direct and indirect influence. Interesting interpretations can also be made of the tallies in individual cells, for example, a relatively large number of tallies in Cell 3–3 indicates a teacher who develops student ideas with considerable care. On the other hand the tallies in Cell 7–7 may identify a teacher given to excessive criticism or self-reference.

---

[21] *Ibid.,* p. 12 (1960).

[22] *Ibid.,* Appendix F, p. 19 (1960), p. 39 (1965).

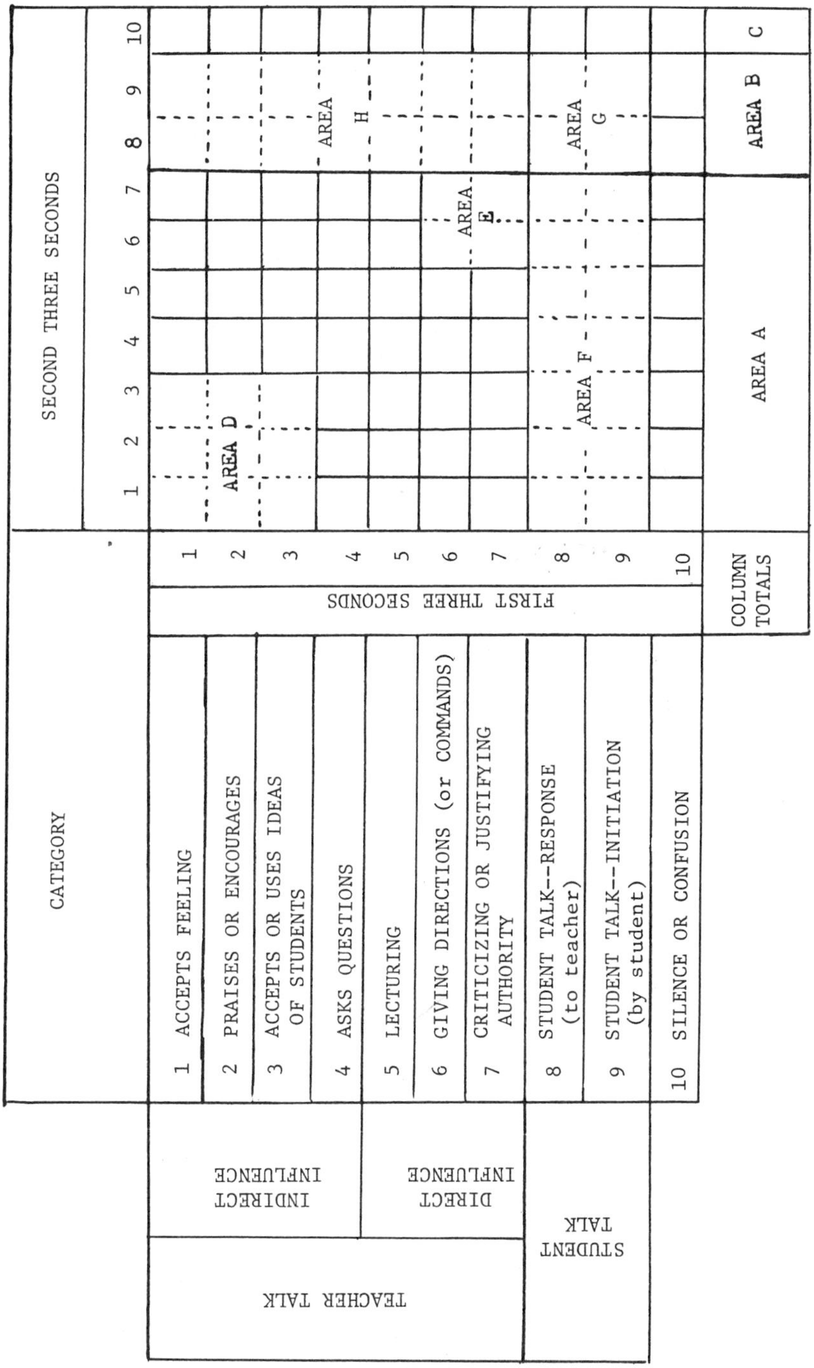

Figure 6.1 Flanders' categories and matrix for interaction analysis. [Adapted from Flanders, Appendix F, p. 5 and p. 60 (1960) or p. 20 and p. 80 (1965).]

Three more observational systems for obtaining data relevant to classroom climate or teacher-pupil interactions are more briefly summarized below.

Marie Hughes and her associates developed "The Provo Code for the Analysis of Teaching" by analyzing narrative records of teacher behaviors first recorded in shorthand by trained observers. Numerous specific behaviors or "teaching functions" are classified according to seven major categories: "Controlling Functions, Imposition of Teacher, Facilitating Functions, Functions That Develop Content, Functions That Serve as Response, Functions of Positive Affectivity, and Functions of Negative Affectivity."[23] This observation system reflects the influence of Withall, although it is not restricted to verbal behaviors.

In the research reported in 1965, a system was developed for obtaining and analyzing observational data relevant to teacher-pupil "transactions" in the affective domain and "the kinds of behavior of boys and girls which elicit specific types of overt teacher controlling and instructional behavior."[24] Both observation in the classroom and tape recording were employed. More recently, Spaulding has developed "The Coping Analysis Schedule for Educational Settings (CASES)" and "The Spaulding Teacher Activity Rating Schedule (STARS)."[25] The first schedule focuses on the overt behavior of children while the second focuses on the overt efforts of teachers to bring about cognitive, social, and motor changes in pupils.

A 20-channel impulse event recorder having 20 pens connected to a 20-button microswitch was used in the continuous recording of the frequency and duration of behavioral occurrences.

Wallen's study has greatly modified the Flanders observation system for use in the first and third grades. The categories are made more suitable for these grades, they apply to teacher behaviors only, and no effort is made to classify behaviors in sequence or to use the Flanders matrix. Wallen's observation system includes categories ranging from "acknowledges student's raised hand," "praise and encouragement,"

---

[23] Marie M. Hughes and others, *Development of the Means for the Assessment of the Quality of Teaching in Elementary Schools* (Salt Lake City: University of Utah Press, 1959).

[24] Robert L. Spaulding, *Achievement, Creativity, and Self-Concept Correlates of Teacher Pupil Transactions in Elementary Schools*, 2nd ed. U. S. Department of Health, Education, and Welfare, Office of Education, Cooperative Research Project No. 1352 (Hempstead, New York: Hofstra University, 1965).

[25] Robert L. Spaulding, "The Durham Education Improvement Program" in David W. Brison and Jane Hill, eds., *Psychology and Early Childhood Education* (Toronto: The Ontario Institute for Studies in Education, 1968), pp. 37–50. CASES and STARS are also included in the first volume of the Simon and Boyer anthology cited in the selected references at the end of this chapter.

through "explaining or problem structuring," to "hostility and repri-mands," thus reflecting teacher behaviors Flanders classified as indi-rect and direct influence. Such nonverbal teacher behaviors as "putting arm around child" and "physically striking a child" are appro-priately categorized.[26]

The importance of classroom climate studies

Studies of teacher-student interactions or of classroom climate of the types summarized above have seldom revealed significant relationships between the behaviors observed and measures of achievement in the cognitive domain. Medley and Mitzel state, "A principal defect in OScAR is its failure to get at any aspect of classroom behavior related to pupil achievement of cognitive objectives."[27] Flanders, however, was able to report significant differences supporting the generalizations that "the teaching methods we have called indirect produce more achievement," "direct influence decreases learning except when goals have initially been clarified and made acceptable by the use of indi-rect influence," and "the students who achieved most and had signifi-cantly higher scores on our revised classroom attitude instrument were in classes which were exposed to flexible patterns of teacher influ-ence. This flexible pattern included periods of predominantly direct influ-ence as well as other periods of predominantly indirect influence."[28]

These and similar studies have served to develop methods of col-lecting, recording, and interpreting classroom observational data. They have provided a basis for the creation of more effective observation systems, apart from their contribution to methodology; they have also made important contributions to a better understanding of the factors and conditions motivating classroom learning and the attainment of instructional objectives in the affective domain. The studies we turn to now differ in their greater emphasis on the cognitive or ideational aspects of instruction and learning. These studies are concerned with the logic and strategies of teaching and with thought processes of stu-dents. Observational studies using categories relevent to thought

---

[26] Normal E. Wallen, *Relationships Between Teacher Characteristics and Student Be-havior—Part III.* U. S. Department of Health, Education, and Welfare, Office of Educa-tion, Cooperative Research Program No. SAE OE5-10-181 (Salt Lake City: University of Utah, 1966).

[27] Medley and Mitzel, "Measuring Classroom Behavior," in *Handbook of Research,* p. 286.

[28] Flanders, pp. 107–09 (1960), pp. 108–10 (1965). See also Edmund Amidon and Ned A. Flanders, "The Effects of Direct and Indirect Teacher Influence on Dependent-Prone Students Learning Geometry," *Journal of Educational Psychology* 52 (December 1961), pp. 286–91.

processes may also employ categories relevant to affective attributes of instruction and learning, and to the routine of instruction.

Studies using cognitive systems

B. O. Smith and his associates in 1962 and in 1967 reported basic studies on the logic and strategies of teaching.[29] Both of these studies on the natural history level of inquiry, involved observation, description, and classification of cognitive elements of the content of classroom discourse. The first study dealt with the logical attributes of smaller elements or units termed "episodes." An episode is a verbal exchange between at least two persons focused on a single point or item. For example, the teacher may ask "What does sublimation mean?" The student replies "A solid substance when heated changes to a gas without melting." The teacher closes the episode by saying "That is correct." Many episodes are much more complex. Several students may talk to the same point. Episodes are viewed as logical operations, a form of rule-guided behavior. The example given is a defining episode and there are several logical rules to be obeyed in the process of defining. One of the rules specifies that the term defined should not appear in the definition. In this study, a lengthy discourse on the part of either teacher or student, without the intervention of another person, was classified as a monolog. These were not analyzed. Episodes were classified in terms of their entries, or opening phrases, since these are indicative of the kind of correct response logically demanded. The categories of entries and, hence, of episodes were: defining, describing, designating, stating, reporting, substituting, evaluating, classifying, comparing and contrasting, conditional inferring, and explaining (subdivided into six different types). Each category was defined in a paragraph or more and criteria formulated for its application.

The study of the strategies of teaching dealt with "larger maneuvers having to do with the control of the subject matter of instruction." The units of discourse analyzed are "ventures" within which strategies may occur. Ventures in general contain more than one episode. A venture consists of several utterances dealing with a single topic and having one overarching objective. By "objective" is meant the central point of the unit of discourse, the conclusion to which the verbal exchanges lead, rather than an instructional objective as usually consid-

---

[29] B. Othanel Smith, Milton Meux, and others, *A Study of the Logic of Teaching.* U. S. Department of Health, Education, and Welfare, Office of Education, Cooperative Research Project No. 258 (7257) (Urbana: University of Illinois, 1962); B. Othanel Smith and others, *A Study of the Strategies of Teaching.* U. S. Department of Health, Education, and Welfare, Office of Education, Project No. 1640 (Urbana: University of Illinois, 1967).

ered. The types of ventures identified according to their objectives were: causal, conceptual, evaluative, particular, procedural, reason, and rule. As in the case with episodes, each venture was defined and illustrated in detail. In addition to carefully defined criteria for the identifying of ventures, each venture was broken down into "moves." These are the units of content and their manipulations that, with their sequences, characterize the strategy underlying a venture which leads to the obtaining of its objective.

In both of these studies, transcripts of the same 85 tape recordings supplemented by the notes of a live observer were obtained in all four grade levels of five high schools of varying type, and in the subject fields of English, Mathematics, Science, History, and Social Studies. The analyses of the data thus collected resulted in the units of classroom discourse described above, their categorization, and the criteria to be used in application of the criteria. Another notable characteristic of both reports is the attention given to the development of the conceptual framework within which the research was conducted. (See especially the fourteenth chapter in the report of each study: "Logic, Language, and Psychology" and "Teaching as Rule Behavior in a System."

Both studies are on the natural history level of inquiry contributing to better understanding of cognitive attributes of classroom learning and instruction. They suggest a need for similar studies with somewhat modified methodology dealing with both cognitive and affective attributes. What elements in episodes and ventures, for example, constitute praise, feedback, and other motivational factors? Both studies make a contribution to the theory of instruction, suggesting hypotheses about variables worthy of study by means of correlation analysis and school experimentation.[30]

Two other studies similar to those of Smith and his associates are noteworthy with reference to their methods of analyzing transcripts of classroom discourse.

Arno Bellack and his associates were "influenced by recently developed concepts in the study of language and meaning by contemporary philosophers and psychologists, including Brown, Feigl, White, and Wittgenstein."[31] They developed four major categories: Structuring, Soliciting, Responding, and Reacting. The first two are moves which are initiating while the last two are reflexive. A "teaching cycle" begins

---

[30] See Chapters 11 and 12.

[31] Arno A. Bellack and others, *The Language of the Classroom* (New York: Teachers College Press, 1966), pp. 1–2. The references cited are included among the suggested references at the end of this chapter.

with an initiating move or maneuver and ends with a reflexive one. The analysis was also concerned with the dimensions of meaning of classroom discourse, including "Substantive-logical meanings," which refer to the cognitive processes derived from the episodes of Smith's *Study of the Logic of Teaching:* defining, interpreting, explaining, and so on. The content analysis system applied to transcripts of classroom discourse is most ingenious.

Wright and Proctor have contributed a category system for classifying verbal behaviors in high school mathematics classes.[32] Two of the three major categories concern the logical and cognitive aspects of verbal behaviors, but the subcategories of this major category, "Attitude Frame," classify behaviors having to do with both the directing and motivating of learning. Use of this category system requires both considerable training and superior knowledge of mathematics.

During their research on gifted children initiated in 1959, Gallagher and Aschner developed a category system deriving four of their five primary categories from Guilford's theory of the operations of thinking. The four categories are *Cognitive-Memory* (C-M), *Convergent Thinking* (CT), *Divergent Thinking* (DT), and *Evaluative Thinking* (ET).[33]

The Cognitive-Memory category is concerned with such thought processes as recognition, rote memory, and recall. "Facts, ideas, and other remembered materials are *reproduced* not produced in this primary category." The Convergent thinking category relates to "thought processes that are both analytic and integrative within a closely structured framework." The thinking is productive, but it is reasoning based on given/or remembered data.[34] One is Explanation which has the subcategories of Narrative Explanation, Rational Explanation, and Value Explanation. The first may be exemplified by an historical account of a sequence of events, the second by a citation of evidence supporting a conclusion, and the third by reasons supporting or justifying a value judgment.

[32] Muriel J. Wright and Virginia H. Proctor, *Systematic Observation of Verbal Interaction as a Method of Comparing Mathematics Lessons.* U. S. Department of Health, Education, and Welfare, Office of Education, Cooperative Research Project, No. 816 (St. Louis, Mo.: Washington University, 1961).

[33] James J. Gallagher, *Productive Thinking in Gifted Children.* U. S. Department of Health, Education, and Welfare, Office of Education, Cooperative Research Project No. 965 (Urbana: University of Illinois, 1965). Gallagher cites J. P. Guilford, "Structure of Intellect," *Psychological Bulletin* 53 (July 1956), pp. 267–93, and "Three Faces of Intellect," *American Psychologist* 14 (August 1959), pp. 469–79.

[34] Mary Jane McCue Aschner, "The Analysis of Verbal Interaction in the Classroom," in Arno A. Bellack, ed., *Theory and Research in Teaching* (New York: Bureau of Publications, Teachers College, Columbia University, 1963), p. 61.

Under Divergent Thinking, the subcategories include Elaboration, Divergent Association, Implication, and Synthesis. Students may elaborate or develop a point already made, suggesting novel instances or examples. Under Divergent Association a student may sharpen and give unexpected perspective to some central idea by suggesting comparisons and analogies. Under Implication, the student extrapolates beyond what is given, suggesting antecedents or consequences. Under Synthesis, a student may, on his own initiative and starting with a central idea, create a new point of view or frame of reference. He may provide a complex integration of many ideas.

The fourth of the categories stemming from Guilford's theory is Evaluation. It relates to value-based judgments requested or expressed by students. The student may be restricted or unrestricted in his choice of criteria. Contrast, for example, "Why is Leonardo da Vinci considered a genius?" with "Which was the greater artist, Leonardo or Michelangelo?"

Routine, the fifth category, in addition to the managerial and structuring aspects of instruction, includes the subcategory Verdict under which were classified instances of praise or reproof usually directed toward an individual student rather than toward the group. Obviously, this category is in the affective domain.

In this study, tape recordings of each class session were supplemental by the notes made by two live observers. Transcripts of the tape recordings were edited by the observers and the transcripts thus revised were subjected to analysis of their content. Symbols from the coded transcripts were entered in flow charts, "so that recurrent patterns of thought production in teacher-student and student-student interaction could more readily be traced."[35]

The four observational systems briefly characterized below are also useful in collecting data relevant to the affective and cognitive attributes of classroom behavior.

Oliver and Shaver reported categories useful in the classification of socio-emotional, cognitive, and procedural aspects of teaching behavior. Each specific procedural or cognitive verbal behavior of the teacher is also classified according to one of a scale of affective or socio-emotional subcategories. This system was used in an experiment comparing two "styles" in the teaching of a unique problems-type curriculum in high school social studies.[36]

Amidon has recently revised the "Verbal Interaction Category Sys-

---

[35] Aschner, "Analysis of Verbal Interaction," p. 68.

[36] Donald W. Oliver and James P. Shaver, *Teaching Public Issues in the High School* (Boston: Houghton Mifflin, 1966).

tem (VICS)" developed with Hunter.[37] Both systems mentioned are modifications of the Flanders system, but the revision noted above gives even greater emphasis to the cognitive. One major category requires the classification of teacher questions into the subcategories of cognitive-memory, convergent, divergent, and evaluative thinking.

David Denny has contributed an observation schedule designed to record data relevant to classroom climate and to such cognitive attributes as the amount of divergent thinking stimulated by the teacher and the occurrence of unusual or creative responses made by the pupils.[38]

Tyler developed a unique observation system whose categories are derived from psychoanalytic theory. The major categories are intervention (interpretation), transference, counter transference, resistance, and discoverance. While most of the categories and subcategories are in the affective domain, the first set of subcategories of the first major category are cognitive. The questions and comments of the instructor are coded under the categories of the first volume of the *Taxonomy of Educational Objectives* by Bloom and others—Knowledge, Comprehension, Application, Analysis, Synthesis, and Evaluation.[39] Tape recordings were listened to while analyzing transcripts of the tapes better to interpret what was said. "The meanings that sentences have depend upon intonation, speed, quality of voice, emotion, and the like... Yes can be said in an encouraging accepting manner or in a defensive manner."[40]

Problems in collection and analysis of classroom observational data

The degree of skill required in collecting data by direct observation in classrooms depends on the kinds of data collected and the method used in collecting them. Obviously less skill is required when observational schedules or record forms have been so planned that the observer merely records and categorizes or "codes" instances of clearly defined specific behaviors. The skill and training required greatly in-

---

[37] Edmund J. Amidon and Elizabeth Hunter, *Improving Teaching: Analyzing Verbal Interaction in the Classroom* (New York: Holt, Rinehart and Winston, 1966). The revised schedule appears in the Simon and Boyer anthology cited in the selected references concluding this chapter.

[38] David A. Denny, "Identification of Teacher-Classroom Variables Facilitating Pupil Creative Growth," *American Educational Research Journal* 5 (May 1968), pp. 365–83.

[39] Louise L. Tyler, "The Utilization of Psychoanalytic Concepts for Assessing Classroom Transactions," *Journal of Educational Research* 60 (February 1967), pp. 260–66. A complete reference to the *Taxonomy* is given on page 190.

[40] *Ibid.,* p. 264.

crease, however, with an increase in the extent to which the observer must make inferences. One of the great advantages of using tape recorders and kinescopes is that the observer can postpone making inferences until the data recorded are analyzed.

It is often claimed that the observer in the classroom may bias the data collected. One means of controlling such bias is for the observer to be adequately trained and to have acquired the appropriate attitudes. The actual process of collecting observational data may also bias the data collected, but this is not now considered an important problem. Pupils and teachers are so frequently observed nowadays that the presence of observers seldom affects their classroom behavior. Principals, supervisors, student teachers, and visiting educators come and go in the classrooms of city school systems. After the first two or three visits, the presence of an observer no longer seems threatening. Pupils and teachers quickly become accustomed not only to observers, but to the presence of tape recorders and even kinescopes. It is important, however, to reassure teachers that the observations recorded or ratings made will be used only for the purposes of the research, will be treated confidentially, and will not in any way affect their status as teachers. Teachers should be informed that observation of usual teaching is anticipated and that it is best for them not to know just what behaviors are to be observed in order to obviate self-consciousness about such behaviors.

While administrators and teachers may be reluctant to have classroom observational data collected, such reluctance can often be overcome by tactfully demonstrating that the problem is clearly defined and important, and that the data will not be used to evaluate their efficiency. Clearance should be obtained from the chief administrator, the observer should adhere strictly to the schedule of periods of observation, and should be considerate in his relations with teachers and pupils.

One of the major problems in preparing to collect observational data or to analyze them is the formulation of categories. The categories of a given set should be so exhaustive that each behavior of a class of behaviors is relevant to one of the categories. The categories should also be mutually exclusive so that a given behavior is not relevant to more than one category. There should be only a few categories in a given set and each should receive appreciable use in the coding of observations. Frequently, categories need to be divided into subcategories for the more adequate classification of behaviors within a major category. (What is said above also applies to sets of subcategories.) Where numerous, but infrequently occurring, behaviors are to be observed and classified, it is preferable to use a "sign" system instead of or in addition to a category system. The sign system can be a numbered list of infrequent, but actually occurring, behaviors. The signs may appear in abbreviated form on the observation schedule.

It is often desirable to modify or adapt categories used in earlier studies and to combine parts of two or more observation systems. Sometimes, as in the studies reported by Smith and his associates, categories must develop as analysis proceeds.

The phraseology labeling a category—its more elaborate description—must be chosen with care, otherwise an observer or analyst has difficulty in determining whether a particular behavior is relevant or not.[41] Observers and analysts should be carefully trained—memorizing categories, becoming familiar with signs, and receiving practice in the use of the observation system—before collecting or analyzing data in earnest.

Another important problem is that of deciding what observational units and periods of observation should be used. The observational units may be time units (for example, the three-second intervals of Flanders and the five-minute intervals of Medley and Mitzel). Periods of observation may be 20 minutes in an elementary school or an entire class period in high school. In some observational studies, such as the episodes and ventures of Smith and his colleagues, "natural" units are more appropriate than time units.

While reliability and validity of data are discussed in greater detail in Chapter 7, which deals with collection of data by means of tests and other measuring instruments, these attributes apply also to observational data. This is true not only of the data obtained through use of rating scales by observers of classroom behaviors, but also to other observational data observed and coded, such as counts or combinations of counts, relevant to specific behaviors, or groups of behaviors. Determinations of observer agreement with reference to behaviors observed and recorded concurrently are estimates of one type of reliability. Determinations of reliability, based on data collected on different occasions, by one or more observers, in a number of classrooms are much more useful estimates of reliability than indices of agreement between two observers in a single classroom on one occasion.[42]

Validity is concerned with the extent to which a test or other measuring instrument measures what the test or instrument is designed

---

[41] For a useful discussion of the writing of categories and the construction of category and sign systems, see Medley and Mitzel, "Measuring Classroom Behavior," *Handbook of Research,* pp. 297–305.

[42] Medley and Mitzel have also made a truly important contribution to the general problem of reliability estimation. The procedure described is applicable to observational and other measurement data. *Ibid.,* pp. 309–25.

to measure. In the case of observational data one criterion is relevance to the research problem. It should be obvious that the validity of observational data varies with the kinds of behaviors observed and with the amount of inference required in coding and interpreting them. Reliable counts of numbers of pupils asking questions during a class hour are readily seen to be valid measures of this type of behavior. (Reliability of observations seems to be a necessary, but not sufficient, condition for validity. Reliable data can be invalid if observers are all making the same errors—which is improbable but not impossible.) Determination of the validity of counts of pupils whose answers to questions are to be coded separately as instances of convergent and divergent thinking is a much more difficult task.

Another important technical problem concerns the legitimacy of generalizations inferred from data in studies of the kinds described. The collecting of data by classroom observation requires such time and effort that samples may not be adequately large and representative. To what kind of a population does the researcher generalize given one score per classroom for each variable? To what kind of a population does one generalize given scores in terms of occurrences per units of time whether three-second or five-minute intervals?[43] While it is essential to obtain representative data to justify generalizations, obtaining representativeness may be quite a different problem in the case of classroom observational data than in test data for survey-type studies. A universe of classroom behaviors may be adequately represented in a relatively few classrooms. How many instances of teacher sarcasm and of concomitant pupil responses need be observed to conclude that such teacher behavior is negatively motivating? Surely such observations need not be made in classrooms scattered from coast to coast. Repetition or replication of a well-designed observational study involving relatively few classes may also suffice in describing the patterns of logical teaching behaviors and the strategies occurring with different kinds of content. Larger samples selected at random from some well-defined population are needed in the testing of hypotheses and the inferring of generalizations relevant to relationships between the observational variables and variables measured in other ways.

OBTAINING DATA THROUGH CONTENT ANALYSIS

Analysis of the content of visual, oral, and written communications yields data useful in the study of a variety of problems in the behavioral sciences. Such communications include pictures and gestures; kine-

---

[43] Meux, "Studies of Learning," pp. 547–49.

scopes and tape recordings of lessons; books; editorials and articles in newspapers and magazines; movies and radio or television programs; student writings and other products of student behavior.

Examples of early use of content analysis

Data relevant to educational problems have long been obtained through analysis of some of the sources mentioned above. J. M. Rice, sometimes called the founding father of educational research, analyzed pupil written compositions in one of his tests for spelling and language errors. He analyzed pupil answers to arithmetical problems on another of his tests for errors and thought processes. His challenging articles based on such data were published between 1897 and 1903 in *Forum* magazine.[44]

Shortly after World War I, interest developed in analysis of the textbook content, as for example, estimating vocabulary difficulty.[45] Other early analyses of content relevant to curriculum development include Finley and Caldwell's analysis of newspapers to determine the amount of attention given to biology[46] and W. W. Charters' analysis of 7,337 sales checks to ascertain the characteristics of arithmetical computations performed by salespeople.[47] Interest in curriculum objectives also motivated the analyses made by Bobbitt and others to identify the "major fields of human concern." Topics covered in *Encyclopaedia Brittanica, Readers' Guide, Literary Digest,* and newspapers were classified and tabulated.[48]

Characteristics of contemporary content analysis

In more recent years, analyses have continued to be made of oral and written communications of pupils, textbooks and other instructional materials, and of articles in newspapers and magazines relevant to educational problems. For a number of years, analyses have also been made of the content of movies, radio programs, and TV broadcasts. Content analysis has had its greatest developments in techniques and in variety of applications in behavioral science fields other than educa-

---

[44] See Max D. Engelhart and Macklin Thomas, "Rice as the Inventor of the Comparative Test," *Journal of Educational Measurement* 3 (Summer 1966), pp. 141–45. Rice's articles are listed in the bibliography.

[45] B. A. Lively and S. L. Pressey, "A Method for Measuring the Vocabulary Burden of Textbooks," *Educational Administration and Supervision* 9 (October 1923), pp. 389–98.

[46] C. W. Finley and O. W. Caldwell, *Biology in the Public Press* (New York: Columbia University, 1923).

[47] W. W. Charters, *Curriculum Construction* (New York: Macmillan, 1923), pp. 231–36.

[48] Franklin Bobbitt and others, "Curriculum Investigations," *Supplementary Educational Monographs,* No. 31 (Chicago: University of Chicago Press, 1926).

tion. These include analyses of public opinion, of propaganda, of civilian morale in times of war (as evidenced in captured civilian letters), and of military and political intentions of hostile nations.[49]

Certainly, contemporary leading authorities on content analysis would object to classifying all of the early and many of the recent analyses of content relevant to educational problems as examples of content analysis. They would object to the lack of testing of hypotheses derived from theory. Another major objection would be to the absence of effort to measure variables other than by counts of easily identifiable characteristics. Nevertheless, many educational researches of the kinds mentioned have exerted significant influences on educational practices and similar studies will continue to do so.

Berelson defined content analysis as "a research technique for the objective, systematic, and quantitative description of the manifest content of communication."[50] This definition is applicable to many of the educational researches earlier mentioned. Some authorities object to the word "manifest" in Berelson's definition. Concern for only what is manifest would restrict content analysis to things readily observed and classified and would not extend it to the constructs inferred from these things. Kerlinger omits "manifest" from his modification of the definition. He emphasizes the measurement of variables, and the testing of theories and of hypotheses.[51] Current expert opinion concerning the scientific characteristics of content analysis may be summarized by Cartwright's point that its purpose is to transform recorded "raw" phenomena into reproducible or objective data which can be subjected to measurement and quantitative treatment. The data thus treated should contribute to the development of systematic theory and yield generalizations which apply beyond the materials analyzed.[52]

In summarizing several chapters of an important book on content analysis, Pool describes how "qualitative" content analysis can be useful in discovering hypotheses and in developing categories useful in their quantitative testing. Qualitative analysis serves to identify the categories later used when making the frequency counts of quantitative

---

[49] See Bernard Berelson, "Content Analysis," in Gardner Lindzey, ed., *Handbook of Social Psychology,* Vol. I (Cambridge, Mass.: Addison-Wesley, 1954), Chapter 13. This chapter is a summary of Berelson's *Content Analysis in Communication Research* (Glencoe, Ill.: Free Press, 1952). For a similar discussion of the uses of content analysis, see Dorwin P. Cartwright, "Analysis of Qualitative Material," in Leon Festinger and Daniel Katz, eds., *Research Methods in the Behavioral Sciences* (New York: Holt, Rinehart and Winston, 1953), Chapter 10.

[50] Berelson, "Content Analysis," p. 489.

[51] See Fred N. Kerlinger, *Foundations of Behavioral Research: Educational and Psychological Inquiry* (New York: Holt, Rinehart and Winston, 1965), pp. 544–45.

[52] Cartwright, "Analysis of Qualitative Material," p. 435.

analysis. In this connection Pool points out, however, that "it should not be assumed that qualitative methods are insightful, and quantitative ones merely mechanical methods for checking hypotheses. The relationship is a circular one; each provides new insights on which the other can feed."[53] He describes contingency analysis as a means of studying relationships between variables. "Contingency analysis asks not how often a given symbolic form appears in each of several bodies of text, but how often it appears in conjunction with other symbolic units."[54] Frequency counts are discussed by Pool as measures of variation or intensity of attitudes expressed in the content analyzed and he briefly discusses "evaluation assertion analysis," a technique for measurement of attitudes developed and more fully explained by Osgood.[55]

It should be evident to the reader that there are a number of parallels between data collecting through content analysis and data collecting by procedures earlier described. As a matter of fact, the term content analysis does apply to the analysis of responses to open-end questions included in questionnaires or in interviews and to transcripts of tape recordings of classroom discourse.

Useful content analysis techniques in educational problems

As in all research, the problem should be clearly defined and its definition should include the specific questions to be answered or the hypotheses to be tested by the data.

Following the statement of the problem and a decision to collect data by content analysis, there should be specification of the "universe" to be sampled. By universe in this context is meant the "population" of communications to which the conclusions or generalizations derived from the analysis are to apply. Examples of such universes are all texts in elementary school physics published since 1950, all compositions written by sixth-grade pupils in a large elementary school at some specified time, or all editorials appearing in the newspapers of some city during a period of controversy over programed instruction. In such instances the entire universe may be analyzed. On the other hand, sampling will need to be employed when the volume of content to be analyzed is large. There may be a sampling of communications representative of the universe, for example, a random sample of 500 of the

---

[53] Ithiel De Sola Pool, "Trends in Content Analysis Today: A Summary," in Ithiel De Sola Pool, ed., *Trends in Content Analysis* (Urbana, Ill.: University of Illinois Press, 1959), Chapter 7, p. 192. Reprinted with permission of author and publisher.

[54] *Ibid.,* p. 196.

[55] Charles E. Osgood, "The Representational Model and Relevant Methods," *Trends in Content Analysis, op. cit.,* Chapter 2.

10,000 pupil compositions written at the specified time by all the pupils completing the sixth grade in a large city school system. All of the communications of a universe may be obtained, but the content of each systematically sampled. Such sampling occurs in "readability" studies where, for example, in using the Dale-Chall formula it was recommended:

> Take approximately 100 words about every tenth page for books. For articles, select about four 100-word samples per 2000 words. Space these samples evenly. For passages of about 200 to 300 words analyze the entire passage. Never begin or end a sample in the middle of a sentence.[56]

The goal of a sampling plan should be such as to give each relevant element in the universe of content equal chance of being observed and recorded. While the total sample analyzed should be large and representative to justify generalizations, it is unwise to decide how large a sample to analyze until trial of the analytical procedure to be used reveals the amount of time, effort, and expense that will be required.

Another crucial step in undertaking a content analysis is the formulation of a set of categories. Categories may be dichotomies such as "creative" and "noncreative," "favorable" and "unfavorable," and "authoritarian" and "democratic." If the analyst identifies and records only instances of one of the two attributes thus paired, he must assume absence of the other. In some studies unordered categories are used. An analysis of basic high-school physics texts could involve the use of such subject-matter content categories as "mechanics"; "work and energy"; "kinetic theory and heat"; "electrostatics, electricity, and magnetism"; "sound"; "light"; and "atomic and nuclear phenomena." In many studies, the categories are in serial order. They are often used to measure the intensity of attitudes expressed in the content analyzed, for example, "very favorable," "favorable," "neutral," "unfavorable," and "very unfavorable." Such sets of categories promote measurement of variables even though they may not meet the rigorous requirements of interval or ratio scales.[57] The following ordered categories were used, in addition to the Dale-Chall formula, to judge the readability of selections adapted for publication in seventh and eighth grade readers.[58]

---

[56] Edgar Dale and Jeanne S. Chall, "A Formula for Predicting Readability: Instructions," *Educational Research Bulletin* 27 (February 18, 1948), p. 37.

[57] Cartwright, "Analysis of Qualitative Material," pp. 442–43. See also pages 198–201 of Chapter 8 of this book.

[58] Seventh and eighth grade readers of the *Companion Series* of *Adventures in Literature* published in 1962 by Harcourt, Brace & World.

*Easy; within the range of nearly all students.

**Moderately simple; most students can handle with little difficulty.

***May be challenging, but offers no severe difficulties.

****Definitely challenging; will require sustained effort.

Often major categories will themselves be divided into subcategories. Ideally, the categories and subcategories should be clearly and operationally defined and should be exhaustive and mutually exclusive. The objectivity or reproducibility, the reliability and the validity of the data obtained through content analysis depend on the extent to which the categories meet the ideal requirements mentioned.

In addition to categorization of the content to be analyzed, decisions have to be made with reference to the units of analysis—words, sentences or paragraphs, or entire communications such as editorials, newspaper and magazine articles, telecasts, or student compositions.[59] These are recording units when they represent the smallest segments of content given a single characterization. A single sentence assertion or an entire editorial may be recorded by a tally adjacent to the category label "very favorable." In analysis of textbooks, single words may be appropriate recording units in studies of vocabulary. Words may be appropriate units in analyses of pupil writings. They may be indicators of certain attitudes or values. Sentences, paragraphs, or longer segments of content such as editorials or student compositions may increase the difficulty of categorization because of complexity and the necessity to make difficult judgments as to just what category is relevant. Utterances, episodes, and ventures have already been noted as units in the content analysis of classroom discourse.

Space-time units such as column-inches can be used in the analysis of news articles and editorials. Column-inches could be used as the unit in analyzing the space given to various topics in the educational news section of *Time* magazine over a period of a year or more. Counts of sentences or column inches of editorials may answer the question of what proportion of editorial comment is favorable to some controversial decision without, however, answering the question of what proportion of individual editors, or newspapers, are favorable. In the analysis of the elementary physics texts earlier mentioned, numbers of pages devoted to each of the topics listed should serve the purpose, although column-inches or sentences would be more precise. In analyzing

---

[59] Bernard Berelson, in "Content Analysis," pp. 507–09 of *Handbook of Social Psychology,* proposed such recording units as words, themes, characters, and items. Except for "characters" these parallel those given above. He also proposed the term "space-time measures," but these are "enumeration" units. Also see Cartwright, "Analysis," pp. 440–41 in *Research Methods in Behavioral Sciences.*

movies, radio programs, and television broadcasts numbers of minutes devoted to specific topics can be the enumeration units used.

It is most important that whichever categories and recording or enumeration units are used be clearly defined, and that they be employed systematically and objectively. A carefully planned recording form with appropriate marginal labels will facilitate this aim. If the data are to be key punched, a computer expert should be consulted. Estimates should be made of the reliability[60] and validity of the data. If the data are relevant to constructs, the legitimacy of such labels as "creative" and "need satisfying" is a problem of construct validity.[61] The adequacy of the sampling of the "class of behaviors" to which the generalizations are to apply should be a matter of concern. The generalizations derived from the data should usually apply only to the universe of which the sample of content analyzed is a representative sample. If, however, the analysis serves to establish a theory, or the hypothesis tested becomes a general principle, applications going beyond the content sampled may be justified. The above statement refers also to research in which the data are collected by means other than content analysis. It is not presumed, of course, that theories and general principles are necessarily permanently established.

---

[60] The procedure outlined by Medley and Mitzel can be used with content analysis data. *Handbook of Research,* pp. 310–20.

[61] See pages 165 to 168 of Chapter 7.

Questions for
Study and Discussion

1. To what extent was the teaching of Socrates characterized by "indirect influence?"

2. What kinds of questions asked by teachers are most likely to stimulate divergent thinking?

3. How might Flanders' observational system be employed in the training or supervision of teachers?

4. How could content analysis be applied in the study of current controversial educational issues?

5. Would a sign system be more useful in studying the affective or the cognitive attributes of classroom behaviors?

6. Which of the classroom observation systems give attention to the sequence of teacher and pupil behaviors?

7. In what ways can the philosophy of language contribute to the study of classroom learning?

8. How can a live observer contribute to a classroom research in which tape recordings are made of classroom discourse?

9. Which of the observational studies briefly summarized includes categories that exemplify a "scale"?

10. What are the differences between "episodes" and "ventures"?

Suggestions
for Further Study

A variety of methods of obtaining, categorizing, and analyzing classroom observational data have been described in this chapter. The student seriously interested in one or more of these methods should locate the original reports of those that interest him. Apart from the opportunity this avails him to examine observation schedules in their entirety, the original reports contain much more of interest. The student can find discussions of conceptual frameworks, statements of problems often listing hypotheses, information concerning other variables measured in relation to the observational ones, and inferences drawn from the data.

The student should be alert to the future publication of reports of research using classroom observational data. These appear in the professional educational, psychological, and sociological journals. They also appear in reports of Cooperative Research Projects funded by the U.S. Office of Education. Future issues of the *Review of Educational Research* on the "Methodology of Educational Research" and on "Growth, Development, and Learning" should be useful in locating new reports and writings about new methodological developments. The anthology volumes on classroom observation instruments edited by Anita Simon and E. Gil Boyer, cited among the references, is an excellent source of information on observation systems. It can be found in research and development centers and regional laboratories funded by the U.S. Office of Education.

The selected references list a number of books containing discussions of the methods of obtaining and analyzing observational data. The chapters of the issues of the *Review of Educational Research* earlier cited are listed again. They should be read in their entirety. The same is true of the Medley and Mitzel, and the Withall and Lewis chapters in the *Handbook of Research on Teaching* and of the anthology *Interaction Analysis* edited by Amidon and Hough. Also listed are references to important writings on the philosophy of language and of science that can be useful in acquiring a proper conceptual framework. The books by Abraham Kaplan and by Hilgard and Bower should also be studied in this connection. Chapter 2 of this text is also relevant.

Much of the research in which classroom observational data are collected is concerned with teacher effectiveness. For a comprehensive summary of such research see "Teacher Effectiveness" by Ned A. Flanders and Anita Simon and published in the Fourth Edition of the *Encyclopedia of Educational Research*. See also *Analyzing Teaching Behavior* by Flanders.

Only brief mention has been made in this chapter of observational studies concerned with group dynamics, and with social factors of home and school environments influencing pupil learning and adjustment. The *Review* chapter of Boyd and DeVault refers to a number of researches in this field and to publications on the methodology of such research. One has only to read articles dealing with controversial issues in current newspapers and magazines to realize its very great importance.

Selected References

Amidon, Edmund J. and John B. Hough, eds. *Interaction Analysis: Theory, Research, and Application.* Reading, Mass.: Addison-Wesley, 1967.

Bales, Robert F. *Interaction Process Analysis.* Cambridge, Mass.: Addison-Wesley, 1950.

Bellack, Arno A., ed. *Theory and Research in Teaching.* New York: Bureau of Publications, Teachers College, Columbia University, 1963.

Berelson, Bernard. *Content Analysis in Communication Research.* Glencoe, Ill.: Free Press, 1952.

————. "Content Analysis." In *Handbook of Social Psychology,* edited by Gardner Lindzey, Vol. I. Cambridge, Mass.: Addison-Wesley, 1954. Chapter 13.

A condensation of the book cited above.

Boyd, Robert D., and M. Vere DeVault. "The Observation and Recording of Behavior," in "Methodology of Educational Research." *Review of Educational Research* 36 (December 1966): 529–51.

Brown, Roger. *Words and Things.* New York: Free Press (Macmillan), 1958.

Cartwright, Dorwin P. "Analysis of Qualitative Material." In *Research Methods in the Behavioral Sciences,* edited by Leon Festinger and Daniel Katz. New York: Dryden, 1953. Chapter 10.

Feigl, Herbert. "Logical Empiricism." In *Readings in Philosophical Analysis,* edited by Herbert Feigl and Wilfrid Sellars, pp. 3–26. New York: Appleton-Century-Crofts, 1949.

Flanders, Ned A. *Analyzing Teaching Behavior.* Reading, Mass.: Addison-Wesley, 1970.

Heyns, Roger W., and Ronald Lippitt. "Systematic Observational Techniques." In *Handbook of Social Psychology,* edited by Gardner Lindzey, pp. 370–404. Vol. I. Reading, Mass.: Addison-Wesley, 1954.

Holsti, Ole R. "Content Analysis." In *The Handbook of Social Psychology,* edited by Gardner Lindzey and Elliott Aronson, pp. 596–602. Vol. I. 2nd ed. Reading, Mass.: Addison-Wesley, 1968.

Hudgins, Bryce B. *The Instructional Process.* Chicago: Rand McNally, 1971.

Kerlinger, Fred N. *Foundations of Behavioral Research, Educational and Psychological Inquiry.* New York: Holt, Rinehart, and Winston, 1965. Chapters 28 and 30.

Medley, Donald M., and Harold E. Mitzel. "Measuring Classroom Behavior by Systematic Observation." In *Handbook of Research on Teaching,* edited by N. L. Gage. Chicago: Rand McNally, 1963. Chapter 6.

Meux, Milton O. "Studies of Learning in the School Setting," in "Growth, Development, and Learning." *Review of Educational Research* 37 (December 1967): 539–62.

Pool, Ithiel De Sola, ed. *Trends in Content Analysis.* Urbana, Ill.: University of Illinois Press, 1959.

Selltiz, Claire and others. *Research Methods in Social Relations,* rev. ed. New York: Holt, Rinehart, and Winston, 1959. Chapter 6.

Simon, Anita and E. Gil Boyer. *Mirrors for Behavior, An Anthology of Classroom Observation Instruments.* Philadelphia: Research for Better Schools, Inc. 1970. Volumes I–XV. Summarized as *Mirrors for Behavior II.* 2 Volumes.

Weick, Karl E. "Systematic Observational Methods." In *The Handbook of Social Psychology,* edited by Gardner Lindzey and Elliot Aronson, pp. 357–451. Vol. II. 2nd ed. Reading, Mass.: Addison-Wesley, 1968.

White, Alan R. *The Philosophy of Mind.* New York: Random House, 1967.

Withall, John. "Research Tools: Observing and Recording Behavior" in "The Methodology of Educational Research." *Review of Educational Research* 30 (December 1960): 496–512.

——— and W. W. Lewis. "Social Interaction in the Classroom." In *Handbook of Research on Teaching,* edited by N. L. Gage. Chicago: Rand McNally, 1963. Chapter 13.

Wittgenstein, Ludwig. *Philosophical Investigations.* (Translated by G.E.M. Anscombe.) New York: Macmillan, 1953.

7

Collecting Data: Tests and Other Measuring Instruments

For many educational research problems, the most appropriate data are those which may be collected by means of tests, or other measuring instruments. Such data include measures of aptitude, achievement, interests, attitudes, and other personality traits. The data may be obtained to test hypotheses or to answer questions in survey-type investigations. In studies of growth or development, equivalent forms of the same test, or test battery, may be administered at intervals of several months. Similarly, in educational experimentation, equivalent forms of the same test or battery may be administered at the beginning and end of the experimental instruction to measure the comparative effects of different methods or materials of instruction. In addition to the collection of measurement data directly relevant to a problem, other test data may be obtained, as earlier noted, to define or characterize the samples of students participating in the research in order to facilitate application of the findings to populations other than the one sampled.

CHARACTERISTICS OF TESTS ESSENTIAL TO EFFECTIVENESS

The characteristic of a test most fundamental to its effectiveness and which is contributed to by all other desirable characteristics is its *validity*—how well it measures what it is designed to measure. To be valid, a test must be relevant to the purpose for which it is used and must be reliable. In simplest terms, validity may be thought of as the extent to which test scores are related to some criterion external to the test itself. This criterion may be the scores on another test concurrently or subsequently given. Or the criterion may be definitions of instructional objectives in behavioral terms. Finally, the criterion may be a concept, or construct, concerning some ability or trait. Similarly, reliability most simply refers to the consistency with which the scores on a test are related to scores on the same test when given a second time, to scores on an equivalent form given at nearly the same time, or to scores on a hypothetical test given at the same time. The contrast between validity and reliability is, somewhat loosely, a contrast between consistency evaluated in terms of external and internal criteria. Reliability is first discussed because understanding of reliability facilitates understanding of validity, and because, as noted earlier, just as reliability contributes to validity, objectivity contributes to reliability, and hence, indirectly to validity. This does not mean, of course, that only objective tests are reliable and valid. It does imply that objectivity of scoring contributes to reliability and validity, whether a test is of the objective or essay type. The same is true of attitude inventories, rating scales, projective techniques and any measuring instruments whatever.

Other important characteristics of tests which influence their effectiveness include adequate norms, optimum length, clarity and effectiveness of expression, appropriate organization, and legibility and attractiveness of format. Adequate norms, whether in terms of percentile ranks or standard scores, are advantageous in educational research. See Chapter 8, pages 225 to 233. Such norms facilitate comparisons of samples of pupils tested with norm populations and thus aid in specifying the types of populations to which it may be held that generalizations apply. This is true not only for descriptive studies in which tests are used to collect data (see Chapter 10), but also for studies of the relationships between variables through use of various kinds of correlation coefficients (see Chapters 8 and 11) and through experimentation (see Chapter 12). In growth or development studies, and in experimentation, the researcher may wish to analyze gains in scores. When this is the case, it is especially important that equivalent forms of the tests used are available.

In selecting or constructing tests or other measuring instruments consideration must be given to such practical matters as the testing time required, the skill needed in administration, and the method of scoring. Most published tests and many locally constructed ones are designed for use with machine scorable answer sheets. It is necessary to anticipate what kind of a scoring machine will be used—the old IBM 805, the new IBM 1230 or 1231, Digitek, or some similar new machine. A locally constructed test can be designed so that a "standard" answer sheet can be purchased that is suitable for any of the machines just mentioned. Locally constructed objective tests can be hand scored, using scoring strips or stencils conforming to a hand score answer sheet. Often, it is an economy to order or duplicate fewer book-lets than the number of students tested so long as the booklets are checked to see whether students observed the instruction *not* to write in them.

The preparation of tests by the researcher himself that can satisfy the criteria suggested above requires planning; planning prior to the writing of exercises and, after they have been written, planning that insures adequate evaluation of exercises by means of item analysis.[1] Planning is also required in organizing a test, in obtaining adequate reproduction of the test material, in giving and scoring the test, and in interpreting the scores.

The characteristics mentioned above may be used as criteria in selecting published standardized tests or other measuring instruments for the purpose of collecting data in educational research studies of the types noted at the beginning of this chapter. Such criteria should be kept in mind when reading test reviews in the Buros *Mental Measurements Yearbooks,* in catalogs of test publishers, and when examining sample copies of tests and their manuals. For fuller understanding of the criteria consult the new *Standards for Educational and Psychological Tests and Manuals.*[2]

RELIABILITY

Physical measurements compared with educational or psychological measurements

When the length of an object is measured two or more times with a footrule, it is possible to determine the length precisely enough for practical purposes. A second measurement may suffice if it checks the first, or the average of several measurements may be taken as the precise length. Deviations of each of the several measurements from their average, or from the length accepted as precise, are random errors. They reflect the fact that some of the lengths as measured are too long and some too short. If the footrule is accurately scaled and appropriately applied to the object, and the object does not change in length while being measured, the distribution of random errors testifies to the accuracy or reliability of such measurement. The smaller the range or spread of such errors, the greater the confidence in the reliability of any single measurement of length. Such measurement of physical objects has certain advantages over measurement by educa-

---

[1] See Chapter 11, pages 361 to 366.

[2] *Standards for Educational and Psychological Tests and Manuals* (Washington, D.C.: American Psychological Association, 1966).

tional and psychological tests: the object measured is not typically affected by the process of being measured and, normally, the object does not change in length while being measured.

The true score and error components of an observed test score

If we suppose that a test score has two components, first, a hypothetically true measure of whatever ability or abilities the test measures and, second, a part or component of the score which is error, we have imagined a situation analogous to measurement of length as described above. If a student could be tested repeatedly with the same or parallel tests without being affected by the testing and without change in his abilities from other causes, his average score would be his "true" score and the spread of the deviations of all of his scores from this average would be a means of determining the reliability of the test. Again, the narrower the spread, the greater confidence we might have in a single testing and the higher the reliability of the test. Perfect reliability would occur if there were complete freedom from such errors. Note, however, the restriction to whatever abilities the test *measures,* not whatever abilities the test *is designed* to measure. Use of the latter phrase is more relevant to a discussion of validity.

Correlation coefficients as indices of test reliability

A comparison to physical measurements also provides another approach to the concept of reliability. Suppose that the length of each of several objects is measured but once and the objects are arranged in order of length and numbered accordingly. Then let us suppose that the objects are thoroughly mixed, spread out with the numbers on their bottoms, and measured again. If they are then arranged in order of size according to the second series of measurements, the extent to which the second order is consistent with the first is evidence of the reliability of the measurements. Similarly, if a large group of students is tested twice *without being influenced on the second occasion by the first testing or by other causes,* the consistency with which they are ranked on both occasions is a measure of the reliability of the test. A method frequently used in summarizing such evidence is to compute the coefficient of correlation between the paired scores of the students tested twice, this being one type of coefficient of reliability.

Although coefficients of correlation will be explained more fully later in this text (Chapters 8, 9 and 11), a brief explanation is needed here. The coefficient of correlation which can vary from -1.00, through zero, to $+1.00$ is an index of the extent to which paired measures (for example, pairs of test scores of the same pupils on two tests) are associated. If pupils are tested twice with a long and well-constructed test, the correlation between the pairs of scores may be as high as

+ .90 or + .95. In the case of a shorter test, for example, a test of 75 multiple-choice exercises, the correlation coefficient—a coefficient of reliability—may be + .80.

The standard error of measurement as an index of test reliability

Coefficients of reliability can also be obtained from an estimate of the spread of the distribution of errors in test scores, more technically, the error variance. Conversely, estimates of the error variance can be obtained from coefficients of reliability computed by correlating scores (as well as in other ways). The coefficient of reliability is a measure of the part of the variation, or variance, in actual test scores of a sample of students attributable to variation, or variance, of their "true" scores. The variation in errors, the error variance, accounts for the balance of the variation or variance in actual scores. The square root of the error variance, the standard error of measurement,[3] is, theoretically, the standard deviation of the distribution of errors in the scores of an individual student tested many times under the ideal conditions earlier mentioned. Think of a true score as the mean of very numerous ordinary scores portrayed by the familiar bell-shaped normal curve, and errors as the deviations of the ordinary scores from the true score or mean at the center of the base line of the curve. In theory, approximately 68 percent of the ordinary scores of this hypothetical student fall between one standard error of measurement below the true score and one standard error of measurement above the true score. The higher the coefficient of reliability, the smaller the standard error of measurement. Suppose, for example, that three tests have the coefficients of reliability of .95, .90, and .80 and assume the same standard deviation of 10 score units for each. The standard errors of measurement are approximately 2, 3, and 4.5 score units. In the case of the third test, 68 percent of the observed scores of the hypothetical student mentioned above would have a range of 9 units centered about his hypothetical true score.

The preceding paragraphs present an idealized view of test reliability. The coefficient of reliability usually obtained and the corresponding standard error of measurement are approximations. The measuring instrument—the test—influences what is measured, and what is measured changes from one measurement to the next. Let us consider, first, estimations of reliability obtained by testing students twice with the same test.

---

[3] See the discussion of the standard error of measurement in Chapter 9, pages 256 to 259. The explanation given above applies more precisely to *estimated* true scores corresponding to observed scores.

The test-retest coefficient of reliability

When the same educational or psychological test is given twice to the same students, instability of student performance is one source of chance errors. Students may respond differently on each occasion to some of the items or exercises. Some scores on the second administration may be relatively higher because learning has intervened. Other scores may be lower, because of forgetting. Instability or lack of consistency in performance may be due to differences in motivation. Students may do their best on one occasion but have little interest in exerting themselves on another. Deviations in actual scores from scores which would precisely measure whatever abilities the test measures may also include errors due to carelessness or subjectivity in scoring, guessing, lapses of attention, misinterpretation of directions or of items, and the like.

Consistent misinterpretation on two occasions and recall of answers previously given, whether correct or incorrect, may spuriously increase correlation of the scores and thus yield a coefficient of reliability which is an overestimate. "The same answers may be repeated not because the individual is consistent in his behavior, and arrives at the same conclusion in the same way, but because he has a memory of his previous response."[4] All factors mentioned above through which the first administration of a test influences scores the second time the same test is given affect the dependability of such a coefficient of reliability. Most often the coefficient is an overestimate.

Any test contains but a sample of all the items or exercises which might be written in an effort to measure whatever abilities are measured by the test. The test-retest coefficient of reliability does not take into account error due to lack of representativeness of the items. An individual student's score, especially on a short essay or objective test, may be affected by what he has emphasized or neglected in study. The given test may not adequately sample his knowledge or skills. If he is lucky in the items presented, he may receive a higher score than he deserves. If unlucky he may receive a lower score. Test-retest coefficients of reliability do not take into account this type of error.

---

[4] Robert L. Thorndike, "Reliability," in E. F. Lindquist, ed., *Educational Measurement* (Washington, D.C.: American Council on Education, 1951), Chapter 15, p. 579; and Julian C. Stanley, "Reliability," in Robert L. Thorndike, ed., *Educational Measurement,* 2nd ed. (Washington, D.C.: American Council on Education, 1971), Chapter 13. These references are excellent sources of information with respect to the meaning of test reliability, the factors influencing it, and methods used in its estimation. For an earlier comprehensive discussion of different types of reliability coefficients and their determination, see Lee J. Cronbach, "Test 'Reliability': Its Meaning and Determination," *Psychometrika* 12 (March 1947), pp. 1–16.

The equivalent forms coefficient of reliability

The kind of errors just described may be taken into account by testing students on two occasions with *equivalent forms* of the same test. Reliability coefficients thus obtained should be and often are lower than the coefficients which might be obtained by testing students twice with the same test.

The dependability of a reliability coefficient obtained by correlating scores on two equivalent forms may be adversely affected in somewhat the same ways as the test-retest reliability coefficient. The content of the exercises in the two forms may be too much alike in specific details. Each form may not be an adequately independent and representative sample of all of the items which might be written to test the ability in question. Furthermore, the taking of the first form may influence the taking of the second. Students may learn from the first testing how better to attack the problems of the second. Or students may similarly misinterpret directions on both occasions. The operation of such factors tends to result in a reliability coefficient which is an overestimate. Conversely, if students are unequally motivated on the two occasions, or if the two forms are given a relatively long time apart, variation in learning or practice or in forgetting or loss of skills may intervene. These factors will lower the coefficient of reliability obtained.

In spite of the possible limitations mentioned above, the equivalent forms reliability coefficient is generally accepted as the most accurate and meaningful of the types of reliability coefficients. Such coefficients are estimates of how reliably the test measures individual differences in the abilities contributing to performance on both forms (apart from highly specific abilities whose functioning is unique to each form). Like test-retest coefficients they also take into account the stability of measurement from one occasion to the next. The time between testings should be reported to facilitate interpretation of the reliability coefficient thus obtained.

Reliability estimates based on a single testing

Reliability coefficients are probably most often computed from data collected from a single administration of a test. The scores correlated are the scores on parallel half-tests later reorganized as a single test, or they may be the scores obtained by separate scoring of two halves of randomly selected items, most often the scores obtained by separate scoring of alternate, or odd and even, items.

The coefficient of correlation between the scores of two half-tests or for odd and even items is entered in the Spearman-Brown formula to obtain an estimate of the coefficient of reliability of the *whole* test:

$$r_{xx} = \frac{2r_{12}}{1 + r_{12}} \qquad (7.1)$$

Here r_{xx} is the coefficient of reliability and r_{12} refers to the correlation between the half-tests. Suppose that the correlation between the two half-tests is .80. Then

$$r_{xx} = \frac{2 \times .80}{1.00 + .80} = \frac{1.60}{1.80} = .89$$

When an odd-even split results in independent, equivalent, parallel halves and responding to one item does not influence response to the next (thus increasing the correlation between halves), defensible estimates of the coefficient of reliability are obtained. Similar reliability coefficients can also be derived from one administration of a test if the percents of students responding correctly to each item are obtained in addition to their total scores. Use can then be made of the Kuder-Richardson Formula 20, or Hoyt's analysis of variance method.[5]

All reliability coefficients derived from data obtained from a single administration of a test are estimates of the reliability of measures of individual differences at the time of testing. They do not account for day-to-day instability in performance nor for errors due to lack of representativeness of the items. They are often called "coefficients of internal consistency" or of "homogeneity."

Speed as a factor in reliability estimates

In closing this discussion of reliability coefficients it should be emphasized that where speed is an important factor in taking a test, reliability coefficients should *not* be determined from data obtained on a single administration. Omission of items toward the end tends spuriously to increase the consistency, for example, of odd and even scores and leads to overestimates of reliability. In the case of the Kuder-Richardson Formula 20 and in Hoyt's analysis of variance method, the percentages of correct response to the items of the test used in obtaining these estimates may similarly be too consistent from item to item with the items of a hypothetical second test, with which the given test is presumed to be correlated. In a speeded test the percents progressively decrease, not necessarily from increase in difficulty but because time is a factor. More dependable estimates of the reliability of tests where speed is a factor in performance are obtained by

---

[5] For the original papers on the methods referred to above, see G. F. Kuder and M. W. Richardson, "The Theory of the Estimation of Test Reliability," *Psychometrika* 2 (September 1937), pp. 151–160; and Cyril Hoyt, "Test Reliability Estimated by Analysis of Variance," *Psychometrika* 6 (June 1941), pp. 153–160. An elementary explanation of analysis of variance is given in Chapter 13. Analysis of variance designs for estimating reliability coefficients are increasingly being applied, not only to test scores, but to ratings and other measurement data. See Medley and Mitzel's chapter in the *Handbook of Research on Teaching*.

correlating scores from two administrations of the test, or, better still, from administration of equivalent forms.

Group heterogeneity and reliability estimates

A researcher often compares published coefficients of reliability of standardized tests when deciding what tests to use. He should know that the size of such coefficients is in part directly determined by the range of individual differences in ability within the groups tested. Other things equal, the greater the range or heterogeneity of the group tested in obtaining data to estimate the reliability of a test, the higher the coefficient of reliability. Testing pupils in a succession of school grades will result in a higher coefficient of correlation than testing pupils all on the same grade level. In a single grade the paired scores of two forms of the same test may so scatter as to be indicative of low correlation, a low coefficient of reliability. (See Figure 8.2 on page 206 of Chapter 8.) In successively higher grades, similar scattering occurs, but the paired scores are generally higher. This general increase in scores from grade to grade enlarges their range and, hence, the greater the correlation between them. If diagramed, the points depicting the correlation would seem to be relatively closer to a diagonal.

Reliability coefficients can be adjusted for such heterogeneity if the standard deviations of the different groups are known. Suppose that r and s are the reported reliability coefficient and the standard deviation for the group or sample used in obtaining r. Suppose also that s' is the standard deviation of a group differing in heterogeneity and that r' is the reliability coefficient we wish to estimate for this group. Then on the assumption that the standard errors of measurement are equal for both groups, applying to any student regardless of the group of which he is a member:

$$s'\sqrt{1-r'} = s\sqrt{1-r} \text{ and solving for } r':$$

$$r' = 1 - \frac{s^2}{s'^2}(1-r) \tag{7.2}$$

Suppose that for a range of three grades the standard deviation, s, and reliability coefficient, r, are 15 score units and .90. Suppose also that the standard deviation for a single grade is 10. Then r', the reliability coefficient for the single grade, may be estimated,

$$r' = 1 - \frac{225}{100}(1-.90)$$
$$= .775 \text{ or } .78$$

Thus a test with a reliability coefficient of .90 may be actually less reliable than a test with a reliability coefficient of .80 where the latter is based on testing in a single grade. Better comparisons can be made by studying the standard errors of measurement of the two tests, since these take into account the variability of the pupil or student populations.

Factors promoting test reliability

It may be helpful to list the factors that research has shown tend to increase test reliability:

1. Assuming that items or exercises are of reasonably comparable quality, the longer the test, in other words, the greater the number of items, the higher the reliability.

2. Assuming that the incorrect answers or distracters of multiple-choice exercises are all reasonably plausible to less able students, item reliability and, hence, reliability of objective tests increases with numbers of choices per exercise. True-false or two-choice items are least reliable, and reliability increases predictably, though at a diminishing rate, for three, four, and five or more choices.

3. Items should have an optimum range of difficulty. Very difficult or very easy items tend to lower the reliability of a test from the level it would be if such items were replaced by items of more appropriate difficulty.

4. Items should discriminate between superior students and inferior students as classified by the part or total scores on the test or some other appropriate criterion used in item analysis.[6]

5. Directions for series of items should be free from ambiguous phraseology and needlessly technical terms. If correction for guessing is to be used, the directions should include a statement to this effect.

6. Time limits should be ample in most achievement tests to insure that speed is not a factor. (Where speed of performance is one of the objects of measurement, this does not apply.)

7. The test should be administered under appropriate testing conditions—providing adherence to time limits where time limits are specified, freedom from distractions, precautions to prevent cheating, and the like.

8. The scoring key should be correct for all items. Errors due to carelessness in scoring should be nonexistent or minimal. In the case of essay examinations, high "reader reliability" should be sought since this contributes to the reliability of essay tests.

---

[6] See page 168 of this chapter, page 205 of Chapter 8, and the discussion of item analysis in Chapter 11, pages 361 to 366.

Where the purpose is to evaluate "level of mastery," the items may be so easy that most pupils respond correctly. Such a test may show what proportion of a group of pupils has attained the objectives of a learning experience. This purpose may be served satisfactorily without reliably discriminating among the pupils who make perfect scores.[7]

VALIDITY

A test is said to be valid if it measures what it is stipulated to measure. (In research, what is stipulated is a variable specified in the statement of the problem.) As has been shown earlier, a test does not measure what it is expected to measure unless it does so consistently, that is, reliably. In past years a number of different kinds of validity including "face" validity, "curricular" validity, and "empirical" validity have been identified. More recently the terms "concurrent," "predictive," "content," and "construct" validity have become widely used. Concurrent validity (important when the purpose is that of assessing the present status of ability, achievement, or other traits) and predictive validity are now referred to and discussed under the heading of "criterion-related" validity.[8] Attention is first directed to the meanings of the terms identifying the different kinds of validity. While content validity (which has tended to supplant curricular validity for achievement tests) is possibly of the greatest concern in the evaluation of the attainment of educational objectives, concurrent, predictive, and even construct or "trait" validity are of importance also and are well worth understanding by persons seriously interested in testing.

Face validity

The term "face validity" is no longer in good repute.[9] Face validity pertains to immediate judgment of the validity of a test in terms of its content. A test is assumed to be valid if it appears to be valid. For example, a test made up of addition, subtraction, multiplication, and division exercises is assumed to be a valid measure of these aspects of computational ability in arithmetic with no more than a quick look at the exer-

---

[7] See "Learning for Mastery" in Benjamin S. Bloom, J. Thomas Hastings, and George F. Madaus, *Handbook on Formative and Summative Evaluation of Student Learning* (New York: McGraw-Hill, 1971), Chapter 3.

[8] For the earliest published discussion of concurrent, predictive, content, and construct validity see "Technical Recommendations for Psychological Tests and Diagnostic Techniques," *Psychological Bulletin* (Supplement) 2 (March 1954), pp. 13–28. For a later one introducing the term criterion-related validity (*not* criterion-referenced) see *Standards for Educational and Psychological Tests and Manuals, op. cit.*, pp. 13, 16–23.

[9] Charles I. Mosier, "A Critical Examination of the Concepts of Face Validity," *Educational and Psychological Measurement* 7 (September 1947), pp. 191–205.

cises it contains. Such judgments of tests like the one just described may not be far from the truth, even though unsupported by other evidence. On the other hand, however, consider the dependability of a similar evaluation of a test of creativity.

Empirical or criterion-related validity

The term "empirical" in general refers to knowledge derived from observation, experience, or experimentation. In essence, it is knowledge based on observational data, although subjective factors function in their interpretation. What is meant by empirical, or criterion-related, validity may be illustrated by considering what has often been done by the author of a new test, for example, a new group intelligence test. The new test may be given along with an established test, possibly the Stanford-Binet, to the same group of students. A high correlation between the paired scores on both tests is interpreted as evidence of the concurrent validity of the new test, although the validity of the criterion test itself is ultimately based on judgment as to the nature of intelligence. Empirical validity evaluated by this method is termed "concurrent" validity. Or, the predictive validity of aptitude tests may be empirically determined by correlating their scores with subsequent measures of achievement. Here again, the validity of the criterion is a problem and ultimately is a matter of judgment.

A teacher who studies the scores of his students on a test just administered to them in relation to his present estimates of their ability is performing a rudimentary estimate of concurrent validity. Another teacher, for example a teacher of English composition, likewise estimates concurrent validity when he compares the scores his students make on an objective English test with his current ratings of the writing ability of the students. Occasionally, teachers with elementary knowledge of statistical method may compute coefficients of correlation between different tests administered at about the same time to their students and thus obtain more adequate indices of concurrent validity. Similarly, a teacher may study the scores his students earn on a proficiency test given at the start of a semester, in relation to scores on subsequent tests given during the semester or on the final examination administered at the end of the semester. He may thus estimate the predictive validity of the proficiency test in terms of how well his students conform to earlier measures of their ability. Again, more adequate indices may be obtained through computation of correlation coefficients. A group of teachers, concerned with the adequacy of marks assigned in sequences of courses, may assess the predictive validity of marks by correlating first semester marks with second or later semester marks in the sequence. This, of course, represents interest beyond the call of duty. Having gone this far, the test-minded teacher may also obtain a regression equation for use in predicting measures of subsequent achievement from the proficiency test scores, and the standard error of estimate useful as an index of the probable accuracy of such predictions. Correlations are similarly obtained as estimates of the concurrent and the predictive validity of tests developed in prediction research and reported in the manuals of published aptitude tests. (See Chapter 11.)

Content validity

Until comparatively recently the type of validity most often discussed with reference to achievement tests was their curricular validity—the validity with which a certain achievement test measured instructional or educational objectives, too often defined merely by the subject matter of a course. In recent years, the term curricular validity has tended to be replaced by the term content validity, though the latter term has not been restricted only to achievement tests. "Content validity is evaluated by showing how well the content of the test samples the class of situations or subject matter about which conclusions are to be drawn."[10] If, in the case of achievement tests and other evaluation instruments, "class of situations" refers to the *behaviors* defined as the objectives of instruction, the concept of content validity is a useful one.

Content validity as contrasted with construct validity is the more empirical. It is assessed in terms of behavior, or observable evidences of behavior, and does not involve the kind of inferences with respect to traits or abilities underlying behavior characteristic of efforts to assess construct validity. Unfortunately, as Ebel[11] has emphasized, content validity is likely to be thought of as referring to the merely informational objectives of instruction, to the materials of instruction, or to the subject matter of instruction. To say that a test is valid with respect to the content of instruction, or to the subject matter of instruction, is to limit validity estimates to only a part of the range of desirable instructional objectives. A truly effective achievement test or other evaluation instrument should be relevant to behavioral objectives beyond those on the level of knowledge, as well as being reliable.

Just how is the content validity of an achievement test to be deter-

---

[10] "Technical Recommendations," *op. cit.,* p. 13, or *Standards,* pp. 12–13 and 15–16.

[11] Robert L. Ebel, "Obtaining and Reporting Evidence on Content Validity," *Educational and Psychological Measurement* 16 (Autumn 1956), pp. 269–82. This is a valuable source of information concerning practical means of estimating the validity of exercises with respect to instructional objectives ranging from knowledge through intellectual skills. See also the *Taxonomy of Educational Objectives* by Benjamin Bloom and others, *Basic Principles of Curriculum and Instruction* by Ralph W. Tyler, and *Improving Classroom Testing* by Max D. Engelhart, listed in the bibliography of this chapter.

mined? Given an adequately detailed list of behavioral objectives on the level of knowledge, the estimation of validity with respect to such objectives seems comparatively easy. One can, for example, enter a check mark, or marks, after each objective to indicate that there are one or more exercises relevant to the objective. A judgment can then be made concerning how representative the questions or exercises are of all the items listed in the statement of such objectives. Of course, the dependability of such an estimate is also a function of the extent to which the objectives listed are representative of the content actually taught, or that which should be taught in terms of acceptable ultimate aims of education. Furthermore, the validity of test exercises, considered individually, involves more than relevance to some word or phrase symbolizing knowledge of a topic like Avogadro's principle in elementary chemistry, for example. A single exercise may require merely that the student match the name of the principle with its definition. Other items not present in the test could pertain to knowledge of the history of the principle, evidence supporting its truth, and its applications. This raises the question of how well the item or items actually sample the knowledge that is important for students to acquire concerning this principle on the level of elementary chemistry.

If a test or other device is to be used in evaluating attainment of instructional objectives not restricted to those on the level of knowledge, the estimation of its content validity is much more difficult. The problem is one of estimating how well the test samples and measures classes of student behaviors other than assimilation of knowledge, such as applications of knowledge, intellectual skills, and appropriate attitudes when seeking solutions to novel problems.

Let us consider the content validity of objective exercises designed to measure skills listed by social science instructors as aspects of "critical thinking." Again it is not difficult by study of their content to identify test items relevant to each of these skills. For example, consider the objective, "identification of a central issue or problem" and the following exercise:

The basic problem of all government implied in the argument quoted above is
A. free enterprise vs. socialism.
B. democracy vs. dictatorship.
C. individual freedom vs. the welfare of society.
D. rule by an élite or by the people.

It is easy to see that the content of this exercise is relevant to the objective stated.

Thus while it is very worth while to associate test items with objectives, one should also make judgments as to whether the skills listed are satisfactorily representative of all the skills which might appropriately be listed; whether the skills listed are adequately represented or sampled by test items; and whether the test behavior corresponds reasonably well to student behavior in other than the testing situation.

Construct validity

To go beyond the identifying of exercises with defined behavioral objectives and to seek understanding of the underlying personal factors determining test scores is to enter the domain of construct or trait validity. According to Cronbach, evaluation of the content validity of achievement tests requires both logical analysis with reference to objectives and empirical evidence with respect to the psychological processes determining test scores. He urges that "for many objectives construct validity must also be investigated."[12] Earlier, in a classic paper, Cronbach and Meehl state *"Content validity* is ordinarily to be established deductively, by defining a universe of items and sampling systematically within this universe to establish the test. *Construct validation* is involved whenever a test is to be interpreted as a measure of some attribute or quality, which is not operationally defined."[13]

There are, of course, informal ways by which a teacher may gain insights concerning the factors influencing test scores. For example, consider the test item presented earlier. Suppose that relatively few students responded by giving answer "D," the correct answer. Questioning may reveal that the word "élite" was not understood. Further questioning of the few who responded correctly may indicate that they arrived at answer D through a process of elimination. The teacher may then conclude that this item is not a valid measure of the ability of these students to identify a central issue or problem. A more formal approach is to have students recall the steps taken mentally while attempting to solve exercises, or to think aloud when in the process of solving exercises, using a technique developed by Bloom and Broder.[14]

Other ways of going beyond the identifying of items with definitions of instructional objectives include estimations of concurrent validity whether informal or through calculation of coefficients of correlation. A teacher or researcher may study the scores students earn on a critical thinking test of the type described, in relation to observations of incidents of critical thinking on the part of certain students during class

[12] Lee J. Cronbach, "Validity," in C. W. Harris, ed., *Encyclopedia of Educational Research* (New York: The Macmillan Co., 1960), pp. 1553–1554.

[13] Lee J. Cronbach and Paul E. Meehl, "Construct Validity in Psychological Tests," *Psychological Bulletin* 52 (July 1955), pp. 281–302.

[14] Benjamin S. Bloom and Lois J. Broder, *Problem-Solving Processes of College Students* (Chicago: University of Chicago Press, 1950).

discussion, or in written work.[15] Another approach may be to rate students with a scale like the following and to correlate the ratings with the critical thinking scores:

Is eager to obtain new ideas or to formulate hypotheses, but invariably suspends judgment with respect to them until evidence has been obtained and evaluated.	5 Points
Is receptive to new ideas or hypotheses and shows willingness to suspend judgment on numerous occasions, but is sometimes reluctant to seek data or consider alternative hypotheses.	4 Points
Is passive with respect to new ideas or hypotheses and shows only occasional willingness to suspend judgment or to seek necessary data.	3 Points
Preconceived ideas and prejudices usually preclude acceptance of new ideas or hypotheses even when evidence adequate to support them is provided.	2 Points
Always clings to his own ideas and is actively intolerant toward evidence which disproves them or which adequately supports opposing ideas or hypotheses.	1 Point

Identification of exercises relevant to specific skills listed under the heading of "critical thinking" is clearly content validation. The concurrent validation procedures described above are also means directed toward the goal of construct or trait validation. Certainly, a question of construct or trait validation arises when the class of behaviors defined by the skills listed and the exercises relevant to them are given the label "critical thinking." The test maker may claim that the objectives listed collectively constitute an operational definition of just what is meant, and all that can be meant, by the term "critical thinking."[16] Others would argue that critical thinking is a construct, a *conception* of an ability, trait, or attribute functioning in behavior, rather than the observed behavior itself.

Recall in this connection Plato's "Allegory of the Cave." Gulliksen has likened the shadows seen on the walls to test scores, and the world outside inferred by the persons facing the walls to traits or attributes measured by the scores. Students of philosophy may also recall that

---

[15] For an excellent discussion of using students' writing as a means of exploring their patterns of thinking and attitudes, see Vernor M. Sims, "The Essay Examination is a Projective Technique," *Educational and Psychological Measurement* 8 (Spring 1948), pp. 15–31.

[16] There is philosophical support for this point of view. For discussion of the issue read H. P. Bechtoldt, "Construct Validity: A Critique," *American Psychologist* 14 (September 1959), pp. 619–29.

the scholastic philosopher Abelard in mediating between realism and nominalism proposed conceptualism, which teaches that universals exist in the mind as concepts and are not real in the Platonic sense. Possibly, test scores belong to the real world of particular individuals, or events, while the title of the test refers to a concept, or construct!

When a test or another kind of evaluation instrument, for example, an attitude inventory, is proposed as a measure of such constructs as "scientific attitude," "love of truth," and "racial tolerance," it is evident that the validation of such an instrument is construct validation. To hypothesize that the trait named in the title of the test or inventory is the trait actually measured by the instrument does not suffice; evidence to test the hypothesis must be obtained. To continue the example of critical thinking, data may be obtained as earlier described or through the use of informational, reading, and reasoning tests and the scores on these tests correlated with the critical thinking scores. If the hypothesis is true, or the title "critical thinking" justified, the critical thinking scores and reasoning scores should be more highly correlated than the critical thinking and informational scores or the critical thinking and reading scores. Even better evidence to support the hypothesis would be a substantial coefficient of partial correlation between the critical thinking and reasoning scores, with the effect of the other variables eliminated. The procedures just suggested are not without limitations. More effective tests of such hypotheses may be obtained through utilization of the more complex techniques of correlation analysis and factor analysis (see Chapter 11).

One also might hypothesize, or theorize, that certain instructional techniques will develop critical thinking skills, and through experimentation determine whether the groups of students subjected to such instruction obtain significantly higher scores than control students.[17] Such experimentation tests both the validity hypothesis and the hypotheses or theory relevant to the instructional techniques. The efficiency with which the validity hypothesis is tested depends on the soundness of the learning theory from which the instructional techniques are derived. But at the present stage of development of psychology as a science, it suffices if the evidence is consistent for both the validity hypothesis and the theory relevant to the instructional techniques.[18] Obviously, if the experimental students do not achieve more of what-

---

[17] An example of experimentation of this kind is reported in Hymen M. Chausow, *The Organization of Learning Experiences to Achieve More Effectively the Objective of Critical Thinking in the Social Science General Course of Junior College Level.* Doctoral dissertation, University of Chicago, 1955.

[18] The experiment described above is somewhat analogous to the nomological validation recommended by Cronbach and Meehl with reference to psychological tests. See Cronbach and Meehl, "Construct Validity."

ever is measured by the test than the control students, the data challenge the legitimacy of the title, "A Test of Critical Thinking," while a significant difference in favor of the experimental students would support acceptance of the title pending further investigation.

How efforts to increase test reliability can decrease validity

When the purpose of a test is to measure a single ability, total scores on a long trial form of the test can be used as the criterion in item analysis to identify the items having satisfactory discriminating power. Items unsatisfactory in this respect are eliminated. Application of this procedure results in a more homogeneous test, a more reliable test, and hence, a more valid test of the single ability. If, however, the test is to measure more than one type of ability or achievement, use of total scores as the criterion can lower validity for this purpose. For example, if the trial form of a test of general scholastic aptitude has many more verbal than quantitative items, item analysis will favor the verbal ones. Similarly, if the trial form of a social studies test has numerous factual items and relatively few critical-thinking items, use of the total scores as the criterion will favor the factual ones and the test will be a less valid measure of general achievement in the social studies. In such situations, use of part scores as criteria is recommended. The homogeneity of the parts, their reliability, and their validity is increased. Appropriately weighted part scores may then yield more valid measures of general scholastic aptitude or general achievement. What has just been said is possibly more relevant to the production of standardized tests. In the case of item-analyzed teacher-made objective achievement tests, total score discrimination indices usually suffice in identifying questionable items. Prior to the elimination of such items, however, their content validity should be considered. Some of them may pertain to concepts or skills inadequately represented in the test or too little emphasized in instruction.

Norm-referenced vs. criterion-referenced interpretations of test data

In recent years the term *criterion-referenced* has been contrasted with *norm-referenced* in discussing the interpretation of test data.[19] The term criterion-referenced should not be confused with the criterion-related validity earlier explained, which concerns the efficiency of pre-

---

[19] See Robert Glaser, "Instructional Technology and Measurement of Learning Outcomes," *American Psychologist* 18 (August 1963), pp. 510–22; W. James Popham and T. R. Husek, "Implications of Criterion-Referenced Measurement," *Journal of Educational Measurement* 6 (Spring 1969), pp. 1–9, and Robert Ebel, "Content Standard Test Scores," *Educational and Psychological Measurement* 22 (Spring 1962), pp. 15–25.

diction of criterion scores, marks, or grade-point averages. Criterion-referenced interpretation is more akin to content validity where test scores are interpreted in terms of behaviors, or construct validity where they are interpreted with reference to some construct. When test scores are interpreted with reference to norms, pupil scores are compared to the scores of other pupils in a representative norm sample or population. When stating a criterion-referenced interpretation, one might say "John correctly solved 70 percent of a series of simultaneous linear equations . . ." and, in the case of norm-referenced interpretation, "The percentile rank of John's score is 62 according to the ninth-grade norm data."

Criterion-referenced interpretations are useful in the case of mastery tests where the distributions of test scores are not normal ones. They are useful when interpretating the data of teacher-made tests and in interpretating data obtained during computer-assisted instruction. Criterion-referenced interpretations are also useful as a supplement to norm-referenced interpretations of standardized tests. They give concrete meaning to total, part, or item scores for teachers, parents, and concerned laymen.

Item analysis revealing that a given item is both very easy and non-discriminating indicates generally satisfactory mastery of the relevant knowledge or skill. An item shown by the data to be both very difficult and nondiscriminating provides evidence suggesting increased emphasis in instruction. An item of moderate difficulty and considerable positive discriminating power provides evidence suggesting remedial instruction for the less able pupils who responded incorrectly.

The data pertaining to very easy items may indicate that further instruction is superfluous while the data for very difficult items may imply elimination or postponement of effort to teach the relevant knowledge or skill. Such interpretations of item data obtained from locally constructed objective achievement tests have been extremely valuable to teachers of the City Colleges of Chicago engaged in cooperative production of instructional materials, particularly in the courses of the general education program.

USING TEST DATA IN RESEARCH

In the preceding section of this chapter, criteria useful in the selection or construction of tests were discussed. In planning a research where test data are to be collected, all of the criteria should be applied in deciding which tests to use. It is most important to select or construct tests which will yield valid measures of the variables relevant to the problem of the research. (The fact that so many tests and other instruments are of dubious and uncertain validity complicates the problem of test selection.) It is also necessary to consider such characteristics of tests as reliability, adequacy of norms, suitability to educational level, time required for administration, methods of scoring, and other practical matters.

Types of research using test data

Test data are used in descriptive and analytical surveys. They are used in correlation studies of relationships between traits and in experimental research. The kind of test data collected depends on the problem of the research. A general aptitude test, an achievement battery, or an attitude inventory is useful in each of the types of research mentioned above.

Administrators, counselors, and teachers need to know the level and variability of pupil aptitudes and achievements in the various schools and grades. City-wide testing programs where test data are routinely collected in the various schools do not constitute educational research. The data thus obtained may be helpful, however, in efforts to solve local educational problems. When this is the case the process can be called institutional research.

The data routinely collected may also be the source of all or a part of the data needed in conducting research of the types earlier mentioned. Such data have the advantage of being unobtrusively collected. The pupils are unaware that they are subjects of research. Another advantage of city-wide or even more widely obtained data is that they afford opportunities to study the representativeness of samples of classes or pupils drawn at random from the available data. A possible disadvantage is that research problems may be selected in terms of the available data instead of having the problem define the data to be collected.

For the graduate student or other neophyte researcher a brief characterization of various types of tests and measuring instruments may be helpful. Suggestions for sources of information which should be studied before the researcher makes final selection of tests and other measuring instruments to be applied in his study of a particular problem may be useful as well.

Two major categories are tests of "ability or maximum performance" and instruments designed to measure "typical performance."[20] The first category includes tests of general ability or aptitude, tests of special aptitudes, and achievement tests and test batteries. The second

---

[20] These categories are those suggested by Cronbach. The subcategories mentioned above roughly parallel his. See Lee J. Cronbach, *Essentials of Psychological Testing*, 3rd ed. (New York: Harper & Row, 1970), p. 35.

category includes attitude scales, interest inventories, self-report or structured tests of personality, projective techniques, trait rating scales, and sociometric and other observational techniques.

TESTS OF GENERAL ABILITY OR APTITUDE

While the word "intelligence" appears in the titles of a number of the tests which will be discussed, the terms "general mental ability," "general scholastic ability," or "general scholastic aptitude" are tending to supplant the label "intelligence test." As Cronbach points out:

> Much misuse or misinterpretation of mental tests arises simply from the labels "intelligence" and "capacity," as they suggest that inborn potentiality is being measured. Performance on the tests is influenced by many things not included in this concept of "intelligence." Each test calls for knowledge, skills, and attitudes developed in Western culture, and better developed in some Western environments than in others. A mental test gives only indirect evidence on "potentialities," as we can observe potentiality only when it has flowered in performance. We cannot assume that all children in the culture or all those who have attended the same school have had equal opportunities to develop the abilities we test.[21]

It is exceedingly important to recognize the significance of Cronbach's statement. Typical tests of general scholastic aptitude are truthful in predicting relatively low academic achievement for environmentally disadvantaged minority group pupils. They predict quite accurately the relatively low levels of achievement that will be attained in instruction inappropriate to the needs of these pupils and inadequately motivating.[22]

While construct validity has received much attention in factor analysis and other studies, more needs to be known concerning the mental processes underlying "intelligence" test scores. High correlations between paired scores on group tests of intelligence and school achievement test batteries do raise questions concerning the validity of the former as measures of "native" or "innate" capacity.[23] While serious efforts have been made (as exemplified by the *Davis-Eells Games* and the *IPAT Culture Free Intelligence Test*) to produce tests that are

---

[21] *Ibid.*, p. 205. Reprinted with permission of author and publisher.

[22] *Ibid.*, pp. 305–06.

[23] William Coleman and Edward E. Cureton, "Intelligence and Achievement: The 'Jangle' Fallacy Again," *Educational and Psychological Measurement* 14 (Summer 1954), pp. 347–51.

at least "culture fair," opinion and evidence provided by research are controversial concerning the success of such efforts.

Individual intelligence tests

As the reader undoubtedly knows, there are both individual and group tests of "intelligence" or general mental ability. The leading individual tests are the *Stanford-Binet Intelligence Scale,* the *Wechsler Intelligence Scale for Children,* and the *Wechsler Adult Intelligence Scale* (for ages 16 and over). While such tests are undoubtedly the best measures of general mental ability available, the skill, time, and effort they require tend to restrict their use where a large number of pupils or students are to be tested. In educational or sociopsychological research where the problem concerns maladjusted pupils whose traits are to be studied intensively and in relation to environmental factors, one of the individual intelligence tests mentioned above is a better choice than a group test of intelligence.

Group tests of intelligence

As earlier noted, intelligence or general scholastic aptitude test data are useful in survey, prediction, and experimental studies. Group tests require less skill to administer than individual intelligence tests; they can be machine scored; the expense of testing per pupil is much less than it is with individual pupils; and city-wide group test data are much more likely to be available.

Examples of widely used group tests are the *California Test of Mental Maturity,* the *Cooperative School and College Ability Tests* (SCAT), the *Kuhlmann-Anderson Measure of Academic Potential,* the *Lorge-Thorndike Intelligence Tests,* and the *Otis-Lennon Mental Ability Test.* (For discussion of numerous other tests of general academic aptitude see the texts by Anastasi, by Cronbach, and by Thorndike and Hagen as well as the Buros *Mental Measurements Yearbooks* cited elsewhere in this chapter or among the selected references at the end.)

The problem of an educational research and the characteristics of the pupil population may suggest what type and level of group test will be appropriate. The trend in group testing of general ability is away from the traditional effort to measure a single global ability. Some of the tests named above yield separate verbal and nonverbal scores or verbal and quantitative scores in addition to their total scores. One might expect the quantitative scores to be useful in educational research in physics and mathematics and the nonverbal scores to be useful in studies of educationally disadvantaged pupils.

The *Cooperative School and College Ability Tests* (SCAT) differ most from the others in emphasis on "school-learned abilities," although the *Scholastic Aptitude Test* (SAT) also puts considerable emphasis on verbal and mathematical abilities developed in schools below the college level. Interestingly, such tests contain exercises similar to those found in achievement tests on the elementary or high school level. It is possible that the farther away a student gets from his elementary or high school instruction involving the knowledge and skills required to give correct responses to such exercises, the more he must depend on his intelligence.

MULTIPLE AND SPECIAL APTITUDE TESTS

Multiple aptitude and special aptitude tests should be useful in prediction research. The former should be especially useful in the differential prediction of abilities. A student may earn scores revealing greater mechanical than clerical aptitude. Examples of multiple aptitude batteries are the *Differential Aptitude Test* (DAT) and the *General Aptitude Test Battery*. John Carroll and Norman Frederiksen have commented on the wealth of validity studies reported with reference to the DAT.[24] Both are enthusiastic concerning the technical excellence of the tests, the manual, and the booklet, *Counseling From Profiles: A Casebook for the Differential Aptitude Tests*. Both, too, are critical of the differential validity of the tests, but Carroll stresses the difficulty of attaining high differential validity:

> Of course, any multifactor battery like the DAT tends to be handicapped by the fact that even if truly independent aptitudes exist, the differences between them are obscured by common educational experiences and by degrees of motivation for school learning and for test taking which more or less uniformly make for a high, medium, or low level of performance on a series of tests. There is not much chance that *any* set of differential tests designed chiefly for general educational guidance, as DAT is, would not be substantially affected by these influences.[25]

Closely second in quality among multiple-aptitude tests is the *General Aptitude Test Battery* (GATB) developed and used by the United States Employment Service and also used by State Employment Services which have collaborated in validating this battery in local work situations. Some reviewers have commented that more validity studies are needed. In his excellent comparison of the DAT and the GATB, Lee

---

[24] *Fifth Mental Measurements Yearbook*, pp. 669–76.

[25] *Ibid.*, p. 673. Reprinted with permission of author and publisher.

Cronbach has commented with respect to the latter that "one cannot expect to measure with the precision of the DAT, which uses subtests five times as long."[26]

Other multiple-aptitude batteries include the *Academic Promise Tests,* the *Flanagan Aptitude Classification Tests,* the *Guilford-Zimmerman Aptitude Survey,* the *Multiple Aptitude Tests,* and the *SRA Primary Mental Abilities.* The graduate student or other researcher interested in selecting one of these or a similar battery to collect data in his research should read the relevant reviews in the *Yearbooks* mentioned above.

Some of the best tests of special aptitudes are included in the aptitude batteries, for example, the *Mechanical Reasoning and Clerical Speed and Accuracy* tests of the DAT. Again, the major problem is the devising of tests that will measure skills whose functioning requires unique rather than general abilities or aptitudes. Otherwise, prediction may be more effective when based on measurement of general aptitude and evaluation of actual proficiency in the special field.

Prediction studies using published aptitude tests or batteries and other locally collected data offer a valuable kind of institutional research. The data may be the basis of expectancy tables for use in guidance and placement. Such tables may be more satisfactory than published ones because they are derived from local student populations. Summaries of the data characterizing the groups of students tested are an aid in making instructional decisions.

ACHIEVEMENT TESTS AND TEST BATTERIES

Published achievement tests and test batteries are used extensively in city-wide testing programs and school surveys. Such tests are most often administered along with a group test of general aptitude. The tests may be scored by machines in the central office of the schools or by a scoring service provided by a test publisher.

Examples of widely used achievement test batteries are the *California Achievement Tests,* the *Cooperative General Achievement Tests,* the *Essential High School Content Battery,* the *Iowa Tests of Educational Development,* and the *Metropolitan Achievement Tests.*

In a large school system the local test and curriculum experts spend hours debating the relative merits of widely used tests and batteries with reference to dependable norms and curricular or content validity. Usually, the group will include classroom teachers who are experienced in the use of the tests in different areas of the city.

Dependable norms are important in the selection of published tests and test batteries for use in educational research. They help in char-

---

[26] Cronbach, *Essentials of Psychological Testing,* p. 358.

acterizing the representativeness of the pupils participating in an experiment or in some other kind of educational research. Of crucial importance is the content validity of the tests. Identification of the test items with listed behavioral objectives is most desirable. This is especially so if the objectives guided writing of the exercises and were also the actual objectives of instruction as shown by observational records.

Objectives and their sources are summarized in the manuals of the better published tests. A two-dimensional chart may reveal what test items are relevant to each behavioral and content objective.[27] The *Iowa Test of Basic Skills* has been praised for its relating of its items to the "skill processes" tested. The following paragraph is quoted from the late Vergil Herrick's review in the *Fifth Mental Measurements Yearbook:*

> A major strength of this new battery is its curricular validation. Besides the usual widespread administration of sample test items and the establishment of discrimination and difficulty indexes, extremely careful identification and definition of the skill processes being tested was done before test items were devised. This aspect of test development is not usually undertaken with such care, and the authors are to be commended for the way the curricular validation of their test items was done. School staffs attempting to improve their curriculum in the skill areas could use with profit the definitions of the skill objectives developed by the Iowa staff. These curricular analyses are found in the *Teacher's Manual* and form a basis for helping teachers plan remedial or corrective instruction following evaluation. Here each basic skill is analyzed, the test items related to it identified, and corresponding teaching suggestions made.[28]

A number of tests and batteries, seemingly valid with respect to objectives generally accepted as desirable, are uneven in this quality. Several of the newer batteries have been criticized for too great an emphasis on evaluation of intellectual skills to the neglect of evaluation of basic concepts or knowledge of a field. An example of such criticism occurs in Robert W. B. Jackson's review of the *Sequential Tests of Educational Progress* (STEP). Although he states that this series "is undoubtedly one of the best available," he contends that many test users will not consider it appropriate, "since for many school people the acquirement of knowledge of subject matter is still deemed to be a primary and even laudable aim of education."[29] On the other hand, certain of the batteries listed above have been criticized for not giving

---

[27] See the references cited on page 163.

[28] *Fifth Mental Measurements Yearbook*, p. 32. Reprinted with permission of publisher.

[29] *Ibid.*, p. 67.

sufficient emphasis to measurement of modern content and intellectual skills transcending knowledge.

More than one achievement test or battery has been found wanting in evaluation of English skills. It is contended that knowledge of grammatical terms and rules receives more attention in test items than functional skills relevant to standard usage. Furthermore, items often require, for "correct" responses, knowledge of usage no longer considered the exclusively accepted usage by authorities on English expression. A similar situation prevails in the neglect of the understandings of modern mathematics.

Tests are not equally valid in all situations. Validity of standardized achievement tests for local purposes, or for use in educational research, presents certain peculiar issues. A given test or battery may be judged valid with respect to the instructional objectives which directed its production, and these objectives may be deemed to be in harmony with generally accepted aims of education, but, even so, the test or battery may not be satisfactorily valid with reference to local instructional objectives, or with the objectives of instruction in an educational experiment. In such cases, and often in educational research other than experimental, the researcher will need to construct his own achievement test or tests.

The Taxonomy of Educational Objectives, Handbook I, Cognitive Domain by Benjamin Bloom and others will be especially helpful in accomplishing this task since it contains numerous exercises relevant to different instructional objectives. Also useful in the writing of achievement exercises are *Measuring Educational Achievement* by Robert Ebel, *Measurement and Evaluation in Psychology and Education* by Robert Thorndike and Elizabeth Hagen, and *Improving Classroom Testing* by Max Engelhart.

Series of objective items of the kinds first developed in the Progressive Eight Year study are useful in analytical survey research and in experimentation where the interest is in thinking processes exhibited by students. Each series of items refers to quoted material containing information or data to be interpreted. Certain of the part scores indicate overgeneralization, overcaution, and the tendency to confuse value judgments with factual statements. Also appropriate in studying thought processes of students is analysis of the thinking aloud of students while responding to objective exercises. This was mentioned in the section on construct validity, as was the recommendation by Vernor Sims that an analysis be made of the thought processes of students exhibited in their responses to essay exercises.

When an achievement or other test has been selected or constructed for an analytical survey or an experiment, the researcher is obligated to report evidence of its reliability, its content validity, and its construct validity.

MEASURES OF ATTITUDES, INTERESTS, AND OTHER PERSONALITY TRAITS

When we say that a person is characterized by scientific attitude, is interested in art, is tolerant, or is authoritarian—we may in each case be referring to a class of behaviors, the person's typical behavior, or to the corresponding construct. We observe and measure behavior in a variety of situations and, in fact, we must do so in order to infer that a person is characterized in any of the ways listed above. B. F. Green admirably expresses in more detail what has just been said. Although he discusses attitude measurement, the same ideas apply to other typical behaviors or traits:

> To be able to understand how attitudes can be measured, we first need to examine the concept of attitude. Like many psychological variables, attitude is a hypothetical or latent variable, rather than an immediately observable variable. The concept of attitude does not refer to any one specific act or response of an individual, but is an abstraction from a large number of related acts or responses. For example, when we state that individual A has a less favorable attitude toward labor organizations than individual B, we mean that A's many different statements and actions concerning labor organizations are consistently less favorable to labor than are B's comparable words and deeds. We are justified in using a comprehensive concept like attitude when the many related responses are consistent. That is, if people who disapprove of the closed shop are also likely to want to outlaw strikes, and to oppose minimum wage laws, then it seems reasonable to speak of an antilabor attitude.[30]

Types of attitude scales

Efforts to develop objective measures of attitudes go back to 1925.[31] Two types of attitude scales are most widely known: the Thurstone and the Likert. In the construction of attitude scales of the Thurstone type, a series of statements of varying degrees of favorableness and

---

[30] Bert F. Green, Jr., "Attitude Measurement," in Gardner Lindzey, ed., *Handbook of Social Psychology* (Reading, Mass.: Addison-Wesley, 1954), p. 335. Reprinted with permission of author and publisher.

[31] For a brief review of history of attitude scales beginning with the work of Allport and Hartman in 1925, Thurstone and his associates between 1929 and 1933, and Remmer's "generalized" scales developed during the '30s, see John E. Horrocks, *Assessment of Behavior* (Columbus, Ohio: Merrill, 1964), pp. 682–91. For discussions of procedures used in developing attitude scales see Bert F. Green, Jr., Chapter 9 in *Handbook of Social Psychology; J. P. Guilford, Psychometric Methods*, 2nd ed. (New York: McGraw-Hill, 1954), pp. 456–69; Allen L. Edwards, *Techniques of Attitude Scale Construction* (New York: Appleton-Century-Crofts, 1954); Jum C. Nunnally, *Psychometric Theory* (New York: McGraw-Hill, 1967), pp. 529–34, and Gene Summers, *Attitude Measurement* (Chicago: Rand McNally, 1970).

unfavorableness toward such attitudinal objects as war, communism, and capital punishment are sorted by several judges to establish scale values. Finally, the selected statements are listed in random order. The examinee responds by checking the statements with which he agrees. His score is the mean, or preferably the median, of the scale values of the statements with which he agrees. In a Likert type attitude scale, preliminary trial is given to a series of statements, half of which are favorable and half of which are unfavorable. After analysis of the trial data has revealed the discriminating power of the statements, a final scale of twenty to twenty-five items is selected. An examinee is expected to respond to each statement indicating whether he strongly agrees, agrees, is undecided, disagrees, or strongly disagrees. Where three choices are specified, they are "Yes," "?," and "No." His score is the sum of the weights assigned to his responses. The weights are 1 to 5 for five choice items and 2 to 4 for three choice ones.

The following three items from Ruth C. Peterson's attitude scale toward war, developed under Thurstone's direction, illustrate the kind of items included in such scales, whether of the Thurstone or Likert types:

War brings out the best qualities in men.

I never think about war and it doesn't interest me.

There is no conceivable justification for war.

Applications of the use of Likert type scales are to be found in the Eight Year Study of Progressive Education[32] and the Cooperative Study of General Education. The *Scale of Beliefs* of the Eight Year Study lists 100 statements to be marked agree, disagree, and uncertain. Separate scores evaluate attitudes toward democracy, economic relationships, labor and unemployment, nationalism, race, and militarism. The total score is indicative of position on a continuum ranging from conservatism to liberalism. A second scale of 100 items where each statement is a reversal of one in the first form can be administered to secure *consistency* scores. (If the examinee agreed to a particular statement on one form he should, to be consistent, disagree with it on the second.) A similar instrument constructed by Albert W. Levi for use in the Cooperative Study of General Education provides for two uncertainty scores, "warranted uncertainty" and "unwarranted uncertainty."[33] For example, one *should* be uncertain concerning such a statement as

---

[32] E. R. Smith, R. W. Tyler, and the Evaluation Staff, *Appraising and Recording Student Progress* (New York: Harper, 1942).

[33] Albert W. Levi, *General Education in the Social Studies* (Washington, D.C.: American Council on Education, 1948).

"today's teenagers are more immoral than teenagers of the 1920s." The scales referred to in this paragraph, or similar locally constructed ones, are worth considering when planning institutional evaluation studies. The *Scale of Beliefs* was used on several occasions in the Chicago City Junior College to evaluate changes in student attitudes thought to be the effect of social science instruction. The student responses recorded on standard answer sheets were quickly tabulated with the "graphic item counter" of the old IBM 805 electric scoring machine. More modern equipment should accomplish the tabulation much more rapidly.

Limitations of attitude scales

Attitude measurement as described above has certain limitations. Responses to an attitude scale may not be honest expressions of the examinee's convictions nor reliable predictions of how the examinee will behave in a real life situation. Attitudes vary in stability as situations change. In an instrument such as the *Scale of Beliefs,* knowledge may be a factor. One of the items has to do with "conscientious objectors." Chicago junior college students' attitudes were much more favorable toward such persons in June 1942, than in September 1941, possibly because they had acquired a better understanding of the problem. While all such attitude data should be interpreted with reservations, data obtained from *groups* of students in other than threatening situations may be more reliable and valid than the data relevant to an individual student. Students who have learned about the scientific method and the scientific attitude in social science, or other sciences, may be so motivated as to try to give honest answers.

Measurement of values

Values are related to both attitudes and interests. According to Horrocks, values may be thought of as "generalized and dominant interests conditioned by attitudinal components. A value defines for an individual those means and ends which are desirable."[34] He describes the Allport-Vernon Study of Values—an inventory containing 120 items based on six categories of values—theoretical, economic, aesthetic, social, political, and religious. In one part of the test the student indicates alternative preferences and in the other he ranks four choices at a time. The preferences or choices are indicative of values in the areas just listed. While this instrument was developed before 1931, it is still highly regarded. Another extremely interesting instrument for the measurement of values is the *Inventory of Student's General Goals*

---

[34] Horrocks, *Assessment of Behavior,* p. 691.

in Life developed for use in the Cooperative Study in General Education by Harold B. Dunkel.[35] The student compares each of such goals as "making a place for myself in the world; getting ahead," "self-sacrifice for the sake of a better world," and "living for the pleasure of the moment," with each of the other listed goals, an application of the method of paired comparisons. The student's score would seem to be an estimate of his position along the scale between complete selfishness and extreme altruism.

Measurement of interests

It seems quite well established that such interest inventories as the *Strong Vocational Interest Blank* and the *Kuder Preference Record* yield measures of interests that are reasonably stable if obtained beyond the early high-school years. Interest scores discriminate fairly well between men in various occupations and between men satisfied or dissatisfied with their occupations. It has been shown that interest scores obtained from college students on the *Strong Blank* were quite effective in predicting actual occupational area almost 20 years later. Interest inventories have shown, however, small predictive value for occupational success, for success in vocational training, or for academic grades, and the fact that interest can be "faked" makes the prospect unfavorable for the usefulness of interest measures in competitive selection situations. Although of limited value in predicting academic or vocational achievement, interest inventories are valuable in high school and college counseling. They may aid the counselor in establishing rapport, and the student in better evaluating his own potentialities in relation to the opportunities open to him.[36] Factor analysis of the *Strong Blank* and the development of inventories based on factor analysis such as the *Kuder Preference Record* and the *Guilford-Schneideman-Zimmerman Interest Survey* have promoted progress in the growth of a theory of interests. The *Kuder* and the *Guilford* inventories exemplify efforts to obtain scores relevant to areas of interests such as "outdoor," "mechanical," "linguistic," and so on, rather than for specific vocational fields.

An important aspect of the measurement of interests is pointed out in T. L. Kelley's comment: "Interest without achievement is counterfeit, deceiving both the possessor and the observer. Only if it leads to accomplishment has it merit, but if it does so lead then achievement it-

---

[35] Harold B. Dunkel, *General Education in the Humanities* (Washington, D.C.: American Council on Education, 1947).

[36] See Cronbach, *Essentials of Psychological Testing,* p. 481.

self is the measure of its merit and no further measure is needed."[37] Consider in this connection the difference in interests between a student who can correctly associate "laser" with its brief characterization and a student who can correctly associate *Mene, Mene, Tekel,* and *Parsin* with the prophet Daniel. An informational test containing a variety of such items was used in Project Talent.[38]

Self-report or structured measures of personality

A reading of reviews of self-report personality inventories in successive volumes of the *Mental Measurements Yearbook* offers only very limited support for the generalization that there has been "some" success in increasing the validity of such instruments. Comments like "the total impression is that adequate validity has not been demonstrated," "no evidence of predictive validity is presented," and "the reviewer at this time can see no good reason why a test user should want to obtain the scores," occur with distressing frequency. Also distressingly frequent are adverse criticisms of the techniques used in obtaining validity data and condemnations of exaggerated claims for validity. A number of reviewers are laudatory in their comments on the efforts made to develop self-report inventories on the basis of factor-analysis studies and in terms of personality theories, but Cronbach's comment in this connection is apt: "There is less consensus as to the number of personality factors reliably identified, the best organization of them, or their most appropriate names than there is regarding ability factors."[39]

In the development of self-report personality inventories there has been no lack of formulation of constructs pertaining to personality traits, but there has been a paucity of well-designed efforts toward construct validation. Even factor-analysis studies do not contribute much in cases in which factors derived from one study cannot be identified as the same factors in another study. Concurrent validation resulting in numerous correlations between scores obtained from various inventories contributes little or nothing if the validity of none of the instruments has been satisfactorily established. Defensible studies of predictive validity are badly needed since the ultimate justification of such instruments is their effectiveness in predicting behavior. Finally, the validity of self-report inventories, including interest inventories, is limited by the contamination of scores through deliberate or un-

---

[37] Truman Lee Kelley, "The Future Psychology of Mental Traits," *Psychometrika* 5 (March 1940), pp. 1–15.

[38] Briefly described in Chapter 10 of this book. See page 300.

[39] Cronbach, *Essentials of Psychological Testing,* p. 523.

conscious falsification, or "faking." The respondent may have imperfect insight into self or he may misinterpret the items. He may intentionally seek to portray the way he hopes others think he feels or the way he wishes he could feel.[40]

Examples of self-report inventories

Examples of self-report inventories include: The *Allport-Vernon-Lindzey Study of Values,* the *Billet-Starr Youth Inventory,* the *Kuder Preference Record–Personal,* the *Mooney Problem Check Lists,* and the *SRA Youth Inventory.* Other notable self-report personality inventories are: the *California Personality Inventory,* the *California Test of Personality,* the *Edwards Personal Preference Schedule,* the *Gordon Personal Profile,* the *Gordon Personal Inventory,* the *Guilford-Zimmerman Temperament Survey,* the *IPAT Children's Personality Questionnaire,* and the *Minnesota Multiphasic Personality Inventory.* A number of these inventories and especially the *Minnesota Multiphasic Personality Inventory* should be used only by those who have adequate training and experience in the use of such instruments.

Unstructured or projective measures of personality

What has been said with reference to such nonprojective personality instruments as the *Minnesota Multiphasic* applies with possibly greater force to such projective techniques as the *Rorschach,* the *Thematic Apperception Test,* the *Bender-Gestalt Test,* and other such instruments. Study of reviews in recent volumes of the *Mental Measurements Yearbook,* of the texts by Anastasi, Cronbach, and Thorndike and Hagen listed at the end of this chapter under suggestions for further study, support the view that in general the validity of such instruments remains to be established.[41]

Although the validity of self-report and projective measures of personality has been seriously questioned, their use in research and in the practice of education and psychology by persons with adequate training and critical attitudes should *not* be discouraged. Only through research and through experience in their use can progress be made toward determination of their predictive and construct validity.

---

[40] W. Scott Gehman, "A Study of Ability to Fake Scores on the Strong Vocational Interest Blank for Men," *Educational and Psychological Measurement* 17 (Spring 1957), pp. 65–70.

[41] See reviews in recent volumes of the *Annual Review of Psychology* on such topics as "Assessment of Individual Differences," "Theory and Techniques of Assessment," and "Personality," or pertinent reviews in recent issues of the *Review of Educational Research* on "Educational and Psychological Testing." The reviews in these sources and the sources earlier cited, especially the *Mental Measurements Yearbooks,* include extensive bibliographies.

Rating scales and other miscellaneous measuring instruments

In concluding this discussion of measures of typical behavior or performance, mention should be made of trait rating scales, sociometric devices, and other miscellaneous instruments. Examples of rating scales include the man-to-man or *Army Rating Scale,* developed by Walter Dill Scott and his associates in World War I,[42] the *Haggerty-Olson-Wickman Behavior Rating Schedule* published first in 1930, and, among other more recent scales, the *Purdue Rating Scale for Administrators and Executives,* and the *KD Proneness Checklist* developed by Kvaraceus to be used by teachers in identifying potential delinquents.

In a typical "graphic" rating scale each trait or behavior to be rated is the label of a line which has 5 to 7 points above very brief descriptive statements. This example is from the Haggerty-Olson-Wickman Schedule B:

27. Is he generally depressed or cheerful?   Score

Dejected, Melancholic, In the dumps	Generally dispirited	Usually in good humor	Cheerful, Animated, Chirping	Hilarious
(3)	(4)	(1)	(2)	(5)

Types of errors often mentioned with reference to rating scales include those due to "halo effect," i.e., ratings of specific traits being influenced by general impressions of the person rated; "logical error," where similar ratings are given to traits which seem logically related; and "proximity error," where similar ratings are given to adjacent traits on the rating scale.[43] Other types of errors include "stereotype error" (all persons of a certain kind are believed to be generally superior or inferior by the rater), "leniency or generosity error," and "error of central tendency," where average ratings predominate when the rater is uncertain.

In closing, mention should also be made of the usefulness of sociograms in studying social relationships among children and such instruments or techniques for assessing personality dynamics as the *Bender-Gestalt,* the *Semantic Differential,* and the Q-sort. The interested reader can find discussion of such techniques in the texts of Cronbach, Guilford and Horrocks earlier cited. The selected references at the end of this chapter should also be consulted.

---

[42] For a description of this and other rating scales see Horrocks, *Assessment of Behavior,* Chapter 18; Cronbach, *Essentials of Psychological Testing,* Chapter 17; and Guilford, *Psychometric Methods,* pp. 263–301.

[43] Guilford, *Psychometric Methods,* pp. 278–80.

RESEARCH ON PROBLEMS OF MEASUREMENT

The problems and issues of test reliability and of test validity are far from solved or settled. The concept of the true score is still debated. How best to obtain indices of reliability, validity, item difficulty, and item discriminating power are still among the goals of measurement research. The same is true of techniques to be used in constructing parallel tests, in equating the scores on different tests, and in obtaining composite scores. These are among the major problems of measurement research. There is also a "cultural lag" between the findings of research on such problems and test practices.

Research on problems of measurement is a legitimate field for thesis research of graduate students with the requisite interest and training. In addition to purely theoretical studies, there is a definite need for empirical studies testing presumably well-established theories. Further research is needed, even on so seemingly mundane a problem as correction for guessing. It is still worth studying whether or not scoring procedures other than the counting of only correct answers to multiple-choice items increase test reliability and validity.

While there are numerous published tests of scholastic and other aptitudes and of various kinds of educational achievement, improvements are needed as the purposes of testing change. For example, the evaluation of computerized instruction and of modern mathematics demand new types of achievement tests. Contemporary social conditions suggest needs for new kinds of aptitude tests and for more acceptable practices in testing. The whole field of personality measurement is open to research on theory, development of new instruments, and empirical studies of reliability and validity. Much has been accomplished, but much more remains to be done.

Questions for
Study and Discussion

1. What factors tend to cause a test-retest coefficient of reliability to be an overestimate of the reliability of a test?

2. What types of reliability coefficient take into account instability of performance over a period of time?

3. Why are reliability coefficients obtained through correlating scores on equivalent forms of a test likely to be lower than test-retest coefficients or coefficients based on the administration of a single form?

4. Study pages 25–32 of the *Standards for Educational and Psychological Tests and Manuals* to supplement what is said in this chapter about test reliability.

5. How should knowledge of their construct validity aid in selecting tests likely to have satisfactory predictive validity?

6. A researcher has devised a test of "creative ability." In what type of validity should he be most interested? How should he go about determining whether or not his test has such validity?

7. A number of widely used group intelligence tests are highly correlated with each other. The high correlation coefficients are evidence of what types of validity?

8. Study pages 12–24 of the *Standards for Educational and Psychological Tests and Manuals* to supplement what is said in this chapter about test validity.

9. How can adequate test norms contribute to the formulation of meaningful generalizations in educational research of the descriptive and experimental types?

10. What important factors limit the validity of self-report personality inventories?

11. What are the important factors limiting the reliability and validity of rating scales?

12. Compare essay and objective achievement tests with respect to reliability and validity.

13. Prepare a brief report on the early history of the testing movement. (One good source is *Ten Years of Educational Research* cited in Chapter 2.)

14. Assume that an achievement battery is to be selected for a survey-type study on the eighth-grade level. Outline the steps that should be followed in deciding what battery should be used.

15. What types of achievement other than knowledge of subject-matter content can be measured by objective exercises? Characterize appropriate exercises.

16. What is meant by the terms "formative evaluation" and "summative evaluation"?

17. What characteristics of tests are relevant to "performance contracts" and "accountability"?

18. What are the advantages and limitations of "mastery" testing? Can motivation be a problem?

Suggestions
for Further Study

The student seriously interested in educational and psychological testing will find it very much to his advantage to supplement what has been said in this chapter by studying such texts as *Psychological Testing* by Anne Anastasi (Macmillan), *Essentials of Psychological Testing* by Lee J. Cronbach (Harper), *Measurement and Evaluation in Psychology and Education* by Robert L. Thorndike and Elizabeth P. Hagen (Wiley).

Among other texts of interest to students are *Educational Measurements and Their Interpretation* by Frederic B. Davis (Wadsworth), *Measuring Educational Achievement* by Robert L. Ebel (Prentice-Hall), *Introduction to Educational Measurement* by Victor H. Noll (Houghton Mifflin), *Measurement in Today's Schools* by Julian C. Stanley (Prentice-Hall), and *Measurement and Evaluation in Education, Psychology, and Guidance* by Georgia S. Adams in consultation with Theodore L. Torgerson (Holt, Rinehart, and Winston). *Assessment of Behavior* by John E. Horrocks (Merrill) is encyclopedic in the variety of tests listed and discussed. The text by Ebel referred to above contains elementary derivations of the Kuder-Richardson Formula 20 and of the Spearman-Brown formula. Mention should also be made of *Measurement and Evaluation in Teaching* by Norman E. Gronlund (Macmillan).

Theory of Mental Tests by Harold Gulliksen (Wiley), *Psychometric Methods* by J. P. Guilford, and the more recent *Psychometric Theory* by Jum Nunnally (McGraw-Hill), and *Statistical Theories of Mental Test Scores* by Frederic M. Lord and Melvin R. Novick (Addison-Wesley) are without peer with reference to the statistical and mathematical aspects of testing.

Among the references listed at the end of this chapter are several anthologies to which attention should especially be directed: *Testing Problems in Perspective, Twenty-Fifth Anniversary Volume of Topical Readings from the Invitational Conference on Testing Problems* edited by Anne Anastasi (American Council on Education), *Problems in Human Assessment* edited by Douglas N. Jackson and Samuel Messick (McGraw-Hill), *Principles of Educational and Psychological Measurement, A Book of Readings* edited by William A. Mehrens and Robert L. Ebel (Rand McNally), and *Educational and Psychological Measurements,*

Contribution to Theory and Practice edited by David A. Payne and Robert F. McMorris (Blaisdell).

Medley and Mitzel's chapter in the *Handbook of Research on Teaching* (Rand McNally) has already been cited in this chapter and in Chapter 6. Other chapters especially relevant to measurement are those entitled "Rating Methods in Research on Teaching" by H. H. Remmers, "Testing Cognitive Ability" by Benjamin S. Bloom, and "Measuring Noncognitive Variables in Research on Teaching" by George G. Stern.

In E. F. Lindquist and others, *Educational Measurement* (American Council on Education), examples of chapters to be seriously studied include "Writing the Test Item" by Robert L. Ebel, "The Essay Type of Examination" by John M. Stalnaker, "Reliability" by Robert L. Thorndike, "Validity" by Edward E. Cureton, and "Units, Scores, and Norms" by John C. Flanagan. The second edition of *Educational Measurement,* edited by Robert L. Thorndike and published in 1971, includes chapters on "Reliability" by Julian C. Stanley, on "Validity" by Lee J. Cronbach, and numerous other chapters paralleling those in the first edition that are also worthy of serious study. (See page 317.)

In the 1960 *Encyclopedia of Educational Research,* the articles on "Reliability" by Cyril J. Hoyt, "Validity" by Lee J. Cronbach, and "Tests and Examinations" by Robert L. Ebel and Dora E. Damrin are relevant to this chapter.

The fourth edition of the *Encyclopedia of Educational Research,* edited by Robert L. Ebel and published in 1969 includes nine articles relevant to educational measurement. They are "Achievement Tests" by William E. Coffman, "Intelligence and Special Aptitude Tests" by Martin J. Nelson, "Marks and Marking Systems" by Robert L. Thorndike, "Measurement in Education" by Robert L. Ebel, "Measurement Theory" by Edward E. Cureton, "Scaling" by Norman Cliff, "Scores and Norms" by Roger T. Lennon, and "Test Use" by Frank E. Womer and N. Kishor Wahi. The article entitled "Prediction" by William B. Michael is cited in Chapter 11.

Other sources of information which should be mentioned include *The Impact and Improvement of School Testing Programs* by Warren G. Findley and others, the Sixty-second Yearbook of the National Society for the Study of Education, Part II. Bert F. Green's chapter on "Attitude Measurement" in the *Handbook of Social Psychology* was cited earlier. Among other chapters in this *Handbook* well worth studying is "Sociometric Measurement" by Gardner Lindzey and Edgar F. Borgatta.

Oscar Buros' *Mental Measurements Yearbooks* are essential in identifying and evaluating published educational and psychological tests of all kinds. Reading the reviews is among the very best of ways to enhance one's knowledge of measurement. The issues of the *Review of Educational Research* entitled "Educational and Psychological Testing," augment such knowledge and keep one up to date in the field. The same is true of the *Proceedings of the Invitational Conferences on Testing Problems* sponsored by the Educational Testing Service, and the *Test Service Bulletins* of such publishers of standardized tests as Harcourt, Brace.

Attention should again be directed to *Standards for Educational and Psychological Tests and Manuals,* the *Taxonomy of Educational Objectives* by Benjamin S. Bloom and others, and to such journals as *Educational and Psychological Measurement, American Educational Research Journal, Journal of Educational Measurement* and *Psychometrika.*

Many of the items cited above, or cited as footnotes in this chapter, or listed among the selected references concluding this chapter require a considerable background in mathematics and statistical method to read with understanding, but they are included for their importance as contributions to the theory and practice of measurement.

Selected References

American Psychological Association, American Educational Research Association, and National Council on Measurement in Education. *Standards for Educational and Psychological Tests and Manuals.* Washington, D.C.: American Psychological Association, 1966. (Copies sell for one dollar).

Anastasi, Anne, ed. *Testing Problems in Perspective, Twenty-Fifth Anniversary Volume of Topical Readings from the Invitational Conference on Testing Problems.* Washington, D.C.: American Council on Education, 1966.

Bechtoldt, H. P. "Construct Validity: A Critique." *American Psychologist* 14 (September 1959): 619–29.

Bloom, B. S., D. R. Krathwohl, and B. B. Masia. *Taxonomy of Educational Objectives, The Classification of Educational Goals: Cognitive and Affective Domains.* New York: McKay, 1969.

———, J. Thomas Hastings, George F. Madaus and others. *Handbook on Formative and Summative Evaluation of Student Learning.* New York: McGraw-Hill, 1971.

Campbell, Donald T. "Recommendations for APA Test Standards Regarding Construct, Trait, or Discriminant Validity." *American Psychologist* 15 (August 1960): 546–53.

——— and Donald W. Fiske, "Convergent and Discriminant Validation by the Multitrait-Multimethod Matrix." *Psychological Bulletin* 56 (March 1959): 81–105. Reprinted in Gene Summers, *Attitude Measurement.* Chicago: Rand McNally, 1970.

Cronbach, Lee J., "Test 'Reliability': Its Meaning and Determination." *Psychometrika* 12 (March 1947): 1–16.

———. "Coefficient Alpha and the Internal Structure of Tests." *Psychometrika* 16 (September 1951): 297–334.

——— and Paul E. Meehl. "Construct Validity in Psychological Tests." *Psychological Bulletin* 52 (July 1955): 281–302.

——— and others. *The Dependability of Behavioral Measurement.* New York: Wiley, 1971.

Dressel, Paul L., ed. *Evaluation in General Education.* Dubuque, Ia.: Wm. C. Brown, 1954. (Includes rating scale reprinted on page 166.)

DuBois, Philip H. "Varieties of Psychological Test Homogeneity." *American Psychologist* 25 (June 1970): 532–36.

Ebel, Robert L. "Estimation of the Reliability of Ratings." *Psychometrika* 16 (December 1951): 407–24.

————. "Obtaining and Reporting Evidence on Content Validity." *Educational and Psychological Measurement* 16 (Autumn 1956): 269–82. *See also the adjacent articles by Edith Huddleston and Roger Lennon.*

Engelhart, Max D. "A Method of Estimating the Reliability of Ratings Compared with Certain Methods of Estimating the Reliability of Tests." *Educational and Psychological Measurement* 19 (Winter 1959): 579–88. *An effort to relate methods of reliability estimation proposed by Horst, Ebel and Tryon.*

————. *Improving Classroom Testing.* What Research Says to the Teacher, No. 31. Washington, D.C.: National Education Association, 1964.

Fishbein, Martin, ed. *Readings in Attitude Theory and Measurement.* New York: Wiley, 1967.

French, John W. "The Description of Aptitude and Achievement Tests in Terms of Rotated Factors," *Psychometric Monograph* No. 5. Chicago: University of Chicago Press, 1951.

Guilford, J. P. *The Nature of Human Intelligence.* New York: McGraw-Hill, 1967. *See the excellent review of this important book by John B. Carroll in the March, 1968, issue of the* American Educational Research Journal.

Gulliksen, Harold. "Intrinsic Validity." *American Psychologist* 5 (October 1950): 511–17.

Horst, Paul. "A Generalized Expression for the Reliability of Measures," *Psychometrika* 14 (March 1949): 21–31.

Jackson, Douglas N., and Samuel Messick, eds. *Problems in Human Assessment.* New York: McGraw-Hill, 1967.

Lindquist, E. F., ed. *Educational Measurement.* Washington, D.C.: American Council on Education, 1951.

Lindvall, C. M., Richard C. Cox and others. *Evaluation as a Tool in Curriculum Development: The IPI Evaluation Program.* AERA Monograph Series on Curriculum Evaluation 5. Chicago: Rand McNally, 1970.

Lord, Frederic M., and Melvin R. Novick. *Statistical Theories of Mental Test Scores.* Reading, Mass.: Addison-Wesley, 1968.

Mehrens, William A., and Robert L. Ebel, eds. *Principles of Educational and Psychological Measurement, A Book of Selected Readings.* Chicago: Rand McNally, 1967.

Nunnally, Jum C. *Psychometric Theory.* New York: McGraw-Hill, 1967.

Osgood, Charles E., George J. Suci, and Percy H. Tannenbaum. *The Measurement of Meaning.* Urbana: University of Illinois Press, 1957. *The Semantic Differential.*

Payne, David A., and Robert F. McMorris, eds. *Educational and Psychological Measurement, Contributions to Theory and Practice.* Waltham, Mass.: Blaisdell, 1967.

Scott, William A. "Attitude Measurement." In *The Handbook of Social Psychology,* edited by Gardner Lindzey and Elliot Aronson, pp. 204–73. Vol. II. 2nd ed. Reading, Mass.: Addison-Wesley, 1968.

Snider, James G., and Charles E. Osgood, eds. *Semantic Differential Technique, A Source Book.* Chicago: Aldine, 1969. *A comprehensive anthology of 52 papers on the origin, methodology, validity, and applications of the Semantic Differential.*

Stephenson, William. *The Study of Behavior: Q-Technique and Its Methodology.* Chicago: University of Chicago Press, 1953.

Summers, Gene F., ed. *Attitude Measurement.* Chicago: Rand McNally, 1970.

Thorndike, Robert L., ed. *Educational Measurement.* 2nd ed. Washington, D.C.: American Council on Education, 1971.

Tryon, Robert C. "Reliability and Behavior Domain Validity; Reformulation and Historical Critique." *Psychological Bulletin* 54 (May 1957): 229–49.

Tyler, Ralph W. *Basic Principles of Curriculum and Instruction.* Chicago: University of Chicago Press, 1950.

————, ed. "Educational Evaluation: New Roles, New Means." *Sixty-eighth Yearbook of the National Society for the Study of Education,* Part II. Chicago: University of Chicago Press, 1969.

Wesman, Alexander G. "Intelligent Testing." *American Psychologist* 23 (April 1968): 267–74.

8

Summarizing Data: Elementary Descriptive Statistics

The organization and summarization of data are essential steps between the collection of data and their interpretation. Effectively done, these steps give meaning to the data both for the researcher and the reader of the research report. The report of the research may end with a summary and a statement of conclusions, but organizing and summarizing precede the writing of such formal statements.

This chapter introduces the student to the organization and summarization of numerical data—data pertaining to attributes or characteristics which vary in magnitude. These matters are given further treatment in Chapters 10–13 which deal successively with descriptive studies of present practices and conditions, studies of relationships or concomitant variation and prediction, and studies of relationships for which educational experimentation is appropriate. The treatment of data useful in historical, curriculum, and philosophical research is discussed in Chapters 14 and 15.

Anticipating the organization and summarization of data

When defining an educational research problem, the kinds of data to be collected and their organization, summarization, and interpretation should be anticipated. The forms used in copying data from records, in tabulating questionnaire responses, in coding classroom observations, and in making a content analysis should be so designed as to promote summarization and interpretation. Test score data may be initially recorded as lists of pupils' names and their scores. Alternatively, several scores and other items of information may be entered on individual data cards in a uniform order. The scores and other items should be briefly and appropriately labeled and the dates of testing given.

When it is expected that the data will be the input of a computer, they should be recorded in a manner approved by an expert in data processing. The forms used in recording may provide such classification of data that keypunching or the production of paper or magnetic tape is more quickly and accurately accomplished. This was illustrated with reference to questionnaire data on page 105 of Chapter 5. The questions were numbered to conform with the columns of a punched card and the answers were numbered in terms of the potential holes within columns.

Where the graduate student, or other researcher, must do the tabulating of the data by hand from individual data cards or lists, the forms or tables used in tabulating should be designed both with reference to the individual data cards or lists and with reference to the tables to appear later in a report of the research. The data should be so organized as to facilitate computation of percentages or the calculation of such statistics as means, standard deviations, and coefficients of correlation. The explanations of calculation procedures appearing in later pages of this chapter will shed light on how this is done.

The values of tables and graphs

Tables are a very effective means of summarizing data. They enable a reader to comprehend and interpret data which might otherwise be scattered about in a research report. Counts or frequencies and their corresponding percentages should be listed in appropriately labeled columns and rows. *N,* the total number of cases, should be entered at the bottom of each column. When the data are the frequencies of a frequency distribution, medians and quartiles or means and standard deviations can similarly be reported. The meaning of data presented in tables can be enhanced by graphs of various types such as the bar or pie graph. While tables occur most frequently in reports of research of the survey type, they are also useful in reports of other types of research. For example, a table of intelligence test scores may characterize the groups of pupils participating in an experiment. Examples of various types of tables and graphs are given later in this chapter and, with more detail, in Chapter 10.

The role of descriptive statistics

Means, medians, standard deviations, and coefficients of correlation are descriptive statistics. Also in the realm of descriptive statistics are counts and percentages classified in various ways, distributions of test scores, tables, and graphs. All of the above are useful in summarizing data so as to facilitate their interpretation.

The problem of an educational research requiring numerical data for its solution implies, but does not make explicit, the kinds of descriptive statistics most appropriate in the summarizing and interpreting of the data. In order to select appropriate statistics, it is essential to acquire understanding of the different kinds of variables and what different statistics reveal about data relevant to them. The next section of this chapter contains explanations which should contribute to such understanding. Methods of calculating the earlier-explained statistics are then described, followed by discussion of percentiles, percentile ranks, and standard scores including methods of deriving them from observed or "raw" scores.

At appropriate intervals in this chapter (and Chapters 9, 10, 11, and 13), practice exercises useful in facilitating learning of the computational procedures are discussed. Solve the exercises before turning to the answers which appear on pages 530 to 534 of the Appendix.

The role of statistical inference

One or more kinds of descriptive statistics may suffice on the descriptive level of inquiry. When, however, data pertain to samples, preferably random ones, and interpretation includes the formulation of generalizations which are to apply to the populations from which the samples are drawn, application should be made of the techniques of statistical inference. Chapter 9 provides an elementary introduction to such techniques. They are also given further attention in Chapters 10–13.

DIFFERENT KINDS OF VARIABLES

Nominal variables

Where data are counts of cases in unordered classes or categories, it is possible to list the numbers in each class or category. Such counts can also be changed to percentages or proportions. The data may pertain, for example, to students attending some university and enrolled in various engineering curricula. Within a particular category it cannot be inferred from the data that one student is more of a civil engineer than another. Nor can it be said that civil engineering is higher or lower as a class than mechanical engineering. It can only be observed that the numbers, percentages, or proportions are different. Within a category, without other data, individuals cannot be ranked. Numerals may be used to identify the various classes or categories without intending that the numerals signify any particular order. Such variables as just described are called *nominal* variables and they are said to have a nominal scale, although the scaling is limited to discriminating members of one class or category from members of another. Data having a nominal scale are often referred to as "qualitative" data although the counts in various categories are a type of quantification.

Ordinal variables

When it is possible to rank the individuals in a group, class, or category in order of possession of some trait, it is legitimate to report that one individual has more or less of the trait than another. It is not legitimate, however, to specify how much more or how much less. A difference of 10 units in rank above the average does not necessarily represent the same difference in ability, or in the possession of some other trait, as a difference of 10 units of rank below the average. Here, even the average should properly be a median rather than a mean. This type of variable is called an *ordinal* variable and the scale an ordinal scale. The data are in the form of numbers identifying positions along the scale in rank order only.

Interval variables

With an *interval* variable, the units of the scale are equal, or are assumed to be equal. With such a variable it is legitimate to compare differences at different points along the scale. While we cannot say with assurance that the difference between 35 and 40 on an achievement test stands for the same difference in ability as the difference between 65 and 70, we do treat test scores as if they truly had an interval rather than an ordinal scale. Successful response to an easy objective test item usually contributes as much to a high course mark as successful response to a very difficult item. We seldom hesitate to treat the standard scores discussed later in this chapter as if their units were truly equal along the scale of a given test or from subtest to subtest of a test battery. It is assumed that the standard deviations of the raw scores represent equal ranges of ability since they are obtained from the same pupil populations. Standard score units are contrasted with percentile rank units which *do* decrease in size along the scale of observed score units of a test the further they are from mean or median.

Ratio variables

Without a true zero point, it is not legitimate to conclude that one individual has twice as much of a trait as another. In the case of a *ratio* variable such a statement can legitimately be made. Chronological age is a ratio variable. One child can be twice as old as another. Although such statements cannot be made about typical standard score scales, use of means as reference points serves somewhat the same function as true zero points. There is some analogy in this respect to Centigrade or Fahrenheit temperature scales which have arbitrary zero points. Temperatures in absolute degrees range down to a true zero at approximately $-273°C$ (or $-459°F$). Their scale is a ratio scale. Five hundred and forty-six degrees on the absolute scale (in units equivalent to

Centigrade units) is twice as hot as 0°C. For most purposes, however, the conventional Centigrade and Fahrenheit scales suffice. Similarly, although test score data do not satisfy the purist with reference to ratio or even interval scales, meaningful interpretations are made of such data using procedures explained in later pages. Finally, it should be noted that effort has been made and is being made to establish ratio scales in psychological measurement.

Discrete and continuous variables

Although counts of pupils are discrete numbers or integers there is no hesitation in summarizing such data by computing means and standard deviations to one or two decimals. Percentages or proportions are similarly treated.[1] Although, as indicated above, test score scales are, strictly speaking, ordinal scales, there is somewhat better logic in calculating means, medians, and standard deviations to one or more decimals since it can be assumed that given more precise instruments, the ability underlying the trait could be measured more finely than in integral score units. Hence, we treat test scores as representing *continuous* rather than discrete variables and an average of 37.68 in score units makes more sense than an average of 37.68 in units of children.

SIGNIFICANT FIGURES AND ROUNDING OFF

While the counts of individuals referred to above may be exact and, therefore, completely accurate data, most numerical educational and psychological data are approximations. If you learn that there are 4,500 sixth-grade pupils in a city school system, only the first two digits are *significant*. You can best assume that there are between 4,450 and 4,550 pupils. If, however, there are exactly 4,500 pupils and a decimal point is placed after the second zero, the number 4,500. has four significant figures. Zeros used merely to locate decimal points, however, are not counted as significant. Each of the following has three significant figures: 654, 6.54, .0654 and .000654. However, if the 5 is replaced by a zero each of the numbers still has three significant figures. The zero is also significant in such a number as 6.540, ended as indicated. In adding or subtracting numbers of varying decimal places, the sum or difference should be rounded off to the number of decimal places of the least precise number. For example, if 5.2, 7.87, and 1.2846 are added, the sum should be rounded

---

[1] The word "percent" is used only when preceded by a specific value, for example, 10 percent. Percent is preferably spelled as one word. A percentage of 53, or 53 percent, is a proportion of .53.

off to one decimal place. In multiplication or division the number of significant figures in the product or quotient is the number of significant figures in the least accurate number entering the computation. A square root has the same number of significant figures as the number whose square root is obtained. It has been recommended that one should first round off the other numbers involved in a computation to one more digit than the least precise number, and then round off the result to the same number of significant figures as the least precise number. In the case of division and obtaining of square roots, it is also a good rule to perform the computations to at least two more decimal places than are to be retained in the result of the computation.

Rules in rounding off

When rounding numbers, if the digit eliminated is more than 5, change the preceding digit to the next higher digit. Thus 8.67 rounded to one decimal becomes 8.7, while .00867 and .008673 become .009 when rounded to three decimals. However, successive rounding such as the following should be avoided: 4.347 changed first to 4.35 and then to 4.4. The number reported should be 4.3. Similarly, when the number eliminated is less than 5, no change is made in the preceding digit: 7.4 and .074 become 7 and .07. Likewise, .074362 rounded to three decimals becomes .074 and, to two decimals, .07. If the number to be eliminated is *exactly* 5, no change in the preceding digit should be made if the number is even, but increase it one digit if it is odd. For example, 7.850 may be rounded to 7.8, but 6.350 rounded to one decimal place becomes 6.4. This last rule is presumed to prevent a systematic increase due to rounding in the result of a computation.

Means, medians, and standard deviations usually are reported to no more than one or two decimal places. Coefficients of correlation ordinarily are reported to no more than two decimal places unless they are likely to be used in further statistical analysis. Given relatively small samples, it suffices to report means, medians, standard deviations, and percentages to no more than one decimal. To report a statistic to more decimals than is justified is to give a false impression of accuracy.

SUMMARIZING NOMINAL OR QUALITATIVE DATA

Nominal data are counts in unordered categories. In summarizing such data the counts are usually converted to percentages although this is not particularly meaningful when N, the total number of cases, is small. Some suggestions can be made concerning the computing of percentages that will also be useful when it is desired to compute percentages for the frequencies in a frequency distribution. If the number of counts or frequencies is small, each can be divided by N and multiplied by 100. If, however, the number of different categories or number of class intervals of a frequency distribution is large, computation of percentages by multiplication of each count or frequency by the reciprocal of $N \times 100$ can be done much more rapidly. If a desk calculator is available, divide 1 by N. Then transfer the reciprocal from the counting dials of the calculator to its keyboard. Multiplication by N should yield 1 followed by a series of zeros or 9 followed by a series of 9's in the product dials. The decimal point can then be marked along the product dials indicating 100.000. . . 99.99. . . . After clearing the counting and product dials *only,* multiplication successively by the counts or frequencies will result in the corresponding percentages appearing successively in the product dials. This procedure is illustrated in Table 8.1.

Table 8.1   Computing Percentages

School Grade	Numbers* of pupils enrolled	Percentage in the counting dials**	Percentage rounded to one decimal
First	115,487	13.2863. . . -	13.3
Second	109,847	12.6375. . .	12.6
Third	109,599	12.6089. . .	12.6
Fourth	107,200	12.3329. . .	12.3
Fifth	105,223	12.1055. . .	12.1
Sixth	104,747	12.0507. . .	12.1
Seventh	103,340	11.8889. . .	11.9
Eighth	100,601	11.5737. . .	11.6
Ungraded	13,169	1.5150. . .	1.5
N	869,213	99.9999. . .	100.0

$1/N \times 100 = .0001150465$
* Data from page 43 of the *Biennial Report: Part One,* 1964–66 of the North Carolina Public Schools. Reprinted with permission of the Department of Public Instruction, Raleigh, N. C.
** The percentages were actually calculated to the same number of decimal places as $1/N \times 100$, or 10 places. Four places should suffice for later rounding to one or two.

The sum of percentages should equal 100., 100.0, or 100.00 if two decimal places are carried, but, because of rounding error, it may not quite equal such a figure. It has been argued on logical grounds, that the sum should be reported as 100, 100.0, or 100.00 even in cases where it is not precisely that amount. Adjustment of certain percentages so that their total exactly equals 100, 100.0, or 100.00 reduces their accuracy and is undesirable when the adjusted percentages are given individual interpretations. Increasing the last digit of the reciprocal by one often contributes to obtaining 100 or 100.00 as the sum of the percentages.

A slide rule can also be used conveniently with 100 times the reciprocal of N when precision to one decimal place suffices.

Percentages from incomplete data

Frequently the data collected relevant to some sample of size N are incomplete. For example, questionnaire and interview respondents may not answer all of the questions asked. In computing percentages, N cannot be used uniformly as the base. In such cases a percentage should have as its base the number reporting usable information. If the number of omissions is small relative to N, the representativeness of the sampling is probably not significantly impaired. If, however, the number of omissions is relatively large, it is desirable to exclude the data pertaining to such questions altogether, or to make further effort to obtain them.

Percentages for data where individuals are represented in more than one category

Another case that requires special attention occurs when individuals are included in two or more counts in the same set of categories. For example, consider data collected from students concerning their participation in several extracurricular activities. Many of the students will report participation in more than one activity, so that when the total number of students is used as the base, the percentages will total more than 100. When this happens the sum of the percentages is without meaning and, hence, should not be given in the table reporting the data. N should still be used as the base, but the fact of multiple participation should be noted with reference to the table, either in the context of the research report explaining the table or in a footnote to the table.

Combining percentages from different samples

When combining percentages from several samples of different size, the items should be weighted in terms of the sizes of the samples. The simple average of 15, 25, and 50 percent is 30 percent. Suppose, however, that the sizes of the three samples are respectively 100, 500, and 1000. Then:

$$
\begin{array}{rcr}
100 \times .15 = & 15 \\
500 \times .25 = & 125 \\
1000 \times .50 = & 500 \\
\hline
1600 & & 640
\end{array}
$$

and 640 is 40 percent of the cases in the total sample. (The same process can be used with means, but not with other sample statistics.) This is an effective way of checking the entries in a table whose last column concerns a total sample.

Using tables to report percentages

Counts or frequencies accompanied by percentages are effectively reported in appropriately labeled tables. As earlier noted, where the frequencies and the percentages are those of a frequency distribution, the bottom rows of the table may report, in addition to *N,* such summary descriptive statistics as the mean and standard deviation or the quartiles and the median. The presentation of data in tables of the type just described may suffice. It is often useful, however, to supplement tables with graphs. Bar graphs and pie graphs are especially useful in enhancing the meaning of percentages. An example of the former appears on page 305 of Chapter 10.

Using percentages as bases for generalizing and in study of relationships

Percentages and differences in percentages obtained from samples are frequently used in generalizing to the populations from which the samples were drawn. In making such generalization or inferences sampling errors must be considered. Counts or frequencies and percentages or proportions are also used in obtaining indices of the strength of relationships between nominal variables, or between such variables and continuous ones like test scores. The sampling errors of percentages and proportions are explained in Chapter 9 as are tests to determine whether probably significant relationships exist between the nominal variables to which the data are relevant. A significant relationship is not necessarily a high degree of relationship. Indices of the strength of relationships between nominal variables, or between nominal and continuous variables, are explained in Chapter 11.

SUMMARIZING QUANTITATIVE DATA

The term "quantitative" is used here to designate data relevant to variables which have interval or ratio scales, or are treated as if they had such scales. The interpretation of quantitative data in the form of ranks which have an ordinal scale is dealt with in the concluding section of Chapter 11.

Adding to the meaning of quantitative data by summarizing

Test scores and other kinds of quantitative data are not very meaningful until summarized. Lists of pupils' names and their test scores do not clearly reveal the average score nor the spread or variability among the scores. Such characteristics of the test score data are somewhat more readily seen if the scores are listed in order of size. Halfway down the list is a score of average size. The range of scores from the lowest score to the highest score gives some indication of the variability. An average thus identified is not likely to be a precise average, nor is the range a very satisfactory estimate of variability, depending as it does only on the magnitudes of the lowest and highest scores. Either or both of these may differ considerably from scores less extreme.

Frequency distributions

Suppose that scores instead of being listed as described above, are tallied yielding counts of the pupils whose scores fall within such intervals as 35–39, 40–44, 45–49, and so on until, for example, 85–89 includes the highest score. The numbers of scores, or frequencies, in these intervals characterize collectively the score data much more meaningfully than does the original list of scores. For example:

Table 8.2 A Frequency Distribution

Class interval	f
85–89	2
80–84	3
75–79	7
70–74	12
65–69	15
60–64	11
55–59	8
50–54	4
45–49	3
40–44	0
35–39	1
N	66

A frequency distribution of the kind illustrated in Table 8.2 with score or class intervals of 5 units (or other than 5 units) immediately reveals the approximate position of the average score since this is most often in a centrally located interval with a relatively high frequency. Some idea of the spread of variability of the scores can be gained by observing how they cluster in and about the central interval and how rapidly the frequencies decrease in size above and below this interval. The data in such a frequency distribution can be made even more meaningful by presenting them in graphic form as a "histogram" or a "frequency polygon." How to tally frequency distributions and to construct such graphs is explained on pages 208 to 211.

Measures of central tendency

Listed scores may be summed and divided by N, their total number, to obtain the arithmetic average, the mean symbolized by M or $\overline{X}$. (The symbols $\overline{X}$ and $\overline{Y}$ are used in this text rather than the still widely used

M_x and M_y.) The mean and the median symbolized by *Md* can be obtained from scores which have been tallied in a frequency distribution.

The median is the *point* on the scale of the test scores above which there are half the scores and below which there are also half. An advantage of the median as compared with the mean is that it is less affected by the extremely high or low scores of a badly skewed distribution. (See page 204.) The median is also preferable to the mean in obtaining the average of an ordinal variable, for example, rankings of students. Usually, however, the mean is the more appropriate measure of central tendency when dealing with an interval or a ratio variable. A sample mean is a better estimate of the population central tendency than the median of the same sample. The mean also better lends itself to algebraic manipulation. It appears in numerous statistical formulas. Another measure of central tendency is the mode. It is, for example, the scale value of the most frequently occurring score. (There may be more than one mode.) The mode is seldom used in educational research.

From a frequency distribution one can also easily calculate Q_1 and Q_3, the first and third quartiles. These are also *points* on the scale of scores. The first and third quartiles, with the median (Q_2), divide the distribution into four sections each containing one-fourth of the scores.

Measures of variability

The quartile deviation, or *Q*, equals one-half the range of scores between Q_1 and Q_3. *Q* and the standard deviation of the sample of scores, symbolized by the small letter *s*, are measures of variability. When the same test is given to two or more groups of pupils, comparison of the quartile deviations, or comparison of the standard deviations, may reveal differences in variability or heterogeneity. They may indicate, for example, that providing for individual differences in one group of pupils will be more difficult than in another, more homogeneous, group.

The quartiles and the quartile deviation can be calculated from scores listed in order of size or, more readily, when tallied in a frequency distribution. The standard deviation can be computed from listed scores which need not be listed in order of size, or from a frequency distribution. Essentially, the standard deviation is the square root of the sum of the squares of the differences between the scores and their mean divided N or $N - 1$. A standard deviation can be visualized as a distance along the score scale measured above and below the mean. The same thing is true of the quartile deviation, although it is measured above and below the median.

Graphic representation of measures of central tendency and of variability

Figure 8.1 is the familiar bell-shaped normal curve with the mean, median, and the mode in the center of the base line. The quartile

Figure 8.1   Normal curve illustrating quartile deviation and standard deviation

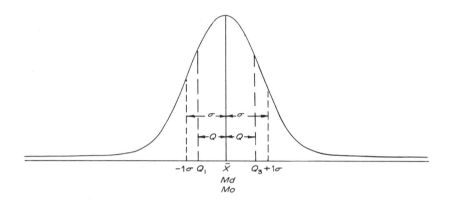

deviation and the standard deviation are shown both above and below the mean, median, and mode. The area between the vertical dashed lines above Q_1 and Q_3 comprises 50 percent of the total area of the curve. The vertical dotted lines above -1σ and $+1\sigma$ enclose 68.26 percent of the total area, or if we think in terms of test scores, 68.26 percent of the scores. The symbol for the standard deviation in Figure 8.1 is the small Greek letter σ (sigma) rather than s. The use of σ is appropriate in discussing a normal curve and when the standard deviation referred to is a population standard deviation; its estimate, a sample standard deviation, is given the symbol s. μ could replace $\overline{X}$ as the mean for the same reasons, but $\overline{X}$ is probably more meaningful in this figure.

If the data in a frequency distribution are used in drawing a histogram or a frequency polygon one can see from such a graph whether or not the distribution resembles a normal one. Often a distribution is skewed. In such cases its graph is asymmetrical. If extended excessively to the right, the skewness is positive and the mean is larger than the median. If extended to the left the skewness is negative and the mean is smaller than the median. In either case when there is much skewness, the median is preferable to the mean as a measure of central tendency. If a curve of a distribution is more peaked than normal, it is said to be leptokurtic and, if less peaked, platykurtic. A normal curve is mesokurtic. Mere inspection of a histogram or frequency polygon will not suffice to identify such departures from normal since change of units of the coordinate axes can change the appearance of the graph. Computation of "moments" about the mean and their substitution in simple formulas yield measures of skewness and kurtosis which are effective indices of how closely a frequency distribution of observed measures approximates a normal one.[2] Another means of testing the normality of a distribution is the χ^2 (Chi square) test explained in Chapter 9.

Too hard a test will yield a *positively* skewed distribution of scores having a relatively large proportion of low scores and a long "tail" of relatively few high scores extending toward the upper or positive end of the score scale. The mean is greater than the median. Too easy a test will yield a *negatively* skewed distribution having a relatively large proportion of high scores with a long tail of relatively few low scores falling toward the lower or negative end of the score scale. The median is larger than the mean. A test of average difficulty will yield a flattened or platykurtic distribution instead of a normal one. (Remember the appearance of a duckbill platypus.) The more platykurtic a distribution of test scores, the greater the discrimination among students ranging widely in ability.

The product-moment coefficient of correlation

The Pearson product-moment coefficient of correlation summarizes the extent of relationship between two continuous variables. An abstract definition of the correlation coefficient states that it is an index which summarizes the extent to which the scores vary concomitantly from their respective means. The variables may be the paired scores of students taking the same test. Usually, with such data the relationship is positive with both scores in each pair of scores tending to deviate in the same direction above or below the mean of its series of scores. For example, in a given pair of relatively high or relatively low reading and arithmetic scores, both scores most often will be above the two means or below the two means. A moderate negative coefficient of correlation will usually be obtained between chronological ages and intelligence or achievement scores of pupils in the same grade, since the younger pupils tend to be the brighter ones.

If the scores in each pair of scores are equal, their concomitant variation is identical, and the coefficient is $+1.00$. If the highest score in one series pairs with the lowest score in the other, the next highest with the next to lowest and so on for all the pairs, the coefficient is -1.00. (More than rank is involved here. The paired scores must be equal or proportional and opposite in sign.) If the scores in the two series are only randomly related the coefficient is zero.

---

[2] See, for example, George A. Ferguson, *Statistical Analysis in Psychology and Education,* 3rd ed. (New York: McGraw-Hill, 1971), pp. 67–68.

Graphic representation of correlations differing in size

In Figure 8.2 the small graphs illustrate such correlations as $+ 1.00$, $+ .60, 0, - .60$ and $- 1.00$:

Figure 8.2   Graphs illustrating correlations of varying size

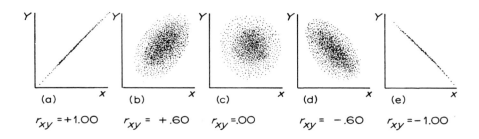

(a) $r_{xy} = +1.00$ (b) $r_{xy} = +.60$ (c) $r_{xy} = .00$ (d) $r_{xy} = -.60$ (e) $r_{xy} = -1.00$

Each point on the graphs represents a pair of scores. Suppose that the two series of X and Y scores are normal distributions to be portrayed graphically. This has to be done in three dimensions. For graphs (a) and (e) imagine a plane vertical to the page and along the dotted lines shown. On these planes would appear normal curves. In the case of graph (c) the paired scores would be represented by a circular mound which if sliced *horizontally* would reveal a succession of circles of decreasing size from the page. Sliced vertically, however, the cross sections would be normal curves. Horizontal slices of the mounds imagined for (b) and (d) would be ellipses. Slices of these mounds parallel to the X or the Y axes would again yield normal curves defining the surface of each mound. The technical terms applied to the distributions thus depicted is "normal bivariate distribution" and to their graphic presentation, as imagined, "normal bivariate surface." On page 352 of Chapter 11 a normal bivariate distribution of 7,010 cases is given. A solid could be constructed to represent it, but the solid would be analogous to a histogram of numerous columns rather than a surface whose cross sections are perfectly normal.

The advantages of scattergrams or correlation charts (unfortunately decreasingly used in calculating correlation coefficients) are that through their study one gains conceptions of correlation coefficients of varying size.

Assumptions concerning the coefficient of correlation

One of the assumptions relevant to the interpretation of the product-moment correlation coefficient is that the relationship is linear. If the points shown scatter, they should scatter about a straight line rather than a curve. When the latter is the case, the product-moment coefficient is inappropriate. The "correlation ratio" should be calculated as explained in the more advanced texts in statistical method. Fortunately, the need to do so is comparatively rare when dealing with educational or psychological data. Another assumption with reference to the correlation coefficient is that of "homoscedasticity." The curves in the imagined vertical slices of the correlation surface should exhibit equal variability. In a correlation chart, the scores tabulated in the different rows of the chart should be equally variable. The same should be true of the data in the various columns. Departures from this assumption tend to limit the general applicability of the standard error of estimate to predicted scores of varying size. A normal bivariate distribution as described above can occur in the absence of normal distributions of X and Y, but skewness of either or both of these "marginal" distributions may be associated with failure to satisfy the assumptions of linearity and homoscedasticity.[3]

Applications of the coefficient of correlation in education and psychology

Pearson product-moment coefficients are used as indices of the relationship between measures of achievement in various school subjects and between measures of abilities and other traits. The variables thus compared should be continuous variables. Special types of correlation coefficients or other indices of relationship are needed in estimating the association between nominal or ordinal variables or between nominal variables and continuous ones. Such indices and their applications are discussed in Chapter 11.

The reliability and validity coefficients described in Chapter 7 are, of course, product-moment correlation coefficients. Two of the types of reliability coefficients are obtained by calculation from paired scores of students tested twice with the same test or a second time with an equivalent form of the test. A validity coefficient may be evidence that two different tests are measuring much the same achievements, abilities, or other traits. Validity coefficients are also among the statistics needed in obtaining the regression equations used in predicting future academic or vocational achievement.

Correlation coefficients between the scores on numerous tests given to the same individuals may be the data used in factor analysis in efforts to identify the "primary" abilities underlying the scores on the tests.

---

[3] See, for example, Quinn McNemar, *Psychological Statistics,* 4th ed. (New York: Wiley, 1969), pp. 152–53. See also page 332 in this book.

Interpretation of coefficients of correlation

Something should be said here about the interpretation of product-moment coefficients of correlation, although this is discussed more fully in Chapters 9 and 11. A coefficient of correlation cannot be interpreted as a percentage, although its square may be interpreted as an estimate of what proportion of the variance—or standard deviation squared—of one of the variables can be attributed to variation in the other. The correlation coefficient, of course, does not identify which variable is cause and which is effect. To say that a coefficient is significant is merely to indicate what the probability is that the association is a positive one if the sign of the coefficient is positive, or how probable it is that the association is negative if the coefficient has a negative sign. This is important when investigating traits where the observed measures yield relatively low coefficients. For coefficients of substantial size obtained from relatively large samples, it is usually more important to ascertain the significance of differences between the coefficients, a matter treated in the next chapter. Where the problem is one of prediction, the nearer a correlation coefficient is to $+ 1.00$ or $- 1.00$, the more accurate are the predictions that can be made from the data using a regression equation involving the coefficient. Then the interest is in the standard error of estimate rather than in the standard error of the coefficient of correlation itself. As one gains experience with coefficients of correlation between measures of various abilities or traits, concepts develop from comparisons which may justify conclusions that a given coefficient is high or low. A coefficient of correlation of $+ .23$ may be considered a high coefficient if the variables are generally thought to be independent or unrelated. A coefficient of $+ .65$ between scores on two tests designed to measure intelligence would be considered comparatively low. In this connection it should be emphasized that the correlations are between the traits or abilities *as measured,* rather than between the traits or abilities themselves.

METHODS OF CALCULATING DESCRIPTIVE STATISTICS

Methods of calculating means, standard deviations, medians, quartiles, quartile deviations, and coefficients of correlation are described in the pages following an explanation of the symbol, Σ. Also included in these pages is an explanation of how to tally frequency distributions since these are useful in calculating most of the statistics mentioned above and in preparing tables and graphs. Frequency distributions are also of use in obtaining percentiles and percentile ranks.

Tallying frequency distributions

The scores listed at the left in Table 8.3 are tallied to obtain the frequency distribution first shown in tallies and then changed to numbers at the right.

Table 8.3   Tallying Listed Scores to Obtain a Frequency Distribution

Listed Scores						Class Interval	f	Class Interval	f
47	64	82	74	67	71	85–89	𝍲𝍲	85–89	2
66	82	76	61	64	69	80–84	𝍲𝍲𝍲	80–84	3
73	57	65	70	86	75	75–79	𝍳𝍲𝍲	75–79	7
54	67	71	66	53	66	70–74	𝍳𝍳𝍲𝍲	70–74	12
88	71	68	84	73	62	65–69	𝍳𝍳𝍳	65–69	15
57	58	64	68	68	56	60–64	𝍳𝍳𝍲	60–64	11
63	77	78	73	45	71	55–59	𝍳𝍲𝍲𝍲	55–59	8
77	63	58	65	59	51	50–54	𝍲𝍲𝍲𝍲	50–54	4
49	61	67	79	64	70	45–49	𝍲𝍲𝍲	45–49	3
36	53	62	63	72	59	40–44		40–44	
68	69	75	70	65	56	35–39	𝍲	35–39	1
								N	66

It is advisable to make two tallies in order to check each frequency and the total N.

Choosing a class interval and its midpoint

Before tallying it is necessary to select a class interval of such size that there will not be too few or too many intervals. There should seldom be less than 8 or more than 16. It is also necessary to identify the actual limits and the midpoints of intervals for use in later calculations. If we assume, for example, that a score of 65 ranges from 64.5 up to 65.5 the lower limit of the interval 65–69 is 64.5 and the upper limit is 69.5. (The upper limits of the score of 65 and of the interval 65–69 are more precisely 65.499... and 69.499..., in other words, up to 65.5 and 69.5 as limits.) The midpoint of the class interval 65–69 is shown in Figure 8.3:

Figure 8.3   The midpoint of a class interval

64	65	66	67	68	69	70
	↑		↑		↑	
	64.5		67		69.5	
	Lower Limit		Midpoint		Upper Limit	

Making the same assumption, the limits and midpoints of intervals of 1, 3, 10, 15, and 25 units are illustrated in Table 8.4.

The rule for finding the midpoint is to add one-half of the units in the interval to the actual lower limit. An exception to this procedure occurs where a score, or other measure, does not range from one-half unit below to one-half unit above the score, but ranges from exactly the score up to just short of the next score. For example, children of age 11 range from exactly 11 up to just less than 12. Here the midpoint

Table 8.4   Illustrative Limits and Midpoints

Units in Interval	As Listed	Actual Limits	Midpoint
1	7	6.5– 7.5	7
3	12–14	11.5–14.5	13
10	80–89	79.5–89.5	84.5
15	45–59	44.5–59.5	52
25	75–99	74.5–99.5	87

of the interval 10–14 is 10 + 2.5 or 12.5, rather than 12. Where this assumption is made the midpoints are always .5 units greater than those listed above. The class interval of 1 characterizes frequency distributions where frequencies are obtained of the numbers of pupils earning *each* score. "As listed" refers to the way class intervals are usually given when tallying or in tables. In Table 8.4 only single intervals of varying numbers of units are given as examples.

Graphs of frequency distributions

Two graphs of the frequency distribution are shown. Figure 8.4 is a histogram or column diagram and Figure 8.5 is a frequency polygon:

Figure 8.4   Histogram

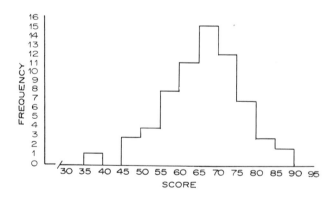

Note that the height of each column of the histogram corresponds to the frequency in each class interval—1 in the interval 35–39, 0 in the interval 40–44, 3 in the interval 45–49, etc. The columns are located precisely between the actual limits 34.5–39.5, . . . , 44.5–49.5, etc., since this is more correct than between 35–40, . . . , 45–50, etc., although such locating of columns is probably more usually done. Sometimes each column is set off with vertical lines from the horizontal axis, but omission of such lines within the histogram has become conventional. In the case of the frequency polygon dots are located above the midpoints

Figure 8.5 Frequency polygon

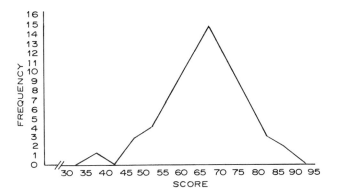

of intervals having frequencies and the heights of these dots, in terms of the scale of the vertical axis, correspond to the frequencies in the intervals. The dots are located above 37, . . . , 42, 47, etc., rather than above 37.5, . . . , 42.5, 47.5, etc. Note that the dots are connected with straight lines and that the lines are brought down to the horizontal axis at 32 and 92, the midpoints of intervals just below and just above the lowest and highest intervals containing frequencies. Lines are also brought down at 42 since the 40–44 interval has a zero frequency. Where two or more frequency distributions are presented in the same graph, either as histograms or as frequency polygons, and the N's differ, the frequencies in each distribution should be changed to percentage frequencies by dividing the original frequencies by the corresponding N and multiplying by 100. Then, both or all of the figures will have the same area and their comparison will be facilitated.

The meaning of Σ

Before discussing the calculation of means and standard deviations it is desirable to explain the meaning of Σ which occurs in numerous formulas. It is, of course, the Greek capital letter "sigma" and is not to be confused with the lower case σ (sigma) used to designate the standard deviation of measures of a population from which samples are drawn. As used here and in formulas presented later, Σ is a "summation operator" and most simply specifies that a series of scores, a series of squares of scores, or a series of products of scores are to be summed. Such summations are symbolized by ΣX or ΣY, ΣX^2 or ΣY^2 and ΣXY. The meaning of ΣX^2 differs from the meaning of $(\Sigma X)^2$. The former indicates the sum of the squares of scores while the latter indicates the square of the sum of scores. Given three scores 4, 5, and 6: ΣX^2 equals 77, while $(\Sigma X)^2$ equals 15^2 or 225. A similar distinction holds for products, ΣXY differing from $\Sigma X \Sigma Y$. The former refers to the sum of the individual products of pairs of X and Y scores while the latter designates the product of the two sums ΣX and ΣY.

Frequently, which scores, squares of scores, or products of scores are to be summed is self-evident. Often, however, it is desirable to designate by superscripts and subscripts just what is to be summed. For example, if the nX_i scores of group j are to be summed this may be specified by:

$$\sum_{i=1}^{nj} X_i.$$

Sometimes one first sums the scores, the squares of scores, or the products of scores of several, or k, groups separately and then obtains the sum of such sums. This process is indicated by a double summation sign. For example, if there are n_j students in each of k groups, the summation of *all* the X_{ij} scores may be indicated:

$$\sum_{j=1}^{k} \sum_{i=1}^{nj} X_{ij}.$$

Some authorities use n's exclusively to designate the numbers of subjects in each group. In this text, N's are used where there are two (or relatively few groups) or to designate the size of a total sample. In Chapter 13, $n_1 + n_2 + n_3 + \ldots + n_k = N$.

Calculating means and standard deviations from listed scores

When there are relatively few listed scores it is easy to obtain their mean simply by summing the scores and dividing by N, the total number of scores. It is also relatively easy to obtain the standard deviation if the mean is a whole number, in other words, an integer. It is first necessary to obtain the differences, or deviations, of each score from the mean. For example, if the mean is 63, scores of 68 and 59 deviate $+5$ and -4 from the mean. (Such deviate measures are symbolized by small letters x and y rather than X and Y.) Each of the deviate measures is squared, the sum of the squares divided by $N-1$, and the square root obtained. Division by $N-1$ rather than N provides a sample standard deviation that is a better estimator of the standard deviation of the population from which the sample was drawn. The sample variance, the square of the standard deviation, is an "unbiased" estimator of the population variance. The sample standard deviation, although not entirely unbiased, is more nearly unbiased when $N-1$ rather than N is used. ,

The computation procedures just described are summarized by the formulas:

$$\overline{X} = \frac{\Sigma X}{N}. \tag{8.1}$$

$$s_x = \sqrt{\frac{\Sigma X^2}{N-1}}. \qquad (8.2)$$

When one has numerous listed scores and the mean is not an integer, Formula 8.1 may still be used, but it is more convenient to use a formula for the standard deviation involving the squares of ordinary scores rather than the squares of deviate measures. The squares may be obtained from a table of squares, or they may be computed on a desk calculator, listing each square for later summing, or permitting the squares to cumulate in the product dials. Using the 66 scores listed in Table 8.2:

$$\Sigma X = 4,361.$$

$$\Sigma X^2 = 294,539.$$

$$\overline{X} = \frac{\Sigma X}{N} = \frac{4361}{66} = 66.0758 \text{ or } 66.08.$$

$$s_x = \sqrt{\frac{N\Sigma X^2 - (\Sigma X)^2}{N(N-1)}}, \qquad (8.3)$$

$$= \sqrt{\frac{66 \times 294,539 - (4361)^2}{66(66-1)}},$$

$$= \sqrt{\frac{19,439,574 - 19,018,321}{4290}},$$

$$= \sqrt{98.1942},$$

$$= 9.9093 \text{ or } 9.91.$$

Even for no more than 66 scores ranging in size from 36 to 88, the calculations illustrated involve numbers of considerable size. Hence, when a desk calculator is not available, the following formula may be preferred:

$$s_x = \sqrt{\frac{\Sigma X^2}{N} - \overline{X}^2}, \qquad (8.4)$$

$$= \sqrt{\frac{294,539}{66} - 66.08^2},$$

$$= \sqrt{96.1457},$$

$$= 9.8054 \text{ or } 9.81.$$

The formula just given yields slightly less accurate values because of greater rounding error. In order to obtain a better estimate of the population standard deviation, $\frac{N}{N-1}$ should be used as a multiplier of, for example, 96.1457 before taking the square root. When this is done $s_x = 9.88$, differing from the 9.91 earlier obtained only because of rounding error.

Tables of squares and square roots are helpful in applying Formulas 8.2, 8.3, and 8.4. Many texts on statistical method contain such tables. They are also found in the book *Barlow's Tables*. A desk calculator is also useful in obtaining sums of scores, sums of squares of scores, and in computing square roots. See pages 534 to 535 of the Appendix for aid in computing square roots.

Methods of calculating descriptive statistics from frequency distributions still worth studying

Since electronic computers have become increasingly available, some authorities are critical of efforts to explain computation of means and standard deviations from frequency distributions and coefficients of correlation from correlation charts. They are especially critical of explanations of methods applicable to data tallied or coded in other than unit class intervals. Nevertheless, some experience in computing from such frequency distributions and correlation charts contributes to student understanding in ways that computing only from listed scores cannot do. Many graduate students and school personnel interested in educational research do not have ready access to desk calculators or computer equipment. Whether or not a desk calculator is used, where scores and N's are large, calculation of means and standard deviations from frequency distributions and of coefficients of correlation from correlation charts can be accomplished with less effort than calculations from listed scores.

Calculating the mean of a frequency distribution

In calculating the mean from a frequency distribution, the midpoint of one of the intervals is used as a reference point or arbitrary origin, AO. The term arbitrary origin is meaningful since AO can be the midpoint of any class interval.

Under x' in Table 8.5 are listed the extent to which, *in intervals as units,* the class intervals deviate above and below the class interval 65–69 containing the selected arbitrary origin, the AO of 67.00. (No matter what interval is chosen as the location of the arbitrary origin, the calculation will always result in the same value for the mean.) Each frequency is multiplied by the corresponding x' to obtain each fx', for example, $2 \times +4 = 8$ and $4 \times -3 = -12$. The arbitrary origin in the 65–69 interval is the *midpoint* of that interval, 67.00. The formula *adjusts* 67.00 to the correct value of the mean 65.94 giving greater weight to scores below 67 than above, since there are more of them and some of them deviate further below than do those above. This is indicated by the fact that $\Sigma fx'$ equals -14. The value of i would be 1, 3, 10, 15, or 25 if class intervals of such size are used. $\dfrac{\Sigma fx'}{N}$ must be multiplied by i to make the adjustment in *score units.* Using Formula 8.1, summing actual scores and dividing by N will often give a slightly different mean where the scores are not evenly distributed within each interval. The procedure illustrated above assumes that they are evenly distributed. The arbitrary origin for a distribution of chronological ages may, for example, be 12.50 rather than 12.00. *Be sure to check your computations.*

Table 8.5 Calculation of the Mean of a Frequency Distribution

Class interval (i)	f	x′	fx′
85–89	2	+4	8
80–84	3	+3	9
75–79	7	+2	14
70–74	12	+1	12
65–69	15	0	(+43)
60–64	11	−1	−11
55–59	8	−2	−16
50–54	4	−3	−12
45–49	3	−4	−12
40–44	0	−5	0
35–39	1	−6	− 6
	N = 66		(−57)

$$\overline{X} = AO + i\left(\frac{\Sigma fx'}{N}\right), \qquad (8.5)$$

$$= 67.00 + 5\left(\frac{43 - 57}{66}\right),$$

$$= 67.00 + 5\left(\frac{-14}{66}\right),$$

$$= 67.00 + \left(\frac{-70}{66}\right),$$

$$= 67.00 - 1.06,$$

$$= 65.94.$$

Calculating the standard deviation of a frequency distribution

In order to compute the standard deviation for the data in Table 8.5 the column headed fx'^2 has been added in Table 8.6. Its sum is $\Sigma fx'^2$ or

Table 8.6 Calculation of the Standard Deviation of a Frequency Distribution

Class Intervals	f	x′	fx′	fx′²
85–89	2	+4	8	32
80–84	3	+3	9	27
75–79	7	+2	14	28
70–74	12	+1	12	12
65–69	15	0	(+43)	
60–64	11	−1	−11	11
55–59	8	−2	−16	32
50–54	4	−3	−12	36
45–49	3	−4	−12	48
40–44	0	−5	0	0
35–39	1	−6	− 6	36
			(−57)	262

262. Each of the values in this column should be obtained in two ways for a check, for example, $+ 4 \times 8 = 32$ or $2 \times 4^2 = 32$. Similarly, $- 3 \times - 12 = 36$ and $4 \times - 3^2 = 4 \times 9 = 36$. All the numbers in this column are positive.

The values of i, N, $\Sigma fx'^2$, and $\Sigma fx'$ are then substituted in Formula 8.6 and the standard deviation, s_x, calculated:

$$s_x = i \sqrt{\frac{N\Sigma fx'^2 - (\Sigma fx')^2}{N(N-1)}} \qquad (8.6)$$

$$= 5 \sqrt{\frac{66 \times 262 - (-14)^2}{66(66-1)}}$$

$$= 5 \sqrt{\frac{17{,}292 - 196}{4{,}290}}$$

$$= 5 \sqrt{3.9851} = 5 \times 1.9963$$

$$= 9.9815 \text{ or } 9.98.$$

Observe that $\Sigma fx'$, $43 - 57$, or -14, is divided by N, here 66, before squaring. Its square, $+196$, is subtracted from 17,292. Also note that the square root is taken of 3.9851 *before* multiplying by the size of the class interval, here 5.

If you have a desk calculator available, take the arbitrary origin as 32.00, the midpoint of the interval just below the interval having a frequency. Consider the x' values to range upward from 1 in the 35–39 interval, to 11 in the 85–89 interval. Suppose each x' value to have a corresponding x'^2 value ranging from 1 to 121. Place each x' and x'^2 successively at the left and right in the keyboard of the calculator (1 and 1, 2 and 4, ... 11 and 121) multiplying each pair of x' and x'^2 values by the corresponding f. Use the first two columns of keys at the left side of the keyboard to provide for 2 digit values of x' and use the three columns at the right for values of x'^2 ranging from 1 to 3 digit numbers. Do not clear the product dials until $\Sigma fx'$ and $\Sigma fx'^2$ have accumulated at the left and right in them. For the data given above, these sums are 448 and 3,300. When substituted in Formulas 8.5 and 8.6, precisely the same mean and standard deviation are obtained.

Sheppard's correction

The standard deviation of 9.98, although the square root of an unbiased estimator of the population variance, differs from the 9.91 first obtained from the listed scores. The scores in class intervals are *not* evenly distributed. (This is true also of normal distributions of scores when tabulated in class intervals.) Below the mean, more scores are above the midpoint of an interval than below. Above the mean, more scores are below the midpoints than above. The difference of each midpoint from the mean, each x' used in computation, is therefore slightly larger than the average deviation of the scores. Hence, the standard deviation is also slightly larger. As the number of class intervals *decreases,* the greater the difference of the standard deviation from the one computed using listed scores. An adjustment can be made for the discrepancy through use of Sheppard's correction for "coarseness of grouping." In the case of Formula 8.6, 1/12 or .0833... is subtracted before obtaining the square root and multiplication by *i*. Sheppard's correction is actually $i^2/12$. When *s* has been already computed from a frequency distribution in other than unit intervals and has been changed to score units through multiplication by *i,* such a standard deviation should be squared, $i^2/12$ subtracted, and the square root taken again. When Formula 8.6 is used and Sheppard's correction is anticipated, subtraction of 1/12 or .0833... suffices. Since *i* precedes the radical, this is equivalent to multiplying both the uncorrected s^2 in units of class intervals and 1/12 or .0833... by i^2 before taking the square root. When the correction is applied to the data above, 9.98 becomes 9.88, a value closer to the 9.91 first obtained with the listed scores.

When the range of scores is small, for example, when letter marks have been coded from 1 to 5, or stanines, are used, the correction should also be applied in calculating standard deviations (see pages 221–222).

Calculating the median, the quartiles, and the quartile deviation of a frequency distribution

The same frequency distribution of 66 scores is used to illustrate the computation of a median in Table 8.7 on page 218.

Unlike the calculation of the mean, one must identify the interval in which the median actually falls. To do this add frequencies up from the bottom until the next frequency will yield more than half the cases. Here $1 + 3 + 4 + 8 + 11 = 27$ and adding 15 will exceed 33. Note in the formulas that *l.l.* and *u.l.* refer to the *actual* lower and upper limits of the interval in which the median must be located, while f_{md} is the frequency in this interval. The first formula adds to the actual lower limit, 64.50, a *fraction of the score units* sufficient to mark off enough more scores to increase 27 to 33, or half the scores. (Recall that the median is the point on the scale below which half the scores fall.) If you will return to the list of 66 scores on page 209, you will find 6 of the 15 between 64.5 and the median 66.5 These are three scores of 65 and three of 66. They occupy $\frac{6}{15}$ of 5, or 2 scale units. Hence, 2 is added to 64.50 to obtain the median 66.50. Similarly, the second formula subtracts $\frac{9}{15}$ of 15, or 3 scale units, from the upper limit 69.50 to obtain the median 66.50. (Not all data will so nicely illustrate the above.)

Table 8.7 Calculation of the Median
of a Frequency Distribution

Class intervals	f		
85–89	2		
80–84	3	s_{down}24	
75–79	7		
70–74	12		
65–69	15	f_{md}	15
60–64	11		
55–59	8		
50–54	4	s_{up}	27
45–49	3		
40–44	0		
35–39	1		
	$N = 66$		

$$Md = l.\ l.\ + \frac{\dfrac{N}{2} - s_{up}}{f_{md}} \, i, \qquad (8.7)$$

$$Md = 64.50 + \frac{\dfrac{66}{2} - 27}{15} \, 5 = 66.50.$$

CHECK

$$Md = u.\ l.\ - \frac{\dfrac{N}{2} - s_{down}}{f_{md}} \, i, \qquad (8.8)$$

$$Md = 69.50 - \frac{\dfrac{66}{2} - 24}{15} \, 5 = 66.50.$$

Formulas 8.7 and 8.8 are easily modified to compute the quartiles Q_1 and Q_3. For Q_1 substitute $\dfrac{N}{4}$ in the first formula and $\dfrac{3N}{4}$ in the second. For Q_3 substitute $\dfrac{3N}{4}$ in the first formula and $\dfrac{N}{4}$ in the second. Similar formulas can easily be written for deciles and percentiles. In every case, s_{up} and s_{down} must be less than the figures from which they are to be subtracted. *Always use both formulas to check.*

Calculating medians and quartiles with a desk calculator

The following steps may be used in computing Q_1, Md, and Q_3:

1. Calculate $N/4$, $N/2$, and $3N/4$ by multiplying N successively by .25, .50, and .75.
2. To calculate Q_1, for example, insert $N/4$ at the left in the keyboard of the calculator and transfer it to the product dials as for division.
3. Successively subtract frequencies upward until inspection of the

next higher frequency in the distribution indicates that its value is greater than the value remaining in the dials.

4. Divide by this next higher frequency and add the quotient to two decimals to the exact lower limit of the interval containing the divisor. Where i differs from 1, multiply by i before adding.

5. To check Q_1, for example, put $3N/4$ in the keyboard and subtract frequencies successively *downward* until the "next higher frequency" is reached and divide by this frequency. The quotient, or the quotient times i, is then subtracted from the exact upper limit of the interval in which Q_1 falls.

Applying the procedure to the data earlier given, $Q_1 = 59.50 + .23 = 59.73$ or $64.50 - 4.77 = 59.73$. Similarly calculated, $Md = 66.50$ and $Q_3 = 72.625$ or 72.62. (The number preceding 5 is even.)

Obtaining Q, the quartile deviation

Q_1, Md, and Q_3 are also respectively the 25th, 50th, and 75th percentiles. (See pages 228–229.) When the difference between Q_3 and Q_1 is divided by 2 the quartile deviation Q, here 6.45, is obtained. It is sometimes called the semi-interquartile range. Measured above and below the median it includes the middle 50 percent of the cases and, like the standard deviation, is often used as a measure of variability.

Practice Exercise   8.1

Assume that you have tallied the scores of 70 students on a 100 item objective test. Compute each of the following:

90–94	1	(1)	the mean
85–89	3		
80–84	6	(2)	the median
75–79	9		
70–74	11	(3)	Q_1 and Q_3
65–69	13		
60–64	8	(4)	Q
55–59	7		
50–54	5	(5)	the standard deviation
45–49	4		
40–44	1		
35–39	2		
N	70		

Carry computations to four decimal places, if you use a desk calculator, but later round off the mean, median, etc., to two places. Calculate the standard deviation dividing by N ($N - 1$). Next prepare a histogram and a frequency polygon for the same data. Then, and only then, compare your answers with those given on page 530.

CALCULATING COEFFICIENTS OF CORRELATION

There are a number of formulas for computing the Pearson product-moment coefficient of correlation. Among the easiest to use is the following one:

$$r_{xy} = \frac{\Sigma XY - N\overline{X}\overline{Y}}{Ns_x s_y}. \tag{8.9}$$

When using this formula pairs of scores are listed and these may be ordinary raw scores, standard scores including stanines, or letter marks converted to numbers from 1 to 5.

Each X and Y is squared and listed under X^2 and Y^2. Each X and Y is multiplied and the product listed under XY. The sums of the five columns ΣX, ΣY, ΣX^2, ΣY^2, and ΣXY are then substituted in the appropriate formulas to obtain $\overline{X}$, $\overline{Y}$, s_x, s_y, and r_{xy}. (See page 221.) The five columns are illustrated in Figure 8.6:

Figure 8.6 Sums of scores, squares of scores, and products of scores

X	Y	X^2	Y^2	XY
25	20	625	400	500
21	23	441	529	483
.	.	.	.	.
.	.	.	.	.
9	7	81	49	63
ΣX	ΣY	ΣX^2	ΣY^2	ΣXY

Where the scores are large and N is also large a table of squares or a desk calculator is almost a necessity. Where the measures are stanines or marks expressed from 1 to 5 no aids are necessary in listing the values in the columns.

A scattergram for marks or stanines

An alternative procedure is to tally the paired marks, paired stanines, or paired marks and stanines in a "scattergram" or simple correlation chart as shown in Figure 8.7. (Where stanines are involved it is necessary to increase the rows, columns, or both to 9.) Assume that 45 pairs of marks have been tallied and the tallies changed to frequencies, for example, in the first row of the chart two students earning X marks expressed as 4's earned Y marks expressed as 5's and three students earned both X and Y marks expressed as 5's:

Figure 8.7 Correlation chart for coded letter marks and the sums of the coded marks, their squares, and products

	X						X	Y	X²	Y²	XY
	1	2	3	4	5		8	10	32	50	40
							15	15	75	75	75
5				2	3		6	12	12	48	24
Y							12	16	36	64	48
4		3	4	7	1		28	28	112	112	112
							5	4	25	16	20
3	1	3	8	2			1	3	1	9	3
							6	9	12	27	18
2	1	4	3				24	24	72	72	72
							8	6	32	18	24
1	2	1					1	2	1	4	2
							8	8	16	16	16
							9	6	27	12	18
							2	2	2	2	2
							2	1	4	1	2
							135	146	459	526	476
							ΣX	ΣY	ΣX^2	ΣY^2	ΣXY

In making the entries in each row of the table at the right multiply the number in the cell by the number above it outside the correlation chart to secure X, by the number on the same level outside the chart to secure Y, by the square of the number above to secure X², by the square of the number to the left to secure Y², and by the product of the two outside numbers to secure XY. Do this successively from left to right and row by row as one would do in reading a page. Only occasionally will it be necessary where the cell frequency is high to resort to pencil-and-paper computation. Repeat the process described checking each entry in the table. Check also the sums of the columns.

The sums of the columns are then substituted in the following formulas for the means, standard deviations, and coefficient of correlation:

$$\overline{X} = \frac{\Sigma X}{N} = \frac{135}{45} = 3.0000 \text{ or } 3.00,$$

$$\overline{Y} = \frac{\Sigma Y}{N} = \frac{146}{45} = 3.2444 \text{ or } 3.24.$$

$$s_x = \sqrt{\frac{\Sigma X^2}{N} - \overline{X}^2 - .0833},$$

$$= \sqrt{\frac{459}{45} - 3.0000^2 - .0833} = 1.0567 \text{ or } 1.06.$$

$$s_y = \sqrt{\frac{\Sigma Y^2}{N} - \overline{Y}^2 - .0833},$$

$$= \sqrt{\frac{526}{45} - 3.2444^2 - .0833} = 1.0390 \text{ or } 1.04.$$

$$r_{xy} = \frac{\Sigma XY - N\overline{X}\,\overline{Y}}{Ns_x s_y},$$

$$= \frac{476 - 45 \times 3.0000 \times 3.2444}{45 \times 1.0567 \times 1.0390} = .7693 \text{ or } .77.$$

Sheppard's correction was applied in the calculation of the coefficient of correlation just illustrated. It will also be observed that N rather than $N - 1$ was used in calculating the standard deviations. Had $N - 1$ been used, as in Formula 8.3, N in the denominator of Formula 8.9 should be changed to $N - 1$.

It has been my experience that correlations between paired marks obtained as illustrated above agree closely with correlations between the paired test scores on which the marks were based, if the distributions of scores and marks are reasonably normal. It may be inferred from this that correlations between paired marks are somewhat dubious where one or both of the mark distributions are skewed. The same is true of correlations between marks and stanines, or between stanines.

A formula for use with a desk calculator

If you have a desk calculator available, Formula 8.10 is preferable to Formula 8.9, since there will be less rounding error:

$$r_{xy} = \frac{N\Sigma XY - \Sigma X\Sigma Y}{\sqrt{[N\Sigma X^2 - (\Sigma X)^2][N\Sigma Y^2 - (\Sigma Y)^2]}} . \qquad (8.10)$$

This formula can be used with pairs of listed scores, pairs of listed marks coded from 1 to 5, pairs of listed stanines, and such data tallied in correlation charts exemplified by Figures 8.7 and 8.8. In the case of a chart like Figure 8.8, as will be explained in detail later, the rows and columns labeled with code numbers with a wider range than 1 to 9 can designate the class intervals of frequency distributions of scores.

If the standard deviations are also desired, the terms in the brackets of the denominator of Formula 8.10 should be divided by $N(N - 1)$ before taking their square roots. (This is equivalent to using Formula 8.3 twice.) If the coefficient of correlation and each standard deviation are to be corrected by Sheppard's correction, insert $- N^2/12$ within each bracket before obtaining the one square root necessary in computing the coefficient of correlation and before dividing by $N(N - 1)$ in computing the standard deviations as explained above. If the divisor were N^2, rather than its close approximation $N(N - 1)$, cancellation of each N^2 would change $- N^2/12$ to precisely $1/12$ or $.0833 . . .$

A useful correlation chart

If you have a number of correlations to calculate, if the numbers of students are large and if computer equipment is not available, you may find it efficient to mimeograph charts similar to Figure 8.8 omitting from the charts only the numbers in italics, which are data similar to those you would enter and use in actual computation:

Figure 8.8   Correlation chart

$$X$$

	1	2	3	4	5	6	7	8	9	(f)	(g)	(h)	(i)	(j)	(k)
9	9	18	27	36	45	54 (1)	63	72 (1)	81 (2)	4	9	81	36	324	288
Y 8	8	16	24	32	40 (1)	48	56 (2)	64 (3)	72 (1)	7	8	64	56	448	416
7	7	14	21	28 (1)	35	42 (3)	49 (5)	56 (1)	63	10	7	49	70	490	455
6	6	12	18 (2)	24	30 (4)	36 (7)	42 (2)	48 (1)	54	16	6	36	96	576	540
5	5 (1)	10 (2)	15 (3)	20 (5)	25 (9)	30 (4)	35 (2)	40	45	26	5	25	130	650	585
4	4 (1)	8 (2)	12 (8)	16 (3)	20 (2)	24	28	32	36	16	4	16	64	256	268
3	3 (1)	6 (6)	9 (2)	12	15	18	21	24	27	9	3	9	27	81	84
2	2 (1)	4 (2)	6 (1)	8 (1)	10	12	14	16	18	5	2	4	10	20	26
1	1 (1)	2 (1)	3	4	5	6	7	8	9	2	1	1	2	2	3
(a)	3	7	14	16	18	17	11	6	3	95 = N	491	2847	2665		
(b)	1	2	3	4	5	6	7	8	9	ΣY	ΣY^2	ΣXY			
(c)	1	4	9	16	25	36	49	64	81						
(d)	3	14	42	64	90	102	77	48	27	$467 = \Sigma X$					
(e)	3	28	126	256	450	612	539	384	243	$2641 = \Sigma X^2$					

When each pair of scores has been tallied and the tally checked (possibly on a separate form having only the scattergram) the tallies should be changed to corresponding numerals, the frequencies. Then ΣX, ΣY, ΣX^2, ΣY^2, and ΣXY can be obtained in the following steps:

1. Sum the frequencies in the columns of the scattergram to secure the values in Row (a) just below the scattergram. Sum the frequencies in the rows of the scattergram to secure the values in Column (f) to the right of the scattergram. Sum the values in Row (a) and in Column (f) to obtain N, the number of pupils.

2. Obtain the figures which sum to ΣX and ΣX^2 by multiplying each frequency in Row (a) just below the scattergram by the printed figures in Rows (b) and (c) just below it. For example, 14 is multiplied by 3 and by 9 to obtain 42 and 126. Sum Row (d) to obtain ΣX and Row (e) to obtain ΣX^2.

3. Similarly obtain the figures which sum to ΣY and ΣY^2 by multiplying each frequency in Column (f) just to the right of the

scattergram by the printed figures beside it in Columns (g) and (h). For example, 4×9 equals 36 and 4×81 equals 324. Sum Column (i) to obtain ΣY and Column (j) to obtain ΣY^2.

4. The values in Column (k) which sum to ΣXY are obtained row by row, cumulating the sum of the products of each cell frequency in the scattergram with the printed number in the cell. For example, $(1 \times 54) + (1 \times 72) + (2 \times 81)$ equals 288 and $(1 \times 40) + (2 \times 56) + (3 \times 64) + (1 \times 72)$ equals 416. Sum column (k) to obtain ΣXY. Be sure to check all computations.

If a desk calculator is available, the entries need not be made in Rows (d) and (e) nor in Columns (i), (j), and (k) of the chart illustrated by Figure 8.8. In order to obtain ΣX and ΣX^2, place 1 from Row (b) in the keyboard of the calculator in the first row of keys at the left and 1 from Row (c) in the keyboard in the last row of keys at the right. Multiply by the first frequency in Row (a), here 3, using the multiplier bar or, if the calculator has automatic multiplication, using the appropriate key. The value 3 will then appear at either side in the product dials. Clear the keyboard and the counting dials, but not the product dials. Put 2 and 4 from Rows (b) and (c) in the keyboard and multiply by the next frequency in Row (a), here 7; then 17 and 31 will appear in the product dials at the left and right respectively. Continue this process for all the frequencies in Row (a) and then enter ΣX and ΣX^2 in the appropriate blanks. Repeat for a check. ΣY and ΣY^2 are computed similarly and can begin at the top with 9 and 81 in the keyboard at the left and at the right. This is essentially the procedure explained on page 216.

The correlation chart presented in Figure 8.8 can be modified by substituting class intervals of both variables for the numbers 1 to 9 in the scattergram part of the form. There may be more than nine rows and columns. It should be easy to see how to extend the series of numbers in each row and column including Rows (b) and (c) and Columns (g) and (h). For each variable the lowest class interval should be the lowest one having one or more frequencies. The class intervals need not be the same for each variable. The formulas previously given may be used in calculating the correlations and standard deviations. Where a variable has more than 9 intervals Sheppard's correction need not be applied. The standard deviations used in calculating the correlation coefficient are in class intervals as units. Each should be multiplied by the number of units in the class interval of the given variable to express them in raw score units. If means are desired $i \dfrac{\Sigma X}{N}$ and $i \dfrac{\Sigma Y}{N}$ will need to be added to the midpoints of the class intervals next below the lowest shown in the modified form. For example, if the lowest X interval having one or more frequencies is 35–39, $i \dfrac{\Sigma X}{N}$ is added to 32.00. If the lowest Y interval is 10–19, $i \dfrac{\Sigma Y}{N}$ is added to 4.5.

One limitation of the correlation chart illustrated by Figure 8.8 is that it does not provide the checks characteristic of more elaborate and less easily understood charts. Hence, it is essential to check the tallying and *all* steps in the computations.

Practice Exercise   8.2

The course marks of 100 students have been converted to numbers from 1 to 5 and these marks are paired with the stanines earned by the same students on a test of general scholastic aptitude administered at the beginning of the term. Considering the stanines as variable X and the course marks as variable Y, the paired measures have been tallied in the correlation chart given below:

		1	2	3	4	5	6	7	8	9
									X	
Y	5						1	1	2	3
	4			1	2	5	6	7	2	1
	3		1	2	9	15	8	3		
	2	1	7	3	8	3	2			
	1	3	1	2	1					

Obtain $\overline{X}, \overline{Y}, s_x, s_y$, and r_{xy}. (In your calculations compute to 4 decimal places and round off to 2. Apply Sheppard's correction in computing both s_x and s_y.)

TRANSFORMING RAW SCORES TO PERCENTILES, PERCENTILE RANKS, AND STANDARD SCORES

There are numerous occasions in instruction, in guidance, in placement, and in educational research requiring interpretation of test scores. A student's "raw" score, the number of test items answered correctly, or this number corrected for guessing, has little meaning. Raw scores on different tests cannot legitimately be compared where the tests differ in numbers of items and in difficulty. A raw score of 61 on one test may represent a higher level of achievement than a score of 83 on another. Raw scores need to be transformed to such derived measures as percentile scores or ranks, or standard scores. Such transformed scores facilitate comparisons.

Most test manuals of standardized tests contain tables listing for each raw score the corresponding percentile score or standard score. Where the test manual pertains to a test battery, numerically equal percentile scores, or standard scores, are presumably comparable measures and, as such, indicative of comparable levels of ability. A student's differing percentile scores, or differing standard scores, yield insights concerning his relative levels of achievement or aptitude as measured by the various tests in a test battery. Such transformed scores are obviously useful in instruction, in guidance, and in placement. They also have value in educational research, especially in institutional studies. For example, suppose that a survey is needed of the characteristics of the students entering a particular high school or college. The median raw scores of a group of entrants when transformed to norm percentile scores, or standard scores, may provide data useful in making institutional decisions. Such decisions may be made even more wisely if the administrator also knows what proportions of the entrants exceed the norm 25th, 50th, and 75th percentiles. One type of local norm that may also be valuable to obtain is local percentile scores. These scores are a means of estimating what proportion of entrants are likely to be enrolled in some remedial course, assuming a given local percentile score has been set as the critical one. In instruction and guidance, local norms facilitate comparison of an individual student with his fellow students.

An educational researcher may construct one or more tests, possibly for use with standardized tests, in collecting his data. Tables of percentile scores or standard scores equivalent to the raw scores on each test derived from his data will again facilitate comparisons. Whether locally derived percentile score or standard score equivalents are used or not, the educational researcher who uses tests to collect data should understand the meaning of percentile scores and standard scores. An explanation of how such scores are obtained should contribute to a better understanding of their meaning. Attention is directed first to percentile scores, after which standard scores are considered.

Percentiles and percentile ranks

The reader has learned that the quartiles Q_1, Q_2 (the median) and Q_3 divide a distribution of scores into four sections, each containing one-fourth the total number of students tested. Similarly, the percentiles are *points* dividing the distribution into 100 equal parts. Suppose that there are 1,000 raw scores in a distribution. Ten scores will fall between any two successive percentile points. On the raw score scale, however, the distances between the points are *not* equal. This is illustrated in Figure 8.9:

Figure 8.9   Normal curve illustrating score scale differences between percentiles

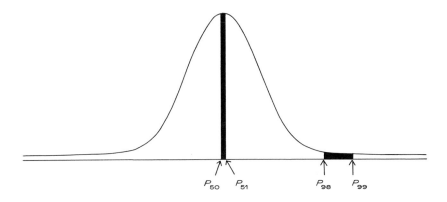

In the normal curve shown above, the two areas in black each represent 1 percent of the total area or 1 percent of the total number of scores. P_{50} is at the mean and P_{51} is $+ .025$ standard deviations from the mean. Taking one standard deviation as the unit, the difference between P_{50} and P_{51} along the score scale is .025 such units. P_{98} and P_{99} are respectively $+ 2.054$ and $+ 2.326$ standard deviations from the mean and differ .272 standard deviation units, over ten times as great a difference as the one between P_{50} and P_{51}. If this were a distribution of intelligence quotients having a mean of 100 and a standard deviation of 16, then $P_{50} = 100$, $P_{51} = 100.4$, $P_{98} = 132.9$, and $P_{99} = 137.2$. The standard scores explained later in this chapter differ from percentile scores in that the units along the scale of measurement can be assumed as equal. Percentile scores or percentile ranks do have the advantage, however, of being much more readily understood by school administrators, counselors, teachers, students and parents. It is easy to understand what is meant by the statement that 67 percent of the students received scores lower than this one. It is not easy to explain, however, the relation between percentile and percentile rank.

A raw score of 43 ranges between 42.5 and 43.5 (more precisely 43.499...). The midpoint of the score is exactly 43. Suppose that of 320 students taking a test, 188 receive scores less than 43 and that 20 receive scores of 43. If we assume that the ability of these students ranges between 42.5 and 43.5, then 10 are below the midpoint—exactly 43—and the total number of students below this midpoint is $188 + 10$ or 198. This is 61.875 percent of 320 students and this percentage rounds off to 62, the percentile *rank* of the score of 43. The percentile rank of a score is thus a measure of the percentage of cases receiving a lower score, plus one-half the cases receiving the given score.

Only occasionally does a percentile such as P_{30}, P_{48}, or P_{60} exactly correspond to the midpoint of a raw score. We may say that the score of 43 is at $P_{61.875}$ and that it also has a percentile rank of 61.875, but it is usual to round off such values to whole numbers. Whole numbers suffice in counseling and some authorities recommend percentile bands, a combination of several percentile units, or ranks, as precise enough because of errors of measurement.

Obtaining percentiles or percentile ranks

In order to obtain percentiles or percentile ranks calculated by the method explained below it is necessary to tally the frequencies of each raw score as is illustrated by the first two columns of Table 8.8.

Table 8.8   Calculation of Percentiles or Percentile Ranks

Raw Score	f	Cum. f	$f/2$	Cum. f'	Percentile or Percentile Rank
44	1	193	.5	193.5	99.74 or 99.7
43	3	190	1.5	191.5	98.71 99
42	8	182	4.0	186.0	95.88 96
41	19	163	9.5	172.5	88.92 89
40	42	121	21.0	142.0	73.20 73
39	47	74	23.5	97.5	50.26 50
38	35	39	17.5	56.5	29.12 29
37	24	15	12.0	27.0	13.92 14
36	10	5	5.0	10.0	5.15 5
35	3	2	1.5	3.5	1.80 2
34	2	0	1.0	1.0	.52 .5
N	194		$1/194 \times 100 = .51546$ after Gulliksen, 1950		

The next step is to make the entries in the column headed *Cum. f,* a column of the cumulative frequencies *below* each score. In the row which begins with raw score 37, $10 + 3 + 2$ equals the *Cum. f* 15. The column headed $f/2$ lists one-half the frequency of each raw score. For example, $24/2 = 12.0$. In the column headed *Cum. f'* are listed each *Cum. f* plus its corresponding $f/2$. For example, $15 + 12.0 = 27.0$.

Each value in the *Cum. f'* column may be divided by N and multiplied by 100, or, after placing $1/N \times 100$ in the keyboard of a desk calculator, successive multiplication by each *Cum. f'* without clearing the keyboard will yield the percentiles or percentile ranks. A desk calculator may be used, but a slide rule will suffice.

Using a desk calculator

The procedure described below can be accomplished with a desk calculator given only a list of raw scores in order of decreasing size and their frequencies, *f*. (Where the range of raw scores is large, their tally in a table rather than a list is recommended, each row of cells corresponding, for example, to 35, 36, 37, 38, 39 or even to 30, 31, 32, . . . , 39.)

1. Calculate $\dfrac{100}{2N}$.

2. Place $\dfrac{100}{2N}$ in the keyboard, making the last digit one unit higher, for example, .25774 rather than .25773.

3. Multiply by 2N and set the decimal point marker in the product dials. (For example, 100.00. . . or possibly 99.99. . . .) Clear the dials, but not the keyboard.

4. Multiply by the frequency nearest the bottom of the scale and record the rounded-off value in the product dials as the percentile rank of the score corresponding to this frequency. Clear counting dials only.

5. Multiply again by the frequency nearest the bottom of the scale, clear counting dials only and multiply by the next higher frequency in the scale. Record the rounded-off value in the product dials as the percentile rank of the midpoint of the score corresponding to the "next higher" frequency. Clear counting dials only.

6. Multiply successively by the second and third frequencies from the bottom of the scale to secure the percentile rank of the score corresponding to the third frequency up from the bottom.

The process is repeated, multiplying each time by the frequency corresponding to the score for which the percentile rank is being computed and by the next lower frequency in the scale. (The latter is most conveniently the first of the two multipliers.) When the percentile rank of the highest score in the scale has been obtained and the counting dials cleared, multiplication again by the frequency of the highest score should result in a number that equals, or rounds off, to 100 in the product dials—thus checking the entire calculation except for very improbable compensating errors. The procedure just described is a simplification of one devised by Thurstone.[4]

When either of the two methods explained above are applied to frequency distributions with class intervals greater than unity, percentiles of the midpoints of the intervals are obtained. The midpoints and their percentiles can be used in drawing percentile graphs or ogives from which the percentile ranks of individual scores can be esti-

---

[4] L. L. Thurstone, "Note on the Calculation of Percentile Ranks," *Journal of Educational Psychology* 18 (December 1927), pp. 617–20.

mated. It is usually less effort and more accurate to tally each score as suggested above.

Standard scores

If two tests are given to the same pupils—unless the tests are equivalent forms—one cannot compare a pupil's raw score on one of the tests with his raw score on the other. The score units are unequal and are not measured from the same reference point. If, however, it is assumed that the test means represent the same levels of ability and the standard deviations represent the same spreads in ability, reference points and a basis for equal units are established. One type of standard score is the z score for which the standard deviation itself is the unit. If the raw score on one test is .5 standard deviation above the mean of that test, the z score is + .5. If the raw score is 1.3 standard deviations below the mean the z score is − 1.3. A distribution of such z scores for the population of pupils or students used in determining z scores necessarily has a mean of 0 and a standard deviation of 1. Since the z score unit is comparatively coarse (68 percent of pupils may earn z scores between + 1 and − 1) and many people dislike dealing with negative numbers, standard scores are usually based on arbitrary means and standard deviations other than 0 and 1. Probably the most frequently used values are 50 and 10, although other values are used rather widely. Examples are the 500 and 100 of College Board scores and the 5 and 2 of stanines.

Obtaining linear standard scores

If the primes stand for standard scores X' and X stands for raw scores, according to the assumption earlier stated,

$$\frac{X - \bar{X}}{s_x} = \frac{X' - \bar{X'}}{s'_x}. \tag{8.11}$$

A given standard score X' deviates as much from its mean $\bar{X'}$ in terms of its standard deviation s'_x as the corresponding raw score X deviates from its mean $\bar{X}$ in terms of its standard deviation. This is a *linear* relationship, and the standard scores obtained are called *linear* standard scores. If corresponding values of X and X' are plotted on graph paper with X one axis and X' the other, the graph is a straight line.

If we use 50 and 10 as the arbitrary values for $\bar{X'}$ and s'_x the equality given above becomes

$$\frac{X - \bar{X}}{s_x} = \frac{X' - 50}{10},$$

and if we solve for X'

$$X' = \frac{10}{s_x} X + (50 - \frac{10}{s_x} \bar{X}).$$ (8.12)

Where $\bar{X} = 94.35$ and $s_x = 13.52$

$$X' = \frac{10}{13.52} X + (50 - \frac{10}{13.52} 94.35),$$

$$X' = .74X - 19.79.$$

Formula 8.12 is convenient for setting up a conversion table. (Arbitrary values other than 50 and 10 can, of course, be used.) Each raw score X is successively substituted in the equation to obtain and list the corresponding standard score values. This can readily be done with a desk calculator, putting the multiplier .74 in the keyboard, multiplying by the highest score X, subtracting (or adding) the constant (here -19.79), replacing the highest score in the counting dials without clearing the product dials, placing .74 back in the keyboard, and then successively touching the proper key, or keys, to reduce the value of X in the counting dial one unit at a time without clearing the keyboard or product dials. The standard scores appear one after the other in the product dials and can be rounded off and listed for each X score. The same procedure may be used with simple regression equations which differ from the linear conversion equation illustrated above only in including a coefficient of correlation. See page 330 of Chapter 11.

Obtaining normalized standard scores

Normalized standard scores differ from linear standard scores in that having converted a distribution of raw scores to normalized standard scores, the distribution is normal. If the procedure is applied to distributions of raw scores on two or more tests given the same students which are skewed differently, the normalized standard scores are more comparable than linear standard scores would be. Like linear standard scores, the advantage of normalized standard scores over percentile ranks is that one can more legitimately assume equality of units along the scale of measurement.

Given a tally of the frequencies of each score and their corresponding percentile values from Table 8.7, the normalized standard scores listed in the last column of Table 8.9 on page 232 were obtained through use of the table of the areas of the unit normal curve given as Table B in the Appendix.

Two examples should suffice to illustrate the process of obtaining normalized standard scores having an arbitrary mean of 50 and a standard deviation of 10. To the left of the percentile 73.20 is 73.20 percent

Table 8.9   Determination of Normalized Standard Scores

Raw Score	f	Percentile	$\dfrac{X}{\sigma}$ or z	Normalized Standard Scores	
44	1	99.74	+2.80	78.0 or	78
43	3	98.71	+2.23	72.3	72
42	8	95.88	+1.74	67.4	67
41	19	88.92	+1.22	62.2	62
40	42	73.20	+ .62	56.2	56
39	47	50.26	+ .01	50.1	50
38	35	29.12	− .55	45.5	46
37	24	13.92	−1.08	39.2	39
36	10	5.15	−1.63	33.7	34
35	3	1.80	−2.10	29.0	29
34	2	.52	−2.56	24.4	24

of the area of a normal curve. Between this percentile and the mean is 73.20 − 50.00 percent of the area or a proportion of .2320. Entering the table of the areas and ordinates of the unit normal curve on page 522 with this proportion of area reveals that it lies between the mean and an $\dfrac{X}{\sigma}$ or a z of + .62. This is illustrated in Figure 8.10.

Figure 8.10   Normalized standard score above the mean

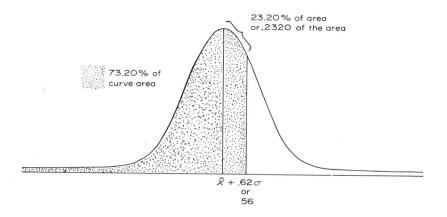

23.20% of area or .2320 of the area

73.20% of curve area

$\bar{X} + .62\sigma$
or
56

The value of + .62 is a standard score where the arbitrary mean is 0 and the arbitrary standard deviation 1, in other words, a normalized z score. To convert to a standard score scale with a mean of 50 and standard deviation of 10, each such z score is multiplied by 10 and 50 is added, for example, .62 × 10 + 50 = 56.2 or 56.

To obtain normalized standard scores for raw scores below the mean, the percentile must be *subtracted* from 50 and the result expressed as a proportion of the area of the curve. For example, $50 - 13.92 = 36.08$ or .3608. Again, using the normal curve table with .3608 as the proportion of area between the mean and $\frac{x}{\sigma}$ we find .3599 the nearest approximation to .3608 and the corresponding $\frac{x}{\sigma}$ or z of 1.08. It is taken as $- 1.08$ since the raw score is below the mean. This is illustrated in Figure 8.11.

Figure 8.11   Normalized standard score below the mean

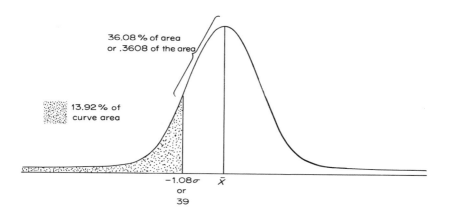

Again, $- 1.08 \times 10 + 50 = 39.2$ or 39. It is easy to see from these examples how the other normalized standard scores are obtained. It also is easy to see how arbitrary means and standard deviations other than 50 and 10 can be used.

Given percentiles of midpoints of class intervals other than unity, the midpoints and their corresponding standard score values may be plotted on fine cross section paper and connected with a line graph. This may be used in estimating for each raw score its corresponding standard score.

The procedures explained in this section should be useful to any-one interested in establishing local norms for standardized tests as an aid to placement and counseling in any school or college, or in convert-ing scores on a test especially constructed for use in educational research.

Practice Exercise   8.3

Given the following unit tally of raw scores, determine the percentile ranks which would usually be listed for each score and for the raw scores of 43 and 36, and determine the corresponding linear standard scores and the normalized standard scores having an arbitrary mean of 50 and a standard deviation of 10. The raw score mean and standard deviation are given for your convenience.

Raw Score	f	
46	1	
45	3	
44	5	
43	8	
42	13	$\overline{X} = 40.13$
41	12	
40	19	$s_x = 2.55$
39	14	
38	9	
37	5	
36	4	
35	3	
34	2	
N	98	The answers to this exercise are on page 530.

The answers to this exercise are on page 530.

Questions for
Study and Discussion

1. Until recent years, intelligence quotients were obtained by computing the ratio between mental age and chronological age. Was *IQ* thus calculated a ratio variable?

2. How many significant figures are there in each of the following numbers?

    6300,   630.,   6.30,   and   .063

3. An excessively difficult test is given to students and a frequency distribution obtained. Will the distribution be positively or negatively skewed? Will the mean be lower or higher than the median?

4. When is it desirable to change the frequencies of frequency distributions to percentages?

5. What is the percentile rank of a standard score of 60 where the arbitrary mean of the standard scores is 50 and the standard deviation 10?

6. Pairs of Centigrade and Fahrenheit readings are obtained daily for 90 days. Estimate the correlation between these paired measures. Are they ratio or interval variables?

7. After calculating a coefficient of correlation between scores on a reading and an arithmetic test, it was discovered that the scoring of the latter was characterized by numerous random errors. What effect did this have on the computed coefficient?

8. A counselor tells a student that his score on an aptitude test is in the top quartile. What is wrong with this statement?

9. Five units are added to each of the scores on Test X and these scores are correlated with scores on Test Y. Which of the following will be affected?

$$\bar{X} \quad Md_x \quad Q \quad s_x \quad r_{xy}$$

10. If a distribution of observed scores has a normal distribution, what three measures mentioned in this chapter are numerically equal to each other and what two measures, though numerically unequal, are measures of variability?

11. An office of institutional research has converted the scores on a test to percentile ranks. After the scores have thus been converted, a frequency distribution of the percentile ranks is tallied using class intervals of 10. A histogram is drawn to portray the distribution. What will it look like?

12. One formula for the coefficient of correlation is $r_{xy} = \dfrac{\Sigma z_x z_y}{N}$ or $\dfrac{\Sigma z_x z_y}{N-1}$.

    Explain why this formula is algebraically equivalent to Formula 8.9 on page 220. Why not use it instead of Formula 8.9?

13. In what ways are stanines preferable to percentile ranks in the interpretation of test scores?

14. There is a low correlation between the scores on reliable tests of clerical aptitude and of mechanical aptitude. How does this influence the interpretation of the scores?

15. Discuss the early history of the coefficient of correlation. If it is available to you in your institutional or public library consult *Studies in the History of Statistical Method* by Helen M. Walker.

Suggestions
for Further Study

The student interested in continuing his study of descriptive statistics will find it useful to consult certain of the texts listed among the selected references at the end of Chapter 9. For those who feel a lack of basic mathematical skills the appendix of Edwards' *Statistical Methods for the Behavioral Sciences* and Walker's *Mathematics Essential for Elementary Statistics* will be especially helpful. The texts by Edwards, Blommers and Lindquist, Downie and Heath, Ferguson, Guilford, McNemar, and Tate are all excellent sources of information with reference to descriptive statistics. Most of these texts are also among the sources recommended in supplementing Chapters 9, 10, 11 and 13.

9

Interpreting Data: Elementary Statistical Inference

Educational data are frequently and routinely reported for local consumption in schools, school systems, and colleges. Much use is made of the techniques explained in Chapter 8. Often the data are relevant to entire pupil populations, for example, frequency distributions of the scores of all sixth-grade pupils on general scholastic aptitude and achievement test batteries administered in a local testing program. Scores may be converted to standard scores or percentile ranks and comparisons made with published norms. Such summaries of data, useful as they are, do not deserve to be called "educational research." As emphasized earlier, educational research is concerned with problems and the data are collected to answer questions or to test hypotheses. When the data are from random samples, inferences or generalizations derived from the testing of hypotheses are applicable to the populations from which the samples were drawn. Some of the concepts and procedures of statistical inference which evaluate the dependability of such generalizations will be introduced in this chapter.

THE IMPORTANCE OF RANDOM SAMPLING

Random sampling is fundamental to statistical inference. Unless samples are chosen at random from the populations to which generalizations are to apply, the use of interval estimates and significance tests is questionable. When random sampling is used, each element of a population has an equal and independent chance of being included in the sample. A random sample may not be a representative one, but the techniques of statistical inference make it possible to take into account chance departures from representativeness in deriving generalizations from the data.

Selecting representative samples of schools or pupils within schools without randomization results in biased samples. The possibility of adequately accounting for the effect of bias in generalizing is rare. Randomization is of special importance in experimental research both in the selection of samples of pupils to participate and in their assignment to different treatments. Random assignment to different groups promotes control of those factors which can bias experimental findings.

Unfortunately, random sampling is not always feasible. The researcher must collect his data from schools or pupils which are available. In such cases, as has been emphasized, it is especially desirable to describe the characteristics of the sample so that the reader of the research report is better able to judge the kind of population to which the findings apply. Although, strictly speaking, the techniques of statistical inference should not be used in the absence of random sampling, their use has become conventional. Obviously, such use does not eliminate biases which can occur when other than a random sample is selected.

Frequently, even when a random sample is obtained, a researcher will generalize to a hypothetical population or universe, typified by the population actually sampled, but assumed to be indefinitely larger—"all" seventh-grade pupils.

While it often seems impractical to obtain a random sample of pupils or schools, the researcher should not give up too easily. A school superintendent or a college administrator can be convinced that random sampling is a basic requirement for excellence in research. The administrator may be assured that he can have greater confidence in generalizations derived from survey or experimental data where pupils or schools are selected at random. Random sampling will also be more acceptable to the administrator when careful planning eliminates or greatly reduces disruption of usual school activities. For example, pupils or schools may be selected at random prior to the start of a school year. In conducting an experiment, pupils may be assigned at random to classes which will receive different methods of instruction before classes are organized in the usual way.

SELECTING A RANDOM SAMPLE

Statistics and parameters

Given the data obtained from a sample, one can calculate a mean, a standard deviation, a coefficient of correlation, or a percentage. These are "statistics" while the unknown values in the population or universe to which the generalizations are to apply are "parameters." The symbols used are:

	SAMPLE STATISTIC	POPULATION PARAMETER
Mean	$\overline{X}$	μ (mu)
Standard deviation	s	σ (sigma)
Coefficient of correlation	r	ρ (rho)
Proportion	p	ϕ (phi)

Note that small Greek letters are used to designate parameters. The symbols $\overline{X}$ and $\overline{Y}$ or $\overline{X}_1$ and $\overline{X}_2$ are increasingly used to designate sample means rather than M_x and M_y or M_1 and M_2. The symbol $\overline{D}$ is used to designate the mean of the individual differences between pairs of scores. The symbols s and σ suffice to designate a standard deviation of scores or other measures of a sample or population when only one variable is under consideration. Where there is more than one variable such subscripts as 1 and 2, x and y, or x_1 and x_2 are used. When, however, lettered subscripts are below a short vertical bar, a standard error is designated, for example, $s_{\overline{x}}$ designates the standard error of the mean of the sample scores, $\overline{X}$, while $s_{\overline{x}_1 - \overline{x}_2}$ or $s_{\overline{D}}$ designates the standard error of a difference.

The summation sign Σ should not be confused with s or σ. It is unfortunate that ρ is also the conventional symbol for a coefficient of rank correlation and that ϕ is also used for the phi coefficient. The symbols for neither of these statistics are needed in this chapter.

Point estimates and interval estimates

Given a statistic relevant to a sample, a point estimate or an interval estimate may be made. The former is an estimate of some specific value of a population parameter. The mean of a random sample is an unbiased estimator of the mean of the population from which the sample was drawn. According to the Law of Large Numbers, the larger the size of the sample the more probable it is that the sample mean approximates the population mean. An interval estimate, or more specifically a confidence interval, based on the data of a sample, is a range of scores or other measures within which a parameter is presumed to fall at a specified level of probability or confidence. The sample statistic may be the mean, its standard error, and the confidence interval obtained from them. This is explained in greater detail in later discussion of the standard error of the mean and the standard errors of other statistics.

Sample statistics also include differences between means, correlation coefficients, and percentages or proportions. In interpreting such differences, it may be hypothesized that the population difference is zero, a null hypothesis often given the symbol H_0. In the case of two means, for example, it may be hypothesized that $\mu_1 = \mu_2$ and an interval estimate ranging equally above and below zero obtained from the data. As will be explained in more detail later, the observed difference is then compared with this range of measures. If it extends from zero beyond the limits of the range, either positively or negatively, the null hypothesis is rejected. When this occurs it is inferred at a specified level of probability that the population difference is other than zero. It may be concluded, for example, that the observed difference is "statistically significant" at the 1 percent or the 5 percent level. Frequently, these levels are referred to as the .01 level and the .05 level.

The interval estimate used in testing a null hypothesis should not be called a confidence interval. A confidence interval can be used with reference to a difference, however, in estimating the range within which the population difference can be presumed to fall at a given level of confidence. This is especially useful in evaluating the "practical" importance of a highly significant difference. A small difference of little practical importance may be highly significant primarily because large samples were used.[1]

Sampling distributions as models

In understanding the making of interval estimates or in testing the significance of differences, a mathematical model is needed. The type of mathematical model referred to here is a sampling distribution. Such a frequency distribution can be obtained empirically. For example, in the case of the standard error of the mean, very numerous random samples can be drawn and a frequency distribution of the means obtained. According to the Central Limit Theorem, such distributions of means for large samples tend to approximate a normal distribution. Hence, the normal curve defined by a complex equation is accepted as the model. Both the curve and its equation are presented in Figure 9.1.

The symbol Y stands for the height of the curve at any value of X along the horizontal axis; e equal to 2.718 . . . is the base of natural logarithms; and π is, of course, 3.1416. . . . The standard deviation of X, σ, and the mean, μ, are appropriately in Greek letters since they pertain to a theoretical distribution rather than to sample data.

In the case of differences between means of large samples, the sampling distribution is also normal, but for relatively small samples,

---

[1] Quinn McNemar, *Psychological Statistics,* 4th ed. (New York: Wiley, 1969), p. 105.

Figure 9.1 Normal curve and equation of the normal distribution

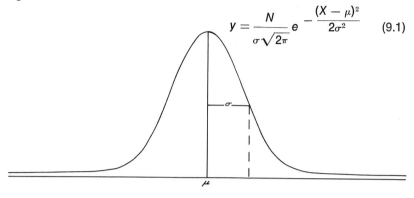

$$y = \frac{N}{\sigma\sqrt{2\pi}}\, e^{\, -\frac{(X - \mu)^2}{2\sigma^2}} \qquad (9.1)$$

the sampling distributions depart from the normal. They may be represented by a family of curves, one curve for each sample of different size or numbers of degrees of freedom. All the curves have the same area and are similar to the normal curve in shape, but decrease slightly and progressively in height while increasing slightly in spread, thus increasing the area in each tail. These curves are the curves of the sampling distributions of *t,* a ratio useful in testing the significance of differences. Such tests are explained later in this chapter.

The sampling distributions of coefficients of correlation, especially of those of considerable size, whether positive or negative, are not normal. This contingency is met by converting the correlation coefficient to another statistic which is approximately normally distributed. A percentage or proportion (a percentage of 76 is a proportion of .76) has a sampling distribution which is a binomial distribution.[2] If, however, the number of individuals in the sample (*N*), is reasonably large and the population proportion (ϕ), is not close to zero or one, the sampling distribution approximates the normal. Tables of the ordinates and areas of the unit normal curve are useful in obtaining interval estimates or in testing the statistical significance of sample differences in percentages, or in percentages changed to proportions. If samples are small, use is made of the binomial distribution and "exact" probabilities are obtained. Two other types of sampling distributions may be mentioned: those of χ^2 (chi square), useful when observed frequencies or proportions are compared with each other or with theoretical frequencies or proportions, and *F* distributions useful in comparing

---

[2] See pages 269 and 270 for curves representing particular binomial and χ^2 distributions.

variances (essentially squared standard deviations). The *F* distributions are the basis of tables of *F* especially useful in analysis of variance. Both χ^2 and *F* distributions may be depicted by whole families of curves whose shapes are a function of the sample size, or more precisely, the degrees of freedom.

As earlier suggested, sampling distributions may be obtained empirically. This is usually done to illustrate concretely the kind of curve, or kinds of curves, representing the sampling distribution. The tables of values actually used to obtain critical values in setting limits to interval estimates within which a parameter may be expected to occur with a given probability, or in testing the significance of differences, are obtained from computations using complex algebraic equations. These equations correspond to curves approximated by the empirically obtained curves. The theoretical curves are mathematical models. The normal curve is such a model, an abstraction having no more real existence than a perfect circle. Consider in this connection the following quotation from Kenneth Rexroth's discussion of Plato's *Republic:* "It was intended as a model in the mathematical sense, a Platonic Form of the Perfect State, which even an actualized state, as perfect as could be conceived, would resemble no more than a plate does the circle in Euclid."[3]

Degrees of freedom

The number of degress of freedom, rather than *N,* occurs in the denominator of formulas used in computing unbiased estimators of population variances (for example, *N* −1 as noted in Chapter 8). The number of degrees of freedom also occurs in formulas for computing standard deviations, standard errors, coefficients of correlation, and other estimators of parameters. In addition, degrees of freedom are used when consulting tables of *t,* χ^2, and *F* in making tests of significance. Where *N* is the number of observations in a sample, *N* − 1 may be the number of degrees of freedom of values of the observations which are free to vary. Given the five scores 12, 15, 19, 23, and 26, the mean is 19. The deviations from the mean are respectively − 7, − 4, 0, + 4, and + 7. If any four of these deviations are known, the fifth is determined, because the sum of the deviations from the mean must equal zero. Only four of the deviations or scores corresponding to them are free to vary, hence the number of degrees of freedom is 4. If you were asked to list three numbers whose sum is to be 15, as soon as you

---

[3] Kenneth Rexroth, "Plato's 'Republic'," *Saturday Review,* 33, February 19, 1966. A Platonist might object, however, that the Platonic Forms alone are real.

name two numbers the third is fixed. Hence, here the number of degrees of freedom is 2.[4]

USING A TABLE OF RANDOM NUMBERS
TO OBTAIN A RANDOM SAMPLE

It is fundamental in random sampling that each member of the population from which the sample is drawn has the same probability or chance of being included in the sample. The selection of each member of the sample should be independent of the selection of any other member. The selection of one member of the sample should not in any way influence the selection of any other member of the sample if it is truly random. Such samples are most readily obtained through the use of tables of random numbers.

If, for example, 12 of 85 elementary schools in a school system are to participate in a survey-type study or in an experiment, the 85 schools should be numbered from 1 to 85. Then, turning to a table of random numbers the researcher starts at some randomly selected point in the table and successively observes pairs of digits moving horizontally or vertically and lists the first twelve pairs of digits, no single pair exceeding 85 numerically. When a given pair of digits recurs, the pair is ignored. The process can be illustrated using random numbers from Table A in the Appendix. Let us start with the eleventh

70997
49626
88974
48237
77233

77452
89368
31273
23216
42698

09172
47070
13363
58731
19731

line of the fifth column and use the first pair of digits in each group of five digits. The random numbers with which we are concerned are listed at the left. Using the first two digits, the twelve schools randomly chosen are those numbered 70, 49, 48, 77, 31, 23, 42, 9, 47, 13, 58, and 19. Note that numbers 88 and 89 are not used since they are greater than 85. Note also that 77 recurs. It may seem a little strange that schools 47, 48, and 49 are among those chosen, but the "die was cast" when the starting point was randomly selected. Further, it is probably a matter of chance also that these schools were serially numbered 47, 48, and 49. If the number of schools in the population of schools to be sampled is between 100 and 999, three digit random numbers would be successively considered. Suppose that the population consists of 815 schools and that 12 are to be selected at random. If the same starting point is randomly chosen and the first three digits of each group of five considered, the sample of 12 schools would be those numbered 709,

---

[4] For a classic discussion of degree of freedom, see Helen Walker, "Degrees of Freedom," *Journal of Educational Psychology* 31 (April 1940), pp. 253–60.

496, 482, 772, 774, 312, 232, 426, 91, 470, 133, and 587. Normally, one would not randomly twice select the same starting point.

The same process may be employed in selecting a simple random sample of pupils. All the pupils in the population must be numbered serially. The number of the highest numbered pupil has the number of digits of each of the succession of random numbers considered. (Three digit numbers include, of course, such numbers as 007, 029, and 307.) If the pupil population to be sampled is, for example, all of the seventh-grade pupils in several similar elementary schools, each school may be assigned a range of serial numbers sufficient to cover all the seventh-grade pupils in that school. If the schools differ materially in types of pupil population, it will be desirable to classify them by types or "strata." A random sample is then chosen for each stratum and these samples studied both separately and as an appropriately weighted total sample. Stratified sampling, cluster sampling, and multistage sampling are all characterized by randomization. Such sampling techniques are discussed briefly in Chapter 10 and in greater detail in the texts cited in that chapter.

Sampling with and without replacement

It was stated earlier that if a random number recurs, it is ignored. This is random sampling without replacement. Suppose that small disks were numbered from 1 to 85, placed in a container and 12 disks drawn successively, shaking the container well between each draw. Obviously no given number of the 85 would recur. Again, this is sampling without replacement. Both procedures are sampling without replacement and from a relatively small or finite population. The number of different samples that could be drawn in this way, the number of combinations of 85 taken 12 at a time, or C_{12}^{85}, is almost 132,000 billion. The variability of the means of even this large number of possible samples is slightly restricted so that in computing the standard error of the mean, the finite population correction explained on page 263 should appropriately be applied. (In the sample of 12 of 85 pupils the standard error as usually computed should be multiplied by .93.)

If, however, as each disk is drawn it is replaced in the container or a recurring random number is not ignored, we have random sampling with replacement. Since in theory disks may be drawn in this way an infinite number of times and a large table of random numbers may be used an indefinitely large number of times, the drawing of a single sample is, in effect, sampling from an infinite population. (Where a population of schools is sampled in either of these ways, the occurrence of the same school more than once may be difficult to explain to a school superintendent.)

When the sample is relatively large in comparison with the population from which it was drawn using a table of random numbers, it is appropriate to ignore an occasional recurring random number and to use the finite population correction. When, however, the population is relatively large as compared with the size of the sample, random numbers recur less frequently and the finite population correction need not be applied. If, for example, the population and the sample were 815 and 12, rather than 85 and 12, the correction of .99+ is negligible. Furthermore, it is quite customary in such cases to generalize, not to the population actually existing here and now, but to a more hypothetical indefinitely large population of which the population sampled is assumed to be representative.

STANDARD ERRORS OF MEANS AND OF DIFFERENCES BETWEEN MEANS

It was mentioned earlier that data obtained from a sample are frequently used as a basis for generalizations applying to the population from which the sample was drawn. One kind of a generalization is an inference with respect to the population mean derived from a sample mean and its standard error.

The standard error of the mean

The standard error of the mean of a *random* sample is an estimate of the standard deviation which would be obtained if one drew a large number of such random samples, calculated the means of all these samples and, treating them like ordinary scores, calculated the standard deviation of this distribution of means. The standard error of the mean is the standard deviation of such a sampling distribution. In practice, however, the standard error of the mean of a single sample is calculated from the formula:

$$s_{\bar{x}} = \frac{s_x}{\sqrt{N}} \tag{9.2}$$

where s_x is the standard deviation of the scores in the sample.[5]

Suppose that a sample mean $\bar{X}$ is 85, the sample standard deviation s_x is 24, and N is 256. Then the standard error of the sample mean $s_{\bar{x}}$ is 1.5.

---

[5] When s_x is calculated, the squared deviations of the scores from the sample mean should be divided by $N - 1$ rather than N. If this was not done, use $N - 1$, rather than N, in the formula given above. If the first N in the denominators of Formulas 8.3 and 8.6 for standard deviations is replaced by N^2, $s_{\bar{x}}$ is directly obtained and with less rounding error. See Chapter 8, pages 213 and 216.

If we hypothesize that the population mean μ_x is 82.06 and use $s_{\bar{x}}$ as an estimate of $\sigma_{\bar{x}}$, the standard error we could obtain if we knew σ_x, the population standard deviation, the sample mean of 85 is 1.96 × $s_{\bar{x}}$ or 2.94 score units above the *hypothesized* population mean. If the population mean were 82.06, a sample mean as large or larger than 85 would occur only 2.5 percent of the time. By consulting a table of the areas of the unit normal curve,[6] it will be found that only 2.5 percent of the area is beyond 1.96 standard deviation units from the mean. Use of this area as one "tail" of the normal curve is illustrated in Figure 9.2.

Figure 9.2   Population mean hypothesized below the sample mean

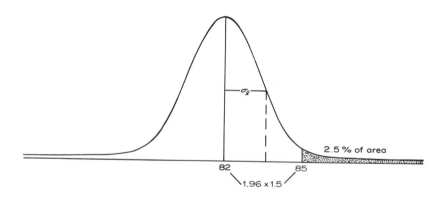

If we hypothesize that the population mean is 88, or more precisely 87.94, a sample mean as low, or lower than 85 would occur 2.5 percent of the time.[7] This is illustrated in Figure 9.3.

Note that the curves representing the distributions of the many samples that could be drawn are centered about hypothesized values of the population mean rather than about the observed mean of 85. The usual estimate of $\sigma_{\bar{x}}$, the standard deviation of the curves, is the standard error $s_{\bar{x}}$ of 1.5 obtained from a single sample.

---

[6] See Table B in the Appendix. The columns headed $\dfrac{x}{\sigma}$ list values which are in standard deviation units. For example, .50 is one-half standard deviation.

[7] "Would occur some specified percent of the time" on this and later pages means "on the average" in an infinite number of trials. It does *not* mean 1, 2.5, 5, 95, or 99 times in any given 100 trials.

Figure 9.3   Population mean hypothesized above the sample mean

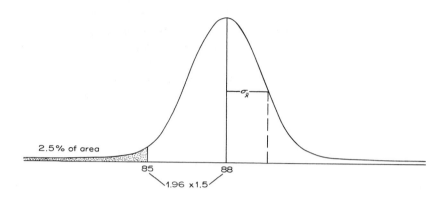

If successive random samples were drawn from a population and their means calculated, they would vary from sample to sample. If, for each of these means we estimate intervals analogous to 82–88, the probability is that 95 percent of the time these intervals will include the population mean. On the other hand, if we wish to be confident that we will be correct 99 percent rather than 95 percent of the time, the limits should be determined by using 2.58 rather than 1.96 so that the shaded areas will each be .5 percent of the area of the normal curves illustrated above. In this case, the confidence interval is approximately 81–89. Such intervals are often expressed in one of the following ways:

$$M_x - 1.96s_{M_x} \leq \mu \leq M_x + 1.96s_{M_x}$$
$$\overline{X} - 1.96s_{\overline{x}} \leq \mu \leq \overline{X} + 1.96s_{\overline{x}}$$

These inequalities imply that the chances are 95 in 100 that the population mean μ falls between the limits $M_x \pm 1.96s_{M_x}$ or $\overline{X} \pm 1.96s_{\overline{x}}$. In case of the illustrative data, 85 ± 3, or 82–88. If 99 percent confidence limits are specified, 2.58 is used instead of 1.96

In order to obtain such values as 1.96 and 2.58 from Table B in the Appendix it is necessary to locate .4750 and .4951 in the columns headed "Area." These are the areas expressed as proportions between the mean and the distances from the mean expressed in basic standard score units expressed as $\dfrac{x}{\sigma}$ as well as z. The proportions of area beyond 1.96 and 2.58 are .5000 − .4750 or .025 and .5000 − .4951 or .005, corresponding to 2.5 percent and .5 percent. In many tables of the unit normal curve it is necessary to interpolate. The 1.96 and 2.58 can more readily be obtained from the bottom row of a table of t.[8] These values are in the columns headed .05 and .01 for a two-tailed test, twice the proportion of area in each tail. It is usually best to use the table of t in the interpretation of standard errors of means and of differences between means since this table is applicable to samples, or more precisely, degrees of freedom of varying size.

The standard error of a difference

A somewhat similar procedure is used in making inferences with respect to differences between the means of samples. Suppose that one sample mean, $\overline{X}_1$, is 91 and the other sample mean, $\overline{X}_2$, is 85 and that the standard error of each mean is 1.5. If the samples are independent random samples, the standard error of the difference is computed using Formula 9.3 or its equivalent:[9]

$$s_{\overline{x}_1 - \overline{x}_2} = \sqrt{s_{\overline{x}_1}^2 + s_{\overline{x}_2}^2} = \sqrt{1.5^2 + 1.5^2} = 2.12. \qquad (9.3)$$

For simplicity let us say that this standard error of the difference between the means equals 2.0. Let us also assume that it is a good estimate of $\sigma_{\overline{x}_1 - \overline{x}_2}$ or σ_D, the standard deviation of all the differences between the means which would be obtained from a succession of pairs of independent random samples drawn from the population to which we wish to generalize—a sampling distribution of such differences. Let us hypothesize that there is no population difference, or that this difference is zero. As mentioned earlier, it is hypothesized that $\mu_1 = \mu_2$. This is a null hypothesis. If the population difference is zero, how often as a result of *chance* would a difference as large as 91 − 85, or 6, occur?

If a difference as large as 6 would thus occur less than 1 percent of the time, we reject the null hypothesis and say that the observed difference is significant at the 1 percent or .01 level. The sampling distribution of differences may be drawn with the hypothetical population or universe difference of 0 at the center.

One can see from Figure 9.4 that a difference equal to, or greater than, 5.16 above or below 0 will occur 1 percent or less than 1 percent of the time as a result of the operation of chance. Since the observed difference of 6 is somewhat larger than 5.16, it too is significant at the

---

[8] See Table C in the Appendix.

[9] Formula 9.3 is modified as Formula 13.1. In effect the standard errors of each mean are averaged. See page 406.

Figure 9.4 Curve illustrating a two-tailed test of the significance of a difference

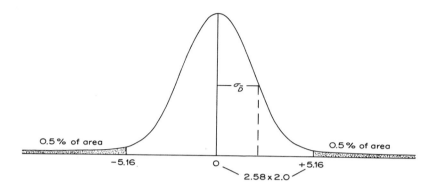

1 percent level and the null hypothesis is rejected. In thus rejecting a null hypothesis we can assume that in the long run the decision to reject will be correct 99 percent of the time. One percent of the time when we so reject a null hypothesis and infer that a real difference exists, we will be in error. This is called an *error of the first kind.* On the other hand, if the observed difference, though real in the population to which we wish to generalize, is not large enough to be significant, an *error of the second kind* occurs. The higher the standard set for significance, the more often errors of the second kind occur. This will be discussed further with reference to the specifying of levels of significance.

An observed difference has been previously expressed as a multiple of its standard error to see whether or not it extends into the critical area at either end of the curve. Usually this purpose is accomplished by computing the ratio between a difference and its standard error. The ratio is labeled z for large samples, or degrees of freedom, and t for smaller ones. For example,

$$z \text{ or } t = \frac{\bar{X}_1 - \bar{X}_2}{s_{\bar{x}_1 - \bar{x}_2}}, \tag{9.4}$$

$$= \frac{6}{2} = 3.00.$$

For large samples this ratio can be as small as 2.58 or 1.96 for significance at the 1 percent and 5 percent levels. For degrees of freedom as small as 14, the t of 3.00 is still significant at the 1 percent level. When formula 9.3 is used to obtain $s_{\bar{x}_1 - \bar{x}_2}$ the number of degrees of freedom with which to enter a table of t is $N_1 + N_2 - 2$ where the N's are the numbers of subjects in each sample.

Often $-(\mu_1 - \mu_2)$ or some hypothesized population value other than 0 concludes the numerator of Formula 9.4. For a null hypothesis that states $\mu_1 = \mu_2 = 0$, $\bar{X}_1 - \bar{X}_2$ should suffice.

Formulas for the standard error of a difference when samples are not independent

Formula 9.3 is applicable in testing the difference between two means where the samples are independently chosen at random. If a sample of pupils is tested twice with the same test, or equivalent forms of the same test, and the intention is to test the significance of a difference between the two means, Formula 9.5 may be used.

$$s_{\bar{x}_1 - \bar{x}_2} = s_{\bar{D}} = \sqrt{s_{\bar{x}_1}^2 + s_{\bar{x}_2}^2 - 2s_{\bar{x}_1} s_{\bar{x}_2} r_{12}} \qquad (9.5)$$

where r_{12} is the correlation between the paired scores of the same pupils and the standard error of each mean is obtained as earlier explained.

The same standard error can be obtained from the individual differences between the pairs of scores. Let D represent such an individual difference. Then $\dfrac{\Sigma D}{N}$ equals $\bar{X}_1 - \bar{X}_2$, or $\bar{D}$, the mean of the differences. Some of the differences between the pairs of scores will be positive and some negative. Their sum and their mean will be negative if $\bar{X}_2$ is greater than $\bar{X}_1$. Their squares and, of course, the sum of their squares will be positive. Given the sum of these ΣD^2 and the square of the sum of the differences $(\Sigma D)^2$, Formula 9.6 may be used to obtain the standard error.

$$s_{\bar{D}} = \sqrt{\frac{N \Sigma D^2 - (\Sigma D)^2}{N^2(N - 1)}} . \qquad (9.6)$$

Here N is the number of pairs. (Note that this formula with X—a score—instead of D—a difference—is the formula suggested in footnote 5 for the standard error of a mean of scores or other measures.)

If the z or t ratio is desired, it is most readily obtained by placing ΣD instead of $\bar{D}$ in the numerator of Formula 9.4 and by replacing $N^2(N - 1)$ with $(N - 1)$ in Formula 9.6 to obtain the denominator of the ratio. These changes result in Formula 13.3 as given on page 407.

When Formula 9.5, 9.6, or 13.3 is used, the number of degrees of freedom is one less than the number of pairs of scores. These formulas may be used in testing the significance of differences between the posttest means or mean gains of two groups in experiments where the subjects have been paired on the basis of their pretest scores prior to the introduction of the experimental instruction. Formulas 9.5, 9.6, and

13.3 will result in the same value of z or t for the same data. Another formula, the matched groups formula, involves the correlation between the measures used in matching or pairing and the gains or posttest scores. This is discussed further in Chapter 13.

Two-tailed versus one-tailed tests

The significance test illustrated by Figure 9.4 and discussed in relation to this figure is called a "two-tailed" test since two "tails" of the curve representing the sampling distribution of differences are involved. For some problems a "one-tailed" test may be made. We still form a null hypothesis that the true difference is zero, but we wish to estimate the probability that one population mean is greater than the other, in other words, that the difference is in a specified direction. When the research hypothesis is $\mu_1 > \mu_2$, the null hypothesis is $\mu_1 \leq \mu_2$. When the research hypothesis is $\mu_1 < \mu_2$, the null hypothesis is $\mu_1 \geq \mu_2$. In the case of a one-tailed test applied to a difference based on data from large samples, the difference must be equal to or greater than $2.33s_{\bar{x}_1 - \bar{x}_2}$, or $2.33s_{\bar{D}}$, for significance at the 1 percent level or equal to or greater than $1.64s_{\bar{x}_1 - \bar{x}_2}$ or $1.64s_{\bar{D}}$ for significance at the 5 percent level. This is illustrated for the 5 percent level by Figure 9.5 using the same error of 2.0.

Figure 9.5 Curve illustrating a one-tailed test of the significance of a difference

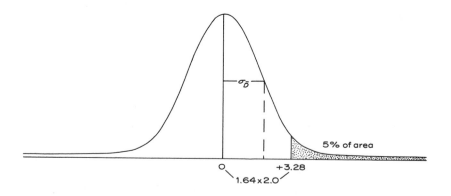

Obviously, the standards for significance are lower for a one-tailed test than for a two-tailed one. Smaller differences are significant. Some authorities object to one-tailed tests for this reason. Their use seems logical when, for example, the research hypothesis is that some new method of instruction is more effective than the method previously used. It should be emphasized, however, that it is not an acceptable practice to decide to use a one-tailed test after discovering that a difference is nonsignificant when a two-tailed test is made. It is also not good practice to make a one-tailed test "where samples of unequal size have been drawn from a badly skewed population."[10]

The specification of significance levels

The higher the level of significance specified, the less likely it is that errors of the first kind will occur. When the consequences of making an error of the first kind are truly serious, it is better to specify the 1 percent level, or even higher, than a lower level. If, for example, the problem calls for the testing of a research hypothesis whose affirmation will support its acceptance as an important general principle, the corresponding null hypothesis should not be rejected except at a relatively high level of significance. If a new method of instruction will be much more expensive than the method presently in use, a relatively high level of significance should also be specified.

It was earlier noted, however, that the higher the level of significance specified, the more likely the occurrence of errors of the second kind. The rejection of a null hypothesis at the 5 percent level may justify tentative acceptance of a research hypothesis pending further research on the problem. Similarly, rejection of a null hypothesis at the 5 percent, or even the 10 percent, level may justify a decision to change to some new method of instruction which requires no more effort and expense than the one now used. A decision not to change, though the new method is in fact more effective, will occur less often since the probability of an error of the second kind is smaller.

The probability of errors of the first kind is indicated by the level of significance chosen for the rejection of an hypothesis. For the 5 percent level it is an α (alpha) of .05 and for the 1 percent level an α of .01. (α is the proportion of the total area blackened in the curves shown in Figures 9.4 and 9.5.)

The probability of errors of the second kind

The probability of not rejecting a null hypothesis is designated by β (beta). In estimating such probabilities it is necessary to consider hypotheses alternative to H_0, the null hypothesis. Each alternative hypothesis pertains to a population difference having its own sampling distribution. The curve at the left in Figure 9.6 is the kind of curve used

---

[10] Bela O. Baker, and others, "Weak Measurements vs. Strong Statistics," *Educational and Psychological Measurement* 26 (Summer 1966), pp. 291–309.

Figure 9.6   Curves illustrating a β of .10

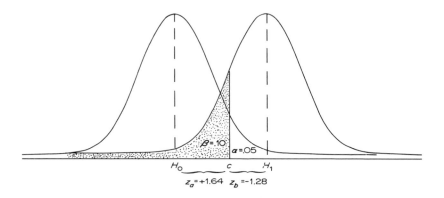

in Figure 9.5 to illustrate a one-tailed test. The curve at the right is so placed that, if H_1 were true in the population, no more than 10 percent of observed differences would result in failure to reject the null hypothesis H_0, a β of .10.

Since the curve at the left pertains to a one-tailed test with an α of .05, the distance H_0 to the critical ordinate at c is the z_a of + 1.64 in units of the standard error of the difference. The distance c to H_1, needed in locating the curve at the right, is obtained by entering a table of the areas and ordinates of the normal curve. In a detailed

table the area in the smaller portion .1003 corresponds to a $\frac{x}{\sigma}$ or z of

1.28. In Table B on page 522 of the Appendix the area .3997 from the mean must be subtracted from .5000 to obtain .1003, the β corresponding to the z_b of − 1.28. Disregarding the negative sign added to z_b, the scale distance in units of the standard error of the difference is $z_a + z_b$. This is the difference corresponding to the alternative hypothesis H_1.

A practical application of the process described above is in deciding what size random samples to use in order to preclude more than a specified proportion of errors of the second kind, for example, .10. The experimenter needs to estimate the standard deviation of his posttest scores or gains and he must also specify in *score* units a difference to correspond to H_1, usually a difference large enough to have practical or scientific importance. Suppose, for example, that the estimate of the standard deviation is 12 score units and the specified difference $\mu_1 - \mu_2$, or δ, is 4 score units. Then Formula 9.7[11] may be used to estimate N.

---

[11] For a derivation of this formula see Allen L. Edwards, *Statistical Methods*, 2nd ed. (New York: Holt, Rinehart, and Winston, 1967), pp. 239–42.

$$N = \frac{2 \sigma^2 (z_a + z_b)^2}{\delta^2},$$ (9.7)

$$= \frac{2 \times 12^2 (1.64 + 1.28)^2}{4^2},$$

$$= 153.48 \text{ or } 153.$$

Here $N = N_1 + N_2$. Two groups of 153 individuals each are needed. The symbols σ, δ (delta), μ_1, and μ_2 all pertain to population parameters.

In the case of a two-tailed test at the 5 percent level, the z_a of 1.64 is replaced by 1.96 corresponding to an $\alpha/2$ of .025. Since the alternative hypothesis specifies a difference in a particular direction, only one tail of the curve for the sampling distribution of H_0 is involved.

Formula 9.7 is actually a "backward" solution of Formulas 9.2, 9.3, and 9.4, solving for N. If these formulas are applied using a standard deviation of 12, N's of 153, and the difference of 4 score units, the z of Formula 9.4 equals 2.92, the sum of z_a and z_b.

Suppose the curve of the sampling distribution of H_1 in Figure 9.6 is shifted further and further to the right to represent larger and larger hypothesized differences. The β's and the shaded area to the left of c decrease toward 0. If the curve is shifted so that its mean at H_1 coincides with c, $\beta = .50$, and half the differences observed lead to errors of the second kind. Further shifting of the curve to the left for smaller and smaller hypothesized differences is accompanied by increase in β from .50 to .95. When the alternative hypothesized difference is 0, the hypothesis becomes the null hypothesis. Although $\beta = .95$, there can be no errors of the second kind. If the population difference is truly zero, the null hypothesis should *not* be rejected. In a one-tailed test, if the shifting described above continues so that H_1 is to the left of H_0, β increases to 1.00, but there can still be no errors of the second kind. The alternative hypothesis is compatible with the null hypothesis more precisely expressed as $\mu_1 \leq \mu_2$ when the *research* hypothesis is $\mu_1 > \mu_2$, but a two-tailed test would have been preferable. In the case of a two-tailed test, as we suppose H_1 to continue to the left of H_0, β decreases from .95 toward 0. For such a test, the null hypothesis is $\mu_1 = \mu_2 = 0$ and differences may be significant whichever sample mean is the greater. The reader will find it helpful to sketch a series of figures to illustrate this.

The power of a test

Where β represents the probability of making errors of the second kind, the probability of *not* making such errors is $1 - \beta$. (It is the probability of rejecting a null hypothesis when it is not true and should, therefore, be rejected.) This probability, $1 - \beta$, is the *power* of a test. Careful study of the preceding section should prepare the reader better to understand curves of the power functions of one-tailed and two-tailed tests presented in texts on statistical method. The heights of these curves, their ordinates, are in units of $1 - \beta$.

When planning a research requiring tests of significance it is important to consider ways of reducing the probability of errors of the second kind. One means of doing this is to select the more powerful among alternative tests. *If* an observed difference is in the hypothesized direction, a one-tailed test is more powerful than a two-tailed test. When the design of an experiment justifies use of either Formula 9.5 or 9.6 for the standard error of a difference, a test resulting from their use is generally more powerful than one based on Formula 9.3. The standard error of the difference will be smaller, the ratio z or t will be larger, and the chances greater that the observed difference is significant.

Given the additional estimate of ρ—the correlation between paired posttest scores or gains—the $2\sigma^2$ of Formula 9.7 could be multiplied by $(1 - \rho)$ in obtaining an estimate of the size of each group.[12] It should be noted, however, that the number of degrees of freedom associated with Formulas 9.5 and 9.6—one less than the number of pairs of subjects—rather than the $N_1 + N_2 - 2$ associated with Formula 9.3 requires a larger t for significance. For quite small samples the test involving Formula 9.3 will be the more powerful. If the number of subjects in each group is 25 and t equals 2.00, the difference is significant at the 5 percent level for 48 degrees of freedom, but not for 24.

THE STANDARD ERROR OF MEASUREMENT

In discussing test reliability in Chapter 7 it was stated that the square root of the error variance of test scores is the standard error of measurement. Note the following proof[13] of this statement:

An observed score X equals a "true" score plus a random error of measurement, or

$$X = X_T + e. \tag{9.8}$$

If we assume that these components of X are uncorrelated with X and with each other, their variances in the *population* are

$$\sigma_x^2 = \sigma_T^2 + \sigma_e^2. \tag{9.9}$$

---

[12] Formula 9.5 becomes $\sqrt{2\,s_{\bar{x}}^2\,(1 - r_{12})}$ when the error variances of the two means are equal.

[13] For more detailed proof see one of the advanced texts cited in this chapter.

Then, if X_1 and X_2 for two randomly parallel forms are expressed as deviate measures x_1 and x_2, their *population* correlation, the coefficient of reliability

$$\rho_{xx} = \frac{\Sigma x_1 x_2}{N \sigma_{x_1} \sigma_{x_2}}$$

$$= \frac{\Sigma (x_T + e_1)(x_T + e_2)}{N \sigma_{x_1} \sigma_{x_2}}.$$

Multiplying the terms in the numerator, omitting terms in the product containing e_1 and e_2 which correlate 0 with x_T and with each other, dividing by N, assuming $\sigma x_1 = \sigma x_2$, and knowing that the true score of each person tested is the same on each form

$$\rho_{xx} = \frac{\sigma_t^2}{\sigma_x^2}. \tag{9.10}$$

Since σ_t^2 equals $\sigma_x^2 - \sigma_e^2$, Formula 9.10 may be written

$$\rho_{xx} = \frac{\sigma_x^2 - \sigma_e^2}{\sigma_x^2} \text{ or } 1 - \frac{\sigma_e^2}{\sigma_x^2}. \tag{9.11}$$

Application of simple algebra to Formula 9.11 yields the equation $\sigma_e^2 = \sigma_x^2 (1 - \rho_{xx})$ and its square root is the formula for the standard error of measurement in the population $\sigma_e = \sigma_x \sqrt{1 - \rho_{xx}}$, (9.12) or in the case of a sample

$$s_e \text{ or } s_{meas} = s_x \sqrt{1 - r_{xx}}. \tag{9.13}$$

Let us assume that a test is known to have a reliability coefficient of .90 and that the scores have a standard deviation of 15. Because this test is not perfectly reliable, we need to obtain a confidence interval in order to infer for a given observed score and for a specified level of confidence the limits within which the corresponding true score may be located. The center of such a confidence interval is the *estimated* true score rather than the observed score.[14] It is obtained by multiplying the observed score—expressed as a deviate from the mean of the observed scores—by the coefficient reliability. Suppose that the mean of the

[14] See Jum C. Nunnally, *Psychometric Theory* (New York: McGraw-Hill, 1967), p. 220, and, for a recent critical treatment, Julian C. Stanley "Reliability" in R. L. Thorndike, ed., *Educational Measurement,* 2nd ed. (Washington, D.C.: American Council on Education, 1971), pp. 356–442.

scores including one of 105 is 75. Then the estimated true score is a deviate score of $+ 27$, or 102 in score units of the test. If the observed score was 45, the estimated true score, as a deviate, is $- .27$ and in score units 48. (The standard deviation of a distribution of estimated true scores is equal to the observed standard deviation times the square root of the coefficient of reliability.) For the illustrative data the standard error of measurement

$$s_{meas} = s_x \sqrt{1 - r_{xx}},$$
$$= 15 \sqrt{1 - .90},$$
$$= 4.74.$$

For a student whose observed score is 105 and for the 95 percent level of confidence, it may be hypothesized that *if* the student's true score is as high as 111, or $102 + 1.96 \times 4.74$, an observed score of 105 or smaller would occur less than 2.5 percent of the time. Similarly, *if* a true score of 93 is hypothesized, an observed score of 105 or greater would occur less than 2.5 percent of the time. Hence, in this instance, we can be confident at the 95 percent level that the true score is between 93 and 111. The chances are about 68 in 100, or approximately 2 to 1 that the true score is between 97 and 107. It would seem that a test whose reliability coefficient is .90, a relatively high coefficient of reliability, is not very accurate—a fact to be recalled when interpreting the test scores of individual students or in assigning letter marks.

The statement that we can be confident at the 95 percent level that the true score of the student will fall between 93 and 111 needs qualification. We cannot be even so confident. The standard error of measurement is an approximation. It is an approximation in part because the coefficient of correlation used in computing it is an approximation. While it is used to evaluate the accuracy of scores of varying size on a test, recent research has shown that the dependability of a standard error of measurement decreases for scores so low that guessing affects their reliability. Very high scores, too, on an easy test are less accurate than is indicated by the standard error of measurement.[15] In Chapter 11, the standard error of measurement is further discussed in relation to the standard error of estimate used in evaluating the accuracy of predicted scores.

Fortunately, the standard error of measurement of a mean is usually very much smaller than the standard error of measurement of an in-

---

[15] Lee J. Cronbach, *Essentials of Psychological Testing*, 3rd ed. (New York: Harper, 1970), pp. 164–65.

dividual score. The value computed with Formula 9.13 can be divided by $\sqrt{N-1}$. This is seldom done because the usual standard error of a mean, as earlier noted, accounts for both variable errors of sampling and of measurement.

Practice Exercise 9.1

For a sample of 121 cases the estimate of the population standard deviation is 13. If the mean is 105, what is the interval estimate for the population mean at the 95 percent level of confidence and for the 99 percent level? Round off to whole numbers. See page 530 for the answer.

Practice Exercise 9.2

Two random samples of 61 students each are given an achievement test. The mean and the standard error of the mean of the first group are respectively 63 and 1.4, while the mean and the standard error of the mean of the second group are 59 and 1.2. What is the value of t? Is the difference between the two means significant, and, if so, at what level? Suppose that the students in the two samples were paired on a pretest and that their paired posttest scores correlate $+ .60$. Assume also that the posttest scores have the means and standard deviations previously given. What is the value of t? Is the difference between the final means significant and, if so, at what level? See page 531 for the answers to this exercise.

Practice Exercise 9.3

A test has a mean of 57, a standard deviation of 8, and a coefficient of reliability of .84. What is the standard error of measurement? A student receives a score of 68. Between what two scores (expressed as integers) can it be estimated, at the 95 percent level of confidence, that his true score is located?

Practice Exercise 9.4

An experimenter has estimated 10 score units as the standard deviation of the posttest scores of each of two groups he plans to use in an experiment. He presumes that a difference of 5 score units significant at the 5 percent level would justify change to whichever method of instruction is favored by such a difference. If errors of the second kind are not to have a probability greater than .10, what size groups should he use? If instead of using a two-tailed test as implied above, he plans a one-tailed test with an α of .05 and a β of .10, what size groups should he use? Explain the difference in the sizes of the groups.

STANDARD ERRORS OF COEFFICIENTS OF CORRELATION AND OF DIFFERENCES BETWEEN COEFFICIENTS OF CORRELATION

It was mentioned that the standard error of a mean could be obtained by calculation of the standard deviation of very numerous random samples drawn from the same population. A similar point was made with reference to the standard error of a difference. Such statements are justified on the assumption that the sampling distributions of means or differences are normal distributions. One cannot make such an assumption concerning the sampling distribution of a coefficient of correlation, especially with reference to positive or negative correlations markedly different from zero. Suppose that the correlation between two variables in the population is + .85. The correlations for samples drawn from this population may have a median of + .85, but the distribution will be skewed since none of the sample correlations can exceed 1.00, even though they may have an unrestricted range below + .85.

The transformation of r to z_r

To meet this difficulty Sir Ronald Fisher proposed the transformation of coefficients of correlation by an equation to values of z_r whose sampling distribution is very nearly normal. (This z_r is not to be confused with the z applied to the basic type of standard scores.) Table D on page 525 of the Appendix lists corresponding values of r and z_r. (The equation used is given below the table.) For an r of .10, z_r is .100. For an r of .16, z_r is .161. For an r of .70, z_r is .867. For an r of .80, z_r is 1.099. Formula 9.14 is used in computing the standard error of a z_r of any size.

$$\sigma_{z_r} = \frac{1}{\sqrt{N-3}}. \tag{9.14}$$

This standard error has the symbol σ_{z_r} rather than s_{z_r} since it is a theoretical value and is not estimated from a sample.[16] Since the sampling distribution of z_r is so nearly normal, 1.96 and 2.58 can be used in obtaining the 5 percent and 1 percent confidence intervals of z_r and, hence, of r for samples of varying size.

In interpreting r, the confidence limits for z_r are first computed and then converted to values of r. For example, if for 103 cases the observed correlation is + .80, the z_r of 1.099 has a standard error of .10. The 95 percent confidence limits are $1.099 - .10 \times 1.96 = 903$ and $1.099 + .10 \times 1.96 = 1.295$. The corresponding values of r are .72 and .86.

---

[16] McNemar, *Psychological Statistics*, p. 157.

Testing the significance of a difference between two coefficients of correlation

When it is desired to test the significance of a difference between two r's the *squared* standard errors of the corresponding z_r's, both 1 divided by $N - 3$, are used in Formula 9.15 for the standard error of a difference.

$$\sigma_{z_{r_1} - z_{r_2}} = \sqrt{\frac{1}{N_1 - 3} + \frac{1}{N_2 - 3}}. \qquad (9.15)$$

The difference between the z_r's is the numerator of the z ratio used in testing the significance of differences, a z analogous to t and not to be confused with z_r. When testing the significance of differences between two z_r's and therefore of two r's at the 5 percent and 1 percent levels, 1.96 and 2.58 are used for large or small N's. If the correlations to be compared are obtained from data relevant to the same subjects, a more complex formula for t should be used than Formula 9.15.[17]

Testing the significance of a small coefficient of correlation

When the problem is one of determining whether a relatively small correlation coefficient is significantly different from zero and N is large, the observed correlation can be compared with a standard error of

$$1/\sqrt{N} \text{ or } 1/\sqrt{N - 1}. \qquad (9.16)$$

The ratio of a small r to a standard error thus calculated has an approximately normal sampling distribution. In order to be significant at the 5 percent or 1 percent levels, the ratio should equal or exceed 1.96 or 2.58 in a two-tailed test. When, however, both r and N are relatively small

$$t = \frac{r}{\sqrt{1 - r^2}} \sqrt{N - 2} \qquad (9.17)$$

and Table C in the Appendix can be used with $N - 2$ degrees of freedom. Several of the texts on statistical method listed at the end of this chapter have tables in their appendices giving the values of r required for significance at several levels and for various degrees of freedom.

Practice Exercise 9.5

Suppose that for a sample of 226 children the correlation between their intelligence test scores and their fathers' incomes is $+ .16$. Make a

---

[17] *Ibid.*, p. 158.

one-tailed test to determine at what level the coefficient of correlation of + .16 may be significant.

Suppose that a correlation coefficient is + .30 for a sample of 32 pupils. Make a one-tailed test to determine at what level this coefficient may be significant.

Practice Exercise 9.6

For a sample of 203 first-year college students the correlation between their high school grade point average and first-year college grade-point averages is + .55. For another sample of 181 first-year students the correlation between their scores on a general scholastic aptitude test and their grade point averages is + .63. Are these correlations significantly different? If so, at what level?

MAKING INFERENCES CONCERNING NUMBERS, PERCENTAGES, OR PROPORTIONS OF OBSERVATIONS

The variables for which we compute means, differences between means, and coefficients of correlation and their standard errors are treated as continuous variables. While test scores, ages of children, numbers of pupils in classes ranging in size, are discrete whole numbers, calculating means to one or more decimals is to deal with such variables as if they can have values between successive whole numbers. With nominal data such as counts of cases falling in specified categories, for example, counts of heads and tails in tossing coins, or numbers of students responding "yes," "no," or "uncertain" to an attitude item, use may be made of the numbers or frequencies of observations, or these may be changed to percentages or proportions.

Given a random sample and a count of the number of individuals in the sample having some specific characteristic, the problem may be one of estimating the number possessing the characteristic in the population from which the sample was drawn. Often the number or frequency is converted to a percentage or proportion of the sample, and the number in the population having the characteristic is later estimated from the sample proportion or percentage. A superintendent may estimate from such a percentage the number of classes needed to provide for educable mentally handicapped pupils. It should be obvious that in interpreting a sample percentage or proportion, its standard error is needed so that the interval or range in which the population value is likely to fall can be specified with a defined level of confidence.

Standard errors of proportions or percentages

The sampling distribution of the parameter ϕ is a binomial distribution. In the case of very small samples, and extremely small or large values of p, exact or direct probabilities should be computed in order to estimate from proportions and percentages.[18] To use Formula 9.18 given below for the standard error of a proportion, Np or Nq, whichever is smaller, should be greater than 5. (If p is .65, q equals $1 - p$, or .35.) For p or q equal to .5, a sample of 10 suffices for use of the formula. If p is .2 and q is .8, or the converse is true, a sample of 25 is the smallest for which Formula 9.18 is appropriate. For a p or q of .1 or .9 a sample of 50 cases is the minimum. When this criterion is satisfied, the binomial distribution so closely approximates the normal distribution that $\pm 1.96\ s_p$ for the 95 percent level and $\pm 2.58\ s_p$ at the 99 percent level can be used to identify the limits within which the population value ϕ probably occurs. s_p should be multiplied by 100 if the interval is to be reported in percentages.

Suppose for a random sample of 92 seventh-grade pupils, the percentage of pupils reading below grade level is 36, or a proportion of .36. Then

$$s_p = \sqrt{\frac{pq}{N}} \tag{9.18}$$
$$= \sqrt{\frac{.36 \times .64}{92}}$$
$$= .05.$$

Using the same procedure as in estimating confidence intervals for a mean, the interval limits for the 95 percent level are $.36 + 1.96 \times .05$ which round off to .26 and .46, or in percentages 26 and 46. The limits for the 99 percent level are $.36 + 2.58 \times .05$ which round off to .23 and .49, or 23 and 49. Larger samples would, of course, yield shorter confidence intervals. If the inference drawn from the sample is to apply, not to "all" seventh-grade pupils but strictly to the population of 368 seventh-grade pupils in the school system from which the 92 pupils were drawn at random, ignoring any recurring random numbers, multiplication of s_p by

$$\sqrt{\frac{M - N}{M - 1}} \quad \text{or} \quad \sqrt{\frac{368 - 92}{368 - 1}} = .87$$

where M represents the size of the population. For these data, the s_p when multiplied by the finite population correction of .87, reduces it to .04 and the confidence intervals to 28–44 and 26–46 in percentages. The same correction can be applied to other standard errors, but as earlier noted, unless the sample is a comparatively large fraction of

---

[18] Where .64 is a proportion, 64 is the corresponding percentage, or 64 percent.

See one or more of the texts on statistical method listed among the selected references at the end of this chapter.

the pupil or other population from which the sample was drawn, the adjustment makes little difference in the interpretation of the data.

This discussion could immediately extend to standard errors of differences between proportions and percentages, but since the x^2 statistic can be used to accomplish the same (and other) purposes, both are considered together.

Using chi square to test differences between frequencies

Chi square symbolized by x^2 is used in many problems where comparison is made between observed and theoretical frequencies. For example, suppose that it is hypothesized that art students have no real preference for abstract art as contrasted with representational art. If a random sample of 100 art students were consulted, the expected[19] or theoretical frequencies are 50 favoring the former and 50 favoring the latter. Suppose further that the observed frequencies symbolized by O are 62 and 38. Then

$$x^2 = \sum \frac{(O - E)^2}{E} = \frac{(62 - 50)^2}{50} + \frac{(38 - 50)^2}{50} = 5.76. \qquad (9.19)$$

There is only one degree of freedom. When 62 is known 38 is determined. In order to learn whether the null hypothesis should be rejected, the sampling distribution of x^2 for one degree of freedom is needed. Such a sampling distribution can be obtained by tossing 100 coins numerous times counting heads and tails and tallying the frequency distribution of the values of $\frac{(O - E)^2}{E}$ such as $\frac{(62 - 50)^2}{50}$, $\frac{(38 - 50)^2}{50}$, $\frac{(48 - 50)^2}{50}$, $\frac{(52 - 50)^2}{50}$, and so on. The sampling distribution for five degrees of freedom can be similarly determined by tossing a single die very numerous times, calculating a x^2 for each toss, and tallying the x^2 values thus obtained. For varying degrees of freedom a family of x^2 curves can be obtained, the curve becoming more and more normal as the number of degrees of freedom nears 30. Through the use of a complex equation, tables have been derived which list values of x^2 for various probability levels and numbers of degrees of freedom from 1 to 30. (Where the number of degrees of freedom exceeds 30, compute $\sqrt{2x^2} - \sqrt{2df - 1}$ which has a nearly normal sampling distribution, and compare the result with 1.64 and 2.33 as critical values for significance at the 5 percent and 1 percent levels respectively.) For one

---

[19] The term "expected" refers to what would occur if a null hypothesis were true, for example, a difference of zero or some other theoretical value. In Formula 9.19 its symbol is E.

degree of freedom χ^2 must exceed 3.84 for significance at the 5 percent level and 6.64 for significance at the 1 percent level.

The χ^2 of 5.76 indicates that the null hypothesis can be rejected at the 5 percent level and we infer that art students in general prefer abstract art to representational art.

Testing differences when nominal variables are categorized in two or more ways

An important application of χ^2 is with reference to two variables from independent samples, each categorized in two ways. The frequencies are entered in a fourfold contingency table. Let us suppose that in a questionnaire study of alumni of a junior college, one of the questions asks the graduates whether in the future development of the junior college curriculum, college preparatory or terminal vocational offerings should receive the greater emphasis. Suppose further that the data are divided between alumni who were fulltime and parttime students. The null hypothesis is that there is no difference between former fulltime and former parttime students in attitude toward the types of curricula thus evaluated.

Suppose the data obtained are classified and recorded as follows in a fourfold or 2 × 2 table:

	Favoring college preparatory	Favoring terminal vocational	Total
Fulltime	73 A	42 B	115 A + B
Parttime	52 C	68 D	120 C + D
Total	125 A + C	110 B + D	235 N

χ^2 can be obtained from such data by subtracting expected frequencies from the observed frequencies, squaring the differences, dividing each by the corresponding expected frequency and summing. Each expected frequency can be obtained by dividing the product of the marginal frequencies in the same row and column by N: for example, for cell A, $\dfrac{115 \times 125}{235} = 61.17$. The expected cell frequencies, proportional to the marginal totals, are those which would be expected if the variables have no association with each other. (Enter the expected frequencies and marginal totals in a 2×2 table and the proportionality is apparent.) For such a fourfold table there is one degree of freedom. Given specific marginal totals, as soon as one expected frequency has been obtained the other three are determined. For example, $115 - 61.17 = 53.83$ for cell B, $125 - 61.17 = 63.83$ for cell C, and $110 - 53.83$ or $120 - 63.83 = 56.17$ for cell D. Then, using Formula 9.19:

$$\chi^2 = \frac{(73 - 61.17)^2}{61.17} + \frac{(42 - 53.83)^2}{53.83}$$
$$+ \frac{(52 - 63.83)^2}{63.83} + \frac{(68 - 56.17)^2}{56.17} = 9.57.$$

All four differences in the numerators are equal.

Instead of calculating χ^2 for data in a fourfold table as just suggested, Formula 9.20 may be used.

$$\chi^2 = \frac{N(AD - BC)^2}{(A + B)(C + D)(A + C)(B + D)}, \tag{9.20}$$
$$= \frac{235 \ (73 \times 68 - 42 \times 52)^2}{(73 + 42)(52 + 68)(73 + 52)(42 + 68)},$$
$$= 9.57.$$

For one degree of freedom, this χ^2 is significant beyond the 1 percent level for which 6.64 is required. This justifies rejection of the null hypothesis and supports the conclusion that graduates who were fulltime students are more favorable toward the development of college preparatory curricula than are graduates who were parttime students. The latter are just as significantly more favorable to the development of terminal curricula.

The procedure immediately following the fourfold table can be extended to data classified in more than two categories for each variable. For example, if one variable has three categories and the other four, the expected frequencies can be obtained as indicated above from the marginal totals and use made of Formula 9.19, adding as many terms as there are cells in the table of data. The following formula is also applicable:

$$\chi^2 = N \left[\sum \left(\frac{f^2_{rc}}{f_r f_c} \right) - 1 \right]. \tag{9.21}$$

where for a given cell of the table, f^2_{rc} is square of the frequency in that cell, f_r is the sum of the frequencies in the same row of cells, and f_c is the sum of the frequencies in the same column. If the data just given were in such a table, the first term summed would be $73^2 \div 115 \times 125$ or .3707. As many such terms will be summed as cells in the table. N is, of course, the number of individuals in the total sample. The number of degrees of freedom is $(c - 1)(r - 1)$ where c and r are the numbers of rows and columns.

Using the standard error of a difference between independent proportions instead of chi square

Formula 9.22 for testing the significance of a difference between *independent* proportions can be applied to the data in the fourfold table earlier given, after the frequencies have been changed to proportions.

$p_1 = \dfrac{73}{115} = .63$ a	$q_1 = \dfrac{42}{115} = .37$ b
$p_2 = \dfrac{52}{120} = .43$ c	$q_2 = \dfrac{68}{120} = .57$ d

$$p = \frac{125}{235} = .53 \qquad q = \frac{110}{235} = .47.$$

$$z = \frac{p_1 - p_2}{\sqrt{pq\left(\dfrac{1}{N_1} + \dfrac{1}{N_2}\right)}}, \qquad (9.22)$$

$$= \frac{.63 - .43}{\sqrt{.53 \times .47\left(\dfrac{1}{115} + \dfrac{1}{120}\right)}},$$

$$= 3.07.$$

Formula 9.22 provides for a single estimate of the error variance. In effect, the two standard errors which could be computed for the compared proportions are averaged. This is analogous to the change of Formula 9.3 to Formula 13.1.[20]

The N's are large enough to use the table of the areas and ordinates of the normal curve or the bottom row of the table of t. Since 3.07 exceeds the 2.58 required for significance at the 1 percent level, the null hypothesis is rejected. It may be noted that the square of 3.07 approximates the x^2 of 9.57 earlier obtained. If enough decimal places are used they are exactly equal.[21] x^2 has the advantage of similar application to data classified in more than two categories for each variable.

---

[20] See McNemar, *Psychological Statistics*, p. 62.

[21] If more decimal places are carried, 3.07 becomes 3.0938 whose square rounds off to 9.57.

Suppose with reference to the junior college, or similar data, one of the questions asked is whether those alumni unclassified with reference to previous type of attendance favor emphasis on development of college preparatory offerings or favor emphasis on the development of terminal curricula. In accordance with the null hypothesis, the expected frequencies are each 235/2 or 117.50 while the observed frequencies for the total sample are 125 and 110. Hence, using Formula 9.19.

$$\chi^2 = \frac{(125 - 117.50)^2}{117.50} + \frac{(110 - 117.50)^2}{117.50} = .96.$$

Now $p_1 = \frac{125}{235} = .53$ and $p_2 = \frac{110}{235} = .47$, and, for this problem, p and q have the same values as before.

$$z = \frac{.53 - .47}{\sqrt{.53 \times .47 \left(\frac{1}{125} + \frac{1}{110}\right)}} = .92.$$

Both the χ^2 and the z are obviously nonsignificant.[22]

Sampling distributions and Yates' correction

When N's, or more correctly, expected frequencies are relatively large, the sampling distributions of proportions or differences in proportions though binomial distributions so closely approximate the normal that tables of the normal curve can be used in making interval estimates or tests of significance. Similarly, sampling distributions of χ^2 may be represented by continuous curves. When, however, expected frequencies are small, continuity is impaired. Consider first in this connection the histogram of a binomial distribution as compared with a smooth normal curve. The histogram in Figure 9.7 portrays the *expected* frequencies of heads for six coins tossed 64 times: 1, 6, 15, 20, 15, 6, 1. In obtaining the probability of 6 or more heads the *expected* frequencies of 6 + 1 or 7 is divided by 64 and equals .1094. The 7 possible outcomes of a single toss of six coins range from 0—or no—heads to 6.

The mean of both the normal and the binomial distributions is 3.00. The standard deviation of the binomial distribution equals $\sqrt{npq}$ where n is the number of coins, here 6, and p and q both equal .5, the probability of a head or tail when a single coin is tossed once. The standard deviation equals 1.2247. Let us use this standard deviation as if it also applied to the continuous normal distribution although it came

---

[22] Again, if enough decimal places are carried, .92 becomes .9785 whose square rounds off to .96.

Figure 9.7   Normal curve fitted to binomial distribution

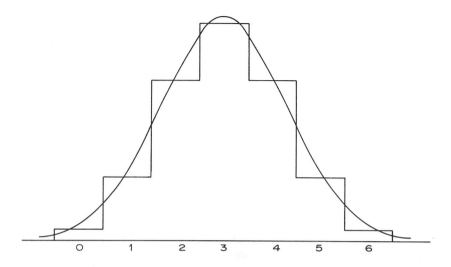

from a discrete series. Let us shift from the scale value of 5 to 4.5—
one application of Yates' *correction for continuity*—and calculate
the proportion of the area of the normal curve beyond 4.5. It is approximately .1103, not very different from the *exact* probability of
.1094. Had Yates' correction not been made, the area beyond the scale
value of 5 approximates .0516, considerably different from the .1094
obtained from the binomial distribution. As the number of coins tossed
increases, the correction becomes more and more negligible and normal curve values are increasingly justified in estimating exact probabilities.[23]

For an appropriate χ^2 curve to be applicable or more closely approximated as exemplified by the *smooth* curve in Figure 9.8, Yates'
correction for continuity is also used. When obtaining χ^2 by the procedure defined by Formula 9.19 and the smallest expected frequency is
between 5 and 10, subtract .5 from *each observed* frequency which is
greater than the corresponding expected frequency and add .5 to each
observed frequency which is less than the expected one before sub-
tracting and squaring the differences. For example, $\dfrac{(9-7)^2}{7} + \dfrac{(5-7)^2}{7}$
becomes $\dfrac{(8.5-7)^2}{7} + \dfrac{(5.5-7)^2}{7}$. In the case of Formula 9.20, first
determine the smallest expected frequency by dividing the product of

---

[23] For an example of this and more detailed explanation, see McNemar, *Psychological Statistics*, pp. 46–48.

Figure 9.8 Empirical and theoretical curves for χ^2 distributions with four degrees of freedom

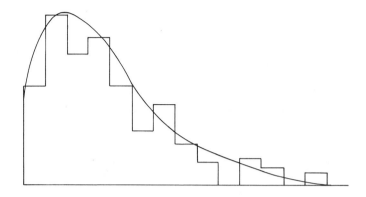

the two smallest marginal frequencies by *N*. (In the case of the data in the fourfold table on page 267 the smallest marginal frequencies are 110 and 115, therefore 54 is the smallest expected frequency.) Given an expected frequency between 5 and 10, $N/2$ is subtracted from the absolute difference[24] between *AD* and *BC* before squaring. In the case of Formula 9.22 multiply N_1 or N_2, whichever is smaller, by *p* or *q*, whichever is smaller, for a product which should exceed 5. For the data illustrating Formula 9.22, $.47 \times 115 = 54$. If the product is between 5 and 10, the quantity $\frac{1}{2}\left(\frac{1}{N_1}+\frac{1}{N_2}\right)$ should be subtracted from the absolute value of $p_1 - p_2$. Formulas 9.19, 9.20 and 9.22 should not be used where expected frequencies of less than 5 occur. Exact or direct probabilities should be computed.[25] Yates' correction need not be applied in computing χ^2 where there is more than one degree of freedom. This is the case for data to which Formula 9.21 is applicable.

Testing differences when the frequencies, percentages, or proportions are not independent

It is assumed in using the procedures discussed above that the frequencies, percentages, or proportions categorized are *independent*. When the data in the cells of a fourfold table have been obtained from the same individuals, or the individuals have been paired or matched

---

[24] Absolute difference implies a disregard for the sign of the difference. For example, if the difference between 72 and 6 below Table 9.2 on page 280 were -66, the result of the correction would be -55, not -77.

[25] McNemar, *Psychological Statistics,* pp. 62–63 and 262–63. For further discussion, see the texts by Edwards, Ferguson, Glass and Stanley, Guilford, or Walker and Lev.

as in controlled experimentation, the calculation of χ^2 or the test of the significance of a difference between proportions must be modified.[26] One type of problem for which such modification is necessary involves comparison of responses of the same group of students to two test items in order to test the significance of a difference in their difficulty. Another application occurs where the problem concerns change in attitudes from one time to another. Suppose the pupils enrolled in a course in contemporary social problems are administered an attitude inventory at the beginning and end of the course. The pupils are asked on both occasions to indicate agreement or disagreement with reference to such an item as:

The race of a prospective buyer should not be considered in selling a house.

Suppose that the frequencies of the responses are entered in the following fourfold table:

| | | Final testing | |
		Disagree	Agree
Initial testing	Agree	26 A	42 B
	Disagree	39 C	48 D

The same 39 pupils disagreed with the item on both testings and the same 42 pupils agreed with the item on both occasions. However, 26 of the 155 pupils changed their responses from agree to disagree and 48 changed theirs from disagree to agree. Hence, $A + D$ or 74 represents the number of pupils changing in attitude from agree to disagree and from disagree to agree. If the intervening instruction was without effect we would expect as many changes of agree to disagree as changes of disagree to agree. In each case, the expected frequency would be $\dfrac{A + D}{2} = 37$. Given 26 and 48 as the observed frequencies, χ^2 can be computed in the basic way by Formula 9.19.

$$\chi^2 = \frac{(O - E)^2}{E} = \frac{(26 - 37)^2}{37} + \frac{(48 - 37)^2}{37} = 6.54.$$

---

[26] Recall the modification of Formula 9.3 to Formula 9.5.

In general, it is more convenient to use Formula 9.23 or 9.24.[27]

$$\chi^2 = \frac{(A - D)^2}{A + D},$$ (9.23)

$$= \frac{(26 - 48)^2}{74},$$

$$= 6.54.$$

Formula 9.24 for the testing of differences between correlated proportions may be applied to the same data.[28] Let $a = \dfrac{A}{N} = \dfrac{26}{155} = .17$ and $d = \dfrac{D}{N} = \dfrac{48}{155} = .31$.

$$z = \frac{d - a}{\sqrt{\dfrac{a + d}{N}}},$$ (9.24)

$$= \frac{.31 - .17}{\sqrt{\dfrac{.17 + .31}{155}}},$$

$$= 2.56.$$

Both the χ^2 of 6.54 and the z of 2.56 are significant at almost the 1 percent level.[29] Assuming that the attitude inventory obtains valid data, after rejecting the null hypothesis, it may be concluded that the type of instruction evaluated is effective in changing pupil attitudes with reference to "open occupancy."

Yates' correction may be applied in using Formula 9.23 by subtracting 1 from the absolute difference between D and A in the numerator before squaring. In the case of Formula 9.24, subtract $1/N$ from the absolute difference between d and a in the numerator. Formulas which include the correction are often written with short vertical lines on either side of the expression designating the difference from which the correction is subtracted.

It was noted that Formulas 9.23 and 9.24 are useful in interpreting categorized data obtained from a single sample of the same or matched

[27] McNemar shows the equivalence of Formulas 9.23 and 9.24 and their analogy to Formulas 9.5 and 9.6. See McNemar, *Psychological Statistics*, pp. 54–58, 90–92, and 261–62.

[28] The $d - a$ in the numerator of the formula is equivalent to $p_2 - p_1$, the difference in proportions of agreement obtained from initial to final testing. The denominator is the standard error of the difference between correlated proportions. See McNemar, *ibid.*, p. 57.

[29] If z is computed to more decimal places, its square rounds off to 6.54 while z itself rounds off to 2.56.

individuals from one testing to another in order to evaluate, for example, attitude change. The same formulas are useful in comparing responses to two items on the same test taken by the same or matched individuals. McNemar reports and discusses a formula useful in similarly evaluating responses by the same or matched individuals to more than two items responded to on the same occasion or the responses to a single item on more than two occasions.[30]

The preceding paragraphs had to do with correlated frequencies or proportions where the correlation was attributed to data obtained from the same or matched individuals. Correlation may also underlie the frequencies or proportions where the data obtained from different samples are classified in some ordered fashion, for example, levels of education and levels of vocational aspiration. There may be an underlying ability variable. The χ^2 technique provides a test of whether or not some significant association is present. Phi coefficients and coefficients of contingency are evidences of the strength of association though neither can safely be compared to product-moment coefficients of correlation in this respect.[31]

Using chi square to test "goodness of fit"

One of the important uses of χ^2 is that of testing the "goodness of fit" of a frequency distribution of observation to a theoretical distribution, or to a distribution known to exist in the population from which a sample was drawn. For example, one might have for a sample of pupils, data concerning their parents' occupations and census data for the city, giving the percents of persons employed locally in certain occupational categories. Another such application is to use χ^2 to test the goodness of fit of a sample distribution of test scores to a different or larger distribution of scores. The latter may be scores pertaining to a much larger sample and the problem is that of determining how representative the smaller sample is of the larger one. Where both distributions are basically observational, the computation of χ^2 does not differ essentially from use of Formula 9.19, the population frequencies, percentages, or proportions serving as the expected ones. The number of degrees of freedom is one less than the number of categories, such as occupational classifications or class intervals of test scores. Where, however, a sample distribution of scores is compared with a normal distribution or other theoretical distribution, the procedures for obtaining expected frequencies and degrees of freedom differ from those earlier explained. In the column labeled "O" of Table 9.1 are the actual or observed frequencies of a distribution of Otis Gamma intelligence test

---

[30] *Ibid.*, pp. 263–64.

[31] These coefficients are discussed in Chapter 11. See pages 355 to 358.

scores of 883 students entering one of the larger branches of Chicago City Junior College.[32] In the column labeled "E" are the theoretical or expected frequencies. The process of determining how well a normal curve fits the observational or Otis data should be easily understood from the explanation of the numbered notes which follow the table.

Table 9.1 Goodness of Fit of Normal Frequencies to Frequency Distribution of Otis Scores

Score intervals	O	(2) $\dfrac{x}{\sigma}$	Proportion of normal curve area	(8) E	$O-E$	$(O-E)^2$	$\dfrac{(O-E)^2}{E}$
75–80	1 ⎫ (1)						
70–74	25 ⎬ 26		.0384 (3)	34	− 8	64	1.88
		1.77					
65–69	54 ⎭		.0517 (4)	46	8	64	1.39
		1.34					
60–64	90		.0913	81	9	81	.00
		.91					
55–59	117		.1342	118	− 1	1	.01
		.48					
50–54	155		.1645	145	10	100	.69
		.05					
45–49	133		.1679 (5)	148	−15	225	1.52
		− .38					
40–44	130		.1430 (6)	126	4	16	.13
		− .81					
35–39	80		.1015	90	−10	100	1.11
		−1.24					
30–34	55		.0600	53	2	4	.08
		−1.67					
25–29	22 ⎫		.0296	26	− 4	16	.62
		−2.10					
20–24	12 ⎬ 21		.0179 (7)	16	5	25	1.56
15–19	7 ⎪						
10–14	2 ⎭						
5–9							
0–4							
N $\overline{X}$ s	883 48.96 11.63		1.000	883			$\chi^2 = 8.99$

(1) Observed frequencies less than 10 are combined.
(2) Precise lower limits of class intervals as deviates from the ob-

---

[32] Max D. Engelhart, "Obtaining Comparable Scores on Two Tests," *Educational and Psychological Measurement* 19 (Spring 1959), pp. 55–64.

served mean in units of the observed standard deviation. For example, $\dfrac{69.50 - 48.96}{11.63} = 1.77$ and $\dfrac{39.50 - 48.96}{11.63} = -.81$.

(3) Proportion of area of the unit normal curve *beyond* $\dfrac{X}{\sigma}$ of 1.77 equals .0384. From Table B in the Appendix, .5000 − .4616 = .0384. (The area .4616 is, of course, the area between $\dfrac{X}{\sigma} = 1.77$ and the mean of 0.00.)

(4) The area between $\dfrac{X}{\sigma}$ of 1.34 and $\dfrac{X}{\sigma}$ of 1.77 equals .4616 − .4099 where the latter corresponds to $\dfrac{X}{\sigma} = 1.34$. Continue with similar subtractions.

(5) The area between $\dfrac{X}{\sigma} = .05$ and the mean of .00 equals .0199; between .00 and $\dfrac{X}{\sigma} = -.38$ equals .1480; hence, the area between $+.05$ and $-.38 = .0199 + .1480 = .1679$. (Supply your own negative signs for values of $\dfrac{X}{\sigma}$.)

(6) Here, .1480 is subtracted from .2910, the area between $\dfrac{X}{\sigma} = -.81$ and the mean of .00 to obtain .1430. Next, .2910 is subtracted from .3925 corresponding to $\dfrac{X}{\sigma} = -1.24$. Continue with similar subtractions.

(7) The area beyond $\dfrac{X}{\sigma} = -2.10$ equals .5000 − .4821 or .0179.

(8) The proportions of the area of the unit normal curve are each multiplied by *N*. For example, .1342 times 883 equals 118. The sums of the two columns should equal, or very closely approximate, 1.000 and 883.

(9) The computations in the last three columns of Table 9.1 should require no explanation. Because of the combining of small observed frequencies the number of categories of classification is 11. Since the theoretical normal distribution is made to agree with the *N, X,* and *s* of the observed distribution, 3 degrees of freedom are lost. Hence, 11 − 3 equals 8 degrees of freedom.

(10) Between 30 and 50 percent of the time in random sampling for 8 degrees of freedom and a χ^2 of 8.99, a worse fit to the normal curve would be obtained.[33]

---

[33] See Table D in the Appendix. In the columns for $P = .50$ and $P = .30$ and in the row for 8 degrees of freedom, 8.99 is between the listed values of 7.34 and 9.52.

We can conclude that the Otis score data are characterized by only chance departures from a normal distribution. If the P's were between .05 and .01, a hypothesis that the normal or any other theoretical distribution characterizes the universe would be questionable, and if P equals .01, or is less than .01, the hypothesis would be rejected. On the other hand, if the P is greater than .95 or especially .99, the fit is so good as to create suspicion of a computational error or operation of some factor other than chance in the selection of the sample. Values of P between .05 and .95 are evidence of a satisfactory fit supporting the inference stated at the beginning of this paragraph.

The use of measures of skewness and kurtosis as a means of testing how well a distribution approximates a normal distribution was mentioned on page 204 of Chapter 8. Such a test and the one explained below are said to be more sensitive than the χ^2 test in indicating whether an observed distribution is significantly different from a normal distribution.

The Kolmogorov-Smirnov Test

The data in Table 9.1 can be used to explain this test. The frequencies in the column headed "O" are cumulated upward as proportions. (This can most readily be done on a hand calculator by multiplying the successive frequencies by $1/N$, clearing the counting dials, but not the keyboard or product dials.) The proportions under the heading "Proportion of normal curve area" are also cumulated upward, adding one proportion after another. Differences are next computed between the observed and expected cumulated proportions and the largest difference identified. In the 45–49 row, the cumulated proportions are .4994 and .5199. Their difference of − .0205 is the largest one. In this test, its symbol is D, a statistic whose sampling distribution is known.

At the .05 level, D must exceed $1.36/\sqrt{N}$ and, at the .01 level, $1.63/\sqrt{N}$ to justify rejection of the hypothesis that the observed distribution is normal, or that it could be obtained through random sampling of a normal population. The D of − .0205 is less than the .0458 or .0549 calculated in this way. The Kolmogorov-Smirnov test can also be used in testing the goodness of fit of an observed distribution to some theoretical distribution other than a normal distribution. Furthermore, it can be used to test the hypothesis that two random samples are from the same population.[34]

---

[34] For more detailed discussion of the Kolmogorov-Smirnov test see Guilford, *Fundamental Statistics in Psychology and Education,* 4th ed. (New York: McGraw-Hill, 1965), pp. 260–66, or other texts treating this test.

Practice Exercise 9.7

For a random sample of 136 seventh-grade pupils, 68 percent have mothers who are members of the PTA. Assuming this sample was drawn from a population so large that the finite sampling adjustment can be ignored, what are the confidence limits for the percentage of 68 at the 95 percent level?

Practice Exercise 9.8

Assume that frequencies for two *independent* samples have been recorded in the following fourfold table:

	Yes	No
Group 1	35	21
Group 2	18	26

Compute χ^2 and also test the significance of the difference between proportions responding "Yes" in the two groups. How significant are the results?

Practice Exercise 9.9

A sample of 35 high school students of social studies were tested at the beginning and end of the semester with an attitude inventory containing the item "A good citizen should criticize the policies of his government." The same 6 students disagreed with the item on both occasions and the same 8 students agreed on both occasions. Five students changed their response from agree to disagree and 16 changed theirs from disagree to agree. Construct the appropriate 2 × 2 table and then compute both χ^2 and z using Yates' correction. Square the z obtained for a check. How significant are the findings?

Practice Exercise 9.10

Test the goodness of fit to a normal distribution of the frequency distribution of 100 scores given below. The mean is 22.5 and the standard deviation 12.0.

50 – 54	2
45 – 49	4
40 – 44	6
35 – 39	7

30 – 34	8
25 – 29	9
20 – 24	11
15 – 19	27
10 – 14	16
5 – 9	7
0 – 4	3

NONPARAMETRIC OR DISTRIBUTION-FREE TESTS

Parametric tests are used in testing hypotheses relevant to means and differences between means of variables which have, or are assumed to have, interval or ratio scales. An estimate is made of a parameter— a population value of a mean or of a difference. It is assumed that the populations from which the samples are drawn have normal distributions or that the sampling distributions of the means or differences are normal. Nonparametric methods do not require such assumptions. They are appropriate in interpreting data relevant to variables having nominal or ordinal scales. Nonparametric methods include the procedures earlier discussed with reference to nominal data, those pertaining to percents or proportions or involving χ^2. Frequently data concerning variables usually assumed to have interval or ratio scales are subjected to nonparametric tests. Test scores may, for example, be split at the median and the number of scores above or below the median counted. Alternatively, test scores or similar measures may be assigned ranks positioned on an ordinal scale. Usually this is done because of relatively small numbers of cases or reluctance to make the assumptions cited above. The nonparametric methods require less computation than the parametric methods. This is an asset where prompt analysis of data is desired. However, the nonparametric methods are less powerful than the parametric ones. They are somewhat less likely to reject a null hypothesis when it should be rejected.

In general, the null hypothesis tested by nonparametric methods states that the samples are drawn from populations having identical distributions of measures of the variable studied. Note the use of the term "identical" rather than "normal." Note also the absence of any mention of a parameter such as a mean. In the following paragraphs four widely used nonparametric methods are briefly explained and illustrated.

The median test

In the case of the first nonparametric method to be discussed, the *median test,* the null hypothesis just stated requires some qualification.

Failure to reject this hypothesis does not necessarily imply that the samples were drawn from identical distributions. The expectation is that as many measures in one sample will be above as below the common median as in the other samples. The test assumes that the underlying variable is continuous and that the probability of ties in the precise values of this variable is zero. Actually, ties do occur in measures of the variable studied.[35]

The first step in applying the median test to two independent samples is to compute the common median. The second step is to identify the measures *above* and those *at* and *below* this median in each sample. This is illustrated by the columns of + and − signs in Table 9.2. (Disregard the columns of ranks for the present.) The third step is to enter the numbers of + and − signs in a 2 × 2 or fourfold table. The final step is to apply a χ^2 test. Formula 9.20 is used here, but with Yates' correction. The χ^2 of 4.58 is significant at the 5 percent level and the null hypothesis of identical population distributions is rejected at that level. For one degree of freedom a χ^2 of 3.84 is required at this level for a two-tailed test. The 2 × 2 table and the calculation of χ^2 follow Table 9.2. The common median is 28.

Table 9.2   Data for Two Independent Samples

Measures		Above Median + Below Median −		Ranks	
Sample 1	Sample 2	Sample 1	Sample 2	Sample 1	Sample 2
20	18	−	−	3	1
25	19	−	−	8	2
26	22	−	−	9	4
29	23	+	−	12	5.5
30	23	+	−	13	5.5
31	24	+	−	14	7
35	27	+	−	16	10
39	28	+	−	18	11
42	34	+	+	19	15
44	37	+	+	20	17
45		+		21	
49		+		22	
$N_1=12$	$N_2=10$			$R_1=175$	$R_2=78$

---

[35] For a more comprehensive discussion of the points made in this paragraph, see William L. Hays, *Statistics for Psychologists* (New York: Holt, Rinehart, and Winston, 1963), pp. 620–23.

	Above Median	Below Median
Sample 1	9 A	3 B
Sample 2	2 C	8 D

$$\chi^2 = \frac{N\left(|AD - BC| - \frac{N}{2}\right)^2}{(A + B)(C + D)(A + C)(B + D)},$$

$$= \frac{22\left(|72 - 6| - \frac{22}{2}\right)^2}{(9 + 3)(2 + 8)(9 + 2)(3 + 8)},$$

$$= 4.58.$$

Application of the median test to data relevant to two small independent samples has been illustrated above. Had the cell frequencies of the 2×2 table been smaller[36] Yates' correction would not suffice and exact or direct probabilities should be calculated.

The median test can be similarly applied to data relevant to more than two independent samples. Again, a common median is computed. Counts are entered in a table with two columns of cells and as many rows of two cells each as samples. The number of degrees of freedom is $(k - 1)(2 - 1)$ for k samples. Formula 9.21 may be used to compute χ^2.

The rank sum tests

The Wilcoxon rank sum test and the equivalent Mann-Whitney U test can be applied to measures expressed as ranks to test the hypotheses that the samples are from a common population or from populations with the same distributions of measures. These tests are almost as powerful as the t test when applied to normal distributions and may be more appropriate when the distributions are other than normal.[37]

From a finite population of $N_1 + N_2 = N$ measures ranked from 1 to N, the number of equiprobable samples of size N_1 equals $C_{N_1}^N$. Suppose that N_1 is 3 and N is 5 and that the measures are ranked from 1 to 5; then the 10 equiprobable samples possess the following sets of ranks where the order within a sample is immaterial:

1,2,3; 1,3,4; 1,4,5; 2,1,4; 2,1,5; 2,3,4; 2,4,5; 3,1,5; 3,2,5; 3,4,5

The distribution of the sums of the ranks within the 10 samples ranges from 6 to 12 and has a mean of 9. It is with the means of such

---

[36] The smallest expected frequency for the illustrative data is $11 \times 10 \div 22 = 5$, the minimum for use of Yates' correction.

[37] Except for some modifications, the discussion of these tests parallels George A. Ferguson, *Statistical Analysis in Psychology and Education*, 3rd ed. (New York: McGraw-Hill Book Company, 1971), pp. 326–29. The original contributions are Frank Wilcoxon, "Individual Comparisons by Ranking Methods," *Biometrics Bulletin* 1 (1945) 80–82; and H. B. Mann and D. R. Whitney, "On a Test of Whether One of Two Random Variables is Stochastically Larger than the Other," *Annals of Mathematical Statistics* 18 (1947) 50–60.

sampling distributions that the sums of the ranks of two independent samples are compared in testing the hypotheses stated above. For samples larger than the one in the illustration given above, Formula 9.25a and Formula 9.25b may be used to calculate the means $\bar{R}_1$ and $\bar{R}_2$, the expected sums of the ranks.

$$\bar{R}_1 = \frac{N_1(N_1 + N_2 + 1)}{2} \qquad (9.25a)$$

$$\bar{R}_2 = \frac{N_2(N_1 + N_2 + 1)}{2} \qquad (9.25b)$$

Ranks corresponding to the measures listed in Table 9.2 are given at the right in the table. The lowest measure is given a rank of 1 and the highest a rank of 22. Two tied measures of 23 are given ranks of 4.5 rather than 4 and 5.[38] (If ties are numerous a modification of Formula 9.24 should be used.[39]) R_1 and R_2, here 175 and 178, are the sum of the ranks of each sample. Using Formulas 9.25a and 9.25b the expected sums of the ranks, the means $\bar{R}_1$ and $\bar{R}_2$ are equal respectively to 138 and 115. If the null hypothesis of common or identical distributions is true, R_1 should not differ from $\bar{R}_1$, and R_2 should not differ from $\bar{R}_2$. The -1 in the numerator is a continuity correction to be subtracted from the absolute difference between R_1 and $\bar{R}_1$ or between R_2 and $\bar{R}_2$. Its purpose is the same as that explained with reference to Yates' correction. The denominator is the standard deviation of the sampling distribution earlier discussed. It is the standard error of the difference expressed in the numerator.[40]

$$z = \frac{|R_1 - \bar{R}_1| - 1}{\sqrt{\dfrac{N_1 N_2(N_1 + N_2 + 1)}{12}}} \quad \text{or} \quad \frac{|R_2 - \bar{R}_2| - 1}{\sqrt{\dfrac{N_1 N_2(N_1 + N_2 + 1)}{12}}}. \qquad (9.26)$$

Using the data[41] of Table 9.2:

$$z = \frac{|175 - 138| - 1}{\sqrt{\dfrac{12 \times 10(12 + 10 + 1)}{12}}} \quad \text{or} \quad \frac{|78 - 115| - 1}{\sqrt{\dfrac{12 \times 10(12 + 10 + 1)}{12}}},$$

---

[38] Three identical measures, for example, the 7th, 8th, and 9th would all receive a rank of 8. The next higher measure, if untied, would receive a rank of 10. N_1, R_1, and $\bar{R}_1$ usually, but not necessarily, refer to the smaller sample.

[39] Ferguson, *Statistical Analysis*, 3rd ed., p. 328.

[40] For a derivation see Edwards, *Statistical Methods*, pp. 356–57.

[41] For the same data, $R_1 - \bar{R}_1$ and $R_2 - \bar{R}_2$ are always numerically equal, but opposite in sign. The divisor of $N_1 N_2(N_1 + N_2 + 1)$ is always 12. Ferguson now gives only the first of the above formulas for z. *Op. cit.* p. 327.

$$= \frac{36}{15.1659} \text{ or } - \frac{36}{15.1659},$$

$$= 2.37 \text{ or } -2.37.$$

This z is significant at the 5 percent level. The square of z is a χ^2 of 5.62. This is higher than the χ^2 of 4.58, and indicates the greater power of the rank sum test as compared with the median test.

When the samples have less than 8 cases, the statistic U should be computed and its significance determined by consulting tables prepared by Mann and Whitney. These tables and their extension by Auble to samples ranging up to 20 for either or both variables may be found in the text by Siegel.[42]

$$U_1 = N_1 N_2 + \frac{N_1(N_1 + 1)}{2} - R_1. \tag{9.27}$$

$$U_2 = N_1 N_2 + \frac{N_2(N_2 + 1)}{2} - R_2. \tag{9.28}$$

For our data $U_1 = 23$ and $U_2 = 97$. The smaller of these values is taken as U. Entering Table K on page 276 of Siegel's text for $N_1 = 12$ and $N_2 = 10$, the value 29 is given. Since 23 is *less* than 29, the null hypothesis is again rejected at the 5 percent level for a two-tailed test.

When there are more than two independent samples, application can be made of the Kruskal-Wallis one-way analysis by ranks.[43]

The sign test and the matched-pairs signed rank test

The nonparametric methods previously discussed are applicable only to *independent* samples. When the individuals sampled have been tested twice, or are paired as is often done in experimentation, either the *sign test* or the *matched-pairs signed-ranks test* developed by Wilcoxon[44] may be used. Both of these methods are applied to the data of Table 9.3, data employed by Palmer Johnson to illustrate the *t* test using Formulas 9.5 and 9.6.[45]

---

[42] Sidney Siegel, *Nonparametric Statistics for the Behavioral Sciences* (New York: Mc-Graw-Hill, 1956), pp. 270–77. Siegel recommends computation of U and use of tables taken from Donovan Auble, "Extended Tables for the Mann-Whitney Statistic," *Bulletin of the Institute for Educational Research* (Bloomington: Indiana University, 1953).

[43] See Ferguson, *Statistical Analysis*, pp. 301–33, or W. H. Kruskal and W. A. Wallis, "Use of Ranks in One-Criterion Variance Analysis," *Journal of the American Statistical Association* 47 (December 1952), pp. 583–621.

[44] Frank Wilcoxon, *Some Rapid Approximate Statistical Procedures* (Stanford, Conn.: American Cyanamid Company, 1949).

[45] Palmer O. Johnson, *Statistical Methods in Research*, © 1949, Prentice-Hall, Inc., Englewood Cliffs, New Jersey, pp. 75–79. Reprinted by permission of publisher.

Table 9.3 Test Score Data for Two Paired Samples

X	Y	X — Y signs	X — Y d	Signed Ranks of d	Rank with Less Frequent Sign
73	58	+	15	12.5	
52	37	+	15	12.5	
100	53	+	47	25	
60	77	−	−17	−16	16
75	51	+	24	20.5	
67	62	+	5	3	
61	55	+	6	5.5	
59	30	+	29	23	
33	39	−	− 6	− 5.5	5.5
19	16	+	3	1.5	
32	15	+	17	16	
27	37	−	−10	− 9.5	9.5
68	44	+	24	20.5	
54	27	+	27	22	
26	43	−	−17	−16	16
30	27	+	3	1.5	
69	53	+	16	14	
43	29	+	14	11	
23	13	+	10	9.5	
11	17	−	− 6	− 5.5	5.5
26	20	+	6	5.5	
30	9	+	21	19	
28	35	−	− 7	− 8	8
53	21	+	32	24	
23	42	−	−19	−18	18
$N_1 = 25$	$N_2 = 25$				$T = 78.5$

In using the sign test, differences between the paired scores favoring variable X are given a + sign while those favoring Y are given a − sign. (If a difference is zero, a zero is entered and the N reduced one unit.) Under the null hypothesis, the number of + signs equals the number of − signs. The expected numbers are equal. After the numbers of + signs and − signs have been counted, x^2 can be computed using Formula 9.19, preferably with Yates' correction. (When the numbers of pairs is less than 10, exact probabilities should be computed using the binomial expansion.) An alternative is to use Formula 9.29 as recommended by Ferguson.[46] D is the difference between the numbers of + and − signs, − 1 is the continuity correction, and N is the number of paired measures.

---

[46] Ferguson, *Statistical Analysis*, pp. 324–25.

$$z = \frac{|D| - 1}{\sqrt{\dfrac{}{N}}}, \qquad (9.29)$$

applied to the data of Table 9.3:

$$z = \frac{|11| - 1}{\sqrt{\dfrac{}{25}}} = 2.00.$$

Using a table of the unit normal distribution this z is significant at the 5 percent level.

In applying the Wilcoxon matched-pairs signed-ranks test, differences between the paired measures are ranked from lowest to highest without regard to sign, but the ranks are then given the signs of the differences. (Again, if a difference is zero, it is excluded and N reduced one unit.) Under the null hypothesis the samples come from the same population, or from populations with identical distributions, and the sum of the positive ranks should equal the sum of the negative ranks. This is obviously half the sum of the total ranks. As earlier explained, the sum of N ranks is $N(N + 1)/2$. Hence, the expected sum $E(T)$ equals $N(N + 1)/4$. The test is applied to the sum of the ranks of the *less* frequent sign, and this sum, T, is substituted as positive in the numerator of Formula 9.30. The standard deviation of its sampling distribution, a standard error, is the denominator.[47]

$$z = \frac{T - E(T)}{\sqrt{\dfrac{N(N + 1)(2N + 1)}{24}}}. \qquad (9.30)$$

Applied to the data of Table 9.3:

$$z = \frac{78.5 - 162.50}{\sqrt{\dfrac{25(25 + 1)(2 \times 25 + 1)}{24}}},$$

$$z = -2.26.$$

This z, significant at the 5 percent level, is a little higher than the 2.00 of the signs test. It is lower, however, than the 2.75 reported by Palmer Johnson. A t of 2.75 is almost significant at the 1 percent level for 24 degrees of freedom.

The two-way analysis of variance for ranks developed by Friedman[48]

---

[47] Tables giving the magnitudes of T required for significance with reference to N's ranging from 6 to 25 are reported in the texts by Siegel, Ferguson, and in other sources.

[48] Milton Friedman, "The Use of Ranks to Avoid the Assumption of Normality Implicit in the Analysis of Variance," *Journal of the American Statistical Association* 32 (December 1937), pp. 675–701.

should be used where there are more than two samples of matched individuals. This method is discussed in most texts devoting chapters to nonparametric methods.

Practice Exercise   9.11

X	63	55	55	50	49	45	41	39	33	32	29	24
Y	54	56	48	28	38	18	27	42	21	19	30	15

(1) Assume that the two samples are independent. Then apply the median test ($Md = 38$) and the Wilcoxon rank sum test.
(2) Assume that the two samples are paired individuals. Then apply the sign test and the Wilcoxon matched-pairs signed-ranks test.

Questions for
Study and Discussion

1. Prepare a glossary of brief definitions of each of the following symbols, words, or phrases:

σ	Level of significance
β	Model
Binomial distribution	Nonparametric test
Central Limit Theorum	Null hypothesis
Confidence interval	Parameter
Error of the first kind	ϕ
Error of the second kind	One-tailed test
Expected value	Power of a test
Finite population correction	Random sampling
Interval estimate	Two-tailed test
Law of Large Numbers	χ^2
Level of confidence	z (three definitions)

2. The t distribution is frequently called "Student's" distribution. Who was "Student"?

3. For what contributions to statistical method is Sir Ronald Fisher noted?

4. What aspects of statistical inference discussed in an elementary fashion in the first part of this chapter reflect the contributions of Jerzy Neyman and Egon Pearson?

5. Two differences between means on the same achievement test are significant at the 5 percent level. The first two means were computed for samples of 50 pupils each and the second two means from samples of 100 pupils each. Which difference was the larger?

6. If $\bar{X} - \mu$ were written in the numerator of Formula 9.4, what symbol should appear in the denominator? How does the ratio thus written relate to the inequality given on page 248 of this chapter? See page 138 of the text by Ferguson or other advanced texts.

7. Write out the proof of Formula 9.10 on page 257 from the brief description above the formula. Compare your effort with the proofs given on pages 164–65 of McNemar's text or with the one on page 365 of Ferguson.

8. List a number of problems for which a χ^2 test is applicable. Indicate for which of these problems a test of differences between proportions can result in a z whose square equals χ^2.

9. What are the advantages and limitations of nonparametric tests?

10. There has been considerable controversy concerning the testing of null hypotheses in recent years. Summarize the pros and cons after reading the references by Bakan, Kruskal, LaForge, Nunnally, and Rozeboom.

11. What are Bayesian statistics? See the writings on Bayesian methods listed among the selected references at the end of this chapter.

Suggestions
for Further Study

Many of the questions just listed are suggestions for further study. The student will find it useful to supplement what is said in this chapter by further study of statistical inference in one or more of the texts listed among the selected references. The student will also find it useful to read the 1960 and 1969 *Encyclopedia of Educational Research* articles by Chester W. Harris. The *Review of Educational Research* article by Cherry Ann Clark and similar chapters in later issues of the same publication on "Methodology of Educational Research" will acquaint the student with recent developments in statistical inference.

The student will also find it useful to relate the various techniques of statistical inference to research problems by reading reports of research published in such journals as *The American Educational Research Journal, Journal of Educational Measurement, Journal of Experimental Education, Journal of Educational Psychology,* and *Journal of Educational Research.* These journals and *Psychological Bulletin, Psychological Review,* and the *Annual Review of Psychology* typically contain discussions of statistical techniques or summaries of recent developments with respect to them. Later chapters of this book also contain further applications of both the procedures of descriptive statistics and of statistical inference to different kinds of educational research problems.

Selected References
For Chapters 8 and 9

Bakan, David. "The Test of Significance in Psychological Research." *Psychological Bulletin* 66 (December 1966): 423–37.

Blommers, Paul, and E. F. Lindquist. *Elementary Statistical Methods in Psychology and Education.* Boston: Houghton Mifflin, 1960.

Bohrnstedt, George W. "Reliability and Validity Assessment in Attitude Measurement." In *Attitude Measurement* edited by Gene F. Summers, pp. 80–91. Chicago: Rand McNally, 1970.

Clark, Cherry Ann. "Hypothesis Testing in Relation to Statistical Methodology," in "Statistical Methodology." *Review of Educational Research* 33 (December 1963): 455–73.

Dixon, Wilfrid J., and Frank J. Massey, Jr. *Introduction to Statistical Analysis.* 3rd ed. New York: McGraw-Hill, 1968.

Downie, N. M., and R. W. Heath. *Basic Statistical Methods.* 3rd ed. New York: Harper and Row, 1970.

DuBois, Philip H. *An Introduction to Psychological Statistics.* New York: Harper and Row, 1965.

Edwards, Allen L. *Statistical Methods.* 2nd ed. New York: Holt, Rinehart, and Winston, 1967.

Edwards, Ward, Harold Lindman, and Leonard J. Savage. "Bayesian Statistical Inference for Psychological Research." *Psychological Review* 70 (May 1963): 193–242.

Ferguson, George A. *Statistical Analysis in Psychology and Education,* 3rd ed. New York: McGraw-Hill, 1971.

Glass, Gene V and Julian C. Stanley. *Statistical Methods in Education and Psychology.* Englewood Cliffs, N.J.: Prentice-Hall, 1970.

Guenther, W. C. *Concepts of Statistical Inference.* New York: McGraw-Hill, 1965.

Guilford, J. P. *Fundamental Statistics in Psychology and Education.* 4th ed. New York: McGraw-Hill, 1965.

Harris, Chester W. "Statistical Methods." In *Encyclopedia of Educational Research,* edited by C. W. Harris, pp. 1397–1410. 3rd ed. New York: Macmillan, 1960. (Also in the 4th ed., 1969, pp. 1307–18.)

Hays, William L. *Statistics for Psychologists.* New York: Holt, Rinehart and Winston, 1963.

Heermann, Emil F., and Larry A. Braskamp. *Readings in Statistics for the Behavioral Sciences.* Englewood Cliffs, N.J.: Prentice-Hall, 1970. (Parts Two, Three, and Four are relevant to our Chapter 9 while Part Six is relevant to Chapter 11 and Part Five to Chapter 13.)

Johnson, Palmer O., and Robert W. B. Jackson. *Modern Statistical Methods: Descriptive and Inductive.* Chicago: Rand McNally, 1959.

Kaiser, Henry F. "Directional Statistical Decisions." *Psychological Review* 67 (May 1960): 160–67.

Kruskal, William H. "Tests of Significance." In *International Encyclopedia of the Social Sciences,* Vol. 14, edited by David L. Sills, pp. 238–50. New York: Macmillan and Free Press, 1968.

LaForge, Rolfe. "Confidence Intervals or Tests of Significance in Scientific Research?" *Psychological Bulletin* 68 (December 1967): 446–47.

McNemar, Quinn. *Psychological Statistics.* 4th ed. New York: Wiley, 1969.

Meyer, Donald L. "A Bayesian School Superintendent." *American Educational Research Journal* 1 (November 1964): 219–28.

———— and others, "Statistics," in "Methodology of Educational Research." *Review of Educational Research* 39 (December 1969): 723–47.

———— and Raymond O. Collier, Jr. (eds.). *Bayesian Statistics.* Ninth Annual Phi Delta Kappa Symposium on Educational Research. Itasca, Illinois: F. E. Peacock, 1970.

Michael, William B. "Selected Contributions to Parametric and Nonparametric Statistics," in "Statistical Methodology." *Review of Educational Research* 33 (December 1963): 474–489.

Mood, A. M., and F. A. Graybill. *Introduction to Theory of Statistics.* 2nd ed. New York: McGraw-Hill, 1963.

Nunnally, Jum. "The Place of Statistics in Psychology." *Educational and Psychological Measurement* 20 (Winter 1960): 641–50.

Rozeboom, W. W. "The Fallacy of the Null-Hypothesis Significance Test." *Psychological Bulletin* 57 (September 1960): 415–28.

Siegel, Sidney. *Nonparametric Statistics for the Behavioral Sciences.* New York: McGraw-Hill, 1956.

Tate, Merle W. *Statistics in Education and Psychology, A First Course.* New York: Macmillan, 1965.

Walker, Helen M., and Joseph Lev. *Statistical Inference.* New York: Holt, Rinehart and Winston, 1953.

———— and ————. *Elementary Statistical Methods.* 3rd ed. New York: Holt, Rinehart and Winston, 1969.

10

Studying Present Practices and Conditions

The research techniques applicable to a variety of education problems that have been discussed in preceding chapters of this book follow a general pattern from the selection and definition of a problem, through the collection of data, to their summarization and interpretation. Now different types of educational research will be considered, classified in terms of kinds of problems and in terms of differing techniques.

SURVEYS AND SURVEY RESEARCH

Surveys that are not accepted as research

In his scholarly discussion of survey research method, Robert Herriott has cited authors of studies of introductory texts on educational research who are extremely critical of "survey research."[1] This critical attitude is exemplified in a statement by Monroe and Engelhart:

> The designation of "educational research," is frequently given to relatively simple and routine investigations such as surveys of current conditions or practices. This custom is unfortunate. The usage of the term should be limited so that research in education will be comparable in its essential characteristics with research in other fields.[2]

---

[1] Robert E. Herriott, "Survey Research Method," in R. L. Ebel, *Encyclopedia of Educational Research,* 4th ed. (New York: Macmillan, 1969), p. 1400. The studies cited are by Sam D. Sieber and by Martin Trow. See the references at the end of this chapter.

[2] Walter S. Monroe and Max D. Engelhart, *The Scientific Study of Educational Problems* (New York: Macmillan, 1936), p. 2.

Herriott is among those who have noted the reluctance of social scientists to accept as *research,* surveys in which a hastily written questionnaire is administered to some readily accessible group of pupils or teachers to collect data relevant to some problem of local interest. He points out, however, that the survey method has proved useful to social scientists in the study of social and social-psychological relationships, including those relevant to formal education. Sociologists, educational sociologists, and social psychologists value both *descriptive* survey research and *explanatory* or *analytic* survey research.[3] Before discussing research of these types, however, something more should be said about educational surveys, particularly the city or state school survey, whether accepted as research or not.

Educational surveys

Survey methods are widely used to obtain data useful in evaluating present practices and in providing a basis for decisions. The typical city or state school survey may be characterized by application of some of the techniques of educational research, but there are a number of differences from genuine research. A city school survey is usually characterized by a multiplicity of purposes rather than by a relatively specific problem, statements of one or more hypotheses, and other involvement with theory. In a city or state school survey a wide variety of data relevant to many aspects of the school system are collected. Such data may include pupil enrollments, training and experience of teachers, summaries and analyses of test scores, and characteristics of school buildings and other facilities. Given adequate definitions such data can be collected objectively. The same is true of the collection of attitudes of teachers and pupils, although these data are more difficult to interpret validly. A city or state school survey is expected to include appraisals and recommendations. These can be the most valuable aspects of a survey report if they are based on evidence and are not unduly influenced by the climate of public opinion.

Most school surveys have been conducted by experts from outside the school system. Often the experts are resented by local administrators. The use of outside experts is sometimes necessary when the local administrators and other staff members are blind to local conditions and problems. In general, however, there should be cooperative effort and all those who have responsibility for the successful conduct of a survey should possess scientific attitudes and use scientific methods. Especially helpful will be the training of local specialists so

---

[3] Herriott, "Survey Research," p. 1400.

that they will be able, with some advice from outside experts, to conduct dependable self-surveys. The increasing availability of data-processing equipment should promote the trend in this direction.

Routine collection of data in the schools is not research, but the data thus collected can be useful in research. While it is true that institutional research using survey methods may solve immediate practical problems without contributing generalizations to the science of education, consider the effects on educational theory and practice of the survey-type studies exemplified by W. H. Maxwell's pioneer city-wide age-grade tables,[4] E. L. Thorndike's survey study of pupil elimination from schools,[5] and Leonard Ayres's early survey of retardation.[6] Prior to these reports of survey data there was little understanding of the range and significance of individual differences in school pupils.

Descriptive survey research

In a descriptive survey research, data specified in the problem are obtained from a sample selected from a clearly defined population to describe the population in terms of the variables studied. Some kind of random sampling is necessary to justify use of statistical inference estimates of the sampling error of the descriptions. Reasoning is required in identifying the population to be described and the variables by which it is to be described.[7]

The last sentence suggests a paradox. How can a population be defined if its characteristics are not known? If the characteristics are known, why conduct a descriptive or other sampling survey? Suppose a survey is to be made of the attitudes and other traits of high-school dropouts. The fact of having dropped out of high school should suffice in identifying the population to be sampled and later to be further described by the sample data.

Descriptive survey research is characterized by classification of the data relevant to the variables studied. The data may be terms descriptive of the population as inferred from the sample or they may be univariate frequency distributions, for example of ages, weights, test scores, or of other measures. They may be counts of different

---

[4] W. H. Maxwell, *Sixth Annual Report of the City Superintendent of Schools* (New York, 1904), pp. 42–49.

[5] E. L. Thorndike, "The Elimination of Pupils from School," *U.S. Bureau of Education Bulletin,* No. 4 (Washington, D.C.: Government Printing Office, 1907).

[6] L. P. Ayres, *Laggards in Our Schools* (New York: Charities Publishing Company, 1909).

[7] Herriott, "Survey Research," p. 1400. See also Palmer O. Johnson, "Development of Sample Survey as a Scientific Methodology," *Journal of Experimental Education* 27 (March 1959), pp. 167–76.

answers given in interviews or to a questionnaire. When summaries of such data result in statements or inferences concerning the population, these statements are *descriptive* generalizations, or laws. (If relationships are inferred between the variables which may be assessed by such indices as correlation or contingency coefficients, the survey becomes an explanatory research.)

Descriptive survey research is in the second stage of scientific inquiry. Recall from Chapter 2 that the first stage, identification of a problem, is followed by the second or natural history stage in which observation, induction, description, and classification predominate. These earlier stages are prerequisite to the third stage: that of deductively formulated theory. Unless the third stage is preceded by the second, according to Northrop "the result inevitably is immature, half-baked, dogmatic, and for the most part worthless theory."[8]

Many more appropriately conducted descriptive surveys and survey researches are needed. Much of our knowledge of educational practices and conditions is both undependable and fragmentary.

Explanatory or analytic survey research

It has been suggested that a descriptive generalization may initiate the building of a theory. Such a generalization may be a summary of numerous isolated facts classified together because of some common characteristic. As such, the generalization suggests no hypothesis to be tested. For this to occur there must be the insight that the facts summarized may have some kind of relationship with another set of facts. A conjecture of this kind may be stated as a hypothesis of the form "If A, then B . . . ." The hypothesis identifies a relationship between variables that may be tested.

Given a hypothesis, a theory exists even prior to the testing of the hypothesis. Of course, theory building need not and does not stop with a single hypothesis which, when adequately tested, may become a law. Complex theories stem from simpler theories earlier proposed and tested in research. It can be argued that the research which contributes most effectively to educational practice most closely parallels scientific research. "If A, then B . . ." has its analog, "If we decide to do this . . . , then the consequences will be . . . ."

Like descriptive survey research, explanatory or analytic survey research requires definition of a population and the use of probability sampling, that is, some kind of random selection to justify use of the methods of statistical inference in the interpretation of data. Some-

---

[8] F. S. C. Northrop, *The Logic of the Sciences and the Humanities* (New York: Macmillan, 1947), pp. 37–38. See also Abraham Kaplan, *The Conduct of Inquiry* (San Francisco: Chandler, 1964), p. 114.

times probability sampling can appropriately be supplemented by *purposive sampling* to select subjects having characteristics uniquely relevant but less likely to be selected in sufficient number by random sampling of a larger population.

In his explanatory survey research reported in 1955 Stauffer used a *multistage* probability sample of about 4500 citizens and a *purposive* sample of approximately 1500 community leaders.[9]

The hypotheses in explanatory survey research, as in other theory related research, may contain constructs. These should be operationally defined by specifying how they are to be observed and measured. Recent research in school administration is of the explanatory survey type. There have been considerable recent developments in administrative theory. The hypotheses tested in such research contain such constructs as "initiating structure," "consideration," and "role conflict." Interest in theory is increasingly characteristic of *non*-experimental research in education, in psychology, and in sociology on problems relevant to education. In addition to problems in the field of school administration, non-experimental and frequently explanatory survey research is concerned with problems of growth and development, characteristics of atypical children—the culturally disadvantaged, the socially disadvantaged, the mentally handicapped, the physically handicapped and the gifted. In the suggestions for further study at the end of this chapter the reader will be directed toward important sources relevant to some of these problem areas.

THE EX POST FACTO CHARACTER OF EXPLANATORY SURVEY RESEARCH

The meaning of "ex post facto"

The term *ex post facto* is derived from the fallacy *post hoc, ergo propter hoc* which means: "after this, therefore caused by this."[10] It has come to be applied to research in which causal inferences are based on reasoning retrospectively from effects to causes. The effect exists and the circumstances or conditions surrounding it seem to be a logical place to look for the cause. We may know which circumstances or conditions antedate the effect. Therefore we feel justified in attributing the effect to the most plausible of the circumstances or conditions.

---

[9] Samuel A. Stauffer, *Communism, Conformity and Civil Liberties* (New York: Doubleday, 1955). See Herriott's summary, "Survey Research," p. 1406.

[10] Fred N. Kerlinger, *Foundations of Behavioral Research* (New York: Holt, Rinehart and Winston, 1965), p. 359.

Can phenomena be explained in other than causal terms?

In descriptive research factual data relevant to many variables are collected and, as earlier noted, the data are summarized as descriptive generalizations. We leave descriptive research when the generalizations suggest hypotheses concerning relations among the variables. Are all relationships concomitant, or are there causal ones? The diffidence with which scientists and philosophers use the word "cause" would seem to imply that the certainty of causes is questionable. If this is true, how can experimentation yield more dependable conclusions than correlational methods? (As a matter of fact, such methods are acquiring greater acceptability in causal studies.[11]) But turning away from the issue raised above, let us assume that it is not reprehensible to talk about causes in the sense accepted by the practical man and consider the ways in which explanatory survey research can avoid the limitations of ex post facto research.

Campbell and Stanley,[12] in their very important writings on experimental research, have contrasted ex post facto research with "true" experiments in which the researcher is able to manipulate the causal or independent variable and to exert control of other variables by random assignment of subjects to treatments. They also discuss *quasi-experiments* at considerable length. These range from classroom experiments in which pupils are not assigned to treatments at random and the experimenter may have only partial control, to those in which the causal variable of interest is not introduced by the experimenter, but may have operated for a long time. Examples of such *pseudo-experiments* include, as Stanley has emphasized, research on cancer and on brain-damaged children. The research of Dr. J. M. Rice has been called quasi-experimentation and "comparative" survey. It may also be referred to as explanatory survey. Dr. Rice tested thousands of elementary pupils to obtain data which supported his hypothesis that the amount of time given daily to spelling drill is not a crucial factor in spelling achievement. The amount of time varied from school to school, but was not controlled by Dr. Rice (see page 377).

It has been suggested that some possibly causal variables must be studied in a non-experimental context because of their very nature. Such variables cannot be actively manipulated nor can subjects be

---

[11] See pages 339 to 342 of Chapter 11, and Stanley Rickard's review of Robert M. Blalock's *Causal Inference in Nonexperimental Research* in *Psychometrika* 33 (June 1968), pp. 253–54.

[12] See Donald T. Campbell and Julian C. Stanley, "Experimental and Quasi-Experimental Designs for Research in Teaching," in N. L. Gage, ed., *Handbook of Research on Teaching* (Chicago: Rand McNally, 1963), pp. 171–246; also separately published as *Experimental and Quasi-Experimental Designs for Research* (Chicago: Rand McNally, 1966).

assigned at random to their influences. These variables include sex, social class, measured aptitude, and present attitudes.

Kerlinger[13] and others have emphasized the importance in ex post facto studies of testing several atlernative plausible hypotheses rather than a single hypothesis, or none. This is compatible with the proposal of "multiple working hypotheses" by Thomas Crowder Chamberlin and the "strong inference" of John R. Platt (see page 18). Mention of the great geologist Chamberlin brings to mind the Chamberlin-Moulton planetesimal hypothesis of the origin of the solar system as contrasted with the nebular hypothesis proposed by the Marquis de Laplace. Some version of the former is held today and is supported by *observation* and *reasoning*. It is an excellent example of ex post facto research. Observations of the retrograde motion of certain satellites of Jupiter, Saturn, and Uranus, the great differences in mass of the inner and outer planets, and greater angular momentum of the planets compared to that of the sun support a planetesimal hypothesis rather than a nebular one. If we may return to earth, observation and reasoning in testing multiple hypotheses are crucial in non-experimental research. Recall the very definite contributions of classroom research on teaching discussed in Chapter 6. Non-experimental explanatory survey may not be as dependable in the study of causal factors as true experimentation, but given the testing of multiple hypotheses, the utilization of the best of observational procedures in the collecting of data, and the necessary critical thinking in analysis of the data and their limitations, so-called ex post facto research can contribute dependably to decision-making in educational practice and, when especially well done, add to scientific knowledge in education.

It is generally accepted that true experimentation with its greater control of causal or independent variables and random assignment of subjects to treatments can yield more dependable identification and measurement of causal factors, but, as earlier noted, correlational techniques are used to study causal factors. The analysis of variance techniques, employed primarily in experimental research, are increasingly being used in non-experimental studies of causal factors. These techniques are explained in Chapter 13.

SURVEYS OF GROWTH OR DEVELOPMENT

Studies of growth or development are considered here as a type of survey research. Such studies differ from the kinds of survey research earlier explained in that the changes investigated occur over a period of time. They differ from time-series experiments in that no experimen-

---

[13] Kerlinger, *Foundations*, p. 373.

tal variable is introduced at some point in the series of observations or measurements.[14] The two general types of growth studies are the cross-sectional and the longitudinal.

Cross-sectional growth studies

In cross-sectional studies the data are collected at one time from samples of subjects of various ages. For example, in a city which has a well-organized testing program, pupils in a series of grades may be tested *simultaneously* with the same test or test battery analyzing the data of modal-age pupils. This procedure eliminates pupils who deviate substantially in age, especially the overage or retarded pupils (who should be separately studied). If the data were so sorted as to yield groups of pupils of the same age, the pupils would be heterogeneous with respect to grade. Restriction to modal-age pupils facilitates comparisons with modal-age norms. Such comparisons are useful in defining the populations sampled. Where the problem calls for the observation or measurement of a variable or variables other than those measured by the test with modal-age norms, the testing of pupils simultaneously in a sequence of grades is desirable. Cross-sectional studies of growth would be much more meaningful if an "anchor" test or battery were used.

One major advantage of the cross-sectional type of growth study is that the findings are more quickly obtained than in a longitudinal research which may last for several years. It is also less expensive than a longitudinal study based on the same number of variables and subjects. The cross-sectional study is not as effective as the longitudinal study in revealing individual variations in growth. It does not lend itself to the preparation of individual growth curves.

The cross-sectional study is often adversely affected by selection. I recall drawing a smooth curve based on semester medians of *Chicago Reading Test D* given to pupils in grades 6, 7, 8, 9, 10, 11, and 12. The slope characteristic of grades 6, 7, and 8 was maintained through the high school grades. It was at first concluded that increase in reading ability continued at the same rate through high school until an expert critic suggested that student elimination could be the major factor. In longitudinal studies, selection is also a limitation.

Longitudinal growth studies

The longitudinal study requires repeated measurements of the same subjects over an extended period. An advantage of this type of study is

---

[14] Campbell and Stanley, *Experimental and Quasi-Experimental Designs*, p. 37f. or p. 207f. in Gage's *Handbook*.

the possibility of examining individual variations in the growth of traits, for example, the erratic growth patterns of adolescents. As noted, longitudinal studies also suffer from selection. It is very difficult to collect data semester after semester or year after year. Pupils who drop out of high school are usually unavailable for testing. Such elimination, as noted above, can produce spurious growth records since the more able pupils remain in school. If a longitudinal study is continued over a considerable period other changes may occur in the sample repeatedly tested. Subjects become averse to testing and do not exert themselves. On the other hand, the fact of repeated observation, interviewing, and testing may create a situation marked by Hawthorne effect, presumably the motivation resulting from participation in a study, rather than from some causal factor of interest to the researcher. The term comes from an experiment conducted at the Hawthorne plant of the Western Electric Company.

Longitudinal studies are time consuming, require considerable financial support, and continuity of personnel over a period of years.[15] In spite of such difficulties there have been a number of notable longitudinal studies. Two of these are described below:

(1) *The Genetic Studies of Genius*[16]

In 1921, Lewis M. Terman and his associates selected 1500 "gifted" children with the Stanford-Binet intelligence test as the final criterion. This group was investigated with respect to many characteristics including racial and social origin; intellectually superior relatives, school progress and intellectual history; play interests; reading interests; intellectual, social, and activity interests; character and personality traits. Comparisons were made with a group of average children.

Data were collected from this sample at intervals, the latest data collecting occurring between 1950–1952 and in 1955. Ninety-five percent of the 1437 living subjects participated in the 1950–52 field study. The achievements of this group of subjects is evidence of the predictive validity of the intelligence test. Far greater percentages of this group earned higher degrees, were in the professions, and received high honors than average persons.

---

[15] For further discussion, see Deobold B. Van Dalen, *Understanding Educational Research,* 2nd ed. (McGraw-Hill, 1966), pp. 228–31.

[16] L. M. Terman and others, "Mental and Physical Traits of a Thousand Gifted Children," *Genetic Studies of Genius,* Vol. I (Stanford, Cal.: Stanford University Press, 1925); L. M. Terman and Melita Oden, "The Gifted Group at Mid-Life: Thirty-five Years' Follow-Up of the Superior Child," *Genetic Studies of Genius,* Vol. 5 (Stanford, Cal.: Stanford University Press, 1959).

Data were also obtained relevant to intellectual and social interests and to personality traits. Some skeptical person has noted that the knowledge of being a member of so superior a group has been an important factor in motivating the achievements of the group—a persistent Hawthorne effect.

(2) *Project Talent*[17]

Almost half a million students in grades 9, 10, 11, and 12 in 1,353 schools in all parts of the country were given the Project Talent paper-and-pencil tests and inventories in the spring of 1960. In 1963, about 10,000 12th-grade students in over 100 public high schools of the original sample were tested with an abridged Project Talent battery. About 7500 of the 10,000 had been tested as 9th graders in 1960. These students thus provided the data for a longitudinal study of cognitive growth.

In the analysis of the data a variety of statistical techniques were used: canonical correlation between grade 9 and grade 12 scores, factor analysis, univariate and multivariate analysis of variance, multiple discriminant analysis, part and partial correlation, partial canonical correlation, and step-wise multiple regression analysis. (Obviously, electronic data processing equipment was indispensable in a research of such magnitude.)

Among the findings of this research were important and statistically significant gains in cognitive skills, especially in curriculum related fields with the two sexes revealing somewhat different patterns of growth. The report includes a very interesting analysis of the factors producing the changes in cognitive growth, a discussion of aptitude versus achievement and, under *Implications for Education:* "The Disadvantaged Child," "General Education versus Vocational Education" and "Effective and Ineffective High Schools."

In concluding this discussion of longitudinal studies mention should be made of Benjamin Bloom's very scholarly and influential work in which numerous longitudinal studies have been summarized and interpreted.[18]

---

[17] This summary is largely based on *Cognitive Growth During High School,* Bulletin No. 6, Project Talent (Palo Alto, Cal.: American Institute for Research, 1967). See also John C. Flanagan and others, *The American High School Student* (Pittsburgh: University of Pittsburgh, 1964); Marian F. Shaycoft, *The High School Years: Growth in Cognitive Skills* (American Institute for Research and University of Pittsburgh, 1967).

[18] Benjamin S. Bloom, *Stability and Change in Human Characteristics* (New York: Wiley, 1964).

SUGGESTIONS FOR CONDUCTING A SURVEY RESEARCH

Most masters' and doctoral theses in education are research of the survey type. One need only study the education section of a recent volume of *Dissertation Abstracts* to recognize that this is the case. It is also true of most institutional research studies. In the general fields of educational psychology and educational history, survey-type research is much less often encountered. As earlier noted, however, there should be more exploratory descriptive survey research in educational psychology, suggesting hypotheses for experimental testing. Studies in educational history, especially recent educational history, should also be characterized by research of the descriptive survey type.

In reviewing the steps the graduate student, or other survey researcher, should take in conducting a survey research, a considerable amount of time and thought should be given to the discovery of an appropriate problem and to its definition as explained in Chapter 3. To accomplish this it is essential to locate and study the previous research on the problem. Such study helps to formulate a problem and to suggest techniques useful in attacking a problem. Usually it is desirable to prepare a critical summary of the previous research.

If the contemplated research is to be a descriptive survey, it is appropriate to state the problem as a declarative statement or general question and follow this with a series of subordinate questions. If the survey research is of the explanatory or analytic type, the general statement of the problem may be supplemented by a series of hypotheses.

A well defined problem should suggest the kinds of data to be collected and the sources of the data. In survey research, relevant data may be collected by copying from records, by means of questionnaires or interviews, by systematic observations, by content analysis, and by means of tests or other measuring instruments. (Chapters 5, 6, and 7 suggest procedures for planning.) The planning stage should also include deciding upon the populations to be sampled, the sampling procedures to be used, the methods of summarizing and organizing the data, and, finally, the techniques appropriate for interpreting the data. Chapters 8, 9, and the next sections of this chapter should be helpful in making these decisions, as will the more advanced texts cited.

Explanatory or analytic survey research is concerned with the study of relationships between variables. Hence, appropriate indices of relationship should be used. For relationships between continuous variables the indices include product-moment coefficients of correlation and coefficients of partial correlation. For relationships between nominal variables use is made of such indices as phi coefficients and coefficients of contingency. The graduate student should familiarize himself with the assumptions which need to be met to justify use of any of these indices and also with how the indices are interpreted. The computer may do the calculations, but it will not provide the necessary thinking.

The next sections of this chapter discuss topics focused on survey research—the general aspects of summarizing and interpreting survey data, the kinds of tables and graphs applicable to the summarizing of survey data, and an elementary introduction to such survey sampling methods as stratified random sampling and cluster sampling. (Multi-stage sampling is too technical to explain in an introductory text.) It is to be hoped that future graduate students after diligent study of this text and more advanced ones will promote a more satisfactory "image" for survey research in education. It badly needs a better reputation.

SUMMARIZING AND INTERPRETING SURVEY DATA

In preparing the report of a survey study the audience for whom the report is being written should be considered. A critical reader is likely to be interested in details which will enable him to evaluate the dependability of the study. If most of the readers are going to be school administrators and teachers whose interests will be limited to the principal findings and their interpretation, fewer details should be reported and the phraseology of the report should be as simple as possible. Where technical terms necessarily must occur, they should be defined. When the audience is likely to be researchers as sophisticated as the author, or even more sophisticated, the phraseology and other aspects of the report may be relatively more technical, but not needlessly so. The author should strive to communicate with, rather than to impress, his audience.

Classifying and tabulating survey data

The tabulating of measures pertaining to a continuous variable such as test scores was explained in Chapter 8. When the data are relevant to several variables and to several groups, it is necessary to anticipate—even before they are collected—how they are ultimately to be organized, summarized, and interpreted. It may be desirable to have separate tabulations of data from several subgroups, for example, different school grades, different high schools, elementary schools of different sizes, and so on. If there are likely to be sex differences, boys and girls should be tallied separately. The methods of classification should be compatible if comparisons are to be made with earlier survey studies. Provision will need to be made for cross classification if it is anticipated that relationships between the variables are to be evaluated by coefficients of correlation. If the formulas appropriate to stratified sampling are to be applied, the classification should reflect the strata defined. In any case, effort should be made to have the data partitioned into relatively homogeneous subgroups. If, after the data have been tabulated, the classification is more elaborate than necessary, the data of different groups may be combined. It is better to have this happen than to regret later that subdividing the data was not done.

When the data are such quantitative measures as test scores, teachers' salaries, size of classes, and the like, it is relatively easy to select appropriate categories. When, however, categories are needed prior to the classification or coding of observations of pupil and teacher behaviors, of responses to open-end questions from questionnaire or interviews, there needs to be considerable trial of categories in pilot studies before engaging in any final classification. If, in a trial, items occur which do not fit any previously stated category, then a new category is added.

In minor studies, data relevant to several variables may be tallied in the columns of a locally constructed form. It is usually more efficient to use individual 3″ × 5″ or 4″ × 6″ index cards. The items of data may be recorded in a uniform sequence at the left of each card. The balance of the card may be used to record squares and products and, if called for by the problem, nonnumerical items. Each card should include information necessary to identify the subject. This procedure suffices when the numbers of subjects and variables are small and the computations can be done on a desk calculator. For survey studies involving numerous variables, numerous subjects, and many groups, it is desirable to use the usual 80-column punched card. Such cards are an excellent means of recording data even though the analysis of the data may not involve the use of a computer. Long before the development of the electronic computer, machines have sorted such cards and tabulated the data automatically, using the 80-column punched card (see page 508). Now punched cards are widely used to record the data which will become computer input. A major advantage of even the earlier sorting and tabulating machines is that frequency distributions are tabulated rapidly and a printed record of them obtained. The investigator can also have what cross classifications he needs. The computer offers the additional advantage of doing all the computation, although none of the thinking, required for a successful research.

Tables and graphs

In preparing a report of a survey research for publication in a journal the researcher is wise to examine several recent issues of the journal to study examples of tables and graphs. If the report is a thesis the student should study earlier theses having tables and graphs. If the report is that of an institutional research directed to relatively unsophisticated readers, titles and captions should be phrased in language as simple as possible. Where technical terminology must be used, the terms should be defined in a note below the table or below the graph.

A number of methods of summarizing data were explained in Chapter 8. Where the data pertain to continuous variables, frequency distributions are especially useful. The meaning of the data is enhanced when such statistics as the mean, standard deviation, and the standard error of the mean are listed below the *N*. (For a relatively unsophisticated audience, the 25th, 50th, and 75th percentiles can be more readily explained and understood.) A single frequency distribution may be effectively accompanied by a frequency polygon or histogram.[19] If there are two or three frequency distributions of data pertaining to the same variable and having class intervals of the same size, converting the ordinary frequencies to percentage frequencies will make it possible to draw frequency polygons of the same area, thus facilitating comparison of one group with another. Consider in this connection the comparison of a local distribution of two or three hundred cases with a norm distribution of several thousand.

Data are often summarized graphically by means of bar graphs, a modification of the histogram.[20] The bars may be vertical, separated somewhat from each other, and colored black. The horizontal axis may be the score scale of a test in ordinary, or derived, scores. The vertical axis at the left may be in ordinary or percentage frequencies. Vertical bars in pairs, or in threes, may be drawn in contact with each other and with differing symbols to represent different groups. The individual bars may differ in the frequency or percentage frequency portrayed, but each set of two or three such bars will have the same horizontal scale value, while the different sets will have different values. Often the bars, whether singly, in pairs, or in threes, may run horizontally from a vertical axis at the left. The lengths of the bars may represent the frequencies of values of a continuous variable, or counts in the categories of an unordered series. Whether frequencies or counts, the data may be expressed as percentages. The order of the bars may be in terms of decreasing counts or percentages in the categories. This is illustrated by Figure 10.1.

The frequencies, counts, or percentages should be represented by the *lengths* and not by the areas of the bars. The bars should be in the same units and should be measured from the same zero point. If the lengths of the bars are not proportional to the frequencies, the graph will be misleading.

It is unwise to use circles of various sizes to indicate relative magni-

---

[19] See pages 210–211 in Chapter 8 for an explanation of the drawing of a frequency polygon or histogram.

[20] This discussion of graphs is based on Monroe and Engelhart, *Scientific Study,* pp. 239–42.

Figure 10.1 Percentages of twelfth-grade students enrolled in various high school courses. [Based on Project Talent data reported in Table 9 of John C. Flanagan, "Student Characteristics: Elementary and Secondary," in R. L. Ebel, ed., *Encyclopedia of Educational Research,* 4th ed. (New York: Macmillan, 1969), p. 1334.]

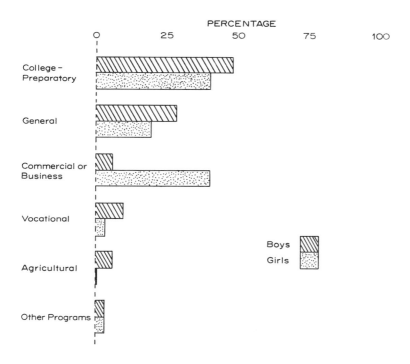

tudes because it is difficult to make accurate comparisons of such areas. Circles may be used, however, to illustrate the proportions of a population which fall into different categories. The area of the circle represents 100 percent and the sectors represent the percentages of each category. A circle divided in this way is known as a pie graph, often used to portray a breakdown of educational expenditures. Line graphs are useful in indicating trends in enrollment, costs, and the like and in illustrating the growth or development of traits. Figure 2.4 on page 30 contains two line graphs or learning curves of white rats.

When there are several frequency distributions of measures of the same variable, as often occurs in surveys and survey research, the data may be reported as illustrated by Table 10.1 and by Figure 10.2.

While Table 10.1 makes use of a scale of ordinary scores, the intervals of a standard score scale, for example, the stanine scale, can be given in the left column or *stub.* When percentage frequencies are computed, the columns of tabulated data are split with the subheads *f*

Table 10.1 Distributions of Total Scores of September ——— Junior College Entrants on the ——— Edition of the American Council on Education, Psychological Examination for College Freshmen

Total Scores	College A		College B		College C		All Three Colleges	
	f	%	f	%	f	%	f	%
150–159					1	.1	1	.0
140–149					6	.4	6	.2
130–139	7	1.4	4	.4	12	.9	23	.8
120–129	5	1.0	6	.6	27	2.0	38	1.4
110–119	17	3.4	22	2.4	58	4.3	97	3.5
100–109	26	5.1	43	4.6	98	7.2	167	6.0
90–99	38	7.5	53	5.7	164	12.1	255	9.1
80–89	57	11.3	80	8.6	205	15.1	342	12.3
70–79	60	11.9	123	13.3	184	13.5	367	13.2
60–69	74	14.6	171	18.5	224	16.5	469	16.8
50–59	77	15.2	157	17.0	190	14.0	424	15.2
40–49	74	14.6	123	13.3	108	7.9	305	10.9
30–39	41	8.1	88	9.5	57	4.2	186	6.7
20–29	17	3.4	45	4.9	19	1.4	81	2.9
10–19	9	1.8	10	1.1	6	4	25	.9
0–9	4	.8	0	0.0	0	0.0	4	.1
N	506	100.0	925	100.0	1359	100.0	2790	100.0
Q_3	83.6	(67)	77.6	(59)	91.1	(76)	86.3	(70)
Md	63.7	(37)	61.8	(34)	73.6	(52)	67.4	(42)
Q_1	47.0	(14)	46.7	(14)	57.4	(26)	51.8	(20)
Q	18.3		15.4		16.8		17.2	

and % at the top of the columns. Just below the N, near the bottom of the stub are listed the symbols Q_3, Md, and Q_1. If the researcher prefers, these symbols may be replaced by the captions 75th percentile, 50th percentile, and 25th percentile. Note the order of the symbols and the equivalent captions. Below Q_1 is listed Q, the quartile deviation, or semi-interquartile range. It is a measure of the variability of each sample and equals $\dfrac{Q_3 - Q_1}{2}$. Note that the score intervals of the test range from 0–9 to the highest interval containing a score. (It would be generally preferable to include the interval which terminates in the perfect score, but the norm data contain no score as high as 160.)

Instead of the sample statistics mentioned above, the symbols listed at the left in the table may be N, $\overline{X}$, s_x, and $s_{\overline{x}}$. Use of mean, standard deviation, and standard error of the mean implies a somewhat sophisticated audience for the survey report. (Most institutional researchers soon learn this.)

To the right of each Q_3, Md, and Q_1 in Table 10.1 are listed in parentheses, the national norm percentiles of the local quartiles. Note that the quartiles of College C are above the national 75th percentile, *Md,* and 25th percentiles.

If a table or figure requires a footnote, it should be given immediately below the table or figure and should start with an asterisk rather than a small number which, within a table or figure containing numerical data, can be mistaken for an exponent.

Titles and subtitles in a table, and captions to a figure should be brief and unambiguous. A table or·figure should explain itself without much dependence on the context in which it appears. Tables such as 10.1 are most often printed today with few if any vertical lines, horizontal lines sufficing.

In the title of Table 10.1, blanks appear and the names of the col-

Figure 10.2 ACE total score data of September ——— junior college entrants. The wide vertical bars range from Q_1, the 25th percentile, to Q_3, the 75th percentile, with the medians or 50th percentiles, shown by horizontal lines. The heavy vertical lines range up to the 90th percentile and down to the 10th percentile. Note that the top 10 percent and the bottom 10 percent of students are in the ranges indicated by the broken lines.

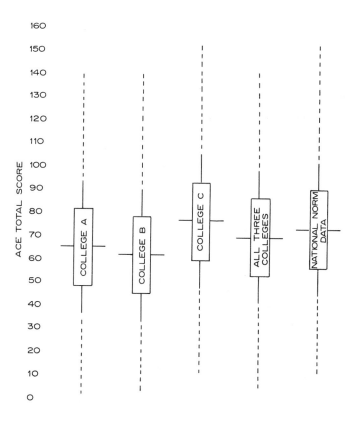

leges are changed to College A, College B, and College C to prevent their identification. (The data are real rather than fictitious.) Often, such name changes are made to forestall invidious comparisons, with only the head of each school knowing how *his* school is labeled.

Figure 10.2, based on the same test data, is a unique type of bar graph. If narrower bars are used, data from 15 to 20 institutions could appear on the same page. The wider bars could range from $+ 1$ standard deviation down to $- 1$ standard deviation. Horizontal dotted lines could identify the critical scores used in placement of students in accelerated or in remedial classes. The footnote below the title of the figure suffices to explain it.

The preceding paragraphs have been largely concerned with summarizing and interpreting data by using the methods of descriptive statistics. In the next section consideration is given to some of the methods of statistical inference as applied to both descriptive and explanatory survey research.

AN ELEMENTARY INTRODUCTION TO SURVEY SAMPLING METHODS

Simple random sampling

The use of a table of random numbers in selecting a simple random sample and the interpretation of the standard error of the mean of such a sample was explained in Chapter 9. In the absence of other knowledge about a population, but where the population can be enumerated, a random sample selected as earlier explained is a type of probability sample. Each member of the population has an equal and independent chance of being selected. A major problem in accomplishing such random sampling is the difficulty of enumerating a scattered population serially so that selection by the use of random numbers can be done. Further difficulties are involved in obtaining data from such a scattered sample. These difficulties and the need to reduce costs led to the development of improved sampling procedures such as stratified random sampling, cluster sampling, and multistage sampling.[21] Each of these types of sampling is described briefly in the following sections and formulas are given which are useful in interpreting data obtained in stratified and in cluster sampling. No formulas are given for multistage sampling since knowledge of analysis of variance is prerequisite

---

[21] For an excellent introduction to survey sampling, see Palmer O. Johnson, "Development of the Sample Survey as a Scientific Methodology," *Journal of Experimental Education* 27 (March 1959), pp. 167–76.

for understanding this technique. After study of Chapter 13 the student should be better prepared to study multistage sampling in one of the advanced texts on survey statistics.

Stratified random sampling

Stratified random sampling can provide greater precision in estimating population values. Its use requires prior knowledge of the characteristics of the population studied so that it can be divided into relatively homogeneous subpopulations or strata. Independent random samples are then drawn from each stratum. While subpopulation within the strata should be relatively homogeneous, the strata should "differ from one another in the mean of the characteristic under measurement."[22] The sizes of the samples drawn at random from each stratum may be proportional to the numbers in each stratum of the population. When this occurs, as will be explained later, computation of the mean of the total sample and its standard error is much simplified. It is not necessary, however, for the samples to be proportionate to the sizes of the strata in the population. Where one stratum in the population is known to be more variable than others, its sample optimum size may be larger than would otherwise be the case. One rule specifies that sample size for optimum allocation may be proportional to the product of the size of the stratum in the population and its standard deviation. Often, costs of sampling the various strata are taken into consideration in deciding on the sizes of the samples.

In educational research, a stratified sample may be drawn from such strata as pupils of defined levels of ability or different types of schools—urban and rural, inner city and suburban—where there are real differences between the strata.

Cluster sampling

In one type of cluster sampling the population of individuals is divided into groups which may or may not be of the same size. Heterogeneity within the clusters tends to increase the precision of the estimates of the population mean and of its standard error. For total samples of the same numbers of individuals, stratified sampling may have greater precision than simple random sampling, but simple random sampling may yield more precise estimates than cluster sampling. Cluster sampling is the least precise but least costly type of sampling of a large population, since numerous individuals are located in the same clusters. One example of cluster sampling is the random selection of sixth-grade

---

[22] *Ibid.,* p. 172.

classes of pupils from a population of all the sixth-grade classes in a large public school system. Such sampling on a nationwide basis may be used in establishing national norms for a test.

Multistage sampling

A two-stage process of sampling may involve cluster sampling within the strata of a stratified sample. In three-stage sampling the primary units may be the strata of a stratified sample or some other type of unit selected at random. The second-stage units are selected at random from the primary units and the tertiary units are selected at random from the secondary ones. The tertiary units may be the ultimate units, for example, individual pupils. An example of three-stage sampling could be (1) the selection of a random sample of cities in some state, (2) a random selection of elementary schools within the cities, and (3) a random selection of fifth-grade classes within the schools.

Systematic sampling

Often it is easier to obtain a systematic sample than a simple random one. For example, if one has a card file of the individuals to be sampled and one-tenth are to be chosen, the first individual is randomly selected from the first ten. Suppose that this random selection is the 7th card, then the later cards to be drawn are the 17th, the 27th, the 37th, and so on. While such sampling may yield a more representative sample than simple random sampling, a systematic sample occasionally can be biased. For example, the same first letters may characterize the names of numerous members of certain nationality groups and such a group may be overrepresented in a systematic sample.[23]

The remainder of this discussion of survey sampling presents formulas for the means of stratified random samples and cluster samples and for the error variances of these means. Their square roots are, of course, the standard errors which may be used in obtaining confidence intervals for the population means (or proportions).

Notation and formulas for stratified random sampling

N =   number of individuals in the total population

N_h =   number of individuals in one of the k strata or levels of the population

n_h =   number of individuals in one of the k samples

n =   number of individuals in the total sample

$$n_1 + n_2 + n_3 + \ldots + n_h + \ldots + n_k = n$$

---

[23] For a more detailed discussion of systematic sampling, consult William G. Cochran, *Sampling Techniques,* 3rd ed. (New York: Wiley, 1963), or other advanced text.

X_{ih} = one of the individual measures

$\bar{X}_h$ = mean of the individual measures in one of the k samples

$$\bar{X}_h = \frac{\sum_{i=1}^{n_h} X_{ih}}{n_h}. \tag{10.1}$$

s_h^2 = variance of the X_{ih} in one of the k samples:

$$s_h^2 = \frac{\sum_{i=1}^{n_h}(X_{ih} - \bar{X}_h)^2}{n_h - 1}. \tag{10.2}$$

$\bar{X}_{st}$ = mean of the entire sample:

$$\bar{X}_{st} = \frac{\sum_{h=1}^{k} N_h \bar{X}_h}{N} \quad \text{or} \quad \frac{\sum_{h=1}^{k} n_h \bar{X}_h}{n}. \tag{10.3}[24]$$

Both expressions give the same estimate of μ, the population mean, when all $\dfrac{n_h}{n} = \dfrac{N_h}{N}$.

$s_{\bar{x}_{st}}^2$ = the error variance of $\bar{X}_{st}$:

$$s_{\bar{x}_{st}}^2 = \frac{1}{N^2} \sum_{h=1}^{k} N_h^2 (1 - f_h) \frac{s_h^2}{n_h}, \tag{10.4}$$

or

$$s_{\bar{x}_{st}}^2 = \frac{1}{N^2} \sum_{h=1}^{k} N_h(N_h - n_h) \frac{s_h^2}{n_h}.$$

The finite population correction $(1 - f_h)$ equals $\dfrac{N_h - n_h}{N_h}$.

Formulas 10.1, 10.2, 10.3, and 10.4 are general. The N_h, n_h, and $(1 - f_h)$ may vary from stratum to stratum. When $\dfrac{n_h}{n} = \dfrac{N_h}{N} = W_h$—the stratum weight is the same for all strata—we have *proportional allocation* and a *self-weighting* sample. Formulas 10.3 and 10.4 may be written:

---

[24] See Helen M. Walker and Joseph Lev, *Statistical Inference* (New York: Holt, Rinehart and Winston, 1953), pp. 174–78; and Cochran, *ibid.*, pp. 82–92. The formulas given above can also be found in other texts on survey sampling statistics, sometimes in symbols unfamiliar to educational and psychological researchers.

$$\bar{X}_{st} = \frac{\sum\limits_{h=1}^{k} \bar{X}_h}{k}, \text{ or } \frac{\sum\limits_{h=1}^{k} \sum\limits_{i=1}^{n_h} X_{ih}}{n},$$ (10.5)

$$s_{\bar{x}_{st}}^2 = \frac{(N-n)}{nN} \sum\limits_{h=1}^{k} W_h s_h^2.$$ (10.6)

If the samples from each stratum are equal in size, their means can be summed and the sum divided by k to obtain $\bar{X}_{st}$. If, however, the samples are not equal in size, but are proportional to the sizes of the population strata, the X_{ih} must be separately summed, these sums combined, and their total divided by n.

In Formula 10.4, $\dfrac{nN_h}{N}$ is substituted for n_h to obtain Formula 10.6. If, in all strata, the finite population correction is negligible, Formula 10.4 simplifies to

$$s_{\bar{x}_{st}}^2 = \sum\limits_{h=1}^{k} \frac{W_h^2 \, s_h^2}{n_h}.$$ (10.7)

This simple formula for the error variance of the mean of a stratified sample makes it easier to see that $s_{\bar{x}_{st}}^2$ is, in general, a kind of weighted average of the error variances, $s_{\bar{x}_h}^2$.

If the stratified random sampling data are proportions, substitute p_{st} and p_h for $\bar{X}_{st}$ and $\bar{X}_h$ in Formula 10.3. Substitute $s_{p_{st}}^2$ and $p_h q_h$ for $s_{\bar{x}_{st}}^2$ and s_h^2 in Formulas 10.4 and 10.6.

Notation and formulas for cluster sampling

M = the number of clusters in the population
m = the number of clusters in the total sample
n_i = the number of individuals in a cluster
N = the number of individuals in the total sample
X_i = one of the individual measures in a cluster

$\bar{X}_i$ = the mean of one of the clusters

$$\bar{X}_i = \frac{\sum\limits_{i=1}^{n_i} X_i}{n_i}$$ (10.8)

$\bar{n}_i$ = the average size of the clusters

$$\bar{n}_i = \frac{\sum_{i=1}^{m} n_i}{m}. \tag{10.9}$$

$\bar{X}_c =$ the sample estimate of the mean μ of the population

$$\bar{X}_c = \frac{\sum_{i=1}^{m} n_i \bar{X}_i}{N}. \tag{10.10}$$

$s_{\bar{x}_c}^2 =$ the error variance of $\bar{X}_c$.

$$s_{\bar{x}_c}^2 = \frac{M - m}{Mm} \frac{\sum_{i=1}^{m} n_i^2 (\bar{X}_i - \bar{X}_c)^2}{(m - 1)(\bar{n}_i)^2} \tag{10.11}[25]$$

If the clusters are all of equal size Formula 10.11 simplifies to

$$s_{\bar{x}_c}^2 = \frac{M - m}{Mm} \frac{\sum_{i=1}^{m} (\bar{X}_i - \bar{X}_c)^2}{m - 1}. \tag{10.12}$$

Since $\dfrac{M - m}{M}$ equals the finite population correction, if m is so small compared with M that this correction is negligible, Formula 10.11 further simplifies to

$$s_{\bar{x}_c}^2 = \frac{\sum_{i=1}^{m} (\bar{X}_i - \bar{X}_c)^2}{m(m - 1)}. \tag{10.13}$$

In this form "it is easy to see" that this formula is analogous to one of the ways of computing the error variance of the mean of a simple random sample. It differs in that the computation is based on cluster *means* rather than individual scores.

When the cluster sample data are proportions, substitute $s_{p_c}^2$ for

---

[25] For a derivation of Formula 10.11 see Eli S. Marks, "Sampling in the Revision of the Stanford-Binet Scale," *Psychological Bulletin* 44 (September 1947), pp. 413–34. For the simplification of Formula 10.11 and an excellent treatment of various methods of sampling a finite population see Helen M. Walker and Joseph Lev, *Elementary Statistical Methods*, 3rd ed. (New York: Holt, Rinehart and Winston, 1969), pp. 327–50. Stratified and cluster sampling are similarly treated in *Statistical Inference*, pp. 174–78, by the same authors.

$s_{\overline{x}_c}^2$ and p_i for $\overline{X}_i$ and p_c for $\overline{X}_c$ where these refer respectively to a cluster proportion and the proportion in the total sample.

Errors other than those accounted for by standard errors

It should be remembered that standard errors account for variable errors of sampling and of measurement. In random sampling the process tends to control some of the factors that bias the data. Chance may occasionally deal out samples that are not representative, but the standard errors computed for simple random sampling, stratified random sampling, cluster sampling, and multistage sampling take such chance limitations of the data into account. We can be confident in the long run that 95 percent of the time (or 99 percent of the time) the population mean is between ——— and ———.

It is unfortunately true that systematic errors can not be so easily dealt with. A high reliability coefficient of a test used to collect data, although necessary, is insufficient to tell us whether the test collects valid data where the problem is the criterion and the constructs are abstract. Systematic errors of validity may so bias the findings in a comparative survey that they are undependable. When data are collected by questionnaire or interview, failure of a proportion of the members of a sample to respond is a well recognized factor in biasing. When data are obtained by systematic observation, prejudices and preconceptions may bias data. It is extremely difficult to deal with systematic errors of the kinds mentioned. Careful planning, replication of studies, and the maintaining of objective or scientific attitudes are essential.

Practice Exercise 10.1

A proportional allocation or self-weighting stratified random has each n_h equal to 30 and n equal to 90. The total population has an N equal to 900. The top stratum has stanine scores of 7, 8, and 9. The middle stratum has stanine scores of 4, 5, and 6. The lowest stratum has stanine scores of 1, 2, and 3. The distribution of scores is

Stanine	f	Stanine	f	Stanine	f
9	8	6	12	3	11
8	11	5	10	2	10
7	11	4	8	1	9

Round off the stanine means of each stratum to whole numbers and compute each stratum variance to two decimal places. Compute the mean and the error variance of the mean of the total sample to four decimal places.

(a) What is $\bar{X}_{st}$?   (b) What is $s^2_{\bar{x}_{st}}$?

Practice Exercise 10.2

A random sample of 100 clusters of 25 high school entrants each was given a reading test. The cluster *means* are given in the following frequency distribution. Assume that the finite population correction can be ignored.

Stanine Mean	f
9	4
8	7
7	12
6	17
5	20
4	17
3	12
2	7
1	4
$\overline{m}$	$\overline{100}$

(a) What is $\bar{X}_c$?

(b) What is $s^2_{\bar{x}_c}$?

Questions for Study and Discussion

1. Discuss the early history of the school survey movement.

2. What characteristics justify calling a descriptive survey "descriptive survey research"?

3. In what ways does an explanatory or analytic survey research differ from a purely descriptive one?

4. What is an *ogive?* How might one be used in reporting survey research?

5. What are the uses of case studies in educational, psychological, and sociological research? Locate research reports utilizing case studies.

6. What characteristics of the individual strata make stratified random sampling most effective?

7. What is needed in addition to survey data to justify the making of appraisals and recommendations?

8. In what journals are you likely to find reports of research relevant to administrative theory in education?

9. What are the advantages of cluster sampling? What are its limitations?

10. In what ways can tables and graphs distort the meaning of data?

11. Select a problem for a descriptive survey research and write a proposal for conducting it.

12. What are the distinctions between a comparative survey, a quasi-experiment, and a "true" experiment (See the Campbell and Stanley citation in footnote 12.)

13. In what ways can data-processing equipment contribute to conducting survey research?

14. What are the advantages of a longitudinal survey research? What are the difficulties in conducting such research?

15. What difficulties are likely to be encountered in conducting a survey of city schools or a higher institution under present conditions?

Suggestions
for Further Study

The selected references of this chapter include discussions of survey research methodology and a few examples of reports of survey
research. Brief annotations have been added to some of the references
where the titles do not suffice to indicate their relevance. The student
interested in undertaking a survey research will find it useful to consult
Reviews of Educational Research, having such titles as "Education for
Socially Disadvantaged Children," "Education of Exceptional Children," and "Educational Organization, Administration and Finance."
The Yearbooks of the *National Society for the Study of Education* and
the 1969 and earlier editions of the *Encyclopedia of Educational Research* contain many summaries and references to survey research in
education. See William H. Angoff's chapter in the second edition of
Educational Measurement for further discussion of sampling, especially
cluster sampling.

Selected References

Bayley, Nancy. "On the Growth of Intelligence." *American Psychologist* 10 (December 1955): 805–18.

————. "A New Look at the Curve of Intelligence," *Proceedings of the 1956 Invitational Conference on Testing Problems*. Princeton, N.J.: Educational Testing Service, 1957. Pp. 11–25.
These two references discuss findings of the Berkeley Growth Study directed by Nancy Bayley.

Bloom, Benjamin S. *Stability and Change in Human Characteristics.* New York: Wiley, 1964.

Campbell, Roald F., and Russell T. Gregg, eds. *Administrative Behavior in Education.* New York: Harper, 1957.

Carlson, Richard O. *Adoption of Educational Innovations.* Eugene, Oregon: The Center for Advanced Study of Educational Administration, University of Oregon, 1965.

Cochran, William G. *Sampling Techniques.* rev. ed. New York: Wiley, 1963.

Coladarci, Arthur P., and Jacob W. Getzels. *The Use of Theory in Educational Administration.* Stanford: Stanford University Press, 1955.

Coleman, James S., and others. *Equality of Educational Opportunity.* Washington, D.C.: Government Printing Office, 1966.
A very important and controversial analytic survey research.

Cooper, Dan H. "School Surveys." In *Encyclopedia of Educational Research,* edited by C. W. Harris, pp. 1211–16. 3rd ed. New York: Macmillan, 1960.

Cornell, Francis G. "Sampling Methods." In *Encyclopedia of Educational Research,* edited by C. W. Harris, pp. 1181–83. 3rd ed. New York: Macmillan, 1960.

Erickson, Donald A. "The School Administrator," in "Educational Organization, Administration, and Finance." *Review of Educational Research* 37 (October 1967): 417–32.

Getzels, Jacob W., and Egon G. Guba. "Role, Role Conflict, and Effectiveness: An Empirical Study." *American Sociological Review* 19 (April 1954): 164–75.

Goslin, David A. *Teachers and Testing.* New York: Russell Sage Foundation, 1967.

Appendix I describes the random sampling of schools from a U.S. Office of Education. Directory of Public Secondary Day Schools.

Griffiths, Daniel E. "Administrative Behavior." In *Encyclopedia of Educational Research,* edited by Robert L. Ebel, pp. 17–24. 4th ed. New York: Macmillan, 1969.

Gross, Neal, Ward S. Mason, and Alexander W. McEachern. *Explorations in Role Analysis: Studies of the School Superintendency Role.* New York: Wiley, 1958.
Hypotheses derived from theory are tested.

Halpin, Andrew W. *Theory and Research in Administration.* New York: Macmillan, 1966.

Hansen, Morris H., William N. Hurwitz, and William G. Madow. *Sample Survey Methods and Theory.* New York: Wiley, 1953.

Harris, Chester W., ed. *Problems in Measuring Change.* Madison: University of Wisconsin Press, 1963.

Havighurst, Robert J. and others. *Growing Up in River City.* New York: Wiley, 1962.
An interesting and important longitudinal study.

Hemphill, John K., Daniel E. Griffiths, and Norman Fredericksen. *Administrative Performance and Personality: A Study of the Principal in a Simulated Elementary School.* New York: Teachers College, Columbia University, 1962.

Herriott, Robert E., "Survey Research Methods." In *Encyclopedia of Educational Research,* edited by Robert L. Ebel, pp. 1400–1419. 4th ed. New York: Macmillan, 1969.

Johnson, Palmer O. "Development of the Sample Survey as a Scientific Methodology." *Journal of Experimental Education* 27 (March 1959): 167–76.

Kish, Leslie. *Survey Sampling.* New York: Wiley, 1965.

Lipham, James M. "Leadership and Administration," *Behavioral Science and Educational Administration.* The Sixty-third Yearbook of the National Society for the Study of Education, Part II. Chicago: University of Chicago Press, 1964, pp. 119–41.

Lord, Frederic M. "The Measurement of Growth." *Educational and Psychological Measurement* 16 (Winter 1956): 421–37.
Study of this paper should be followed by study of Quinn McNemar's "On Growth Measurement."

———. "Further Problems in the Measurement of Growth." *Educational and Psychological Measurement* 18 (Autumn 1958): 437–51.

McNemar, Quinn. "On Growth Measurement." *Educational and Psychological Measurement* 18 (Spring 1958): 47–55.
Describes use of a simpler regressed score method for estimating true gain from observed gain.

Marks, Eli S. "Sampling in the Revision of the Stanford-Binet Scale." *Psychological Bulletin* 44 (September 1947): 413-34.

Sieber, Sam D. "Survey Research in Education: The Case of the Misconstrued Technique." *Phi Delta Kappan* 49 (January 1968): 273–76.

Trow, Martin. "Education and Survey Research." In *The Uses of Survey Research,* edited by Charles Glock and others, pp. 315–75. New York: Russell Sage, 1967.

Tucker, Ledyard R., Fred Damarin, and Samuel Messick. "A Base-Free Measure of Change." *Psychometrika* 31 (December 1966): 457–73.

Walker, Helen M., and Joseph Lev. *Elementary Statistical Methods.* 3rd ed. New York: Holt, Rinehart and Winston, 1969.

White, Kinnard. "Personality Characteristics of Educational Leaders: A Comparison of Administrators and Researchers." *School Review* 73 (Autumn 1965): 292–300.

11

Studying Relationships: Concomitant Variation and Prediction

The next three chapters are concerned with study of relationships. Correlation techniques, including the product-moment coefficient of correlation and other indices of "concomitant variation" are useful in investigating the extent to which variation in one variable is associated with variation in one or more other variables. Many of the variables studied are interval variables or, occasionally, ratio ones. Often, however, the variables are nominal variables whose association with other nominal variables, or with interval ones, are of interest to the researcher. One aim of this discussion is to aid the graduate student or other educational researcher in selecting types of correlation coefficients or other measure of association appropriate to his problem. The purpose of the research may be that of developing an effective means of predicting academic or vocational success, or the purpose may be one of estimating the extent to which abilities, achievements, and other traits are associated with one another or with educational and other environmental variables.

The role of correlation techniques in the study of causal relationships

Which variables are causes and which effects cannot be ascertained by correlation techniques alone. This is best accomplished by experimentation where the experimenter can introduce or otherwise manipulate the variables hypothesized as causes.

It is possible, for example, to study the relationship between attendance and nonattendance in after-school reading classes of culturally deprived pupils and subsequently obtained reading test scores by computing the appropriate type of correlation coefficient. An alternative is to evaluate such instruction experimentally, pretesting and posttesting groups of pupils who received and did not receive the instruction. Assuming that the groups are equivalent at the start of the experiment in all important relevant factors, or that initial differences are taken into account statistically, a significant difference in reading achievement test means, or mean gains, at the end of the experiment may favor the after-school instruction. This difference would be more dependable evidence that the instruction caused the greater achievement than would the correlation coefficient earlier mentioned. Where, however, causal factors have been dependably identified, correlation techniques are useful in estimating their strength or importance.

The role of correlation techniques in the study of problems of prediction

In the case of prediction problems, the predictor variable or variables may be measures of causal factors of the achievement predicted, but the interest is not in their identification as causes. It suffices to know that variation in the predictor variable, or variables, is closely associated with variation in the variable to be predicted.

Intelligence test scores or scores on tests of general scholastic aptitude, scores on tests of special aptitude or proficiency in some special field, achievement test scores, school marks, grade-point averages, and, more recently, measures of personality traits are used singly, or in various combinations, as bases for predicting future academic or vocational success. Predictions from such variables may be made in different ways. Very frequently predictions are made informally on the basis of available data. This occurs, for example, when a counselor studies a student's record of test scores, course marks, participation in activities, and offers advice with reference to further academic training. Often predictions are made that the mark earned in the first of a sequence of courses forecasts a similar mark in the second. In dealing with practical problems of guidance and placement, increased use should be made of more efficient methods involving correlation techniques. Furthermore, while predictions of the types just mentioned are widely made, understanding of correlation techniques contributes to more intelligent applications of these informal ways of predicting.

The correlation coefficient obtained from paired scores on an aptitude test given on entrance to a college and grade-point averages earned after a semester or more of attendance is an index of the predictive validity of the aptitude test. The correlation coefficient, the means, and the standard deviations of both variables are used in obtaining an equation, termed a "regression equation," useful in predicting grade-point averages from the aptitude scores. Substituting an aptitude score for X and solving the equation yields Y', the predicted grade-point average. Regression equations may use scores from a single predictor test or they may use appropriately weighted scores from more than one test. The predictor variables may be or include aptitude and achievement test scores, course marks earned on a lower level, and measures of personality traits. A regression equation involving more than one predictor variable is a "multiple" regression equation.

The criterion problem

In undertaking research on a prediction problem culminating in a simple or multiple regression equation, measures of the academic or vocational achievement must be defined and later obtained. Such measures are termed the "criterion" variable. It is important to obtain measures as reliable and valid as possible. Equally important is the selection or construction of reliable tests or other instruments for which substantial predictive validity for the criterion variable can be hypothesized. It is desirable that the predictor variables have low correlations among themselves to avoid duplication of effort. (An exception is a "suppressor" variable—measures obtained from a test having low correlation with the criterion variable, but whose correlation with another predictor test enhances the predictive efficiency of the combination.) In seeking or constructing promising tests for use in a prediction study, the student or other researcher should consult reports of previous similar research. He should also study sources of information on tests and other measuring instruments, especially the *Mental Measurements Yearbooks.*

The sampling problem

Another major phase in a prediction study is the selection of an adequate sample of the individuals to be tested at the start with the predictor tests and later with the criterion test. (Of course, the predictor variables may be, or include, course marks and the criterion similarly may be marks earned some time later, or grade-point averages.) One difficulty in predictive studies is loss of cases from the initial testing to the time the criterion measures are obtained. Such losses tend to lower the measures of correlation used in obtaining a regression equation.[1] It should be noted that a regression equation predicts most efficiently when applied to populations most closely comparable to the sample providing the data on which it is based. Since there is likely to be some

---

[1] For a discussion of ways of dealing with this problem see Harold Gulliksen, *Theory of Mental Tests* (New York: Wiley, 1950), Chapters 12 and 13; and Frederic M. Lord and Melvin R. Novick, *Statistical Theories of Mental Test Scores* (Reading, Mass.: Addison-Wesley, 1968), pp. 140–48.

loss in predictive efficiency when, for example, it is applied to later groups of college entrants or of prospective employees, the prediction research should be replicated, a procedure known as "cross validation."

Measures of association and means of prediction

An elementary discussion of theory concerning the coefficient of correlation, regression equations, standard errors of estimate and standard errors of measurement should contribute to the reader's understanding of why regression equations are effective in making predictions and how the accuracy of predictions can be evaluated. Explanations follow on how to estimate the chances for a given predictor score X, that students or other individuals will receive a criterion score Y, below (or above) some specified level, and how to determine the corresponding predictor score for a specified risk of failure or chances of success. Included also are explanations of methods useful in constructing an expectancy table and in selecting a cutting score.

Regression equations are usually employed in predicting a "fallible" criterion—a criterion variable that is to some extent unreliable. It is comforting to know that a predictor test more effectively predicts "true" achievement than it does the criterion measures of achievement. A student of English composition may acquire more skill (or less) than his course mark in this subject indicates. The prediction may be a better estimate of his skill than the one made by his teacher.

Attention is next directed to the comparative efficiency in predicting future achievement by means of regression equations and the more informal use of test scores or marks for the same purpose.

Brief discussion of multiple and partial correlation is followed by a very elementary discussion of factor analysis. Apart from their use in prediction, multiple correlation coefficients and the "regression coefficients" of a multiple regression equation have applications in estimating the association between one "dependent" variable and two or more "independent" variables in combination, and in estimating the relative contributions each of the latter makes to variation in the former. Partial correlation coefficients are useful in estimating the remaining correlation between two variables when other variables are held constant or eliminated. *If* valid measures of innate child intelligence, innate parental intelligence, and environment were available, partial coefficients could answer the old question about the relative importance of heredity and environment! There are, of course, more tangible, but similar problems, that partial coefficients do help to solve. Factor analysis is useful in studying traits underlying test and other measurement variables; it contributes to establishment of the construct validity of tests and other measuring instruments; it aids in the selection of tests for use in prediction; and it has greatly contributed to our knowledge of human abilities and traits.

Measures of relationship other than Pearson product-moment coefficients of correlation or their derivatives, multiple and partial coefficients are then dealt with. These include rank correlation coefficients, tetrachoric coefficients of correlation, biserial and point biserial coefficients, ϕ (phi) coefficients, and coefficients of contingency. Some of these are reasonably efficient estimates of the more familiar Pearson product-moment coefficients. They are often the only appropriate indices for studying relationships among ordinal and nominal variables, or between such variables and others assumed to be interval or ratio ones.

The final major section of this chapter is concerned with item-analysis procedures useful in test construction, whether the tests are produced for research purposes, or for use in more routine evaluations of ability, achievement, or other traits. Most of the indices mentioned in the preceding paragraph have applications in item analysis. This section contains a number of suggestions and explanations of great practical value to the graduate student who constructs a test for use in collecting his data. The suggestions may also aid the expert in a city school or college office of research concerned with test construction or with analysis of tests locally constructed by teachers, or groups of teachers working cooperatively under the direction of the expert.

AN ELEMENTARY MATHEMATICAL EXPLANATION OF CORRELATION AND REGRESSION

In the physical sciences there are a number of cases in which variation in one factor is accompanied by such variation in the other that the relationship between the two may be represented by a straight line. For example, if X is the temperature expressed in absolute degrees (degrees Centigrade $+ 273$) the volume Y of a given mass of gas increases or decreases in such a way that the changes of volume with temperature may be portrayed as a straight line drawn through points which are the X and Y values of simultaneous observations of the temperature and volume of the gas. All of the points representing the observations, except for minute observational or measurement errors, are on the same straight line. This is illustrated by Figure 11.1.

Linear relationships in education and psychology

In education and psychology and other fields where measurements are less exact, or the underlying relationship between two variables less perfect, a plotting of the points which represent paired values of X and Y yields a scatter of points in which the less perfect the relationship, the greater the scatter. For example, where the values of X and Y are

Figure 11.1   Graph of a linear equation—physics data

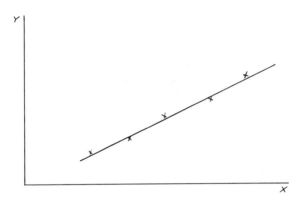

scores on two tests administered to the same sample of pupils, the plotting of points representing paired values of X and Y may yield an elliptical scatter of points extending from the lower left corner of a chart toward the upper right corner. If the two tests are highly correlated this elliptical scatter may be much more elongated and narrow than the scatter one would obtain from tests which are much less correlated. In order to use the Pearson product-moment correlation coefficient as an index of the amount of relationship between the two variables X and Y, it is most desirable that the relationship be linear. This does not mean the points representing the paired observations of X and Y all fall on the same line. It does mean that if one draws a line for use in predicting a Y value from an X value, or a line for predicting an X value from a Y value, with the least error, that these lines will be straight lines through the points representing the paired observations of X and Y scattered about the lines. Such a line with the scatter of points about it is shown in Figure 11.2. Where the correlation is less than perfect two separate lines may be drawn, one for predicting Y from X and one for predicting X from Y. These lines will later be referred to as regression lines. For simplicity only the line for predicting values of Y is shown. The Y distances labeled "d" are explained on page 327.

A plot of points which tends to curve significantly would not justify attempts to draw straight lines, nor the use of the Pearson product-moment correlation as an index of the amount of relationship. There are, of course, techniques for fitting a curve where the relationship is curvilinear, but these are seldom used with psychological or educational data.

The best fitting straight line

Assuming the relationship of X and Y is linear, the line useful in predicting values of Y from values of X with the least error, is the line from

Figure 11.2 Graph of a linear equation—educational or psychological data

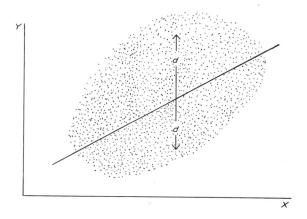

which the sum of the squares of the deviations of the points which represent the paired values of observations of X and Y are a minimum. Above each value of X is a point on the line. The Y value of each such point is the value of Y that would be predicted from the given value of X. Above the same value of X, there may be other points located in terms of the original data. The distances in units of Y of these points from the line are the deviations just referred to. Note in Figure 11.2 the deviations labeled "d." One could sum these distances to obtain a measure of how well the line fits the observations, but the deviations above the line would be positive while those below would be negative. Summing the squares of the distances or deviations gives a measure, untroubled by positive and negative values, of how well the line fits the observations. The problem is to so locate a line for predicting Y from X, or a line for predicting X from Y, that the sum of the squares of the deviations explained above is a minimum.

The equation of the best fitting line

In elementary algebra the equation for such a line to be used in predicting Y from X is $Y = AX + B$ where A and B are determinable constants. In statistics we call such an equation a regression equation and we change Y to Y' to indicate that the values of Y estimated by means of the equation are predictions. Such values of Y differ from the observed values of Y in the original data in that they are all on the line. Given N pairs of observations of X and Y, we may transform these observations or scores to standard scores having means of zero and standard deviations of unity. Each standard score replacing an X score equals $\dfrac{X - \bar{X}}{s_x}$ and each standard score replacing an original Y score is equal to $\dfrac{Y - \bar{Y}}{s_y}$

where $\bar{X}$ and $\bar{Y}$ are the means and s_x and s_y are the standard deviations of the X and Y scores. Such standard scores are here represented by the symbols z_x and z_y. (When we say a pupil is .5 of a standard deviation above the mean of test X we are giving him a standard or z_x score of $+ .5$.) Predicted Y scores on the standard score basis may be given the symbol z'_y. The linear equation mentioned above may be written in standard score form as $z'_y = az_x$. (No term corresponding to B in $Y = AK + B$ is needed since the coordinate axes replacing X and Y axes in Figure 11.3 are located at the means of the z_x and z_y scores which equal zero.)

The theory of least squares

The deviations, such as those labeled "d" in Figure 11.2, are equal to $z_y - z'_y$ and, since each z'_y is equal to az_x, each $z_y - z'_y$ is equal to $z_y - az_x$. According to the theory of "least squares," it is the sum of the squares of such deviations that must be a minimum for the regression line to be the best fitting line and for the regression equation $z'_y = az_x$ to predict values of z_y, or Y, with the least error. The sum of squares to be minimized may be written:

$$\Sigma(z_y - az_x)^2 =$$
$$\Sigma(z_y^2 - 2az_xz_y + a^2z_x^2).$$

Determining the value of "a"

We need to determine the value of a. Using differential calculus, this is done by taking the derivative of the expression just given with respect to a, setting the derivative equal to zero, and solving it for a. (Recall from calculus that the derivative of ka^2 and ka are respectively $2ka$ and k. Also recall that in obtaining a derivative only terms involving the variable with which the derivative is concerned are differentiated and that terms involving other variables are considered constant.) Following this procedure the derivative with respect to a is:

$$\Sigma(2az_x^2 - 2z_xz_y).$$

Distributing the "summation operator," Σ, setting the derivative equal to zero, and dividing by 2,

$$a\Sigma z_x^2 - \Sigma z_xz_y = 0.$$

Since the standard deviation of z scores equals $\sqrt{\dfrac{\Sigma z_x^2}{N-1}} = 1.00$,

$\Sigma z_x^2 = N - 1$. Substituting $N - 1$ for Σz_x^2, $a\Sigma z_x^2 - \Sigma z_xz_y = 0$,

becomes $\qquad a(N - 1) - \Sigma z_xz_y = 0 \qquad$ and

$$a = \frac{\Sigma z_xz_y}{N-1}.$$

"a" is the coefficient of correlation. In the equation $z'_y = az_x$, "a" defines the slope of the line representing the equation.[2] This is illustrated in Figure 11.3.

Figure 11.3 Graph of $z'_y = az_x$

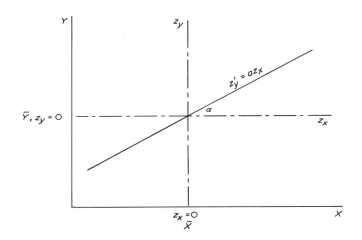

a, the slope of the line is equal to the tangent[3] of the angle shown in the diagram. It is a measure of the rate of change of variable z_y with respect to change in variable z_x. It is also equal to the Pearson product-moment coefficient of correlation between the paired scores of z_x and z_y.

$$r_{xy} = \frac{\Sigma z_x z_y}{N - 1}. \tag{11.1}$$

When x and y are deviate measures equal to $X - \overline{X}$ and $Y - \overline{Y}$, z_x equals $\dfrac{x}{s_x}$ and z_y equals $\dfrac{y}{s_y}$. Substituting these in Formula 11.1 yields:

---

[2] For a similar, but more detailed derivation of "a" see M. D. Nefzger and James Drasgow, "The Needless Assumption of Normality in Pearson's r," *American Psychologist* 12 (October 1957), pp. 623–25.

The authors claim that only the assumption of linearity of two continuous variables is necessary for the computation of the product-moment coefficient of correlation. No assumption is needed for computation, but the satisfying of this and the other assumptions mentioned on pages 206–207 of Chapter 8 promotes interpretation and use. See also Arnold Binder, "Considerations of the Place of Assumptions in Correlational Analysis," *American Psychologist* 14 (August 1959), pp. 504–10.

[3] The tangent of α in this right triangle is the ratio of the vertical opposite side to the horizontal adjacent one:

$$r_{xy} = \frac{\Sigma xy}{(N-1)s_x s_y}, \text{ usually written } r_{xy} = \frac{\Sigma xy}{Ns_x s_y}. \qquad (11.2)$$

This is equivalent to Formula 8.9 on page 220:

$$r_{xy} = \frac{\Sigma XY - N\bar{X}\bar{Y}}{Ns_x s_y}. \qquad (8.9)$$

and Formula 8.10, the two formulas most often used with paired raw or ordinary scores.

The regression equation

When r_{xy} is substituted for "a" in $z'_y = az_x$, we have the regression equation in z or standard score form:

$$z'_y = r_{xy} z_x. \qquad (11.3)$$

and when $\dfrac{Y' - \bar{Y}}{s_y}$ and $\dfrac{X - \bar{X}}{s_y}$ are substituted for z'_y and z_x, Formula 11.3 becomes the more familiar regression equation for predicting values of Y from values of X:

$$Y' = r_{xy} \frac{s_y}{s_x} X + (\bar{Y} - r_{xy} \frac{s_y}{s_x} \bar{X}). \qquad (11.4)$$

A similar equation may be written for predicting values of X from values of Y, but such equations are seldom used since X most often refers to the predictor test. In using such an equation, substitute the values of r_{xy}, s_x, s_y, $\bar{X}$, and $\bar{Y}$. Simplified, for example, Y' may equal $.54X + 16.42$ or $.54X - 16.42$. Then substitute successively the various possible values of X and record the corresponding values of Y', preferably listing both series of scores in order of decreasing size. This can be done rapidly and accurately with a desk calculator as explained on page 231 of Chapter 8.

DERIVATIONS OF THE STANDARD ERRORS OF ESTIMATE AND OF MEASUREMENT

The deviations from the regression line labeled "d" in Figure 11.2 are equal to $z_y - z'_y$. For a given predictor score z_x, the predicted z'_y is the mean of numerous z_y scores later received by the students who earlier earned the given z_x. The standard deviation of the differences between the z_y scores and z'_y (the $z_y - z'_y$), is the standard error of estimate, $s_{y \cdot x}$.

Since z'_y is a mean, a $z_y - z'_y$ difference is analogous to an ordinary deviate measure x obtained from the difference, $X - \bar{X}$. Formula 8.2 for an ordinary standard deviation can be written for the square of such a standard deviation as $\dfrac{\Sigma(X - \bar{X})^2}{N - 1}$. Hence, by analogy, the squared standard error of estimate:

$$s^2_{y \cdot z} = \frac{\Sigma(z_y - z'_y)^2}{N - 1},$$

$$= \frac{1}{N - 1} \Sigma(z_y - r_{xy}z_x)^2. \qquad \text{(since } z'_y = r_{xy}z_x)$$

Squaring, distributing Σ, and multiplying by $1/N - 1$, this equation becomes

$$s^2_{y \cdot x} = \frac{\Sigma z^2_y}{N - 1} - 2r_{xy} \frac{\Sigma z_x z_y}{N - 1} + r^2_{xy} \frac{\Sigma z^2_x}{N - 1}.$$

Since the squared standard deviations of z scores equal 1.00 and $\dfrac{\Sigma z_x z_y}{N - 1}$ equals r_{xy}, the last equation becomes

$$s^2_{y \cdot x} = 1 - 2r^2_{xy} + r^2_{xy},$$

$$= 1 - r^2_{xy}, \text{ and}$$

$$s_{y \cdot x} = \sqrt{1 - r^2_{xy}} \text{ or} \qquad (11.5)$$

$$s_{y \cdot x} = s_y \sqrt{1 - r^2_{xy}}. \qquad (11.6)$$

Formula 11.5 is the standard error of estimate of z'_y scores while Formula 11.6 is the standard error of estimate of Y' scores where s_y differs from 1.00.

The squares of $s_{y \cdot x}$ thus obtained are not unbiased estimators of $s^2_{y \cdot x}$. Where N is small, $(1 - r_{xy})$ or $s^2(1 - r^2_{xy})$ should be multiplied by $\dfrac{N - 1}{N - 2}$ and the square root taken.[4]

The standard error of measurement

The formula for the standard error of measurement may be similarly derived. For $z_y - z'_y$ we substitute $z_x - X_{x_T}$, the difference between an observed score X, in standard score form, and the theoretical true score X_T, also in standard score form—true scores being the average of numerous X scores of the same individual in the absence of practice effect. The derivation yields:

$$s_e = s_x \sqrt{1 - r^2_{xx_T}}.$$

---

[4] See Allen L. Edwards, *Statistical Methods*, 2nd ed. (New York: Holt, Rinehart and Winston, 1967), p. 111.

However, $r^2_{xx_T}$, the square of the correlation between observed scores and true scores of the same variable, equals r_{xx} the coefficient of reliability of the variable.[5] Hence, this formula becomes Formula 9.13 on page 257:

$$s_e = s_{meas} = s_x \sqrt{1 - r_{xx}}. \tag{9.13}$$

It was explained in Chapter 9 that the standard of measurement can be used to indicate for a specified level of confidence what range of estimated true scores relevant to a given observed score will include the student's true score. Similarly, as explained in the next section, the standard error of estimate indicates how later obtained criterion scores will range about a predicted criterion score, Y'.

The applicability of the standard error of estimate depends on how well the assumptions of linearity and homoscedasticity are satisfied. (Homoscedasticity is defined as equal variability of the measures in the various rows or various columns of a correlation chart.) If values of X deviating widely from $\overline{X}$ are avoided and N is reasonably large, the standard error of estimate can usually be applied with comparative safety. The same is true of the standard error of measurement.

INTERPRETING PREDICTED SCORES

In Figure 11.4, Y' as a point on the regression on line is a prediction from the given X. Its level on the Y scale is also indicated. The small normal curve above X represents the numerous actual Y scores which might be obtained by a very large number of students receiving the score X on the aptitude or proficiency test. The mean of this distribution is the predicted Y' and its standard deviation is the standard error of estimate:

$$s_{y \cdot x} = s_y \sqrt{1 - r^2_{xy}}.$$

The ellipse in the figure represents the scatter of frequencies in the correlation chart from which r_{xy} was calculated. If Figure 11.4 were an elliptical model in three dimensions, as described on page 206 of Chapter 8, the error of estimate curve would be a vertical cross section. A similar curve, or cross section, could be located above each score X within the range for which $s_{y \cdot x}$ is safely applicable.

---

[5] For proof see Charles C. Peters and Walter R. Van Voorhis, *Statistical Procedures and Their Mathematical Bases* (New York: McGraw-Hill, 1940), pp. 204–08. Another proof is explained in Jum C. Nunnally, *Psychometric Theory* (New York: McGraw-Hill, 1967), pp. 183–84. This proof is somewhat analogous to the one on page 346 of this chapter.

Figure 11.4 Graph illustrating a regression line and the standard error of estimate

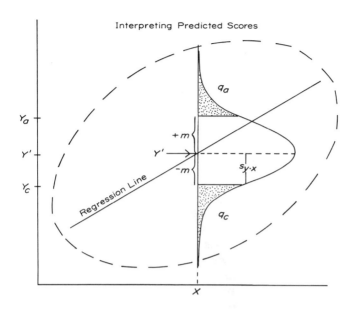

Y_c represents a specified status of Y measures, for example, the lowest score given a mark of **C**. Higher on the scale and above Y' the specified status Y_a may represent the lower limit of a mark of **A**. The distance m portrays the difference between a specified status and the predicted status. In the case of the first example given, $Y_c - Y'$ or m, is negative since Y' is greater than Y_c. In the second example, m is positive since Y_a is higher on the scale than Y'.

In Figure 11.4, q_c is the proportion of the normal curve representing the distribution of errors of estimate indicative of the risk of obtaining a mark below **C** (or other unsatisfactory status) for students earning the given score X. Similarly, q_a is an estimate of the chances of success, that is, the probability of students obtaining a given X exceeding the specified Y_a. To determine what proportion or percentage q is of the area of the curve one must first express m in units of the standard error of estimate:

$$m = \frac{Y_c - Y'}{s_{y \cdot x}} \quad \text{or} \quad \frac{Y_a - Y'}{s_{y \cdot x}}. \tag{11.7}$$

An illustration of the procedure

Assume that Y_c, the critical score for a mark of **C**, or higher, is a Y score of 100 and that we are interested in what proportion, or percentage, of students obtaining an X score of 50 will receive Y scores below the Y_c of 100. Assume further that

$$\overline{X} = 43, \ \overline{Y} = 107, \ r_{xy} = 60, \ s_{y \cdot x} = 14\sqrt{1 - 60^2} = 11.20,$$

$$s_x = 8, \ s_y = 14, \text{ and } r_{xy}\frac{s_y}{s_x} = b_{y \cdot x} = 60\frac{14}{8} = 1.05.$$

Substituting $b_{y \cdot x}$ for $r_{xy}\dfrac{s_y}{s_x}$ in Formula 11.4 the regression equation becomes[6]

$$Y' = b_{y \cdot x} X + (\overline{Y} - b_{y \cdot x} \overline{X}), \tag{11.8}$$

$$= 1.05X + (107 - 1.05 \times 43),$$

$$= 1.05X + 61.85.$$

Substituting 50 for X, $Y' = 114.35$ and

$$m = \frac{Y_c - Y'}{s_{y \cdot x}} = \frac{100 - 114.35}{11.20} = -1.28.$$

From the table of the normal curve, the area beyond $\dfrac{X}{\sigma} = 1.28$, or q, here q_c, equals .1003. Ten percent of the students receiving an X score of 50 will probably receive Y scores below 100.

Assume now that a Y_a score of 130, or above, is required for a mark of **A**. The chances of receiving such a mark by a student whose X score is 50 are similarly obtained. The predicted score Y' is still 114.35, but m is positive:

$$m = \frac{130 - 114.35}{11.20} = +1.40.$$

From the table of the normal curve the area beyond $\dfrac{X}{\sigma} = 1.40$, or q_a is .0808, or 8 percent of the entire area of the curve of errors of estimate.

The procedure explained above can be modified to answer such a question as "What aptitude or proficiency test score should a student obtain so that the probability of his failing to reach some specified level of achievement is .10?" To continue with the illustrative data, suppose that the Y_c of 100 is retained and that now we wish to know for what proficiency test score X, no more than 10 percent should fail to earn a mark of **C** or higher. Then X can be computed by Formula 11.9.

---

[6] $b_{y \cdot x}$ is a regression coefficient.

$$X = \frac{Y_c - m\, s_{y \cdot x} - \overline{Y} + b_{y \cdot x}\, \overline{X}}{b_{y \cdot x}}, \qquad (11.9)$$

$$= \frac{100 - (-1.28)\, 11.20 - 107 + 1.05 \times 43}{1.05},$$

$$= 50.$$

Formula 11.9 is obtained from Formula 11.7 by substituting the right hand member of Formula 11.8 for Y' and solving for X.

Expectancy tables and cutting scores

The procedures explained above could be used in advising students, applying Formula 11.8 to a range of representative proficiency or aptitude test scores. Similarly, Formula 11.9 could be used for a sequence of proportions, or risks, of failure in order to identify the corresponding proficiency or aptitude scores. However, some efforts of this kind would probably be of less practical value in the counseling or placement of students than in giving a counselor a better understanding of regression equations and standard errors of estimate.

Estimation of chances of surpassing various levels of achievement or of risk of failing to achieve these levels for a range of proficiency or aptitude test scores can be estimated from expectancy tables. Many such tables appear in the manuals of standardized aptitude tests. It is an excellent practice to develop expectancy tables based on local data when sufficient data have accumulated. Predictor and criterion scores can be tallied as one tallies a correlation chart. Horizontal lines, possibly the lower limits of the class intervals of the criterion or Y distribution may correspond to specified levels of achievement grade-point averages of 1.0, 1.5, 2.0, etc., or to the lower limits of marks in some single subject field. The columns of the chart may correspond to class intervals of the predictor test. One can then change the frequencies in each column to proportions or percentages of the total frequencies in each column. If desired, the frequencies can be cumulated downward in a column before converting them to proportions or percentages. The lowest frequency may be excluded from the cumulation and converted to a proportion or percentage. Then, for a given class interval of the aptitude scores, one may note what proportions of the students receiving aptitude scores within a given interval are likely to exceed the various levels of achievement or to fall below the lowest level of achievement.[7]

---

[7] For an excellent discussion of expectancy tables, see W. B. Schrader, "A Taxonomy of Expectancy Tables," *Journal of Educational Measurement* 2 (June 1965), pp. 29–35.

The same tally of paired predictor and criterion measures may be the means of selecting a cutting score. A horizontal line may be drawn across the chart to represent some specified level of achievement, a level comparable to the Y_a or Y_c earlier discussed. The frequencies below the line may then be studied in order to locate a vertical line whose X score value can serve as a cutting score. The further to the right this vertical line is placed, the higher the percentage of students who might achieve satisfactorily, but who would be rejected because of X scores lower than the cutting score. On the other hand, as the vertical line is shifted to the left, the percentage of students exceeding the cutting score, but who do not achieve satisfactorily, increases. Look at the vertical line in Figure 11.6 on page 352 and visualize the change in percentages in the upper left and lower right quadrants which would occur if the line were shifted first to the right and then to the left.

The procedures just described will be more efficient than application of Formulas 11.8 and 11.9 when the relationship between variables X and Y is curvilinear rather than linear. They will be more efficient if the distributions are skewed because the predictor or criterion measures have too high or too low average levels of difficulty for the sample of students tested. The variability in the columns may be seriously unequal from column to column thus limiting the applicability of the standard error of estimate. The expectancy table and the cutting score procedure take the data limitations noted above into account. It is decidedly important, however, to construct expectancy tables and identify cutting scores only when a comparatively large number of pairs of X and Y scores are available. Cross validation is also important since the data relevant to future groups of students may possess different characteristics. Furthermore, the specified levels of achievement may change. These levels are standards and value judgments are made in setting them. Value judgments also characterize the choosing of a cutting score. Decisions must be made with reference to what proportions of students it is justifiable to reject who might have succeeded or to accept who are likely to fail.[8]

Practice Exercise 11.1

Assume that an English proficiency test is given at the beginning of a term and after course marks are reported analysis of the data yields the following statistics where X pertains to the proficiency test scores and Y pertains to the English marks. Assume also that the English marks exhibit the following standards in terms of basic standard

[8] For further discussion, see Lee J. Cronbach, *Essentials of Psychological Testing*, 3rd ed. (New York: Harper, 1970), pp. 421–25.

scores. **A** ($+ 1.5$ and above); **B** ($+ .5 - + 1.5$); **C** ($+ .5 - - .5$); **D** ($- .5 - - 1.5$); **F** (below $- 1.5$).

$$\overline{X} = 35 \qquad \overline{Y} = 0.0 \qquad r_{xy} = + .65$$
$$s_x = 7 \qquad s_y = 1.0$$

(a) What is the standard error of estimate of the marks?

(b) What is the risk of an **F** mark for a student obtaining a proficiency test score of 28?

(c) What are the chances that the given student will obtain a mark of **B** or **A**?

(d) What cutting score should be set on the proficiency test so that no more than 5 percent of the students earning this score should be expected to receive a mark *less* than **B**?

(e) Draw diagrams similar to Figure 11.4 to illustrate your results.

PREDICTIONS BASED ON COMPARABLE MEASURES

It was mentioned earlier that predictions are often made using a mark in one course as a forecast of the mark likely to be earned by the student in a succeeding course. Frequently standard scores on one test are taken as indicators of the level of achievement to be expected of a student on a comparably scaled second test. Where the two tests do not have comparable scales, scores on both tests can be converted to a common scale. This was explained in Chapter 8 with reference to standard scores.

An alternative is to convert the scores on one of the tests to the scale of the other. In converting scores on test X to the scale of test Y, Formula 11.4 can be used omitting r_{xy} or considering it equal to 1.00. The Y' values obtained are transformed values of X. They have the same mean and standard deviation as the observed Y scores. Using the illustrative data: $Y' = 1.75X + 31.75$. Substituting for X, 43, $43 + 8$, $43 - 8$ yields Y' values equal to 107, 121, and 93. These values equal $\overline{Y}$, $\overline{Y} + s_y$, and $\overline{Y} - s_y$.

After substituting the observed means and standard deviations in Formula 11.4 as described above a facilitating table can be obtained (see page 231 of Chapter 8) and the Y' values used as predictions. Such Y' scores are not as accurate predictions as those obtained when the equation includes r_{xy}. If r_{xy} is known, though not used, the standard error of estimate of the predictions is

$$s_{y \cdot x} = s_y \sqrt{2(1 - r_{xy})}. \tag{11.10}$$

Using the illustrative data earlier given

$$s_{y \cdot x} = 14 \sqrt{2(1 - .60)} = 12.52.$$

as compared with the 11.20 obtained with Formula 11.6.

The derivation of Formula 11.10 parallels that given for Formula 11.6. One simply substitutes $(z_y - z_x)^2$ for $(z_y - r_{xy}z_x)^2$. Formula 11.10 can be used where both tests have a common scale, for example, a mean of 50 and a standard deviation of 10, and the correlation between the tests is known. The standard error obtained with Formula 11.10 was named the standard error of substitution by Marion W. Richardson.

MULTIPLE CORRELATION AND MULTIPLE REGRESSION EQUATIONS

The coefficient of multiple correlation is an estimate of the relationship between one variable and two or more others in combination. If X_1 is the criterion, or dependent variable, and X_2 and X_3 are the predictor, or independent variables, the coefficient of multiple correlation may be given the symbol $R_{1.23}$ or, in general, $R_{1.234\ldots n}$. In a multiple regression equation each of the independent or predictor variables are so weighted that the sum of the squares of the deviations from the regression *plane* are a minimum.[9] For only two independent variables the regression equation for ordinary scores may be written:

$$X_1' = b_{12\cdot3}X_2 + b_{13\cdot2}X_3 + (\bar{X}_1 - b_{12\cdot3}\bar{X}_2 - b_{13\cdot2}\bar{X}_3). \qquad (11.11)$$

If the variables are expressed as standard scores with a mean of 0 and a standard deviation of 1.00 the constant term in the parenthesis becomes zero and the equation becomes

$$z_1' = \beta_{12\cdot3}z_2 + \beta_{13\cdot2}z_3. \qquad (11.12)$$

The regression coefficients in both equations are called partial regression coefficients and those in the standard score equation or equations are referred to as β (beta) coefficients.[10] The relationship between ordinary regression coefficients is exemplified by the equation:

$$b_{12\cdot3} = \beta_{12\cdot3}\frac{s_1}{s_2}. \qquad (11.13)$$

Formula 11.14, analogous to Formula 11.6, is the standard error of estimate of scores predicted by means of a multiple regression equation:

$$s_{x_1 \cdot x_2 x_3}\ldots n = s_1 \sqrt{1 - R_{1.23\ldots n}^2}. \qquad (11.14)$$

---

[9] For a discussion of the geometry of this, see George A. Ferguson, *Statistical Analysis in Psychology and Education*, 3rd ed. (New York: McGraw-Hill, 1971), pp. 396–397.

[10] Such coefficients have nothing in common with the probability of errors of the second kind except the symbol β.

Procedures for computing coefficients of multiple correlation and obtaining multiple regression equations are given in most standard texts on statistical method. Computer programs have long been available for obtaining multiple correlation coefficients and regression equations.

Improving the efficiency of prediction

It is worth repeating that a regression equation, whether a simple or a multiple one, becomes less efficient when applied to a different population of students than the one used in establishing it. It is desirable to check it with a new population, the procedure called cross validation. As earlier mentioned, when two or more predictor tests are used their contribution to predictive efficiency is enhanced if the predictor tests are each substantially correlated with the criterion, but have low correlations among themselves. For example, r_{12}, r_{13}, etc., should be substantial, but ideally, r_{23}, r_{24}, r_{34}, etc., should be low. It was mentioned earlier that the efficiency of prediction can sometimes be increased through use of a "suppressor" variable—a variable which does not have significant correlation with the criterion, but because of its relationship to some predictor variable increases the predictive efficiency of the combination. Finally it should be mentioned that as successive predictor variables are added, a multiple correlation coefficient increases more and more slowly and the same is true of the predictive efficiency of a multiple-regression equation. For an additional variable to make a contribution, it should be relatively uncorrelated with the other predictors. Adding such a variable can contribute more to the efficiency of prediction than increasing the reliability of one or more of the original predictors. In this connection it is urged again that consideration be given to traits less easily measured such as motivation. It should also be emphasized again that in prediction studies serious concern needs to be given to the reliability and validity of the criteria. More should be done to promote the reliability and validity of teachers' marks, grade point averages, and other criteria of achievement.

Evaluating variables identified as causes

The square of $R_{1.23...n}$ is an estimate of the proportion of the variance (standard deviation squared) to be credited to the predictor variables in combination. If there are several predictor variables which are themselves uncorrelated, the beta coefficients of these variables equal the correlation coefficients of the variables with the dependent variable, and the sum of the squares of the beta coefficients is equal to the squared multiple correlation coefficient obtained from the same data. The relative importance of the predictor variables as "causes" of the dependent variable is indicated by the magnitudes of the squared betas. When, however, the predictor variables, in addition to their correlation with the criterion variable—the "effect"—are correlated among themselves, the interpretation described is limited by the presence of "product terms" analogous to the $2s_{\bar{x}_1}s_{\bar{x}_2}r_{12}$ of Formula 9.5 on page 251 of Chapter 9. There will be as many such product terms as pairs of correlated predictor, or causal, variables. Suppose that there are three correlated predictor variables X_2, X_3, and X_4 hypothesized as causes of X_1. Then $R^2_{1.234}$ is equal to the sum of the following:

$$\beta^2_{12\cdot34}$$

$$\beta^2_{13\cdot24}$$

$$\beta^2_{14\cdot23}$$

$$2\beta_{12\cdot34}\beta_{13\cdot24}r_{23}$$

$$2\beta_{12\cdot34}\beta_{14\cdot23}r_{24}$$

$$2\beta_{13\cdot24}\beta_{14\cdot23}r_{34}$$

The first three terms have been called coefficients of "direct" determination and the last three, coefficients of "joint" determination. Sometimes negative coefficients of joint determination make the drawing of meaningful causal inferences difficult or impossible.

The path coefficients technique: a brief history

The procedure outlined above was originated by Sewall Wright and first reported in 1921.[11] Wright drew diagrams showing the hypothetical relationships between the variables and calculated path coefficients later shown to be equivalent to beta coefficients.[12] Early applications of the path coefficient technique in the field of educational psychology were made by Burks,[13] Heilman,[14] and Engelhart.[15] Burks obtained a

---

[11] Sewall Wright, "Correlation and Causation," *Journal of Agricultural Research* 20 (January 1921), pp. 557–85.

[12] See E. L. Kelly, "The Relationships Between the Techniques of Partial Correlation and Path Coefficients," *Journal of Educational Psychology* 20 (February 1929), pp. 119–24.

[13] B. S. Burks, "The Relative Influence of Nature and Nurture on Mental Development," *The Twenty-Seventh Yearbook of the National Society for the Study of Education,* Part I (Chicago: University of Chicago, 1928), pp. 299–301. See also Mordecai Ezekiel, *Methods of Correlation Analysis* (New York: Wiley, 1930), pp. 181–84, 379–80. (The coefficients *first* termed part correlation and determination.)

[14] J. D. Heilman, "Factors Determining Achievement and Grade Location," *Journal of Genetic Psychology* 36 (September 1929), pp. 435–56. A briefer account is given in Part II of the *Yearbook* cited above.

[15] Max D. Engelhart, "The Relative Contributions of Certain Factors to Individual Differences in Arithmetical Problem Solving Ability," *Journal of Experimental Education*

coefficient of part determination. Heilman, and Engelhart later, prorated the coefficients of joint determination in proportion to the magnitudes of the coefficients of direct determination. It was conjectured that the independent variable with the larger coefficient of direct determination should be credited with a greater share of the relevant coefficient of joint determination. Heilman and Engelhart added the splits obtaining total coefficients of determination for each independent variable whose sum equaled the coefficient of multiple determination. Heilman went further. He also prorated the unknown variance, $1 - R^2$, between his measured variables and arrived at .81 and .19 as estimates of the proportions of the variance of school achievement—as measured—to be attributed to heredity and environment. Strangely enough, these estimates are not very different from those of a more sophisticated, but controversial, recent research.[16]

Splitting or prorating coefficients of joint determination as earlier described is now considered indefensible unless more is known from other data about the causal relations among the variables. Furthermore, different causal assumptions call for different procedures and kinds of partitioning.

Modern path analysis: a brief introduction

In recent years, the term path analysis has come to designate not only the method of path coefficients but also analysis involving causal interpretation of ordinary and beta regression coefficients. This type of analysis can be most simply explained in terms of the beta, or standard score regression coefficients as exemplified by those in Formula 11.12. These coefficients can be interpreted as indicating how much each predictor variable contributes to the value of the variable predicted in standard score form. For example, if in Formula 11.12, $\beta_{12 \cdot 3} = .60$ and $\beta_{13 \cdot 2} = .40$, then .60 or $\beta_{12 \cdot 3}$ is the hypothesized increase in z_1 for a unit increase in z_2, assuming that z_3 remains constant as indicated by the subscript to $\beta_{12 \cdot 3}$. Similarly, .40 is the hypothesized increase in z_1 to be attributed to unit increase in z_3. A number of examples of similar, but much more complex, analyses using ordinary regression coefficients, beta coefficients, and sometimes their squares, are reported in several

---

1 (September 1932), pp. 19–27. For a derivation and further summarization of early applications, see Max D. Engelhart, "The Technique of Path Coefficients," *Psychometrika I* (December 1936), pp. 287–93; and Walter S. Monroe and Max D. Engelhart, *The Scientific Study of Educational Problems* (New York: Macmillan, 1936), pp. 395–99.

[16] Arthur R. Jensen, "Social Class, Race, and Genetics," *American Educational Research Journal* 5 (January 1968), pp. 1–42. On page 16 he states ". . . heritability studies based on Stanford-Binet on samples from essentially the same population show that about 80 percent of the variance in IQ is attributable to hereditary factors and 20 percent or less to environmental factors."

of the educational, psychological, and sociological research journals. Especially interesting are the diagrams depicting chains of hypothesized causal relations.

It should be noted that the techniques mentioned are all drawn from the general linear model which means that their interrelationships are specifiable. The path coefficients of Sewall Wright are the beta coefficients of regression equations. They are interpreted as suggested above or their squares may be used. When multiple measures of each underlying variable are used and the variables assumed to be causes are uncorrelated with each other, although correlated with the variable assumed to be the effect, their path coefficients are equivalent to the "factor loadings" of an "orthogonal solution" in factor analysis (see page 348). There are also similar relationships with "fixed effects" analysis of variance and analysis of covariance techniques (see Chapter 13).

The references listed below are relevant to recent discussion or use of path analysis.[17]

PARTIAL CORRELATION

Many years ago, Terman[18] reported a correlation of + .582 between mental age and depth of chest for a large group of gifted boys ranging in age from nine to fourteen. The correlation between chronological age and depth of chest was + .618 and between chronological age and mental age + .941. Let us designate these correlations as r_{12}, r_{13}, and r_{23} respectively assigning 1, 2, and 3 as the symbols for mental age, depth of chest, and for chronological age. Then Formula 11.15 may be used to compute a coefficient of partial correlation, an *estimate* of the correlation between mental age and depth of chest for gifted boys homogeneous with respect to chronological age. It is an *estimate* of the correlation for gifted boys of the same age:

---

[17] Hubert M. Blalock, *Causal Inference in Nonexperimental Research* (Chapel Hill: University of North Carolina Press, 1961); R. B. Darlington, "Multiple Regression in Research and Practice," *Psychological Bulletin* 69 (March 1968), pp. 161–82; Otis D. Duncan, "Path Analysis: Sociological Examples," *The American Journal of Sociology* 72 (July 1966), pp. 1–16; John W. Tukey, "Causation, Regression, and Path Analysis," in Oscar Kempthorne and others, eds., *Statistics and Mathematics in Biology* (Ames, Iowa: Iowa State College Press, 1954), pp. 35–66; Charles E. Werts and Donivan J. Watley, "Analyzing College Effects; Correlation vs. Regression," *American Educational Research Journal* 5 (November 1968), pp. 585–98; and Charles E. Werts and Robert L. Linn, "Path Analysis: Psychological Examples," *Psychological Bulletin* 74 (September 1970), pp. 193–212.

[18] L. M. Terman and others, *Genetic Studies of Genius,* Vol. I (Stanford, California: Stanford University Press, 1925), p. 168.

$$r_{12\cdot3} = \frac{r_{12} - r_{13}r_{23}}{\sqrt{1 - r_{13}^2}\sqrt{1 - r_{23}^2}}, \qquad (11.15)$$

$$= \frac{.582 - .618 \times .941}{\sqrt{1 - .618^2}\sqrt{1 - .941^2}},$$

$$= +.002.$$

Since the partial coefficient is so nearly zero, it is evident that there is no significant relationship between depth of chest and mental age. However, for the same group of boys heterogeneous with respect to chronological age, the correlation between mental age and standing height was + .835, between chronological age and standing height + .845, and between chronological age and mental age the same + .941. The coefficient of partial correlation calculated in the same way was + .220. One should not infer, of course, that standing height is among the causes of mental age or that mental age is among the causes of standing height. The relatively low, but probably significant, relationship between standing height and intelligence as measured by mental age may be due to physiological factors influencing both variables.

Other applications of partial correlation coefficients

The computation of a coefficient of partial correlation may be appropriately calculated as a means of eliminating, or holding constant, one or more variables other than chronological age although the procedure works best when the variable, or variables, eliminated are reasonably pure measures. For example, suppose that the problem is to estimate the relationship between reasoning ability as measured by some valid psychological test of reasoning and arithmetical problem-solving ability as measured by an achievement test consisting of a number of verbal problems in arithmetic. Given scores of the same pupils on such tests and on tests of computational ability, general reading achievement or ability, and possibly other measures of variables likely to contribute to arithmetical problem-solving achievement, the appropriate partial correlation, $r_{12\cdot34\ldots\cdot n}$, would be an estimate of the net correlation between reasoning ability and problem-solving ability as measured. The partial correlation coefficient would thus yield some indication of the importance of reasoning in solving arithmetical problems.

Correlation of residuals

The error of estimate, or deviation from a regression line $z_y - r_{xy}z_x$, is also termed a "residual." It represents that part of variable Y which is independent of, or uncorrelated with, variable X. Similarly, $z_1 - r_{13}z_3$

and $z_2 - r_{23}z_3$ are residuals, the parts of variables 1 and 2 which are independent of variable 3. The correlation between these residuals is the partial correlation $r_{12 \cdot 3}$.

The residuals themselves are deviate measures comparable to the deviate measures, x and y. The formula for the product-moment coefficient of correlation for deviate measures is

$$r_{xy} = \frac{\Sigma xy}{\sqrt{\Sigma x^2}\sqrt{\Sigma y^2}}. \tag{11.16}$$

By analogy:

$$r_{12 \cdot 3} = \frac{\Sigma(z_1 - r_{13}z_3)(z_2 - r_{23}z_3)}{\sqrt{\Sigma(z_1 - r_{13}z_3)^2}\sqrt{\Sigma(z_2 - r_{23}z_3)^2}}.$$

This simplifies to

$$r_{12 \cdot 3} = \frac{r_{12} - r_{13}r_{23}}{\sqrt{1 - r_{13}^2}\sqrt{1 - r_{23}^2}}.$$

Writing out the intervening steps of the proof and solving Practice Exercise 11.2 will increase the student's understanding of the coefficient of partial correlation.

Practice Exercise 11.2

Suppose that 7 fives, 24 fours, 38 threes, 24 twos and 7 ones were listed as one variable, analogous to the normal distribution of marks in a five-letter system. (I actually did this exercise some years ago.) Then these one hundred numbers were entered on index cards, the cards thoroughly shuffled, and the numbers listed as a second series beside the first. The cards were then shuffled again and a third series of numbers entered. The three series of numbers are labeled a, b, and c. Except for chance, the correlations between these series should be zero. Actually they were $r_{ab} = -.02$, $r_{ac} = -.05$, and $r_{bc} = +.01$. Then three new series of numbers were listed. Variable 1 is $a + b$. Variable 2 is $b + c$. Variable 3 is b alone. Below are given the data for first, second, and one hundredth rows of the table listing the six series of numbers just mentioned:

a	b	c	1	2	3
5	2	4	7	6	2
5	5	3	10	8	5
.	.	.	.	.	.
.	.	.	.	.	.
1	3	2	4	5	3

Three correlation coefficients were then computed. They were $r_{12} = .5436$, $r_{13} = .7455$, and $r_{23} = .7559$. Calculate $r_{12 \cdot 3}$. With which of the correlations given above should it be compared? Why?

FACTOR ANALYSIS

Factor analysis had its origin in 1904 when Charles Spearman proposed his two-factor theory of mental abilities.[19] He hypothesized that the correlation between two mental tests is due to a factor common to both tests which he named "g." Each of the two tests was also presumed to be characterized by a specific factor "s," unique to each.

In support of this theory, Spearman noted that when he entered all of the correlations between several mental tests in a table so that the sums of the rows and of the columns were in order of rank, the coefficients in any pair of rows or columns decreased proportionately. This is illustrated by Table 11.1. Each correlation coefficient appears twice in such a table, a specially organized "correlation matrix." How the proportionality mentioned above supports the two-factor theory is explained below the table.

Table 11.1 Intercorrelations of Six Hypothetical Variables Having One Common Factor*

	d	b	f	e	a	c	Sums
d		.72	.63	.54	.45	.18	2.52
b	.72		.56	.48	.40	.16	2.32
f	.63	.56		.42	.35	.14	2.10
e	.54	.48	.42		.30	.12	·1.86
a	.45	.40	.35	.30		.10	1.60
c	.18	.16	.14	.12	.10		.70
Sums	2.52	2.32	2.10	1.86	1.60	.70	

* Adapted from J. P. Guilford, *Psychometric Methods*, 2nd ed. (New York: McGraw-Hill, 1954), p. 474. Reprinted with permission of publisher. Chapter 16 is among the best introductions to factor analyses, as is Ferguson's chapter 27.

In illustration of the proportionality consider the correlations of tests d and b listed in the first two columns of the table:

[19] Charles Spearman, "General Intelligence Objectively Determined and Measured," *American Journal of Psychology* 15 (1904), pp. 201–93.

$$\frac{r_{df}}{r_{bf}} = \frac{r_{de}}{r_{be}} = \frac{r_{da}}{r_{ba}} = \frac{r_{dc}}{r_{bc}}$$

$$\frac{.63}{.56} = \frac{.54}{.48} = \frac{.45}{.40} = \frac{.18}{.16}$$

Each numerator is 1.125 times each denominator. These are hypothetical correlations. Even if the correlations could be attributed to a single common factor, errors of measurement and sampling would tend to cause deviations from strict proportionality or perfect "hierarchical order."

The tetrad difference and the tetrad equation

For a pair of such ratios pertaining to no more than four tests at a time, Spearman multiplied the extremes of the proportion by its means to obtain what he called a "tetrad difference" and postulated that, if such a difference equaled zero, except for chance deviations, one common factor was sufficient to account for the correlations. Writing such a difference for tests, 1, 2, 3, and 4 to promote ease in reading what follows, one of three tetrad differences for these tests becomes the tetrad equation:

$$r_{12}r_{34} - r_{13}r_{24} = 0. \tag{11.17}$$

It is easy to prove that the tetrad difference equals zero, *if* the magnitude of the correlations is due to a single common factor. The partial coefficients $r_{12 \cdot g}$, $r_{34 \cdot g}$, $r_{13 \cdot g}$, and $r_{24 \cdot g}$ must equal zero if g is the only factor contributing to the correlation between tests 1, 2, 3, and 4. Hence, considering only variables 1 and 2,

$$r_{12 \cdot g} = \frac{r_{12} - r_{1g}r_{2g}}{\sqrt{1 - r_{1g}^2}\sqrt{1 - r_{2g}^2}} = 0.$$

Since the denominator times zero is zero, $r_{12} - r_{1g}r_{2g} = 0$ and $r_{12} = r_{1g}r_{2g}$. Similarly, $r_{13} = r_{1g}r_{3g}$, $r_{24} = r_{2g}r_{4g}$, and $r_{34} = r_{3g}r_{4g}$. Substituting these products of coefficients in the tetrad difference stated above, the difference becomes

$$r_{1g}r_{2g}r_{3g}r_{4g} - r_{1g}r_{3g}r_{2g}r_{4g}.$$

and is obviously equal to zero. A single common factor suffices to make the tetrad difference vanish.[20]

---

[20] See Charles Spearman, *The Abilities of Man* (New York: Macmillan, 1927), Appendix, p. iii.

Group factors

For a number of years, the frequency with which such tetrad differences equaled or approximated zero tended to support Spearman's two-factor theory of intelligence. The tests studied were relatively homogeneous ones. After a time, however, tetrad differences accumulated significantly different from zero. Spearman and others then explained such nonvanishing tetrads in terms of "group" factors. Such factors differ from *g* in that they are considered common to several tests, but not to all of the tests analyzed. (Even today British psychologists, particularly, retain *g*, group factors, and specific factors.)[21]

Development of more systematic methods

In the late 1920s and early 1930s, T. L. Kelley, Harold Hotelling, K. J. Holzinger, L. L. Thurstone and others began the development of more systematic methods of factor analysis. It should suffice here to describe in an elementary fashion some aspects of the methods developed by Thurstone. To avoid the calculation of numerous tetrad differences and to provide for the possible existence of several factors, he devised the "centroid" method. Given a table of all the intercorrelations of numerous tests and with no special concern for a general factor, the centroid method extracts one centroid factor after another. In a manner somewhat similar to partial correlation, the original correlations are successively reduced until they do not differ significantly from zero. Each factor is represented by a series of "factor loadings"—correlations of that factor with each of the tests. The factor loadings of the first factor thus extracted are all positive and most are relatively large, larger on the average than the loadings of factors subsequently extracted. Some have argued that this factor is *g*. The factor loadings of factors other than the first are positive and negative in about equal numbers. Factors are continuously extracted until the "residual" correlations in the successive correlation matrices do not differ significantly from zero. The factor loadings of each centroid factor are listed in a "factor matrix" with columns labeled for each factor I, II, III, etc. The rows are labeled with reference to the tests. A factor loading in a given cell is the correlation between a given test and a particular centroid factor, for example, r_{3II}. The centroid solution, with the possible exception of the first factor, has little if any psychological meaning. How can negative loadings be meaningful when all tests of desirable mental abilities are positively correlated? Furthermore the centroid solution is not a mathematically unique one. It can, however, be transformed to a psychologically meaningful one by "rotation of axes."

---

[21] For example, see Philip Vernon, *The Structure of Human Abilities* (New York: Wiley, 1950).

Rotation of axes in factor analysis

This is best explained if we think of the tests mentioned above as vectors radiating from an origin in a graph having axes at the start representing two of the centroid factors, for example, axes I and II. Two highly correlated tests have vectors with only a small angular separation. Two tests with little correlation between them have a large angular separation. A test having a high factor loading with reference to a given factor may be represented by a vector with a small angle between it and the given factor axis. In drawing such a graph, the size of each angle needed is obtained by entering a table of cosines with the factor loading, or correlation between a test and a factor, as a cosine and noting the corresponding angle.[22] If the factor loading is .5 the angle is 30° If the factor loading is 0 the angle is 90° and it is 0° if the loading is 1.00. Negative loadings correspond to angles greater than 90°. Even though the factor or reference axes are rotated to obtain psychological meaning the angular separations of the test vectors among themselves do not change. In Figure 11.5 axes I and II are centroid axes. Vectors 1, 2, 3, 4, 5, and 6 are test vectors. Axes I' and II' are the coordinate axes after rotation.

The new axes I' and II' have been drawn so that the angles between them and the test vectors in each set of such vectors are as small as possible. Tests 1, 2, and 3 now have high correlations with axis I' and low correlations with axis II'. The converse is true for tests 4, 5, and 6. If tests 1, 2, and 3 are verbal tests, axis I' may designate a verbal factor. If tests 4, 5, and 6 are arithmetical tests, axis II' may designate a number factor. If there are several factors, such rotations are done for two factors at a time since there are as many dimensions as factors. A plane of two dimensions suffices for two factors. Three factors can be—and have been—represented by points on a sphere. More than three factors and a variety of test vectors radiate from an origin in hyperspace— space of more than three dimensions.

Orthogonal solutions, oblique solutions, and simple structure

If, after rotation, the coordinate or factor axes are all at right angles to each other the solution is said to be "orthogonal." If this is not the case, the solution is called "oblique." Thurstone discarded effort to obtain

---

[22] The cosine of an angle of a right triangle is the ratio of the opposite side to the hypotenuse of the triangle. The cosine for angle α in this triangle is a/b:

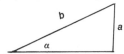

It is assumed above that the test vectors have been adjusted to unit length.

Figure 11.5   Graph illustrating rotation of axes in factor analysis

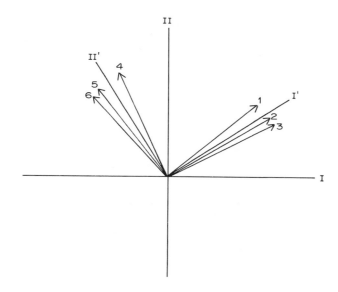

orthogonal solutions in favor of what he termed "simple structure," a type of oblique solution of maximum psychological meaning. The factor axes of such a solution are correlated among themselves and these correlations can be analyzed for one or more "higher order" factors. It has been suggested that the first of such factors, common to all of the tests, is a rebirth of *g*.

In recent years much in factor analysis has changed, even though much remains the same. John Carroll, Raymond Cattell, Harry Harman, Chester Harris, Paul Horst, Louis Guttman, Henry Kaiser, Ledyard Tucker, and others have greatly increased the effectiveness of factor analysis techniques as the student will discover if he studies some of the references cited at the end of this chapter.

Applications of factor analysis

One major use of factor analysis in psychological and educational research is that of testing hypotheses concerning the nature of human abilities and other traits. Another major use is in testing hypotheses concerning the validity of tests. A new reasoning test may be devised and its validity studied by including it in a battery of tests of reasoning whose validity has been established. Certain tests may be included with the expectation that they will measure a certain factor, with the result being the discovery of a new factor. Thurstone discovered the factor "word fluency" in this way. Factor analysis contributes knowledge about tests that is useful in their selection for prediction of academic or vocational success. Factorially pure tests have low intercorrelations. They may be valid with reference to abilities basic to success in certain subject fields or vocations. The use of multiple-regression equations involving such tests are most effective in prediction. Such tests are "univocal"; they "speak with one voice."

If factorially pure psychological tests are administered to students along with one or more achievement tests, factor analysis of the data may reveal what "primary abilities" or factors contribute to achievement as measured. Such analyses might resolve the old issue of essay versus objective tests and also reveal the types of objective achievement test exercises most effective in measuring intellectual skills transcending recall of information.[23] It has been suggested that factor analyses be used in testing experimental hypotheses. The effects of the teaching methods could be assessed by factor analyses of data obtained before and after different methods of instruction or other treatments have been used. Factor analyses could also be made of data obtained from samples of pupils on different age levels to study prolonged effects of environmental influences.

Factor analysis and data processing

As a result of the development of electronic computers in recent years and of improved techniques, factor analyses, including rotations of axes, are rapidly and more objectively accomplished. Given the scores of the same individuals on numerous tests, the computer quickly calculates all of the intercorrelations and subjects them to whatever type of factor analysis is specified in the computer program. This frees the graduate student, or other researcher, from much arduous labor. One disadvantage is that the student is all too likely to acquire little understanding of what has been done for him. Hence, it is strongly urged that the student, planning to have his data factor analyzed, seriously study the references concerning factor analysis cited in suggestions for further study, in the last section of this chapter as well as those works cited as footnotes and in the selected reference list.

OTHER MEASURES OF RELATIONSHIP

The familiar product-moment coefficient of correlation is used to estimate the amount of association between two continuous variables

---

[23] For an example of such research, see John W. French, "The Description of Aptitude and Achievement Tests in Terms of Rotated Factors," *Psychometric Monograph* No. 5 (Chicago: University of Chicago Press, 1951).

having, or assumed to have, interval or ratio scales. Where the variables are measured in terms of ranks, or one or both variables are counts in two or a very few categories, indices other than the usual product-moment coefficient are obtained. Each of these indices is briefly discussed and illustrated. Attention is given to the comparative advantages and limitations of the indices at the end of this section.

The Spearman rank-difference coefficient of correlation

When the paired measures are ranks or are pairs of test scores for a small sample converted to ranks, the Spearman rank-difference coefficient of correlation ρ (rho) may be computed using Formula 11.15,

$$\rho = 1 - \frac{6\Sigma D^2}{N(N^2 - 1)}. \qquad (11.15)$$

where D is the difference in ranks. When changing scores to ranks, equal scores should receive the same rank. For example, suppose each of two persons is sixth in position from the top, then each would be given the rank of 6.5 and there would be no rank of 7. If each of three persons are sixth in position, each receives a rank of 7 and there are no ranks of 6 and 8. The next rank is 9, if the next scores are not tied. In applying Formula 11.15 to the X and Y score data in Table 9.3 on page 283, ranks were assigned to each series of scores separately. The differences in ranks of the paired scores were obtained and squared. The sum of the squares equals 811.50.

$$\rho = 1 - \frac{6\Sigma 811.50}{25(25^2 - 1)},$$

$$= + .69.$$

The product-moment coefficient of correlation for paired X and Y scores computed with Formula 8.10 is $+ .67$. Formula 11.15 is easily derived from one of the formulas for product-moment r.[24]

A coefficient similar to ρ or rho is Kendall's τ (tau). Where ranking is done by several raters, Kendall's coefficient of concordance, W, is the appropriate one to obtain.[25]

A normal bivariate frequency distribution

The normal bivariate frequency distribution in Figure 11.6 is presented here for use as a model, possibly too ideal a model, in explaining tetra-

---

[24] Such a derivation is given in Edwards, *Statistical Methods*, pp. 133–34.

[25] For further discussion see such texts as those by Edwards, Ferguson, and McNemar listed among the selected references of Chapter 9.

Figure 11.6   Normal bivariate frequency distribution for a correlation of +.60

```
                                                                      2464
                                           1   1   1   1   1           35%
                                       1   1   1   1   2   1   1   1   1
                                   1   1   2   2   3   3   3   2   2   1   1
                               1   1   2   3   4   5   5   7   5   5   3   2   1   1
        1041                 1   2   3   4   6   8  10  10   9   9   6   5   2   1   1
          15%              1   2   4   6  10  13  16  17  17  14  11   9   5   3   1   1
                        1   2   5   8  13  19  24  27  27  25  20  14   9   7   3   2   1
                    1   3   5  10  17  25  32  38  41  38  32  25  17  10   5   3   1   1
                1   3   6  11  19  29  41  50  56  55  49  38  27  17  10   5   2   1
            1   2   5  11  20  32  47  60  70  72  67  55  41  27  16   8   4   2   1
        1   2   5  10  19  32  49  66  80  86  84  72  56  38  24  13   6   3   1   1
    1   2   4   8  10  29  47  66  84  95  96  86  70  50  32  19  10   4   2   1
────1—3—6—13—25—41—60—80—95—100—95—80—60—41—25—13—6—3—1──────────────
    1   2   4  10  19  32  50  70  86  96  95  84  66  47  29  17   8   4   2   1
1   1   3   6  13  24  38  56  72  85  86  80  66  49  32  19  10   5   2   1
1   2   4   8  16  27  41  55  67  72  70  60  47  32  20  11   5   2   1
1   2   5  10  17  27  38  49  55  56  50  41  29  19  11   6   3   1
1   1   3   5  10  17  25  32  38  41  38  32  25  17  10   5   3   1
1   2   3   7   9  14  20  25  27  27  24  19  13   8   5   2   1                    1041
1   1   3   5   9  11  14  17  17  16  13  10   6   4   2   1                          15%
1   1   2   5   6   9   9  10  10   8   6   4   3   3   2   1
1   1   2   3   5   5   7   5   5   4   3   2   1   1   1
    1   1   2   2   3   3   3   2   2   1   1
        1   1   1   1   2   1   1   1   1
            1   1   1   1   1
2464
  35%
```

choric, biserial, point biserial, and fourfold point coefficients of correlation or ϕ (phi) coefficients.

This normal bivariate distribution has 25 rows and 25 columns.[26] The distributions of frequencies in each row and column closely approximate normal distributions. This also is true of the "marginal" distributions, not listed in the figure of the 7010 X and the 7010 Y "scores." Imagine how the data would appear in three dimensions with columns whose heights are proportional to the frequencies ranging from 1 to 100. Computation of the Pearson product-moment coefficient of correlation results in a coefficient of + .60. Division into the four quadrants, splitting the frequencies in the central row and the central column yields the numbers and percentages indicated.

---

[26] It was constructed by the author using the procedure described in the introductory pages of Leone Chesire, Milton Saffir, and L. L. Thurstone, *Computing Diagrams for the Tetrachoric Correlation Coefficient* (Chicago: University of Chicago Bookstore, 1933).

Tetrachoric coefficients of correlation

The usual product-moment coefficient is the most appropriate coefficient to compute when both variables are continuous, the relationship is linear, and the variables have at least reasonably normal distributions. The tetrachoric coefficient of correlation is often obtained for data which are percentages or proportions such as can be entered in a fourfold or 2 × 2 table. The two variables may be "artificially" dichotomized, for example, ordinary scores on two tests thus classified to avoid the effort required in computing product-moment *r*. Tetrachoric coefficients have also been obtained where the proportions in the 2 × 2 table refer to such traits as "good teaching-poor teaching" and "appreciative-unappreciative," assuming that the traits thus defined and measured correspond to variables satisfying the assumptions mentioned above.[27]

Tetrachoric coefficients can be computed through use of a very complex formula or less closely approximated with a simpler one. Usually, however, computing diagrams called *"abacs"* or tables are used. Figure 11.8 on page 363 is such an abac. It is applicable in obtaining tetrachoric coefficients when equal numbers of cases characterize the two categories of at least one of the two variables. In item analysis this occurs when the tests to be analyzed are classified as above and below the median total test, or other criterion, score. If the 35 and 15 percents at the right in Figure 11.6 are doubled, entering the abac in Figure 11.7 with 70 and 30 yields a tetrachoric *r* of + .60.

When the data for both variables are dichotomized unequally, the *Computing Diagrams* relevant to Figure 11.6 (cited in footnote 26) may be used rather than the abac just mentioned.

A normal bivariate frequency distribution and its smooth surface in three dimensions has an equation analogous to the equation for a normal distribution or a normal curve for one variable. One term in the former equation is the product-moment coefficient of correlation. We can think of the tetrachoric coefficient as an estimate of the product-moment coefficient in the equation of the normal correlation surface best fitting the proportions or percentages in a fourfold table. Normal bivariate distributions, similar to the one in Figure 11.6, for a range of values of product-moment *r* were obtained for use in producing the 46 *Computing Diagrams* earlier cited.

Biserial coefficients of correlation

In the case of tetrachoric coefficients both variables are dichotomies. When one variable is continuous, but the other a dichotomy, the index

---

[27] Max D. Engelhart and Ledyard R. Tucker, "Traits Related to Good and Poor Teaching," *School Review* 44 (January 1936), pp. 28–33. One hundred tetrachoric coefficients were obtained in this study. The time was B.C. (before computers).

of relationship between the variables frequently obtained is the biserial coefficient of correlation here symbolized as r_b. The trait underlying the dichotomized variable, X, is assumed to be normally distributed in the population and linearly related to the continuous variable, Y. Formulas 11.18 and 11.19 are equivalent formulas for the biserial coefficient of correlation:

$$r_b = \frac{\overline{Y}_p - \overline{Y}_q}{s_t} \frac{pq}{y}, \text{ or} \tag{11.18}$$

$$r_b = \frac{\overline{Y}_p - \overline{Y}_t}{s_t} \frac{p}{y}. \tag{11.19}$$

In these formulas, $\overline{Y}_p$ and $\overline{Y}_q$ are the means of the two distributions of Y scores and $\overline{Y}_t$ is the mean of all the Y scores. The symbols p and q refer to the proportions of the Y scores in the Y_p and Y_q distributions. The symbol s_t refers to the standard deviation of all the Y scores and $N-1$ is used in its computation. If the data are given as in Practice Exercise 11.3 on page 360 where $\overline{Y}_p$ is larger than $\overline{Y}_q$, their appearance resembles that of the data in an ordinary correlation chart where the correlation is positive. The unlabeled dichotomized variable X has only two unit intervals 0 and 1, or two otherwise designated, but implied, categories. The symbol y is explained below.

Assume two distributions of scores on some test. In the first distribution are the scores of students classified as "lazy." The mean of their scores, $\overline{Y}_q$, equals 76, and the proportion of such students in the total sample, q, equals .44. In the second distribution are the scores of the students classified as "energetic." Their mean, $\overline{Y}_p$, is 87 and the proportion of such students, p, is .56. The mean and standard deviations of both distributions combined, $\overline{Y}_t$, and s_t, are 82.16 and 12. $\overline{Y}_t$ equals $p\overline{Y}_p + q\overline{Y}_q$ and is given to two decimals better to show the equivalence of Formulas 11.18 and 11.19 and also the equivalence to each other of Formulas 11.20 and 11.21..

Imagine the area of the unit normal curve divided into two parts of area .56 and .44. The symbol y here represents the height of the curve, or ordinate, where the split occurs. Entering the area column of Table B in the appendix with $.56 - .50$ or .06, we find .0596 the nearest area value and .3945 the corresponding ordinate. The height of the curve at this point is .3945. Hence,

$$r_b = \frac{87 - 76}{12} \frac{.56 \times .44}{.3945} = .5725 \text{ or } .57, \text{ or}$$

$$r_b = \frac{87 - 82.16}{12} \frac{.56}{.3945} = .5725 \text{ or } .57.$$

It is assumed above that the variable "lazy-energetic" pertains to a trait which is continuous, normally distributed, and linearly related to the test scores, and these may be reasonable assumptions. The same assumptions are often made with reference to correct and incorrect response on test items. Both tetrachoric and biserial coefficients are frequently obtained in item analysis.

When the X variable of Figure 11.6 is dichotomized, application of Formula 11.18 or 11.19 yields a biserial coefficient of correlation equal to + .60.

Point biserial coefficients of correlation

When one of the variables is a continuous variable, but the variable dichotomized is a "point" variable—a nominal variable where all the individuals in each of the two categories are identically characterized by the trait whose name is given to the category—the point biserial coefficient of correlation, r_b, is the appropriate index of relationship. Let us assume that sex is such a variable and the two score distributions having $\overline{Y}_q = 76$ and $\overline{Y}_p = 87$ are those of boys and girls. Then, for such data, a point biserial coefficient of correlation may be computed by either of the following formulas:

$$r_{pb} = \frac{\overline{Y}_p - \overline{Y}_q}{s_t} \sqrt{pq}, \text{ or} \qquad (11.20)$$

$$r_{pb} = \frac{\overline{Y}_p - \overline{Y}_t}{s_t} \sqrt{\frac{p}{q}}. \qquad (11.21)$$

Applied to the same data:

$$r_{pb} = \frac{87 - 76}{12} \sqrt{.56 \times .44} = .4550 = .46, \text{ or}$$

$$r_{pb} = \frac{87 - 82.16}{12} \sqrt{\frac{.56}{.44}} = .4550 = .46.$$

Although the point biserial coefficient is a product-moment coefficient[28] most appropriately applied where one variable is a nominal or true point variable, when the point biserial coefficient is computed for the data in Figure 11.6, it equals + .48. More is said about this later.

Fourfold point coefficients of correlation or ϕ (phi) coefficients

When both of the variables dichotomized are nominal or point variables, the fourfold point coefficient of correlation can be computed using Formula 11.22 or other equivalent formula.

---

[28] For a derivation of Formula 11.20 see J. P. Guilford, *Fundamental Statistics in Psychology and Education,* 4th ed. (New York: McGraw-Hill, 1965), pp. 537–38. See Allen Edwards for the derivation of algebraically equivalent formulas for both r_b and r_{pb} in terms of listed scores. Calculations are simpler and subject to less rounding error. The height of the ordinate is still needed in computing r_b. *Statistical Methods,* pp. 123–26 and 128–30.

Suppose that in a random sample of 100 voters, 60 are Democrats and 40 are Republicans. Suppose also that these individuals can also be classified dichotomously as liberals and conservatives. (For all we know this may not be a nominal variable.) Finally, suppose that the data have been recorded in the following fourfold table:

	Conservative	Liberal
Democrat	25 A	35 B
Republican	28 C	12 D

$$\phi = \frac{BC - AD}{\sqrt{(A + B)\ (C + D)\ (A + C)\ (B + D)}}, \qquad (11.22)$$

$$= \frac{980 - 300}{\sqrt{(25 + 35)\ (28 + 12)\ (25 + 28)\ (35 + 12)}},$$

$$= .28.$$

Note the similarity of Formula 11.22 to Formula 9.15 for x^2. When x^2 is calculated using the same data, it equals 7.73. If x^2 is obtained first, Formula 11.23 can be used to compute the phi coefficient:

$$\phi = \sqrt{\frac{x^2}{N}} = \sqrt{\frac{7.73}{100}} = .28. \qquad (11.23)$$

Like the point biserial coefficient, the ϕ coefficient is also a product-moment coefficient.[29] Using the data of Figure 11.6 in Formula 11.22, ϕ equals + .40. Let us use the same data with Formula 8.9 for the Pearson product-moment coefficient.

Assume that variables X and Y have scale values of 1 and 0. Assume also that the percentages in Figure 11.6 are frequencies totaling 100. The data thus modified are recorded in the correlation chart below.

		X	
		0	1
Y	1	15	35
	0	35	15

---

[29] See, for example, Edwards, *Statistical Methods*, pp. 126–38, or Guilford, *Psychometric Methods*, pp. 538–39, for derivation of formulas.

Computing as illustrated in Chapter 8 for letter marks: ΣX, ΣY, ΣX^2, ΣY^2 all equal 50 and ΣXY equals 35. $\bar{X}$ and $\bar{Y}$ equal .5. If division is by $N = 100$ rather than by $N - 1$, s_x and s_y also equal .5. Then substituting in Formula 8.9:

$$r_{xy} \text{ or } \phi = \frac{\Sigma XY - N\bar{X}\bar{Y}}{Ns_x s_y} = \frac{35 - 100 \times .5 \times .5}{100 \times .5 \times .5},$$

$$= \frac{10}{25} = .40.$$

The ϕ coefficient .40 differs from the product-moment coefficient of .60 earlier obtained. If, however, application is made of Sheppard's correction for coarseness of grouping r_{xy} or the ϕ coefficient equals $+ .60.$[30]

The coefficient of contingency

When one or both of the nominal or point variables studied have more than two categories, the coefficient of contingency C may be computed as an index of the amount of association between the variables. Like the ϕ coefficient, the coefficient of contingency is similarly related to χ^2.

Assume that a sample of 217 adults ranging in income have been asked to indicate "agreement," "uncertainty or indifference," and "disagreement" with reference to the statement:

Business and industry should be regulated by the Federal government to protect the interests of the general public.

Agreement is indicative of a liberal attitude while disagreement may be regarded as indicative of a conservative one.

Assume that the frequencies of the three types of response for the three groups have been entered in the following contingency table:

	Disagree	Indifferent	Agree
High Income	35	24	17
Average Income	19	26	22
Low Income	12	20	42

Use of Formula 9.16 gives a χ^2 of 25.02 which is significant beyond the one-tenth of one percent level for 4 degrees of freedom. The contingency coefficient is most readily calculated using Formula 11.24.

---

[30] See Guilford, *Psychometric Methods*, pp. 353–54 for discussion of the limited conditions justifying such estimation of the product-moment r normally obtained from continuous variables.

$$C = \sqrt{\frac{\chi^2}{N + \chi^2}},$$ (11.24)

$$= \sqrt{\frac{25.02}{217 + 25.02}},$$

$$= .32.$$

Whether to regard the ϕ coefficient of .28 and the contingency coefficient of .32 as positive or negative is an arbitrary matter. Which end of the variables Republican-Democrat or conservative-liberal are positive and which negative?

Note that while both χ^2 values given above are highly significant, both the phi coefficient and the coefficient of contingency seem to indicate relatively small degrees of association. If the data in the contingency table were other than fictitious, it might be concluded that liberalism-conservatism is only moderately related to economic status. The ϕ of .28 and the C of .32, although actually relatively small, also seem small because we tend to compare them mentally with coefficients of correlations between paired test scores.

Advantages and limitations of the various indices of relationship

When the data are measures of continuous linearly related variables with normal or nearly normal distributions, no other index has the merit of the Pearson product-moment coefficient of correlation. Modern electronic computers make such coefficients no more difficult to obtain than any of the other indices. Programed for Pearson product-moment coefficients and given data from which rank, point biserial, and ϕ coefficients can be computed using formulas earlier given, the computer reports the same values. Where both variables are continuous in the sense that test scores are continuous, Pearson product-moment coefficients are, in general, the coefficients to use in obtaining partial and multiple correlation coefficients, multiple regression equations, and in accomplishing other types of multivariate analysis.[31]

The use of tetrachoric coefficients and biserial coefficients as estimates of product-moment coefficients can be defended in exploratory studies when N's are large and computer equipment is not available. Numerous estimates may be quickly needed and their relative magnitudes may be of major immediate interest in identifying relationships deserving more intensive and sophisticated investigation. Biserial and tetrachoric coefficients are still widely used in item analysis even though some authorities question the assumption that the abilities un-

---

[31] See Nunnally, *Psychometric Theory*, pp. 118–36 or other advanced text.

derlying scores of 1 or 0 on objective test items are normally distributed. Here again it may be argued that it is their relative values that are of interest in item elimination or revision, although standards must be set to identify unsatisfactory items.

Obtaining rank difference coefficients is better justified when the data are actual ranks assigned by judges rather than test scores ranked in order of size. The best justification for the point biserial coefficient is that the variable dichotomized is a nominal or point variable. Such point biserial coefficients can be used with Pearson product-moment coefficients in obtaining multiple regression equations. The use of ϕ coefficients and coefficients of contingency is best justified when the variables studied are nominal or point variables. There is no justification for stating that point biserial and ϕ coefficients are generally lower than product-moment coefficients for the same data. They *are* product-moment coefficients. They should not be obtained from artificially dichotomized continuous variables as estimates of the more appropriate product-moment coefficients. The r_{pb} of .48 and the ϕ of .40 are poor estimates of the r_{xy} of .60 in view of the median splits and normal distributions seldom encountered with real data.

All of the indices of relationship have limitations stemming from the data used in obtaining them. The Pearson product-moment, the biserial, and the tetrachoric coefficients may be based on data which do not satisfy the assumptions earlier noted. The ratio of correlation η (eta) is more appropriate than the Pearson product-moment coefficient when the relationship is curvilinear. Biserial coefficients can exceed 1.00 where distributions seriously depart from normal. Extreme splits in the dichotomizing of both continuous or nominal variables results in indices of uncertain or restricted magnitude. Point biserial coefficients cannot equal 1.00 even for median splits of the continuous variable while ϕ coefficients can do so only where both variables are split 50:50. The more extreme the splits the greater the lowering of r_{pb} and of ϕ. The coefficient of contingency cannot exceed .816 for a 3×3 table. When indices other than Pearson product r must be used because of the nature of the data, it is recommended that the index chosen be obtained in the same way for each of the relationships studied in order to facilitate comparisons and other kinds of interpretation.

Practice Exercise 11.3

A high school counselor concerned about the dropout problem obtained the test records of the students entering four years earlier, selected a random sample of 100, and tallied the achievement battery stanine frequencies listed below under Y_t. He then divided his sample between dropouts and graduates and tallied the frequencies listed under Y_q and Y_p. He also calculated the three means and the standard deviation, s_t.

Stanine	Y_q	Y_p	Y_t
9		3	3
8		6	6
7	1	12	13
6	3	14	17
5	6	16	22
4	9	7	16
3	7	4	11
2	6	3	9
1	3		3
N	35	65	100
$\overline{Y}$	3.6286	5.6769	4.9600
	or	or	or
	3.63	5.68	4.96
s_t			1.9065
			or
			1.91

(1) Assuming that dropout-graduate is a point variable, the counselor calculated a point biserial coefficient of correlation. What is its value rounded off to two decimals?

(2) When his principal saw this coefficient, he argued that one can assume that the dichotomized variable is basically "life adjustment," that it is normally distributed, and that this justifies calculation of a biserial coefficient of correlation. What is its value rounded off to two decimals? What construct validity can be ascribed to the measures of life adjustment?

(3) The counselor then noted the median of the Y_t scores is 5.00 and that he could split the frequencies in the stanine 5 row and thus secure a fourfold table.

	Dropout	Graduate
Above *Md*	7	43
Below *Md*	28	22

He then calculated a ϕ coefficient. What is the value of the ϕ coefficient he obtained?

(4) He showed the ϕ coefficient to the principal who reminded him that, if the dichotomized variable is life adjustment, he could

obtain a tetrachoric coefficient of correlation. The counselor then doubled the percentages in the table and using those in the second column and the abac in Figure 11.8, obtained the tetrachoric coefficient. What is its value?

After discussing the implications of the four coefficients, the principal and the counselor decided that the truly important fact discovered in the research is the high proportion of dropouts. They then concluded that efforts should be made to remedy this situation. They also noted that the achievement battery given on entrance to high school is one means of identifying potential dropouts, but that other traits should also be studied.

ITEM ANALYSIS

When an objective test has been constructed for research or instructional purposes and administered to a reasonably large group of students, the difficulty and discriminating power of each item should be determined in order to identify the items that need to be revised or eliminated before the test is used again to collect data in research, to measure ability or aptitude, or to evaluate achievement.[32] In addition to determining the difficulty of items and their discriminating power from data relevant to correct answers, similar data with reference to the incorrect answers or distracters is also very valuable in item revision and in evaluating instruction.

Item analysis and modern data processing

Test scoring and analysis can be rapidly and routinely accomplished with modern electronic equipment. During or subsequent to test scoring by means of an IBM 1231, a Digitek, or other scoring machine of this type, appropriately programed computer equipment can be subjecting the test data to analysis. The resultant printout may contain, for example, (1) a frequency distribution of the total test scores, their mean, standard deviation, the Kuder-Richardson 20 reliability coefficient and (2) item-analysis data reporting for an upper group and a lower group, where the total sample of tests is split at the median (or into a highest 27 percent and lowest 27 percent) in terms of the total score, the proportions of such groups giving each answer to each item, the proportion of both groups combined giving each answer, and the correlation of the responses to each answer with the total score on the test. This index of

---

[32] Recall what was said in Chapter 7 concerning item analysis in relation to test reliability and test validity. See page 168.

discriminating power may be a biserial coefficient, a point biserial coefficient, or a ϕ coefficient. The proportion of response of both groups combined to the correct answer can be identified as such by an asterisk. Usually the index of discriminating power for this answer will be positive and the other indices negative.

Item analysis by simpler equipment or by hand

When tests are scored and analyzed by less elaborate equipment, or by hand, counts of responses for upper and lower groups can be used in obtaining difficulty and discrimination indices. The latter may be *estimates* of biserial or point biserial coefficients, tetrachoric correlation coefficients, ϕ coefficients, Davis discrimination indices, or the simple discrimination index *D*. To best obtain counts of correct responses by hand it is desirable to mimeograph a tally form such as is illustrated by Figure 11.7. Only the first page need have the heading shown.

Figure 11.7 Tally form for item analysis

Title of Test _____ Date _____

| Item Number | Tallies of Correct Responses | Percentages | | Discrimination Index |
		Upper and Lower Groups	Total Group	
1	⊬⊬ ⊬⊬ ⊬⊬ ⊬⊬ ⊬⊬ ⊬⊬ ⊬⊬ ⊬⊬ ||| 38	76	62	.45
	⊬⊬ ⊬⊬ ⊬⊬ ⊬⊬ |||| 24	48		
2				

First list the item numbers in the left column. Then after separating the test papers or answer sheets into groups above and below the median total test score, tally each test completely, entering a tally for each item answered correctly in the upper cells to the right of the item numbers for each upper group test and in the lower cells for each lower group test. Change the tallies to numbers, entering these frequencies at the ends of the tally cells, for example, 38 and 24. Change the frequencies to percentages by dividing by the number of papers in each group and multiply by 100 to obtain the percentages in the upper and lower groups. This can be done rapidly with a desk calculator or slide rule. Since there are equal numbers of tests in each group, division by 2 gives the percentages for the total group—the item difficulties.

Proportions rather than percentages may be used. The discrimination index entered above is a tetrachoric r. It could be any one of the indices mentioned above and the splits could be the upper and lower 27 percent groups.

An abac for tetrachoric correlation coefficients

In using the abac illustrated in Figure 11.8, enter it from the left with the percent correct response for the upper group and from above with the percent of correct response of the lower group. A ruler or edge of a card may be used to identify the two lines from the left and from above—but make no pencil marks on the abac. Using the fictitious data 76 percent and 48 percent, the lines intersect between the curves labeled $r_t = +\ .40$ and $r_t = +\ .50$. (Where the intercept falls between two curves it is necessary to interpolate.) For the data just given the

Figure 11.8   Abac for tetrachoric coefficients of correlation

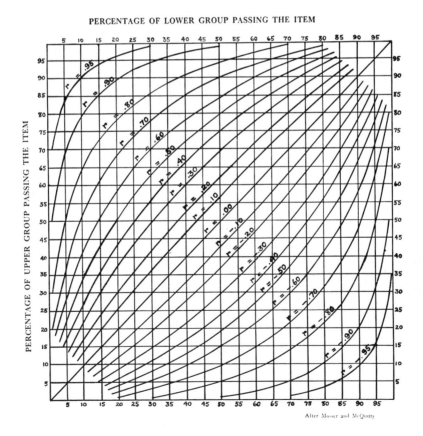

After Mosier and McQuitty

tetrachoric coefficient is estimated as + .45. Assume that the percentages for the upper and lower groups are respectively 47 and 60. The tetrachoric coefficient equals − .20, indicative of an unsatisfactory item. For such items with tetrachoric coefficients less than + .30, it is good practice to obtain counts or tallies of the upper and lower groups to each answer since such data are so useful in item revision and in the evaluation of instruction.

After the tally form has been completed, or the item difficulties and discrimination indices obtained from counts supplied by machine, the indices and the key to each item may be recorded adjacent to each item in one or more copies of the test. An alternative is to record the data on 4″ × 6″ index cards each also containing a copy of the item.

Other item analysis procedures

Many years ago, T. L. Kelley[33] recommended use of upper and lower groups of the 27 percents of the students receiving the highest and lowest scores. It was argued that data from such contrasting groups would yield more sensitive indices of discriminating power than data from samples of tests split at the median total score. More recently a number of abacs and tables have been published for obtaining such indices or estimates of the correlations between whatever is measured by the test items and total test or other criterion scores.[34] Davis discrimination indices, also based on data from upper and lower 27 percent groups, are essentially estimates of product-moment coefficients converted to Fisher's z values and as such have a scale of equal units. The Davis difficulty indices similarly have a scale of equal units.[35]

Although biserial and point biserial coefficients are best obtained through use of formulas earlier given and ϕ coefficients can be obtained through use of Formula 11.25

$$\phi = \frac{P_u - P_l}{2\sqrt{pq}}. \tag{11.25}$$

abacs are given in Guilford's *Psychometric Methods* and *Fundamental*

---

[33] T. L. Kelley, "The Selection of Upper and Lower Groups for the Validation of Test Items," *Journal of Educational Psychology* 30 (January 1939), pp. 17–24.

[34] John C. Flanagan, "General Considerations in the Selection of Test Items and a Short Method of Estimating the Product-moment Coefficient from Data at the Tails of the Distribution," *Journal of Educational Psychology* 30 (December 1939), pp. 674–80; Chung-Teh Fan, *Item-Analysis Table* (Princeton, N.J.: Educational Testing Service, 1952).

[35] Frederick B. Davis, "Item-analysis Data: Their Computation, Interpretation, and Use in Test Construction," *Harvard Education Papers,* No. 2 (Cambridge: Graduate School of Education, Harvard University, 1946).

Statistics. Jurgensen has published a table useful in obtaining ϕ coefficients.[36]

The easiest of all discrimination indices to obtain is the simple index *D*. It is the difference between the proportions of correct response in upper and lower groups whether split at the median or whether upper and lower 27 percents are used. Like point biserial coefficients and ϕ coefficients, *D* favors items of moderate difficulty and does not rise sharply for very easy or very difficult items which actually discriminate between relatively few students. Where item-analysis data are obtained largely for local use, the *D* indices should suffice, especially if they are obtained for each answer.[37] This is illustrated by the following test item and the real data relevent to it. Answer (2) was keyed as the best answer.

According to Madison, a strong executive leadership which violates the principle of separation of power is

		P_u	P_l	D
(1)	impossible because men are not angels and must be restrained	.21	.37	$-.16$
(2)	possible but not desirable	.31	.36	$-.05$
(3)	possible and desirable	.04	.08	$-.04$
(4)	always tyranny	.44	.19	$+.25$

It is evident from the data that more above average than below average students considered answer (4) best. Thoughtful reading of the quotation from *The Federalist* which preceded the item reveals that answer (2) *is* best since Madison used the phraseology "might behave with all the violence of an oppressor" which logically rules out "always tyranny." The next time this item was used, answer (4) was changed to "necessary in times of emergencies," a plausible but irrelevant answer. The analysis then showed that 50 percent of all students gave answer (2) and the *D* rose from $-.05$ to $+.14$. It is likely that substitution of a more plausible answer (3), an unattractive distracter, would have further increased the discriminating power of the item.

Item analysis and the teacher

Item-analysis data are obviously indispensable in the production of standardized aptitude, achievement, and personality tests. Such data are also of great value where research or testing bureaus in city school

---

[36] C. E. Jurgensen, "Table for Determining Phi Coefficients," *Psychometrika* 12 (March 1947), pp. 17–29.

[37] Max D. Engelhart, "A Comparison of Several Item Discrimination Indices," *Journal of Educational Measurement* 2 (June 1965), pp. 69–76. This article also appears in William A Mehrens and Robert L. Ebel's *Principles of Educational and Psychological Measurement* (Chicago: Rand McNally, 1967), pp. 387–94.

systems, or higher institutions, supervise teacher production of tests for widespread local use. Teachers are helped in evaluating attainment of objectives of instruction and in writing better items for widely used future tests or for tests whose use is restricted to individual teachers. The teachers themselves may do the analyses of such tests.[38]

Even elaborate computer printouts accompanied by clearly written statements of explanation are eagerly welcomed by teachers contributing items or using the tests. Such efforts help to fill the gap between test theory and test practice.

---

[38] "How to do it" is explained in these inexpensive booklets: Paul B. Diederich, "Short-Cut Statistics for Teacher-Made Tests," *Evaluation and Advisory Series,* No. 5 (Princeton, N.J.: Educational Testing Service, 1960); Max D. Engelhart, "Improving Classroom Testing," *What Research Says to the Teacher,* No. 31 (Washington, D.C.: National Education Association, 1964).

Questions for
Study and Discussion

1. What is the early history of the theory of "least squares"?

2. Given paired Y and Y' scores, what does their coefficient of correlation equal? (The Y scores are the same Y scores used to obtain the regression equation.)

3. What happens to test reliability and to test validity when items with low item-total test score indices of discriminating power are eliminated during the revision of the test?

4. What is the "correction for attenuation" and how is it used?

5. List a number of problems for which ϕ coefficients and coefficients of contingency might be useful in interpretation of the data.

6. Why does an "oblique" solution in factor analysis imply higher order factors?

7. What is meant by the terms "alpha risk," "average risk," and "maximum risk"? (See the papers by Cronbach and Gleser and by Lord listed among the selected references.)

8. What limitations of the data can limit the effectiveness of the procedures explained on pages 333–335 for estimating chances of success, risk of failure, and the setting of a cutting score?

9. Apart from the uses of χ^2 in testing the significance of ϕ and contingency coefficients, what means are available for testing the significance of or estimating confidence intervals for tetrachoric, biserial, point biserial, and ϕ coefficients?

10. What indices can be used in estimating the correlations between pairs of test items (interitem correlations)? How many would be needed for an objective test of 100 items?

Suggestions
for Further Study

Among the references at the end of Chapter 9 are excellent sources concerning all of the indices of concomitant variation from Pearson product-moment coefficients to coefficients of contingency. Such texts include those by Edwards, Ferguson, Guilford, Hays, McNemar, and Walker and Lev. In view of what has been said in the present chapter, Carroll's article included among the selected references should be of interest.

The student may first supplement his knowledge of prediction techniques by study of Goldine Gleser's article on prediction in the 1960 edition and William B. Michael's article in the 1969 edition of the *Encyclopedia of Educational Research.*

Lavin's analysis of theory and research on the prediction of academic achievement and Bloom's *Stability and Change in Human Characteristics* can aid the student, or other researcher, in deciding what variables to include in a prediction study. Bloom's monograph and Astin's *The College Environment* should be especially helpful in identifying promising environmental variables.

The book by DuBois is notable for its treatment of partial correlation, multiple correlation, and multiple regression equations. It is especially useful in its outlining of computational procedures.

Tucker's *Formal Models for a Central Prediction System* is an important recent contribution to prediction theory and techniques. Bloom and Peters' monograph and Bashaw's article are also concerned with central prediction systems, and procedures to be used to increase the comparability of both predictor and criterion measures where students, coming from a variety of secondary schools, enroll in a variety of higher institutions. These procedures differ from the methods used by the Research Service of the American College Testing Program. A number of regression equations are obtained separately for each participating higher institution. The predictor examinations are common to each prospective entrant and, although high-school marks are also used in regression equations, no effort is made to increase their comparability from one high school to another. This large-scale prediction program is described in my review of the *American College Testing Program Examinations* included in the list of references.

Nothing has been said in this chapter about differential prediction that is concerned with the problem of predicting for an individual what his comparative success might be in two or more educational or vocational fields. Such analysis has applications in advising which field to select and in academic or vocational placement. Discriminant analysis has the purpose of estimating, on the basis of data of the kinds used in obtaining regression equations, to which one of one or more groups an individual should be assigned. Are the abilities and other traits of this college entrant more like those characterizing a group of successful engineers or more like those characterizing a group of successful journalists? Among the texts earlier cited which discuss discriminant analysis are Guilford's *Fundamental Statistics,* which does so briefly, and Nunnally's *Psychometric Theory,* at greater length. Decidedly worth reading are the articles by French, Rulon, and Tiedeman. The most comprehensive recent book on discriminant analysis is Rulon, Tiedeman, Tatsuoka, and Langmuir's *Multivariate Statistics for Personnel Classification.* Cronbach and Gleser's *Psychological Tests and Personnel Decisions* is a major contribution to the theory of decision-making and thus decidedly relevant to prediction.

The student seriously interested in learning more about factor analysis should begin by reading Spearman's 1904 article and his book *The Abilities of Man,* both cited earlier in this chapter. He should next read Wolfle's *Factor Analysis to 1940* and Holzinger's article on factor analysis in the 1950 edition of the *Encyclopedia of Educational Research.* Further study should include the chapter on factor analysis in Guilford's *Psychometric Methods.* Still further study may then be directed toward one or more of the texts by Cattell, Harman, Horst, and, of course, Thurstone. Glass and Taylor's chapter entitled "Factor Analysis Methodology" in the December 1966 issue of the *Review of Educational Research* is an excellent source of information concerning recent developments. Similar chapters will no doubt appear in later issues of the *Review* devoted to the methodology of educational research.

The student of factor analysis and of other multivariate techniques needs to learn matrix algebra. Certain of the references earlier mentioned contain elementary or introductory discussions. For a comprehensive understanding of the subject, Horst's *Matrix Algebra for Social Scientists* should be studied.

Guilford's *Psychometric Methods* and his *Fundamental Statistics,* Davis' monograph cited on page 364 and his chapter in Lindquist and others' *Educational Measurement* are good sources to consult on item analysis. Henrysson's "Gathering, Analyzing, and Using Data on Test Items," Chapter 5 in Thorndike and others, *Educational Measurement,* 2nd ed., is an excellent recent treatment. For other recent developments relevant to item analysis (and to much more) the more advanced student should study Horst's *Psychological Measurement and Prediction,* Nunnally's *Psychometric Theory,* and as he nears the zenith in his preparation for research, Lord and Novick's *Statistical Theories of Mental Test Scores.*

Selected References

Astin, Alexander W. *The College Environment.* Washington, D.C.: American Council on Education, 1968.

Bashaw, Wilbur L. "Central-Prediction-System Models." *American Educational Research Journal* 2 (May 1965): 151–62.

Bloom, Benjamin S. *Stability and Change in Human Characteristics.* New York: Wiley, 1964.

―――― and Frank R. Peters. *The Use of Academic Prediction Scales for Counseling and Selecting College Entrants.* New York: Free Press of Glencoe, 1961.

Carroll, John B. "The Nature of the Data, or How to Choose a Correlation Coefficient." *Psychometrika* 26 (December 1960): 347–72.

Cattell, Raymond B. *Factor Analysis.* New York: Harper and Row, 1952.

Cooley, William W. and Paul R. Lohnes. *Multivariate Procedures for the Behavioral Sciences.* 2nd ed. New York: Wiley, 1971.

Cronbach, Lee J. and Goldine C. Gleser. *Psychological Tests and Personnel Decisions.* 2nd ed. Urbana: University of Illinois Press, 1965.

―――― and ――――. "Interpretation of Reliability and Validity Coefficients: Remarks on a Paper by Lord." *Journal of Educational Psychology* 50 (October 1959): 230–37.

DuBois, Philip H. *Multivariate Correlational Analysis.* New York: Harper and Row, 1957.

Engelhart, Max D. "American College Testing Program Examinations." A review in Buros *Sixth Mental Measurements Yearbook.* Highland Park, N.J.: Gryphon Press, 1965. Pp. 2–7.

French, John W. "The Logic of and Assumptions Underlying Differential Testing." In *Testing Problems in Perspective,* edited by Anne Anastasi, pp. 321–30. Washington, D.C.: American Council on Education, 1966.

Glass, Gene V and Peter A. Taylor. "Factor Analytic Methodology," in "Methodology of Educational Research." *Review of Educational Research* 36 (December 1966): 566–87.

Gleser, Goldine C. "Prediction." In *Encyclopedia of Educational Research,* edited by C. W. Harris, pp. 1038–47. New York: Macmillan, 1960.

Guilford, J. P. *Psychometric Methods.* 2nd ed. New York: McGraw-Hill, 1954.

———. Fundamental Statistics in Psychology and Education. 4th ed., New York: McGraw-Hill, 1965.

Gulliksen, Harold. *Theory of Mental Tests.* New York: Wiley, 1950.

Harman, Harry H. *Modern Factory Analysis.* 2nd ed. Chicago: University of Chicago Press, 1967.

Harris, Chester W. "Bivariate and Multivariate Problems." In *Encyclopedia of Educational Research,* edited by author, pp. 1410–15. 3rd ed. New York: Macmillan, 1960.

Holzinger, Karl J. "Factor Analysis." In *Encyclopedia of Educational Research,* edited by W. S. Monroe, pp. 429–33. 2nd ed. New York: Macmillan, 1950.

Horst, Paul. *Matrix Algebra for Social Scientists.* New York: Holt, Rinehart, and Winston, 1963.

———. *Factor Analysis of Data Matrices.* New York: Holt, Rinehart, and Winston, 1965.

———. *Psychological Measurement and Prediction.* Belmont, Cal.: Wadsworth, 1966.

Lavin, David E. *The Prediction of Academic Performance, A Theoretical Analysis and Review of Research.* New York: Russell Sage Foundation, 1965.

Lord, Frederic M. "The Utilization of Unreliable Difference Scores." *Journal of Educational Psychology* 49 (June 1958): 150–52.

——— and Melvin R. Novick. *Statistical Theories of Mental Test Scores* (with contributions by Allan Birnbaum). Reading, Mass.: Addison-Wesley, 1968.

Mayo, Samuel T. "Toward Strengthening the Contingency Table as a Statistical Method." *Psychological Bulletin* 56 (November 1959): 461–70.

Michael, William B. "Prediction." In *Encyclopedia of Educational Research,* edited by R. L. Ebel, pp. 982–93. 4th ed. New York: Macmillan, 1969.

Nefzger, M. D., and James Drasgow. "The Needless Assumption of Normality in Pearson's r." *American Psychologist* 12 (October 1957): 623–25.

Nunnally, Jum. *Psychometric Theory.* New York: McGraw-Hill, 1967.

Pruzek, Robert M. "Methods and Problems in the Analysis of Multivariate Data." *Review of Educational Research* 41 (June 1971): 163–90.

Rozeboom, W. W. *Foundations of the Theory of Prediction.* Homewood, Ill.: Dorsey Press, 1966.

Rulon, Phillip J. "Distinctions Between Discriminant and Regression Analyses and a Geometric Interpretation of the Discriminant Function." *Harvard Educational Review* 21 (1951): 80–90.

————, David V. Tiedeman, Maurice M. Tatsuoka and Charles R. Langmuir. *Multivariate Statistics for Personnel Classification.* New York: Wiley, 1967.

Thurstone, L. L. *Multiple-Factor Analysis.* Chicago: University of Chicago Press, 1947.

Tiedeman, David V. "A Geometric Model for the Profile Problem." In *Testing Problems in Perspective,* edited by Anne Anastasi, pp. 331–54. Washington, D.C.: American Council on Education, 1966.

Tucker, Ledyard R. "Formal Models for a Central Prediction System." *Psychometric Monograph No. 10.* Richmond, Va.: William Byrd Press, 1963.

Wolfle, Dael. "Factor Analysis to 1940." *Psychometric Monograph No. 3.* Chicago: University of Chicago Press, 1940.

12

Studying Relationships:
Educational Experimentation

The methods of experimental research can yield more dependable conclusions concerning cause and effect relationships than the descriptive or correlation methods explained in Chapters 10 and 11. In an experiment, a hypothesized causal variable can be introduced and manipulated under controlled conditions. Observation of the subsequent change may identify the former as a cause and the latter as its effect. The opportunity to observe such a sequence directly is an advantage unique to experimental research.

Robert S. Woodworth, one of the pioneer leaders of experimental psychology, stated in 1938:

1. The experimenter makes the event happen at a certain time and so is fully *prepared* to make an accurate observation.

2. Controlled conditions being *known* conditions, the experimenter can set up his experiment a second time and repeat the observation; and what is very important in view of the social nature of scientific investigation, he can report his conditions so that another experimenter can duplicate them and check the data.

3. The experimenter can systematically *vary* the conditions and note the concomitant variation in the results.[1]

---

[1] R. S. Woodworth, *Experimental Psychology* (New York: Holt, Rinehart and Winston, Inc., 1938), p. 2. Reprinted with permission of publisher. This quotation appears slightly changed in the revised edition of 1954.

Variables introduced or manipulated by an experimenter are termed *independent* variables while the variables observed for concomitant changes are termed *dependent* variables. This is exemplified by the experimentation which resulted in Boyle's Law. Varying the pressure of the gas (air)—the independent variable—resulted in concomitant, though inverse, variation in the dependent variable—the volume of the gas.[2] For many years, it was considered necessary to obey the "law of the single variable," holding all other variables constant except for the one whose effect is being studied. With the development of the analysis of variance techniques, first introduced in 1923 by Sir Ronald Fisher, two or more independent variables can be varied simultaneously and their separate and joint effects, or interactions, evaluated. This is discussed further on pages 422 to 425.

In the behavioral and certain other sciences, independent variables are called *treatments*. In educational research, methods of instruction compared experimentally are examples of treatments. Ideally, the subjects, or other experimental units, to which treatments are applied should be drawn at random from the population to which the generalizations are to apply. At best, the subjects are drawn at random from some accessible population, for example, all of the sixth-grade pupils in some large school system. The "target" population may be some larger population of which the accessible population is hopefully representative. The subjects drawn at random from an accessible population should be assigned at random to the various treatment groups. Random selection from an appropriate population and random assignment to treatment groups justify the making of significance and other statistical tests in the interpretation of the data. Random assignment to treatment groups also promotes initial equivalence of groups with reference to extraneous factors whose effects on the dependent variable can otherwise mask the true effects of the independent variables, the treatments studied. Such random assignment is an essential characteristic of a "true" experiment in the behavior sciences.

For many years the typical experiment in education involved the use of two groups, an "experimental group" in which an "experimental factor" was introduced and manipulated, and a "control group" in which no change was made in its treatment or method of instruction. While efforts were made to control the extraneous or nonexperimental factors these efforts seldom involved randomization.

Such terms as *experimental factor, nonexperimental factor, experimental group,* and *control group* are not often used with reference to modern experiments involving analysis of data relevant to the simultaneous effects of several independent variables.

---

[2] See Chapter 2, p. 27.

DEVELOPMENT OF EXPERIMENTAL METHODOLOGY

Beginning with the pioneer applications of experimental controls in physical science, this section briefly reviews the development of experimental methodology, including the significance of Mill's Canons, the contributions of the testing movement and the techniques of statistical inference to experimentation, and the changing attitudes toward experimental-type educational research since the turn of the century.

The purposes of experimental controls

Control of variables in experimentation has three major purposes: (1) restraint to keep conditions constant which would otherwise mask the true effect of the independent variable or experimental factor on the dependent variable, (2) guidance or manipulation of the independent variable to determine if it will have its hypothesized effect on the dependent variable, and (3) arrangement of conditions such that checks or comparisons can be made of a dependent variable in the presence or absence of the independent variable, or of different independent variables.[3] Experimental design may be thought of as the planning of the structure and conduct of an experiment to promote the controls specified above.

Pioneer applications of controls in physical science

Experimenters from the beginning of experimental research have recognized the necessity of controlling variables. In his study of the motion of falling bodies, Galileo rolled a ball down an inclined plane because he could not accurately measure time elapse in free fall. It was necessary to "dilute" the influence of gravity.[4] In Chapter 2 it was noted that in order to control variables other than altitude, Pascal had a barometer observed at the foot of the mountain Puy de Dôme while a number of other observations were made at different heights on the mountain and in sunshine and shade. These were later compared with the control observation. Boyle's manipulation of an independent variable was mentioned earlier in this chapter and also in Chapter 2.

John Stuart Mill's contribution to experimental methodology

Although anticipated in many ideas by Francis Bacon and David Hume, J. S. Mill's *A System of Logic* first published in 1843 and containing "Mill's Canons,"[5] greatly contributed to interest in inductive logic and,

---

[3] See Edwin G. Boring, "The Nature and History of Experimental Control," *American Journal of Psychology* 67 (December 1954), pp. 573–89.

[4] Gerald Holton and Duane H. D. Roller, *Foundations of Modern Physical Science* (Reading, Mass.: Addison-Wesley, 1958), p. 29.

[5] John Stuart Mill, *A System of Logic* (New York: Harper & Brothers, 1846).

hence, to scientific methodology. Especially relevant to the third type of experimental control earlier listed is the Second Canon, defining the Method of Difference:

> If an instance in which the phenomenon under investigation occurs, and an instance in which it does not occur, have every circumstance save one in common, that one occurring only in the former; the circumstance in which alone the two instances differ, is the effect, or cause, or a necessary part of the cause, of the phenomenon.[6]

Although the Method of Difference as stated above serves to identify a cause-and-effect relationship, it does not specify whether the circumstance in which alone the two instances differ is the cause *or* the effect. In discussing this Canon, Mill stated, however, "It is . . . the very nature of an experiment to introduce into the pre-existing state of circumstances a change perfectly definite."[7] It is obvious from the discussion that Mill regarded "a change perfectly definite" as a cause.

The Method of Difference, because of its emphasis on a single circumstance in which two instances differ, has been called the "law of the single variable." Educational experimenters and experimenters in other fields long believed in conformity with it. It is interesting to note, however, that Mill himself thought the Method of Difference and his other Canons inapplicable to social problems because of the multiplicity of causes.[8] With the development of the techniques of multivariate analysis of variance it has become accepted, as earlier noted, that two or more independent variables can be varied simultaneously or successively and their separate and joint effects evaluated. With reference to the entire methodology proposed by Mill it is contended by Tiedeman that "there is ample room not only for the law of the single variable but also for the law of multiple variables operating conjointly not only simultaneously but also successively."[9]

Experimentation in psychology and education prior to 1900

Ernst Weber between 1834 and 1839 and Gustav Fechner between 1855 and 1859 conducted the experimentation leading to their psychophysical laws relating stimulus intensities to sensory judgments. Between 1879 and 1900 numerous psychological experiments were undertaken

---

[6] *Ibid.,* p. 225.

[7] *Ibid.,* p. 226.

[8] *Ibid.,* pp. 552–55.

[9] David V. Tiedeman, "Experimental Method," in C. W. Harris, ed., *Encyclopedia of Educational Research,* 3rd ed. (New York: Macmillan, 1960), p. 490. For criticism of Mill's Canons, see Morris R. Cohen and Ernest Nagel, *An Introduction to Logic and Scientific Method* (New York: Harcourt, Brace, 1934), Chapter 13.

by Wilhelm Wundt, Francis Galton, Hermann Ebbinghaus, William James, and J. McKeen Cattell. Usually this laboratory experimentation was undertaken using one subject, often the experimenter himself. Many of the experiments were concerned with problems of reaction time, associations and memory, and attention span.[10]

Dr. J. M. Rice began his testing in spelling in 1895. In 1897 he reported his investigation in *Forum* under the title "The Futility of the Spelling Grind." Three different tests were constructed and 33,000 pupils in grades 4 through 8 in 21 cities were tested by one or more of these tests. The best established conclusion to be derived from Rice's data would seem to be the lack of relationship between minutes per day devoted to drill in spelling and achievement in spelling. A correlation of − .12 between averages on one of Rice's spelling tests and minutes per day of spelling drill for the 82 classes for which such data are reported has been calculated. This research is best termed a comparative survey, or possibly, a "quasi-experiment" since Rice did not manipulate the independent variable, time per day devoted to spelling, nor did he assign the very numerous school classes at random to the various levels of the variable.[11] A subsequent spelling investigation reported in 1902 by O. P. Cornman is more deservedly considered a controlled experiment. Spelling drill was eliminated for a three-year period in two "experimental" schools and the resulting spelling achievement was somewhat superior to that of classes in other Philadelphia schools continuing the traditional instruction.[12]

Earliest use of experimental and control groups

R. L. Solomon states that "we have not been able to find a single case of the use of control group design, as we use it today, before the year 1901."[13] He credits E. L. Thorndike and R. S. Woodworth[14] with earliest

---

[10] For further discussion of Weber's and Fechner's laws and the experimentation mentioned above, see Henry E. Garrett, *Great Experiments in Psychology,* 3rd ed. (New York: Appleton-Century-Crofts, 1951); E. G. Boring, *A History of Experimental Psychology,* 2nd ed. (New York: Appleton-Century-Crofts, 1950); J. P. Guilford, *Psychometric Methods,* 2nd ed. (New York: McGraw-Hill, 1954); and R. S. Woodworth and Harold Schlosberg, *Experimental Psychology,* rev. ed. (New York: Holt, 1954).

[11] See Julian C. Stanley, "Rice as Pioneer Educational Researcher," *Journal of Educational Measurement* 3 (Summer 1966), pp. 135–40; Max D. Engelhart and Macklin Thomas, "Rice as the Inventor of the Comparative Test," *Journal of Educational Measurement* 3 (Summer 1966), pp. 141–45.

[12] O. P. Cornman, *Spelling in the Elementary School: An Experimental and Statistical Investigation* (Boston: Ginn, 1902).

[13] R. L. Solomon, "An Extension of Control Group Design," *Psychological Bulletin* 46 (March 1949), p. 137.

[14] Edward L. Thorndike and Robert S. Woodworth, "The Influence of Improvement in One Mental Function Upon the Efficiency of Other Functions," *Psychological Review* 8 (1901), pp. 247–61, 384–95, 553–64.

use of experimental and control groups and W. H. Winch of the London schools with the first thorough use of such groups.

In the experiments on "transfer of training" conducted by Thorndike and Woodworth, the experimental groups had no more than six subjects while the control group given the same tests, but no intervening training, consisted of eight subjects. The control group was used to determine whether any of the gains of the experimental group should be attributed to the initial testing. The type of control briefly described by Thorndike and Woodworth is widely used today.

It is a little disconcerting to discover that this extremely influential experimentation, one of the major factors in the elimination of faculty psychology and the doctrine of formal discipline, had so few subjects participating. Possibly the recognition of the importance of larger and representative samples of subjects arose with increased understanding of the range of individual differences.

Winch also was concerned with the problem of transfer of training. He used two groups of 17 pupils each in a London elementary school. In his 1908 report, he states:

> With the aid of the teacher, the girls were now placed in two equal groups. This was not easy to arrange, but we finally succeeded in getting two groups, A and B, which had an equal aggregate of marks and which were thought by the teacher to be equal.[15]

Winch's conclusions were largely based on small groups of pupils on the same levels of ability as shown by the initial testing. According to Solomon, it is evident that Winch had no realization that he was innovating quite modern experimental design.[16]

During the years prior to 1930 the desirability of using control groups in school experimentation was increasingly recognized. Such groups were employed in 35 out of 72 experimental investigations reported in the *Journal of Educational Research* from January 1920 to June 1927, and in 17 of 26 experiments reported as *Teachers College, Columbia University Contributions to Education* from 1918 to 1926. It is evident that although the use of control groups was widely recognized as desirable, a large proportion of contemporary experimenters failed to use them.[17]

---

[15] W. H. Winch, "The Transfer of Improvement in Memory in School Children," *British Journal of Psychology* 2 (January 1908), pp. 284–93.

[16] Solomon, "An Extension of Control," p. 138.

[17] For more of this early history, see Walter S. Monroe and Max D. Engelhart, *Experimental Research in Education,* Bureau of Educational Research Bulletin No. 48 (Urbana: University of Illinois, 1930), pp. 7–17.

The contribution of the testing movement to experimental educational research

The development of intelligence tests and of achievement tests was accompanied by increasing interest in experimentation under school conditions. In 43 percent of the learning experiments reported in the *Journal of Educational Research* from January 1920 to December 1928, intelligence tests were used to obtain pupil data for the purpose of obtaining "equivalent" groups. Standardized achievement tests, first developed in 1908 and 1909 by C. W. Stone and S. A. Courtis, were also employed to collect data used in equating groups and in measuring experimental achievement. In 58.3 percent of the learning experiments reported in the *Journal of Educational Research* from January 1920 to December 1928 standardized achievement tests were used for the latter purpose.

By 1930 a multitude of achievement tests had been developed in almost all elementary and secondary school subjects, in some college subjects, and progress was being made "in development of measurements of character and personality." In the years since 1930 new tests and types of tests have continued to proliferate and, in addition to their other uses, have contributed to experimental research in education.[18]

Statistical method and experimental educational research

Such mathematicians as Laplace, Gauss, and Bravais had developed some ideas of correlation before Galton, but the first clear statement of the theory and the term must be credited to him. Further development of correlation methods by Pearson, Yule, Spearman, and others made possible the use of correlation techniques described in Chapter 11.[19] In experimental research, correlation techniques were immediately useful in evaluating the validity and reliability of intelligence tests and achievement tests used to equate groups and to measure gains in achievement. The error of difference formulas first used in the interpretation of differences in achievement in educational experiments evolved as a result of the work of Encke and Airy (astronomers) and Sheppard and Yule, mathematical statisticians associated with Karl Pearson. In 1908, "Student" (W. S. Gosset) contributed the *t* ratio and its sampling distribution.[20] The analysis of variance was first introduced in 1923 by R. A. Fisher in an agricultural journal and in 1925 in the first edition of his *Statistical Methods for Research Workers*. The first edition of his *Design of Experiments* appeared in 1935.

---

[18] *Ibid.,* p. 10.

[19] Helen M. Walker, *Studies in the History of Statistical Method* (Baltimore: Williams and Wilkins, 1929), pp. 92–115.

[20] Student (pseud.), "The Probable Error of a Mean," *Biometrika* 6 (1908), pp. 1–25.

Cultural lag is well illustrated by the length of time it took for the ideas of "Student" and Fisher to have an impact on educational experimentation in the United States. There is little evidence of their application in reports of experiments published in our research literature prior to 1940.

School experimentation was greatly stimulated in the 1920s by W. A. McCall's *How to Experiment in Education.* In this, "an undervalued classic,"[21] McCall explains one-group, equivalent group, and rotation experimental designs. He indicates understanding of the importance of random samples when using the standard error formulas and of random assignment of treatments in the obtaining of equivalence of groups:

> Just as representativeness can be secured by the method of chance, when the subjects involved are sufficiently numerous, so equivalence may be secured by chance, provided the number of subjects to be used is sufficiently numerous.[22]

In this and in his development of the rotation technique, a Latin-square design, he anticipated Fisher.

McCall presented formulas for the standard error of a difference (our Formulas 9.3 and 9.5) as well as formulas for partial and multiple correlation and regression equations. He provided excellent schemas for summarizing experimental data and for computing standard errors. It is evident that he was familiar with degrees of freedom since he suggested subtracting 1, 2, and 3 from n's equal to or less than 30.

McCall is probably best remembered for the "Experimental Coefficient" which he introduced as a criterion for the significance of a difference:

$$EC = \frac{\text{Difference}}{2.78 \text{ SDD}}$$

When this ratio equals 1.0 for a one-tailed test, the chances are 369 to 1 that the difference is in the specified direction. When the difference is 3.0 times its standard error the chances are 369 to 1 "that the true

---

[21] So judged by Donald T. Campbell and Julian C. Stanley, "Experimental and Quasi-Experimental Designs for Research on Teaching," in N. L. Gage, ed., *Handbook of Research on Teaching* (Chicago: Rand McNally, 1963), p. 172. Also separately published as *Experimental and Quasi-Experimental Designs for Research* (Chicago: Rand McNally, 1966), p. 2.

[22] W. A. McCall, *How to Experiment in Education* (New York: Macmillan, 1923), p. 41.

D lies between obtained D minus 3 SDD and obtained D plus 3 SDD."[23] (As explained in Chapter 9, such multiples of the standard error are measured from zero rather than from the scale value of the observed difference. The outcome is the same, but the logic is better!)

McCall understood that a sample could not give "absolute" certainty, so he considered 369 to 1 as indicative of "practical certainty." However, his statements that "an EC of 0.5 means that we can be only half certain that the true D is above zero. An EC of 2.0 means that we can be doubly certain that the true D is above zero, and similarly for other sizes of EC,"[24] are absurd since it is impossible to divide or to multiply certainty. The chances corresponding to an EC of 0.5 are 11 to 1, to an EC of 1.0 are 369 to 1, and to an EC of 2.0 approximately 400,000 to 1. (Compare the area beyond $2 \times 2.78 \, \sigma$, or $4.56 \, \sigma$, with the area of the rest of a unit normal curve.)

McCall's criteria for the significance of differences are comparable to those recommended by other educational statisticians of his time—generally a difference should be three times its standard error or four times its probable error. Fisher, however, recommended twice the standard error as a minimum, a criterion approximately equivalent to the .05 level. In tables for use in interpreting analysis of variance data in the 1925 and later editions of *Statistical Methods for Research Workers* critical values are listed for the .05 and .01 levels. It should be noted that Fisher was accustomed to using more valid and reliable data than McCall and other educational experimenters.

Although the analysis of variance and other techniques were further reported in Fisher's *Design of Experiments* (1935) and in later editions of this book and of *Statistical Methods for Research Workers,* application of these techniques came slowly.[25] Their adoption was promoted indirectly by Snedecor's text (1937) and more directly by Lindquist's earlier text (1940). It is almost impossible to find in the research literature of education applications of analysis of variance prior to World War II. Following World War II an increasing number of texts appeared especially applicable to the design of experiments relevant to psychological and educational problems. These texts include those by Johnson (1949), McNemar (1949), Edwards (1950), Walker and Lev (1953), Lindquist (1953), Ferguson (1959), and Winer (1962). Complete references

---

[23] *Ibid.,* pp. 163–64. SDD is McCall's symbol for the standard error of a difference, *D.*

[24] *Ibid.,* p. 155. In spite of this amusing lapse, the text as a whole is still an "undervalued classic."

[25] For more detail, see Julian C. Stanley, "The Influence of Fisher's 'The Design of Experiments' on Educational Research Thirty Years Later," *American Educational Research Journal* 3 (May 1966), pp. 223–29.

to these or later editions of these texts are given on pages 449–450. Educational experimenters are also turning increasingly to advanced books on mathematical statistics.

Stanley reported that about half of the 26 articles in the first volume of the *American Educational Research Journal* in 1964 were experiments.[26] Actually, there are reports of 14 experiments and in 8 of these application was made of analysis of variance. Seventeen of the 40 articles in the 1968 volume are reports of one or more experiments, 16 are reports of other, but sophisticated types of research, and 7 are discussions of research methodology including Bracht and Glass's notable "The External Validity of Experiments." In *all* 17 reports of experiments, use was made of analysis of variance techniques ranging from simple analysis of variance through such complex designs as repeated measures, Graeco-Latin squares and complex factorial designs. In 14 of the reports, random assignment to treatments is explicitly mentioned.

Changing attitudes toward experimental research in education

Between 1910 and 1914 such distinguished educational psychologists as E. L. Thorndike, W. F. Dearborn, and G. M. Whipple were urging that learning experiments conducted under laboratory conditions using adults as subjects should be repeated under school conditions using children as subjects.[27] J. C. Bell in 1918 and W. A. McCall in 1923 revealed a sublime faith in the value of experimentation as a means of solving educational problems:

> Now comes the experimentalist, and with clear, unfaltering eye and steady relentless tone, he demands of each subject the justification for its existence.[28]

> Everywhere there are evidences of an increasing tendency to evaluate educational procedures experimentally.[29]

In 1928, Carter V. Good exhibited a similar attitude:

> It is to the experimental method that education must look for the solution of many of its most vexing problems. It is upon this basis that the ultimate establishment of education as a science must rest.[30]

---

[26] *Ibid.,* p. 225.

[27] Monroe and Engelhart, *Experimental Research,* p. 12.

[28] J. C. Bell, "A New Humanism Needed," *Journal of Educational Psychology* 9 (March 1918), p. 165. [An editorial] Transfer of training was a problem of major interest.

[29] W. A. McCall, *How to Experiment,* p. 2.

[30] C. V. Good, *How to Do Research in Education* (Baltimore: Warwick and York, 1928), p. 146.

Between 1925 and 1930, however, such leaders as M. R. Trabue, V. A. C. Henmon, C. H. Judd, W. S. Monroe, M. E. Haggerty, G. M. Whipple and Clifford Woody had become increasingly critical of the quality of contemporary educational research.[31] With reference to the 72 experiments reported between 1920 and 1927 in the *Journal of Educational Research,* Monroe gave the following critical evaluation:

> Thirty-five of these studies, or slightly less than half, were controlled experiments. Only seven were definitely built upon previous investigations and in only seventeen others was any comparison made with the results of previous investigations. Thus forty-eight, or two-thirds of the total number, may be considered relatively isolated studies.[32]

He then listed nine conclusions as representative of the disappointing nature of the conclusions. "Some of them approach being platitudinous; others deal with relatively unimportant details of instructional procedure." For example:

> Improvement in comprehension in reading will result from drill, the children of lesser ability profiting most.
> Knowledge that there may be a final examination will produce worthwhile results.[33]

Monroe and his associates considered approximately 47, or nearly two-thirds, of the 72 experiments to be open to such serious criticism that the conclusions could not be accepted as dependable. One of the chief reasons for this judgment was that

> In several instances, the improvement in achievement noted appeared to have been due to the enthusiasm of the teacher for the procedure rather than to any inherent worth. The fact that a procedure is new frequently results in unusual enthusiasm on the part of the teacher which is communicated to the pupils. In fact, the pupils themselves are likely to be stimulated directly by a procedure that lifts their work out of the usual deadly routine.[34]

After citing several leaders recently critical of educational experi-

---

[31] Monroe and Engelhart, *Experimental Research,* pp. 13–15.

[32] Walter S. Monroe and others, *Ten Years of Educational Research, 1918–1927.* Bureau of Educational Research Bulletin No. 42 (Urbana: University of Illinois, 1928), pp. 79–80.

[33] *Op. cit.*

[34] *Ibid.,* p. 81.

mentation and while noting that pessimism in the 1930s followed the overoptimism of the 1920s, Carter V. Good states:

> We must always remember, however, that experimentation is the only valid procedure for settling disputes concerning educational practice, for verifying educational improvements, and for establishing a tradition ... in which improvements can be introduced without the danger of a "faddish discard of old wisdom in favor of inferior novelties."[35]

Despite the dilemmas noted by Monroe in 1928 and others since then, increasing numbers of experiments under school conditions are being conducted today. With superior training and improved techniques experimenters should be capable of functioning in harmony with the 1928 and 1966 expectations of Carter Good.

EXPERIMENTATION AND THE THEORY AND PRACTICE OF EDUCATION

Considerable emphasis was put on experimentation in introducing the student to various methods of scientific inquiry in Chapter 2. Like other types of scientific research, experimental research begins with a problem. One or more research hypotheses are derived from experience and observation or deductively from theory (antecedent generalizations or laws). They, and the problem to which they pertain, may be produced by creative or insightful thinking. In any case, each hypothesis is a prediction of what will happen when it is subjected to experimental test. Many hypotheses are tested mentally and rejected. The more promising hypotheses may be tested through collection and analysis of data. If actual experiment results in rejection of the null hypothesis, the corresponding research hypothesis may be tentatively accepted as a generalization or law since it was not disconfirmed. Hypotheses thus accepted become a part of theory useful in explanation, in prediction, and in intelligent control of events in the practice of education. They retain this status until superseded by more acceptable laws or generalizations.

This type of experimentation is likely to be directed by experts in psychological or educational research affiliated with universities. An experiment thus directed may be a "laboratory" experiment or a "field" experiment using school pupils as subjects. An experiment conducted

---

[35] Carter V. Good, *Essentials of Educational Research* (New York: Appleton-Century-Crofts, 1966), p. 370. This quote also appears in his *Introduction to Educational Research* of 1959 and 1963.

as described is "conclusion oriented."[36] Educational experiments are also conducted by the research bureaus of city school systems, bureaus of institutional research of colleges and universities, and federally financed research and development centers. The experiments conducted by staff members of such organizations are more properly concerned with the solution of immediate practical problems, such as the relative merits of differing instructional methods or materials. The solutions of such problems may be of help to administrative officers in deciding what methods or materials should be used. An experiment of this type is "decision oriented."

Decision-oriented experiments conducted in local school systems or bureaus of institutional research in higher institutions could be much more effectively conducted given better-trained research personnel who devote themselves to research rather than to promotion. The effectiveness of these experiments would also be enhanced given administrative officers with better understanding of the basic requirements of research, especially the importance of randomization and of integrity in the interpretation of data. The local research expert can increase the effectiveness of his experimental research if he relates it to previous relevant research and theory. His replication of such research under somewhat different local conditions or subjects may contribute to the generalizability of a principle earlier reported in a conclusion-oriented study.

It has been recommended in recent years that an exploratory type of experimentation termed *aexperimentation* [sic] precede the more formal kind. Such research efforts are considered appropriate in situations where relevant variables cannot be defined in advance, when it is premature to define hypotheses, and where it is impossible or undesirable to introduce controls. According to E. G. Guba:

> The aexperimental approach yields information about relationships as they actually occur in nature, focuses attention on many variables at once, provides a certain flexibility for adjusting to situations rigid controls of experimentalism make impossible, and yields a rich and detailed supply of information . . .[37]

When this approach is used the instructional procedure or procedures can be modified as time passes and the thinking processes of the pupils can be observed or measured by brief diagnostic-type tests

---

[36] See Lee J. Cronbach and Patrick Suppes, eds., *Research for Tomorrow's Schools: Disciplined Inquiry for Education* (New York: Macmillan, 1969).

[37] Egon G. Guba, "The Expanding Concept of Research," *Theory Into Practice* 6 (April 1967), pp. 57–60.

which the pupils understand are not a basis of marks. The processes observed or the products produced can provide "periodic feedback to project administrators and others responsible for continuous control and refinements of plans and procedures."[38]

Research of the type described above may be considered on the second level of inquiry as defined by Northrop (see Chapter 2, pages 12 to 14); and it is compatible with Medley and Mitzel's recommendation that direct and systematic observation occur in experimentation (Chapter 6, page 121). It may provide the information needed to prepare adequate behavioral definitions of experimental treatments useful in planning more rigorously conducted experiments. It could also be the best way to introduce innovations.

PROCEDURES AND PROCEDURAL PROBLEMS IN EDUCATIONAL EXPERIMENTATION

The basic design in educational experimentation involves an experimental group and a control group, or two groups subjected to different treatments. A pretest may or may not be given, but some kind of observation or testing is done during the experiment or at its end. Much of what is said in this chapter about experimentation using relatively few groups also applies to experiments of more complex design.

We start with selections from a 1931 discussion[39] which is followed by current comments of the junior author.

Procedures and problems circa 1930

The numbered selections quoted are followed in their source by explanation of standard error of difference formulas, including the matched groups formula:

1. *Equivalent groups.* The groups of pupils used in the experiment should be equivalent in all respects that will affect their achievement during the experiment. This requirement can be approximated by pairing pupils on the basis of intelligence test scores and then comparing the groups thus formed with respect to chronological age, to previous achievement in the school subject, and to measures of reading ability. If the differences between the means and the standard deviations of the groups with re-

---

[38] Daniel L. Stufflebeam, "The Use and Abuse of Evaluation in Title III," *Theory Into Practice* 6 (June 1967), pp. 128–33.

[39] Walter S. Monroe and Max D. Engelhart, *A Critical Summary of Research Relating to the Teaching of Arithmetic*, Bureau of Educational Research Bulletin No. 58 (Urbana: University of Illinois, 1931), pp. 98–100. Very minor changes have been made so that the quoted material applies to arithmetic and to other school subjects.

spect to these three characteristics are relatively small, the groups may be considered approximately equivalent. It is desirable that the groups also be approximately equivalent with respect to personality traits, physical conditions, sex, and race.

2. *Specification of experimental factor and control of nonexperimental factors.* The experimental factor should, if possible, be restricted to a single phase or detail of instructional procedure. The method used with the experimental group should vary from that used with the control group in only this single phase, and if other variations are permitted, their effect must be accurately measured or a plan of neutralization must be devised. (This requirement is sometimes designated as the Law of the Single Variable.) The total instructional procedure to be used in both groups should be specified in writing, or at least a detailed record should be kept of what is done.[40]

The teacher factors whose control in experiments appears to be the most important are (1) instructional techniques employed during the recitation period, especially those relating to the assignment, and motivation; (2) skill of the teacher in carrying out instructional techniques and classroom-management procedures; (3) zeal of the teacher; (4) personality traits of the teacher. In addition, care should be exercised to avoid marked differences in the minor teacher factors—physical condition, sex, and age.

The important factors under the head of general and extra-school factors are (1) materials of instruction, (2) environment in which learning activity takes place, and (3) minutes per day devoted to learning activity in the subject. The materials of instruction, desks, chairs, light, heat, ventilation, and other aspects of the learning environment should be identical for both groups. Study and recitation periods should be of equal length in the experimental and control groups. Parents should be urged to refrain from influencing the learning activity of the pupils, and, possibly, should be asked to cooperate in restricting the activity to the classroom.

It should be noted that the precise prescription of an instructional procedure and the strict control of nonexperimental factors is incompatible with good teaching. A teacher should adapt her techniques to the needs of her pupils as they become apparent. Hence, conformity to the requirements for precise experimentation will, in many cases, tend to reduce the effectiveness of the teaching, and this in turn will introduce an element of uncertainty in the interpretation of the results of the experiment.

Current comments

The preceding paragraph and numerous similar criticisms probably contributed to the disillusionment with experimental research in the 1930s.

The two paragraphs on control of nonexperimental factors seem as

---

[40] See p. 388.

sensible today as when they were written. Note the emphasis on the equating of groups and the lack of any recommendation of random assignment to treatments. Monroe believed, however, that, when used on a comparatively large scale, equivalence could be secured by randomization.[41] He conducted an experiment in which a comparison was made of pupil responses to different kinds of arithmetical problem statements on four tests passed out in alternate order—1, 2, 3, 4; 1, 2, 3, 4; etc. in each classroom. A total of 9,526 sixth-, seventh-, and eighth-grade pupils in 41 Illinois cities participated. (In 1958, E. B. Page reported an experiment employing the same technique of randomization.[42])

Given random selection and matching of pairs *followed* by random assignment to treatment groups, the statements under equivalent groups, *if feasible,* would be applicable today.

The restriction of the experimental factor to a single phase or detail of instructional procedure in conformity with the Law of the Single Variable now strikes one as archaic. What is said, however, does suggest that each of the variables of a present-day experiment should be carefully specified and the instructional procedures for all groups outlined in detail. Furthermore, the actual instruction in the compared groups should be observed as suggested on page 121 of Chapter 6. Descriptive observational records akin to those used in sociology and anthropology have been urged to accomplish this aim. The precise specification and control of instructional procedures is often incompatible with good teaching as was suggested above. The production of a comprehensive observational record of what was actually characteristic of instruction should permit the teacher to have the freedom to teach effectively and to reduce uncertainty in interpreting the experimental data. It may also be recommended that the problem statements include operational definitions of what the pupils do as outcomes of the compared instructional procedures. Observations of what the pupils do are as important as observations of what the teachers do. Let us turn now to important recent analyses of the validity or dependability of experiments.

Contemporary analyses of procedural problems

Since 1957, Donald Campbell, Julian Stanley, Glenn Bracht, and Gene Glass have reported comprehensive analyses of factors or threats

---

[41] Walter S. Monroe, *How Pupils Solve Problems in Arithmetic,* Bureau of Educational Research Bulletin No. 44 (Urbana: University of Illinois, 1929).

[42] Ellis B. Page, "Teacher Comments and Student Performance: A Seventy-four Classroom Experiment in School Motivation," *Journal of Educational Psychology* 49 (August 1958), pp. 173–81.

jeopardizing the validity of experiments.[43] Campbell and Stanley emphasize that the threats they list are usually of less concern in "true" experiments where subjects have been assigned at random to treatments and the treatments and measurements are under the control of the experimenter. The threats are of much greater concern in "quasi-experiments" where random assignment is not feasible and the experimenter has less or no control of the variables studied.

The following list is derived from the sources cited rather than directly quoted. The material has been expressed less technically and with more emphasis on school experimentation.

Threats to internal validity

1. *History:* events, other than the experimental treatments, occurring between pretest and posttest producing effects mistakenly attributed to the difference in treatments.

2. *Maturation:* processes within the experimental subjects during an experiment producing effects mistakenly credited to the difference in treatments. These processes include fatigue, hunger, loss of interest, and in a prolonged experiment, unequal acquisition of relevant knowledge or skill from sources external to the experiment.

3. *Instability:* unreliability of measures, fluctuations in sampling, instability of repeated or "equivalent" measures. These are the *only* threats to which statistical tests of significance are relevant. They account for variable errors of measurement and sampling only.

4. *Irrelevant effects of testing:* If a pretest or other tests are given during an experiment, the scores on the posttest may be affected by this testing apart from the effects of the treatments administered to each group. This is especially likely to occur when attitude measurements are obtained with a suitable pretest and a posttest, but only the experimental group is expected to grow in the attitudes measured.

5. *Instrumentation:* Changes may occur in raters or in the basis of ratings from one group to another or testing conditions may not be uniform from group to group. The posttest may not be equally valid or fair with reference to the instruction in the compared groups. Two groups may have different but equally desirable objectives.

---

[43] Donald T. Campbell, "Factors Relevant to the Validity of Experiments in Social Settings," *Psychological Bulletin* 54 (July 1957), pp. 297–312; Donald T. Campbell and Julian C. Stanley, "Experimental and Quasi-Experimental Designs for Research on Teaching," in N. L. Gage, ed., *Handbook of Research on Teaching* (Chicago: Rand McNally, 1963), pp. 175–76 and 204, or their separate publication with the same title, pp. 16–17 and 34; and Glenn H. Bracht and Gene V Glass, "The External Validity of Experiments," *American Educational Research Journal* 5 (November 1968), pp. 437–74; and Donald T. Campbell, "Reforms as Experiments," *American Psychologist* 24 (April 1969), pp. 409–29.

6. *Statistical regression:* Below-average pupils drawn from a superior population tend to receive higher scores on a second testing. Their scores tend to "regress" upward toward their population mean. Above-average pupils drawn from a less able population tend to obtain lower scores on a second testing.

Figure 12.1   An illustration of statistical regression

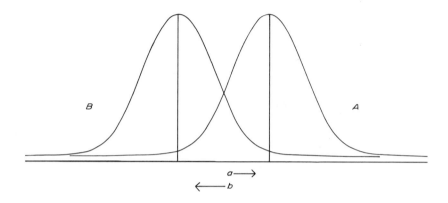

In Figure 12.1, pupil *a* is a member of the population represented by Curve A and Pupil *b* is a member of the population represented by Curve B. Both Pupils *a* and *b* have received the *same* score on the pretest and are selected as one pair of subjects in setting up an experimental and a control group. All *a* pupils located in the same school constitute one group and all *b* pupils in another school constitute the other group. (Within each pair the scores are equal or approximately so, but the scores vary from pair to pair. They are generally above the B average and below the A average on the pretest.) Obviously, the experimental findings will favor Group A, possibly leading to the conclusion that the treatment administered to this group is significantly better than the treatment received by the other group when, in fact, this treatment is not inherently more effective. Conversely, if this treatment is actually more effective and is administered to Group B, the conclusion is likely to be that it is less effective than the other treatment.

The *a* pupils, because of their regression toward the *posttest* mean of Group A, tend to raise this mean spuriously. Conversely, the *b* pupils, because of their regression toward the posttest mean of Group B, tend to lower this mean spuriously. If the pretest scores and the posttest scores were perfectly correlated there would be no such regression effects. The lack of perfect correlation is due to variable errors of measurement (the unreliability of the tests) and to variable effects of extraneous factors unique to each group.[44]

7. *Selection:* biases resulting from differences in the selection of subjects in the compared groups. The subjects may have had, for example, quite different past instruction which contributes unequally to the achievement of the compared groups. The biases due to differences in selection may "interact" or combine with history, maturation, or other irrelevant factors to introduce effects confused with those of the compared treatments.

8. *Experimental mortality:* The loss of subjects during an experiment may differ from group to group because of a *priori* differences in the abilities or differences in the compared treatments. Unless the treatments actually used and the conditions characterizing their use are adequately described, one treatment may be much more rigorous than another.

Threats to external validity

External validity pertains to the extent to which the findings of an experiment can be generalized. To what extent can the conclusions be applied to other populations or conditions? Threats to external validity may limit the generalizations to a restricted population and to specific conditions.[45]

1. *Inadequate description of the independent variable.* In order to state valid generalizations the experimenter must describe the independent variable explicitly. Others cannot judge what applications of finding are justified nor can the given experiment be satisfactorily replicated unless the treatments and conditions characterizing their use are adequately described.[46] This limitation occurs all too frequently in the proposal or plan for an experimental research and the report of the experiment after completion.

2. *Inadequate representativeness of the accessible and target populations.* The subjects participating in an experiment may be adequately representative of an accessible population without being representative of the target population to which the generalizations are expected to

---

[44] For further discussion, see Campbell and Stanley, *Experimental and Quasi-Experimental Design,* pp. 10–12 in their book, pp. 180–82 in Gage's *Handbook,* and especially the Allen Edwards and Robert Thorndike references listed at the end of this chapter. Quinn McNemar recommends matching on the basis of regressed or estimated true scores. *Psychological Statistics,* 4th ed. (New York: Wiley, 1969), pp. 179–80.

[45] See Campbell and Stanley, *Experimental and Quasi-Experimental Design,* pp. 5–6 or pp. 175–76 in Gage's *Handbook;* and Bracht and Glass, "External Validity," p. 438.

[46] Bracht and Glass, *ibid.*

apply. Accessible populations may differ in a variety of ways which interact with treatments. These may be unrecognized when conclusions are stated as if applicable to "all fourth-grade pupils in the United States." Samples can also be inadequately representative of the accessible population.[47] There may be both random and systematic errors of sampling.

3. *Departures from usual school conditions.* The subjects participating in an experiment may be motivated by the knowledge that they are participating in an experiment (the Hawthorne effect). The relatively superior achievement of an experimental group when contrasted with that of a control group may be attributable to the novelty of the method of instruction appealing to the interest of the pupils and stimulating greater zeal on the part of the teacher.[48] When two or more different methods or treatments are compared and this is known to the pupils and their teachers, an experiment may take on the attributes of a competition, creating abnormal school conditions.

4. *Pretest and posttest sensitization.* As earlier noted under internal validity, a pretest may have effects confused or "confounded" with treatment effects. This is especially true of attitude measurement. It is less true where the pretest is similar to tests routinely given. According to Bracht and Glass, a posttest can also engender attitudes and intellectual skills which would remain latent without the occurrence of the posttest.[49]

5. *Inadequate measurement of the dependent variable.* The experimental testing of hypotheses in an experiment requires "the conceptualization of the dependent variable and its operational definition" so that appropriate measuring instruments can be selected or constructed.[50] Often thorough analysis will reveal that more than one dependent variable should be defined where the objectives of instruction are not restricted to knowledge alone but include critical thinking skills and attitudes.

6. *Interactions of various extraneous factors with treatments.* All threats to external validity, including those briefly described above, are interactions of various irrelevant factors with treatments. In addition to interaction effects attributable to selection, artificial instructional conditions, pretest and posttest sensitization, and biased measurement of

---

[47] Bracht and Glass, *op. cit.,* pp. 438–43; Campbell and Stanley, *op. cit.,* pp. 19–20 or 189–90.

[48] Lee J. Cronbach, "Course Improvement Through Evaluation," *Teachers College Record* 64 (May 1963), p. 672–83.

[49] Bracht and Glass, *op. cit.,* pp. 463–64.

[50] *Ibid.,* p. 465.

dependent variables, interaction effects also may be due to history, maturation, expectations of teacher or experimenter, and time of measurement. A treatment effect may appear differently when measured immediately than when measured after a lapse of time.[51]

There are two kinds of interactions between "personological" variables and treatments, "ordinal" and "disordinal." Pupils of differing levels of ability may respond differently to the compared treatments. In the case of ordinal interaction, one treatment may be relatively more effective than the other at all levels, but considerably more effective at certain levels. Thus, all pupils may profit from a certain type of drill with below-average pupils receiving much more benefit from this treatment than from the other. For the interaction to be disordinal the relative effectiveness of the treatments must differ from level to level. Treatment A may be relatively more effective than Treatment B for pupils of above-average aptitude while for pupils of below-average aptitude Treatment B may be more effective than Treatment A. Disordinal interactions are a threat to generalizations concerning the comparative effectiveness of treatments, but they may be meaningful on their own account since they indicate that the effectiveness of the treatments varies with other characteristics of populations. Graphs with two lines connecting the posttest means of different level subgroups for each treatment are often drawn to illustrate interaction. If the lines do not cross, the interaction is ordinal, while if they do cross, the interaction *may* be disordinal. The reliability of such evidence has been questioned.[52]

DESIGNING AND CONDUCTING EXPERIMENTS TO MAXIMIZE INTERNAL AND EXTERNAL VALIDITY

It would be pleasant to think that one can suggest a completely satisfactory antidote for every threat. Random selection of samples from a well-defined accessible population followed by random assignment of subjects to treatments makes possible the conduction of "true" experiments. Such randomizations eliminates, except for the operation of chance, the threats of statistical regression and selection. The other threats to internal validity—history, maturation, instability, irrelevant effects of testing, instrumentation, and experimental mortality may, or may not, be adequately controlled. They are more likely to be controlled given random assignment to groups. Randomly selected pupils are more

---

[51] *Ibid.,* pp. 439 and 465–66.

[52] *Ibid.,* pp. 444–52. See also E. F. Lindquist, *Design and Analysis of Experiments in Psychology and Education* (Boston: Houghton Mifflin, 1953), pp. 123–27; Ardie Lubin, "The Interpretation of Significant Interaction," *Educational and Psychological Measurement* 21 (Winter 1961), pp. 807–17.

likely on the average to react similarly to irrelevant aspects of testing, instrumentation, and to be similarly persistent in participating. On the average they may be expected to mature at similar rates. History should be checked by observation in both experimental and control groups. Extraneous events may disrupt instruction in one group rather than both or all groups. Experimental mortality may be accounted for by comparing the pretest scores of the treatment groups. If mortality and chance factors in selection result in significant differences between the pretest scores of the groups, application of analysis of covariance can supply approximate adjustments for the initial inequality of the groups completing the experiment.

Let us consider in greater detail antidotes to certain important threats to both internal and external validity.

1. *Adequate description of the independent variable and the experimental conditions.* Unless the compared treatments are defined in detail along with the conditions which characterized their use, it is difficult to ascertain the causes of the variation in effects. Given an adequately defined research problem as noted in Chapter 3, a guide is supplied for data collection and for the experimental instruction. Such material should also appear in the report of the experiment so that others may know just what was done. This aids generalization and replication. Incidentally, replication and trial of treatments with other populations and other conditions, including different settings and even different instruments for measuring the dependent variable, or variables, is probably the best antidote to threats of invalidity of this nature.

2. *Adequate characterization of the experimental samples, the accessible population, and the target population.* Traits of the pupils participating in an experiment can be compared with those of the accessible population and often with those of a target population, provided the school or school system has an adequate local testing program. The report of the experiment may contain a table, or tables, paralleling frequency distributions of scores on both aptitude tests and achievement tests of the pupils participating in the experiment, of their peers in the school and in the school system, along with norm data for similar pupils in a representative sample throughout the United States. A local research bureau should routinely collect the data with which samples can be readily compared.

3. *Maintenance of normal school conditions.* Experiments of the type reported by Monroe in 1929 and by Page in 1958 where the treatments are assigned at random in the materials distributed, without the teacher constituting an instructional factor, surely do not create abnormal classroom conditions. This was especially true of Page's experiment since routinely given objective tests were the pretest and posttest. In 1925, E. H. Reeder used mimeographed sheets of study questions as

the experimental treatment contrasted with the absence of such questions, rotating the questions or their absence. In spite of the possibility of carryover of study habits from experimental learning to control learning which could reduce differences in achievement, the results were significantly favorable to the experimental treatment.[53] At the present time, programmed materials of different types or methods of administration can be compared experimentally without causing pupils to realize that they are the subjects in an experiment. Random assignment to equivalent groups on the basis of test data obtained from routinely administered tests can be done without disrupting present class organization. An alternative is to follow Reeder's example and use a rotation technique or even the Latin square technique which insures random assignment of treatments to the same pupils without creating unbalanced Hawthorne effects.

Random assignment to treatments necessitating the breakup of extant classes is sure to seem abnormal to students and to be an annoyance to school administrators. Sometimes it is possible to make assignments at random to treatments before classes are organized at the beginning of a term. An alternative in experiments conducted in a random sample of schools is to use *intact* classes as the experimental unit and class *averages,* as on pretests and posttests or posttests alone, as the data.[54] Classes can be randomly assigned to treatments. Given pretest or other initial data already available, a factorial type of analysis of covariance with more than one covariate can be used to adjust posttest means for relevant initial differences and to provide an appropriate measure of error in testing the significance of the adjusted differences.[55]

Where the compared methods or treatments are administered by one or more teachers it is obviously difficult to avoid the existence of departures from normal school conditions as noted by Cronbach and much earlier by Monroe. Probably the best antidote to this threat is for the expert in experimentation to provide detailed instruction to teachers with reference to the daily application of the compared treatments, meanwhile stressing the importance of objective attitudes toward the treatments and the necessity for not disclosing to students that an experiment is taking place. In most city public schools the frequent pres-

---

[53] E. H. Reeder, *A Method of Directing Children's Study of Geography,* Columbia University Contributions to Education No. 193 (New York: Bureau of Publications, Teachers College, 1925).

[54] How to do this is explained in Chapter 13, pages 427 to 429. See Campbell and Stanley, *Experimental and Quasi-Experimental Design,* p. 22 or p. 192 in Gage's *Handbook.* These authors cite Lindquist, *Design and Analysis,* and his 1940 *Statistical Analysis in Educational Research.*

[55] See pp. 441–442 of Chapter 13 for further discussion.

ence of observers and even the occurrence of changes in instruction at the beginnings of school terms tend to make experimental instruction no special novelty. The large-scale experimentation of the type referred to here offers a measure of control of teacher zeal and skill in administering a particular treatment. In an experiment with one group per treatment, teacher zeal and skill may produce systematic errors in the dependent variable. In the data for all schools combined, such errors become compensating variable errors and thus do not change the treatment means of the posttest data. Finally, replication and trial of treatments in ordinary rather than experimental instruction may offer a final pragmatic test of the efficacy of a treatment.

4. *Meeting the problems of pretest and posttest sensitization.* The typical two-group experiment, whether a true experiment or a quasi-experiment, is characterized by the giving of a pretest to both groups followed by application of different treatments. In order to avoid the unequal effect of the pretest which is especially characteristic of attitude measurement, although not restricted to such measurement, it was suggested by Solomon[56] and by Campbell and Stanley[57] that four groups be used and that a pretest be given in only two of these groups. If we let R stand for random assignment to treatments, O_1 and O_3 for pretest means of two of the groups, O_2, O_4, O_5, and O_6 for the posttest means of the groups, and X for the treatment administered in the experimental groups, and let the absence of an X stand for the treatment in the control groups (presumably the usual kind of instruction), the Solomon Four-Group Design is portrayed by Campbell and Stanley as follows:

$$
\begin{array}{cccc}
R & O_1 & X & O_2 \\
R & O_3 & & O_4 \\
R & & X & O_5 \\
R & & & O_6
\end{array}
$$

Campbell and Stanley point out that in the Solomon Four-Group Design, the effect of X can be studied by comparing the test means O_2 with O_1, O_2 with O_4, O_5 with O_6, and O_5 with O_3. If these comparisons agree, all favoring the effectiveness of X or all questioning its effectiveness "the strength of the inference is greatly increased." Comparisons of O_6 with O_1 and O_3 yield evidence of the combined effects of maturation and history unconfounded with the effect of X.

---

[56] Richard L. Solomon, "An Extension of Control Group Design," *Psychological Bulletin* 46 (March 1949), pp. 137–50.

[57] Campbell and Stanley, *Experimental and Quasi-Experimental Design*, pp. 24–25 or pp. 194–95 in Gage's *Handbook*.

If the *posttest* means are listed in a 2 × 2 table:

	No X	X
Pretested	O_4	O_2
Unpretested	O_6	O_5

Analysis of variance can be used to estimate from the column means the main effect of X, from the row means the main effect of the pretest, and from the cell means the interaction of the testing with X. If the main and interactive effects of the pretesting are negligible, the pretest and posttest data of the first two groups can be subjected to analysis of covariance, the pretest data being used as the covariate. This would adjust for any chance lack of equivalence as measured by the pretest and provide an error estimate of greater power. For the analysis of variance first mentioned one needs, in addition to the posttest means, the posttest scores of the subjects in each of the four groups. The variability of the posttest scores within the groups provides some of the data used in obtaining a measure of error. In the analysis of covariance both the individual pretest and posttest scores are also needed.

An alternative to the Solomon Four-Group Design as a means of dealing with the problem of pretest sensitization is to use no pretest. Where the subjects have been assigned to treatments at random, the groups are reasonably large, and nonexperimental factors carefully controlled, the Posttest-Only Control Group Design is recommended by Campbell and Stanley:

$$R \qquad X \qquad O_1$$
$$R \qquad\qquad O_2$$

It may not be necessary to depend on chance alone to produce equivalence in pupil characteristics where earlier and routinely collected test and other data are available which can "be used for blocking or leveling, or as covariates."[58] In analysis of variance, *blocking* and *leveling* are means of promoting equivalence of individuals or subgroups analogous to pairing or matching. The meaning of covariate has already been suggested.

In their discussion of posttest sensitization Bracht and Glass[59] note that the posttest may so change the pupils thus tested that they become less representative of the population sampled. The solution to this problem, they suggest, is to employ valid unobtrusive measures. In an ex-

---

[58] *Ibid.*, pp. 25–26 or pp. 195–96.

[59] Bracht and Glass, "External Validity," pp. 463–64. These authors cite Eugene J. Webb and others, *Unobtrusive Measures: Nonreactive Research in the Social Sciences* (Chicago: Rand McNally, 1966).

periment to promote more tolerant attitudes toward members of a different racial or religious group, observation of behavior or study of pupil personnel records could yield more valid data than a posttest of the character of an attitude inventory. It is assumed that no pretest of this nature is given. In the case of experimentation concerned with treatments or methods of instruction, a posttest may provide the crucial factor in the acquisition of concepts or skills. Unobtrusive measures may not adequately measure the effects of different treatments whether these are materials or methods of instruction. Given valid measures of these outcomes, even though reactive or obtrusive, one solution is to regard such testing as an integral part of the treatment.

5. *Promoting adequate measurement of the dependent variable.* According to Monroe and Engelhart under the heading *Measuring the dependent variable:*

> When an experimental problem is adequately defined, the nature and scope of the dependent variable will be specified. The research worker faces the task of selecting or devising an instrument to measure the specified variable, or more specifically the change in it. . . .
>
> In devising a test for use in an experiment, an attempt should be made to formulate exercises that will call for the functioning of the abilities or traits specified as the dependent variable. It is relatively easy to approximate direct measurement of the more specific abilities such as motor skills and fixed associations. It is more difficult to secure satisfactory measures of knowledge achievement and generalized controls of conduct, such as skill in reflective thinking, attitudes, ideals, and interests. The real test of a pupil's knowledge achievement is his ability to deal with difficulties and new situations. Hence, an instrument for the measurement of knowledge achievement should consist of thought questions. The test of general patterns of conduct (now classified as behaviors in the affective domain) is the consistency of conformity to the pattern. Hence, a single formal test cannot be expected to furnish adequate evidence of such achievement. . . . The real test of the acquisition of study habits (methods of learning) is to be found in the conformity of the students to the procedures after the completion of the period of instruction. . . . Usually the requirements of an experiment are highly specialized, and hence a test that is reported as satisfactory for a general survey of pupil achievement may be a very poor instrument for measuring the dependent variable of an experiment.[60]

This passage suggests many of the concepts now expressed in critical writings on the measurement of the dependent variable, for ex-

---

[60] Walter S. Monroe and Max D. Engelhart, *Scientific Study of Educational Problems* (New York: Macmillan, 1936), pp. 301–05.

ample, the desirability of multiple measurement and of unobtrusive measures. Today's experimenter has advantages not possessed by his predecessors of a third of a century ago—the great variety of tests and other measuring instruments now available, the data useful in judging their reliability and validity, and the improved methods of obtaining and analysing test score data.

Nevertheless, there still are major problems which have not been satisfactorily resolved. While it is usually not too difficult to select or construct a test which is equally fair to both groups when the compared treatments can be expected to differ only in how much of some relatively specific achievement they produce, real dilemmas are encountered when the treatments, methods or materials of instruction, were developed for attaining quite different instructional goals. Consider the difficulty of selecting tests of adequate content validity for experimental evaluation of the new curricula in mathematics and in the physical and biological sciences as compared with traditional instruction in these fields. Similar difficulty is encountered in the experimental evaluation of didactic methods as compared with methods expected to foster critical or inductive thinking and discovery. Apart from use of multiple measurements in order to evaluate the extent of attainment of disparate goals by different treatments, it has been urged that there be "more attention to comparisons of different inductive procedures than to further studies with a didactic contrast group."[61]

Multiple measurement where treatments foster the attainment of disparate goals and experimentation restricted to treatments which differ, but not in goals, may contribute understanding of the extent to which various goals are attained and what means promote their attainment on different levels of ability and maturity. What goals should be sought, however, raises questions of values. According to many, but not all philosophers, such questions cannot be answered by experimentation or other empirical methods alone. But while experimentation may not be sufficient, it *is* necessary.

---

[61] Lee J. Cronbach, "The Logic of Experiments on Discovery" in Lee S. Shulman and Evan R. Keislar, eds., *Learning by Discovery: A Critical Appraisal* (Chicago: Rand McNally, 1966), p. 85. See also the chapters entitled "Variables in Discovery Learning" by Robert Glaser and "The Learning by Discovery Hypothesis" by M. C. Wittrock.

Questions for
Study and Discussion

1. Could McCall's experimental coefficient have contributed to the disillusionment with experimental research in the 1930s?

2. What factor tends to limit the *rotation* (or *Latin square*) type of experiment in school experimentation?

3. Discuss the relationships between a *sample,* the *accessible* population from which it was drawn, and the target population.

4. Give some example of *unobtrusive* measures which might be useful in school experimentation.

5. What type of experimental design is most likely to be threatened by regression effects. How can such effects be avoided?

6. How does a *quasi-experiment* differ from a *true experiment?*

7. How does a *pseudo-experiment* differ from a *quasi-experiment* or from a *true experiment?*

8. Seek definitions of these variables among the references cited:
   organismic variable
   ecological variable
   personological variable
   nuisance variable

9. What is the technical meaning of the term *confounded?*

10. What threats to internal and external validity are likely to become increasingly serious the longer an experiment continues?

11. What are the essential differences between *conclusion-oriented* and *decision-oriented* educational research?

12. What are the two meanings of *replication* in the discussion of experimentation?

13. Draw simple diagrams illustrating ordinal and disordinal interactions.

14. Just what is the Hawthorne effect? How did it get this name?

15. Consult recent issues of the *Journal of Educational Psychology, American Educational Research Journal,* and *Journal of Experimental Education* for examples of "conclusion oriented" and "decision oriented" experiments. What phrase in a problem statement most often suggests the latter?

Suggestions
for Further Study

It will be especially desirable for the student to begin by thoughtful study of Campbell and Stanley's chapter in the *Handbook of Research on Teaching* entitled "Experimental and Quasi-Experimental Designs for Research on Teaching," or their separately published book with the same title, and the other works by Campbell or Stanley listed among the references concluding this chapter. This reading should be extended to the notable paper by Bracht and Glass, "The External Validity of Experiments." Each of these publications concludes with bibliographies containing references to other important relevant materials.

The student will find Edwards' "Experiments: Their Planning and Execution" and Aronson and Carlsmith's "Experimentation in Social Psychology" in the first and second editions of the *Handbook of Social Psychology* excellent summaries of experimental methodology. The same thing is true of the parts of Chapter 4 in Selltiz and others, *Research Methods in Social Relations,* entitled "The Logic of Testing Hypotheses about Causal Relationships" and "Causal Inference from Experiments," and of Tiedeman's "Experimental Method" in the 1960 edition of the *Encyclopedia of Educational Research.* Two recent anthologies can be highly recommended: *Learning by Discovery, A Critical Appraisal* edited by Lee S. Shulman and Evan R. Keislar and *Educational Research, Selected Readings* compiled by William J. Gephart and Robert B. Ingle. The chapters in *Learning by Discovery* by Robert Glaser, M. C. Wittrock, and Lee J. Cronbach which are especially relevant to experimental methodology have already been cited. Students of education and psychology will also profit greatly through study of the chapters by Jerome Bruner, Robert B. Davis, Robert M. Gagné and Jerome Kagan. A number of the selections in *Educational Research, Selected Readings* are cited earlier or listed among the references to this chapter. Other selections most directly relevant to experimentation include those by John R. Platt, John B. Carroll, T. C. Chamberlin, Jum Nunnally, Robert E. Chandler, Joseph Weitz, and Fred N. Kerlinger.

Students interested in the history of experimental research in education and of psychological experimentation will find it interesting to study the paper by Edwin G. Boring, "The Nature and History of Experimental

Control," W. A. McCall's "How to Experiment in Education," and Monroe and Engelhart's University of Illinois Bureau of Educational Research Bulletins 48 and 58 and the *Scientific Study of Educational Problems* as a means of evaluating the progress that has been made in experimental methodology, as well as sources of ideas that should not be forgotten.

Chapter 12 has given little emphasis to the techniques used in summarizing and interpreting experimental data. Before going on to Chapter 13 which deals further with these techniques and extends the discussion to the analysis of variance and the analysis of covariance the student should review Chapters 8 and 9. There is real danger that the student completing his study of Chapters 12 and 13 will conclude that he need merely apply the procedures described to conduct an experiment successfully. Study transcending the material in Chapters 8, 9, 12, and 13 is necessary to conduct a school experiment, but the chapters just mentioned should make such advanced study less formidable.

Selected References

More technical publications on experimental design and the analysis of experimental data are listed at the end of Chapter 13.

Aronson, Elliot and J. Merrill Carlsmith. "Experimentation in Social Psychology." In *The Handbook of Social Psychology,* edited by Gardner Lindzey and Elliot Aronson, pp. 1–79. Vol. 2. 2nd ed. Reading, Mass.: Addison-Wesley, 1968.

Boring, Edwin G. *A History of Experimental Psychology.* 2nd ed. New York: Appleton-Century-Crofts, 1950.

Bracht, Glenn H. and Glass, Gene V "The External Validity of Experiments." *American Educational Research Journal* 5 (November 1968): 437–74.

Campbell, Donald T. "Factors Relevant to the Validity of Experiments in Social Settings." *Psychological Bulletin* 54 (July 1957): 297–312.

————. "Administrative Experimentation, Institutional Records, and Nonreactive Measures." In *Improving Experimental Design and Statistical Analysis,* edited by Julian C. Stanley, pp. 257–91. Chicago: Rand McNally, 1966.

————. "Reforms as Experiments." *American Psychologist* 24 (April 1969): 409–29.

———— and Julian C. Stanley. "Experimental and Quasi-Experimental Designs for Research on Teaching." In *Handbook of Research on Teaching,* edited by N. L. Gage, pp. 171–246. Chicago: Rand McNally, 1963.
Also published separately with the same title by Rand McNally in 1966.

Cook, Desmond L. "The Impact of the Hawthorne Effect in Experimental Designs in Educational Research." *Cooperative Research Project* No. 1757. U. S. Office of Education. June 1967.

Cronbach, Lee J. "The Two Disciplines of Scientific Psychology." *The American Psychologist* 12 (November 1957): 671–84.

————. "Course Improvement Through Evaluation." *Teachers College Record* 64: 672–83; March 1963.

————. "The Logic of Experiments on Discovery." In *Learning by Discovery: A Critical Appraisal,* edited by Lee S. Shulman and Evan R. Keislar, pp. 76–92. Chicago: Rand McNally, 1966.

————— and Patrick Suppes, eds. *Research for Tomorrow's Schools: Disciplined Inquiry for Education.* New York: Macmillan, 1969.

Edwards, Allen L. "Experiments: Their Planning and Execution." In *Handbook of Social Psychology.* Vol. I. Edited by Gardner Lindzey, pp. 259–88. Reading, Mass.: Addison-Wesley, 1954.
Includes an excellent explanation of statistical regression.

Entwisle, Doris R. "Interactive Effects of Pretesting." *Educational and Psychological Measurement* 21 (Autumn 1961): 607–20.

Garrett, Henry. *Great Experiments in Psychology.* 3rd ed. New York: Appleton-Century-Crofts, 1951.

Gephart, William J. and Robert B. Ingle, eds. *Educational Research, Selected Readings.* Columbus, Ohio: Merrill, 1969.

Guilford, J. P. *Psychometric Methods.* 2nd ed. New York: McGraw-Hill, 1954.

Lana, Robert E. "Pretest-interaction Effects in Attitudinal Studies." *Psychological Bulletin* 56 (July 1959): 293–300.
See also his papers on the same topic in the December 1959 and June 1960 issues of the Journal of Applied Psychology *and in the Spring 1966 issue of* Educational and Psychological Measurement.

Selltiz, Claire, and others. "The Logic of Testing Hypotheses About Causal Relationships" and "Causal Inference from Experiments." In *Research Methods in Social Relations,* pp. 80–127. rev. ed. New York: Holt, Rinehart and Winston, 1966.

Shulman, Lee S., and Evan R. Keislar, eds. *Learning by Discovery: A Critical Appraisal.* Chicago: Rand McNally, 1966.

Solomon, Richard L. "An Extension of Control Group Design." *Psychological Bulletin* 46 (March 1949): 137–50.

Stanley, Julian C. "Quasi-experimentation." *School Review* 73 (Autumn 1965): 197–205.

————. "A Common Class of Pseudo-Experiments." *American Educational Research Journal* 3 (March 1966): 79–87.

Tatsuoka, Maurice M. "Experimental Methods." In *Encyclopedia of Educational Research,* edited by Robert L. Ebel, pp. 474–81. 4th ed. New York: Macmillan, 1969.

Thorndike, R. L. "Regression Fallacies in the Matched Groups Experiment," *Psychometrika* 7 (1942): 85–102.

Tiedeman, David V. "Experimental Method." In *Encyclopedia of Educational Research,* edited by C. W. Harris, pp. 486–90. 3rd ed. New York: Macmillian, 1960.

13

Studying Relationships: Analysis of Experimental Data

The discussion of experimental methodology and of statistical inference begun in earlier chapters continues with an elementary introduction of analysis of variance and covariance.

The first section of this chapter deals with the analysis of data where there are two to four groups and decisions have been made a priori with reference to which differences between means are to be tested for significance by the conventional *t* tests (see page 418 with reference to multiple *t* tests).

The types of analysis of variance explained include simple one-way classification or *randomized group* analysis of variance and two-way classification analysis of variance where the entries in a double-entry table are single scores, $n = 1$, or several scores or other measures, $n > 1$. Such analysis of variance is often called *randomized block*. The explanation of analysis of covariance is restricted to the analysis that might be applied in evaluating the relative effectiveness of two treatments where the pretest or other initial data indicate that the groups depart somewhat from equivalence.

The discussions of the types of analysis of variance mentioned above include a list of relevant assumptions and explanations of the partitioning of total sums of squares, expected values of mean squares, and analysis of variance models. Study of these topics contributes to the understanding of how the analysis of variance "works."

Among the suggestions for further study at the end of the chapter mention is made of more complex analyses of variance and covariance which, on occasion, can be useful in school experimentation.

ANALYSIS OF DATA FROM TWO TO FOUR GROUPS

The standard error of the difference between the means of two independent groups

On page 249 of Chapter 9, Formula 9.3 was stated as $s_{\bar{x}_1 - \bar{x}_2} = \sqrt{s_{\bar{x}_1}^2 + s_{\bar{x}_2}^2}$. According to this formula, the error variances of each mean are separately obtained from two unbiased estimators of the population variance, one for each sample. If these estimators are not so different as to challenge the assumption of the homogeneity of variance and the two groups are of equal or approximately equal size, averaging the two unbiased estimators, $s_{\bar{x}_1}^2$ and $s_{\bar{x}_2}^2$, will give a single and better estimate of the population variance. To accomplish this the two sums of squares Σx_1^2 and Σx_2^2 are combined as Σx^2 and used in Formula 13.1. Division of Σx_1^2 and Σx_2^2 respectively by $N_1 - 1$ and $N_2 - 1$ is replaced by $N_1 + N_2 - 2$. The fraction having this as its denominator is actually s_x^2 the single estimator of the population variance. Multiplication by $\left(\dfrac{1}{N_1} + \dfrac{1}{N_2}\right)$, here written as $\left(\dfrac{N_1 + N_2}{N_1 N_2}\right)$ is analogous to the division of the s_x^2 applying to a single group to obtain the $s_{\bar{x}}^2$ whose square root is $s_{\bar{x}}$, the standard error of the mean $\bar{X}$.

$$s_{\bar{x}_1 - \bar{x}_2} = \sqrt{\frac{\Sigma x^2}{N_1 + N_2 - 2}\left(\frac{N_1 + N_2}{N_1 N_2}\right)}. \qquad (13.1)$$

When the two variance estimates are significantly different (this is more likely to happen when the N's are quite different), it is best to use Formula 9.3 and adjust[1] the degrees of freedom used in consulting the table of the t distribution. It has been emphasized by Edwards, however, that if two independent random samples of 25 or more subjects each are used, there is little need to worry about normality of score distribution and of homogeneity of variance. When the N's are equal the t is a "robust" test.[2]

The Σx^2 in Formula 13.1 may readily be obtained by substituting the sums and sums of squares of the scores in the equations:

---

[1] George A. Ferguson, *Statistical Analysis in Psychology and Education,* 3rd ed. (New York: McGraw-Hill, 1971), pp. 155–57.

[2] Allen L. Edwards, *Statistical Methods,* 2nd ed. (New York: Holt, Rinehart and Winston, 1967), pp. 214–15.

$$\Sigma x_1^2 = \Sigma X_1^2 - \frac{(\Sigma X_1)^2}{N_1} \quad \text{and}$$

$$\Sigma x_2^2 = \Sigma X_2^2 - \frac{(\Sigma X_2)^2}{N_2}. \tag{13.2a}$$

$$\text{Then} \quad \Sigma x^2 = \Sigma x_1^2 + \Sigma x_2^2. \tag{13.2b}$$

If there is both a pretest and a posttest you may prefer to use the letters Y and y instead of X and x. The sums of squares in deviate measures for the separate groups, Σx_1^2 and Σx_2^2, when divided respectively by $N_1 - 1$ and $N_2 - 1$ yield the variances of the two groups. The square roots of these are, of course, the two standard deviations.

The standard error of a difference when subjects have been paired or matched

In Chapter 9 on page 251, Formulas 9.5 and 9.6 were given for use in calculating the standard error of a difference where the subjects have been paired in terms of their pretest scores or other initial measures. If the pretest and posttest are equivalent forms of the same test, gains can be computed and either formula just mentioned can be used to obtain the standard error of difference between the mean gains of the two groups. The same formulas can also be used to obtain the standard error of the difference between the two means on the test given at the close of the experimental instruction, whether or not gains are computed. Instead of using either Formula 9.5 or 9.6 to obtain the standard error of the difference used in computing t, a more convenient and equivalent procedure is to list the individual differences D between the gains or posttest scores of the paired pupils summing these differences (ΣD may be negative), summing the squares of the differences, ΣD^2, and squaring the sum of the differences, $(\Sigma D)^2$. Then

$$t = \frac{\Sigma D}{\sqrt{\dfrac{N\Sigma D^2 - (\Sigma D)^2}{N - 1}}}. \tag{13.3}$$

The number of degrees of freedom to use with this formula is $N - 1$ where N is the number of pairs. Unless N and the correlation between the paired scores is reasonably large, a t test based on Formula 13.1 (or 9.3) will be more powerful than one based on Formula 13.3 (or either 9.5 or 9.6).

If, as earlier explained, the pupils have been drawn at random from the *same* population and the members of each matched pair are assigned at random to two groups, Formula 13.4, the "matched groups" formula of E. F. Lindquist and S. S. Wilks[3] can legitimately be used in obtaining the standard error of the difference between posttest means or mean gains:

$$s_{\bar{y}_1 - \bar{y}_2} = \sqrt{\frac{\Sigma y^2}{N_1 + N_2 - 3}\left(\frac{N_1 + N_2}{N_1 N_2}\right)(1 - r_{xy}^2)}. \qquad (13.4)$$

Here x refers to the scores on a pretest or other initial test while y refers to posttest scores or gains. The number of degrees of freedom is $N_1 + N_2 - 3$.

Steps prior to use of Formula 13.4

There will be two sets of pretest or other initial scores and two sets of posttest or other final scores. Let us refer to the initial scores as X_1 in the class which was taught by Treatment A, and X_2 in the class which was taught by Treatment B. Let us refer to the final scores respectively as Y_1 and Y_2. Prepare a table with columns headed by the following symbols:

Class 1 (Treatment A)   Class 2 (Treatment B)

X_1 X_1^2 Y_1 Y_1^2 $X_1 Y_1$ X_2 X_2^2 Y_2 Y_2^2 $X_2 Y_2$

List the X_1, Y_1, X_2, Y_2 scores of the pupils or students in both classes, recording the data of the paired pupils or students in the same row and in the appropriate columns. Enter the squares and products of the scores in the columns headed by X_1^2, Y_1^2, $X_1 Y_1$, X_2^2, Y_2^2, and $X_2 Y_2$. (A table of squares or a desk calculator is helpful here.)

The next step is to sum the columns, labeling these sums ΣX_1, ΣX_1^2, ΣY_1, ΣY_1^2, $\Sigma X_1 Y_1$, ΣX_2, ΣX_2^2, ΣY_2, ΣY_2^2, and $\Sigma X_2 Y_2$.

Calculate the means $\bar{X}_1$, $\bar{Y}_1$, $\bar{X}_2$, $\bar{Y}_2$ dividing ΣX_1, ΣY_1, ΣX_2, and ΣY_2 by the number of pupils in each group N_1 or N_2 (equal since the pupils have been paired). The mean $\bar{X}_1$ should equal $\bar{X}_2$. If equal or approximately equal initial means are not obtained, the analysis of covariance procedure described on pages 436 to 442 should be used.

The next step is to compute the sums of squares and the sums of products of the scores Σx_1^2, Σy_1^2, Σx_2^2, Σy_2^2, $\Sigma x_1 y_1$, $\Sigma x_2 y_2$, and Σx^2, Σy^2 and Σxy in deviate measures repeatedly using Formulas 13.2a and

---

[3] E. F. Lindquist, "The Significance of a Difference between 'Matched' Groups," *Journal of Educational Psychology* 22 (March 1931), pp. 197–204; and S. S. Wilks, "The Standard Error of the Means of Matched Samples," *Journal of Educational Psychology* 22 (March 1931), pp. 205–08.

13.2b and, for the sums of products of scores, Formulas 13.4a and 13.4b. The formulas are:

$$\Sigma x_1^2 = \Sigma X_1^2 - \frac{(\Sigma X_1)^2}{N_1}.$$

$$\Sigma y_1^2 = \Sigma Y_1^2 - \frac{(\Sigma Y_1)^2}{N_1}.$$

$$\Sigma x_2^2 = \Sigma X_2^2 - \frac{(\Sigma X_2)^2}{N_2}.$$

$$\Sigma y_2^2 = \Sigma Y_2^2 - \frac{(\Sigma Y_2)^2}{N_2}.$$

$$\Sigma x_1 y_1 = \Sigma X_1 Y_1 - \frac{\Sigma X_1 \Sigma Y_1}{N_1}. \qquad (13.4a)$$

$$\Sigma x_2 y_2 = \Sigma X_2 Y_2 - \frac{\Sigma X_2 \Sigma Y_2}{N_2}.$$

$$\Sigma x^2 = \Sigma x_1^2 + \Sigma x_2^2.$$

$$\Sigma y^2 = \Sigma y_1^2 + \Sigma y_2^2.$$

$$\Sigma xy = \Sigma x_1 y_1 + \Sigma x_2 y_2. \qquad (13.4b)$$

The values of Σx_1^2, Σy_1^2, and $\Sigma x_1 y_1$, and of Σx_2^2, Σy_2^2, and $\Sigma x_2 y_2$ are then inserted in the formula below to obtain $r_{x_1 y_1}$ and $r_{x_2 y_2}$ for the two groups. If these coefficients are not significantly different when tested as explained on page 261 of Chapter 9 or in a more sophisticated test of "homogeneity of regression," values of Σx^2, Σy^2, and Σxy, obtained as shown above, are substituted in the formula to secure the coefficient of correlation between the initial and final scores of all the subjects.

$$r_{xy} = \frac{\Sigma xy}{\sqrt{\Sigma x^2}\sqrt{\Sigma y^2}}. \qquad (11.16)$$

The coefficient of correlation thus obtained, the means of the final scores of the two classes $\overline{Y}_1$ and $\overline{Y}_2$, the Σy^2 used in the formula above, and the numbers of pupils in each class N_1 and N_2 are then substituted in Formula 13.4 to obtain the denominator of the t based on the matched groups formula.

When pupils are paired or matched the generalizations derived from the data should be applied to pupil populations of the same level and range in ability. On pages 443–444 near the end of this chapter comparisons are made between the standard error of difference Formulas 13.1, 13.3, and 13.4 and the equivalence of these formulas to different types of analysis of variance and covariance. Recall from page 391 of Chapter 12, McNemar's recommendation that pupils be matched on the basis of estimated true scores.

Practice Exercise 13.1

Pretest *X* and Posttest *Y* have been given to two groups of pupils paired on the basis of their pretest scores. The pretest and posttest scores are listed below. (If this were other than a practice exercise there would be more cases and there would have been randomization and other characteristics of a properly conducted experiment.) Small numbers are given to facilitate computation.

	X_1	X_2	Y_1	Y_2
1	7	7	8	9
2	5	5	7	8
3	4	4	5	6
4	4	4	6	9
5	3	3	5	9
6	3	3	7	7
7	3	3	4	10
8	2	2	7	7
9	2	2	2	5
10	1	1	3	4

Calculate *t* using the matched groups formula. If time permits compute gains from pretest to posttest using the two series of gains correlating the pretest scores with the gains.

See page 533 for answers.

ANALYSIS OF VARIANCE

When the number of groups employed in an experiment is small, *t* tests based on appropriate standard error of difference formulas suffice in testing the significance of differences. The analysis of variance techniques may be used as earlier suggested when there are as few as two groups, but they can be applied to many more than two groups. Standard errors of differences and *t* tests deal with one variable at a time. Analysis of variance can deal with problems characterized by more than one causal variable. The variables may be treatment variables, or they may include other variables whose concurrent effects should be evaluated or controlled.

In order to introduce the basic concepts of analysis of variance let us suppose that a number of samples of pupils have been drawn at random from the same general population and have been tested. Two estimates of the variability of the population can be made from the test data. These estimates could be in terms of the standard deviation, but it is customary to use the square of the standard deviation, or "variance" rather than the standard deviation itself. One such squared standard deviation can be obtained by calculating the squared standard deviations of all of the samples 'and averaging them. This estimate of the population variability is called the "within-groups variance." The other estimate is obtained by tallying the distribution of means of all the samples, calculating the squared standard deviation of this distribution, and multiplying it by the number of pupils in each sample. This estimate is called the "between-groups variance." If the samples have been drawn at random, these two estimates of the population variability will tend to be equal. If some factors other than chance have operated, for example, treatments of varying effectiveness, the estimates will not be equal. The between-groups variance will be greater than the within-groups variance. The ratio between the two variances is called "*F*" and its interpretation is similar to that of *t*. Given a significant *F*, modified *t* tests may be used to identify significant differences between the numerous pairs of group means.

Obtaining equations for between-groups, within-groups, and other estimators of population variances involves partitioning of a measure of the total variance, a "total sum of squares" into separate sums of squares whose division by appropriate degrees of freedom yields the estimators just mentioned. This will be demonstrated in some detail for simple analysis of variance after a brief discussion of assumptions relevant to analysis of variance and covariance.

Assumptions relevant to the analysis of variance

It is assumed that the variables in the populations from which the samples are drawn have normal distributions, equal variances (the assumption of homogeneity of variance), and that the components of an observation attributed to different factors identified and measured are additive and, hence, linearly related. In the case of analysis of covariance, it is further assumed that there is homogeneity of regression in the populations sampled. One would expect, for example, that the correlations between pretest and posttest scores would tend to be equal. Finally, it is assumed that the samples drawn at random are independent samples. It is possible to test sample data for violation of these assumptions, but this is too seldom done. Fortunately, however, quite large departures from assumptions are required to seriously affect inferences drawn from the data. When, for example, the distributions have small *N*'s and are quite different from normal, it may be best to use a nonparametric type of analysis. In the case of serious violation of the assumption of homogeneity of variance, transformation of the scores to some other scale or units may resolve this difficulty. Large interaction variances are indicative of serious violation of the additivity assumption and of excessive departures from homogeneity of regression. They may suggest the appropriateness of some other type of analysis, possibly the Johnson-Neyman technique.

Partitioning a total sum of squares in simple one-way or randomized groups analysis of variance

Let X_{ij} equal the ith score in the jth group. Then the deviation of this score from the mean of the group is $(X_{ij} - \overline{X}_j)$ and its deviation from the mean of the total sample is $(X_{ij} - \overline{X})$ or $(X_{ij} - \overline{X}_j) + (\overline{X}_j - \overline{X})$. Suppose that X_{ij} is 75, $\overline{X}_j$ is 60, and $\overline{X}$ is 50. Then $(75 - 50) = (75 - 60) + (60 - 50) = 15 + 10 = 25$. The deviation of the score from the general mean has been broken down into two parts—its deviation from the mean of the group and the mean of the group from the general mean. In other words,

$$(X_{ij} - \overline{X}) = (X_{ij} - \overline{X}_j) + (\overline{X}_j - \overline{X}). \tag{13.5}$$

We need to convert each of these terms to sums of squares from which mean squares or variances can be computed. Squaring both sides of the equation just given:

$$(X_{ij} - \overline{X})^2 = (X_{ij} - \overline{X}_j)^2 + 2(X_{ij} - \overline{X}_j)(\overline{X}_j - \overline{X}) + (\overline{X}_j - \overline{X})^2.$$

Summing all such n_j measures in group j:

$$\sum_{i=1}^{n_j}(X_{ij} - \overline{X})^2 = \sum_{i=1}^{n_j}(X_{ij} - \overline{X}_j)^2 + 2\sum_{i=1}^{n_j}(X_{ij} - \overline{X}_j)(\overline{X}_j - \overline{X}) + n_j(\overline{X}_j - \overline{X})^2.$$

The second term at the right can be omitted since the sum of the scores X_{ij} about the mean of their own group equals zero. The last term begins with n rather than Σ because $(\overline{X}_j - \overline{X})$ is constant for all the n_j scores in group j. Summing for all k groups:

$$\sum_{j=1}^{k}\sum_{i=1}^{n_j}(X_{ij} - \overline{X})^2 = \sum_{j=1}^{k}\sum_{i=1}^{n_j}(X_{ij} - \overline{X}_j)^2 + n_j\sum_{j=1}^{k}(\overline{X}_j - \overline{X})^2. \tag{13.6}$$

Thus we have the sum of squares of the deviations of all the scores from the general mean, in other words the sum of squares for "total," partitioned into (1) the sum of squares of the deviations of the scores from the group means, and (2) the sum of squares of the deviations of the group means from the general mean. The first is called the "within-groups or within-treatments sum of squares," and the second the "between-groups or between-treatments sum of squares." The degrees of freedom associated with the total sum of squares is $N - 1$, with the within-groups sum of squares $k(n - 1)$ or $N - k$, and for the between-groups sum of squares $k - 1$. The $k(n - 1) + k - 1$ equals $N - 1$.

When the within-groups and between-groups sums of squares are divided by their respective degrees of freedom they become unbiased estimators of the population variance. They are called the within-groups variance or mean square symbolized by s_w^2 and the between-groups variance or mean square symbolized by s_b^2. They may be calculated by means of the formulas given below or by the "computing formulas" listed later.

$$s_w^2 = \frac{\sum\limits_{j=1}^{k} \sum\limits_{i=1}^{n_j} (X_{ij} - \overline{X}_j)^2}{k(n - 1)}. \tag{13.7}$$

$$s_b^2 = \frac{n_j \sum\limits_{j=1}^{k} (\overline{X}_j - \overline{X})^2}{k - 1}. \tag{13.8}$$

If the n's vary from group to group Formulas 13.7 and 13.8 are somewhat different. The denominator of the first becomes $N - k$ and the n_j follows the summation sign in the second.

Expected values of the within-groups and between-groups mean squares or variances

Recall from Chapter 9 what is meant by the "expected" value of a parameter. When $N - 1$ is used in calculating the variance of a sample, s^2 is an unbiased estimator of σ^2, the variance of the population from which the sample was drawn at random.[4] When Formula 13.1 is used in testing the significance of the difference between the means of two independent random samples, the sums of squares of the deviations of the scores from each mean are in effect averaged to obtain a better estimator of the population variance. Division is by $n_1 + n_2 - 2$, the degrees of freedom. In the analysis of variance, the within-groups mean square, or the within-groups variance, s_w^2, is similarly obtained to produce a better unbiased estimator of σ^2, the population variance:

$$E(s_w^2) = \frac{\Sigma x_1^2 + \Sigma x_2^2 + \Sigma x_3^2 + \cdots + \Sigma x_k^2}{n_1 + n_2 + n_3 + \cdots + n_{k-k}} = \sigma^2. \tag{13.9}$$

or

---

[4] For a proof that $\overline{X}$, s_x^2, and $s_{\overline{x}}^2$ are unbiased estimators of μ_x, σ_x^2, and $\sigma_{\overline{x}}^2$ see Edwards, *Statistical Methods*, pp. 204–205 or other advanced text.

$$E(s_w^2) = \sum_{j=1}^{k} \sum_{i=1}^{n_j} \frac{(X_{ij} - \bar{X}_j)^2}{N - k} = \sigma^2. \qquad (13.10)$$

When k samples are of equal size, the expected value of the between-groups mean square or variance, s_b^2, can be shown[5] to be

$$E(s_b^2) = \sigma^2 + \frac{n \sum_{1}^{k} (\mu_j - \mu)^2}{k - 1}. \qquad (13.11)$$

The symbol μ_j designates each of the *population* means corresponding to the k sample means $\bar{X}_j$. The symbol μ designates the mean of the population means and corresponds to $\bar{X}$, the grand or total mean of all the samples. If the null hypothesis is true, all of the μ_j are equal, all of the differences $\mu_j - \mu$ equal zero, and the second term at the right equals zero. Then, $E(s_b^2) = \sigma^2$.

If, however, the null hypothesis is false, there are real differences among the population means μ_j, the second term at the right is not equal to zero, and $E(s_b^2)$ equals a quantity greater than σ^2. If significantly reflected in data, we should conclude that the samples are from different populations. The populations may differ because of the effects of the different treatments.

Models for simple one-way or randomized groups analysis of variance

A variable is considered *random* if the levels of the variable are a simple random sample from a normally distributed population of levels. A variable is considered finite if the population of levels is finite. If all of the levels of a variable of concern to an experimenter are included in the study—for example, three methods of instruction, four specified school grades *not* selected at random, and the like—then the variable is *fixed*. In the analysis of variance, generalizations relevant to a random variable apply to the population levels sampled. In the case of a fixed variable, generalizations are restricted to the levels of the variable studied in the experiment.[6]

---

[5] *Ibid.*, pp. 262–64. For derivations also see E. F. Lindquist, *Design and Analysis of Experiments in Psychology and Education* (Boston: Houghton Mifflin, 1953), pp. 59–62; and Quinn McNemar, *Psychological Statistics*, 4th ed. (New York: Wiley, 1969), pp. 292–300, or other advanced text.

[6] Jason Millman and Gene V Glass, "Rules of Thumb for Writing the Anova Table," *Journal of Educational Measurement* 4 (Summer 1967), p. 43.

Suppose that the sample means $\bar{X}_j$ are relevant to a random variable, for example, the means of k samples of students rated by a random sample of raters, where the ratings are treated like observed test scores. An observed test score, X_o equals a true score, X_T, plus an error of measurement, e, or $X_o = X_T + e$. Assuming that the components of X_o are uncorrected with each other and with X_o, the observed variance equals the true score variance plus the error variance whose square root is the standard error of measurement. Similarly, we can consider $\bar{X}_j$ as a random variable equal to $\mu_j + e_j$ where e is a sampling error rather than merely an error of measurement. If we had $\bar{X}_j$ means from random samples of very numerous possible populations, the variance of the distribution of these means—the expected variance —would be

$$\sigma_{\bar{x}_j}^2 = \sigma_{\mu_j}^2 + \frac{\sigma^2}{n}. \tag{13.12}$$

The last term is the sampling variance of the means, the variance attributable only to sampling errors, and equivalent to the usual standard error of sampling squared. The $\sigma_{\mu_j}^2$ is the component of the total variance attributable to real differences between the μ_j corresponding to very numerous differences between the $\bar{X}_j$. When the terms of the equation just given are multiplied by n, the number of individuals in each group, and the order of terms at the right is changed to parallel the order in Formula 13.11:

$$n\sigma_{\bar{x}}^2 = \sigma^2 + n\sigma_{\mu_j}^2.$$

The term at the left is the expected variance among the means, hence, we can write

$$E(s_b^2) = \sigma^2 + n\sigma_{\mu_j}^2. \tag{13.13}$$

It seems plausible to think of the $\sigma_{\mu_j}^2$ in equation 13.13 and the corresponding last term of 13.11 as a variance estimate when these equations apply to a random variable. When however, the $\bar{X}_j$ are fixed effects variables, relatively few in number, equation 13.11 is still applicable, but it is less plausible to think of the last term as a variance estimate. Often in writing equations for expected mean squares for fixed effects variables, the symbol Θ^2 is used instead of a variance symbol in such last terms. When the null hypothesis is true, the last term in 13.11 or 13.13 vanishes and $E(s_b^2)$ equals σ^2, the population variance. When this is the case, it is easy to see that $n\sigma_{\bar{x}}^2$ is $E(s_b^2)$ since $\sigma_{\bar{x}}^2 = \frac{\sigma^2}{n}$. When the null hypothesis is false, it is because of real variation among the μ_j which, for both models, augment the estimate of the population variance provided by s_b^2.

The models discussed above and the equations given for $E(s_b^2)$ contribute to understanding of the between-groups variance estimate s_b^2 and the test described below to determine whether the null hypothesis $H_0 : \mu_1 = \mu_2 = \ldots \mu_j \ldots = \mu_k$ should be accepted or rejected. The models described and a mixed model to be discussed later are especially important in complex analysis of variance. They aid in the selection of an appropriate denominator when making F tests.

The F test in simple analysis of variance

Whether the model is the fixed effects or random one, in simple analysis of variance where only s_b^2 and s_w^2 are obtained from data relevant to several samples, the F ratio is $\frac{s_b^2}{s_w}$. When this ratio approximates unity the null hypothesis $H_0 : \mu_1 = \mu_2 = \mu_3 = \mu_k$ is not rejected and we conclude that there are no significant differences among the treatment or methods means. When, however, the ratio is significantly greater than unity as shown by the F test, the null hypothesis is rejected. There are significant differences among the means, though just which of the differences between the means are significant is not evident from the F test alone.

A worked example

The numerical example in Table 13.1 illustrates the application of the simple variance techniques to four groups of pupils taught by four different methods in a single school. (Since this is an illustrative example, the groups are much smaller than would actually be used.) Compu-

Table 13.1 Illustrative Data for Simple One-Way or Randomized Group Analysis of Variance

Subject	Treatment Groups				
	1	2	3	4	
1	8	6	4	4	
2	9	8	3	5	
3	7	9	4	4	
4	6	7	6	3	
5	5	2	5	1	
n_j	5	5	5	5	$N = 20$
T_j	35	32	22	17	$T = 106$
$\bar{X}_j$	7.0	6.4	4.4	3.4	$\bar{X} = 5.3$

tation is on the basis of raw scores rather than on the basis of deviate measures. The computation formulas can be easily derived from formulas earlier given. In these formulas ΣX and$(\Sigma X)^2$ are written as T and T^2.

Computations of sums of squares

1. *The sum of squares for total*

$$\sum_{j=1}^{k} \sum_{i=1}^{nj} (X_{ij} - \bar{X})^2 = \sum_{j=1}^{k} \sum_{i=1}^{nj} X_{ij}^2 - \frac{T^2}{N}. \qquad (13.14)$$

$$SS_t = 8^2 + 9^2 + 7^2 + \cdots + 3^2 + 1 - \frac{106^2}{20} = 96.2$$

2. *The sum of squares for between groups*

$$n_j \sum_{j=1}^{k} (\bar{X}_j - \bar{X})^2 = \frac{T_1^2 + T_2^2 + \cdots + T_k^2}{n_j} - \frac{T^2}{N}. \qquad (13.15)$$

$$SS_b = \frac{35^2 + 32^2 + 22^2 + 17^2}{5} - \frac{(106)^2}{20} = 42.6$$

When the groups vary in size, divide each T_j^2 by its own n_j before summing and subtracting $\frac{T^2}{N}$.

3. *The sum of squares for within groups*

$$\sum_{j=1}^{k} \sum_{i=1}^{nj} (X_{ij} - \bar{X}_j)^2 = \sum_{j=1}^{k} \sum_{i=1}^{nj} X_{ij}^2 - \sum_{j=1}^{k} \frac{T_j^2}{n_j}. \qquad (13.16)$$

Use of Formula 13.16 is equivalent to $SS_t - SS_b = SS_w$. $\qquad (13.17)$
Hence, $SS_w = 96.2 - 42.6 = 53.6$.

The sum of squares for within groups can also be calculated directly by summing the squares of the deviations of the raw scores from their respective group means:

$$SS_w = \sum [1^2 + 2^2 + 0 + (-1)^2 + \cdots + .6^2 + (-.4)^2 + (-2.4)^2] = 53.6$$

The sum of squares for between groups can also be obtained directly from the deviations of the group means from the general mean.

$$SS_b = \sum [(1.7)^2 + (1.1)^2 + (-.9)^2 + (-1.9)^2] = 42.6$$

Usually, Formulas 13.14, 13.15, and 13.17 are easiest to use in computing the sums of squares for total, between groups, and within groups. The same formulas may also be used with ordinary standard scores, for example, those with a mean of 50 and a standard deviation of 10 in the norm population.

The sums of squares for between-treatment groups and within groups, when divided by the appropriate degrees of freedom $k - 1 = 3$ and $k(n - 1) = 16$ are the desired estimates of the population variance, the mean squares used in the F test. The results of the analysis are summarized in Table 13.2. Such tables are all that are usually given in reporting the results of an analysis of variance.

Table 13.2 Summary of One-Way Analysis of Variance

	Sum of Squares	Degrees of Freedom	Mean Square or Variance
Treatments	42.6	3	14.20 $\left(s_b^2\right)$
Within groups	53.6	16	3.35 $\left(s_w^2\right)$
Total	96.2	19	

$$F = \frac{14.20}{3.35} = 4.24$$

When Table F in the Appendix is consulted, we find that for 3 degrees of freedom relevant to the larger variance, or mean square, and for 16 degrees of freedom relevant to the smaller variance, or mean square, the critical values for the .05 and .01 levels are 3.24 and 5.29. Since the F above is between these values, it is significant at the .05, but not at the .01 level.

t tests following a significant F test

When an F is significant, tests can then be made of the significance of the differences between pairs of sample or group means. Formerly, the within-groups variance was generally used in making a single determination of the standard error of the means and its square was used twice in Formula 9.3 to obtain the standard error of the differences used as the denominator for each t test. For example,

$$s_{\bar{x}} = \sqrt{\frac{3.35}{5}} = .819$$

$$s_{\bar{x} - \bar{x}} = \sqrt{.819^2 + .819^2} = 1.158$$

and t for $\bar{X}_1 - \bar{X}_4 = \dfrac{3.5}{1.158} = 3.11$ which is significant at the .01 level, entering Table C in the Appendix with the 16 degrees of freedom of the within-groups variance. The critical value is 2.921. It is now considered better to use more sophisticated techniques in testing differences between several pairs of means. In 1953, Scheffé[7] proposed the computation of t' for testing the significance of different pairs of treatment means:

---

[7] Henry Scheffé, "A Method for Judging All Contrasts in the Analysis of Variance," *Biometrika* 40 (1953), pp. 87–104.

$$t' = \sqrt{(k-1)F}. \qquad (13.18)$$

For 3 and 16 degrees of freedom and at the .05 level, F equals 3.24. The corresponding t' is 3.12. For the data in Table 13.1 only the difference $\bar{X}_1 - \bar{X}_4$, the largest of the six differences between the four means, is almost significant at the .05 level when its t of 3.11 is compared with the t' of 3.12. This procedure can be extended to comparisons other than those just mentioned. It can be used, for example, to test the significance of a difference between the average of two treatment means and a third mean. One can be confident in making all possible comparisons that the probability of making errors of the first kind will not exceed .05. This is not true when using the t test earlier described. Tests based on t', computed as explained above, are much more rigorous than other methods proposed for making multiple comparisons.[8] Hence, Scheffé has suggested use of the critical value of the .10 level of F. If this is done with the illustrative data, the F of 2.46 yields a t' of 2.72. The differences $\bar{X}_1 - \bar{X}_4$ and $\dfrac{\bar{X}_1 + \bar{X}_2}{2} - \bar{X}_4$ are significant when their t's of 3.11 and 2.85 are compared with the t' of 2.72.

Practice Exercise 13.2

For the data in the following table obtain the F for between-groups variance compared with the within-groups variance (computing to two decimals):

	A	B	C	D	E
1	2	7	3	5	3
2	8	8	2	9	4
3	6	6	5	4	2
4	1	6	4	5	4
5	9	5	3	2	4
6	7	2	6	8	2
7	8	6	6	4	2

Are any t tests justified?

[8] The various methods are discussed by H. A. Scheffé, *Analysis of Variance* (New York: Wiley, 1959), pp. 55–83; Allen L. Edwards, *Experimental Design in Psychological Research*, 3rd ed. (New York: Holt, Rinehart and Winston, 1968), pp. 130–54; George A. Ferguson, *Statistical Methods*, pp. 268–75; B. J. Winer, *Statistical Principles in Experimental Design*, 2nd ed. (New York: McGraw-Hill, 1971), pp. 185–204.

Partitioning the total sum of squares in two-way analysis of variance

In discussing the partitioning of the total sum of squares in simple one-way analysis of variance, the derivation leading to Formula 13.6 and ultimately to Formulas 13.7 and 13.8 for s_w^2 and s_b^2 began with the identity:

$$(X_{ij} - \overline{X}) = (X_{ij} - \overline{X}_j) + (\overline{X}_j - \overline{X}). \qquad (13.5)$$

A given score as a deviation from the general mean is divided into two additive components, the deviation of the score from the mean of its group and the deviation of the group mean from the general mean. In the case of two-way classification analysis of variance, a similar but more complex identity may be written in deviate measures:

$$(X_{rc} - \overline{X}..) = (\overline{X}_{r.} - \overline{X}..) + (\overline{X}_{.c} - \overline{X}..) + (X_{rc} - \overline{X}_{r.} + \overline{X}_{.c} + \overline{X}..) \quad (13.19)$$

The X_{rc} refers to any score in a table such as Table 13.5 on page 426. The symbol $\overline{X}..$ refers to the general mean; all the rc scores in the rows and columns of the table of data have been summed and divided by rc. The dot after the subscript r of the row, mean $\overline{X}_{r,}$, indicates that the c scores in a row have been summed and divided by c. For example, in the fourth row of Table 13.5, $6 + 5 + 2 + 4 = 17$ and 17 divided by 4 equals 4.25, one of the row means below $\overline{X}_{r.}$. Its symbol, if written, would be $\overline{X}_{4.}$. Similarly, where a dot precedes a c, it means that the r entries in a column have been summed and later divided by r. For example, the 8 entries of the third column of Table 13.5 sum to 36 which divided by 8 equals 4.500. Its symbol is $\overline{X}_{.3}$.

Consider the score of 6 in the second column and third row of the table and the identity just given:

$$(6 - 5.00) = (5.50 - 5.00) + (5.75 - 5.00) + (6.00 - 5.50 - 5.75 + 5.00)$$

The first two terms at the right represent components of the score attributable to the deviation of the row mean of the score from the general mean and to the deviation of the column mean from the general mean. Obviously the magnitude of $\overline{X}_{r.}$ and $\overline{X}_{.c}$ influences the size of any given score in the same row and column. But the size of the score is also influenced by random error and possibly by genuine interaction whose magnitude equals the third term at the right in the identity. In the example it equals $-.25$ as a deviate measure.

Derivation similar to that given for simple one-way analysis of variance leads to a partitioning of the total sum of squares

$$\sum_{r=1}^{r} \sum_{c=1}^{c} (X_{rc} - \overline{X}..)^2$$

into a between-rows sum of squares, a between-columns sum of squares, and an interaction or "residual" sum of squares. Instead of writing this out as an equation these sums of squares are listed in Table 13.3. Each is followed by the expression used in obtaining its degrees

Table 13.3 Sums of Squares, Degrees of Freedom, and Mean Squares or Variance Estimates for Two-Way Classification Analysis of Variance*

	Sum of Squares	Degrees of Freedom	Variance Estimate
		$n = 1$	
Rows	$c\sum_{r=1}^{r}(\bar{X}_{r\cdot} - \bar{X}_{\cdot\cdot})^2$	$r - 1$	s_r^2
Columns	$r\sum_{c=1}^{c}(\bar{X}_{\cdot c} - \bar{X}_{\cdot\cdot})^2$	$c - 1$	s_c^2
Interaction or Residual	$\sum_{r=1}^{r}\sum_{c=1}^{c}(X_{rc} - \bar{X}_{r\cdot} - \bar{X}_{\cdot c} + \bar{X}_{\cdot\cdot})^2$	$(r-1)(c-1)$	s_i^2
Total	$\sum_{r=1}^{r}\sum_{c=1}^{c}(X_{rc} - \bar{X}_{\cdot\cdot})^2$	$rc - 1$ or $N - 1$	
		$n > 1$	
Rows	$nc\sum_{r=1}^{r}(\bar{X}_{r\cdot\cdot} - \bar{X}_{\cdot\cdot\cdot})^2$	$r - 1$	s_r^2
Columns	$nr\sum_{c=1}^{c}(\bar{X}_{\cdot c\cdot} - \bar{X}_{\cdot\cdot\cdot})^2$	$c - 1$	s_c^2
Interaction	$n\sum_{r=1}^{r}\sum_{c=1}^{c}(\bar{X}_{rc\cdot} - \bar{X}_{r\cdot\cdot} - \bar{X}_{\cdot c\cdot} + \bar{X}_{\cdot\cdot\cdot})^2$	$(r-1)(c-1)$	s_i^2
Within Cells	$\sum_{r=1}^{r}\sum_{c=1}^{c}\sum_{i=1}^{n}(X_{rci} - \bar{X}_{rc\cdot})^2$	$rc(n-1)$	s_w^2
Total	$\sum_{r=1}^{r}\sum_{c=1}^{c}\sum_{i=1}^{n}(X_{rci} - \bar{X}_{\cdot\cdot\cdot})^2$	$rcn - 1$ or $N - 1$	

* After Ferguson and others.

of freedom and the symbol for the corresponding mean square, or variance. The computing formulas for the sums of square are listed below the illustrative data in Table 13.5 where totals represented by T's have the kind of subscripts defined above.

When the design of the two-way analysis calls for $n > 1$ cases in each cell, an additional term is added to equation 13.19 above and other minor changes are made. From this equation can be derived expressions for a row sum of squares, a column sum of squares, an interaction sum of squares, and a within-cells sum of squares:

$$(X_{rci} - \bar{X}...) = (\bar{X}_{r..} - \bar{X}...) + (\bar{X}_{.c.} - \bar{X}...) +$$
$$(\bar{X}_{rc.} - \bar{X}_{r..} - \bar{X}_{.c.} + \bar{X}...) +$$
$$(X_{rci} - \bar{X}_{rc.}) \qquad (13.20)$$

The sums of squares referred to above have been listed in the lower half of Table 13.3 and are followed by formulas for the numbers of degrees of freedom, and the symbols for the mean squares or variance estimators. The corresponding computing equations are given on page 433 in connection with the data to which they are applied.

Note the change in the number of dots in the subscripts of the means. The additional dot where $n > 1$ signifies the summation of n measures in each cell prior to further summing. This is also shown by the n's preceding the first term in the first three equations and the

$$\sum_{i=1}^{n}$$ in the last two equations.

Both of the worked examples are preceded by discussion of analysis of variance models now considered essential in choosing the error term or denominator of F when making F tests.

MODELS AND EXPECTED MEAN SQUARES FOR TWO-WAY ANALYSIS OF VARIANCE

In making significance tests in other than simple analysis of variance, the denominators selected for F, the within variance, the interaction variance, or one of several interaction variances in complex designs depends on the nature of the variables, whether random, fixed, or both. In making appropriate selections, equations for various expected mean squares such as those listed in Table 13.4 are indispensable.

The equations of the type listed in the table are derived from such an equation as

$$X_{rci} - \mu = a_r + b_c + (ab)_{rc} + e_{rci}. \qquad (13.21)$$

This equation makes the linearity assumption that the deviation of X_{rci} from the general population mean μ equals the sum of the terms at the right also in deviation form. These terms correspond to the pop-

Table 13.4 General Finite Model: Expected Mean Squares or Variances for Two-Way Classification Analysis of Variance*

Source of Variation	Observed Mean Square or Variance	Expectation of Mean Square or Variance
Rows (a)	s_r^2	$\sigma_e^2 + \left(1 - \dfrac{c}{C_p}\right)n\sigma_{ab}^2 + cn\sigma_a^2$
Columns (b)	s_c^2	$\sigma_e^2 + \left(1 - \dfrac{r}{R_p}\right)n\sigma_{ab}^2 + rn\sigma_b^2$
Rows x Columns Interaction (ab)	s_i^2	$\sigma_e^2 + n\sigma_{ab}^2$
Within Cells (w)	s_w^2	σ_e^2

* This table is adapted from J. Cornfield and J. W. Tukey, "Average Values of Mean Squares in Factorials." *Annals of Mathematical Statistics* 27 (1956), 907–49; M. B. Wilk and O. Kempthorne, "Fixed, Mixed, and Random Models," *Journal of the American Statistical Association* 50 (1955), 1144–67; Julian C. Stanley's review in *Educational and Psychological Measurement* 16 (Winter 1956), 551; and Ferguson, *Statistical Methods*, p. 230. Ferguson's explanation of the models is especially recommended for students.

ulation variances σ_a^2 (rows), σ_b^2 (columns), σ_{ab}^2 (interaction), and σ_e^2 (within cells error).[9]

In a more complete version of this model each σ_e^2 is preceded by $\left(1 - \dfrac{n}{N_p}\right)$ where n refers to the number of entries in each cell of a two-way table which is minute as compared with the number of elements N_p in the target population. Hence, $\left(1 - \dfrac{n}{N_p}\right)$ can be assumed equal to unity and therefore omitted.

When both variables are fixed factors, their sample numbers equal the population numbers, $c = C_p$ and $r = R_p$. Then $\left(1 - \dfrac{c}{C_p}\right)$ and $\left(1 - \dfrac{r}{R_p}\right)$ both equal zero, the interaction terms vanish and the General Finite Model becomes the Fixed Model. The symbols σ_a^2, σ_b^2, and σ_{ab}^2 are replaced by θ_a^2, θ_b^2, and θ_{ab}^2 since there are relatively few levels of each variable. Making the changes just noted:

[9] Ferguson, *Statistical Methods*, pp. 229–30.

Fixed Model

Rows, s_a^2	$\sigma_e^2 \ +$	$cn\theta_a^2$
Columns, s_b^2	$\sigma_e^2 \ +$	$rn\theta_b^2$
Interaction, s_{ab}^2	$\sigma_e^2 \ + \ n\theta_{ab}^2$	
Within, s_w^2	σ_e^2	

The observed mean squares s_a^2, s_b^2, and s_{ab}^2 are the numerators of the three F's, while the denominator for each is the s_w^2 corresponding to σ_e^2. Each numerator differs from this denominator in only one term. This is a general rule.

When both variables are random variables, the random samples of levels of each variable C and R are so much smaller than the possible population levels C_p and R_p that $\left(1 - \dfrac{c}{C_p}\right)$ and $\left(1 - \dfrac{r}{R_p}\right)$ can be taken as equal to unity. Then the General Finite Model becomes the Random Model:

Random Model

Rows, s_a^2	$\sigma_e^2 \ + \ \sigma_{ab}^2 \ +$		$cn\sigma_a^2$
Columns, s_b^2	$\sigma_e^2 \ + \ \sigma_{ab}^2 \ + \ rn\sigma_b^2$		
Interaction, s_{ab}^2	$\sigma_e^2 \ + \ \sigma_{ab}^2$		
Within, s_w^2	σ_e^2		

The observed interaction, s_{ab}^2, is used as the denominator of the F's for testing the significance of the row and column variables, while the within s_w^2 is used in the F for testing the significance of the interaction. Note that each numerator differs from its denominator in only one term.

Where one variable is a random variable and the other a fixed variable, the mixed model is applicable. It is useful, for example, in interpreting the data collected in an experiment where the row variable is a random one—students classified in 13 rows of cells representing the class intervals of frequency distributions of posttest scores or gains and four columns representing methods of instruction or treatments of which there are only a limited number.

Mixed Model

Rows, s_a^2	σ_e^2	$+$	$+ nc\sigma_a^2$
Columns, s_b^2	σ_e^2	$+ n\sigma_{ab}^2$	$+ nr\theta_b^2$
Interaction, s_{ab}^2	σ_e^2	$+ n\sigma_{ab}^2$	
Within, s_w^2	σ_e^2		

The F for the random or row variable is s_a^2/s_w^2; the F for the fixed column or treatment variable is s_b^2/s_{ab}^2; the F for the interaction is s_{ab}^2/s_w^2.

Illustration of two-way classification or "randomized block" analysis of variance where $n = 1$

Suppose that 32 pupils in the 4th grade of a large elementary school have been selected at random and assigned at random to four treatment groups. At the conclusion of the experiment, the pupils are given an achievement test yielding stanine scores which are recorded in Table 13.5. The two columns at the right in the table list for each row the sum of the c scores in that row (T_r), the square of the sum (T_r^2), and the mean of the row $(\bar{X}_r)$. The three rows at the bottom of the table list the sum of the r scores in each column (T_c), the square of the sum (T_c^2), and the mean of the column $(\bar{X}_c)$. At the lower right of the table is the sum of all the scores in the table $(T_{..})$ and the square of this sum $(T_{..}^2)$. Also listed are the sum of squares of the column sums $\sum_1^c T_{.c}^2$ and of the rows sums $\sum_1^r T_{r.}^2$ and the general mean $\bar{X}_{..}$. Here the 1's replace the expressions $c = 1$ and $r = 1$ below the summation signs. In some texts even the 1's are omitted with c's and r's, or other appropriate symbols, given above or below the summation signs, or omitted altogether. Following Table 13.5 are the computing equations and computations of the sums of squares SS_c, SS_r, SS_{rc}, and SS_t—sums of squares for treatments, subjects (or blocks), interaction, and total.

Table 13.5 Illustrative Data for Two-Way or Randomized Block Analysis of Variance where $n = 1$

Subject or Block	Treatments				$T_{r.}$	$T_{r.}^2$	$\bar{X}_{r.}$
	1	2	3	4			
1	5	5	5	3	18	324	4.50
2	9	4	4	5	22	484	5.50
3	8	6	5	3	22	484	5.50
4	6	5	2	4	17	289	4.25
5	7	7	3	3	20	400	5.00
6	7	8	6	2	23	529	5.75
7	6	5	4	4	19	361	4.75
8	5	6	7	1	19	361	4.75
$T_{.c}$	53	46	36	25	$T_{..} = 160$	$T_{..}^2 = 25{,}600$	
$T_{.c}^2$	2809	2116	1296	625	$\sum_{1}^{c} T_{.c}^2 = 6846$	$\sum_{1}^{r} T_{r.}^2 = 3232$	
$\bar{X}_{.c}$	6.625	5.750	4.500	3.125	$\bar{X}_{..} = 5.00$		

Computations of Sums of Squares

The equation for the column sum of squares is listed first since the treatments variable is of greater interest than the row variable.

$$SS_c = \frac{1}{r}\sum_{1}^{c} T_{.c}^2 - \frac{T_{..}^2}{N} = \frac{6846}{8} - \frac{25{,}600}{32} = 855.75 - 800 = 55.75 \ (13.22)$$

$$SS_r = \frac{1}{c}\sum_{1}^{r} T_{r.}^2 - \frac{T_{..}^2}{N} = \frac{3232}{4} - \frac{25{,}600}{32} = 808.00 - 800.00 = 8.00 \ (13.23)$$

$$SS_{rc} = \sum_{1}^{r}\sum_{1}^{c} X_{rc}^2 - \frac{1}{r}\sum_{1}^{c} T_{.c}^2 - \frac{1}{c}\sum_{1}^{r} T_{r.}^2 + \frac{T_{..}^2}{N} = \qquad (13.24)$$

$$910 - 855.75 - 808.00 + 800.00 = 46.25$$

$$SS_t = \sum_{1}^{r}\sum_{1}^{c} X_{rc}^2 - \frac{T_{..}^2}{N} = 910.00 - 800.00 = 110.00 \qquad (13.25)$$

For SS_{rc} and SS_t the first term is the sum of the squares of all the scores. From it is subtracted the sum of all the scores squared, divided by the total number of scores. The results of the computations are then entered in a table of the type that is conventional for reporting the results of an analysis of variance:

Table 13.6 Summary of Two-Way or Randomized Block Analysis of Variance, $n = 1$

Source of Variation	Sum of Squares	Degrees of Freedom		Mean Square or Variance	F
Treatments (c)	55.75	3	$(c - 1)$	18.58 (s_c^2)	8.44 *
Subjects or Blocks (r)	8.00	7	$(r - 1)$	1.14 (s_r^2)	
Interaction or residual (rc)	46.25	21	$(c - 1)(r - 1)$	2.20 (s_i^2)	
Total	110.00	31	$(N - 1)$		

* Significant beyond the .01 level for 3 and 21 degrees of freedom.

The treatment variable is a fixed effects one. An F can legitimately be obtained using s_c^2 in the numerator and s_i^2 in the denominator. Since there is no within variance, s_w^2, no test is possible of the s_r^2 of the random row variable. See the "mixed model" on page 425 imagining $n = 1$ and no line for s_w^2. Then the line for the expected s_r^2 has the same number of terms, not one more term when compared with those for s_i^2.

Note the way in which the numerical value of F is reported. Compare it with the method illustrated in Table 13.2 on page 418. Often, numerical values of t or F, in appropriately labeled columns of a table, are asterisked to indicate their significance level, one for the .05 level and two for the .01 level. The asterisk in Table 13.6 refers, of course, to the footnote below the table.

The class rather than the pupil as the experimental unit

As was noted earlier, it is frequently necessary to use intact classes for school experimentation. Suppose that the schools participating in an experiment have been selected at random and that classes in each have been assigned at random to the compared treatments. If all of the classes are the same size, the computations can be the same as those illustrated for the data in Table 13.5. While n continues to equal 1, the entries in the table are not individual scores, but the means of the participating classes.

If the class size is the same within each school, but varies from school to school, the steps of the procedure are somewhat more complicated. In the cells of the table of data, enter the total of the test scores of each class instead of the class mean. Each column of cells pertains to one of k compared treatments (tr). Below each column enter the sum of the class total scores (T_{tr}), and the square of this sum (T_{tr}^2). Let

n_{tr} equal the number of pupils per treatment (the same number for each treatment). The sum of squares for treatments is

$$SS_{tr} = \frac{1}{n_{tr}} \sum_{k=1}^{k} T_{tr}^2 - \frac{T_{..}^2}{N}. \tag{13.26}$$

Each row of cells pertains to one of the r schools. Let T_s and n_s refer to the sum of the class totals and the number of pupils participating in the given school. The sum of squares for schools is

$$SS_s = \sum_{r=1}^{r} \frac{T_s^2}{n_s} - \frac{T_{..}^2}{N}. \tag{13.27}$$

Note that each T_s^2 is separately divided by the corresponding n_s.

Each T_c^2 is the sum of *squares* of the class totals in each row. Each n_c is the number of pupils per class in the given school; it varies from school to school.[10] The sum of the squares for classes is

$$SS_c = \sum_{r=1}^{r} \sum_{k=1}^{k} \frac{T_c^2}{n_c} - \frac{T_{..}^2}{N}. \tag{13.28}$$

The sum of squares for classes is a total sum of squares. Each T_c^2 for a class is analogous to an X_{rc}^2 for an individual pupil. The sum of the T_c^2 in each row is divided by the pupils per class in that school and the results combined for the r schools.

Even though the size of class varies from school to school the procedure as outlined does not give greater weight to the totals of the larger schools or classes and less weight to the smaller schools or classes. In effect, the means are unweighted.

The interaction, or residual, variance is obtained by subtracting from the sum of squares for classes the sum of squares for treatments and the sum of squares for schools as obtained above:

$$SS_i = SS_c - SS_{tr} - SS_s. \tag{13.29}$$

The mean squares or variances for treatments and for interaction are obtained by dividing SS_{tr} and SS_i by $(k-1)$ and by $(k-1)(r-1)$

---

[10] An example will clarify the computing process. Suppose that the class totals of stanine scores in one of the schools are 150, 210, 180, and 130 and that there are 25 pupils in each of the 4 classes. Then T_s, T_s^2, and T_s^2/n_s are respectively 670; 448,900 and 4,498 while $T_c^2/n_c = \dfrac{150^2 + 210^2 + 180^2 + 130^2}{25} = 4{,}636.$

degrees of freedom. The F is equal to the treatment variance divided by the interaction variance. Its significance is tested using the degrees of freedom just specified.

It is advantageous to conduct school experiments unobtrusively and without disruption of classes. Unless the numbers of schools and classes are quite large, however, failure to reject the null hypothesis may be due to the small numbers of degrees of freedom when the data are correctly analyzed using the residual variance rather than a within-classes variance. This should not be a problem in a comparatively large school system where the numbers of schools and classes are large.[11]

Small departures from uniformity in class size may, as a practical matter, be handled by the random elimination of the data of a very few pupils in the larger classes.

Practice Exercise 13.3

Suppose that the data listed below are the stanines of three groups of pupils assigned at random to three treatments. Use the data to compute a two-way classification analysis of variance where $n = 1$. Assume that the column variable is a fixed variable and that the row variable is a random one.

	A	B	C
1	8	8	6
2	7	6	5
3	6	5	5
4	6	5	4
5	5	4	4
6	4	4	4
7	4	3	3
8	3	2	3

Is the F for the column variable significant?

---

[11] For a lucid explanation of these procedures and of the analysis of covariance applied to data where the class is the experimental unit, see E. F. Lindquist, *Statistical Analysis in Educational Research* (Boston: Houghton Mifflin, 1940), pp. 107–108, 114–23, and 196–203; and by the same author, *Design and Analysis of Experiments in Psychology and Education* (Boston, Houghton Mifflin, 1953), Chapter 8. See also other advanced texts, especially when there is no uniformity in class size.

ILLUSTRATION OF TREATMENTS × LEVELS ANALYSIS OF VARIANCE

A Type of Two-Way Analysis of Variance with $n > 1$

The treatments × levels analysis of variance is essentially an application of the randomized block analysis of variance technique to subgroups or blocks which have been matched on the basis of pretest, or other initial test scores.[12] These may be intelligence test scores, scores on an initial achievement test, or some composite of both. It will usually suffice, however, to match in terms of the one initial test which has the higher correlation with the final measures of achievement. While the procedure is illustrated for two groups, it can easily be extended to more than two groups by using additional columns in computing Table 13.7.

We will assume that a *random* sample of students has been selected for participation in the experiment and that the names of the students and their initial test scores have been entered on 3″ x 5″ cards.

1.   Tally the frequency distribution of initial scores preferably in not more than ten intervals. (As few as three to five intervals may be used so that none of the levels subgroups, or blocks, will be too small. The levels may be, for example, in terms of initial scores—very superior, superior, average, etc.) Classify the cards according to the levels decided upon. Then distribute the cards on each level, *at random,* to the two (or more) groups which are to receive the compared treatments or methods of instruction. The numbers of students in each of the subgroups on a given level may be equal, or *all* of the subgroups given the same treatment may have, for example, one-third more cases. The total number of students may, however, vary from level reflecting the proportions of students thus classified in the population to which the generalizations are to apply. The numbers on each of the five levels of the illustrative data in Table 13.7 progressively decrease above and below the average level.

2.   At the conclusion of the experiment, the final achievement scores (or gains) should be entered on each card and the following steps applied to them. (In outlining the steps, final scores alone will be mentioned.)

3.   Adjacent to the final score on each card enter its square. This is most easily done from a table of squares.

4.   Enter in each cell of the *main* part of the computing table the following data relevant to the cases of the given group in the given class interval or level:

---

[12] For further information about the treatments × levels analysis of variance, see E. F. Lindquist, *Design and Analysis*, pp. 121–55.

    a.   The number of cases.

    b.   The sum of the final scores.

    c.   The sum of the *squares* of the final scores.

    d.   The square of the sum of final scores, $(b)^2$.

    e.   The cell mean, which equals $b \div a$.

    f.   The square of the sum of final scores divided by the number of cases, $d \div a$.

Check each entry in each of the cells.

    5.   In the cells of the column headed "Both (or all) groups" enter the following data computed from data given in cells on same level.

    g.   The total number of cases on that level. *For the first row or level* $11 + 11 = 22$

    h.   The sum of the final scores on that level $1{,}570 + 1{,}493 = 3{,}063$

    i.   The square of the sum of final scores on that level, $h^2 = 3{,}063^2 = 9{,}381{,}969$

    j.   The square of the sum of final scores on that level divided by the number of cases on the level, $i \div g = 9{,}381{,}969 \div 22 = 426{,}453.1$

    6.   In the cells at the bottom of the first two, or groups A and B, columns perform the same operations summing vertically as indicated. For the cell at the bottom of the first column:

    k.   The total number of cases in the group $= 11 + 18 + 26 + 18 + 11 = 84$

    l.   The sum of the final scores for the group $= 1{,}570 + 2{,}380, + \ldots + 753 = 9693$

    m.   The square of the sum of final scores in the given group, or column, $l^2 = 9{,}693^2 = 93{,}954{,}249$

    n.   The square of the sum of final scores of the group divided by the number of cases in the group, $m \div k = 93{,}954{,}249 \div 84 = 1{,}118{,}850.3$

    7.   In the cell at the bottom of the column headed "Both (or all) groups" perform essentially the same procedure.

    o.   Sum the g's in this column to obtain N the total number of cases, sum the k's in this row as a check. Here N is equal to 168.

    p.   Sum the h's of the column and as a check the l's to obtain the sum of all the final scores, here, 19,339.

    q.   Square this sum, here, 373,996,921.

    r.   Divide this square by N, $373{,}996{,}921 \div 168 = 2{,}226{,}172.1$.

    8.   The completion of the computations for the treatments by levels analysis of variance follows Table 13.7. The c, r, and n above are not the *c, r,* and *n* of the equations listed later.

Table 13.7 Computing Table

Initial Score Level	Group A		Group B		Both (or all) Groups	
150–	11(a)	2,464,900(d)	11	2,229,049	22(g)	9,381,969(i)
	1,570(b)	142.73(e)	1,493	135.73	3,063(h)	426,543.1(j)
	225,238(c)	224,081.81(f)	204,121	202,640.81		
120–149	18	5,664,400	18	5,139,289	36	21,594,609
	2,380	132.22	2,267	125.94	4,647	599,850.2
	316,876	314,688.86	287,085	285,516.05		
90–119	26	10,137,856	26	9,634,816	52	39,538,944
	3,184	122.46	3,104	119.38	6,288	760,364.3
	393,456	389,917.45	373,650	370,569.76		
60– 89	18	3,261,636	18	3,775,249	36	14,055,001
	1,806	100.33	1,943	107.94	3,749	390,416.6
	184,425	181,202.00	211,112	209,736.05		
30– 59	11	567,009	11	703,921	22	2,534,464
	753	68.45	839	76.27	1,592	115,202.9
	52,559	51,546.27	64,921	63,992.82		
	84(k)	93,954,249(m)	84	93,045,316	168(o)	373,996,921(q)
	9,693(l)	1,118,850.3(n)	9,646	1,107,682.3	19,339(p)	2,226,172.1(r)

Computations of (1) to (5)

		Summation of 2 n terms
(1)	2,226,532.6	(1,118,850.3 + 1,107,682.3)
		Summation of 5 j terms
(2)	2,292,287.1	(426,453.1 + − − − − − + 115,202.9)
		Summation of 10 f terms
(3)	2,293,891.9	(224,081.81 + − − + 51,546.27 + 202,640.81 + − − − + 63,992.82)
		Summation of 10 c terms
(4)	2,313,443.0	(225,238 + − − − + 52,559 + 204,121 + − − − + 64,921)
(5)	2,226,172.1	r from lowest cell of right-hand column of table

Computing equations

$$SS_c = \sum^c \frac{T_{.c.}^2}{n_{.c.}} - \frac{T_{...}^2}{N} = (1) - (5) = 2{,}226{,}532.6 - 2{,}226{,}172.1 = 360.5.$$

$$(13.30)$$

$$SS_r = \sum^r \frac{T_{r..}^2}{n_{r..}} - \frac{T_{...}^2}{N} = (2) - (5) = 2{,}292{,}287.1$$
$$- 2{,}226{,}172.1 = 66{,}115.0.$$

$$(13.31)$$

$$SS_{rc} = \sum^r \sum^c \frac{T_{rc.}^2}{n_{rc.}} - \sum^c \frac{T_{.c.}^2}{n_{.c.}} - \sum^r \frac{T_{r..}^2}{n_{r..}} + \frac{T_{...}^2}{N} = (3) - (1) - (2) + (5)$$
$$= 2{,}293{,}891.9 - 2{,}226{,}532.6 - 2{,}292{,}287.1$$
$$+ 2{,}226{,}172.1 = 1{,}244.3.$$

$$(13.32)$$

$$SS_w = \sum^r \sum^c \sum^n X_{rci}^2 - \sum^r \sum^c \frac{T_{rc.}^2}{n_{rc.}} = (4 - 3) = 2{,}313{,}443.0$$
$$- 2{,}293{,}891.9 = 19{,}551.1.$$

$$(13.33)$$

$$SS_t = \sum^r \sum^c \sum^n X_{rci}^2 - \frac{T_{...}^2}{N} = (4) - (5) = 2{,}313{,}443.0$$
$$- 2{,}226{,}172.1 = 87{,}270.9.$$

$$(13.34)$$

If the n's were equal, the first three equations would begin with $\frac{1}{nr}$, $\frac{1}{nc}$, and $\frac{1}{n}$ and the $T_{.c.}^2$, $T_{r..}^2$, and $T_{rc.}^2$ would not be separately divided by the appropriate n's prior to summing. Compare these equations with those in the lower half of Table 13.3, recalling that here column equations or terms precede those for rows. Note the further simplification of the notation as suggested on page 425.

The F tests illustrated in Table 13.8 are those specified by the mixed model presented on page 425. Assuming the treatments to be a fixed variable, the interaction variance appears in the denominator of the first F. For 4 degrees and 158 degrees of freedom it is nonsignificant even at the .05 level. The levels variable is assumed to be a random one, hence the within-cells variance appears in the denominator of the second F. It is significant far beyond the .01 level. This was to be expected for such data and is of no scientific interest. In obtaining the third F, the treatments $\times$ levels or interaction variance was divided by the within-cells variance. For 4 and 158 degrees of freedom, it is significant at the .05 level. This indicates that the null hypothesis of no relationship between the effectiveness of the treatments and the level of student ability can be rejected. Study of the means of the subgroups indicates that Treatment A is more effective than Treatment B for above-average students, while for less able students, Treatment B is more effective than Treatment A. If the data were other than fictitious we might claim discovery of a disordinal interaction.[13]

If the data of the subgroups on the two lowest levels are exchanged so that all five subgroup means of group A are higher than the corresponding subgroup means of group B, $(1) = 2{,}227{,}618.7$; $SS_c = 1{,}446.6$; $SS_{rc} = 158.2$. The treatments and treatments $\times$ levels variances become respectively 1,446.6 and 39.6. Since the latter is nonsignificant $(F = 39.6/123.7 = .32)$, it is pooled with the within-cells variance to yield an error variance of $123.7 + 39.6$ or 163.3 with $158 + 4$ or 162 degrees of freedom. The F for treatments then becomes 8.86 which is significant beyond the .01 level.

Table 13.8   Treatments $\times$ Levels Analysis of Variance

Source of Variation	Sums of Squares	Degrees of Freedom		Mean Square or Variance
Treatments (c)	360.5	1	$(T-1)$	360.5
Levels (r)	66,115.0	4	$(L-1)$	16,528.8
Treatments $\times$ Levels (rc)	1,244.3	4	$(T-1) \times (L-1)$	311.1
Within cells (w)	19,551.1	158	$(N - TL)$	123.7
Total	87,270.9	167	$(N-1)$	

$$F = \frac{360.5}{311.1} = 1.19 \qquad F = \frac{16{,}528.8}{123.7} = 133.6 \qquad F = \frac{311.1}{123.7} = 2.51$$

---

[13] See the references cited on page 392 of Chapter 12.

If one wishes to test the significance of differences between means on various levels of ability compute the standard error of these differences,

$$s_d = \sqrt{s_w^2\left(\frac{1}{n_{ij}} + \frac{1}{n_{ij}}\right)}. \tag{13.35}$$

where s_w^2 is the within-subgroups variance and each n_{ij} refers to the number of cases in each of the two cells on the same level. The degree of freedom is that of the within-subgroups variance. For example, on the fourth level from the top

$$t = \frac{107.94 - 100.33}{\sqrt{123.7(\frac{1}{18} + \frac{1}{18})}} = \frac{7.61}{3.71} = 2.05.$$

For 158 degrees of freedom this t is significant at the .05 level. The difference favors group B. It is the only one of the five such differences that is significant.

Given more than two treatments, there can be t tests of the differences between the treatment means of the groups as wholes and between the corresponding means on each level. It would then be desirable to use one of the multiple comparison procedures briefly mentioned on pages 418–419.

Practice Exercise 13.4

Suppose that the final achievement stanines of Groups A and B have been classified on three levels of scholastic aptitude: "Superior," "Average," and "Below Average," with equal numbers on each level.

	A	B
Level 1 Superior	8	7
	7	7
	6	5
	6	4
Level 2 Average	6	6
	5	6
	5	5
	4	5
Level 3 Below Average	3	6
	2	5
	2	4
	1	3

Using the steps outlined for treatment $\times$ levels analysis of variance, test the following null hypotheses:

(1)   The treatments applied to Groups A and B are equally effective.
(2)   The treatment effects are unrelated to the levels of aptitude of the pupils.

ANALYSIS OF COVARIANCE

In simple or randomized groups analysis of variance, a between-groups and a within-groups variance are used to obtain F. It is assumed that prior to the experimental instruction the groups do not differ significantly. When it is known that the groups are different initially with reference to some important measured variable, for example, scholastic aptitude or achievement as measured by some test or tests initially given, such data can be used with the analysis of covariance to make adjustments for the initial inequality. Adjustments are made in the post-test means of the groups and, quite as important, in the measure of experimental error. The equations for sums of squares for between groups, within groups, and for total are supplemented by expressions for sums of products. The basic equation is one partitioning the total product sum into a product sum between treatment groups and a product sum within treatment groups.[14]

The adjustments made in the posttest means are on application of linear regressional although no regression equation need be used to adjust posttest scores. Such adjustment of the posttest means (or mean gains) suffices. Similarly equations based on linear regression are used to obtain adjusted sums of squares for total and for within groups and their difference is the adjusted or reduced sum of squares for between groups. It is presumed that the regression lines are not significantly different from one group to another—the assumption of homogeneity of regression.

In more complex designs, the analysis of variance also involves interaction variances, for example, in an experiment conducted in several schools there may be both treatment $\times$ schools and treatment $\times$ levels variances in the same experiment. It should be noted, however, that a treatment $\times$ levels design can be more effective than a covariance design[15] and the reliability of the tests used to measure covariates is a matter of concern.[16] When use of a treatment $\times$ levels design is

[14] Edwards, *Experimental Design,* Chapter 16; Ferguson, *Statistical Analysis,* Chapter 20; McNemar, *Psychological Statistics,* Chapter 18.

[15] L. S. Feldt, "A Comparison of the Precision of Three Experimental Designs Employing a Concomitant Variable," *Psychometrika* 23 (1958), pp. 335–54.

[16] Frederic M. Lord, "Large Sample Covariance Analysis When the Control Variable Is

not feasible, and when reasonably reliable initial test data have comparatively high correlation with posttest scores and not excessively disparate means from one group to another, covariance analysis may be recommended. In any case the worked example given below will introduce the reader to the method.

Analysis of covariance—a worked example

Let us assume that there are 30 pupils in each group or class. (In order to use the procedure described, the classes should be of equal size. If they are not, discard the data of a few pupils in one of the classes, selecting such pupils at random, or modify the computations as suggested on page 438.) Suppose that the data for both (or all) classes have been entered in a table with such headings as

Class 1 (Treatment A)   Class 2 (Treatment B)

X_1 X_1^2 Y_1 Y_1^2 X_1Y_1 X_2 X_2^2 Y^2 Y_2^2 X_2Y_2

and that the sums of scores, sums of squares of scores have been obtained by totaling the columns. The table will differ from the one suggested for use with Formula 13.4 only in the fact that the pupils have not been paired. In a given row, X_1, X_1^2, Y_1, Y_1^2, and X_1Y_1 will pertain to a given pupil of class 1 while X_2, X_2^2, etc. will pertain to a given pupil of class 2.

Let us assume that such a table yields the following sums:

$$\Sigma X_1 = 482 \quad \Sigma X_1^2 = 7{,}136 \quad \Sigma Y_1 = 734 \quad \Sigma Y_1^2 = 18{,}896 \quad \Sigma X_1Y_1 = 11{,}765$$
$$\Sigma X_2 = 326 \quad \Sigma X_2^2 = 6{,}641 \quad \Sigma Y_2 = 723 \quad \Sigma Y_2^2 = 18{,}621 \quad \Sigma X_2Y_2 = 9{,}703$$
$$\Sigma X = 808 \quad \Sigma X^2 = 13{,}777 \quad \Sigma Y = 1{,}457 \quad \Sigma Y^2 = 37{,}517 \quad \Sigma XY = 21{,}468$$
$$N_1 + N_2 = 30 + 30 = N$$

After the data have been recorded in a table similar to the one illustrated above, consideration should be given to testing the assumptions of homogeneity of variance and homogeneity of regression. Consult one or more of the advanced texts earlier listed.

In order to accomplish the analysis covariance summarized in Table 13.9 it is necessary to express the sums of squares and products in terms of deviations from the means of the scores. This is done for "total," "between groups," and "within groups." Adjustments are then made for the initial inequality of the groups. We first calculate the correction terms listed.

Fallible," *Journal of the American Statistical Association* 55 (1960), pp. 307–21. See also S. H. Evans and E. J. Anastasio, "Misuse of Analysis of Covariance When Treatment Effect and Covariate Are Confounded," *Psychological Bulletin* 69 (May 1968), pp. 225–34; Janet D. Elashoff, "Analysis of Covariance: A Delicate Instrument," *American Educational Research Journal* 6 (May 1969), pp. 383–401.

Correction terms:

For X $\quad \dfrac{(\Sigma X)^2}{N} = \dfrac{808^2}{60} = 10,881.07.$

For Y $\quad \dfrac{(\Sigma Y)^2}{N} = \dfrac{1457^2}{60} = 35,380.81.$

For $XY \dfrac{\Sigma X \Sigma Y}{N} = \dfrac{808 \cdot 1457}{60} = 19,620.93.$

Σx^2, Σy^2, and Σxy for total:

$$\Sigma x^2 = \Sigma X^2 - \frac{(\Sigma X)^2}{N},$$

$$= 13,777 - 10,881.07 = 2,895.93.$$

$$\Sigma y^2 = \Sigma Y^2 - \frac{(\Sigma Y)^2}{N},$$

$$= 37,517 - 35,380.81 = 2,136.19.$$

$$\Sigma xy = \Sigma XY - \frac{\Sigma X \Sigma Y}{N},$$

$$= 21,468 - 19,620.93 = 1,847.07.$$

Σx^2, Σy^2, and Σxy for between groups:

$$\Sigma x^2 = \frac{(\Sigma X_1)^2 + (\Sigma X_2)^2}{N_1} - \frac{(\Sigma X)^2}{N},$$

$$= \frac{482^2 + 326^2}{30} - 10,881.07 = 405.59.$$

$$\Sigma y^2 = \frac{(\Sigma Y_1)^2 + (\Sigma Y_2)^2}{N_1} - \frac{(\Sigma Y)^2}{N},$$

$$= \frac{734^2 + 723^2}{30} - 35,380.81 = 2.02.$$

$$\Sigma xy = \frac{\Sigma X_1 \Sigma Y_1 + \Sigma X_2 \Sigma Y_2}{N_1} - \frac{\Sigma X \Sigma Y}{N},$$

$$= \frac{482 \cdot 734 + 326 \cdot 723}{30} - 19,620.93 = 28.60.$$

N_1 is here the number of pupils in each group. (If classes differ in size do not divide once by N_1, but separately by N_1 and N_2. If there are more than two classes each first numerator will contain as many terms as classes and there will be one or more divisions depending on whether or not the classes are of equal or different size. If N_1 were 35 and N_2 were 25, 482^2 would be divided by 35 and 326^2 by 25, the quotients summed before subtracting 10,881.07. The same procedure would be used for Σy^2. In the case of Σxy $482 \cdot 734$ would be divided by 35 and $326 \cdot 723$ by 25.)

Σx^2, Σy^2, *and* Σxy *for within groups:*

These values are obtained by subtracting the between-groups values from the values for total.

$$\Sigma x^2 = 2{,}895.93 - 405.59 = 2{,}490.34.$$
$$\Sigma y^2 = 2{,}136.19 - 2.02 = 2{,}134.17.$$
$$\Sigma xy = 1{,}847.07 - 28.60 = 1{,}818.47.$$

The sum of squares of the final scores for total is next adjusted in terms of the relationship between the initial and final scores. A similar adjustment is made for the sum of squares for within groups.
These adjustments are as follows:

$$SS'_t = \Sigma y^2 - \frac{(\Sigma xy)^2}{\Sigma x^2} = 2{,}136.19 - \frac{(1{,}847.07)^2}{2{,}895.93} = 958.10. \quad (13.36)$$

$$SS'_w = \Sigma y^2 - \frac{(\Sigma xy)^2}{\Sigma x^2} = 2{,}134.17 - \frac{1{,}818.47}{2{,}490.34} = 806.31. \quad (13.37)$$

The *adjusted* sum of squares for between groups is obtained by subtracting the adjusted sum of squares for within groups from the adjusted sum of squares for total. It is called by some authorities a *reduced* sum of squares.

$$SS'_t - SS'_w = SS'_b = 958.10 - 806.31 = 151.79. \quad (13.38)$$

The reduced sum of squares for between groups is divided by one less than the number of groups to obtain the reduced variance between groups. In this case the division is by one. The adjusted sum of squares for within groups is divided by three less than the total number of pupils in order to obtain the adjusted within-groups variance 14.15. (One less for each group and one for the correlation. If there were three groups, the degrees of freedom for within groups would be four less than the total number of pupils.) The F ratio is the ratio between the reduced between-groups variance and the adjusted within-groups variance. Most of the above is summarized in Table 13.9.

As in the case of the equated groups, we first hypothesize that the true difference between the groups is zero. On consulting a table of values of F for various degrees of freedom, we find for the given numbers of degrees, 1 and 57, that F must equal or exceed 4.00 to be significant at the five per cent level and must equal or exceed 7.08 to be significant at the one per cent level. (The values 4.00 and 7.08 are actually listed for 1 and 60 degrees of freedom.) Hence, we infer that the probability is less than one in a hundred that the difference between these groups is due to the operation of chance. If nonexperimen-

Table 13.9 Analysis of Covariance and Test of Significance of Adjusted Means of Final Scores

	Sums of Squares and Products			Adjusted or Reduced Sum of Squares	Degrees of Freedom	Adjusted or Reduced Variance
	$\sum x^2$	$\sum xy$	$\sum y^2$			
Between Groups	405.59	28.60	2.02	151.79	1	151.79
Within Groups	2,490.34	1,818.47	2,134.17	806.31	57	14.15
Total	2,895.93	1,847.07	2,136.19	958.10		

$$F = \frac{151.79}{14.15} = 10.73.$$

tal factors have been adequately controlled, we may ascribe the difference in achievement, as measured by the final test and adjusted to the difference in methods of instruction.

The unadjusted initial and final means of the two groups are:

$$\bar{X}_1 = \frac{\Sigma X_1}{N_1} = \frac{482}{30} = 16.07. \qquad \bar{X}_2 = \frac{\Sigma X_2}{N_2} = \frac{326}{30} = 10.87.$$

$$\bar{Y}_1 = \frac{\Sigma Y_1}{N_1} = \frac{734}{30} = 24.47. \qquad \bar{Y}_2 = \frac{\Sigma Y_2}{N_2} = \frac{723}{30} = 24.10.$$

The general mean of both groups on the initial test, $\bar{X} = \frac{\Sigma X}{N} = \frac{482 + 326}{60} = 13.47$. The initial mean of the first group is 2.60 above the general mean while the initial mean of the second group is 2.60 below the general mean. If the initial and final tests were perfectly correlated and scores numerically equal on either test were actually equal, 2.60 could be subtracted from the final mean of the first group and 2.60 added to the final mean of the second group to correct for the initial lack of equivalence of the groups. Since this condition does not exist, the value 2.60 must be multiplied by the regression coefficient b which takes into account both the actual lack of perfect correlation and any difference in value of the score units on the two tests. Basically, the procedure is one of predicting what the final means would be if the groups were initially equivalent on the pretest.

$$b = \frac{\Sigma xy}{\Sigma x^2} = \frac{1818.47}{2490.34} = .73. \qquad (13.39)$$

The values of Σxy and Σx^2 are those computed for within groups. Multiplying 2.60 by .73 we obtain 1.90.

24.47 − 1.90 = 22.57. Adjusted final mean of the first group, $\bar{Y}_1'$
24.10 + 1.90 = 26.00. Adjusted final mean of the second group, $\bar{Y}_2'$

The difference in adjusted means 3.43 favors the second and initially inferior group. We have already established the fact that this difference is statistically significant.

If more than two groups or classes are used, some modifications are necessary in handling the data. In obtaining ΣX, ΣX^2, ΣY, ΣY^2, and ΣXY, the appropriate sums for each of the groups are added. In computing Σx^2, Σy^2, and Σxy for between groups more terms such as $(\Sigma X_3)^2$, $(\Sigma Y_3)^2$, and $\Sigma X_3 \Sigma Y_3$ are added to the formulas. The number of degrees of freedom for between groups is one less than the number of groups or classes. The number of degrees of freedom for within groups will be $N - n - 1$ where N is the total number of pupils and n is the number of groups. In the case of more than two groups a significant F shows that the differences between the groups are, with a high degree of probability, to be attributed to factors other than chance, possibly to the variations in methods of instruction compared. Adjustment of the final means (or average gains) are made in much the same way. However, since the differences in initial means from the initial general mean will not be equal and opposite in sign as in the case of two groups, it will be necessary to make the following corrections, retaining the signs of these differences. For example:

Final mean $-$ (b) ($+$ difference) $=$ adjusted final mean.
Final mean $-$ (b) ($-$ difference) $=$ adjusted final mean.

The differences in adjusted final means, or adjusted average gains, may be compared and these differences tested for significance by means of the t test. Some of the differences may be significant while others are not. For example, let us suppose that three methods are being compared. Then there are three differences between *adjusted* final means: $\bar{Y}'_1 - \bar{Y}'_2$, $\bar{Y}'_1 - \bar{Y}'_3$, and $\bar{Y}'_2 - \bar{Y}'_3$. The following formula may be used in computing the denominator of the t ratio. (The numerator is the difference in the adjusted means being compared.) The denominator is the standard error of the $\bar{Y}'_1 - \bar{Y}'_2$, the numerical subscripts changing for other comparisons.

$$s_d = \sqrt{\left[\frac{1}{N_1} + \frac{1}{N_2} + \frac{(\bar{X}_1 - \bar{X}_2)^2}{\Sigma x^2_w} \right] s^2_w}. \qquad (13.40)$$

In this formula N_1 and N_2 are the numbers of pupils in each group or class, $\bar{X}_1$ and $\bar{X}_2$ are the *initial* means of the compared classes, Σx^2_w is the initial sum of squares within groups, and s^2_w is the adjusted variance for within groups. Although for two groups the F test suffices, let us apply this formula to the data of the two groups for the purpose of illustration.

$$s_d = \sqrt{\left[\frac{1}{30} + \frac{1}{30} + \frac{(16.07 - 10.87)^2}{2490.34}\right] 14.15} = 1.05.$$

$$t = \frac{\overline{Y}_2' - \overline{Y}_1'}{s_d} = \frac{3.43}{1.05} = 3.27.$$

The value of t exceeds the value of 2.66 necessary for the difference favoring the second group to be regarded as statistically significant. (While there are 57 degrees of freedom, those of the adjusted within groups variance, the table of t lists 2.66 for 60 degrees of freedom.) As mentioned above, in comparing three different differences between adjusted means, or adjusted average gains, three t's would be computed. Where there are more than three groups use should be made of sophisticated techniques described in recent advanced texts.

If the numerator and denominator of the equation just given for t are both squared the ratio is F for the two groups compared. Whether or not this F is significant may be learned from the table of F using one degree of freedom for the numerator and the degrees of freedom of the adjusted within-groups variance for the denominator. Squaring the t of 3.27 closely approximates the F of 10.73 earlier obtained from the analysis of covariance. If enough decimals are carried, t^2, or the F obtained as suggested above, will equal the F obtained by analysis of covariance for two groups. In this case, use of the equation for t, or the squaring just mentioned, is superfluous, but this procedure is useful where there are more than two groups and the F first obtained is significant.

Practice Exercise 13.5

Below are listed Pretest X and Posttest Y scores for Groups 1 and 2 which are not equivalent. Apply analysis of covariance as explained in the preceding pages. Obtain F and t and interpret them.

	X_1	X_2	Y_1	Y_2
1	7	8	10	9
2	5	6	9	8
3	4	5	7	6
4	4	4	8	9
5	3	4	9	9
6	3	3	9	7
7	3	4	8	5
8	2	3	9	4
9	2	3	6	4
10	1	2	5	3

RELATIONSHIPS BETWEEN THE STANDARD ERROR OF DIFFERENCE FORMULAS AND WITH DIFFERENT TYPES OF ANALYSIS OF VARIANCE

For the same data, Formulas 9.5 and 9.6, or 13.3, and 13.4 will all lead to the same value of t, if the size of the correlation coefficient r_{12} (included in Formula 9.5 and implied in Formulas 9.6 and 13.3) can be attributed to what the paired or matched pupils have in common at the start of the experiment and is measured by the test used in pairing or matching. In explaining the tetrad equation on page 346 of Chapter 11 in terms of a single common factor g, $r_{12} - r_{1g} r_{2g} = 0$ and $r_{12} = r_{1g} r_{2g}$. When $r_{1g} = r_{2g}$, $r_{12} = r_{1g}^2$ or r_{2g}^2. By analogy, the r_{12} of Formula 9.5 and implied in Formulas 9.6 and 13.3 is equivalent to the r_{xy}^2 of Formula 13.4. The sample variances must be equal or a single estimate made of the population variance. Suppose that the sampling variance of each mean is unity. Then Formula 9.5 becomes $\sqrt{2 - 2r_{12}}$ while Formula 13.4, less elegantly $\sqrt{(1 + 1)(1 - r_{xy}^2)}$, becomes $\sqrt{2 - 2r_{xy}^2}$ and the two formulas lead to the same t since $r_{12} = r_{xy}^2$.

When simple or randomized group analysis of variance (see pages 412–418) and Formula 13.4 are applied to the same data for two independent groups, the F obtained from application of the analysis of variance equals the square of the t obtained through use of Formula 13.4. The levels of significance are identical. When the two-way or randomized block analysis of variance with $n = 1$ and Formulas 9.5, 9.6, or 13.3 are applied to the data obtained from two groups of paired subjects, the F obtained in this type of analysis of variance will also equal the square of the t obtained by any one of the formulas just mentioned. Finally, with application of the analysis of covariance and Formula 13.4, to the same data for two groups, the F obtained will again equal the square of the t resulting from use of Formula 13.4. Of course, where the groups have been made initially "equivalent" through matching, analysis of covariance need not be applied.[17]

In view of what has just been said it seems odd to note recommendations of analysis of covariance rather than matching followed by use of the matched groups formula. When subjects are paired from the same population, as earlier noted, use of Formula 13.4 is legitimate. To be effective both this procedure and analysis of covariance require use of highly reliable and valid initial measures and the latter should

---

[17] For proofs see Eugene Shen, "Experimental Design and Statistical Treatment in Educational Research," *Journal of Experimental Education* 8 (March 1940), pp. 346–53; Max D. Engelhart, "The Analysis of Variance and Covariance Techniques in Relation to the Conventional Formulas for the Standard Error of a Difference," *Psychometrika* 6 (August 1941), pp. 221–33.

not be expected to compensate for more than minor lack of equivalence of groups.[18]

Analysis of gains or of posttest scores

Where pretests and posttests are equivalent forms of the same test, it is legitimate to compute gains whether or not the gains or the corresponding posttest scores are the data used with any of the standard error of difference formulas mentioned above. For the same data and the same formula, gains and posttest scores will result in the same t. Similarly, for the same data and the same kind of analysis of variance or covariance, the analysis will result in the same F. The pretest and posttest must yield comparable scores.[19]

It has been argued that measures of "true gains," "true change," "residual gains," "true residual gains," or a "base-free measure of change" should be used. All of these types of true score estimates are discussed in the references listed below.[20] Cronbach and Furby state, however,

> There appears to be no need to use measures of change as dependent variables and no virtue in using them. If one is testing the null hypothesis that two treatments have the same effect, the essential question is whether posttest Y_∞ scores vary from group to group. Assuming that errors of measurement of Y are random, Y is an entirely suitable dependent variable.[21]

This seems compatible with the previous statements. Why compute gains if posttest data alone yield the same t or the same F?

---

[18] See page 437.

[19] Max D. Engelhart, "A Note on the Analysis of Gains and Posttest Scores," *Educational and Psychological Measurement* 27 (Summer 1967), pp. 257–60.

[20] Frederic M. Lord, "The Measurement of Growth," *Educational and Psychological Measurement* 16 (Winter 1956), pp. 421–37; Quinn McNemar, "On Growth Measurement," *Educational and Psychological Measurement* 18 (Spring 1958), pp. 47–55; Frederic M. Lord, "Further Problems in the Measurement of Growth," *Educational and Psychological Measurement* 18 (Autumn 1958), pp. 437–51; Ledyard R. Tucker, Fred L. Damarin, and Samuel Messick, "A Base-Free Measure of Change," *Psychometrika* 31 (December 1966), pp. 457–73; Philip H. DuBois, "Correlational Analysis in Training Research," in Philip H. DuBois and G. Douglas Mayo, eds., *Research Strategies for Evaluating Training,* AERA Monograph Series on Curriculum Evaluation 4 (Chicago: Rand McNally, 1970), pp. 109–16; Charles E. Werts and Robert L. Linn, "Path Analysis: Psychological Examples," *Psychological Bulletin* 74 (September 1970), pp. 193–212.

[21] Lee J. Cronbach and Lita Furby, "How Should We Measure 'Change'—or Should We?" *Psychological Bulletin* 74 (July 1970), pp. 68–80.

Questions for
Study and Discussion

Many of these exercises require supplementary reading in one or more of the selected references.

1. How would you justify application of significance tests to data obtained in a quasi-experiment?

2. What does it mean to say that a statistical test is "robust"?

3. What is a treatment level?

4. What is a "nested" variable? Give an example.

5. When is it necessary to use an "incomplete block design"?

6. For what kinds of problems would it be advantageous to use a Latin square design?

7. What are the major threats to the validity of a repeated measures design?

8. What is the assumption of addivity of treatments? How is it related to interaction variances or mean squares?

9. For what kinds of comparisons between the means of several groups in an experiment is it legitimate to use the ordinary t test repeatedly?

10. What does it mean to say that the variables are completely crossed?

11. What advantage does a randomized block design have as compared with a randomized group design?

12. What is "data snooping"?

13. What might you learn from a significant treatments $\times$ schools variance?

14. What is a "split-plot" experimental design?

15. What may limit the usefulness of analysis of covariance?

Suggestions
for Further Study

Only a very few but widely used analysis-of-variance designs have been explained and illustrated in this chapter. The randomized group and randomized block designs are frequently the basis of *factorial* designs in which the various levels of two or more independent variables concurrently affect a dependent variable. If all possible combinations of the treatment levels are represented by measures of the dependent variable, the experiment may be a completely randomized group factorial or a randomized block factorial. (The treatment-by-levels design earlier discussed is a simple example of the latter having two levels of a treatment and five levels of a classification variable.) Factorial designs are also built from Latin squares and from incomplete blocks. Look for discussions of these designs among the texts and papers cited.

In further study the student should attempt to acquire greater understanding of the testing of assumptions, the making of multiple comparisons, and of the issues concerning estimation of the strength of relationship between an independent variable and a dependent variable in an experiment by means of ϵ^2, η^2, or ω^2 (epsilon squared, eta squared, and omega squared). See the 1953 text by Lindquist, p. 63, the 1963 text by Hays, pp. 381–84 and 406–07, and the May 1969 paper in the *American Educational Research Journal* by Glass and Hakstian.

The texts by Edwards, Ferguson, Lindquist and McNemar are most helpful in the study of experimental designs as is evidenced by the many citations in earlier pages. Lindquist's 1940 text is probably the best with which to begin and Winer's text is among the best for an advanced student. Kirk's text presents a table on page 12 which is a veritable taxonomy of experimental designs. Apart from its other excellences, the text by Walker and Lev contains a lucid explanation of the Johnson-Neyman technique.

The titles of most of the other references are indicative of their content. The second Engelhart reference lists equations for factorial analysis of covariance and diagrams useful in guiding substitution in these equations. It was written before models and electronic computers became generally available.

Improving Experimental Design and Statistical Analysis, edited by Julian Stanley, contains, in addition to Stanley's own paper, "Bayesian Approaches to Some Bothersome Problems in Data Analysis" by George E. P. Box; "Some Important Principles for the Use of Incomplete Designs in Behavioral Research" by Leslie D. McLean; "Experimental Design Considerations Associated with Large Scale Research Projects" by Frank B. Baker; and "Administrative Experimentation, Institutional Records, and Nonreactive Measures" by Donald T. Campbell.

The paper by Rita B. Johnson reports a randomized group experiment in which application is made of Duncan's New Multiple Range Test. Graham Nuthall reports two $4 \times 2 \times 3$ factorial analysis of variance in which there is pooling of the triple interaction with the within-cells error and four interaction diagrams. The experiment reported by Fred L. Pigge is an application of analysis of variance and covariance to weighted criterion means. Tests were made of homogeneity of variance and of regression. Since randomly selected schools were randomly assigned to the methods and the data were means rather than individual scores the schools $\times$ methods interaction was the error term. This is a recommended practice when intact classes must be used as the source of data.

The research reported by William E. Coffman and Dana Kurfman is an outstanding example of application of analysis of variance procedures to a measurement problem. Especially worth noting are the listed estimates of mean squares.

It should be emphasized that the statistical methods discussed in this chapter or those explained in advanced texts, while necessary in the interpretation of experimental data, do not insure that all types of error are taken into account. Systematic errors of measurement due to unequal testing times in giving pretests and posttests may limit the dependability of findings. The test or tests used in measuring achievement may be more valid with reference to one type of instruction than another. They may not range over all of the skills considered appropriate objectives of instruction. The unevaluated skills may be developed more effectively in one group than the other. Teachers are likely not to teach with equal zeal and skill in the different groups or with different methods or materials. In summary, important nonexperimental factors may not be controlled. Furthermore, it should be stressed that one experiment is seldom enough. Replication of the experiment in the same school, or better yet in several randomly selected schools, is strongly urged because the systematic errors referred to above may then become randomized and compensating, thus enhancing the dependability of conclusions.

Given an important experimental problem and a desire to contribute to the development of educational theory, it is essential that the experimenter should refrain from reporting findings until adequate attention has been paid to all important sources of error, and until replication has led to conclusions which justify decisions concerned with changes in instruction. Such conclusions cannot, of course, be "certainly true," but the probability of their truth should be such as to justify decisions of the kind just mentioned and, possibly, a place for them in educational theory—until modified, supplemented, or supplanted by later research.

Selected References

Bock, R. Darrell. "Contributions of Multivariate Experimental Designs in Educational Research." In *Handbook of Multivariate Psychology,* edited by Raymond B. Cattell, pp. 820–40. Chicago: Rand McNally, 1966.

Chen, Martin K. "A Critical Look at the Matching Technique in Experimentation." *Journal of Experimental Education* 35 (Summer 1967): 95–98.

Coffman, William E. and Dana Kurfman. "A Comparison of Two Methods of Reading Essay Examinations." *American Educational Research Journal* 5 (January 1968): 99–107.

Dixon, Wilfred J. and Frank J. Massey, Jr. *Introduction to Statistical Analysis.* 2nd ed. New York: McGraw-Hill, 1957.

Edwards, Allen L. *Statistical Methods.* 2nd ed. New York: Holt, Rinehart and Winston, 1967.

———. *Experimental Design in Psychological Research.* 3d ed. New York: Holt, Rinehart and Winston, 1968.

Elashoff, Janet D. "Analysis of Covariance: A Delicate Instrument." *American Educational Research Journal* 6 (May 1969): 383–401.

Engelhart, Max D. "The Analysis of Variance and Covariance Techniques in Relation to the Conventional Formulas for the Standard Error of a Difference." *Psychometrika* 6 (August 1941): 221–33.

———. "Suggestions With Respect to Experimentation Under School Conditions." *Journal of Experimental Education* 14 (March 1946): 225–44. [Includes the worked example of analysis of covariance with the permission of the publisher, Dembar Educational Research Service, Madison, Wisconsin.]

Feldt, L. S. "A Comparison of the Precision of Three Experimental Designs Employing a Concomitant Variable." *Psychometrika* 23 (December 1958): 335–53.

Ferguson, George A. *Statistical Analysis in Psychology and Education.* 3rd ed. New York: McGraw-Hill, 1971.

Glass, Gene V "Testing Homogeneity of Variance." *American Educational Research Journal* 3 (May 1966): 187–90.

——— and A. Ralph Hakstian. "Measures of Association in Comparative Experiments." *American Educational Research Journal* 6 (May 1969): 403–14.

——— and Julian C. Stanley. *Statistical Methods in Education and Psychology.* Englewood Cliffs, N. J.: Prentice-Hall, 1970. Chapters 15–19.

Hays, William L. *Statistics for Psychologists.* New York: Holt, Rinehart and Winston, 1963.

Johnson, Palmer O. *Statistical Methods in Research.* New York: Prentice-Hall, 1949.

—— and Robert W. B. Jackson. *Modern Statistical Methods: Descriptive and Inductive.* Chicago: Rand McNally, 1959.

Johnson, Rita B. "The Effects of Prompting, Practice and Feedback in Programed Videotape." *American Educational Research Journal* 5 (January 1968): 73–79.

Kirk, Roger E. *Experimental Design: Procedures for the Behavioral Sciences.* Belmont, Cal.: Brooks/Cole (Wadsworth), 1968.

Lindquist, E. F. *Statistical Analysis in Educational Research.* Boston: Houghton Mifflin, 1940.

——. *Design and Analysis of Experiments in Psychology and Education.* Boston: Houghton Mifflin, 1953.

Lord, Frederic M. "Large Sample Covariance Analysis When the Control Variable is Fallible." *Journal of the American Statistical Association* 55 (June 1960): 307–21.

Lubin, Ardie. "The Interpretation of Significant Interaction." *Educational and Psychological Measurement* 21 (Winter 1961): 807–17.

McNemar, Quinn. *Psychological Statistics.* 4th ed. New York: Wiley, 1969.

Millman, Jason and Gene V Glass. "Rules of Thumb for Writing the Anova Table." *Journal of Educational Measurement* 4 (Summer 1967): 41–51.

Nuthall, Graham. "An Experimental Comparison of Alternative Strategies for Teaching Concepts." *American Educational Research Journal* 4 (November 1968): 561–84.

Pigge, Fred L. "Analysis of Covariance in a Randomly Replicated Arithmetic Methods Experiment." *Journal of Experimental Education* 34 (Summer 1966): 73–83.

Stanley, Julian C. "Research Methods: Experimental Design," in "Methodology of Educational Research." *Review of Educational Research* 27 (December 1957): 449–59.

——, ed. *Improving Experimental Design and Statistical Analysis.* Seventh Annual Phi Delta Kappa Symposium on Educational Research. Chicago: Rand McNally, 1967.

Walker, Helen and Joseph Lev. *Statistical Inference.* New York: Holt, Rinehart and Winston, 1953.

Wilson, James W. and L. Ray Carry. "Homogeneity of Regression—Its Rationale Computation and Use." *American Educational Research Journal* 6 (January 1969): 80–90.

Winer, B. J. *Statistical Principles in Experimental Design.* 2nd ed. New York: McGraw-Hill, 1971.

14

Studying the Past: Educational Historiography

Research on events and ideas of the past in education can be a most challenging kind of inquiry. Many of the problems investigated require knowledge, skills, attitudes and ideals only acquired after years of training and experience. Other problems concerning the immediate past and locality seem to necessitate little more than the ability to read and write if one may judge from reports of research on such problems. The range of difficulty of problems and the range of ability of those who research in the history of education are striking.

Scientific characteristics of historical research

Historical research has some characteristics in common with scientific research of other kinds. According to the late Prof. Shotwell of Columbia University ". . . history involves two distinct operations, one of which, investigation, is in the field of science, while the other, the literary presentation, is in the field of art."[1] The scientific or investigatory aspects of historical research include (1) the defining of a problem, or the limiting of the scope of an inquiry; (2) the search for sources and the evaluation of their authenticity (external criticism); (3) the evaluation of the relevance, meaning, and dependability of the data obtained from the sources (internal criticism); (4) organization of data to secure an appropriate sequence which will reveal relationships; and (5) the formulation and testing of hypotheses resulting in generalizations which are accepted until disconfirmed.

---

[1] *Encyclopaedia Britannica*, 11th ed., s.v. "History."

Historical research on other than trivial problems requires critical thinking and scientific attitude. We mean by the latter seeking objectivity and suspending judgment pending adequate collection and evaluation of data.

History as an art

The quotation from Shotwell points out that the second of the two distinct operations involved in history, the literary presentation, is in the field of art. Presumably, the literary presentation should be characterized by clarity, logical organization, and effective style. The manner of presentation should sustain the reader's interest without biasing the meaning of the data in their interpretation.

Philosophies of history

Historical research has in its philosophies of history basic assumptions or postulates which are comparable to the basic assumptions of other sciences, e.g., there is a regularity in nature and its phenomena can be observed. These philosophies of history include the Greek, in which events are attributed to fate (*Qué será, será?*); the Christian, which holds, in part, that the fate of men and of nations is in God's hands,[2] the Great Man theory which credits important events to the magnetism of outstanding individuals; the Marxist materialistic philosophy which assumes that the character of a society depends on economic factors, especially its modes of production, and the philosophy of history associated with pragmatism (Peirce, James, Dewey and progressive education).

Who should do research in the history of education?

According to Merle L. Borrowman, the historians of the 19th century were largely concerned with political and military history. He notes that during the early part of the twentieth century such famous historians as James Harvey Robinson, Carl L. Becker, and Charles A. Beard began to promote "New History" which would include all aspects of culture— the economic, artistic, sociological, psychological, and educational. Thus such distinguished professional historians as Samuel Morison, Marcus Jernegan, and Merle Curti researched and published in the field of the history of education.[3] Examples of their research include:
Harvard College in the Seventeenth Century
by Samuel E. Morison (1936)

---

[2] *Ibid.*

[3] Merle L. Borrowman, "History of Education," in C. W. Harris, ed., *Encyclopedia of Educational Research,* 3rd ed. (New York: Macmillan, 1960), p. 662.

Laboring and Dependent Classes in Colonial America
by Marcus W. Jernegan (1931)
The Social Ideas of American Educators
by Merle Curti (1935)

Meanwhile, beginning about 1900 students of Paul Monroe at Teachers College, Columbia University, initiated research in the history of education, conducted by graduate students or staff members of departments of education. Some of the doctoral theses produced at Teachers College in Paul Monroe's time are

The Seven Liberal Arts by Paul Abelson (1906)

Later Roman Education in Ausonius, Capella, and the Theodosian Code by P. R. Cole (1909)

The Educational Views and Influence of DeWitt Clinton by E. A. Fitzpatrick (1911)

The Secularization of American Education as Shown by State Legislation, State Constitutional Provisions, and State Supreme Court Decisions by S. W. Brown (1912)

Early Quaker Education in Colonial Pennsylvania by Thomas Woody (1920)

Apprenticeship and Apprenticeship Education in Colonial New England and New York by Robert F. Seybolt (1917)

The historical research done at Teachers College and in the departments of education elsewhere was expected to inspire education students with a "sense of professional mission."[4]

Over the years, the professional historians, members of history departments and advocates of the New History, developed a considerable scorn for the "part-time" historians of the departments of education. In the "Foreword" to Bernard Bailyn's challenging *Education in the Forming of American Society,* Lester J. Cappon states that the history of American education "has suffered at the hands of specialists, who with the development of public education at heart, sought historical arguments to strengthen their 'cause.' If there was a story of the past worth writing, it was viewed from the narrow concept of formal instruction."[5] Bailyn's book supposedly illustrates how the early history of American education should be written—all about education and very little about schools.

William W. Brickman has effectively replied to Bailyn, reporting a number of instances in which distinguished academic historians have

---

[4] *Ibid.,* p. 663.

[5] Bernard Bailyn, *Education in the Forming of American Society* (New York: Random House [Vintage Books], 1960).

made use of the writings of the educational historians they have disparaged.[6]

While it is gratifying to see the latter thus defended, it must be admitted that there is need for more professionally-trained educational historians with interest in studying schools and other educational factors in the context of the culture of their time. We need more historians in departments of education like Robert Francis Seybolt, Lawrence Cremin, Newton Edwards, and Herman Richey.

Types of research problems dealing with history of education

The titles of historical educational research reports listed above are reasonably representative of different kinds of research in this field. If, however, one examines the list of titles of doctoral theses in the history of education under the heading "Educational History; Biography" in the Phi Delta Kappa *Research Studies in Education,* 1953–1963, it is evident that the most popular areas of interest are biographies of educators, histories of education in some local area, and histories of educational institutions, or of parts of an institution. Many of the titles indicate interest in the relatively recent past. Often the title includes the name of an educator or of an institution of purely local and ephemeral interest. The problems of such theses would seem to have offered little challenge to the student. The sources of his data were likely to be easily located, abundant, and transparently authentic. The production of the thesis probably required a minimum of critical thinking.

The same list, however, does include a number of titles comparable to those earlier given. For example:

The Massachusetts Schoolmaster, 1635–1775
by Norwood M. Cole (1957)
A Documentary History of Education in Colonial Georgia
by Robert Lawrence McCaul, Jr. (1953)
Horace Mann: The Early Years, 1796–1837
by Jonathan Carl Messerli (1963)

The Phi Delta Kappa list has 238 doctoral theses. Of these, 10 have titles relevant to colonial education and 12 are relevant to education in other countries. About one-third of the titles refer to 19th century education in the United States.

Abilities and other traits required for effective research in the history of education

The graduate student undertaking research in the history of education needs a galaxy of talents if his problem is other than a trivial one. He

---

[6] William W. Brickman, "Revisionism and the Study of History of Education," *History of Education Quarterly* 4 (December 1964), pp. 209–23.

should have interest in and knowledge of general history, United States history, and history of education. This knowledge should cover the relationships between the history of the colonies and the contemporaneous European history. It should include understanding the contributions to educational theory and practice of Protagoras, Socrates, Plato, Aristotle, Quintilian, Abelard, Aquinas, the Jesuits, Comenius, Rousseau, Pestalozzi, Herbart, and Froebel,[7] as well as an understanding of philosophy. Frequently a historical thesis concerns the ideas of some great educator or of one or more philosophers influencing him. In his biography of Colonel Francis Parker, Campbell discusses and documents the influences of Hegel, Herbart, and, particularly, Rousseau.[8] Consider the necessity of understanding scholasticism and pragmatism in order to write a thesis comparing the educational ideas of St. Thomas Aquinas and John Dewey.

Another essential in accomplishing effective research on recent educational history is a knowledge of the changes in our society—in its technology, in its conflicts in other aspects of its culture which have created the serious problems of our troubled times, including those in education.

Finally, if the problem concerns history of education in some other country than our own or in the distant past, language skills are usually required. The general absence of such skills may account for the paucity of research by graduate students and faculty members of departments of education in these areas.

Primary sources of historical data

Primary sources of educational research data include charters, laws, court decisions, institutional records, and minutes of school board meetings. These documents are official and, although generally considered dependable, the educational historian must be alert to the possibility of inconsistency or error. This is even more true of newspapers, magazines, letters, diaries, and autobiographies. Reminiscences and accounts of events written long after the events occurred are usually less reliable than diaries or personal letters. It is related that when General Sherman was told that his *Memoirs* were not accurate he defended them by saying, "These are *my Memoirs.* Events are described as *I* remembered them."

Advertisements in colonial newspapers were the primary source of data for the late Professor Seybolt in his studies of private school

---

[7] All are discussed in Harry S. Broudy, "Historic Exemplars of Teaching Method," in N. L. Gage, ed., *Handbook of Research on Teaching* (Chicago: Rand McNally, 1963), Chapter 1.

[8] Jack K. Campbell, *Colonel Francis W. Parker, The Children's Crusader* (New York: Teachers College Press, Columbia University, 1967), p. 134.

masters who taught evening schools.[9] One can be certain from these advertisements what courses were *offered* by the private school masters. One can infer with reasonable justification what courses were *taught* when advertisements of the same courses recur, since the school masters would not have been likely to continue to advertise if this were not the case. Incidentally, the advertisements pertain to an amazing variety of courses including navigation and "fluxions" (calculus).

While the enactment of a law often legalizes practices that were long current, one cannot be sure that this was the case. It can be inferred from the enactment of the Massachusetts Law of 1647—the "old deluder Satan law"—that the Law of 1642 concerning education had not been effective in insuring that parents and masters of apprentices had fulfilled their educational duties.[10]

In addition to official and unofficial documents, *remains* or *relics* are also primary sources of historical educational data. These include such physical objects as old school buildings and obsolete school equipment. Old school books are also remains so far as their content is concerned. The exercises in an elementary arithmetic text often require what would seem to modern eyes needlessly complex or time-consuming computations. I recall such a text of the 1880s in which an exercise asked the pupils to calculate the cost of several gills of whisky at so much a gill. A recent educational historian has deplored the moralizing in McGuffey Readers. Possibly such moralizing was compatible with aims of education accepted at the time the readers were widely used. Where the context of texts are thus evaluated, the text constitutes a remain. If, however, the text has a preface in which the author defines his goals, the preface constitutes a document since its author is stating a message to future readers.

A student planning to write a historical thesis should not select a problem until he has determined whether or not primary sources exist and will be available to him. Such sources may exist but at such a distance that a student may find it impractical to use them. (This problem is less serious than formerly with the development of duplicating services and machines.) It can be argued that the student or other historical investigator must collect at least a considerable portion of his data from primary sources if the report of his research is to be an "original" contribution.

---

[9] R. F. Seybolt, "The Evening School in Colonial America" and "Source Studies in American Colonial Education, The Private School," *Bureau of Educational Research Bulletins* No. 24 and No. 28 (Urbana: University of Illinois, 1925).

[10] Walter S. Monroe and Max D. Engelhart, *The Scientific Study of Educational Problems* (New York: Macmillan, 1936), pp. 165–66.

Secondary sources of historical data

Secondary sources are discussions of the past written by persons who have had access either directly or indirectly to primary sources. Secondary sources are useful in evaluating the data from primary sources and, conversely, the data from primary sources is similarly useful. The secondary source data, if essentially consistent with the primary source data, may supply details that can be legitimately included in the research report with appropriate citations of their source.

Locating sources of historical educational research data

The student planning a research in the history of education should make use of the aids in locating educational information mentioned in Chapter 4, including the card indexes of the library of his institution or nearby institutions. Libraries often have collections of documents or rare books of which he may remain ignorant unless he inquires. Visiting the stacks to locate some book for which the student has the author and title information may acquaint him with other books on the same shelf, relevant to the subject of interest. A reference librarian can supply welcome professional help when told the nature of the problem.

Recall from Chapter 4 how *Education Index* and *Dissertation Abstracts* may be used to locate earlier research on a problem. *Documentation in Education* by Arvid J. and Mary A. Burke is also extremely valuable in learning how and where to seek bibliographical and other educational information.

The bibliographies of books and articles on history of education have very useful reference lists of recent and earlier reports of historical educational research. Comments on many of these studies in the context of the book or article, or annotations accompanying the references, help the student to evaluate their relevance, importance, and dependability. Brickman's *Guide* is an especially notable aid of this kind.[11] More will be said about it in suggestions for further study.

External and internal criticism

External criticism is concerned with efforts to determine the authenticity of a document. This process involves determining who wrote the document, where he wrote it, when he wrote it, and why. The investigation may attempt to determine whether the document is an original or revised version, or one that contains deletions and additions. In addition there may be study of the physical characteristics—age, type of paper,

---

[11] William W. Brickman, *Guide to Research in Educational History* (New York: New York University Bookstore, 1949).

and so on.[12] External criticism may also make use of evidence *within* a document. For example, in a biography of Thomas Paine it is asserted that he wrote the *Declaration of Independence,* not Thomas Jefferson. The evidence given is the claim that, while Paine frequently used the word "hath" in his writings, Jefferson never used that word which appears frequently in the *Declaration.* Possibly Paine, who was not a member of the committee delegated to write the *Declaration,* said to Jefferson, "Look Tom, do not keep saying 'King George has . . . , say King George hath. . . .' It is much more impressive."

Internal criticism has as its purpose, in contrast with external, determination of the meaning of the statements in the document. External criticism may have shown that the document is genuine, but internal criticism is concerned with the literal and the actual meaning of the statements within the document. Was the author a witness of the events he describes? Was he biased or illogical? Did he immediately record his observations?[13] In his *The Oxford History of the American People,* Samuel Eliot Morison states with reference to the *Declaration:* "The bill of wrongs against George III and Parliament, naturally, is exaggerated. Facts will not sustain many of the 'injuries and usurpations.' "[14]

The *Declaration of Independence* can thus be used to illustrate both external and internal criticism. Many more examples are given in the books and articles on historiography listed among the selected references concluding this chapter.

NOTE-TAKING

Note-taking in general was briefly discussed on pages 74 to 80 of Chapter 4. The distinguished educational historian, H. G. Good, discussed this topic comprehensively in a series of articles on historical research in education. What he said on note-taking deserves further consideration.

> A note-system should be flexible, that is, it should be possible to add to it at any point without disarranging the older material; and it should be possible to rearrange the notes at will. This requires that the notes be taken on separate sheets, slips, or cards. Each piece should as far as possible contain a complete item, but when the matter to be noted is

---

[12] *Ibid.,* pp. 93–95.

[13] *Ibid.,* p. 94.

[14] Samuel Eliot Morison, *The Oxford History of the American People* (New York: Oxford University Press, 1965), p. 223.

too extensive it may be continued on successive pieces and these numbered in series. Not more than one item should ever be placed on a single piece. Each piece should have a subject-heading at the top and a margin for indexing, etc., at the left. For most kinds of historical note-taking two sizes of paper are desirable. . . . Probably the most useful sizes are the 3″ x 5″ or 4″ x 6″ cards for small items and the ordinary letter size paper for larger passages.

About three different kinds of notes are regularly made by historical workers. The first is the bibliographical note which always contains the standard data, author, title, pages, place and date of publication, and other formal facts about a document. It should usually have in addition a brief analysis of the contents and some account indicating the uses and the defects of the document. The second kind is the subject note which contains one item of information about a particular topic, with the source whence it was obtained. The great body of notes collected by any student will usually come under this head. One caution may be given here. Do not copy out long passages in readily available works but rather abbreviate and summarize. A third kind may be called the method notes. In collecting such material one constantly comes across suggestions or thinks of ideas which seem useful to interpreting the facts. Such suggestions or interpretive ideas do not fit into either subject or bibliographical entries, but they must be noted or they will be forgotten. Finally, when any extensive body of information is collected, an index and a more or less elaborate system of cross references become useful.[15]

Notes that are direct quotes should be enclosed within quotation marks to avoid unconscious plagiarism. This was pointed out in Chapter 4, but merits reiteration. While the bibliographical reference should contain inclusive pages of its source, each separate note should record its specific page or pages. The complete reference and each note, including the record of page or pages and quoted material, should be checked as soon as written, and checks entered adjacent to each item. Many libraries now have duplicating machines available to students. Rather than copy a long quotation, the page or pages can be duplicated for a small charge. When this has been done, be sure to enter notations in the margins of the duplicate pages, identifying their source. (Otherwise, you may be unwillingly subjected to external criticism!)

Finally, do not neglect to take notes on both sides of an issue, or on evidence to disprove a tentatively accepted hypothesis. This will be extremely important when future historical research will come to deal with current problems and issues.

---

[15] H. G. Good, "Historical Research in Education," *Educational Research Bulletin* 9 (February 5, 1930), pp. 77–78. Reprinted with permission of publisher.

Organization and interpretation of historical educational research data

Organization of historical data in chronological order may be useful to an educational historian in identifying aspects of the development of some educational movement, institution, or practice. On the other hand, a topical organization may be necessary if the research report is to be broad in scope and is to deal with related but differing events over an extended period. Often it is appropriate to organize in chronological order the data relevent to different topics, even though it necessitates numerous cross references.[16]

Special problems in interpreting historical data

Beyond the basic problems of external and internal criticism, authenticity and literal meaning, the interpretation of historical data in educational research involves some special problems. These include the determination of dates, the sources of an educational idea, primacy, influence, and authorship where the documents themselves do not present evidence concerning these things. Brickman's text presents a very interesting and informative discussion of these and other special problems that should be required reading.[17]

Primacy

Examples of the problems of primacy and influence can be offered from my own experience. In the discussion in Chapter 5 of the early history of the questionnaire, reference is made to its use by the Manchester Statistical Society in a survey of the "State of Education in the County of Rutland in the Year 1838." The search which led to this discovery was motivated by an article on Francis Galton in Paul Monroe's *Cyclopedia of Education* published in 1912. In this article Galton was credited with being the first to use a questionnaire. No such claim was made with reference to the Manchester Statistical Society. For all we know William the Conqueror collected the data used in the *Domesday Book* in this way. (Future historians should not use this as evidence that he did.) Palmer Johnson would seem reasonably safe in saying that "the Book of Numbers in the Old Testament is a simple example of a survey, a written record resulting from an enumeration or counting of the wealth of the tribe in terms of persons and animals.[18] He did *not* state, however, that this survey was the first. It is possible to find

---

[16] Brickman, *Guide to Research,* p. 181.

[17] *Ibid.,* pp. 116–60.

[18] Palmer O. Johnson, "Development of the Sample Survey as a Scientific Methodology," *Journal of Experimental Education* 27 (March 1959), p. 167.

instances in educational research literature of credit being given to persons who did not originate the formula or name of a statistic, for example, "part correlation" formerly called "semi-partial correlation."

Influence

In addition to primacy, the establishment of "influence" is often a difficult matter. I recall a thesis problem concerning the contributions of the Harvard philosophers James, Royce, and Santayana to American education. After its author received his degree a member of his committee commented that the thesis contained three excellent biographies!

After devising a "blueprint" for curriculum construction, an outstanding professor of education was accused in print of not having a philosophy, to which he replied, also in print: "I do have a philosophy. It is the absolute idealism of Josiah Royce."[19] This could have been, and possibly was, used as evidence of influence.

Generalizations, hypotheses, and causal relationships

It is recommended that historians should be cautious in generalizing, restricting their generalizing to the period, the area, the practices, and the type of persons for whom they have data. When stating a descriptive generalization it may be appropriate to say "some," "many," "most," or "few," rather than to say or imply "all" or "none."

Hypotheses should not be proposed until the available data have been thoroughly studied and, of course, facts should not be made to conform to a hypothesis. The investigator should not become unduly attached to a hypothesis and should be prepared to abandon it on discovery of even one contrary fact.[20]

It has been said that "history is not a listing of events. That is the area of the annalist or chronicler. To be history, the events must be brought into causal relationships."[21] While this may apply to history as a discipline, it surely does not apply to many individual historical researches, for example, Seybolt's studies of the private and evening schools in colonial America.

In concluding this discussion of the interpretation of historical data it should be emphasized that caution is essential in attributing effects to causes. While it is often justified to designate certain factors as

---

[19] See William Heard Kilpatrick, "Hidden Philosophies," *Journal of Educational Sociology* 4 (October 1930), pp. 59–68; and C. C. Peters, "Revealed Philosophies; A Reply to Professor Kilpatrick," *Journal of Educational Sociology* 4 (January 1931), pp. 260–71.

[20] See Gilbert J. Garraghan, *A Guide to Historical Method* (New York: Fordham University Press, 1946), pp. 350–67; Brickman, *Guide to Research,* pp. 166–67.

[21] Philip W. Perdew, "Criteria of Research in Educational History," *Journal of Educational Research* 44 (1950), pp. 217–23.

causes, it is usually wise to refer to such factors as "among the causes" rather than to insist on a given cause as *the* cause of a given effect. Finally, and especially with reference to causes, it is imperative to guard against bias.

As earlier noted, the writing of a report of historical research is an art. The student writing a thesis on a historical educational problem will find it useful to study Chapter 16 of this text and materials on this topic in the texts on historiography cited among the suggested references at the end of this chapter.

Questions for Study and Discussion

1. A seven-year-old when asked "What is history?" replied "Things that have happened." After being told there was more to it than that, he added "They must have been remembered." Evaluate his entire definition.

2. What is *argumentum ex silentio?* What are its limitations?

3. What are "canons" of historiography? Give examples.

4. For what types of historical problems could statistical methods be applied?

5. Discuss the possibility of research on the history of the testing movement in American education.

6. In what ways can historical methods be applied in the preparation of a critical summary of research on some non-historical research problem?

7. The names "The War of the Rebellion" and "The War Between the States" are symptoms of what?

8. Give examples of historical educational research for which it is essential to have knowledge of different philosophies.

9. Discuss the contribution of historical research to decision-making in education. Should the historian be involved?

Suggestions
for Further Study

The kinds of study which are suggested for effective research in the history of education are the reading of: (1) general histories, (2) histories of the United States, (3) histories of education, (4) writings on historiography, and (5) examples of historical research in education. No general histories are included among the selected references but a reference librarian, a history teacher, or an educational historian can name some good ones. One of Samuel Morison's histories of the United States is listed, as are several histories of American education. These include those by Bailyn (1960), Butts and Cremin (1953), Cremin (1964), Edwards and Richey (1963), Good (1962), Hofstadter and Smith (1961), Karier (1967), and Meyer (1965). Some other references are given to historical writings, for example, Broudy (1963), Brubacher and Rudy (1958), Good (1960), Handlin (1954), and Park (1965).

No references are listed for such classics on historiography as those of Bernheim, Croce, Fling, Langlois and Seignobos, Teggart, and von Ranke.[22] Among the selected references the student will find useful are Brickman (1949); the chapters in the *Review of Educational Research* by Mehl (1961), by Nash (1964), and by Burgess (1967); and the *Encyclopedia of Educational Research* articles by Borrowman (1960) and by Bayles (1969). All of these writings have very helpful bibliographies. Also concerned with historiography are the books by Bailyn (1960), Cremin (1965), Dow (1924), Garraghan (1946), Gottschalk (1950 and 1963), Hockett (1955), and Nevins (1962); and the articles by Brickman (1964), Good (1930), Nagel (1952), Timothy Smith (1961) and Wilson Smith (1961).

The other references are examples of reports of educational research. Note especially the publication of such reports in the *History of Education Quarterly* and the *Harvard Educational Review.*

---

[22] References to all but the last are given in Monroe and Engelhart, *Scientific Study,* pp. 160 and 164.

Selected References

Bailyn, Bernard. *Education in the Forming of American Society, Needs and Opportunities for Study.* Chapel Hill: University of North Carolina Press, 1960. [Also New York: Vintage Books, 1970.]

Bayles, Ernest E. "History of Education." In *Encyclopedia of Educational Research,* edited by Robert L. Ebel, pp. 602–07. 4th ed. New York: Macmillan, 1969.

Borrowman, Merle L. "History of Education." In *Encyclopedia of Educational Research,* edited by C. W. Harris, pp. 661–68. 3d ed. New York: Macmillan, 1960.

Brickman, William W. *Guide to Research in Educational History.* New York: New York University Bookstore, 1949.

———. "Revisionism and the Study of the History of Education." *History of Education Quarterly* 4:209–23; December 1964.

Broudy, Harry S. "Historic Exemplars of Teaching Method." In *Handbook of Research on Teaching,* edited by N. L. Gage. Chicago: Rand McNally, 1963. Chapter 1.

———, and John R. Palmer. *Exemplars of Teaching Method.* Chicago: Rand McNally, 1965.

Brubacher, Robert S., and Willis Rudy. *Higher Education in Transition.* New York: Harper, 1958.

Burgess, Charles. "History of Education," in "Philosophical and Social Framework of Education." *Review of Educational Research* 37 (February 1967): 21–33.

Butts, R. Freeman, and Lawrence A. Cremin. *A History of Education in American Culture.* New York: Holt, Rinehart and Winston, 1953.

Campbell, Jack K. *Colonel Francis W. Parker, The Children's Crusader.* New York: Teachers College Press, Columbia University, 1967.

Carbone, Peter F. "The School as an Agent of Social Change in the United States During the 1930's." *Pædagogica Historica* (International Journal of the History of Education) 9 (1969): 20–40.

Carpenter, Charles. *History of American Schoolbooks.* Philadelphia: University of Pennsylvania Press, 1963.

Cartwright, William H. "Brainwashing and the American Revolution." *Social Education* 29 (January 1965): 32–34.

Cremin, Lawrence A. *The Transformation of the School: Progressivism in American Education,* 1876–1957. New York: Knopf, 1961. [Vintage Books, 1964.]

————. *The Wonderful World of Ellwood Patterson Cubberley: An Essay on the Historiography of American Education.* New York: Bureau of Publications, Teachers College, Columbia University, 1965.

————. *American Education: The Colonial Experience (1607–1783).* New York: Harper and Row, 1970.

Dow, E. W. *Principles of a Note-System for Historical Studies.* New York: Appleton-Century-Crofts, 1924.

Edwards, Newton, and Herman G. Richey. *The School and the American Social Order.* 2nd ed. Boston: Houghton Mifflin, 1963.

Elson, Ruth Miller. *Guardians of Tradition: American Schoolbooks of the Nineteenth Century.* Lincoln: University of Nebraska Press, 1964.

Engelhart, Max D. "Colonel Francis Parker, the Cook County Normal School, and Dr. J. M. Rice." *Illinois School Journal* 48 (Spring 1968): 3–8.

See my review in the same issue of the Campbell biography cited above and the paper about Dr. J. M. Rice cited on page 377 of Chapter 12.

Garraghan, Gilbert J. *A Guide to Historical Method.* New York: Fordham University Press, 1946.

Good, H. G. "Historical Research in Education," *Educational Research Bulletin* (Ohio State University) 9 (January 8, January 22, and February 5, 1930): 7–18, 39–47, 74–78.

————. *A History of American Education.* 2nd ed. New York: Macmillan, 1962.

————. *A History of Western Education.* 2nd ed. New York: Macmillan, 1960.

Gottschalk, Louis R. *Understanding History: A Primer of Historical Method.* New York: Knopf, 1950.

————, ed. *Generalization in the Writing of History.* Chicago: University of Chicago Press, 1963.

Handlin, Oscar, compiler. *Harvard Guide to American History.* Cambridge: Harvard University Press, 1954.

Hockett, Homer C. *The Critical Method in Historical Research and Writing.* rev. ed. New York: Macmillan, 1955.

Hofstadter, Richard, and Wilson Smith, eds. *American Higher Education: A Documentary History.* Chicago: University of Chicago Press, 1961. 2 vols.

Karier, Clarence J. *Man, Society, and Education, A History of American Educational Ideas.* Glenview, Ill.: Scott, Foresman, 1967.

Mehl, Bernard. "History of Education," in "The Philosophical and Social Framework of Education." *Review of Educational Research* 31 (February 1961): 7–19.

Meyer, Adolph E. *An Educational History of the American People.* New York: McGraw-Hill, 1957.

Morison, Samuel Eliot. *The Oxford History of the American People.* New York: Oxford University Press, 1965.

Nagel, Ernest. "Some Issues in the Logic of Historical Analysis." *Scientific Monthly* 74 (March 1952): 162–69.

Nash, Paul. "History of Education," in "Philosophical and Social Framework of Education." *Review of Educational Research* 34 (February 1964): 5–21.

Nevins, Allan. *The Gateway to History.* rev. ed. Boston: Heath, 1962.

Park, Joe. *The Rise of American Education: An Annotated Bibliography.* Evanston, Ill.: Northwestern University Press, 1965.

Smith, Timothy L. "Progressivism in American Education, 1880–1900." *Harvard Educational Review* 31 (Spring 1961): 168–93.

Smith, Wilson, "The New Historian of American Education." *Harvard Educational Review* 31 (Spring 1961): 136–43.

Woody, Thomas. "Of History and Its Method." *Journal of Experimental Education* 15 (March 1947): 175–201.

15

Studying Problems
of What Should Be:
Curriculum Research

DETERMINING WHAT SHOULD BE

In preceding chapters three questions have been posed: (1) What
has been? (2) What is? (3) What will be? Questions asking what has
been known are historical. The second and third questions imply that
their answers may be found through application of "scientific" techniques of fact-finding, measurement, and prediction. A fourth question:
What *should* be? asks what is desirable in educational planning or
action. A school staff may ask: "What reporting system should we be
using to communicate pupil progress?" The staff may then raise subordinate questions about what percentage of pupils are currently classified at the various levels of a scale in use; how many staff members
favor a shift to a letter scale or a word scale, or combined letter scale
and personal conference; what the effect will be upon pupil motivation
and achievement if a specified change is adopted. Answers to some of
these secondary questions may be derived from objective data and regarded as *facts*. The culminating decision about which system should
be adopted represents a *judgment*.

A judgment is more than a mere opinion; it involves reflective thinking. A problem is defined; data are collected; and consideration is given
to probable consequences of adopting possible courses of action, one
of which is finally chosen as most likely to result in attaining the desired goal. For example, if the problem is to determine whether an
audiolingual course or a grammar-translation course should be employed in the modern language program of a particular elementary
school situation, comprehensive inquiry can be made, pertinent to that

situation. Data should be gathered about aptitudes of the pupils, preferences and professional preparation of the teachers, attitude of the community, and available equipment for instruction—both software and hardware. Descriptive and comparative studies of the two types of instruction can supply useful clues about the kinds of learner achievements and attitudes that can be expected from each of them. A judicious choice can be made after assessing the assembled information.

Problems of purposes

Questions about what should be are asked in many areas of the broad field of education: curriculum, administration and organization, guidance, housing and maintenance of buildings, fiscal provisions, and community relations, to name a few. The following are illustrative of such problems of purposes:

1. What means should be used to tap community resources represented in the adult specialists available to us?
2. What are the merits of flexible scheduling for this high school?
3. To what extent should students participate in our school administration?
4. What is the value of non-graded organization at the primary level?
5. Should direct teaching about environment and natural resources be incorporated into the curriculum?
6. What should be the scope of the physical education program?
7. What should be the relations between the chief administrative and maintenance officers of the school or institution?
8. How should the construction of the proposed new school building be financed?

Such problems involve two types of query: about (1) objectives and (2) means. For example, consider the first question in the preceding list: "What means should be used to tap community resources represented in the adult specialists available to us?" In attempting to answer this question about means, the investigator must first consider the prime objective to be attained. Is promotion of better school-community relations the primary desire? Or enrichment of the instructional program? Or provision for occupational guidance? After a decision about the goals is made, there remains the question of means: when, where, how may adult experts be brought into the school program most effectively and efficiently—and who should they be—according to the defined goals. The question about the value of flexible scheduling in the high school may be analyzed differently: (1) What are the reported learning outcomes of this form of organization? (2) What is contributed by these outcomes to the overall objectives of this school? (3) What are the management factors involved: the use of teacher talent, time, equipment, space, in the interest of effective learning? The second question, of course, implies an established definition of the objectives of the school. The determination of objectives, overall or immediate, requires procedures commonly designated as *philosophical.*

The philosophical method

The procedures employed in dealing with problems of what is or what will be are, in general, those of *scientific inquiry.* Examples are: survey techniques, analysis of validated records, experimentation, dependence on statistical techniques in the analysis of data and in reporting the outcomes of the investigation. Such procedures are useful in searching for answers to questions like these: (1) What are the predominant time allotments given to reading and English in the elementary schools of our state? (2) What is the average pupil-teacher ratio in the middle schools of Center City? Precision and fact-finding are hallmarks of scientific inquiry.

Not all problems of education, however, can be answered by factual inquiry alone. Some draw upon a wide range of data that cannot be collected by means of the techniques described in Chapters 5, 6, and 7. Questions such as the following call for use of the procedures of the *philosophical* method: (1) What should be the pupil-teacher ratio in the middle school? (2) Should chronological age be the sole criterion for initial enrollment in Grade 1? These questions cannot be answered solely by factual inquiry, although facts are used in arriving at answers. Using the procedures of the philosophical method, the investigator includes the results of his own experience and ferrets out the observations and beliefs of other persons. He draws upon principles from related fields. He is especially sensitive to implications, to values,[1] to underlying purposes. As he works with his data his method is not necessarily statistical. In testing his hypotheses he is concerned with the relations of their implication to experience and to general principles. Soltis[2] and others have discussed recently the relation of philosophy of education to educational science.

The method of philosophy is less readily described than are the scientific techniques discussed in preceding chapters. Also, because of its non-overt, subjective nature, its procedures are not easily submitted to the same sort of scrutiny that is possible for a technique such as securing equivalent groups by pairing learners on the basis of significant characteristics. We can, however, consider the principal

---

[1] For an excellent and applicable discussion, see Abraham Kaplan, "Values in Inquiry," in *The Conduct of Inquiry* (San Francisco: Chandler Publishing Company, 1964), pp. 370–87.

[2] Jonas F. Soltis, "Philosophy of Education: A Fourth Dimension," *Teachers College Record* 67 (April 1966), pp. 524–31.

phases of the method of philosophical thinking as it is applied to those problems of education that ask what should be.

Design in philosophical method

In general design the method of philosophy is basically the same as that described as the method of research in Chapter 2. The researcher defines his problem, collects data, formulates hypotheses and tests them. In defining his problem, the philosophical truth-seeker seeks to identify the fundamental questions involved and to formulate the assumptions upon which the solution of the problem is based. He may be guided by his own experience in making these assumptions, but typically he consults sources in related fields.[3] The validity of these assumptions rests on the availability and dependability of existing human knowledge brought to bear on the problem. It is also conditioned by the intelligence of the investigator, his beliefs, his prejudices—in other words, by all factors that influence the quality of his thinking.

In the study of problems of purposes, the interpretation of data is carried out by formulating hypotheses and testing them, in turn, if necessary, by all available criteria until the most satisfactory one is identified. The formulation of hypotheses is conditioned by the investigator's sensitivity to the meaning of the data, his knowledge of the field of the problem, his mental qualifications, and his personal philosophy of life. Some hypotheses are bound to prove unsatisfactory. The important concerns should be that each hypothesis is carefully checked against the criteria and that an acceptable one is eventually found. This tested hypothesis is the conclusion; it is the answer to the problem. However, the critical investigator will regard it as a judgment, subject to modification if discovery of new data so warrants.

In earnest self-examination the researcher using the philosophical method submits to critical scrutiny his entire procedure and his tentative conclusions. He asks himself: (1) "Have I been logical in my thinking about the matter?" (2) "Have I considered all that is relevant to the situation?" (3) "Have I been openminded in arriving at a decision?" (4) "Have I suspended judgment long enough to arrive at a decision that is a reasonably sound basis for action?" One test of the defensibility of a decision is its power to generate further thinking about the problem. The ultimate test of the worth of the decision will be found in the consequences of acting accordingly.

---

[3] Traditionally, favorite fields have been psychology, history of education, and educational sociology. For new trends, note Ernest E. Bayles, *Pragmatism in Education* (New York: Harper and Row, 1966); Thomas Green, "Teaching, Acting, and Behaving," *Harvard Educational Review* 34 (Fall 1964), pp. 507–24; Van Cleve Morris, *Existentialism in Education* (New York: Harper and Row, 1966).

Objective techniques and philosophical procedure

Although solving a problem of purposes depends undeniably on judgment, and the total procedure is markedly subjective, objective techniques may contribute significantly to the solution. Facts and principles are needed for making defensible decisions. For example, a school administrator considering the introduction of computer-aided instruction will surely wish to know the effect of machine-teaching upon student achievement. He will need facts about cost, space requirements, special-teacher availability. He will probably wish to learn about practices in other schools similar in characteristics and resources.

After an assumption or hypothesis is derived, objective techniques often prove useful in data-gathering. If the hypothesis is proposed that students should learn to write notes and letters in the forms that adults currently employ, objective techniques may be used to determine which forms are actually being written by adults today, and the frequency of their composition.

Thus in practice, the distinction between scientific research and "philosophical" research breaks down. A person dealing with purposes frequently needs the aid of objective techniques, and workers in the fields of science must at times engage in philosophizing. The need for philosophizing is especially important in experimental research. When a question is raised about the relative effectiveness of two procedures or practices, the assumption is generally made that an experimental attack upon the problem will lead to an acceptable decision; and yet when the problem is adequately defined, such an assumption may turn out to be unsound.

Dependability

Objectivity of data should not be considered the sole criterion of the *dependability* of a conclusion. If the data are highly objective, some persons declare the conclusion to be scientific and endow it forthwith with dependability. Conversely, if the data are relatively subjective, these persons consider the conclusions to be unscientific and therefore lacking dependability. However, as the discussion on faults of data in Chapter 9 and their significances in specified types of research in Chapters 11–13 pointed out, objectivity of data does not guarantee dependability of conclusions.

When the data are accurate, valid, and adequate for the requirements of the problem, a conclusion derived from them is said to be dependable. Even when the data are not wholly satisfactory, a conclusion derived from them may still be shown to be dependable, in spite of admitted limitations. A conclusion reached by the methods of science is called dependable when it appears strongly probable that a replication of the investigation would result in essentially the same conclusion. Applied to the conclusions reached by the methods of philosophy, the designation of "dependable" requires some modification of meaning. For such conclusions the criteria of dependability are implied in the questions: (1) "Was the problem adequately defined?" (2) "Were the basic assumptions recognized and understood?" (3) "Were there any pertinent data overlooked?" (4) "Was the thinking unbiased and critical?" (5) "Were the probable consequences of the conclusion adequately considered?" It is difficult to foresee the consequences of a conclusion. In some cases they are revealed only as time passes. Hence, the testing of philosophical thinking frequently extends into the future. Like wonder drugs, the wonder tools of education are often declared to have harmful side effects as years pass. For instance, the soundness of the once widely acclaimed conclusion that ability grouping should prevail in our schools has been challenged, not on the grounds of its effect on learning achievement, but rather of its effect upon our society.

Since dependability of conclusions in philosophy does not have the same meaning as dependability of findings in science, a comparison can have limited significance. It seems reasonable to say, however, that the conclusions reached by a competent and critical investigator, relative to a problem of purposes, may be highly dependable, and deserving of as much confidence as that given to reports of scientific findings in the field of education.

RESEARCH TECHNIQUES IN CURRICULUM STUDY

The meaning of curriculum research

Since the field of curriculum research supplies a large number of the questions that ask what should be in education, the application of research techniques in this field needs to be discussed more explicitly. The term *curriculum research* is variously defined. According to Henderson, it is a form of inquiry that "studies the relation between subject matter taught a student and his behaviors subsequent to having been taught it and which are relevant to it."[4] According to Tyler's classic rationale these are the four fundamental questions to be answered in this field:

1. What educational purposes should the school seek to attain?
2. What educational experiences can be provided that are likely to attain these purposes?

---

[4] Kenneth B. Henderson, "Research on Teaching Secondary School Mathematics," in N. L. Gage, ed., *Handbook of Research on Teaching* (Chicago: Rand McNally & Company, 1963), p. 1008.

3. How can these educational experiences be effectively organized?
4. How can we determine whether these purposes are being attained?[5]

Others have heard a different drummer, and stepped to the music they hear, among them Israel Scheffler, who suggests stimulatingly novel criteria for assessing purposes of education.[6]

Although curriculum research has been explained in a number of other ways during the past twenty years, consensus still prevails that the term signifies: (1) systematic inquiry concerning desirable goals students are expected to attain; (2) instructional procedures and materials; and (3) evaluation of the attainment of desired change.[7]

Determination of objectives takes top priority as a curriculum problem, or complex of problems, since learning activities and materials of instruction are essentially means, and evaluation of achievement is keyed to the outcomes specified as the objectives.

Reference is frequently made to "scientific curriculum inquiry," and examination of current curriculum studies reveals many applications of objective techniques. However, judgment is also necessary, in providing objectives which the procedures of science sometimes fail to discover. For example, objectives which have to do with the beautiful and of the good, and those which may be postulated as more important in the future than in the present, will not be revealed by activity analyses of the lives of the adults of this generation. Inquiry in this field demonstrates clearly the usefulness of the complementary services of scientific and philosophical procedures in problem-solving.

The function of curriculum research

The function of curriculum research is twofold: (1) to construct new educational programs—horizontally by "grade" levels, or vertically by subject fields—and (2) to reform or revise existing programs, in order to accommodate to a world changing at whirlwind speed. The well publicized "knowledge and population explosions," international developments, heightened concern about the environment, and technological advances, all have had staggering implications for education. These events have instigated inquiry with reference to extension and placement of curriculum content, additional provision for the socially

---

[5] Ralph W. Tyler, *Basic Principles of Curriculum and Instruction* (Chicago: The University of Chicago Press, 1950), pp. 1–2.

[6] Israel Scheffler, "Philosophical Models of Teaching," *Harvard Educational Review* 35 (Spring 1965), pp. 131–43.

[7] For an innovative plan of curriculum research, see Joseph J. Schwab, "The Practical: A Language for Curriculum," *The School Review* 78 (November 1969), pp. 1–23.

and educationally disadvantaged, individualization of instruction, increased federal aid for developing programs and materials, and undoubtedly will instigate a host of other investigations.

Setting of goals

A statement of the educational philosophy, values, and aims characterizing a school, school system, or college indicate the conduct goals—the *ultimate objectives*—of a curriculum. Statements of content, of instructional and guidance goals constitute the *immediate objectives* of the curriculum, and are expected to be compatible with the broad, ultimate aims. The concern of philosophers and statesmen, as well as teachers, with the purposes of education go back to antiquity. The significance of current aims acquires greater meaning when they are studied in relation to the contrasting cultures of the past as well as of the present. Since 1893, national committees and commissions have disseminated reports of their efforts to define and refine educational aims and goals. The novice in curriculum research should become acquainted with those who delved before him.

Instructional objectives are often suggested in the prefaces of textbooks, and are usually listed in curriculum guides for instruction. Some of the clearest and most specific statements may be found in the writings of experts in educational measurement.[8] These sources are especially helpful in classification and definition of objectives as well as in their descriptions of means of evaluating outcomes of instruction.

One of the most important duties of curriculum study is identification of realizable goals for students who range widely in abilities and personal traits. Study of the nature and range of individual differences in educational psychology contributes greatly to teacher understanding of realizable goals. It should be stressed, however, that desirable objectives should not be hastily condemned as unattainable simply because evaluation indicates that they have not yet been satisfactorily realized. For example, it is a fallacy to assume that students of limited ability cannot acquire many of the skills basic to critical thinking. While their instruction may need modification in order for them to acquire these skills, their goals should not be restricted to that which it is *thought* they can assimilate. Their power may be augmented through research, through experimentation and through the devising of new techniques and procedures.

---

[8] See Benjamin S. Bloom, D. R. Krathwohl, and B. B. Masia, *Taxonomy of Educational Objectives, The Classification of Educational Goals: Cognitive and Affective Domains* (New York: McKay, 1969); Tyler, *Basic Principles*, pp. 58–62; and Benjamin S. Bloom, J. Thomas Hastings, and George F. Madaus, *Handbook on Formative and Summative Evaluation of Student Learning* (New York: McGraw-Hill, 1971).

To illustrate, recent research may influence the future course of differentiating instruction for the individual learner. Theories of learning recently discussed hold promise for the slow learner. Carroll[9] suggests that the key to mastery may be the *pace* of the learning process; Bloom[10] reports on recent laboratory experimentation involving five variables in mastery learning strategy. Both Bruner[11] and Scriven[12] similarly stimulate new thinking about differentiation of instruction tailored to individual needs. In setting up goals for the poor achiever, the curriculum researcher should recognize that the case is far from closed.

Specificity in stating objectives

Often a distinction is made between "content" objectives and "behavioral" ones, even though content objectives can be stated in behavioral terms. An objective of English instruction may be listed: "Rewriting sentences to shift from passive to active voice." Stated in this form the objective specifies how the learner should behave or act. It is thus a *behavioral* definition. Similarly, an objective of science instruction may be "applying general principles in solving novel problems." As a practical matter, however, so long as the corresponding behavior is clearly implied, there is no reason why the objectives just mentioned should not be stated in the more familiar phraseology: "The ability to rewrite sentences to shift from passive to active voice" or "The ability to apply general principles in solving novel problems."

The objective in English instruction just cited has the desirable attribute of *specificity*. It would suggest to a competent English teacher the kind of learning experiences which would implement its attainment. It would also suggest to the test maker, whether teacher or test specialist, the kind of test exercises suitable for appraising the measure of attainment. The science objective cited, however, is much too general to be used without further definition. It needs to be related to the content or content objectives of instruction, to the general principles that

---

[9] John Carroll, "A Model of School Learning," *Teachers College Record* 64 (May 1963), pp. 723–33.

[10] Benjamin S. Bloom, "Learning for Mastery," in Benjamin S. Bloom and others, *Handbook on Formative and Summative Evaluation.*

[11] Jerome S. Bruner, *Toward a Theory of Instruction* (Cambridge: Harvard University Press, 1966).

[12] Michael Scriven, "The Methodology of Evaluation," in Robert E. Stake, ed., *Perspectives of Curriculum Evaluation,* AERA Monograph Series on Curriculum Evaluation 1 (Chicago: Rand McNally & Company, 1967), pp. 39–83. The second monograph in this important series is *Evaluation Activities of Curriculum Projects: A Starting Point* by Hulda Grobman. The third is *Instructional Objectives* by W. James Popham and others. The fourth in the series is cited on page 444 of Chapter 13 and the fifth on page 168 of Chapter 7.

the learners are to be expected to understand and apply, and to the classroom problems to be presented as exemplification of those principles.

Classification of instructional objectives

One way of classifying or ordering instructional objectives is to think of them thus:

1. Knowledge and skills used repetitively in specific situations.
2. Understandings and intellectual skills of applying knowledge or proficiency to novel problems.
3. Attitudes, ideals, interests, and appreciations.

Under the first heading come the concepts students should readily recall and the kinds of skills which should become habitual, with little or no reflective thinking needed in their utilization. In the second category are included the abilities and intellectual skills required in the solution of new or thought-provoking problems. Into the third category go all behaviors, or traits underlying behaviors, that are factors influencing what a learner *will* do in a variety of situations, as contrasted with what he *can* do. The behaviors thus characterized are in order of increasing difficulty for instruction and for evaluation.

In a social science general course, a group of instruction designers, enthusiastic about the general behavioral objectives they designated "critical thinking," drafted more specific objectives:

1. Identification of a central issue or problem
2. Recognition and understanding of assumptions
3. Identification of hypotheses tested by data
4. Analysis of argument in respect to bias, emotional factors, and propaganda devices
5. Distinguishing between facts, opinions, and value judgments
6. Analysis of argument with respect to its logic
7. Evaluation of data or evidence
8. Identification of conclusions or inferences supported or not supported by data
9. Understanding of relationships
10. Prediction of consequences or effects

It can be readily seen that for effective use in instruction and in evaluation these *behavioral* objectives require a complementary outline of *content* objectives.

Selection and organization of learning experiences

An outline of the content of instruction to reflect the order in which the content is to be taught should be organized. Such an outline needs to be quite detailed and should define or imply the behavioral objectives that can be classified under the heading of knowledge or understandings.

In curriculum construction it is essential to identify those learning activities and materials of instruction appropriate to a given educational level and to a given area of instruction. Skills in the fundamentals of mathematics, in reading with comprehension, and in oral and written composition are of prime importance in elementary education; however, need for *remedial instruction* at other levels in the educational system requires suitable modification of activities, materials, and pace. Similarly, the development of skills in understanding and using algebraic symbols and equations, in critically evaluating philosophical ideas, and in understanding and applying advanced scientific principles is not appropriate until students have reached later stages of learning maturity, or higher levels of education.

The importance of appropriate *sequence* of learning opportunities is obvious in the case of *acquisition of knowledge.* For example, students who have earlier learned that light from an object moving away from an observer has the lines in its spectrum shifted toward the red are better able to understand evidence supporting the theory that our universe is expanding.

Appropriate sequence of learning experiences is just as necessary to the *acquisition of intellectual skills.* In learning to interpret data presented in a line graph, students need first to learn about axes at right angles to each other which have scales of units measured from zero at their intersection. They next learn that the trend of the line is defined by points whose positions are fixed by their horizontal and vertical distances, or coordinates, measured from the two axes. The students may learn somewhat later that generalizations should not be based on the data thus presented unless the data are accurate and representative. Still later they may learn that inferences which are extrapolations or predictions are less certain than inferences relevant to the trend within the data portrayed by the line.

Sequences of learning experiences also contribute to *development of desirable attitudes.* For example, the scientific attitude is probably most likely to characterize learners benefiting from a long series of learning experiences in a variety of scientific contexts of increasingly complex nature—experiences through which students gradually come to recognize the merit of the attitude and to show it in their problem solving.

Instructional measurement and curriculum evaluation

Properly, *measurement of achievement* means measurement or *prediction* of what learners can or will do in other than the testing situation. The scope of instructional measurement is wide, encompassing as it does the learners' knowledge, understandings, abilities, skills, attitudes, ideals, and appreciations. Present emphasis on behavior, or behaviors, reflects the realization that assessment of the learners' gains is necessarily inference derived from observation of student behavior or performance.

Curriculum evaluation may be considered a data-gathering process in the interest of decision-making. In current usage it appears to designate three ways in which the data are put to use. At the level of the local school, evaluation stresses (1) measurement of pupil progress toward specified instructional objectives. At the system or state level it commonly means assembling information to be the basis for considering (2) curriculum revision or (3) curriculum adoption. Scriven refers to (2) as *formative* evaluation and to (3) as *summative evaluation*.[13] All three are fertile fields for future research endeavors.

Curriculum inquiry

The prospective investigator seeking a researchable problem for thesis or dissertation is advised to explore the professional literature of the field of his special interest. As a starter, he is urged to examine recent issues of the *Review of Educational Research,* pertinent articles in the *Encyclopedia of Educational Research* and in the *Handbook of Research on Teaching* for identification of major references. A recent compilation of readings such as that by Short and Marconnit[14] offers a comprehensive overview through articles by curriculum specialists. Scanning the writing on the many facets of this broad subject may suggest a hitherto unfamiliar subtopic in need of investigation. Another way of finding a problem to study is through perusal of earlier studies. Sometimes a study is discovered that is in need of replication with improved procedures.

Thoughtful reading of related inquiries will typically serve as a stimulus to the creativity of the would-be researcher, and will help him come up with several possibilities for investigation. In settling upon one of them for his research study, he should weigh several factors: the significance of the problem, his own scholarship and personal qualifications, access to sources of pertinent data, and estimated expenditure of time and money.

For curriculum inquiry the researcher should be able to draw upon

---

[13] Scriven, "Methodology," in AERA Series on Curriculum Evaluation 1, pp. 40–43.

[14] Edmund C. Short and George D. Marconnit, eds., *Contemporary Thought on Public School Curriculum: Readings* (Dubuque: Wm. C. Brown Publishers, 1968). Others of interest are William M. Alexander, ed., *The Changing Secondary School Curriculum* (New York: Holt, Rinehart and Winston, 1967); Robert E. Chasnoff, ed., *Elementary Curriculum* (New York: Pitman Publishing Company, 1964); Forrest E. Conner and William J. Ellena, eds., *Curriculum Handbook for School Administrators* (Washington, D.C.: American Association of School Administrators, 1967).

a goodly fund of *background knowledge* of related behavioral sciences, of societal purposes and concerns, of current preoccupations of children and youth. He should have, or acquire, professional understanding of theories of learning and the learning process, of human growth and development patterns, of the nature of knowledge itself. For any investigator in the field of curriculum, familiarity with formal research methods is a necessity, but if he is interested in controlled experiments, he must have at least basic training in statistics, especially the analysis of variance.

In *selecting a problem* and formulating questions to be answered, or hypotheses to be tested, the researcher should be guided by the rule of the possible: what can be fairly and precisely defined and assessed with the resources at his command? In curriculum studies the significance of the results is too often diminished by the choice of outsize variables. The *research proposal* should make every aspect clear: what the problem is, what the hypotheses mean exactly, how the data are collected, what population is sampled, what statistical treatment is applied to the data. Too often the "population" is not sufficiently specified. The hallmark of a good research study is *specificity.*

In curriculum inquiry, as in all research, the design is of paramount importance. The *research design* or plan devised for any inquiry must control variance and at the same time economically lead, hopefully, to valid, accurate answers to the questions in the research proposal. The procedures and instruments of traditional descriptive research have tended to dominate curriculum inquiry. The systematic process-oriented type of descriptive research and the methods of experimental research involving the instructional procedures and materials actually used, should gain a significant place in curriculum planning and reform. Computer-assisted instruction offers opportunity for experimental evaluation of programmed materials without interference of extraneous teacher factors. The future innovator or reformer in the field of curriculum will have use for his knowledge of the data interpretation content of Chapters 11–13 in this book.

With his particular problem in mind, the researcher should review the data-gathering means at his disposal and reflect on his capabilities in respect to statistics. Rereading Chapter 10 in this book should refresh his memory concerning resources available for studying existing conditions of learning in the particular situation he is studying. I am reminded at this point of a local instance of community survey in progress. A study committee appointed by the board of education of a neighboring community[15] has just distributed questionnaires to parents and

---

[15] Chapel Hill, North Carolina.

students to elicit both opinions and recommendations concerning curriculum change, home-school relations and communication, and issues of discipline. Such canvassing of community opinion and provision for involvement is a commendable preliminary to curriculum revision, and should contribute to acceptance of resulting changes. This questionnaire, as an instrument for collecting data in this case, serves the intended purpose of wide-scale sampling of current opinion. It may have, of course, the limitations of its kind: the quantitative and qualitative nature of the responses returned to the committee will indicate its usefulness as a data-gathering instrument. In general, consensus studies as well as studies of present practices tend to be weighted by tradition. This limitation may be offset somewhat by including in the research design provision for getting recommendations of specialists in the field under study. There are sure to be some among these professionals of innovative orientation, who will have compensating ideas for the future in classrooms.

In devising his research design, the investigator should consider thoughtfully the range of data-collecting methods. Support for this will be found in Chapters 5–7 of this book. He will have opportunity to put into action his acquired knowledge of the processes of descriptive statistics for *summarizing* his data (see Chapter 8 for review), and of *interpreting* his data through statistical inference (Chapter 9).

If the researcher has elected to study a problem of learning difficulty or of instructional method and materials, and his reserve of time and facilities warrant, he may well utilize his knowledge of cross-section and longitudinal techniques discussed in Chapter 10. If his situation and interest permit laboratory or field experimentation, knowledge of the content of Chapters 11–13 is vital to his analysis and *conclusion.*

Finally, mention should be made of the importance of deft use of appropriate instruments in the research study. Not so long ago, only paper-and-pencil tools were available for collecting data on learner performance. Tests, pupil products, and crude forms of note-taking by observers had to suffice in recording responses of subjects. Today, scale items refine response-recording in interviews. Tape recordings preserve the facts of interviewing—for later review and evaluation (see Chapter 5). Kinescopes of observations, Flanders' categories and other observation systems are available for research utilization (Chapter 6). Automation in data-processing, and even in instruction, extends the possibilities for educational research and action. These new devices and machines are welcome instruments in curriculum inquiry—if properly operated by a critical, philosophical human mind.

Questions for
Study and Discussion

1. In seeking answers to the following questions, to which ones would you apply procedures of the *philosophical* method? Why?
   a. Should the school year be lengthened in our system?
   b. How does Teachers Manual A compare with Teachers Manual B in making provision for independent study?
   c. What proportionate place should be given in the junior college to general and specialized education?
   d. Should students be involved in the process of evaluating their individual progress in school?
   e. What special-subject assistance for elementary school teachers is now provided in our state?

2. How should teaching about environment and natural resources be incorporated into the curriculum? (Consider subquestions pertaining to implementation of "environmental sciences," and inter-disciplinary program of study, grade placement, the teacher-training program.)

3. What are the advantages and the disadvantages of *nongrading* at the primary level in our system?

4. What do you think of recent predictions that the pendulum of change is due to swing:
   a. toward a curriculum design combining the discipline-centered and the problem-centered approach?
   b. toward a return of core or broad-field patterns of curriculum organization?

5. In a local school, what are the necessary *administrative arrangements* for comprehensive curriculum revision?

6. In a local school, what are the appropriate *personnel responsibilities* for carrying out proposed curriculum changes?

Suggestions
for Further Study

If this chapter has pointed some directions for the curriculum researcher, it has served its purpose. Because of the vast scope and ramifications of curriculum inquiry the reader is urged to explore the specialized treatments in related fields of educational psychology, subject instruction, and evaluation. He is referred also to more comprehensive treatments such as those suggested in the selected references.

Selected References

The Philosophical Approach

Broudy, Harry S. *Paradox and Promise: Essays on American Life and Education.* Englewood Cliffs, N.J.: Prentice-Hall, 1961.

Peters, Richard S. *Authority, Responsibility, and Education.* London: George Allen and Unwin, 1965.

Scheffler, Israel. "Philosophical Models of Teaching," *Harvard Educational Review* 35 (Spring 1965): 131–43.

Smith, B. Othanel, and Robert H. Ennis, eds. *Language and Concepts in Education.* Chicago: Rand McNally, 1966.

Venable, Tom C. *Philosophical Foundations of the Curriculum.* Chicago: Rand McNally, 1967.

Curriculum Inquiry

Bloom, Benjamin S., D. R. Krathwohl, and B. B. Masia. *Taxonomy of Educational Objectives, the Classification of Educational Goals: Cognitive and Affective Domains.* New York: McKay, 1969.

Bruner, Jerome. *Toward a Theory of Instruction.* Cambridge: Harvard University Press, 1966.

Fraser, Dorothy M. *Current Curriculum Studies in Academic Subjects.* Washington, D.C.: National Education Association, 1962.

Frazier, Alexander, ed. *The New Elementary School.* Washington, D.C.: Association for Supervision and Curriculum Development, 1968.

Gagné, Robert M. *The Conditions of Learning.* New York: Holt, Rinehart and Winston, 1965.

Goodlad, John I. *The Changing School Curriculum.* New York: Fund for the Advancement of Education, 1966.

Inlow, Gail M. *The Emergent in Curriculum.* New York: John Wiley & Sons, 1966.

Michaelis, John V., Ruth H. Grossman, and Lloyd F. Scott. *New Designs for the Elementary School Curriculum.* New York: McGraw-Hill, 1967.

National Society for the Study of Education. *Educational Evaluation: New Roles, New Means.* Sixty-eighth Yearbook, Part II. Edited by Ralph W. Tyler. Chicago: The University of Chicago Press, 1969.

Popham, W. J., and Robert L. Baker, eds. "Curriculum." *Review of Educational Research* 39 (June 1969): 283–375.

Tyler, Ralph W. *Basic Principles of Curriculum and Instruction.* Chicago: The University of Chicago Press, 1950.

———— "The Curriculum—Then and Now," *The Elementary School Journal* 57: April 1957.

Unruh, Glenys G., and Robert R. Leeper, eds. *Influences in Curriculum Change.* Washington, D.C.: Association for Supervision and Curriculum Development, 1968.

16

The Research Report

The purpose

The purpose of the research report is to explain the problem investigated, the procedure used in seeking a solution to that problem, the results observed, and the conclusions formed by the researcher. Ordinarily such a report is read by the expert in the field, not by the casual layman. The report must stand the test of critical scrutiny by a reader who will examine its supporting evidence and its line of reasoning and then proceed to his own conclusions. The report should be so clearly presented that the reader can, if he wishes, check the adequacy of the investigation by repeating the steps taken by the researcher.

Format

Dissertations and research articles follow essentially the same structural patterns. Minor variations in requirements, however, are to be found in the manuals of style prescribed by different graduate schools and research institutions. The researcher should ascertain the format required by his adviser or editor and adhere to it consistently.

Certain practices obtaining in scientific and technical reports that differ in some respects from those commonly preferred in general writing will be indicated. The researcher should become familiar with major sources of pertinent specialized information such as those cited at the close of this chapter.

A GENERAL PATTERN FOR A RESEARCH REPORT

The researcher may present his findings according to this frequently used plan:

I. Preliminaries
      Title page
      Preface
      Acknowledgments
      Table of contents
      Lists of tables and figures
II. Text of the Report
      Statement and definition of the problem
      Procedure in collecting the data
      Presentation and summarization of the data
      Analysis and interpretation of the data
      Conclusions and recommendations
III. Reference Matter
      Appendix (if any)
      Glossary (if any)
      Bibliography
      Index (if any)

THE PRELIMINARY PAGES

In a dissertation, certain preliminary material is usually presented before the body of the report. The title page appears first, in form following the style sheet of the graduate school or institution to which the report is submitted. The title is concisely descriptive of the scope and nature of the investigation. Accordingly, the phrasing may include key terms such as *major factors in, relative effectiveness of, relationship of.* Usually the title is typed in capital letters. Of the other items on the page only initial letters of important words are capitalized. These items include: (1) full name of the candidate, (2) name of the department and institution to which the report is submitted, (3) academic degree for which the researcher is a candidate, (4) year in which the degree is to be conferred. No terminal punctuation marks need be used on the title page.

The table of contents has a twofold purpose for the reader: (1) it serves as a synopsis of the report; (2) it facilitates quick locating of any section of the report. Consequently, the table of contents includes the title and beginning page number of the preliminary material, chapters of the text proper, and reference matter. Subheads within the chapters may also be listed, indented under the chapter titles.

Following the table of contents are separate listings of the titles of any figures and tables to which textual references are made. Included in the list of figures may be graphs, charts, maps, diagrams, photographs—as the study may warrant—consecutively numbered. The list of tables locates for the reader the presentations of quantitative data.

The preface states briefly the purpose and scope of the report. Usually it mentions the method of inquiry employed in the study. It may include appreciative acknowledgment of any substantial aid given by others during the course of the research.

THE TEXT OF THE REPORT

Statement and definition of the problem

The first chapter usually begins with a general statement of the nature of the problem to be investigated. The introductory section serves as orientation for the reader. In a resumé of related studies the researcher reports results of previous research and indicates the significance of the problem in education. He points out the issues demanding further investigation that have moved him to undertake the present study. Through his review of existing literature he aims to demonstrate to the reader the importance of that undertaking.

The researcher's analysis of the problem should result in formulation of a fuller statement of the problem, including questions to be answered or hypotheses to be tested. The researcher notes limitations to the scope of his present study and calls attention to initial assumptions on which hypotheses are predicated. He clarifies the meaning intended for any terms in the statement which are used in an uncommon or restricted sense. In a thesis proposal or other design for a research the definition of the problem more elaborately supplies specific information about the sources of data and the procedures to be used in collecting and interpreting them.

Procedure used in collecting the data

A separate section is usually given to the extensive explanation of the procedure used in an investigation. In this part of the report the researcher aims to enable the reader, if so minded, to check the findings by replicating the whole investigation. To that end the researcher describes in detail: (1) the types of data collected, (2) the investigative instruments used in the data-gathering, and (3) the plan for analysis of the data.

The researcher indicates plainly the sources and nature of his data, acknowledging any unavoidable data limitations. In behavioral studies he explains what population was sampled and what basis of selection was used. He states specifically the number and kind of subjects studied: their age and sex, their experiential status, and other pertinent factors which could affect results of the study. In experimental research he may identify the causal or independent variable, and the effect or dependent variable.

Specific information about all investigative instruments employed in the research is of prime importance. These, of course, vary according to the content of the study, but may include tests, questionnaires, records, interviews, observations of behavior, and content analysis. Tools such as verbal directions given to subjects, pretests, and pilot studies should be duly described in this section of the report. Well-known tests, record forms or apparatus need only be named. New instruments should be described in detail—even in some cases reproduced—in an appendix if their length so warrants.

This section of the report concludes with the researcher's plan for analyzing the data collected. In the case of historical research, discussion of the nature of the evidence is presented. In survey and experimental research studies the method of statistical analysis is indicated as well.

Presentation and summarization of the data

The evidence assembled may be qualitative or quantitative data, depending on the type of research—historical, philosophical, or scientific. If it is scientific, this section will combine supportive tables and figures with the explanatory text. The presentation, which may require one or more chapters, should be balanced, objective, and devoid of emotional appraisal by the researcher.

The data presented in this section are not in the form of the raw evidence originally collected, but rather in the form of statistical summaries of the raw data. This information is classified and arranged to confirm or disconfirm each hypothesis or question in turn, in the order it appeared in the introductory chapter. Data on individual subjects is typically presented only in case-study surveys. More commonly the statistics of groups are employed from simple frequency distribution to descriptions involving means and standard deviations, or medians and interquartile range.

Analysis and interpretation of the data

The researcher's analysis and interpretation of the data show how the findings bear precisely upon the hypotheses or questions. The statistical procedures followed for each hypothesis are specified, and the standard of significance applied in testing the hypothesis. Assumptions made in that application are discussed. This section of the report is essentially a study of relationships in the collected and classified evidence, a veritable exercise in statistical inference, recognizing concomitant variation and prediction. The researcher deliberately discusses *all* reasonable explanations for a particular fact, not just the one he endorses, including those unfavorable to his hypothesis.

In developing this part of the research, the reporter scans his work critically for flaws which he will correct: (1) errors of observation or computation, (2) confusion of fact and judgment, (3) conclusion drawn from defective data, (4) false assumptions, such as: "X causes Y because it precedes Y," or "X and Y are alike in all respects because they are alike in one."

Limitations of the study should be squarely met in the discussion here. The researcher should point out the role of any chance factors in obtaining the present results. He may indicate differences between his results and those of the earlier studies, and endeavor to explain them.

Conclusions and recommendations

In the presentation section the researcher has objectively set forth his data. In the analysis section he has given his interpretation of what the data mean and of how they came to be. Finally, he returns to consideration of the basic problem of the study and states precisely his resulting position regarding the hypotheses that were tested. He announces whether the findings confirmed or disconfirmed the hypotheses. If the results warrant, he may discuss the fact that the findings modify an accepted theory.

It is appropriate to indicate in this section of the report what this investigation implies for educational practice and relevant theory. It is usual for the researcher to make recommendations for future research. Appraisals and recommendations should be based on data, but also on philosophical considerations concerning goals and values.

REFERENCE MATERIALS

The appendix

The appendix, which follows the text, is the repository of materials relevant but so voluminous that they tend to break the continuity of exposition if included in the main text of the report. Summaries of the data, of course, are presented usually as tables or graphs in the text of the report, but the data on which calculations are based may be given in an appendix. Calculations or formulas do not appear in the body of the report unless the formulas are unique. Cross references in the text may direct the reader to the materials in the appendix, for example to lengthy quotations from documents, forms used in data-gathering, locally constructed tests, or raw data. Materials supplied in the appendix are appropriately grouped and are also listed in the table of contents.

DOCUMENTATION

As demonstrated in Chapter 4, a research report depends in some measure upon investigative reports that have preceded it. In proof both of his integrity and his thoroughness the researcher acknowledges borrowings from other writers in his note-taking and again when he uses the notes in the report. Whether he paraphrases or quotes another work directly, he supplies adequate documentation of his indebtedness for ideas and words of others. The rules governing the form of providing documentation are so numerous that only some basic principles may be presented here. Useful comprehensive guides are listed below.[1]

The researcher identifies his source materials in (1) footnotes, or (2) parenthetical textual references to his bibliography. To give credit for ideas paraphrased from others, he places a superscript at the end of his own wording and cites the source in a footnote.

Quotations

The writer of a scholarly report presents his main contentions in his own words. As suggested in Chapter 4, he may wisely quote problem statements and hypotheses in full, as well as statements of findings and conclusions, especially those for which criticism is anticipated.

Direct quotations are brought into textual material in two ways. Short quotations are enclosed in quotation marks and incorporated into the paragraph. Longer quotations—usually five lines or over—are set off as block quotations in separate paragraphs which are indented in entirety. Chapter 2, for example, contains the form of various *run-in* and *block quotations.*

It is impossible to overemphasize the importance of duplicating exactly in direct quotation the wording, spelling, capitalization, and punctuation of the original source. Two alterations in expository writing, however, are accepted practice: change of the form of the initial letter of the quotation or of the final mark of punctuation to fit the quotation into the syntax of the text. The first word of a quotation is not capitalized if it is related grammatically to its introductory phrase, even though in the original it was the first word of a sentence:

> The critic remonstrated that "these pupils were not assigned at random to the compared methods." [Quotation originally an entire sentence.]

Conversely, if the quotation is not incorporated grammatically into the text of the sentence, the first word is capitalized whether or not it was in the original source:

---

[1] American Psychological Association, *Publication Manual,* 1967 rev. (Washington, D.C.: American Psychological Association, 1967); James D. Lester, *Writing Research Papers* (Glenview, Ill.: Scott, Foresman and Company, 1967); *A Manual of Style,* 12th ed., rev. (Chicago: The University of Chicago Press, 1969); Kate L. Turabian, *A Manual for Writers of Term Papers, Theses, and Dissertations* (Chicago: The University of Chicago Press, Phoenix Books, 1960).

As the critic protested: "These pupils were not assigned at random to the compared methods."

The researcher quotes only as much of the source as he needs, and he phrases his own sentence so that quoted passages fit in smoothly as elements in his sentences. Both paraphrase and quotation require adequate introduction. The name of the authority is cited and varied words of explanation are given, for example:

In the words of Conant: ". . . .

According to Hilgard the "papers of Thurstone. . . ."

Madden states that the "way we distinguish. . . ."

This statement from Brodbeck should extend. . . .

Michael and Maccoby summarize their data by. . . .

Jones believes that "feedback is influenced by. . . ."

Among the many expressions which can typically vary introductions are *admit, affirm, contend, declare, deny, insist, point out, report, suggest, verify.*

In earlier discussion of note-taking (see Chapter 4) the use of ellipsis was explained, as were the method of denoting omission in a quotation, and the use of brackets to enclose interpolations. A final reminder of certain other mechanics of direct quotation may be in order here. Words, phrases, or sentences quoted within the text are enclosed in double quotation marks. Quotations within run-in quotations are enclosed in single quotation marks; quotations within these are enclosed in double marks. (British practice sometimes reverses this order.) The original marks remain the same in set-off indented quotations. Before a quotation of more than one sentence the introductory phrase is followed by a colon (*As the summary attested:*). A single mark of punctuation accompanies the closing quotation marks. A period or comma is placed before the terminal quotation marks; a colon or semicolon follows the quotation marks. A question mark or exclamation point is placed inside the quotation marks if it belongs to the quoted material, outside if it applies to the whole sentence.

Footnotes

Footnotes are of two kinds: reference and content. *Reference footnotes* (1) cite the authority for exact quotations or borrowed ideas or facts incorporated into the text, or (2) make cross references. *Content footnotes* extend the researcher's textual discussion through elaboration, or through evaluative comment. This supplemental exposition is used for material deemed significant and yet somewhat incidental to the main course of the discussion.

A footnote is signaled by a simple arabic numeral placed slightly above the line of discourse, and after any mark of punctuation except a dash. It should follow the statement to which it refers. Footnotes are placed in numerical order at the foot of the page on which reference is made in the text, and are separated from the text by spacing and a short line from the lefthand margin. The source of information for a reference footnote, except for page number, is the title page of the book cited.

Footnotes follow consistently the form authorized by the sponsoring institution or publication for which the researcher prepares his work. With a few exceptions, such as references in scientific papers and to some public documents, reference footnotes citing an authority for the first time, in an article or chapter, appear in the following set order and full form (omitting any unneeded items):

Book
1. Author's name in normal order, followed by a comma.
2. Title of the book, underlined (for italics), followed by a comma.
3. Name of the editor or compiler in normal order, followed by "ed." or "comp."
4. Name of a series in which the book is included, with the number in the series.
5. Edition, if other than the first, labeled, for example, as: "3rd ed.," "4th ed., rev."
6. Number of volumes in arabic numerals (only if the reference is to a multivolume work as a whole, and not to a specific passage).
7. Facts of publication: city of publication, followed by a colon; publisher, followed by a comma, and year of publication. All enclosed in parentheses and followed by a comma.
8. Volume number, if any, in arabic numerals.
9. Page number of the citation: "pp. 143–44," followed by a period.

Article in a journal
1. Author's name in normal order, followed by a comma.
2. Title of the article, enclosed in quotation marks, with a comma inside the final quotation marks.
3. Name of the journal, underlined, no comma.
4. Volume number, if any, in arabic numerals.
5. Date of the volume, or issue, enclosed in parentheses and followed by a comma.
6. Page number of the citation, followed by a period.

Unpublished material
1. Title and date of the document.
2. Identifying detail, such as box or folio number.
3. Name of the collection.
4. Depository and its location.

In citation of a book produced by *more than three authors,* the name of the first is used, followed by "and others" or "*et al.*" (*et alii,* "and others"), with no punctuation mark after the cited author's name.

Shortened references

After the first reference to a work, subsequent footnotes for that source, *in the same chapter or article,* should be shortened. Brevity may be gained by the use of the author's last name followed by the abbreviated term *op. cit.* (*opere citato,* "in the work cited") substituting for the title of the source already cited. Where it applies appropriately, *loc. cit.* (*loco citato,* "in the place cited") is also substituted for the title already given fully.

Of late, an alternative method is increasingly used for subsequent references. Often the author's last name and the new page number are considered sufficient (for example, "Norwood, p. 49."). If citation is made to more than one book by a given author, it becomes necessary to add an identifying shortened title as well (for example, "Norwood, *Curriculum,* p. 239").

For reference to a work just previously cited, without intervening notes to other works, the abbreviation *ibid.* (from *ibidem,* "in the same place") is used, to repeat as much of the preceding reference as applies in the new entry. If the full first reference to a work appears many pages removed from the second, the writer may wisely choose to use a shortened reference as noted above rather than *ibid.*

The following sample footnotes illustrate forms used in this book and show some space-saving features in shortened references:

[11] Allen L. Edwards, *Statistical Methods,* 2nd ed. (New York: Holt, Rinehart and Winston, 1967), pp. 214–15. [full book citation]

[12] John B. Carroll, "Basic and Applied Research in Education," *Harvard Educational Review* 38 (Spring 1968), 263–76. [article in a journal]

[13] *Ibid.* [same source and page as 12]

[14] F.S.C. Northrop, *The Logic of the Sciences and the Humanities* (New York: The Macmillan Company, 1947), Chapter III.

[15] May Brodbeck, "Logic and Scientific Method in Research on Teaching," in N. L. Gage, ed., *Handbook of Research on Teaching* (Chicago: Rand McNally, 1963), p. 68. [component part of a book]

[16] Britton K. Ruebush, "Anxiety," *Child Psychology.* The Sixty-second Yearbook of the National Society for the Study of Education, Part I (Chicago: The University of Chicago Press, 1963), pp. 462–63. [numbered series]

[17] Abraham Kaplan, *The Conduct of Inquiry* (San Francisco: Chandler, 1964), p. 114.

[18] *Ibid.,* p. 329. [same reference as 17, but page 329]

[19] Allen L. Edwards, *Experimental Design in Psychological Research,* 3rd ed. (New York: Holt, Rinehart and Winston, 1968), pp. 130–54. [second work cited by Edwards]

[20] Northrop, *op. cit.,* p. 36. [refers to 14, but page 36]

[21] Edwards, *Statistical Methods,* p. 215. [makes clear which of the two Edwards books is meant]

Bibliography

A researcher always includes in his report a list of books and other references treating the subject of study. If it is limited to works referred to in the text, this record is entitled "List of References Cited." A more inclusive list is generally headed "Bibliography." In the sciences, however, such a list is usually entitled "References." Although a comprehensive bibliographical list appears at the end of the book, shorter lists of references placed at the ends of chapters are often helpful.

Usefulness to the reader should govern both the arrangement of the entries in a list and the method of their citation. If many unpublished documents are included, a classified arrangement is favored, listing these entries in a section separate from books and journals. Generally, however, entries are arranged in alphabetical order by authors' surnames, chronologically for any particular author. A single-author entry precedes a multiple-author entry beginning with the same last name. An author's own work precedes a work he has edited. Corporate authorship is alphabetized according to the first important word of the work's title.

However reference lists may differ in stylistic details, they do report for each entry facts of (1) authorship, (2) title, and (3) publication. Usually the style adopted for the footnotes can be converted to bibliographical form with relatively few changes. The chief differences to be noted in bibliographical citation generally are the following:

1. Hanging indentation of entries, instead of the paragraph indention of footnotes.
2. Author's name in inverse order: Jones, Robert (for first author of a multiple authorship).
3. Full bibliographical data (shortened citation often suffices in a footnote).
4. Full title, including the subtitle, if any.
5. Repunctuation using periods between the three basic parts of an entry.

The following sample entries indicate the style adopted for this book:

Brodbeck, May. "Logic and Scientific Method in Research on Teaching." In *Handbook of Research on Teaching,* edited by N. L. Gage. Chicago: Rand McNally & Company, 1963. [contribution to a volume of papers]

Carroll, John B. "Basic and Applied Research in Education." *Harvard Educational Review* 38 (Spring 1968): 263–76. [article]

Chausow, Hymen M. "The Organization of Learning Experiences to Achieve More Effectively the Objective of Critical Thinking in the Social Science General Course of Junior College Level." Unpublished Ph. D. dissertation, University of Chicago, 1955.

Edwards, Allen L. *Statistical Methods for the Behavioral Sciences.* 2nd ed. New York: Holt, Rinehart and Winston, Inc., 1967. [book]

————. *Experimental Design in Psychological Research.* 3rd ed. New York: Holt, Rinehart and Winston, Inc., 1968. [two books by same author]

Kaplan, Abraham. *The Conduct of Inquiry: Methodology for Behavioral Science.* San Francisco: Chandler Publishing Company, 1964. [subtitle included]

Lord, Frederic M., and Melvin R. Novick. *Statistical Theories of Mental Test Scores.* Reading, Mass.: Addison-Wesley Publishing Company, 1968. [two authors; the name of the second in normal order; in facts of publication the state cited to avoid ambiguity]

Northrop, F.S.C. *The Logic of the Sciences and the Humanities.* New York: The Macmillan Company, 1947, or Meridian Books, 1959. [paperback edition included]

Ruebush, Britton K. "Anxiety," *Child Psychology.* The Sixty-second Yearbook of the National Society for the Study of Education, Part I. Chicago: The University of Chicago Press, 1963. [series]

Author-date style of citation

In some fields of the natural sciences the author-date form of citation is widely used. A citation in the text is typically enclosed within parentheses:

One investigator (Weinstock 1969, p. 225) has recently reported corroborative findings.

A citation in the reference list gives the familiar three-part information: authorship, title, facts of publication, but the elements are arranged as follows:

1. Author's last name and initials, the year, followed by a period
2. Title in sentence-style capitalization, period
      Of a book: italic type
      Of an article: roman type
3. Facts of publication
      For a book: city, followed by a colon; publisher's name, period
      For an article: journal name in italic type; volume number, followed by a colon; page location of the article, period

The names of publishers and of scientific journals are often abbreviated, as in these typical entries:

Alexander, R. M. 1969. *Animal mechanics.* Seattle: Univ. of Washington Press. [book]

Weinstock, B. 1969. Carbon monoxide: residence time in the atmosphere. *Science* 166:224–25. [article in a journal]

No single bibliographical style enjoys universal acceptance. To supplement the suggestions given in this section, or for help with specialized citations, the reader is referred to the various publications listed at the close of this chapter.

TABLES

Content

A table focuses attention on a set of facts and facilitates recurring reference to that set, if need be. Tabular presentation is a useful means of summarizing data. It is, in fact, the most effective way of presenting large quantities of single, classified facts in small space. From a well-constructed table the reader can spot quickly some significant point of the data or make a swift survey of the findings.

The style of tabular construction presented here is by no means the only one currently acceptable for research reporting. The recommendations made in this section reflect the preferences of this author and the practices followed in this book.

A table well designed can be understood by the reader without dependence upon the text. In turn, good textual discussion stresses the significant generalizations represented in the tabular material. A table has at least two columns, usually more, headed by brief identification of the data in the columns. The left-hand column, the *stub,* is a vertical listing of the items for which information is given in the body of the table. Of these items only the first word and proper nouns and adjectives are capitalized. The *body* of the table, typically vertical columns of figures, presents the significant information of the table. The space common to one specific column and line is known as a *cell.* A symbol for the total number of cases, *N,* is entered at the foot of each column of counts or frequencies.

Placement

A small table, or figure, is placed within the text; a large one is set on a separate page. Each table follows closely the first mention made of it in the text. The position of a table must be determined by its width. One too long for a page may continue on the next page, with the table number repeated, followed by the word *continued.* The column heads in this case are also repeated on the second page, but the title of the table is not. If the table is too wide for the page—but not very much too wide—the table may be turned and placed broadside.

Information of the table is aligned vertically in the columns and horizontally in each row. A column of figures aligns vertically on the decimal points and the commas marking off thousands. If the word *Total* appears at the foot of the stub, it is indented two spaces.

Triple spacing is used above and below a table inserted into the text, a horizontal line is placed above and below the column captions, and another below the last line of items in the table. Vertical lines and additional horizontal ones are used if they make the table easier to read. Rules are omitted on the sides of tables.

Numbers and captions

Every table is given a number, preferably an arabic numeral. As a convenience for the reader, in research reporting the *double numeration* system is widely used, in which the table number consists of the chapter number, a decimal point, and the number of the table in that chapter. Tables are numbered in the order in which they are first mentioned in the text and are cited in the text always by number, not by some vague term such as "the table below."

The title, or caption, identifies the table briefly and clearly in substantival form, with participles favored over relative clauses:

Freshmen Admitted to State College by Counties—instead of:

Number of Freshmen Who Were Admitted to State College by Counties

Various styles of tabular presentation are acceptable, but consistency of style in any report is a requirement. Traditionally the word *table,* in capitals followed by its number in capital roman numerals, was centered on one line. Double spaced below the table number and also set in caps or small caps was the title of the table, centered and without end punctuation. Current practice sanctions other styles of line arrangement and capitalization. It is not unusual to find table number and title set on the same line, sometimes aligned with the stub, or in capitals and lower case, but the styles are not mixed in the same report (see examples in Chapter 8). A table caption may have a subhead, set in a type style different from that of the caption and usually enclosed in parentheses. The boxheads for columns follow the style of the table title in capitalization, substantival form, and centering. If these headings are long, they may be set vertically, to read from bottom to top. If the stub has a boxhead, it is singular in number. Captions are consistently parallel in grammatical construction.

Footnotes

With a table consisting chiefly of numbers, notes on specific parts of the table require either letters or symbols as indentifying superscripts, not the usual arabic numerals serving in textual material. The asterisk (*) is commonly used as a superscript. Other symbols which serve in turn, if needed, are the dagger (†), double dagger (‡), and section mark (§).

Readers seeking help with special problems in the construction of tables may consult the latest edition of the *Publication Manual* of the American Psychological Association, and *A Manual of Style* published by the University of Chicago Press.

FIGURES

Function

Ideas are often conveyed effectively through illustrations and graphs. A diagram of apparatus may well supplement a verbal description. A chart may clarify for the reader certain relationships not immediately noted in a complicated tabular presentation.

Types

Drawings, photographs, or maps may serve to communicate points in some reports. Typical of illustrative forms widely used in reporting educational research are charts and graphs employed in earlier chapters of this book. Among these are the line graph (see Figure 2.4, page 30), the unique bar graph (Figure 10.1, page 305), the histogram (Figure 8.4, page 210), the frequency polygon (Figure 8.5, page 211), and the correlation chart (Figure 8.7, page 223).

Numbers and Captions

As with tables, illustrations are placed so that each one follows closely the first textual reference to it. Illustrations are numbered consecutively, throughout a section or report, with arabic numerals. The double numeration system is favored also, with sectional or chapter divisions of the text. In contrast, however, each illustrative aid is labeled "Figure" or "Fig.," and both number and caption are placed either above or below the illustration. Generally the capitalization and lettering contrast consistently with the style adopted for the tables in the same report. Sentence capitalization is often used for titles of figures (see Figure 8.1, page 204).

LANGUAGE OF THE REPORT

The research report is essentially expository writing, and as such requires suitable regard for unity, coherence, and emphasis, if it is to achieve effective communication of an investigation. Writing such a report is not easy. Its final draft has its beginnings in the first stage of the investigation, when the researcher identifies major topics to be considered, and casts up his first rough outline. As his analysis of the data progresses, he usually sees the need for persisting restructuring of that outline. He must, as well, accept as routine procedure even ruthless revision of the first draft of the report based on his outline, deleting as he should all verbal deadwood, rearranging words and statements for clarity and forcefulness. In a research report a subject of some significance is treated fully, according to established conventions of scholarship. The subject is delimited precisely, the thesis stated plainly, the evidence evaluated searchingly, and the arguments presented logically.

As the researcher composes and revises his report, he pays heed to certain specifics of expressive style and mechanics.

Tone and style

The tone of an investigation is reported impersonally, objectively, as reflected in the cautious qualifications within declarative statements, in the use of third person throughout. The pronouns *I* and *we* receive no play in the vocabulary of research writing. The style of an investigative paper is more formal than informal, as reflected in the choice of words, the deliberate construction of sentences, the careful attention to transitional devices within parts and between parts of the report.

In formal writing the diction is marked by specific and concrete words, and is free from hackneyed expressions. The sentences are varied in length and grammatical pattern. Key expressions appear in emphatic position, usually at beginning or end of statements. Ideas of coordinate value are presented in grammatically coordinate phrases or clauses. Vigor of expression is further realized by occasional arrangement of ideas in balanced constructions, or in order of climax. Not to be overlooked in report writing is *proportion,* the relative amount of space given to major concepts and to minor points. Proportionate emphasis requires dwelling at fitting length on the major ideas, adding supportive evidence to underdeveloped topics.

The ABC of effective reporting

In a research report cardinal virtues are *accuracy, brevity,* and *consistency.* Accuracy is expected with language, as with evidence or interpretation. Precision in the use of words is so crucial that the careful researcher refrains from using a term in one sense at one point and in a different sense at another. He repeats key words, rather than risk misinterpretation through the substitution of synonyms for those key terms. He is scrupulous in citing the exact thought and language of another writer. He strives for accuracy in assembling and presenting his data.

The importance of brevity in the titles of tables and figures has been discussed earlier in this chapter. Equally important is conciseness in the text of a report. Note the improvement made in the following sentences by omitting the bracketed words, which are repetitive or unnecessary:

1. Muscle activity was first clearly described in 1677 by Descartes, [*who was*] a French philosopher.
2. Kilauea, [*which is*] a very active volcano, was studied at close range because [*the nature of*] most of its eruptions had been nonexplosive.

3. A common feature of these studies is [*concerned with*] a comparison of the creative processes involved in arts and in sciences.
4. I would like to see more emphasis [*in the line of*] new materials such as plastics and their fabrication. (Use *on* instead here.)
5. Our concepts [*in the matter*] of what these basic features are has been expanding for a hundred years.
6. The [*character of the*] curriculum must [*serve to*] reflect current concerns.
7. [*Not many*] examples of inhibition of enzyme formation by an end product have been recorded in [*the case of*] plants. (Begin with *Few.*)

Revision of an initial draft of a report calls for expunging offenders such as the following phrases, wherever they are repetitive or superfluous in the text: *in terms of, as to whether, with reference to, in number, was situated.*

The researcher is ruled by uniformity in his use of formally defined terms in his report. He adheres as faithfully to the format adopted for his communication. He is consistent in his punctuation and in his treatment of numbers and symbols. All headings are consistent in grammatical structure and style of capitalization.

Continuity

To make sure that no break occurs in his line of communication to the reader, the researcher uses deliberate means of achieving *continuity*—constant and logical flow of his ideas. First, the organization of his report is characterized by clearcut divisions, indicated by typographical aids: center headings, side headings, enumerated points, italics and other signaling type forms. Within their divisions paragraphs are comprised of sentences arranged in logical sequences, and these paragraphs are in turn shown to be sequentially related. The connection between ideas is plainly pointed out by transitional words, sentences, and paragraphs throughout the report.

Four helpful devices for linking ideas are (1) transitional words and phrases such as *finally, however, in the meantime, moreover, therefore;* (2) echoing expressions: pronouns referring to elements in preceding sentences or named earlier in the same sentence; (3) repetition of certain key terms within the paragraph; (4) a transitional sentence to close one section of the report or to begin a new section. Skillful incorporation, into the text, of quotations and of cross references also contributes to the continuity of the discourse.

Conversely, important as statistical facts are in a research report, incorporation into the text of statistical tables of considerable length or complexity tends to break the course of the verbal communication so disruptively that these tables should be placed in the appendix, to preserve continuity in the textual matter.

Grammatical usage

In report writing, the researcher must be especially heedful of some aspects of English grammar. Certain conventions of English usage are particularly applicable. For example, standard practice with verbs requires the use of *present tense* for references to the data of the investigation and also in statements of established laws or principles. However, *past tense* is used in references to the literature of the problem, in references to implementation of the investigation, and in the reporting of analysis of the data. The *future tense* carries statements both of hypotheses of the study and of suggestions for further research.

EXAMPLES:

These data *are summarized* in the bar graph of Figure 10.1. (present tense with data)

In this analysis four statistical techniques *were used.* (past tense reporting analysis)

Errors in agreement between subject and verb or pronoun referent are the most common ones that the generality of writers makes. A subject which trips up the unwary researcher is his key term *data,* which is plural in number and calls for agreement with plural forms of verb and pronoun: "Last year *these data were* challenged."

A particular fault in syntax often plagues the first draft of the research report: uncertain reference of a pronoun, especially to a noun which is only implied in the statement. The reference of the pronoun *it* is in such doubt in the sentence: "The candidate had applied about four months ago and had already spent a month of *it* in his internship." This sentence may be recast to read: "The candidate, who had applied about four months ago, had already served one month as intern." The pronouns *this* and *these* are similarly liable to faulty reference. A second common syntactical fault is that of incomplete alternative comparison, as in "This class load was *as* heavy if not *heavier than* the other." Recast, the sentence may achieve a completed alternative comparison: "This class load was *as* heavy *as* the other, if not *heavier.*"

As a noun, the term *percentage* is favored over *percent,* in formal writing at least. Accordingly, a caption should read: "Percentage of Day Camps . . . ," instead of "Percent of Day Camps . . . ." Percentages are set in numerals. In humanistic copy the word *percent* follows the number: "40 percent," but in statistical or scientific copy the symbol % may be used: "40%."

Numbers, symbols, abbreviations

In textual material any number or symbol beginning a sentence is spelled out. Exact numbers of less than one hundred are also spelled out. Exceptions to the rule just given are numbers referring to a year or to parts of a book, or statistics and numbers in a series. In scientific text, physical quantities are also expressed in figures:

    20° C   40 pounds   8 meters   5 inches

Numerals of different categories appearing in succession can be confusing: "Before 1969 155 juniors were enrolled in the program." Rearrangement of the sentence elements can result in clearer communication.

Enumerations within the text are indicated by figures between parentheses. Items without internal punctuation may be separated by commas; complex items should be separated by semicolons.

Abbreviations and symbols are frequently used in the textual material of science and technology. In general writing they are confined to footnotes, bibliographies, lists, and tables.

Questions involving numbers, symbols, and abbreviations are so numerous, and usage is so varied, that each researcher should draw upon his authorized manual for answers to his specific problems.

Practice Exercise

Assume that a thesis has five chapters and an appendix; write *one* letter to indicate that the item should most appropriately *first* appear in the

  A   first chapter of the thesis
  B   second chapter of the thesis
  C   third or fourth chapter of the thesis
  D   fifth chapter of the thesis
  E   pages following the fifth chapter

_____ 1. Tests of one or more null hypotheses.

_____ 2. Definitions of important technical terms.

_____ 3. Lists of test scores of the pupils sampled.

_____ 4. Critical evaluation of numerous previous research studies of the problem.

_____ 5. Recommendation of changes which should be made in educational practices.

_____ 6. Reasons why the study is important.

_____ 7. Generalizations which may be derived from the data.

_____ 8. Tables of data presenting frequencies, percents, means, standard deviations, and the like.

_____ 9. Bibliography.

_____10. Hypotheses relevant to the problem other than null hypotheses.

_____11. Mention of the sources of data and the methods used in collecting them.

_____12. Locally constructed tests or questionnaires.

Selected References

A Manual of Style. 12th ed. rev. Chicago: The University of Chicago Press, 1969.

American Mathematical Society. "Manual for Authors of Mathematical Papers." Reprinted from *Bulletin of the American Mathematical Society* 68 (September 1962): 5.

Bernstein, Theodore M. *The Careful Writer: A Modern Guide to English Usage.* New York: Atheneum, 1965.

Conference of Biological Editors. *Style Manual for Biological Journals,* 2nd ed. Washington, D.C.: American Institute of Biological Sciences, 1964.

Harvard Law Review Association. *A Uniform System of Citation and Abbreviations,* 10th ed. Cambridge, Mass.: Harvard Law Review Association, 1958.

Lester, James W. *Writing Research Papers.* Glenview, Ill.: Scott, Foresman, 1967.

Parker, William Riley, compiler. *MLA Style Sheet,* rev. ed. New York: Modern Language Association of America, 1951.

Perrin, Porter G., Karl W. Dykema, and Wilma R. Ebbitt. *Writer's Guide and Index to English.* Glenview, Ill.: Scott, Foresman, 1968.

Publication Manual of the American Psychological Association, 1967 rev. Washington, D.C.: The American Psychological Association, 1967.

Strunk, K. W., Jr., and E. B. White. *The Elements of Style.* New York: Macmillan, 1959.

Turabian, Kate W. *A Manual for Writers of Term Papers, Theses, and Dissertations.* Chicago: The University of Chicago Press, Phoenix Books, 1960.

United States Government Printing Office. *Style Manual.* rev. ed. Washington, D.C.: Government Printing Office, 1967.

17

The Computer in Education
and Educational Research

Among the revolutions characterizing our times not the least important, and possibly the most important, are the changes in the processing of data. Thousands of electronic computers have been installed in business organizations, government offices, school systems, and institutions of higher learning. Many of the applications are to business data and in school systems and colleges to financial accounting, schedule making, and the recording of student data.

Educational applications of the computer

In addition to the applications of data processing in school systems and higher institutions noted above, there are some purely educational applications. Considerable use is being made of "terminals" in various locations in schools and colleges to train students for positions in the data-processing field. Increasingly the computer is being used to assist instruction, referred to by the acronym CAI. It is used on all grade levels from teaching beginners to read to mathematics and physics on the college level. It is argued that this is a most effective means of individualizing instruction, providing for individual differences, and solving the educational problems of the disadvantaged.

Where thousands of tests are scored per hour as at the Measurement Research Center at the State University of Iowa, at Educational Testing Service, and the Psychological Corporation, large, specially built electric scoring machines feed part and total scores directly into data processing equipment which prints individual student reports, item analyses of the tests and test batteries, and summary reports of the test data. On a smaller scale, these things are done at a number of colleges and universities. Digitek scoring machines transfer the item data into data-processing equipment used for dealing with test and other data. (See page 512.)

Applications of the computer in research

Probably the most important application of data-processing equipment in educational, psychological, and sociological research is in the application of statistical methods to data. Properly programed, a computer can give the researcher anything from means and standard deviations to factor analyses rapidly and accurately done. William Cooley has stressed the need for caution:

> All the fancy computer manipulations known to man will not produce meaningful results out of bad data.
> Unfortunately, too many investigators do not consider data processing until after data collection.[1]

The collecting of "good data" instead of "bad data" is promoted by adequate definition of the problem; care in the selection or construction of tests, questionnaires, and other instruments; some kind of probability sampling and, in experimental research, the selection of an appropriate experimental design. The matter of consulting a computer specialist prior to the collection of data was emphasized earlier. In addition, a bit of practice in computing and in application of statistical methods explained in Chapters 8–11 and 13 will better prepare the student for effective processing of his data. Studying FORTRAN and gaining some familiarity with the "hardware" of data-processing should also be beneficial. There are data-processing specialists quite unfamiliar with the methods of educational research, research in other behavioral sciences, and even with the statistical or mathematical methods applied in such research. The computer expert may, nevertheless, locate a program that suits the problem, but the student will have to judge whether or not it does, or how it will need to be modified.

The computer is being used in psychology and sociology, studying processes which can be *simulated* within the computer. Examples include the cognitive processes or strategies of problem-solving and the simulation of social and political processes.

Another important application of the computer is the generating of tables of random numbers and distributions of measures differing from normal ones. Such distributions are useful in determining the

---

[1] William W. Cooley, "Data Processing and Computing," in R. L. Ebel, ed., *Encyclopedia of Educational Research,* 4th ed. (New York: Macmillan, 1969), pp. 284–85.

robustness of t, χ^2, and F. How skewed can a distribution be without making it hazardous to apply the t test?

A BRIEF DESCRIPTION OF A DIGITAL COMPUTER

The computer itself

The typical digital computer[2] has the five components shown in Figure 17.1:

Figure 17.1 Components of a digital computer [Derived from page 3 of Benjamin Kleinmuntz, ed., *Clinical Information Processing by Computer* (New York: Holt, Rinehart and Winston, 1968), and other sources.]

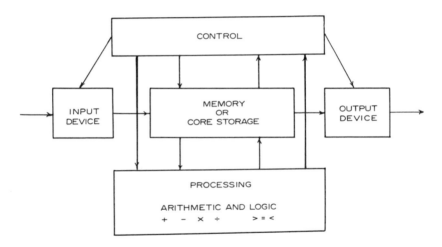

The *control* component coordinates the operations of the other components. It interprets and selects the coded instructions of a program. It controls the sequence of operations and the movements of information from one component to another.

In the *memory* or *core storage* component are stored the program or instructions used by the *processing* component in transforming data stored as sequences of binary units. (For example, 13 as a binary number is 1101 made up of units of 1 or 0.) The memory component may have thousands of cells or "address" locations in which a single sequence of binary digits may designate one of the instructions of the

---

[2] For more detailed and expert discussion of the digital computer and programing, see Paul R. Lohnes and William W. Cooley, *Introduction to Statistical Procedures: With Computer Exercises*, 2nd ed. (New York: Wiley, 1971), Chapter 4; Bert F. Green, Jr., *Digital Computers in Research* (New York: McGraw-Hill, 1963), Chapter 2, or other advanced text.

program, a newly arrived datum, or a transformed datum which may become a part of the results reported.

In the *processing* unit are accomplished such arithmetical operations as addition, subtraction, multiplication, division, raising to a power, and taking a root. In the processing unit the logical operations are also performed of comparing two numbers from the storage unit as to whether one is greater than, equal to, or less than the other. Given the result the computer obeying the next instruction may "branch" to an appropriate sequence of operations.

Input and *output* devices are represented by small rectangles at the left and right in Figure 17.1. The input devices may include card readers, tape readers for paper tape, and tape readers for magnetic tape. The cards read by the card readers are the familiar 80-column punched cards containing data for each subject in the form of appropriately located holes. Other 80-column cards contain the statements of computer programs. Figure 17.2 on page 508 illustrates an IBM card. Paper tape, now less often used as a means of transmitting input, is prepared on a special typewriter and has horizontal rows containing holes while magnetic tape or magnetic discs have similar rows of invisible magnetic spots. Program statements and data can be transmitted to a computer center by telephone. Output devices may include card punches, printers, and tape writers, and, in the case of magnetic tape, "drives" from which such tape is both read and written.

PROGRAMING A DIGITAL COMPUTER

The instructions for a sequence of operations to be performed by a computer may be written in FORTRAN (FORmula TRANslation language) in solving research problems. The instructions thus written constitute a *program.* The program may be one for computing a mean and standard deviation or for the calculations required for a factor analysis. The program in FORTRAN is written on coding sheets and later punched in a series of 80-column cards, one FORTRAN statement to a card. The first cards are *comment* cards. Comment cards always have a C punched in the first column. The statements on these cards are explanations for the human user of the program, for a typical example, C   THIS PROGRAM COMPUTES THE MEAN AND STANDARD DEVIATION OF N SCORES. Such cards may also appear at intervals. The next card is usually one containing a DIMENSION statement which indicates how much space should be reserved in storage for one or more variables, and for a given maximum *N.*

The cards following a DIMENSION statement are usually *input* statements. READ statements may instruct the computer to read data punched in certain columns of the 80-column cards for each of the N

Figure 17.2   An IBM card illustrating how information is coded. [Courtesy International Business Machines Corporation]

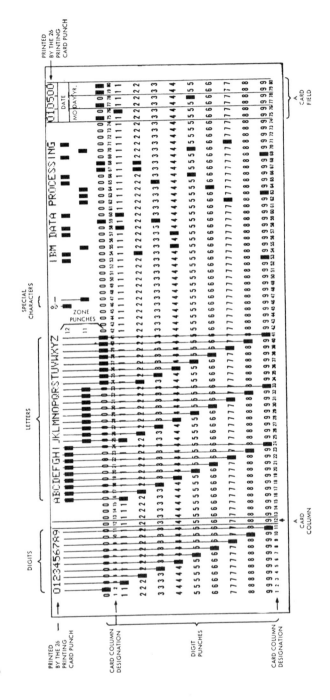

students. The accompanying FORMAT statements specify what columns have been designated for each variable. Later instructions are usually arithmetic statements, for example, to add corresponding values of two variables earlier stored in the memory of the computer. Other types of FORTRAN statements are *control* statements, such as DO statements which may indicate that the operation called for by the next statement is to be repeated from 1 to N times. Examples are included in Figure 17.3 on page 510. The ability to operate such "loops" is one of the most desirable attributes of computers, greatly responsible for their efficiency. WRITE statements accompanied by a FORMAT statement direct the output of the computer whether as punched cards, magnetic tape, or as printout sheets. The last statement in a FORTRAN program is always END.

A program in FORTRAN must be translated by a compiler to a sequence of machine language instructions for storage in the memory of the computer and for use by the computer itself. The machine language corresponding to each instruction is a sequence of binary digits occupying one "word" of storage.

Figure 17.3 is a FORTRAN program for the computation of t by means of Formula 17.1:

$$t = \frac{\bar{X}_A - \bar{X}_B}{\sqrt{\dfrac{\Sigma(X_A - \bar{X}_A)^2 + \Sigma(X_B - \bar{X}_B)^2}{N_A + N_B - 2}\left[\dfrac{1}{N_A} + \dfrac{1}{N_B}\right]}} \qquad (17.1)$$

The denominator of this equation is algebraically equivalent to Formula 13.1 for the standard error of a difference. (See page 406.)

The DIMENSION statement tells the compiler that storage space must be provided for up to 400 values of X_A, or XA, and up to 400 values of X_B, or XB. Line 9 says that N_A, or NA, and N_B, or NB are to be read into the computer with an input format specified by line 2. The values of variable X_A and X_B are to be read in as indicated by the READ statements above and below line 3. The lines beginning with SA, SB, SAA, and SBB refer to storage areas which must be "initialized" to 0. The lines beginning with DO 4 .... and with SA indicate that the N_A values of variable X_A are to be added successively to the SA of O. (SA initially 0 is augmented NA times.) Similarly, the N_B values of X_B are to be added successively to the SB initially of 0. The new SA and SB are equal to ΣX_A and ΣX_B. XBA and XBB are obviously $\bar{X}_A$ and $\bar{X}_B$.

The lines beginning DO 6 .... and SAA indicate the computing of $\Sigma(X_A - \bar{X}_A)^2$ adding its value to the original SAA of 0. Similarly, the lines beginning DO 7 .... and SBB designate the computation of $\Sigma(X_B - \bar{X}_B)^2$.

The line beginning TOP indicates the computation of the numerator,

Figure 17.3 Illustrative FORTRAN program to compute value of *t*-statistic [Quoted from M. Clemens Johnson, *Educational Uses of the Computer: An Introduction* (Chicago: Rand McNally, 1971), p. 186. Reprinted with permission of author and publisher.]

```
        DIMENSION XA(400), XB(400)
9       READ (1, 2) NA, NB
2       FORMAT (2I4)
        READ (1, 3) (XA(I), I = 1, NA)
3       FORMAT (25F3.0)
        READ (1, 3) (XB(I), I = 1, NB)
        SA = 0.
        SB = 0.
        SAA = 0.
        SBB = 0.
        DO 4 I = 1, NA
4       SA = SA + XA(I)
        DO 5 I = 1, NB
5       SB = SB + XB(I)
        XBA = SA/NA
        XBB = SB/NB
        DO 6 I = 1, NA
6       SAA = SAA + (XA(I) − XBA) ** 2
        DO 7 I = 1, NB
7       SBB = SBB + (XB(I) − XBB) ** 2
        TOP = XBA − XBB
        BOT = (SAA + SBB)/(NA + NB − 2)
        BOT = BOT * (1./NA + 1./NB)
        BOT = SQRT(BOT)
        T = TOP/BOT
        WRITE(3, 8) XBA, XBB, T
8       FORMAT (1H2, 'MEANA = ', F8.2, 2X,
    1   'MEANB = ', F8.2, 2X, 'T-RATIO = ', F8.2)
        GO TO 9
        END
```

or top, of the equation for *t*. The three lines beginning BOT should be easily understood by anyone capable of calculating the denominator, or bottom, of the equation for *t*. Obviously, TOP divided by BOT is *t*.

The lines which follow are instructions to WRITE the means $\overline{X}_A$ and $\overline{X}_B$ and the *t* as specified by the format output statement beginning with line 8. It is desirable for the printout to include the particular formula used although this is not specified in this program.

The statement GO TO 9 directs the computer to prepare for another calculation of t, otherwise the process is terminated and the computer is available for other data processing.[3]

THE DATA PROCESSING CENTER OF THE CITY COLLEGES OF CHICAGO

The data processing center of the City Colleges of Chicago is located in the central administrative offices.[4] This third generation IBM 360, Model 40, computer installation serves the seven College campuses, TV College, and the central administration. Terminal devices used for data processing-instructional purposes, computer-assisted instruction, and research are located in four of the seven campuses. The basic functions of the data processing installation of the Colleges can be categorized into two broad areas, namely administrative and academic.

Administrative services

1. *Financial.* The first major computer application was the installation and operation of a payroll system beginning in January, 1967. In 1968, a new appropriation accounting system was implemented resulting in more efficient and accurate internal accounting procedure for the Colleges.

2. *Students.* A computerized registration system was introduced in 1967. Modifications and improvements of this system have been continuous. Similarly, the computerization of the end-of-semester grading process has been accomplished. Students now receive computer-produced mailers which not only contain current semester grades, but cumulative hours and grade point averages as well. A student characteristics report is produced for each College as well as individual profile reports.

3. *Faculty and staff.* The development of a faculty-staff data file was undertaken in April, 1969. The production of campus faculty characteristics reports has aided administrators in meeting the multiple reporting requirements of state, federal, and professional association requests. In addition, analysis reports concerning salary, academic preparation, and work load are now utilized. Department lists, directories, and staff mailing labels have also been generated from this file.

4. *Curriculum.* Information services provided in this area include computerized master schedules, class rosters, section and program

---

[3] This discussion of the FORTRAN program is based on a literal translation of its steps by Ming Szeto of the Data Processing Center of the City Colleges of Chicago.

[4] This section is adapted from a report written by Dr. Henry Moughamian, Coordinator of Instructional Services.

enrollment analyses, class size enrollment reports, and grade distribution analyses.

Academic services

The use of the computer for educational purposes has been a primary goal of the Colleges. To date the following educational applications are made possible by the central data processing installation.

1. *Support of counseling and guidance.* Information describing student characteristics are routinely provided to all campuses through the student accounting system and the student history file.

2. *Research.* The computer center has assembled a library of statistical programs that faculty and staff use for individual, all-college, and funded projects.

3. *Evaluation of instruction.* The test analysis program is recognized as among the best in the country. A Digitek provides central scoring of long objective tests. Since it is wired to the computer, it makes possible the analyses which report for each test the frequency distribution of scores, the mean, the standard deviation, and the data relevant to each item. These include percentages of response for upper and lower groups for *each* answer and the item-test correlations, phi coefficients for the correct and incorrect answers. The printout for each test also includes summary tables. The instructional departments have been provided with brief manuals explaining how to interpret the data described above. During the past year approximately 350 such test analyses were requested by members of the faculties of the Colleges. The analyses are used in the improvement of the objective test material and in evaluating the extent of attainment of instructional objectives.

4. *Instruction in data processing.* Nowhere is the power of the computer more evident than in the training of students for various fields of data processing. During the past year approximately 4,000 students have profited from data-processing instruction using the equipment of the Colleges. About 40 percent of these students have written programs which have been transmitted to the central computer via terminals located on four of the campuses. The value of these experiences for students in obtaining jobs in data processing, as well as for upgrading skills, is demonstrated by the results of recent student follow-up studies. The need for such training is clearly evident in the growing demand for data-processing personnel in the Chicago area.

5. *Computer-assisted instruction.* Funded by a National Science Foundation grant, members of the faculties of the Colleges have been studying the role of the computer in curriculum development. The most practical and economical form of computer-assisted instruction at this time, problem solving, has begun in the academic disciplines of mathe-

matics, physics, and business. In the future, other subject areas will be added.

The computer installation of the Chicago Public Schools, described and illustrated in the next section, has components that are similar in appearance and have much the same functions, but on a larger scale, than those of the data-processing center of the seven City Colleges of Chicago.

THE COMPUTER INSTALLATION OF THE CHICAGO PUBLIC SCHOOLS

This section will give the reader some ideas of the appearance of the data-processing equipment of a large city school system and of the tasks performed by this equipment. In 1970 there were in the Chicago Public Schools, 46 academic high schools, 13 vocational high schools, 447 elementary schools, and 18 special schools for atypical pupils. The total enrollments approximated 435,000 elementary pupils and 138,000 students on the high school level.

Figure 17.4 IBM 360/40 Computer with a 1052 Printer Keyboard Typewriter An IBM 360/40 is currently being utilized in a time-sharing environment to service all Chicago schools offering courses in Computer Education. The system is available for student and teacher use from remote on-line terminal sites in the schools. The software system is a modified version of the IBM Remote Access Computing System (RAX).

The captions of Figures 17.4, 17.5, and 17.6 describe the various data-processing components and the tasks they perform.[5]

Figure 17.5   IBM 2311 Disk Drives, rear left, 2401 Tape Units, rear right, and a 1403 Printer, front right

Components of the IBM 360/40 RAX system include three disk storage drives which allow students and teachers to compile, test, and execute programs on-line from remote locations. In addition, the disk drives allow student programs to be saved and data files to be created and updated. The tape storage drives, card reader, and line printer permit utilization of the system at the central site at the same time service is being given to the schools.

[5] Dr. Eileen C. Stack, Associate Superintendent, Operations Analysis, and Mr. Harry Strasburg, Assistant Superintendent, Chicago Public Schools, in charge of Systems Analysis and Data Processing, supplied the pictures and the information concerning them.

Figure 17.6   IBM 2401 Tape Units, IBM Model 360/50 Computer and a 1052 Printer Keyboard Typewriter

Administrative tasks performed by the IBM 360/50 such as: Daily Finance Transactions, Budget Preparation, Supply Stock Inventory Control, Student Accounting, Student Scheduling, Personnel Position Control, and Payroll Preparation, are performed on an IBM 360/50. The central processing unit contains 512K bytes (characters) of memory. [A *bit* is a binary digit of 1 or 0, while a *byte* is a series of bits, the number varying from one computer to another.] An additional 230,000,000 bytes of storage are accessible through an on-line 2314 Direct Access Storage Device. Eight tape drives provide the ability to manipulate large data files. The Computer System is designed so that several different tasks may be performed concurrently.

Questions for
Study and Discussion

Consult one or more texts on data processing.

1. When were punched cards first used in the processing of data?

2. What is the function of a compiler?

3. How does an analog computer differ from a digital one?

4. What is an accumulator?

5. Give the meaning of the FORTRAN statements:
   READ (5.1) ID, AGE, SEX, SATV, SATQ
   1 FORMAT (15, F3.0, F1.0, 2F5.0)

6. What is a subroutine?

7. How is a flow chart used in data processing?

8. Convert 11 and 13 to binary digits and multiply them.

9. Give an example of a FORTRAN statement which directs the computer to repeat a series of instructions.

10. Describe an example of simulation by a computer.

Suggestions
for Further Study

Among the references listed at the end of this chapter are two which especially deal with simulation, by Abelson (1968) and by Coleman (1961). There are several references listed concerning computer assisted instruction. These include works by Atkinson (1967, 1968), Atkinson and Wilson (1969), by Grubb (1967), and Suppes (1966). The last reference mentioned appears in an issue of the *Scientific American* which is entirely devoted to data processing.

Two of the references are to articles in the *Review of Educational Research* on "Statistical Methodology," by Wrigley (1957) and Baker (1963). The 1960 and 1969 editions of the *Encyclopedia of Educational Research* also contain articles on data processing. The first is by Fattu and the second by Cooley. All of these references are decidedly worth studying, both for the content of the articles and for their well chosen bibliographies. The titles of the other references indicate their content.

Each Spring and Autumn issue of *Educational and Psychological Measurement* contains a section devoted to discussion of computer programs relevant to factor analysis, item analysis, multiple regression techniques, analysis of variance and other procedures of interest to researchers in education and psychology.

Selected References

Abelson, Robert P. "Simulation of Social Behavior." In *The Handbook of Social Psychology,* edited by Gardner Lindzey and Elliot Aronson. Volume II. 2nd ed. Reading, Mass.: Addison-Wesley, 1968. Chapter 12.

Atkinson, Richard C. "CAI-Learning Aspects." In *Computers and Education,* edited by R. W. Gerard, pp. 11–63. New York: McGraw-Hill, 1967.

―――. "Computerized Instruction and the Learning Process." *American Psychologist* 23 (April 1968): 225–30.

―――, and H. A. Wilson, eds. *Computer Assisted Instruction, A Book of Readings.* New York: Academic Press, 1969.

Baker, Frank B. "Computer Course for the Behavioral Scientist." *Educational and Psychological Measurement* 22 (1962): 617–21.

―――. "Use of Computers in Educational Research" in "Statistical Methodology." *Review of Educational Research* 33 (December 1963): 566–78.

―――. "Generalized Item and Test Analysis Program—A Program for the Control Data 1604 Computer." *Educational and Psychological Measurement* 23 (Spring 1963): 187–90.

Borko, Harold, ed. *Computer Applications in the Behavioral Sciences.* Englewood Cliffs, N.J.: Prentice-Hall, 1962.

Coleman, J. S. "Analysis of Social Structures and Simulation of Social Processes with Electronic Computers." *Educational and Psychological Measurement* 21 (Spring 1961): 203–18.

Cooley, William W. "Data Processing and Computing." In *Encyclopedia of Educational Research,* edited by Robert L. Ebel, pp. 283–91. 4th ed. New York: Macmillan, 1969.

―――., and Kenneth J. Jones. "Computer Systems for Multivariate Analysis." *Educational and Psychological Measurement* 24 (Fall 1964): 645–53.

Fattu, Nicholas. "Processing of Data." In *Encyclopedia of Educational Research,* edited by C. W. Harris, pp. 1047–56. 3rd ed. New York: Macmillan, 1960.

Feigenbaum, E. A. and J. Feldman, eds. *Computers and Thought.* New York: McGraw-Hill, 1963.

Flanagan, John C. "Data Processing in Large Scale Research Projects." *Harvard Educational Review* 31 (Summer 1961): 250–56.

Gerard, Ralph W., ed. *Computers and Education.* New York: McGraw-Hill, 1967.

Green, Bert F., Jr. *Digital Computers in Research.* New York: McGraw-Hill, 1963.

————. "The Computer Revolution in Psychometrics." *Psychometrika* 31 (December 1966): 437–45.

Grubb, Ralph E. "CAI-Technical Aspects." In *Computers and Education,* edited by R. W. Gerard, pp. 67–109. New York: McGraw-Hill, 1967.

Johnson, M. Clemens. *Educational Uses of the Computer: An Introduction.* Chicago: Rand McNally, 1971.

Kaiser, Henry F. "Computer Program for Varimax Rotation in Factor Analysis." *Educational and Psychological Measurement* 19 (Autumn 1959): 413–20.

Kleinmuntz, Benjamin, ed. *Clinical Information Processing by Computer.* New York: Holt, Rinehart and Winston, 1969.

Lohnes, Paul R. and William W. Cooley. *Introduction to Statistical Procedures: With Computer Exercises.* 2nd ed. New York: Wiley, 1971.

McCracken, Daniel E. *A Guide to FORTRAN IV Programming.* New York: Wiley, 1962.

Page, Ellis B. "Imminence of Grading Essays by Computer." *Phi Delta Kappan* 47 (January 1966): 238–43.

Suppes, Patrick, "The Uses of Computers in Education." *Scientific American* 215 (September 1966): 206–21.

Veldman, Donald J. *FORTRAN Programming for the Behavioral Sciences.* 2nd ed. New York: Holt, Rinehart and Winston, 1971.

Wrigley, Charles. "Data Processing: Automation in Calculation" in "Methodology of Educational Research." *Review of Educational Research* 27 (December 1957): 528–43.

Appendix

Table A

This is one page of a 30-page table of random numbers. Its use is explained on page 244 of Chapter 9. While a single page suffices for explanation, the page should not be repeatedly used in the selection of random samples. The original or another larger table should be used.

Table B

This table of the areas and ordinates of the normal curve of unit area suffices for most of the purposes explained in this text, but more detailed tables are more convenient. For example, if the area *beyond* $\frac{x}{\sigma}$ or z from the mean or a proportion of the total area of the curve greater than .50 to $\frac{x}{\sigma}$ or z are desired, tables listing area values under the headings "Area in Smaller Portion" and "Area in Larger Portion" make it unnecessary to subtract or add .5000. See Table III in Allen Edward's *Statistical Methods* or other advanced text.

Table C

In this abridged table of *t,* rows relevant to degrees of freedom from 1 to 8 have been omitted. The critical values of *t* usually given in these rows seldom have a legitimate use. Even two groups of 10 pairs of pupils are rather small to justify a parametric test. It is possible, however, to obtain approximate values of *t* for degrees of freedom from 1 to 8 by taking square roots of the values of *F* listed in the first column of the Table of F. One can similarly obtain approximate values of *t* for various degrees of freedom greater than 30 (other than 40, 60, 120, and ∞ in Table C). All the values thus obtained are for the .05 and .01 levels of two-tailed tests. For more precise critical values of *t* other than those listed in Table C, consult Table V of Edward's text.

Table D

The use of Table D in converting coefficients of correlation to values z_r which have an approximately normal sampling distribution is explained on page 260 of Chapter 9. Many texts give z_r values for such *r*'s as .470, .475, .480, etc. Note that the credit for Table D belongs to the present author (and Sir Ronald Fisher).

Table A Random Numbers*

Line\Col.	(1)	(2)	(3)	(4)	(5)	(6)	(7)	(8)	(9)	(10)	(11)	(12)	(13)	(14)
1	10480	15011	01536	02011	81647	91646	69179	14194	62590	36207	20969	99570	91291	90700
2	22368	46573	25595	85393	30995	89198	27982	53402	93965	34095	52666	19174	39615	99505
3	24130	48360	22527	97265	76393	64809	15179	24830	49340	32081	30680	19655	63348	58629
4	42167	93093	06243	61680	07856	16376	39440	53537	71341	57004	00849	74917	97758	16379
5	37570	39975	81837	16656	06121	91782	60468	81305	49684	60672	14110	06927	01263	54613
6	77921	06907	11008	42751	27756	53498	18602	70659	90655	15053	21916	81825	44394	42880
7	99562	72905	56420	69994	98872	31016	71194	18738	44013	48840	63213	21069	10634	12952
8	96301	91977	05463	07972	18876	20922	94595	56869	69014	60045	18425	84903	42508	32307
9	89579	14342	63661	10281	17453	18103	57740	84378	25331	12566	58678	44947	05585	56941
10	85475	36857	53342	53988	53060	59533	38867	62300	08158	17983	16439	11458	18593	64952
11	28918	69578	88231	33276	70997	79936	56865	05859	90106	31595	01547	85590	91610	78188
12	63553	40961	48235	03427	49626	69445	18663	72695	52180	20847	12234	90511	33703	90322
13	09429	93969	52636	92737	88974	33488	36320	17617	30015	08272	84115	27156	30613	74952
14	10365	61129	87529	85689	48237	52267	67689	93394	01511	26358	85104	20285	29975	89868
15	07119	97336	71048	08178	77233	13916	47564	81056	97735	85977	29372	74461	28551	90707
16	51085	12765	51821	51259	77452	16308	60756	92144	49442	53900	70960	63990	75601	40719
17	02368	21382	52404	60268	89368	19885	55322	44819	01188	65255	64835	44919	05944	55157
18	01011	54092	33362	94904	31273	04146	18594	29852	71585	85030	51132	01915	92747	64951
19	52162	53916	46369	58586	23216	14513	83149	98736	23495	64350	94738	17752	35156	35749
20	07056	97628	33787	09998	42698	06691	76988	13602	51851	46104	88916	19509	25625	58104
21	48663	91245	85828	14346	09172	30168	90229	04734	59193	22178	30421	61666	99904	32812
22	54164	58492	22421	74103	47070	25306	76468	26384	58151	06646	21524	15227	96909	44592
23	32639	32363	05597	24200	13363	38005	94342	28728	35806	06912	17012	64161	18296	22851
24	29334	27001	87637	87308	58731	00256	45834	15398	46557	41135	10367	07684	36188	18510
25	02488	33062	28834	07351	19731	92420	60952	61280	50001	67658	32586	86679	50720	94953

* Taken from Statement No. 4914, *Table of 105,000 Random Decimal Digits*, May 1949, prepared by the Interstate Commerce Commission, Bureau of Transport Economics and Statistics. Reprinted with permission.

Table B Areas and Ordinates of the Normal Curve
in Terms of $\frac{x}{\sigma}$ or z*

$\frac{x}{\sigma}$	Area	Ordinate	$\frac{x}{\sigma}$	Area	Ordinate	$\frac{x}{\sigma}$	Area	Ordinate
00	.0000	.3989	.50	.1915	.3521	1.00	.3413	.2420
.01	.0040	.3989	.51	.1950	.3503	1.01	.3438	.2396
.02	.0080	.3989	.52	.1985	.3485	1.02	.3461	.2371
.03	.0120	.3988	.53	.2019	.3467	1.03	.3485	.2347
.04	.0160	.3986	.54	.2054	.3448	1.04	.3508	.2323
.05	.0199	.3984	.55	.2088	.3429	1.05	.3531	.2299
.06	.0239	.3982	.56	.2123	.3410	1.06	.3554	.2275
.07	.0279	.3980	.57	.2157	.3391	1.07	.3577	.2251
.08	.0319	.3977	.58	.2190	.3372	1.08	.3599	.2227
.09	.0359	.3973	.59	.2224	.3352	1.09	.3621	.2203
.10	.0398	.3970	.60	.2257	.3332	1.10	.3643	.2179
.11	.0438	.3965	.61	.2291	.3312	1.11	.3665	.2155
.12	.0478	.3961	.62	.2324	.3292	1.12	.3686	.2131
.13	.0517	.3956	.63	.2357	.3271	1.13	.3708	.2107
.14	.0557	.3951	.64	.2389	.3251	1.14	.3729	.2083
.15	.0596	.3945	.65	.2422	.3230	1.15	.3749	.2059
.16	.0636	.3939	.66	.2454	.3209	1.16	.3770	.2036
.17	.0675	.3932	.67	.2486	.3187	1.17	.3790	.2012
.18	.0714	.3925	.68	.2517	.3166	1.18	.3810	.1989
.19	.0753	.3918	.69	.2549	.3144	1.19	.3830	.1965
.20	.0793	.3910	.70	.2580	.3123	1.20	.3849	.1942
.21	.0832	.3902	.71	.2611	.3101	1.21	.3869	.1919
.22	.0871	.3894	.72	.2642	.3079	1.22	.3888	.1895
.23	.0910	.3885	.73	.2673	.3056	1.23	.3907	.1872
.24	.0948	.3876	.74	.2703	.3034	1.24	.3925	.1849
.25	.0987	.3867	.75	.2734	.3011	1.25	.3944	.1826
.26	.1026	.3857	.76	.2764	.2989	1.26	.3962	.1804
.27	.1064	.3847	.77	.2794	.2966	1.27	.3980	.1781
.28	.1103	.3836	.78	.2823	.2943	1.28	.3997	.1758
.29	.1141	.3825	.79	.2852	.2920	1.29	.4015	.1736
.30	.1179	.3814	.80	.2881	.2897	1.30	.4032	.1714
.31	.1217	.3802	.81	.2910	.2874	1.31	.4049	.1691
.32	.1255	.3790	.82	.2939	.2850	1.32	.4066	.1669
.33	.1293	.3778	.83	.2967	.2827	1.33	.4082	.1647
.34	.1331	.3765	.84	.2995	.2803	1.34	.4099	.1626
.35	.1368	.3752	.85	.3023	.2780	1.35	.4115	.1604
.36	.1406	.3739	.86	.3051	.2756	1.36	.4131	.1582
.37	.1443	.3725	.87	.3078	.2732	1.37	.4147	.1561
.38	.1480	.3712	.88	.3106	.2709	1.38	.4162	.1539
.39	.1517	.3697	.89	.3133	.2685	1.39	.4177	.1518
.40	.1554	.3683	.90	.3159	.2661	1.40	.4192	.1497
.41	.1591	.3668	.91	.3186	.2637	1.41	.4207	.1476
.42	.1628	.3653	.92	.3212	.2613	1.42	.4222	.1456
.43	.1664	.3637	.93	.3238	.2589	1.43	.4236	.1435
.44	.1700	.3621	.94	.3264	.2565	1.44	.4251	.1415
.45	.1736	.3605	.95	.3289	.2541	1.45	.4265	.1394
.46	.1772	.3589	.96	.3315	.2516	1.46	.4279	.1374
47	.1808	.3572	.97	.3340	.2492	1.47	.4292	.1354
.48	.1844	.3555	.98	.3365	.2468	1.48	.4306	.1334
.49	.1879	.3538	.99	.3389	.2444	1.49	.4319	.1315
.50	.1915	.3521	1.00	.3413	.2420	1.50	.4332	.1295

* Reprinted from *Educational Statistics* by J. E. Wert.

Table B Continued

$\dfrac{x}{\sigma}$	Area	Ordinate	$\dfrac{x}{\sigma}$	Area	Ordinate	$\dfrac{x}{\sigma}$	Area	Ordinate
1.50	.4332	.1295	2.00	.4772	.0540	2.50	.4938	.0175
1.51	.4345	.1276	2.01	.4778	.0529	2.51	.4940	.0171
1.52	.4357	.1257	2.02	.4783	.0519	2.52	.4941	.0167
1.53	.4370	.1238	2.03	.4788	.0508	2.53	.4943	.0163
1.54	.4382	.1219	2.04	.4793	.0498	2.54	.4945	.0158
1.55	.4394	.1200	2.05	.4798	.0488	2.55	.4946	.0154
1.56	.4406	.1182	2.06	.4803	.0478	2.56	.4948	.0151
1.57	.4418	.1163	2.07	.4808	.0468	2.57	.4949	.0147
1.58	.4429	.1145	2.08	.4812	.0459	2.58	.4951	.0143
1.59	.4441	.1127	2.09	.4817	.0449	2.59	.4952	.0139
1.60	.4452	.1109	2.10	.4821	.0440	2.60	.4953	.0136
1.61	.4463	.1092	2.11	.4826	.0431	2.61	.4955	.0132
1.62	.4474	.1074	2.12	.4830	.0422	2.62	.4956	.0129
1.63	.4484	.1057	2.13	.4834	.0413	2.63	.4957	.0126
1.64	.4495	.1040	2.14	.4838	.0404	2.64	.4959	.0122
1.65	.4505	.1023	2.15	.4842	.0395	2.65	.4960	.0119
1.66	.4515	.1006	2.16	.4846	.0387	2.66	.4961	.0116
1.67	.4525	.0989	2.17	.4850	.0379	2.67	.4962	.0113
1.68	.4535	.0973	2.18	.4854	.0371	2.68	.4963	.0110
1.69	.4545	.0957	2.19	.4857	.0363	2.69	.4964	.0107
1.70	.4554	.0940	2.20	.4861	.0355	2.70	.4965	.0104
1.71	.4564	.0925	2.21	.4864	.0347	2.71	.4966	.0101
1.72	.4573	.0909	2.22	.4868	.0339	2.72	.4967	.0099
1.73	.4582	.0893	2.23	.4871	.0332	2.73	.4968	.0096
1.74	.4591	.0878	2.24	.4875	.0325	2.74	.4969	.0093
1.75	.4599	.0863	2.25	.4878	.0317	2.75	.4970	.0091
1.76	.4608	.0848	2.26	.4881	.0310	2.76	.4971	.0088
1.77	.4616	.0833	2.27	.4884	.0303	2.77	.4972	.0086
1.78	.4625	.0818	2.28	.4887	.0297	2.78	.4973	.0084
1.79	.4633	.0804	2.29	.4890	.0290	2.79	.4974	.0081
1.80	.4641	.0790	2.30	.4893	.0283	2.80	.4974	.0079
1.81	.4649	.0775	2.31	.4896	.0277	2.81	.4975	.0077
1.82	.4656	.0761	2.32	.4898	.0270	2.82	.4976	.0075
1.83	.4664	.0748	2.33	.4901	.0264	2.83	.4977	.0073
1.84	.4671	.0734	2.34	.4904	.0258	2.84	.4977	.0071
1.85	.4678	.0721	2.35	.4906	.0252	2.85	.4978	.0069
1.86	.4686	.0707	2.36	.4909	.0246	2.86	.4979	.0067
1.87	.4693	.0694	2.37	.4911	.0241	2.87	.4979	.0065
1.88	.4699	.0681	2.38	.4913	.0235	2.88	.4980	.0063
1.89	.4706	.0669	2.39	.4916	.0229	2.89	.4981	.0061
1.90	.4713	.0656	2.40	.4918	.0224	2.90	.4981	.0060
1.91	.4719	.0644	2.41	.4920	.0219	2.91	.4982	.0058
1.92	.4726	.0632	2.42	.4922	.0213	2.92	.4982	.0056
1.93	.4732	.0620	2.43	.4925	.0208	2.93	.4983	.0055
1.94	.4738	.0608	2.44	.4927	.0203	2.94	.4984	.0053
1.95	.4744	.0596	2.45	.4929	.0198	2.95	.4984	.0051
1.96	.4750	.0584	2.46	.4931	.0194	2.96	.4985	.0050
1.97	.4756	.0573	2.47	.4932	.0189	2.97	.4985	.0048
1.98	.4761	.0562	2.48	.4934	.0184	2.98	.4986	.0047
1.99	.4767	.0551	2.49	.4936	.0180	2.99	.4986	.0046
2.00	.4772	.0540	2.50	.4938	.0175	3.00	.4987	.0044

The areas are from the mean to $\dfrac{x}{\sigma}$ or z. For areas beyond $\dfrac{x}{\sigma}$ or z, subtract the listed area from .5000. The ordinate, y, is the height of the curve at $\dfrac{x}{\sigma}$ or z.

Table C   Distribution of t*

Degrees of Freedom	Significance levels for one-tailed tests					
	.10	.05	.025	.01	.005	.0005
	Significance levels for two-tailed tests					
	.20	.10	.05	.02	.01	.001
9	1.383	1.833	2.262	2.821	3.250	4.781
10	1.372	1.812	2.228	2.764	3.169	4.587
11	1.363	1.796	2.201	2.718	3.106	4.437
12	1.356	1.782	2.179	2.681	3.055	4.318
13	1.350	1.771	2.160	2.650	3.012	4.221
14	1.345	1.761	2.145	2.624	2.977	4.140
15	1.341	1.753	2.131	2.602	2.947	4.073
16	1.337	1.746	2.120	2.583	2.921	4.015
17	1.333	1.740	2.110	2.567	2.898	3.965
18	1.330	1.734	2.101	2.552	2.878	3.922
19	1.328	1.729	2.093	2.539	2.861	3.883
20	1.325	1.725	2.086	2.528	2.845	3.850
21	1.323	1.721	2.080	2.518	2.831	3.819
22	1.321	1.717	2.074	2.508	2.819	3.792
23	1.319	1.714	2.069	2.500	2.807	3.767
24	1.318	1.711	2.064	2.492	2.797	3.745
25	1.316	1.708	2.060	2.485	2.787	3.725
26	1.315	1.706	2.056	2.479	2.779	3.707
27	1.314	1.703	2.052	2.473	2.771	3.690
28	1.313	1.701	2.048	2.467	2.763	3.674
29	1.311	1.699	2.045	2.462	2.756	3.659
30	1.310	1.697	2.042	2.457	2.750	3.646
40	1.303	1.684	2.021	2.423	2.704	3.551
60	1.296	1.671	2.000	2.390	2.660	3.460
120	1.289	1.658	1.980	2.358	2.617	3.373
∞	1.282	1.645	1.960	2.326	2.576	3.291

*Table C is abridged from Table III of R. A. Fisher and F. Yates, *Statistical Tables for Biological, Agricultural, and Medical Research,* published by Oliver & Boyd, Ltd., Edinburgh, by permission of authors and publisher.

Table D Transformation of r to z_r*

r	z_r	r	z_r	r	z_r	r	z_r	r	z_r
.00	.000	.20	.203	.40	.424	.60	.693	.80	1.099
.01	.010	.21	.213	.41	.436	.61	.709	.81	1.127
.02	.020	.22	.224	.42	.448	.62	.725	.82	1.157
.03	.030	.23	.234	.43	.460	.63	.741	.83	1.188
.04	.040	.24	.245	.44	.472	.64	.758	.84	1.221
.05	.050	.25	.255	.45	.485	.65	.775	.85	1.256
.06	.060	.26	.266	.46	.497	.66	.793	.86	1.293
.07	.070	.27	.277	.47	.510	.67	.811	.87	1.333
.08	.080	.28	.288	.48	.523	.68	.829	.88	1.376
.09	.090	.29	.299	.49	.536	.69	.848	.89	1.422
.10	.100	.30	.310	.50	.549	.70	.867	.90	1.472
.11	.110	.31	.321	.51	.563	.71	.887	.91	1.528
.12	.121	.32	.332	.52	.576	.72	.908	.92	1.589
.13	.131	.33	.343	.53	.590	.73	.929	.93	1.658
.14	.141	.34	.354	.54	.604	.74	.950	.94	1.738
.15	.151	.35	.365	.55	.618	.75	.973	.95	1.832
.16	.161	.36	.377	.56	.633	.76	.996	.96	1.946
.17	.172	.37	.388	.57	.648	.77	1.020	.97	2.092
.18	.182	.38	.400	.58	.662	.78	1.045	.98	2.298
.19	.192	.39	.412	.59	.678	.79	1.071	.99	2.647

*Computed by the author using the equation:
$$z_r = 1.151293 \, [\log_{10} (1 + r) - \log_{10} (1 - r)].$$

Table E

The table of χ^2 is also abridged, but should suffice for all fourfold tables and contingency tables where $(r - 1)(c - 1)$ is no larger than 15. The abridged table also suffices for testing the goodness of fit of all frequency distributions up to those having as many as 18 class intervals (after combining those with small frequencies and subtracting three degrees of freedom for N, $\overline{X}$, and s_x). See pages 273 to 276 of Chapter 9.

Table F

This table has been abridged by omitting all columns relevant to more than 12 degrees of freedom for the numerator of F, the larger mean square or variance. The critical values in these columns are very rarely used. Anyone needing them is certain to have a text containing the unabridged table. The use of Table F in the analysis of variance and the analysis of covariance is explained in Chapter 13.

Table E Distribution of χ^2*

Degrees of Freedom	Probability, P													
	.99	.98	.95	.90	.80	.70	.50	.30	.20	.10	.05	.02	.01	.001
1	.00016	.00063	.0039	.016	.064	.15	.46	1.07	1.64	2.71	3.84	5.41	6.64	10.83
2	.02	.04	.10	.21	.45	.71	1.39	2.41	3.22	4.60	5.99	7.82	9.21	13.82
3	.12	.18	.35	.58	1.00	1.42	2.37	3.66	4.64	6.25	7.82	9.84	11.34	16.27
4	.30	.43	.71	1.06	1.65	2.20	3.36	4.88	5.99	7.78	9.49	11.67	13.28	18.46
5	.55	.75	1.14	1.61	2.34	3.00	4.35	6.06	7.29	9.24	11.07	13.39	15.09	20.52
6	.87	1.13	1.64	2.20	3.07	3.83	5.35	7.23	8.56	10.64	12.59	15.03	16.81	22.46
7	1.24	1.56	2.17	2.83	3.82	4.67	6.35	8.38	9.80	12.02	14.07	16.62	18.48	24.32
8	1.65	2.03	2.73	3.49	4.59	5.53	7.34	9.52	11.03	13.36	15.51	18.17	20.09	26.12
9	2.09	2.53	3.32	4.17	5.38	6.39	8.34	10.66	12.24	14.68	16.92	19.68	21.67	27.88
10	2.56	3.06	3.94	4.86	6.18	7.27	9.34	11.78	13.44	15.99	18.31	21.16	23.21	29.59
11	3.05	3.61	4.58	5.58	6.99	8.15	10.34	12.90	14.63	17.28	19.68	22.62	24.72	31.26
12	3.57	4.18	5.23	6.30	7.81	9.03	11.34	14.01	15.81	18.55	21.03	24.05	26.22	32.91
13	4.11	4.76	5.89	7.04	8.63	9.93	12.34	15.12	16.98	19.81	22.36	25.47	27.69	34.53
14	4.66	5.37	6.57	7.79	9.47	10.82	13.34	16.22	18.15	21.06	23.68	26.87	29.14	36.12
15	5.23	5.98	7.26	8.55	10.31	11.72	14.34	17.32	19.31	22.31	25.00	28.26	30.58	37.70

*Table E is abridged from Table IV of R. A. Fisher and F. Yates, *Statistical Tables for Biological, Agricultural, and Medical Research*, published by Oliver & Boyd, Ltd., Edinburgh, by permission of authors and publisher.

Table F   Table of F for .05 (roman) and .01 (boldface)
Levels of Significance*

degrees of freedom of numerator

n_2	1	2	3	4	5	6	7	8	9	10	11	12
1	161	200	216	225	230	234	237	239	241	242	243	244
	4,052	**4,999**	**5,403**	**5,625**	**5,764**	**5,859**	**5,928**	**5,981**	**6,022**	**6,056**	**6,082**	**6,106**
2	18.51	19.00	19.16	19.25	19.30	19.33	19.36	19.37	19.38	19.39	19.40	19.41
	98.49	**99.01**	**99.17**	**99.25**	**99.30**	**99.33**	**99.34**	**99.36**	**99.38**	**99.40**	**99.41**	**99.42**
3	10.13	9.55	9.28	9.12	9.01	8.94	8.88	8.84	8.81	8.78	8.76	8.74
	34.12	**30.81**	**29.46**	**28.71**	**28.24**	**27.91**	**27.67**	**27.49**	**27.34**	**27.23**	**27.13**	**27.05**
4	7.71	6.94	6.59	6.39	6.26	6.16	6.09	6.04	6.00	5.96	5.93	5.91
	21.20	**18.00**	**16.69**	**15.98**	**15.52**	**15.21**	**14.98**	**14.80**	**14.66**	**14.54**	**14.45**	**14.37**
5	6.61	5.79	5.41	5.19	5.05	4.95	4.88	4.82	4.78	4.74	4.70	4.68
	16.26	**13.27**	**12.06**	**11.39**	**10.97**	**10.67**	**10.45**	**10.27**	**10.15**	**10.05**	**9.96**	**9.89**
6	5.99	5.14	4.76	4.53	4.39	4.28	4.21	4.15	4.10	4.06	4.03	4.00
	13.74	**10.92**	**9.78**	**9.15**	**8.75**	**8.47**	**8.26**	**8.10**	**7.98**	**7.87**	**7.79**	**7.72**
7	5.59	4.74	4.35	4.12	3.97	3.87	3.79	3.73	3.68	3.63	3.60	3.57
	12.25	**9.55**	**8.45**	**7.85**	**7.46**	**7.19**	**7.00**	**6.84**	**6.71**	**6.62**	**6.54**	**6.47**
8	5.32	4.46	4.07	3.84	3.69	3.58	3.50	3.44	3.39	3.34	3.31	3.28
	11.26	**8.65**	**7.59**	**7.01**	**6.63**	**6.37**	**6.19**	**6.03**	**5.91**	**5.82**	**5.74**	**5.67**
9	5.12	4.26	3.86	3.63	3.48	3.37	3.29	3.23	3.18	3.13	3.10	3.07
	10.56	**8.02**	**6.99**	**6.42**	**6.06**	**5.80**	**5.62**	**5.47**	**5.35**	**5.26**	**5.18**	**5.11**
10	4.96	4.10	3.71	3.48	3.33	3.22	3.14	3.07	3.02	2.97	2.94	2.91
	10.04	**7.56**	**6.55**	**5.99**	**5.64**	**5.39**	**5.21**	**5.06**	**4.95**	**4.85**	**4.78**	**4.71**
11	4.84	3.98	3.59	3.36	3.20	3.09	3.01	2.95	2.90	2.86	2.82	2.79
	9.65	**7.20**	**6.22**	**5.67**	**5.32**	**5.07**	**4.88**	**4.74**	**4.63**	**4.54**	**4.46**	**4.40**
12	4.75	3.88	3.49	3.26	3.11	3.00	2.92	2.85	2.80	2.76	2.72	2.69
	9.33	**6.93**	**5.95**	**5.41**	**5.06**	**4.82**	**4.65**	**4.50**	**4.39**	**4.30**	**4.22**	**4.16**
13	4.67	3.80	3.41	3.18	3.02	2.92	2.84	2.77	2.72	2.67	2.63	2.60
	9.07	**6.70**	**5.74**	**5.20**	**4.86**	**4.62**	**4.44**	**4.30**	**4.19**	**4.10**	**4.02**	**3.96**
14	4.60	3.74	3.34	3.11	2.96	2.85	2.77	2.70	2.65	2.60	2.56	2.53
	8.86	**6.51**	**5.56**	**5.03**	**4.69**	**4.46**	**4.28**	**4.14**	**4.03**	**3.94**	**3.86**	**3.80**
15	4.54	3.68	3.29	3.06	2.90	2.79	2.70	2.64	2.59	2.55	2.51	2.48
	8.68	**6.36**	**5.42**	**4.89**	**4.56**	**4.32**	**4.14**	**4.00**	**3.89**	**3.80**	**3.73**	**3.67**
16	4.49	3.63	3.24	3.01	2.85	2.74	2.66	2.59	2.54	2.49	2.45	2.42
	8.53	**6.23**	**5.29**	**4.77**	**4.44**	**4.20**	**4.03**	**3.89**	**3.78**	**3.69**	**3.61**	**3.55**
17	4.45	3.59	3.20	2.96	2.81	2.70	2.62	2.55	2.50	2.45	2.41	2.38
	8.40	**6.11**	**5.18**	**4.67**	**4.34**	**4.10**	**3.93**	**3.79**	**3.68**	**3.59**	**3.52**	**3.45**
18	4.41	3.55	3.16	2.93	2.77	2.66	2.58	2.51	2.46	2.41	2.37	2.34
	8.28	**6.01**	**5.09**	**4.58**	**4.25**	**4.01**	**3.85**	**3.71**	**3.60**	**3.51**	**3.44**	**3.37**
19	4.38	3.52	3.13	2.90	2.74	2.63	2.55	2.48	2.43	2.38	2.34	2.31
	8.18	**5.93**	**5.01**	**4.50**	**4.17**	**3.94**	**3.77**	**3.63**	**3.52**	**3.43**	**3.36**	**3.30**
20	4.35	3.49	3.10	2.87	2.71	2.60	2.52	2.45	2.40	2.35	2.31	2.28
	8.10	**5.85**	**4.94**	**4.43**	**4.10**	**3.87**	**3.71**	**3.56**	**3.45**	**3.37**	**3.30**	**3.23**
21	4.32	3.47	3.07	2.84	2.68	2.57	2.49	2.42	2.37	2.32	2.28	2.25
	8.02	**5.78**	**4.87**	**4.37**	**4.04**	**3.81**	**3.65**	**3.51**	**3.40**	**3.31**	**3.24**	**3.17**
22	4.30	3.44	3.05	2.82	2.66	2.55	2.47	2.40	2.35	2.30	2.26	2.23
	7.94	**5.72**	**4.82**	**4.31**	**3.99**	**3.76**	**3.59**	**3.45**	**3.35**	**3.26**	**3.18**	**3.12**
23	4.28	3.42	3.03	2.80	2.64	2.53	2.45	2.38	2.32	2.28	2.24	2.20
	7.88	**5.66**	**4.76**	**4.26**	**3.94**	**3.71**	**3.54**	**3.41**	**3.30**	**3.21**	**3.14**	**3.07**
24	4.26	3.40	3.01	2.78	2.62	2.51	2.43	2.36	2.30	2.26	2.22	2.18
	7.82	**5.61**	**4.72**	**4.22**	**3.90**	**3.67**	**3.50**	**3.36**	**3.25**	**3.17**	**3.09**	**3.03**
25	4.24	3.38	2.99	2.76	2.60	2.49	2.41	2.34	2.28	2.24	2.20	2.16
	7.77	**5.57**	**4.68**	**4.18**	**3.86**	**3.63**	**3.46**	**3.32**	**3.21**	**3.13**	**3.05**	**2.99**
26	4.22	3.37	2.98	2.74	2.59	2.47	2.39	2.32	2.27	2.22	2.18	2.15
	7.72	**5.53**	**4.64**	**4.14**	**3.82**	**3.59**	**3.42**	**3.29**	**3.17**	**3.09**	**3.02**	**2.96**

degrees of freedom of denominator

*Abridged reproduction by permission from *Statistical Methods*, 6th edition, by George W. Snedecor and William G. Cochran, © 1967 by the Iowa State University Press.

Table F Continued

degrees of freedom of numerator

n_2	1	2	3	4	5	6	7	8	9	10	11	12
27	4.21	3.35	2.96	2.73	2.57	2.46	2.37	2.30	2.25	2.20	2.16	2.13
	7.68	**5.49**	**4.60**	**4.11**	**3.79**	**3.56**	**3.39**	**3.26**	**3.14**	**3.06**	**2.98**	**2.93**
28	4.20	3.34	2.95	2.71	2.56	2.44	2.36	2.29	2.24	2.19	2.15	2.12
	7.64	**5.45**	**4.57**	**4.07**	**3.76**	**3.53**	**3.36**	**3.23**	**3.11**	**3.03**	**2.95**	**2.90**
29	4.18	3.33	2.93	2.70	2.54	2.43	2.35	2.28	2.22	2.18	2.14	2.10
	7.60	**5.42**	**4.54**	**4.04**	**3.73**	**3.50**	**3.33**	**3.20**	**3.08**	**3.00**	**2.92**	**2.87**
30	4.17	3.32	2.92	2.69	2.53	2.42	2.34	2.27	2.21	2.16	2.12	2.09
	7.56	**5.39**	**4.51**	**4.02**	**3.70**	**3.47**	**3.30**	**3.17**	**3.06**	**2.98**	**2.90**	**2.84**
32	4.15	3.30	2.90	2.67	2.51	2.40	2.32	2.25	2.19	2.14	2.10	2.07
	7.50	**5.34**	**4.46**	**3.97**	**3.66**	**3.42**	**3.25**	**3.12**	**3.01**	**2.94**	**2.86**	**2.80**
34	4.13	3.28	2.88	2.65	2.49	2.38	2.30	2.23	2.17	2.12	2.08	2.05
	7.44	**5.29**	**4.42**	**3.93**	**3.61**	**3.38**	**3.21**	**3.08**	**2.97**	**2.89**	**2.82**	**2.76**
36	4.11	3.26	2.86	2.63	2.48	2.36	2.28	2.21	2.15	2.10	2.06	2.03
	7.39	**5.25**	**4.38**	**3.89**	**3.58**	**3.35**	**3.18**	**3.04**	**2.94**	**2.86**	**2.78**	**2.72**
38	4.10	3.25	2.85	2.62	2.46	2.35	2.26	2.19	2.14	2.09	2.05	2.02
	7.35	**5.21**	**4.34**	**3.86**	**3.54**	**3.32**	**3.15**	**3.02**	**2.91**	**2.82**	**2.75**	**2.69**
40	4.08	3.23	2.84	2.61	2.45	2.34	2.25	2.18	2.12	2.07	2.04	2.00
	7.31	**5.18**	**4.31**	**3.83**	**3.51**	**3.29**	**3.12**	**2.99**	**2.88**	**2.80**	**2.73**	**2.66**
42	4.07	3.22	2.83	2.59	2.44	2.32	2.24	2.17	2.11	2.06	2.02	1.99
	7.27	**5.15**	**4.29**	**3.80**	**3.49**	**3.26**	**3.10**	**2.96**	**2.86**	**2.77**	**2.70**	**2.64**
44	4.06	3.21	2.82	2.58	2.43	2.31	2.23	2.16	2.10	2.05	2.01	1.98
	7.24	**5.12**	**4.26**	**3.78**	**3.46**	**3.24**	**3.07**	**2.94**	**2.84**	**2.75**	**2.68**	**2.62**
46	4.05	3.20	2.81	2.57	2.42	2.30	2.22	2.14	2.09	2.04	2.00	1.97
	7.21	**5.10**	**4.24**	**3.76**	**3.44**	**3.22**	**3.05**	**2.92**	**2.82**	**2.73**	**2.66**	**2.60**
48	4.04	3.19	2.80	2.56	2.41	2.30	2.21	2.14	2.08	2.03	1.99	1.96
	7.19	**5.08**	**4.22**	**3.74**	**3.42**	**3.20**	**3.04**	**2.90**	**2.80**	**2.71**	**2.64**	**2.58**
50	4.03	3.18	2.79	2.56	2.40	2.29	2.20	2.13	2.07	2.02	1.98	1.95
	7.17	**5.06**	**4.20**	**3.72**	**3.41**	**3.18**	**3.02**	**2.88**	**2.78**	**2.70**	**2.62**	**2.56**
55	4.02	3.17	2.78	2.54	2.38	2.27	2.18	2.11	2.05	2.00	1.97	1.93
	7.12	**5.01**	**4.16**	**3.68**	**3.37**	**3.15**	**2.98**	**2.85**	**2.75**	**2.66**	**2.59**	**2.53**
60	4.00	3.15	2.76	2.52	2.37	2.25	2.17	2.10	2.04	1.99	1.95	1.92
	7.08	**4.98**	**4.13**	**3.65**	**3.34**	**3.12**	**2.95**	**2.82**	**2.72**	**2.63**	**2.56**	**2.50**
65	3.99	3.14	2.75	2.51	2.36	2.24	2.15	2.08	2.02	1.98	1.94	1.90
	7.04	**4.95**	**4.10**	**3.62**	**3.31**	**3.09**	**2.93**	**2.79**	**2.70**	**2.61**	**2.54**	**2.47**
70	3.98	3.13	2.74	2.50	2.35	2.23	2.14	2.07	2.01	1.97	1.93	1.89
	7.01	**4.92**	**4.08**	**3.60**	**3.29**	**3.07**	**2.91**	**2.77**	**2.67**	**2.59**	**2.51**	**2.45**
80	3.96	3.11	2.72	2.48	2.33	2.21	2.12	2.05	1.99	1.95	1.91	1.88
	6.96	**4.88**	**4.04**	**3.56**	**3.25**	**3.04**	**2.87**	**2.74**	**2.64**	**2.55**	**2.48**	**2.41**
100	3.94	3.09	2.70	2.46	2.30	2.19	2.10	2.03	1.97	1.92	1.88	1.85
	6.90	**4.82**	**3.98**	**3.51**	**3.20**	**2.99**	**2.82**	**2.69**	**2.59**	**2.51**	**2.43**	**2.36**
125	3.92	3.07	2.68	2.44	2.29	2.17	2.08	2.01	1.95	1.90	1.86	1.83
	6.84	**4.78**	**3.94**	**3.47**	**3.17**	**2.95**	**2.79**	**2.65**	**2.56**	**2.47**	**2.40**	**2.33**
150	3.91	3.06	2.67	2.43	2.27	2.16	2.07	2.00	1.94	1.89	1.85	1.82
	6.81	**4.75**	**3.91**	**3.44**	**3.14**	**2.92**	**2.76**	**2.62**	**2.53**	**2.44**	**2.37**	**2.30**
200	3.89	3.04	2.65	2.41	2.26	2.14	2.05	1.98	1.92	1.87	1.83	1.80
	6.76	**4.71**	**3.88**	**3.41**	**3.11**	**2.90**	**2.73**	**2.60**	**2.50**	**2.41**	**2.34**	**2.28**
400	3.86	3.02	2.62	2.39	2.23	2.12	2.03	1.96	1.90	1.85	1.81	1.78
	6.70	**4.66**	**3.83**	**3.36**	**3.06**	**2.85**	**2.69**	**2.55**	**2.46**	**2.37**	**2.29**	**2.23**
1,000	3.85	3.00	2.61	2.38	2.22	2.10	2.02	1.95	1.89	1.84	1.80	1.76
	6.66	**4.62**	**3.80**	**3.34**	**3.04**	**2.82**	**2.66**	**2.53**	**2.43**	**2.34**	**2.26**	**2.20**
∞	3.84	2.99	2.60	2.37	2.21	2.09	2.01	1.94	1.88	1.83	1.79	1.75
	6.64	**4.60**	**3.78**	**3.32**	**3.02**	**2.80**	**2.64**	**2.51**	**2.41**	**2.32**	**2.24**	**2.18**

degrees of freedom of denominator

Answers to Practice Exercises

8.1 (1) Mean 66.5715   (2) Median 67.5770
              or 66.57   or 67.58

       (3) Q_1 58.4285 Q_3 75.3335   (4) Q 8.4525
              or 58.43   or 75.33   or 8.45

       (5) Standard Deviation 12.2695
              or 12.27

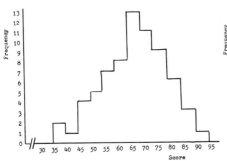 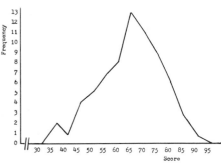

8.2 $\overline{X} = 4.88$ $\overline{Y} = 3.00$ $r_{xy} = .7780$ or .78
       $s_x = 1.8661$ or 1.87 $s_y = .9781$ or .98

Use of Formula 8.10 with Sheppard's correction gives the same value of r_{xy}. The standard deviations obtained as explained with reference to this formula are 1.8755 and .9830. Substitution of these standard deviations in Formula 8.9, with $N - 1$ in the denominator, again yields an r_{xy} of .7780. The slightly higher standard deviations are better estimators of the population standard deviations.

8.3

Raw Score	Percentile Rank
46	99.5
45	97
44	93
43	87
42	76
41	63
40	47
39	31
38	19
37	12
36	7
35	4
34	1

Linear Standard Scores

$X' = 3.9216X - 107.3738$ or
$\quad\quad 3.92X - 107.37$

$X = 43 \quad\quad X' = 61$
$X = 36 \quad\quad X' = 34$

Normalized Standard Scores

$X = 43 \quad\quad X' = 61$
$X = 36 \quad\quad X' = 35$

9.1 103–107 and 102–108. You should take the square root of 121 rather than the square root of 120 since division by $\sqrt{N - 1}$ is implied by the phrase "estimate of the population standard deviation." The degrees of freedom are 120, hence, 1.980 and 2.617 are used.

9.2 $t = 2.17$. For 120 degrees of freedom this t is significant at the .05 level. $t = 3.40$. For 60 degrees of freedom this t is significant at the .01 level. If it were not for the fewer degrees of freedom, t would be significant at the .001 level.

9.3 The standard error of measurement is 3.2 and the 95 percent confidence interval is 60–72, or more precisely, 59.97–72.51. The estimated true score is 66, or 66.24.

9.4 Use of Formula 9.7 first with z_a and z_b equal to 1.96 and 1.28, estimates groups of 84 each for the two-tailed test. Using z_a and z_b equal to 1.64 and 1.28 in Formula 9.7 gives an estimate of groups of 68 each for the one-tailed test. The one-tailed test is the more powerful, hence, the smaller groups needed for the same level of significance.

9.5 Use of Formula 9.16 results in a standard error of .0667. For this large sample, the r of .16 is significant at the .01 level for a one-tailed test.

Use of Formula 9.17 with the r of .30 and the N of 32 yields a t of 1.72 which is significant at the .05 level for a one-tailed test.

9.6 Converting the r's of .55 and .63 to z_r's of .618 and .741, the difference between the z_r's is .123. Use of Formula 9.15 gives a standard error of the difference of .103. The t of .119 is not significant.

9.7 Using Formula 9.18, $s_p = .04$ and the 95 percent confidence interval is 60–76.

9.8 Using Formula 9.20, $\chi^2 = 4.61$.

Using Formula 9.22, $z = 2.15$. Both are significant at the .05 level, $\chi^2 = z^2$, if enough decimals are carried.

9.9 Using Formulas 9.23 and 9.24, $\chi^2 = 4.76$ and $z = 2.18$. Both are evidence of significance at the .05 level.

9.10 For $8 - 3 = 5$ degrees of freedom, the χ^2 of 20.98 is significant at the .001 level for which 20.52 is required. Only once in one thousand times in random sampling from a normal population would a worse fit be obtained. The Kolmogorov-Smirnov D of $+ .1287$ is significant just beyond the .10 level where $1.22/\sqrt{N}$ or .122 is required. Apparently, this test, in this instance, is less powerful. (If your χ^2 equaled 20.99 it is likely that you improperly rounded .125 to .13.)

9.11 For the median test, χ^2 equals 1.50 which is equivalent to a z of 1.22. Both are nonsignificant.

For the Wilcoxon rank sum test, z equals 1.73 which is also nonsignificant.

For the sign test, z equals 2.37 which is significant at the .05 level.

For the Wilcoxon matched-pairs signed-ranks test, $z = 2.59$ which is significant at the .01 level.

When Formula 9.3 was used with the same data, the t of 1.84 is nonsignificant for $N_1 + N_2 - 2$ or 22 degrees of freedom. When Formulas 9.5 and 9.6 were applied, t equaled 3.83 which is significant at the .01 level for 11 degrees of freedom. The nonparametric tests are probably more appropriate for these data, however, than the parametric ones.

10.1   (a)   5.0333

       (b)   .0068

The frequency of each stanine score should be multiplied by its stanine scale value, the stanine stratum mean in integers subtracted, and the $3s_h^2$ substituted in Formula 10.6 with $W_h = \dfrac{1}{3}$, $N = 900$, and $n = 90$.

The variance error for simple random sampling with use of the finite population correction is .0639. The variance error is much smaller because of the limited variability within strata in the case of our stratified random sampling.

10.2   (a)   5.0000

       (b)   .0388

Simple random sampling with the stanines distributed in the same proportions, but with an N of 2500, yields the much smaller error variance of .0015 or .00154. Note that the distribution of stanine means corresponds to the norm distribution of stanine scores, an unlikely event except in a practice exercise!

11.1   (a) $s_{y \cdot x} = .76$

       (b) $q_c = .1314$ or 13 in 100

       (c) $q_a = .0655$ or 7 in 100

       (d)   53.80 or 54 (Five percent or .05 refers to a q_c not a q_a and m is negative.)

       (e)   Two diagrams are needed. See top of page 533.

11.2 $r_{12 \cdot 3} = -.0454$ or $-.05$. The correlation r_{ac} also equals $-.05$. It is the correlation from which variable 3 or b is excluded.

11.3   (1)   Use of either Formula 11.20 or 11.21 results in an r_{pb} of $+.51$.

       (2)   Use of either Formula 11.18 or 11.19 results in an r_b of $+.66$.

       (3)   Using Formula 11.23, the ϕ coefficient is $+.44$.

       (4)   The tetrachoric coefficient obtained through use of the abac in Figure 11.8 approximates $+.68$. Using the *Computing Diagrams* earlier cited, my estimate is $+.66$ which agrees with the biserial coefficient.

Diagrams for answer to Practice Exercise 11.1

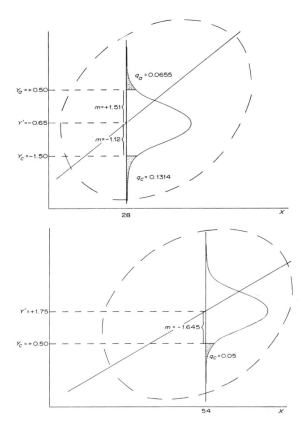

Read Cervantes' *The Dropout: Causes and Cures* cited on page 46 of Chapter 3 before concluding that the measures of "life adjustment" have little construct validity. A complex of traits is involved and life adjustment may be as good a label as Spearman's *g*.

The student should note that the data analyzed are hypothetical but not implausible.

13.1 $t = 2.85$. For 17 d.f. t should exceed 2.11 for significance at the 5% level and 2.90 at the 1% level. The *same* value of t is obtained using gains even though $r_{xg} = -.3044$. One should conclude that the difference is significant at the 5% level, resisting the temptation to say that it is almost significant at the 1% level. The fact that $\Sigma y_1{}^2 = \Sigma y_2{}^2$ suffices to indicate that there is homogeneity of variance of the posttest scores. The correlations $r_{x_1 y_1}$ and $r_{x_2 y_2}$ of .68 and .58 are not significantly different. Conversion to z_r's gives .829 and .663 or a difference of .166. The error of this difference, when computed by Formula 9.15 on page

261, equals $\sqrt{\dfrac{1}{N_1 - 3} + \dfrac{1}{N_2 - 3}} = .5345$. Since $t = .166/.5345$ and is less than unity, the difference in r's is nonsignificant, thus supporting the assumption of homogeneity of regression.

13.2 The F equals 2.25 and for 4 and 30 degrees of freedom is nonsignificant. (2.69 is required for significance at the 5% level.) No t tests are justified since the F is nonsignificant. This result was to be expected since the numbers in the table were drawn from a table of random numbers! If the F turned out to be significant it would be an error of the first kind.

13.3 The F for the treatments or column variable is 9.03 when the treatments variance is divided by the interaction variance. This F is significant beyond the .01 level. For 2 and 14 degrees of freedom 6.51 is required.

13.4 (1) The null hypothesis with reference to the treatments cannot be rejected. $F = \dfrac{2.66}{6.17} = .43$ which is not significant. The 2.66 is the treatments variance and the 6.17 is the interaction variance. (2) The interaction variance is significant at the .05 level. $F = \dfrac{6.17}{1.08} = 5.71$ where 1.08 is the within-subgroups variance. For 2 and 18 degrees of freedom 3.55 is required at the .05 level and 6.01 at the .01 level.

13.5 When computations are carried to four decimals, F rounds off to 9.56 and t to 3.09. Both are significant beyond the 1% level. For 1 and 17 degrees of freedom, 8.40 is required for F and for 17 degrees of freedom, 2.90 is required for t. Since there are only two groups, if enough decimals are carried t^2 equals F. The Σxy for between groups equals -6.4. See the chapter on analysis of covariance in Edwards' *Experimental Design,* McNemar's *Psychological Statistics,* or other advanced text for an explanation.

OBTAINING SQUARE ROOTS

There are various ways of obtaining square roots. Most of the statistics texts earlier cited have tables of squares and square roots of numbers from 1 to 1000. The square roots are given to four decimal places. Square roots can also be obtained to about three significant figures with a slide rule and to four or five using logarithms. One need only divide the complete logarithm, characteristic and mantissa, by 2 and identify the anti-logarithm. Square roots can, of course, be obtained by hand or through use of a desk calculator using the traditional arithmetical method.

The following method of obtaining square roots is credited to Isaac Newton. It is easy to learn, rapid, and accurate. It may be done by hand or on a desk calculator such as the Monroe, Marchant, or Friden. It is a method used by electronic computers.

Given a number, for example, 54.2438, select a round number whose square is nearest the given number. The $7 \times 7 = 49$ is nearest 54.2438. The "iterative" process soon "converges" to the square root.

54.2438 $\div$ 7 = 7.749114. Add this number to 7 and divide by 2 obtaining 7.374557.

54.2438 $\div$ 7.374557 = 7.355533. Add this number to 7.374557 and divide by 2 obtaining 7.365045.

54.2438 $\div$ 7.365045 = 7.365033. Add this number to 7.365045 and divide by 2 obtaining 7.365039.

54.2438 $\div$ 7.365039 = 7.365039. This agreement to six decimal places should suffice![1]

When taking square roots of such numbers as .7486 and .07486, divide first by .8 or .2. In the case of .007486 or .0007486 divide first by .08 or .02.

Tables of "square root multipliers" or "square root divisors" may be used to obtain square roots with any of the desk calculators referred to above. In the case of a table of square root divisors, a three-digit number from the table which most nearly approximates the number whose square root is desired is added to the first three digits of the number, the sum appearing in the lower dials at the left. The sum is then divided automatically by one of two seven-digit numbers given in the same row of the table as the three-digit number earlier identified. Which one of the two seven-digit numbers to select depends on whether or not the number of digits preceding the decimal point, or zeros following the decimal point of the number whose square root is sought, is odd or even. The quotient is the square root to five significant figures. Such tables for obtaining square roots are supplied by the leading manufacturers of desk calculators. The instructions accompanying the tables also include directions on how to increase the accuracy of the square root first obtained to nine or ten significant figures. There are desk calculators which will compute square roots completely automatically.

---

[1] The method is illustrated and explained in Robert L. Thorndike and Elizabeth Hagen, *Measurement and Evaluation in Psychology and Education* (New York: Wiley, 1969), pp. 657–58.

Name Index

Subject Index

Determination, coefficients of, 340
Dictionary of Education, 72
Discriminant analysis, 369
Dissertation Abstracts, 69
 example of, 70
Documentation in Education, 63

Educational Index, 65–67
 excerpt from, 67
Educational research, historical
 abilities required in, 454–455
 aids in locating data, 457
 external criticism, 457
 historians, professional vs. educational, 452–454
 historiography, writers on, 464–467
 internal criticism, 458
 "new" history, 453–454
 note-taking in, 458–459
 and philosophies of history, 452
 primary sources of data in, 455–
  456
 problems of interpretation in, 460–
  462
 remains or relics, 456
 scientific characteristics of, 451
 secondary sources of data in, 457
 types of historical problems, 454
Educational research:
 definition of, 1–2
 and graduate student, 2–3
 federal government and foundation
  support for, 4
 introduction to, 1–7
 role in dynamic society, 1
 and school administrator, counselor
  and teacher, 3
Educational research problems:
 assumptions relevant to, 52–53
 declarative statements vs. questions
  when stating, 44–45
 defining terms in, 49–50
 null vs. research hypotheses in, 47–
  48
 and relevant theory, 50–51
 sources of information, aids in
  locating, 63–73
 specifying scope of, 53–54
 specifying data sources, techniques
  of collection, and interpretation
  for, 54–55

Educational Researcher (AERA), 71–
 72
*Educational Resources Information
 Center* (ERIC) 72
Encyclopedia of Educational Research,
 65
Epistemic correlation, 20
Epistemology, 21
Expected frequency, definition of, 264
Experimental coefficient (McCall's),
 380–381
Experimentation:
 analysis of variance, role in, 374
 and causation, study of, 373–374
 controls, nature and purpose of,
  375–376
 disillusion with, 383–384
 external validity, threats to, 382,
  389–391
 four-group design in, 396
 history of, 377–378, 386–388
 internal validity, threats to, 389–391
 Mill's canons, role in, 375–376
 pseudo, 296
 quasi, 296
 single variable, law of, 376, 387
 statistical methods, contribution of,
  379–382
 statistical regression in, 390
 target population of, 374
 and theory and practice of education, 384–385

Factor analysis:
 applications of, 349–350
 centroid method of, 347–348
 correlation matrix in, 345
 and data processing, 350
 factor loadings, 347–348
 group factors, 347
 hierarchical order in, 346
 orthogonal and oblique solutions
  to, 348–349
 recent developments in, 349
 rotation of axes, explanation and
  graph, 348–349
 simple structure, 349
 Spearman's "g" and "s," 345
 tetrad differences and tetrad equations, 346
Facts on File, 72
Formative evaluation, 161, 186